CW00402202

SOCIAL SECURITY LEGISLATION 2013/14

VOLUME V: UNIVERSAL CREDIT

SOCIAL SECURITY LEGISLATION 2013/14

General Editor
Nick Wikeley, M.A. (Cantab)

VOLUME V:
UNIVERSAL CREDIT

Commentary By

**John Mesher, B.A., B.C.L.
(Oxon), LL.M. (Yale)**
Judge of the Upper Tribunal

Richard Poynter, B.C.L., M.A. (Oxon)
District Tribunal Judge

Nick Wikeley, M.A. (Cantab)
Judge of the Upper Tribunal
Emeritus Professor of Law
University of Southampton

Penny Wood, LL.B., M.Sc.
District Tribunal Judge

Consultant Editor
Child Poverty Action Group

SWEET & MAXWELL      THOMSON REUTERS

Published in 2014 by
Sweet & Maxwell, 100 Avenue Road, London NW3 3PF
Part of Thomson Reuters (Professional) UK Limited
(Registered in England & Wales, Company No 1679046.
Registered Office and address for service:
Aldgate House, 33 Aldgate High Street,
London EC3N 1DL)

Typeset by Servis Filmsetting Ltd, Stockport, Cheshire
Printed and bound in Great Britain by
Ashford Colour Press, Gosport, Hants

For further information on our products and services,
visit www.sweetandmaxwell.co.uk

No natural forests were destroyed to make this product.
Only farmed timber was used and re-planted.

A CIP catalogue record for this book is
available from the British Library

ISBN 978–0–414–03356–6

Crown copyright material is reproduced with the permission
of the Controller of HMSO and the Queen's Printer for
Scotland.

All rights reserved. No part of this publication may be reproduced or
transmitted in any form or by any means, or stored in any retrieval system
of any nature without prior written permission, except for permitted
fair dealing under the Copyright, Designs and Patents Act 1988, or in
accordance with the terms of a licence issued by the Copyright Licensing
Agency in respect of photocopying and/or reprographic reproduction.
Application for permission for other use of copyright material including
permission to reproduce extracts in other published works shall be made
to the publishers. Full acknowledgement of author, publisher and source
must be given.
Material is contained in this publication for which publishing permission
has been sought, and for which copyright is acknowledged. Permission
to reproduce such material cannot be granted by the publishers and
application must be made to the copyright holder.

Thomson Reuters and the Thomson Reuters Logo are trademarks of
Thomson Reuters. Sweet & Maxwell® is a registered trademark of
Thomson Reuters (Professional) UK Limited.

Commentators have asserted their moral rights under the Copyright,
Designs and Patents Act 1988 to be identified as the authors of the
commentary in this Volume.

© 2014 Thomson Reuters (Professional) UK Limited

CONTENTS

PART I
INTRODUCTION

PART II
UNIVERSAL CREDIT: STATUTES

PART III
UNIVERSAL CREDIT: REGULATIONS

PART IV
UNIVERSAL CREDIT: TRANSITIONAL PROVISIONS AND COMMENCEMENT ORDERS

Contents

PART IV
UNIVERSAL CREDIT: CLAIMS & PAYMENTS AND DECISIONS &
APPEALS

Paras

TABLE OF CASES

TABLE OF COMMISSIONERS' DECISIONS

TABLE OF ABBREVIATIONS

1991 Act	Child Support Act 1991
1992 Act	Social Security Contributions and Benefits Act 1992
1995 Act	Jobseekers Act 1995
1998 Act	Social Security Act 1998
2001 Act	Social Security Fraud Act 2001
2007 Act	Welfare Reform Act 2007
2012 Act	Welfare Reform Act 2012
1987 Regulations	Income Support (General) Regulations 1987 (SI 1987/1967); Social Security (Claims and Payments) Regulations 1987 (SI 1987/1968)
1996 Regulations	Jobseeker's Allowance Regulations 1996 (SI 1996/207)
2001 Regulations	Social Security (Loss of Benefit) Regulations 2001 (SI 2001/4022)
2002 Regulations	Tax Credits (Claims and Notifications) Regulations 2002 (SI 2002/2014)
2006 Regulations	Housing Benefit Regulations 2006 (SI 2006/213)
2006 (SPC) Regulations	Housing Benefit (Persons who have attained the qualifying age for state pension credit) Regulations 2006 (SI 2006/214)
2008 Regulations	Employment and Support Allowance Regulations 2008 (SI 2008/794)
2010 Regulations	Employment and Support Allowance (Transitional Provisions, Housing Benefit and Council Tax Benefit) (Existing Awards) (No.2) Regulations 2010 (SI 2010/1907)
AC	Appeal Cases
ADM	*Advice for Decision Making* (DWP)
Claims and Payments Regulations 1987	Social Security (Claims and Payments) Regulations 1987 (SI 1987/1968)
Claims and Payments Regulations 2013	Universal Credit, Personal Independence Payment, Jobseeker's Allowance and Employment and Support Allowance (Claims and Payments) Regulations 2013 (SI 2013/380)
Commencement No.9 Order	Welfare Reform Act 2012 (Commencement No.9 and Transitional and Transitory Provisions and Commencement No.8 and Savings and Transitional Provisions (Amendment)) Order 2013 (SI 2013/983)

Table of Abbreviations used in this Series

Commencement No.11 Order	Welfare Reform Act 2012 (Commencement No.11 and Transitional and Transitory Provisions and Commencement No.9 and Transitional and Transitory Provisions (Amendment)) Order 2013 (SI 2013/1511)
Commencement No.13 Order	Welfare Reform Act 2012 (Commencement No.13 and Transitional and Transitory Provisions) Order 2013 (SI 2013/2657) (c.103)
Commencement No.14 Order	Welfare Reform Act 2012 (Commencement No.14 and Transitional and Transitory Provisions) Order 2013 (SI 2013/2846) (c.114)
Contributions and Benefits Act	Social Security Contributions and Benefits Act 1992
CPAG	Child Poverty Action Group
CTC	child tax credit
DEA	Direct Earnings Attachment
DLA	disability living allowance
DWP	Department for Work and Pensions
Decisions and Appeals Regulations 2013	Universal Credit, Personal Independence Payment, Jobseeker's Allowance and Employment and Support Allowance (Decisions and Appeals) Regulations 2013 (SI 2013/381)
EEA	European Economic Area
EEA Regulations	Immigration (European Economic Area) Regulations 2006 (SI 2006/1003)
ESA	employment and support allowance
ESA(IR)	income-related employment and support allowance
ESA Regulations 2008	Employment and Support Allowance Regulations 2008 (SI 2008/794)
ESA Regulations 2013	Employment and Support Allowance Regulations 2013 (SI 2013/379)
EWCA Civ	Civil Division of the Court of Appeal in England and Wales
Fraud Act	Social Security Fraud Act 2001
HB	housing benefit
HMRC	Her Majesty's Revenue and Customs
IS	income support
Income Support Regulations	Income Support (General) Regulations 1987 (SI 1987/1967)
ITEPA	Income Tax (Earnings and Pensions) Act 2003
Jobseekers Act	Jobseekers Act 1993
JSA	jobseeker's allowance
JSA(IB)	income-based jobseeker's allowance
JSA Regs	Jobseeker's Allowance Regulations 1996 (SI 1996/207)
LCW	limited capability for work
LCWRA	limited capability for work-related activity
NI	National Insurance

Table of Abbreviations used in this Series

PAYE	Pay As You Earn
PAYE Regulations	Income Tax (Pay As You Earn) Regulations 2003 (SI 2003/2682)
PIP	personal independence payment
Rent Officers Order 2013	Rent Officers (Universal Credit Functions) Order 2013 (SI 2013/382)
SPC	state pension credit
SPCA 2002	State Pension Credit Act 2002
SSA 1998	Social Security Act 1998
SSAA 1992	Social Security Administration Act 1992
SSAC	Social Security Advisory Committee
SSCBA 1992	Social Security Contributions and Benefits Act 1992
State Pension Credit Regulations	State Pension Credit Regulations 2002 (SI 2002/1792)
TCA 2002	Tax Credits Act 2002
Transfer Act	Social Security Contributions (Transfer of Functions, etc.) Act 1999
Transitional Provisions Regulations 2010	Employment and Support Allowance (Transitional Provisions, Housing Benefit and Council Tax Benefit) (Existing Awards) (No.2) Regulations 2010 (SI 2010/1907)
Transitional Provisions Regulations 2013	Universal Credit (Transitional Provisions) Regulations 2013 (SI 2013/386)
Tribunal Procedure Rules	Tribunal Procedure (First-tier Tribunal) (Social Entitlement Chamber) Rules 2008 (SI 2008/2685)
UC	universal credit
UKHL	United Kingdom House of Lords
UKSC	United Kingdom Supreme Court
Universal Credit Regulations	Universal Credit Regulations 2013 (SI 2013/376)
WLR	Weekly Law Reports
WRA 2007	Welfare Reform Act 2007
WRA 2012	Welfare Reform Act 2012
WTC	working tax credit

PART I

INTRODUCTION

Universal Credit—An Introduction

If the information technology on which it depends can be made to work, universal credit ("UC") is destined to become the future of working-age social security in Great Britain. Its introduction is the biggest change to the social security system since the abolition of supplementary benefit and its replacement with income support ("IS") by the Social Security Act 1986.

The problem: complexity and disincentives to work

Readers of Volumes I to IV of this work will require no persuasion that the social security system as a whole is complex. However, the changes since 1996—including the introduction of jobseeker's allowance ("JSA") in October 1996, of the new tax credits in April 2003, and of employment and support allowance ("ESA") in October 2008—have destroyed the previous position of IS as a single benefit for all those poor enough to satisfy the means-test and created a system for claimants of working age (i.e., who have yet to attain the qualifying age for state pension credit ("SPC")) that is more than usually Byzantine.

Before the introduction of UC, people of working age who needed to claim benefit because they were not working (or, though working were not earning enough to meet their basic needs) had to choose from a complex array of benefits some of which complemented each other and others of which were mutually exclusive.

Those who were able to work, but could not find a job, generally had to claim JSA, entitlement to which was either "contribution-based", or "income-based" ("JSA(IB)") which was a euphemism for "means-tested". Those who could not work because they were prevented from doing so by illness or disability claimed ESA, which again could be contributory or "income-related" ("ESA(IR)"). Those who could not be expected to work for other reasons (e.g., because they were caring for a young child or for a disabled person) could claim IS, entitlement to which was based on a means-test and had no contributory component.

The three benefits listed above were administered by the Department for Work and Pensions ("DWP") and included elements to help meet a claimant's housing costs if (broadly speaking) the claimant was an owner-occupier. However, for claimants who rented their homes, help for housing costs was provided by a fourth benefit, housing benefit ("HB") which was administered by local authorities.

Moreover, ESA(IR) and—except in a limited class of transitional cases—JSA(IB), and IS were "adults only" benefits. For claimants whose families included children or "qualifying young persons" (people aged between 16 and 20 who are in education or training) state help for the cost of feeding, clothing and bringing up the child or qualifying young person was provided by HM Revenue & Customs ("HMRC") through two further benefits, child benefit and child tax credit ("CTC").

Finally, for some people who were working more than 16 hours a week (and who were thereby excluded from IS, JSA(IB) and ESA(IR)) there was the possibility of claiming working tax credit ("WTC").

The complexity of that system, in which a claimant with children living in rented property might have to claim four different benefits from three different authorities was further aggravated by the fact that entitlement to tax credits was normally calculated with respect to, and paid over, an entire tax year whereas entitlement to IS, JSA(IB), ESA(IR) and HB was calculated weekly and usually paid fortnightly or, in the case of HB, four-weekly or monthly. It was often difficult to ensure that the two different calculation and payment systems meshed together properly, not least because the mechanisms for sharing information between the DWP, HMRC and local authorities were less than perfect. The whole system operated against the background that a mistake, whether by the claimant or the administering authority, could result in an overpayment, leaving the claimant in debt, often for thousands of pounds.

The old system had the further effect of providing financial disincentives to work at certain levels of income. Under the means-tests for IS, JSA(IB) and ESA(IR) only relatively small amounts of earnings were ignored. Claimants whose earnings exceeded those "disregards" had their benefits reduced penny for penny by the amount of the excess and therefore derived no further benefit from their earnings until they earned enough to lose entitlement to benefit altogether.

This is not the place for a detailed discussion of the poverty trap. An example should suffice to make the point:

During 2013/2014, a single claimant aged over 25 on the basic rate of JSA(IB) receives £71.70 per week. The earnings disregard for such a claimant is £5.00. Suppose she does one hour's work a week at the national minimum wage of £6.31 per hour. The first £5.00 of those earnings is disregarded but her JSA(IB) is reduced by £1.31 (the amount by which £6.31 exceeds £5.00) to £70.39. Her total weekly income is thus £76.70 (£6.31 in earnings plus JSA(IB) of £70.39).

Now, suppose she increases her hours to 12 per week. Her weekly earnings are now £75.72 (£6.31 × 12) but her earnings disregard is still £5.00. Therefore her weekly entitlement to JSA(IB) is reduced by £70.72 (£75.72–£5.00) from £71.70 to £0.98, giving her a total weekly income of £76.70 (£75.72 in earnings plus £0.98 in JSA(IB)). In short, her income remains exactly the same whether she works one hour per week or twelve. It is only once she works 13 hours a week, taking her earnings to £82.03 and losing entitlement to JSA(IB) altogether that she begins to be better off. And at that stage, if she is in rented accommodation, she is likely to lose 65 pence in HB for each additional pound that she earns. She will also lose entitlement to "passported" advantages such as free prescriptions, which will provide a further disincentive to work.

Universal credit and the new system

UC is designed to get rid of both the problems outlined above by simplifying the social security system and ensuring that claimants will always be better off in work.

The planned simplification of the system was meant to be achieved by abolishing six of the seven benefits referred to above (IS, JSA(IB), ESA(IR) HB, CTC and WTC) and replacing them with UC. As UC is administered and paid by the DWP, the effect would be to end the role of local authorities in social security administration and to restrict the role of HMRC to the administration of child benefit and guardian's allowance.

In the new system, child benefit continues unaffected and two new benefits, confusingly called "jobseeker's allowance" and "employment and support allowance"—and colloquially referred to as "new-style" JSA and ESA to distinguish them from the older, identically-named, benefits—will be paid without any means-test, but for limited periods, to those who meet the contribution conditions.

The proposed new structure is undoubtedly simpler than the system it will replace.

Unfortunately, the aim of simplification is currently being frustrated by the decision to phase UC in over a period of years. That decision is entirely understandable, given the new benefit's reliance on information technology. It would be a recipe for disaster for UC to be introduced on a general basis before it had been established in pilot areas that it could be properly administered.

However, the effect of a phased introduction is that the two systems continue to co-exist, so that what has been achieved is not a simplification of the benefits system but a significant complication. During the transition, UC is not a *replacement* benefit but an *additional* benefit. Moreover, it is inherent in the design of UC that it overlaps with each of the older benefits it is eventually intended to replace. That overlap means that, in addition to the complication of the old and new systems existing side-by-side (including having two different and mutually exclusive benefits both called JSA and two called ESA), it is also necessary to have legislation defining which set of rules applies to any particular claimant at any given time. That legislation is to be found first, in the Universal Credit (Transitional Provisions) Regulations ("the Transitional Provisions Regulations") which create a "Pathfinder Group" of claimants who, depending on where they live, may have to claim UC rather than one of the "legacy" benefits and, second, in a series of Commencement Orders that, even by the high standards set by past social security legislation, are bewilderingly complex.

Moreover, the need to devote departmental resources to the introduction of UC appears to have delayed the extension of the housing costs element of SPC to cover rent and other payments made by those who are not owner-occupiers. The effect is that local authorities will need to retain their benefits departments—and incur the associated costs and overheads that might otherwise have been saved—to deal with claims for HB from those who are above working age.

All of that might not matter if the transition from the old system to the new were to be relatively swift. However, at the time of going to press, it does not appear that it will be. At present, only certain single people in designated pilot areas who would otherwise have claimed JSA are able to claim UC. Even working with such a limited group of claimants, whose needs are likely to be relatively straightforward, the systems appear to be struggling. And even assuming (as the DWP appears to do) that the initial problems can be overcome, there is no plan to migrate existing recipients of ESA to the new benefit until 2017.

The slow pace of the transition also means that for the vast majority of existing working age claimants the benefits system continues to be as described in the opening paragraphs of this introduction: they will continue to deal with up to three different authorities and to be subject to disincentives to work from the poverty trap.

That having been said, the new scheme has some positive features:

- The drafting of the legislation has a number of eccentricities. For example, the Regulations appear to use the words "claimant" and "person" in an inconsistent and confusing way that assumes that they are precise synonyms for each other; and it is surprising to find what used to be the permitted work rule for those who have limited capability for work hidden away in a regulation (reg.41) that appears to be about when a work capability assessment may be carried out. However, overall—and with the notable exception of the commencement orders—the legislation is better structured and easier to follow than social security lawyers have become accustomed to. Any benefit that replaces six other benefits is inevitably going to be detailed but, by and large, the Regulations and the Transitional Provisions Regulations are not unnecessarily complex.

- The UC scheme embodies political judgments about what claimants should be required to do for their benefit with which it is possible to disagree. However, with the notable and unfortunate exception of owner-occupiers, many of whom will be substantially worse off as a result of working (see below), progress has been made towards eliminating the poverty trap. If we return to the example given above and assume that, instead of claiming JSA, the claimant had been eligible to claim UC then (assuming that she has housing costs) she would have been entitled to a work disregard of £111 per month or £25.62 per week rather than £5.00 per week. She would keep all of her income until she had worked for 4 hours a week at the minimum wage and, were she to work for 12 hours per week (giving a monthly income of £328.12), her entitlement to UC (ignoring the housing costs element) would have been £170.43. She would therefore have a monthly income of £498.55 which is equivalent to £115.05 per week. This compares favourably with the total weekly income of £76.70 (again ignoring housing benefit) that she would have received on JSA (see above).

The relevant law

The UC scheme is established by Pt 1 of the Welfare Reform Act 2012 ("WRA 2012" or "the Act") and by the Schedules to the Act that are given effect by provisions in Pt 1. As is common in social security law, the Act sets out the structure of the scheme and confers extensive powers on the Secretary of State to make regulations prescribing matters of detail. The main regulations are the Universal Credit Regulations 2013 ("the Universal Credit Regulations" or "the Regulations"), but there are others including the Transitional Provisions Regulations and regulations dealing with claims and payments, and decisions and appeals for UC, personal independence payment ("PIP"), new-style JSA and new-style ESA.

So far as we have been able to identify it, this volume contains all the statute law which directly affects entitlement to UC, including procedural issues. Provisions that relate indirectly to UC, i.e., by amending the rules for other benefits so that the refer to UC will be taken into account in the supplement to Vols. I–IV or, depending on when they come into effect, in the 2014/2015 editions of those volumes.

The structure of universal credit

Any description of the structure of UC will involve at least an implicit decision about the level of detail that should be included. Almost any general proposition about social security law will be subject to qualifications and exceptions. Failing to note those qualifications and exceptions risks giving an unhelpfully approximate explanation of how the structure is meant to work. However, dealing with them in full risks obscuring the view of the wood by concentrating on the trees.

We have the advantage that the detailed rules about UC are dealt with in the annotations to the legislation in Pts II to IV. The purpose of this introduction is to give the big picture. It therefore discusses details only where a particular rule is entirely new, or markedly different from the equivalent rules for existing benefits, or is likely to have important practical effects, or to give rise to disputes. There is never any substitute for looking at the actual words of the legislative text. Until they have checked both that text and the commentary to it, readers should assume that everything in this introduction is subject to unstated exceptions, particularly when such exceptions are implied by the use of words such as "normally" and "usually".

UC is a non-contributory, means-tested, working age, social security benefit. That means that it is not "universal". With very limited exceptions people who are not of working age are excluded from entitlement, as are (with no exceptions) those who do not satisfy the means-test. Moreover, as is the case with all non-contributory benefits, the rules contain residence and presence conditions (including a right to reside test) which exclude those who are felt not have a legitimate connection with Great Britain or who have been absent from the UK for an extended period.

In addition, the fact that UC is a social security benefit means that it is not "credit" in the sense in which that word is used in ordinary speech. UC is a *payment*, made as a matter of legal right to those who meet the conditions of entitlement, not a *loan* to tide claimants over a period of reduced income. With the sole exception of the hardship payments made to those who have been sanctioned, UC that has been correctly paid does not have to be repaid.

Couples

At present, the Pathfinder Group is defined so that only single people can make an initial claim for UC. However, one of the basic principles of the benefit is that it cannot usually be claimed by one member of a couple: WRA 2012 s.2(1) provides that a claim for UC may only be made a single person or by members of a couple jointly. It is implicit that any award of UC made on a joint claim will be a joint award to both members of the couple. The "lobster pot" principle, discussed below, means that there may already be joint awards of UC where someone in the Pathfinder Group has become a member of a couple after his or her initial claim for UC.

The basic conditions

Entitlement to UC depends upon satisfying both the "basic conditions" and the "financial conditions" set out in the Act (WRA 2012, s.3(1)). Where a joint claim is made, those conditions must usually be satisfied by both members of the couple (WRA 2012, s.3(2).

The basic conditions are set out in section 4(1) of the Act. They are that the claimant:

- must be at least 18 years old;
- must not have reached the qualifying age for SPC;
- is in Great Britain;
- is not receiving education; and
- has accepted a claimant commitment.

The last three of those conditions are further defined, or partially defined, in regulations. For example, a person who does not have a right to reside in the UK is treated as not being habitually resident here and hence as not being "in Great Britain": see reg.9 of the Universal Credit Regulations. All of those conditions are subject to exceptions which are specified in regulations. In addition, a person who meets the basic conditions cannot acquire entitlement to UC if he or she falls within the restrictions specified in s.6 of the Act and reg.19 of the Regulations.

It should be noted that it is not a condition of entitlement to UC that any claimant should be, or should not be, in remunerative work. The only way in which work affects UC is through the income that is earned from undertaking it.

The financial conditions

The financial conditions are set out in s.5 of the Act. They are that:

- the claimant's capital (or, for couples, joint capital) is not greater than a prescribed amount (currently fixed at £16,000 by reg.18 of the Regulations); and

- the claimant's income (or, for couples, joint income) is "such that, if the claimant were entitled to universal credit, the amount payable would not be less than any prescribed minimum" (currently fixed at one penny by reg.17 of the Regulations).

As is discussed below, entitlement to UC reduces as a claimant's income increases. The effect of the convoluted wording quoted in the second bullet point above is that if, as a result of that reduction, the amount of UC payable would be less than one penny (i.e., nil), the financial conditions are not satisfied. In other words, one cannot be entitled to UC at a nil rate.

As would be expected, the calculation of a claimant's income and capital are the subject of detailed provisions in the Regulations.

Assessment periods

UC is a monthly benefit. Entitlement is normally assessed by reference to the claimant's circumstances during an "assessment period", which is defined by WRA 2012 s.7(2) and reg.21(1) of the Regulations as "a period of one month beginning with the first date of entitlement and each subsequent period of one month during which entitlement subsists". That entitlement is then normally paid monthly in arrears after the end of the assessment period to which the payment relates (see reg.47 of the Universal Credit, Personal Independence Payment, Jobseeker's Allowance and

Employment And Support Allowance (Claims and Payments) Regulations 2013 ("the Claims and Payments Regulations")).

Calculation of entitlement to universal credit

Under s.8(1) of the Act, the amount of an award of UC is the balance of the "maximum amount" less "the amounts to be deducted".

The amount so calculated will normally be reduced by the "benefit cap" (see below) if the claimant's total entitlement to specified social security benefits would otherwise exceed the amount of the cap.

The maximum amount

The maximum amount is a monthly amount. It is conceptually equivalent to the weekly "applicable amount" used in the calculation of entitlement to IS, JSA(IB) and ESA(IR). It is the total of the standard allowance (equivalent to the personal allowances for IS/JSA/ESA) established by WRA 2012, s.9 and reg.36 of the Regulations, and any of the following amounts to which the claimant is (or the joint claimants are) entitled. The amount of the standard allowance and the various elements are specified in a table that forms part of reg.36 of the Regulations.

The child element

Under WRA 2012, s.10 Universal Credit Regulations, regs 24 and 36, an amount is allowed for each child or qualifying young person for whom a claimant is responsible. An additional amount is allowed for each child or qualifying young person who is entitled to disability living allowance ("DLA") or PIP. The amount is higher if entitlement is to the highest rate of the care component of DLA or the enhanced rate of the daily living component of PIP or if the child or qualifying young person is registered blind.

The housing costs element

The housing costs element is payable under WRA 2012, s.11 and regs 25 and 26 of, and Schs 1–5 to the Universal Credit Regulations. The rules are summarised below, but note in particular that owner occupiers who have any earned income are not entitled to housing costs (see Sch.5, Pt 2, para.4)

The LCW element

This is payable where the claimant has limited capability for work. It is equivalent to the work-related activity component of ESA (see WRA 2012, s.12 and regs.27(1)(a) & 36 of the Regulations).

The LCWRA element

This is payable where the claimant has limited capability for work-related activity. It is equivalent to, but paid at a considerably higher rate than, the support component of ESA (see WRA 2012, s.12 and regs 27(1)(b) and 36 of the Regulations)

The carer element

This is equivalent to, and is paid at the same rate as, the carer premium for IS/JSA/ESA (see WRA 2012, s.12 and regs 29 and 36 of the Regulations).

To qualify, a claimant must satisfy the conditions of entitlement to carer's allowance other than having earnings below the prescribed limit and making a claim for that benefit (see regs 30(1) and (2) of the Universal Credit Regulations.

The childcare costs element

The childcare costs element is 70 per cent of the charges incurred by a claimant for relevant childcare (defined in reg.35 of the Regulations) subject to a maximum of £532.29 pcm for one child or £912.50 pcm for two or more children (regs 34(1) and 36) and also to anti-abuse rules in reg.34(2). To qualify, a claimant must satisfy both the work condition (reg. 32) and the childcare costs condition (reg.33)

The childcare costs element is not subject to the benefits cap (reg.81(1) (b) and (2)).

The amounts to be deducted

Once the maximum amount has been ascertained, it is necessary to calculate the amounts to be deducted from it. By WRA 2012, s.8(3) & reg.22 of the Universal Credit Regulations, those amounts are:

- All the claimant's, or the claimants' combined, *unearned* income.

- 65 per cent of the amount by which the claimant's, or the claimants' combined, *earned* income exceeds the work allowance.

The "work allowance" is what is described in IS/HB/JSA/ESA as an "earnings disregard". The higher work allowance is applicable if the award of UC does not include the housing costs element: otherwise the lower work allowance applies. The higher and lower work allowances are each applied at six different rates which are specified in a table that forms part of reg.22 and depend upon the claimant's other circumstances. However, to further the objective of removing disincentives for work all the rates are (much) higher than the earnings disregards to which claimants would be entitled under IS/HB/JSA/ESA. Claimants therefore keep more of their earned income before their benefit is reduced and, if the figure calculated for earned income in the assessment period does not exceed the applicable work allowance, then no earned income is deducted from the maximum amount. Further, once the reduction starts, claimants only lose 65 per cent of the increase in their income rather than 100 per cent. It is these two features of the UC scheme which account for the marked difference in outcome between working claimants on JSA and those on UC that is highlighted above.

Calculation of income

Earned income

Employees

The treatment of the earned income of employees is another new feature of the UC scheme and one of the areas in which the benefit depends heavily upon the efficient operation of information technology. Most employers are now obliged to submit their PAYE returns to HMRC online and on a monthly basis under the "Real-Time Information" system. The idea is that that PAYE information should then be used to calculate the claimant's entitlement to UC for that month. If the system works, it has the advantage that claimants need not report fluctuations in their earnings (and therefore need not fear having to repay overpayments if they omit to do so). The possibility of treating earned income in this way was the main reason for establishing UC as a monthly, rather than weekly, benefit and for providing that payment should be in arrears after the end of the assessment period.

For those advantages to accrue, the way in which earnings from employment are calculated is different from those for IS/HB/JSA/ESA. First, earnings are to be taken as the actual amount received by the claimant during the assessment period (see reg.54(1)). Then, reg.55 defines "earned income" by reference to the income tax definition. Finally reg.61 provides that where the claimant's employer is a "Real Time Information employer", the information on which the Secretary of State bases his calculation of earned income is to be the information reported by that employer through the PAYE system and the claimant is normally treated as having received those earnings in the same assessment period as the Secretary of State received the information.

The self-employed

The principle in reg.54(1) of the Universal Credit Regulations that earnings are to be taken as the actual amount received by the claimant during the assessment period also applies to self-employed earnings. Under reg.57(2), a person's self-employed earnings in respect of an assessment period are to be calculated by taking that person's "gross profits" (defined by reg.57(3) as "the actual receipts in [the assessment] period less any deductions for expenses allowed under regulation 58 or 59") and then deducting any payments of income tax and Class 2 and 4 national insurance contributions actually made to HMRC in that period and any "relievable pension contributions made" (as defined in s.188 of the Finance Act 2004, i.e., contributions to a registered pension scheme for which tax relief is available). Regulations 58 and 59 establish an exhaustive list of the expenses that can be deducted. In particular, reg.59 provides for flat rate deductions for business mileage and the use of the claimant's home for business purposes.

Self-employed earnings are subject to a "minimum income floor" (see regs 62–64). The minimum income floor is usually an amount representing the person's "individual threshold" (see below) converted to a monthly figure and subjected to a notional deduction to reflect the tax and national insurance contributions payable on that level of self-employed earnings. Except during a start-up period (reg.63), self-employed claimants whose earnings in any assessment period are less than their minimum income floor are treated as having earnings equal to that floor.

Unearned income

Unearned income is deducted from the maximum amount without any disregard or taper. However, in contrast to the rules for IS/JSA/ESA and working-age HB, not all types of unearned income fall within the definition.

Those that do are set out in reg.66 of the Universal Credit Regulations and include:

- retirement pension income;

- certain social security benefits (including "new-style" JSA and ESA);

- spousal maintenance payments;

- student income (e.g., student loans and grants: see reg.68);

- payments under permanent health insurance policies and certain mortgage protection policies;

- income from (non-retirement) annuities and from trusts unless disregarded as compensation for personal injury (regs 75 and 76); and

- income treated as the yield from capital under reg.72 (see below); and

- miscellaneous income that is taxable under Pt 5 of Income Tax (Trading and Other Income) Act 2005.

Unearned income is calculated as a monthly amount but—in contrast to earned income—does not necessarily represent the amount actually received by the claimant in the assessment period for which the award is made. Regualtion 73 contains detailed rules for converting unearned income (other than student income) received in respect of periods other than a month into a monthly equivalent. Student income has its own detailed rules, which are set out in regs 69–71.

Treatment of capital

Capital is relevant to UC entitlement in two ways. First, there is a maximum capital limit of £16,000 for both single and joint claimants (see reg.18 of the Universal Credit Regulations). Claimants who have capital in excess of that limit do not satisfy the first financial condition (see WRA 2012, s.5) and are therefore not entitled to benefit. Second, claimants with capital of more than £6,000 but less than £16,000 are treated as receiving an amount of unearned income equal to an "assumed yield" on that income. Regulation 72 of the Universal Credit Regulations provides that that assumed yield is to be £4.35 per assessment period for each £250 (or part thereof). Readers who are familiar with IS/HB/JSA/ESA will recognise the "tariff income" rule under a different name.

The calculation of capital is governed by regs 45–50. By reg.46(1) and (2), the whole of a claimant's capital (other than his or her personal possessions) is to be taken into account unless it is treated as income under regs 46(3) and (4) or disregarded under reg.48 and Sch.10. The valuation rules closely follow those for IS/HB/JSA/ESA and reg.50 contains a notional capital rule which is similar, though not identical to that for the older working age benefits.

The benefit cap

Awards of UC are subject to the "benefit cap" established by ss.96–97 of the Act and regs 78–83 of the Universal Credit Regulations. This means that, subject to limited exceptions, if an award of UC would lead to the claimant's total entitlement to social security benefits exceeding the level of the cap then the amount of UC that the claimant would otherwise be awarded for the assessment period is reduced by the amount of the excess.

The cap is fixed at £2,167 per assessment period—equivalent to £500 per week—for joint claimants or those responsible for a child or qualifying young person, or £1,517 per assessment period—equivalent to £350 per week—for single claimants who are not responsible for a child or a qualifying young person). However, the childcare costs element of UC is not subject to the cap and the cap does not apply at all if the UC award contains the LCWRA element; if a claimant is receiving certain other benefits including new-style ESA with the support component, industrial injuries disablement benefit and attendance allowance; or if any member of the household is receiving DLA or PIP.

Housing costs

Section 8(2)(c) of the Act provides that the maximum amount is to include "any amount included under s.11 (housing costs)". Section 11(1) says that an award of universal credit must include "an amount in respect of any liability of a claimant to make payments in respect of the accommodation they occupy as their home". By s.11(2), the accommodation must be in Great Britain and must be residential accommodation but need not be self-contained. The remainder of s.11 confers powers for the Secretary of State to make regulations, which have been used to make regs 25 and 26 of, and Schs 1–5 to, the Universal Credit Regulations.

Regulation 25 establishes three conditions for eligibility, the "payment condition", the "liability condition" and the "occupation condition" (see reg.25(5)(b)).

The payment condition (reg.25(1)(a) and (2) is that payments must be rent payments (as defined in Sch.1, paras 2 and 3), owner-occupier payments (Sch.1, paras 4–6) or service charges payments (Sch.1, para.7). The inclusion of rent payments is a major change. Previously help with rent was given through HB which was administered by local authorities rather than the DWP. Many—but not all—of the rules about rental payments are similar to those for HB. A further change from IS/JSA/ESA is that for interest payments to count as an owner-occupier payment, it is only necessary that the loan under which the interest is payable should be "secured on the accommodation in respect of which the claimant meets the occupation condition": there is no requirement that the loan should have been taken out to acquire an interest in the accommodation.

The liability condition (reg.25(1)(b) and (3)) is that the claimant (or either joint claimant) must either be liable to make the payments on a commercial basis, or treated as liable to make the payments (Pt 1 of Sch.2) and must not be treated as not liable to make the payments (Pt 2 of Sch.2).

The occupation condition (reg.25(1)(c) and (4)) is that the claimant must normally be treated as occupying the accommodation as his or her home (Pt 1 of Sch.3) and not be treated as not occupying it (Pt 2 of Sch.3)

The rules for the calculation of the housing costs element are set out in Schs 4 (for renters) and 5 (for owner occupiers).

One notable feature of the latter schedule is that if the claimant (or either joint claimant) is an owner-occupier and either of them has any earned income, no housing costs element is payable (Sch.5, para.4). This is a marked change from the old system (where mortgage interest payments could be paid as part of IS or JSA even if the claimant was working for up to 16 hours a week. The following example shows that this rule has the potential to frustrate the stated policy aim that UC will ensure that claimants will always be better off in work:

> The (joint) claimants are a couple with a young daughter. Neither is in work. The mother is the responsible carer for the daughter. She receives child benefit of £20.30 per week (£88.21 per month). However child benefit is not taken into account as unearned income for UC so their unearned income is nil.
>
> They own their home and have eligible housing costs of £500 per month.
>
> Their universal credit entitlement is £1261.14 as follows:

	£	£
Standard allowance for joint claimants where one is aged over 25	489.06	
Child element	272.08	
Housing costs element	500.00	
Maximum Amount	**£1,261.14**	1,261.14
Less Amounts to be deducted		0.00
Entitlement		**£1,261.14**

Their monthly income is £1,349.35 (UC of £1,261.44 + child benefit of £88.21), which leaves them with £848.35 (or £195.47 per week) once their housing costs have been paid.

Suppose the father starts work for 10 hours a week for the minimum wage, so his earnings are £61.90 per week or £268.97 per month.

As the father now has earned income, the couple are no longer entitled to the housing costs element. However, they do get the benefit of the higher work allowance. For joint claimants responsible for a child, that is £536 per month.

To calculate the father's earned income for the purposes of UC, deduct the work allowance of £536 from the earned income of £268.97. As this is less than nil, the couple's earned income for UC purposes remains nil.

The couple's entitlement to universal credit is now £672.93 as follows

	£	£
Standard allowance for joint claimants where one is aged over 25	489.06	
Child element	272.08	
Housing costs element	0.00	
Maximum Amount	**£761.14**	761.14
Less Amounts to be deducted		0.00
Entitlement		**£761.14**

Their monthly income is £1,118.32 (UC of £761.14 + child benefit of £88.21 + earnings of £268.97), which leaves them with £618.32 (or £142.30 per week) once their housing costs have been paid.

The couple is £53.17 (£195.47–£142.30) per week worse off because the father has started work.

Claimant responsibilities and the claimant commitment

The claimant commitment

Under s.4(1)(e) of the Act, it is a basic condition of entitlement to UC that the claimant "has accepted a claimant commitment". By s.14, a claimant commitment is "a record of a claimant's responsibilities in relation to an award of universal credit" and is to include a record of the requirements that the claimant must comply, any prescribed information, and any other information the Secretary of State considers it appropriate to include. However, the claimant commitment does not itself impose requirements on the claimant and the condition that the clamant should accept it appears to have been included so that there is no doubt about what requirements have, in fact, been imposed. Any failure to comply with a requirement is dealt with by a sanction rather than by ending entitlement to benefit.

Claimant responsibilities

Work-related requirements

Section 13(1) of the Act empowers the Secretary of State "to impose work-related requirements with which claimants must comply". There are four different types of work-related requirement:

- The work-focused interview requirement (WRA 2012, s.15):

  As its name suggests, this is a "requirement that a claimant participate in one or more work-focused interviews as specified by the Secretary of State".

- The work preparation requirement (WRA 2012, s.16):

  This is a "requirement that a claimant take particular action specified by the Secretary of State for the purpose of making it more likely in the opinion of the Secretary of State that the claimant will obtain paid work (or more paid work or better-paid work)". Section 16(3) gives the following examples of actions that the Secretary of State may specify:

    o attending a skills assessment;
    o improving personal presentation;
    o participating in training;
    o participating in an employment programme;
    o undertaking work experience or a work placement;
    o developing a business plan; or
    o any prescribed action.

  In addition any claimant with limited capability for work may also be required to participate in a work-focused health-related assessment.

- Work search requirements (WRA 2012, s.17 and reg.95):

  There are two of these. The first is that a claimant must take all reasonable action for the purpose of obtaining paid work (or more paid work or better-paid work). The second is that he or she must also take any particular action specified by the Secretary of State for that purpose. Section 17(3) gives the following examples of actions that the Secretary of State may specify:

o carrying out work searches;
o making applications;
o creating and maintaining an online profile;
o registering with an employment agency;
o seeking references; or
o any prescribed action.

Under reg.95 claimants are treated as not having complied with the first work search requirement unless they have spent at least the "expected number of hours each week minus any relevant deductions" taking action to obtain paid work unless the Secretary of State is satisfied that the claimant has taken all reasonable action for that purpose despite having spent fewer hours taking action.

Regulation 88 provides that the expected number of hours is 35 per week unless the claimant has caring responsibilities or is physically or mentally impaired and the Secretary of State agrees to a lesser number of hours. Regulation 95(2) specifies that relevant deductions means the total of any time agreed by the Secretary of State for the claimant to carry out paid work, voluntary work, a work preparation requirement, or voluntary work preparation in that week or to deal with temporary childcare responsibilities, a domestic emergency, funeral arrangements or other temporary circumstances.

● Work availability requirements (WRA 2012, s.18 and reg.96):

This is a requirement that the claimant be available for work which is defined as "able and willing immediately to take up paid work (or more paid work or better-paid work)"

The work-related requirements which may be imposed on a claimant depend on which of the following groups the claimant falls into—

● Claimants subject to no work-related requirements (WRA 2012, s.19 and regs 89–90):

These include claimants with limited capability for work and work-related activity; claimants with regular and substantial caring responsibilities for a severely disabled person; claimants who are the responsible carer for a child under the age of 1; claimants who have reached the qualifying age for state pension credit (which is possible for a joint claimant if the other joint claimant has not reached that age); pregnant women within 11 weeks of the expected date of confinement and new mothers within 15 weeks of the birth; recent adopters; and certain claimants in education and foster parents of children under 1.

Claimants also fall within this group if they are in work and their earnings equal or exceed the threshold that applies to them. For most people that threshold will be the amount they would earn if they worked for their expected number of hours (usually 35 per week) at the minimum wage. At current rates, that threshold is £220.85 (£6.31 × 35). Lower thresholds apply to those who would otherwise be subject to the work-focused interview requirement only, or the work preparation requirement only, and apprentices. Couples have a joint threshold that applies to their combined weekly earnings.

- Claimants subject to the work-focused interview requirement only (WRA 2012, s.20 and reg.91):

  This group comprises the responsible carers of children who are aged 1 or more but are under 5 and certain foster parents and others caring for children

- Claimants subject to the work-focused interview and work preparation requirements only (WRA 2012, s.21):

  This group comprises claimants who have limited capability for work, but do not also have limited capability for work-related activity.

- Claimants subject to all work-related requirements (WRA 2012, s.22 and reg.92):

  This group comprises every claimant who is not in any of the other groups. The Secretary of State must impose the work search requirement and the work availability requirement on everyone in this group and may also impose the work-focused interview requirement and a work preparation requirement.

  By reg.92, all EEA jobseekers fall within this group even if they would otherwise fall within one of the other groups. It remains to be seen whether this is compatible with EU law.

Regulation 98 establishes special rules for the victims of domestic violence.

Connected requirements

Under s.23 of the Act, the Secretary of State may also impose a "connected requirement". There are three of these. First, claimants may be required to participate in an interview in connection with a work-related requirement. Second, they may be required to provide evidence to verify that they have complied with work-related requirements that have been imposed on them. Finally, they may be required to report specified changes in their circumstances which are relevant to work-related requirements.

Sanctions

It is not a condition of entitlement to UC that claimants should comply with requirements imposed by the Secretary of State under the provisions summarised above. Instead, compliance is enforced by the imposition of sanctions under which the amount of UC payable is reduced. Under regs 110–111 of the Universal Credit Regulations, the maximum reduction is the amount of the standard allowance applicable to the award of UC for the assessment period that is being considered or, where the sanction has only been imposed on one of two joint claimants, half the amount of that standard allowance.

There are four levels of sanction.

Higher-level sanctions are imposed under s.26 of the Act, which specifies that various actions or omissions by the claimant are to be "sanctionable failures". The definition of each of those failures is technical but, in broad terms, higher-level sanctions apply where, for no good reason, a claimant fails to undertake a work placement or apply for a vacancy when required to do so; fails to take up an offer of paid work; or ceases work or loses pay voluntarily or through misconduct (whether before or after claiming UC). The sanction period is fixed by reg.102 of the Universal Credit Regulations. Again the rules are technical but for adults who commit a sanctionable failure during the currency of a claim, the length of the sanction period depends upon whether there has been a previous sanctionable failure within the period of 365 days before the failure that led to the imposition of the current sanction. If not, then the sanction period is 91 days; if there was one previous sanctionable failure within the period, it is 182 days; and, for a third or subsequent sanctionable failure within the 365 day period it is 1095 days (three years). Shorter periods apply if the claimant was under 18 when the sanctionable failure occurred or in the case of a failure that occurred before the claim for UC. Regulation 102 is subject to reg.113 which specifies a number of circumstances in which a sanctionable failure does not result in a reduction of UC.

Medium-level sanctions, low-level sanctions and lowest-level sanctions are imposed under s.27 of the Act. That section provides that it is to be a sanctionable failure for a claimant to fail, for no good reason, to comply with a work-related requirement or a connected requirement unless that failure would also be a sanctionable failure under s.26, in which case the higher-level sanction applies. The level of sanction that such a failure attracts is prescribed in regs 103–105 and depends upon the work-related requirement with which the claimant has failed to comply:

- A failure to take all reasonable action to obtain paid work in breach of a work search requirement under s.17(1)(a) or a failure to comply with a work availability requirement attracts a *medium-level sanction* under reg.103. The sanction period is 28 days for the first such failure in any 365 day period and 91 days for a second or subsequent failure in that period.

- Regulation 104 provides that *low-level sanctions* apply to claimants who are subject to the work preparation requirement or to all work-related requirements and who have failed to comply with a work-focused interview requirement, a work preparation requirement, or a connected requirement, or failed to take a particular action specified by the Secretary of State to obtain work in breach of a work search requirement. The sanction lasts until 7, 14 or 28 days (depending on the number of previous such failures in the preceding 65 days) after the claimant complies with the requirement, or has a change of circumstances so that he or she is not longer subject to any work-related requirements, or the requirement is withdrawn, or the award of UC ends. Again, the period for 16 and 17 year-olds is shorter.

- *Lowest-level sanctions* are governed by reg.105. They apply to claimants who are subject to the work-focused interview requirement only (i.e., under WRA 2012, s.20) and who fail to comply with that requirement. The sanction continues until the claimant complies with the requirement, or has a change of circumstances so that he or she is not longer subject to any work-related requirements, or the award of UC ends.

Although it is counter-intuitive, a low- or lowest-level sanctions can therefore last longer than a high- or medium-level sanction, if the claimant remains non-compliant.

Regulations 103–105 are subject to reg.113, which specifies a number of circumstances in which a sanctionable failure does not result in a reduction of UC.

When deciding whether there has been a previous sanctionable failure within the 365 day period, failures occurring in the 14 days immediately preceding the failure in question are disregarded (reg.101(4)).

The total of all outstanding sanction periods in relation to a particular claimant, cannot exceed 1095 days (reg.101(3)).

Under reg.109, a sanction terminates (irrespective of the length of the unexpired sanction period) if, since the most recent sanction was imposed, the claimant has been in paid work for 26 weeks (not necessarily consecutive weeks) and during each of those weeks his or her earnings were equal to or more that the applicable threshold (see above).

Regulations provide for the date on which the sanction period is to begin. Where a claimant is subject to more than one sanction, they run consecutively (reg.101(2)).

Where a sanction has been imposed, the Secretary of State must make a hardship payment under WRA 2012, s.28 in the (very limited) circumstances prescribed by regs 115–118. Under reg.119, hardship payments are usually recoverable in accordance with section 71ZH of the Social Security Administration Act 1992.

Transitional issues

UC raises two transitional issues. The first is whether a person making a fresh claim for benefit is free to claim IS/HB/JSA/ESA or whether he or she must now claim UC. The second is in what circumstances existing recipients of IS/HB/JSA/ESA will be moved from those benefits to UC. Although the Act contains powers to migrate existing claimants, no detailed regulations have yet been made and migration will probably not take place until UC has been implemented for all new claimants. This introduction will therefore focus on the first issue.

Claimants may (and must) claim UC rather than IS/JSA/ESA if, at the time their claim is made or treated as made, they reside in one of the "relevant districts" and are either in the Pathfinder Group or have formerly been jointly entitled to UC as a member of a former couple.

The relevant districts are set out in the various commencement orders and their number increases as the pilot is extended to new areas. At the time of going to press, the relevant districts are those covered by the Ashton-under-Lyne, Batch Hammersmith, Harrogate, Inverness, Oldham, Rugby, Warrington and Wigan Jobcentres. Those covered by Shotton Jobcentre will be included from April 7, 2014. (The Bath, Harrogate and Shotton districts were, or will be, brought into the scheme by the Welfare Reform Act 2012 (Commencement No.16 and Transitional and Transitory Provisions) Order

2014 (SI No.209/2014) which was made too recently for its text to be included in Pt IV below.).

Membership of the Pathfinder Group is governed by regs 4–12 of the Transitional Provisions Regulations. The requirements are that claimants must be aged over 18 but less than 60 years and 6 months; be single; be British and have been resident in the UK for a continuous period of two years (ignoring absences of up to four weeks); not be pregnant or have been pregnant within the 15 weeks before the claim, meet a number of criteria about their health including making a declaration that they consider themselves fit to work, not be in receipt of existing benefits and tax credits; make a declaration that they have income of less than £270 (if they are under 25) or £330 pcm (if they are aged 25 or over); have capital below £6,000, not be homeless; not live in supported accommodation; not be a carer; make a declaration that they have no self-employed earnings; not be in education or training; not have anyone else acting on their behalf; have a national insurance number; and have a bank account.

One interesting aspect of the rules is that there does not appear to be any power to require the claimant to give the various declarations referred to even if the facts required to be declared exist. To that extent, membership of the Pathfinder Group seems to be voluntary.

Particularly as the above summary represents a considerable simplification of the rules for membership, it will be clear that Pathfinder Group is a very select club and that many of the rules discussed above (for example those about the LCW and LCWRA elements or about self-employed earnings) will not apply to any UC claimant at the time of the claim.

However, that does not mean that those rules cannot apply at all at present. This is because of what is known colloquially as the "lobster pot" principle. The editors of this volume profess no expertise in catching marine crustaceans, but it is understood that the analogy is to the fact that the route into a lobster pot is a narrow one, but that once inside there is more room and, most importantly, the lobster cannot get back out. The principle applies to UC because the commencement orders are structured so that the provisions of the Act that abolish the benefits to be replaced by UC, come into force in relation to a particular claimant when he or she makes a valid claim for, or is actually awarded UC. From that point on, the claimant cannot go back to the former benefits—because they no longer exist for him or her and must therefore continue to claim UC even if he or she no longer lives in a relevant district or has had a change of circumstances that is incompatible with membership of the Pathfinder Group.

Finally, note that claimants who find themselves disadvantaged by having claimed UC will have limited scope for arguing that, objectively, they did not meet the membership criteria for the Pathfinder Group and that therefore they could not lawfully claim, and the Secretary of State could not lawfully award them, UC. Under reg.13 of the Transitional Provisions Regulations, unless the error is discovered before a payment of UC has been made, the claim is treated as one that the claimant was entitled to make and, the award continues in effect as long as the claimant satisfies the conditions of entitlement.

PART II

UNIVERSAL CREDIT: STATUTES

Social Security Administration Act 1992

(1992 c.5)

PART III

OVERPAYMENTS AND ADJUSTMENTS OF BENEFIT

An Act to consolidate certain enactments relating to the administration of social   1.2
security and related matters with amendments to give effect to recommendations of
the Law Commission and the Scottish Law Commission.

[13th February 1992]

GENERAL NOTE

For the main provisions of this Act ("the SSAA 1992") and extensive commen-   1.3
tary, see Vol.III of this series. This Volume only includes certain of the amendments
made to SSAA 1992 by the WRA 2012, namely the insertion of new ss.71ZB to
71ZF inclusive.

Recovery of benefit payments

[¹ Recovery of overpayments of certain benefits

71ZB.—(1) The Secretary of State may recover any amount of the   1.4
following paid in excess of entitlement—
  (a) universal credit;
  (b) jobseeker's allowance;
  (c) employment and support allowance, *and*
  (d) *except in prescribed circumstances, housing credit (within the meaning of
       the State Pension Credit Act 2002).*
(2) An amount recoverable under this section is recoverable from—
  (a) the person to whom it was paid, or
  (b) such other person (in addition to or instead of the person to whom it
       was paid) as may be prescribed.
(3) An amount paid in pursuance of a determination is not recoverable
under this section unless the determination has been—
  (a) reversed or varied on an appeal, or
  (b) revised or superseded under section 9 or section 10 of the Social
       Security Act 1998,
except where regulations otherwise provide.

(4) Regulations may provide that amounts recoverable under this section are to be calculated or estimated in a prescribed manner.

(5) Where an amount of universal credit is paid for the sole reason that a payment by way of prescribed income is made after the date which is the prescribed date for payment of that income, that amount is for the purposes of this section paid in excess of entitlement.

(6) In the case of a benefit referred to in subsection (1) which is awarded to persons jointly, an amount paid to one of those persons may for the purposes of this section be regarded as paid to the other.

(7) An amount recoverable under this section may (without prejudice to any other means of recovery) be recovered—

    (a) by deduction from benefit (section 71ZC);

    (b) by deduction from earnings (section 71ZD);

    (c) through the courts etc (section 71ZE);

    (d) by adjustment of benefit (section 71ZF).]

AMENDMENT

1.5   1. Welfare Reform Act 2012, s.105(1) (April 29, 2013 for certain purposes, but at a date appointed for remaining purposes).

GENERAL NOTE

1.6   This new section marks a fundamental shift in the law relating to the recovery of overpayments of benefit. It deals (at present only) with the recovery of overpaid universal credit, JSA, ESA and the new housing credit element of state pension credit. However, it is not yet fully in force—see further below. Furthermore, so far as ESA and JSA are concerned, the present effect of the commencement provisions is that the new test applies only to overpayments of the new-style contributory versions of ESA and JSA, introduced as part of the universal credit regime.

The Secretary of State is given the power to recover any amount of Universal Credit, JSA and ESA, which has been paid in excess of entitlement (subs.(1)(a)–(c)). The same principle applies also to housing credit which has been paid in excess of entitlement, except in circumstances that will be prescribed in regulations (subs. (1)(d)). There is no requirement on the Secretary of State to establish either a misrepresentation or failure to disclose as a precondition for recovery. It follows that any payment of one of the relevant benefits in excess of the claimant's appropriate entitlement will be a recoverable overpayment, including those overpayments which arise purely as a result of official error. The underlying philosophy is that even the need for the Department to take responsibility for its own mistakes "does not give people the right to keep taxpayers' money that they are not entitled to" (Explanatory Memorandum to the Social Security (Overpayments and Recovery) Regulations 2013, para.7.2).

The overpaid benefit can be recovered from the person to whom it was paid or such other person as is prescribed (subs.(2); see further Security (Overpayments and Recovery) Regulations 2013 (SI 2013/384), reg.4). There must have been a relevant revision, supersession or appellate decision (subs.(3)). This requirement is broadly equivalent to the existing s.71(5A) of the SSAA 1992. However, note that reg.5 of the Security (Overpayments and Recovery) Regulations 2013 provides that "Section 71ZB(3) of the Act (recoverability of an overpayment dependent on reversal, variation, revision or supersession) does not apply where the circumstances of the overpayment do not provide a basis for the decision pursuant to which the payment was made to be revised under section 9 of the Social Security Act 1998 or superseded under section 10 of that Act."

Subsection (5) has the effect that where another income or benefit that would affect the award of universal credit is paid late, any amount of universal credit, which would not have been paid had the other income or benefit been paid on time, is treated as an overpayment and is recoverable from the universal credit recipient.

Where an award of benefit is made to persons jointly, an amount paid to one member of the couple may be treated as paid to the other and so recovered (subs. (6)).

The various methods of recovery are set out in subs.(7), namely deduction from benefit (s.71ZC), by deduction from earnings (s.71ZD) (a new method akin to attachment of earnings), through the courts (s.71ZE) or by adjustment of subsequent benefit payments (s.71ZF).

Note that this section is not fully in force. Article 5(3)(a) of the Welfare Reform Act 2012 (Commencement No.8 and Savings and Transitional Provisions) Order 2013 (SI 2013/358) provided for the amending s.105(1) of the WRA 2012 to have effect in so far as it was not already in force "except in so far as it inserts section 71ZB(1)(d) of the 1992 Act and the word 'and' immediately preceding it" (the italicised text above). The Commencement No.8 Order was then modified by art.23(3) of the Welfare Reform Act 2012 (Commencement No.9 and Transitional and Transitory Provisions and Commencement No.8 and Savings and Transitional Provisions (Amendment)) Order 2013 (SI 2013/983), which provides that new s.71ZB(1)(b) and (c) "come into force on 29th April 2013 only in so far as they relate respectively to a new style JSA award and a new style ESA award".

1.7

Deduction from benefit

[¹ **71ZC.**—(1) An amount recoverable from a person under section 71ZB may be recovered by deducting the amount from payments of prescribed benefit.

1.8

(2) Where an amount recoverable from a person under section 71ZB was paid to the person on behalf of another, subsection (1) authorises its recovery from the person by deduction—

(a) from prescribed benefits to which the person is entitled;

(b) from prescribed benefits paid to the person to discharge (in whole or in part) an obligation owed to that person by the person on whose behalf the recoverable amount was paid, or

(c) from prescribed benefits paid to the person to discharge (in whole or in part) an obligation owed to that person by any other person.

(3) Where an amount is recovered as mentioned in paragraph (b) of subsection (2), the obligation specified in that paragraph shall in prescribed circumstances be taken to be discharged by the amount of the deduction.

(4) Where an amount is recovered as mentioned in paragraph (c) of subsection (2), the obligation specified in that paragraph shall in all cases be taken to be so discharged.]

AMENDMENT

1. Welfare Reform Act 2012, s.105(1) (July 1, 2012 for the purpose only of prescribing under s.71ZC(1) the benefits from which deductions may be made in order to recover penalties, October 1, 2012 to the extent that it inserts s.71ZC(1) for the purpose only of enabling recovery of the penalties to take place by these methods; and April 29, 2013 for remaining purposes).

GENERAL NOTE

This section provides for the recovery of overpayments under the new s.71ZB by deduction from benefit. Thus overpayments of universal credit, JSA, ESA and the housing credit can be recovered by making deductions from payments of

1.9

prescribed benefits (subs.(1)). Where universal credit, JSA, ESA or the housing credit is paid to a third party (e.g. a landlord) on the claimant's behalf, overpayments of those benefits may be recovered from prescribed benefits to which the third party is entitled; ongoing payments of prescribed benefits to the third party being made on the benefit claimant's behalf; or ongoing payments of prescribed benefits paid to the third party on other benefit claimants' behalf (e.g. if a landlord has other tenants who are in receipt of universal credit or housing credit) (subs.(2)). Furthermore, in circumstances to be prescribed by regulations, where deductions are made from payments of prescribed benefits to the third party on the claimant's behalf, then the claimant's obligations to the third party will be discharged, e.g. the landlord would not be able to put the claimant into arrears with their rent (subs.(3)). Similarly, in all cases where deductions are made from payments of prescribed benefits to the third party on behalf of other benefit claimants, the other claimants' obligations to the third party will likewise be discharged (and so the landlord would not be able to hold those other claimants as being in arrears with their rent) (subs.(4)). See further Social Security (Overpayments and Recovery) Regulations 2013 (SI 2013/384), P5 (regs 10–16) and especially reg.15.

Deduction from earnings

1.10   [^{1} **71ZD**.—(1) Regulations may provide for amounts recoverable under section 71ZB to be recovered by deductions from earnings.

(2) In this section "earnings" has such meaning as may be prescribed.

(3) Regulations under subsection (1) may include provision—

(a) requiring the person from whom an amount is recoverable ("the beneficiary") to disclose details of their employer, and any change of employer, to the Secretary of State;

(b) requiring the employer, on being served with a notice by the Secretary of State, to make deductions from the earnings of the beneficiary and to pay corresponding amounts to the Secretary of State;

(c) as to the matters to be contained in such a notice and the period for which a notice is to have effect;

(d) as to how payment is to be made to the Secretary of State;

(e) as to a level of earnings below which earnings must not be reduced;

(f) allowing the employer, where the employer makes deductions, to deduct a prescribed sum from the beneficiary's earnings in respect of the employer's administrative costs;

(g) requiring the employer to keep records of deductions;

(h) requiring the employer to notify the Secretary of State if the beneficiary is not, or ceases to be, employed by the employer;

(i) creating a criminal offence for non-compliance with the regulations, punishable on summary conviction by a fine not exceeding level 3 on the standard scale;

(j) with respect to the priority as between a requirement to deduct from earnings under this section and—

   (i) any other such requirement;

   (ii) an order under any other enactment relating to England and Wales which requires deduction from the beneficiary's earnings;

   (iii) any diligence against earnings.]

AMENDMENT

1. Welfare Reform Act 2012, s.105(1) (July 1, 2012).

DEFINITION

DEFINITION

"earnings"—see subs.(2).

GENERAL NOTE

Under the previous arrangements, the Secretary of State typically recovered overpayment debts through deductions from ongoing benefit entitlement. However, once a claimant subject to an overpayment liability stopped receiving benefit, further recovery relied heavily on the debtor's compliance with repayment. The DWP estimates that about 350,000 people who are no longer in receipt of benefit owe some £500 million (DWP Impact Assessment, *Direct Earnings Attachment to Recover Overpaid Social Security Benefits*, September 2011, p.7). If a former claimant chose not to pay the money owed, then the Department's only option was to take court action, which was not always cost effective. In principle, however, the Department has always been able to apply to the magistrates' court for an attachment of earnings order as a means of recovering outstanding overpayments. Indeed, in the six months from April 2010, the Department obtained 824 orders under the Attachment of Earnings Act 1971, suggesting an annual case load of about 1,650 such cases (DWP Impact Assessment, p.9).   1.11

This new section for the first time empowers both the Department and local authorities to recover debt by attachment of earnings without the need for an application to court. The new Direct Earnings Attachments (DEA) are thus designed to act as an incentive to those liable for overpayments to make arrangements to repay their debts and, if they still refuse to repay, to provide the Department (or local authority) with a simpler alternative means to secure recovery. See further Social Security (Overpayments and Recovery) Regulations 2013 (SI 2013/384), especially Pt 6 (regs 17–30).These Regulations set out the circumstances in which a DEA can be issued, the type of earnings from which a deduction can be taken, the responsibilities of employers and the relevant rates of deduction where a DEA is in place.

The new DEA system may just be an interim measure. The DWP has also considered the possibility of recovering overpayments from former claimants who are now in employment through the PAYE system (DWP Impact Assessment, pp.6–7). However, this method could not be implemented for some years, presumably for operational or technical reasons as much as anything else. But note in this regard the increased powers for information sharing between the DWP and HMRC (see WRA 2012, s.127).

Court action etc.

[¹ **71ZE.**—(1) Where an amount is recoverable under section 71ZB from a person residing in England and Wales, the amount is, if a county court so orders, recoverable—   1.12

(a) under section 85 of the County Courts Act 1984; or

(b) otherwise as if it were payable under an order of the court.

(2) Where an amount is recoverable under section 71ZB from a person residing in Scotland, the amount recoverable may be enforced as if it were payable under an extract registered decree arbitral bearing a warrant for execution issued by the sheriff court of any sheriffdom in Scotland.

(3) Any costs of the Secretary of State in recovering an amount of benefit under this section may be recovered by him as if they were amounts recoverable under section 71ZB.

(4) In any period after the coming into force of this section and before the coming into force of section 62 of the Tribunals, Courts and Enforcement Act 2007, subsection (1)(a) has effect as if it read "by execution issued from the county court".]

AMENDMENT

1. Welfare Reform Act 2012, s.105(1) (October 1, 2012, for the purpose only of enabling recovery of the penalties to take place by these methods and April 29, 2013 for other purposes).

GENERAL NOTE

1.13   This section provides for the recovery of overpayments under new s.71ZB through the courts. Thus overpayments are recoverable through the county courts for claimants residing in England and Wales (subs.(1)) and through the sheriff courts for those residing in Scotland (subs.(2)). The Secretary of State's normal practice is to try and recover court costs when there is a court judgment in his favour. However, under the previous law there was no mechanism for the Secretary of State to recover such associated costs in the same way as if they formed part of the overpayment debt (e.g. by deduction from benefit or by adjustment of subsequent payments of benefit). Accordingly, subs.(3) allows the Secretary of State to recover costs by the same method as the overpayment itself is recovered.

Adjustment of benefit

1.14   [¹ 71ZF. —Regulations may for the purpose of the recovery of amounts recoverable under section 71ZB make provision—
    (a) for treating any amount paid to a person under an award which it is subsequently determined was not payable—
        (i) as properly paid, or
        (ii) as paid on account of a payment which it is determined should be or should have been made,
and for reducing or withholding arrears payable by virtue of the subsequent determination;
    (b) for treating any amount paid to one person in respect of another as properly paid for any period for which it is not payable in cases where in consequence of a subsequent determination—
        (i) the other person is entitled to a payment for that period, or
        (ii) a third person is entitled in priority to the payee to a payment for that period in respect of the other person,
and by reducing or withholding any arrears payable for that period by virtue of the subsequent determination.]

AMENDMENT

1. Welfare Reform Act 2012, s.105(1) (April 29, 2013).

GENERAL NOTE

1.15   This section concerns the recovery of overpayments under new s.71ZB using the method of adjusting subsequent benefit payments. It provides that the Secretary of State may prescribe in regulations that in certain circumstances, amounts paid but subsequently determined as not payable, can be treated as properly paid and be set against future payments of benefit or against certain payments to third parties.

Social Security Act 1998

(1998 c.14)

An Act to make provision as to the making of decisions and the determination of appeals under enactments relating to social security, child support, vaccine damage payments and war pensions; to make further provision with respect to social security; and for connected purposes.

[21st May 1998]

GENERAL NOTE

For the main provisions of this Act ("the SSA 1998"), see Vol.III of this series.   1.17
This Volume only includes the core provisions in the SSA 1998 which are essential to understanding the structure of decision-making and appeals for universal credit. For detailed commentary on these and other provisions, see Vol.III.

CHAPTER II

SOCIAL SECURITY DECISIONS AND APPEALS

Decisions

Decisions by Secretary of State

8.—(1) Subject to the provisions of this Chapter, it shall be for the   1.18
Secretary of State—
   (a) to decide any claim for a relevant benefit;
   (b) [⁶ ...] [¹ and]
   (c) subject to subsection (5) below, to make any decision that falls to be made under or by virtue of a relevant enactment; [¹ ...]
   (d) [¹ ...]
   (2) Where at any time a claim for a relevant benefit is decided by the Secretary of State—
   (a) the claim shall not be regarded as subsisting after that time; and
   (b) accordingly, the claimant shall not (without making a further claim) be entitled to the benefit on the basis of circumstances not obtaining at that time.

(3) In this Chapter "relevant benefit" [² . . .] means any of the following, namely—
    (a) benefit under Parts II to V of the Contributions and Benefits Act;
[⁸(aa) universal credit;]
    (b) a jobseeker's allowance;
[⁵(ba) an employment and support allowance;]
[⁷(baa) personal independence payment;]
[³(bb) state pension credit;]
    (c) *income support*;
    (d) [⁴ . . .]
    (e) [⁴ . . .]
    (f) a social fund payment mentioned in section 138(1)(a) or (2) of the Contributions and Benefits Act;
    (g) child benefit;
    (h) such other benefit as may be prescribed.
(4) In this section "relevant enactment" means any enactment contained in this Chapter, the Contributions and Benefits Act, the Administration Act, the Social Security (Consequential Provisions) Act 1992 [³, the Jobseekers Act] [⁵, the State Pension Credit Act 2002 [⁸, Part 1 of the Welfare Reform Act 2007, Part 1 of the Welfare Reform Act 2012] [⁷ or Part 4 of that Act]], other than one contained in—
    (a) Part VII of the Contributions and Benefits Act so far as relating to housing benefit and council tax benefit; or
    (b) Part VIII of the Administration Act (arrangements for housing benefit and council tax benefit and related subsidies).
[¹(5) Subsection (1)(c) above does not include any decision which under section 8 of the Social Security Contributions (Transfer of Functions, etc) Act 1999 falls to be made by an officer of the Inland Revenue.]

AMENDMENTS

1.19   1. Social Security Contributions (Transfer of Functions, etc.) Act 1999, s.18 and Sch.7, para.22 (April 1, 1999).
2. Welfare Reform and Pensions Act 1999, s.88 and Sch.13 (April 6, 2000).
3. State Pension Credit Act 2002, s.11 and Sch.1, para.6 (July 2, 2002 for the purpose of exercising any power to make regulations or orders and April 7, 2003 for other purposes).
4. Tax Credits Act 2002, s.60 and Sch.6 (April 8, 2003, subject to a saving in respect of outstanding questions concerning working families' tax credit and disabled person's tax credit—see Tax Credits Act 2002 (Commencement No.4, Transitional Provisions and Savings) Order 2003 (SI 2003/962), art.3(1)–(3)).
5. Welfare Reform Act 2007, s.28(1) and Sch.3, para.17(1)(and (3) (March 18, 2008 for regulation-making purposes and July 27, 2008 for other purposes).
6. Welfare Reform Act 2012, s.147 and Sch.14, Pt 8 (April 1, 2013).
7. Welfare Reform Act 2012, s.91 and Sch.9, paras 37 and 39 (February 25, 2013 for regulation-making purposes and April 8, 2013 for other purposes).
8. Welfare Reform Act 2012, s.31 and Sch.2, paras 43 and 45 (February 25, 2013 for regulation-making purposes and April 29, 2013 for other purposes).

1.20   DEFINITIONS

"the Administration Act"—see SSA 1998, s.84.
"claim"—by virtue of SSA 1998, s.39(2), see SSAA 1992, s.191.
"claimant"—see SSA 1998, s.39(1), and by virtue of SSA 1998, s.39(2), see SSAA 1992, s.191.

"the Contributions and Benefits Act"—see SSA 1998, s.84.
"Inland Revenue"—by virtue of SSA 1998, s.39(2), see SSAA 1992, s.191 but
   note that the Inland Revenue has been merged into HMRC (Her Majesty's
   Revenue and Customs) by the Commissioners for Revenue and Customs Act
   2005.
"the Jobseekers Act"—see SSA 1998, s.84.
"prescribed"–*ibid.*
"relevant benefit"—see subs.(3).
"relevant enactment"—see subs.(4).

Revision of decisions

9.—(1) [¹ ...] Any decision of the Secretary of State under section 8   1.21
above or section 10 below may be revised by the Secretary of State—
   (a) either within the prescribed period or in prescribed cases or circum-
      stances; and
   (b) either on an application made for the purpose or on his own initia-
      tive;
and regulations may prescribe the procedure by which a decision of the
Secretary of State may be so revised.

(2) In making a decision under subsection (1) above, the Secretary of
State need not consider any issue that is not raised by the application or, as
the case may be, did not cause him to act on his own initiative.

(3) Subject to subsections (4) and (5) and section 27 below, a revision
under this section shall take effect as from the date on which the original
decision took (or was to take) effect.

(4) Regulations may provide that, in prescribed cases or circumstances, a
revision under this section shall take effect as from such other date as may
be prescribed.

(5) Where a decision is revised under this section, for the purpose of any
rule as to the time allowed for bringing an appeal, the decision shall be
regarded as made on the date on which it is so revised.

(6) Except in prescribed circumstances, an appeal against a decision of
the Secretary of State shall lapse if the decision is revised under this section
before the appeal is determined.

AMENDMENT

1. Welfare Reform Act 2012, s.147 and Sch.14, Pt 8 (April 1, 2013).

DEFINITION

"prescribed"—see SSA 1998, s.84.

Decisions superseding earlier decisions

10.—(1) Subject to [¹ subsection (3)] [⁴ ...] below, the following,   1.22
namely—
   (a) any decision of the Secretary of State under section 8 above or this
      section, whether as originally made or as revised under section 9
      above; [³ ...]
[³(aa) any decision under this Chapter of an appeal tribunal or a
      Commissioner; and]
   (b) any decision under this Chapter [² of the First-tier Tribunal or any
      decision of the Upper Tribunal which relates to any such decision],

may be superseded by a decision made by the Secretary of State, either on an application made for the purpose or on his own initiative.

(2) In making a decision under subsection (1) above, the Secretary of State need not consider any issue that is not raised by the application or, as the case may be, did not cause him to act on his own initiative.

(3) Regulations may prescribe the cases and circumstances in which, and the procedure by which, a decision may be made under this section.

(4) [¹ . . .]

(5) Subject to subsection (6) and section 27 below, a decision under this section shall take effect as from the date on which it is made or, where applicable, the date on which the application was made.

(6) Regulations may provide that, in prescribed cases or circumstances, a decision under this section shall take effect as from such other date as may be prescribed.

[³ (7) In this section—

"appeal tribunal" means an appeal tribunal constituted under Chapter 1 of this Part (the functions of which have been transferred to the First-tier Tribunal);

"Commissioner" means a person appointed as a Social Security Commissioner under Schedule 4 (the functions of whom have been transferred to the Upper Tribunal), and includes a tribunal of such persons.]

AMENDMENTS

1. Social Security Contributions (Transfer of Functions, etc.) Act 1999, s.18 and Sch.7, para.23 (April 1, 1999).
2. Transfer of Functions Order 2008 (SI 2008/2833), art.6 and Sch.3, paras 14 and 148 (November 3, 2008).
3. Welfare Reform Act 2012, s.103 and Sch.12, para.4 (check date, 2013).
4. Welfare Reform Act 2012, s.147 and Sch.14, Pt 8 (April 1, 2013).

DEFINITIONS

"appeal tribunal"—see subs.(7).
"Commissioner"—*ibid.*
"prescribed"—SSA 1998, s.84.

Appeals

Appeal to [² First-tier Tribunal]

12.—(1) This section applies to any decision of the Secretary of State under section 8 or 10 above (whether as originally made or as revised under section 9 above) which—

(a) is made on a claim for, or on an award of, a relevant benefit, and does not fall within Schedule 2 to this Act; [¹ or]

(b) is made otherwise than on such a claim or award, and falls within Schedule 3 to this Act; [¹ . . .]

(c) [¹ . . .]

[¹ (2) In the case of a decision to which this section applies, the claimant and such other person as may be prescribed shall have a right to appeal to [² the First-tier Tribunal], but nothing in this subsection shall confer a right of appeal—

[³(a)] in relation to a prescribed decision, or a prescribed determination embodied in or necessary to a decision;

(b) where regulations under subsection (3A) so provide.]]

(3) Regulations under subsection (2) above shall not prescribe any decision or determination that relates to the conditions of entitlement to a relevant benefit for which a claim has been validly made or for which no claim is required.

[³(3A) Regulations may provide that, in such cases or circumstances as may be prescribed, there is a right of appeal under subsection (2) in relation to a decision only if the Secretary of State has considered whether to revise the decision under section 9.

(3B) The regulations may in particular provide that that condition is met only where—

(a) the consideration by the Secretary of State was on an application;

(b) the Secretary of State considered issues of a specified description, or

(c) the consideration by the Secretary of State satisfied any other condition specified in the regulations.

(3C) The references in subsections (3A) and (3B) to regulations and to the Secretary of State are subject to any enactment under or by virtue of which the functions under this Chapter are transferred to or otherwise made exercisable by a person other than the Secretary of State.]

(4) Where the Secretary of State has determined that any amount is recoverable under or by virtue of section 71[⁴, 71ZB, 71ZG, 71ZH,] or 74 of the Administration Act, any person from whom he has determined that it is recoverable shall have the same right of appeal to [² the First-tier Tribunal] as a claimant.

(5) In any case where—

(a) the Secretary of State has made a decision in relation to a claim under Part V of the Contributions and Benefits Act; and

(b) the entitlement to benefit under that Part of that Act of any person other than the claimant is or may be, under Part VI of Schedule 7 to that Act, affected by that decision,

that other person shall have the same right of appeal to [² the First-tier Tribunal] as the claimant.

(6) A person with a right of appeal under this section shall be given such notice of a decision to which this section applies and of that right as may be prescribed.

(7) Regulations may—

[³(a)] make provision as to the manner in which, and the time within which, appeals are to be brought;

[(b) provide that, where in accordance with regulations under subsection (3A) there is no right of appeal against a decision, any purported appeal may be treated as an application for revision under section 9].

(8) In deciding an appeal under this section, [² the First-tier Tribunal]—

(a) need not consider any issue that is not raised by the appeal; and

(b) shall not take into account any circumstances not obtaining at the time when the decision appealed against was made.

(9) The reference in subsection (1) above to a decision under section 10 above is a reference to a decision superseding any such decision as is mentioned in paragraph (a) or (b) of subsection (1) of that section.

AMENDMENTS

1. Social Security Contributions (Transfer of Functions, etc.) Act 1999, s.18 and Sch.7, para.25 (April 1, 1999).
2. Transfer of Functions Order 2008 (SI 2008/2833), art.6 and Sch.3, paras 143 and 149 (November 3, 2008).
3. Welfare Reform Act 2012, s.102(1)–(4) (February 25, 2013).
4. Welfare Reform Act 2012, s.105(6) (April 29, 2013).

DEFINITIONS

"the Administration Act"—see SSA 1998, s.84.
"claim"—by virtue of SSA 1998, s.39(2), see SSAA 1992, s.191.
"claimant"—see SSA 1998, s.39(1), and by virtue of SSA 1998, s.39(2), see SSAA 1992, s.191.
"the Contributions and Benefits Act"—see SSA 1998, s.84.
"prescribed"—*ibid*.
"relevant benefit"—see s.8(3).

Finality of decisions

1.23   **17.**—(1) Subject to the provisions of this Chapter [¹ and to any provision made by or under Chapter 2 of Part 1 of the Tribunals, Courts and Enforcement Act 2007], any decision made in accordance with the foregoing provisions of this Chapter shall be final; and subject to the provisions of any regulations under section 11 above, any decision made in accordance with those regulations shall be final.

(2) If and to the extent that regulations so provide, any finding of fact or other determination embodied in or necessary to such a decision, or on which such a decision is based, shall be conclusive for the purposes of—

(a) further such decisions;
(b) decisions made under the Child Support Act; and
(c) decisions made under the Vaccine Damage Payments Act.

AMENDMENT

1. Transfer of Functions Order 2008 (SI 2008/2833), art.6 and Sch.3, paras 143 and 155 (November 3, 2008).

DEFINITIONS

"the Child Support Act"—see SSA 1998, s.84.
"the Vaccine Damage Act"—*ibid*.

Section 12(1)

SCHEDULE 2

DECISIONS AGAINST WHICH NO APPEAL LIES

Jobseeker's allowance for persons under 18

1.24   1. In relation to a person who has reached the age of 16 but not the age of 18, a decision—
(a) whether section 16 of the Jobseekers Act is to apply to him; or
(b) whether to issue a certificate under section 17(4) of that Act.

Christmas bonus

2. A decision whether a person is entitled to payment under section 148 of the Contributions and Benefits Act.

Priority between persons entitled to [³ carer's allowance]

3. A decision as to the exercise of the discretion under section 70(7) of the Contributions and Benefits Act.

Priority between persons entitled to child benefit

4. A decision as to the exercise of the discretion under paragraph 5 of Schedule 10 to the Contributions and Benefits Act.

Persons treated as if present in Great Britain

5. A decision whether to certify, in accordance with regulations made under section 64(1), 71(6), 113(1) or 119 of the Contributions and Benefits Act, that it is consistent with the proper administration of that Act to treat a person as though he were present in Great Britain.

[¹ Work-focused interviews

5A. A decision terminating or reducing the amount of a person's benefit made in consequence of any decision made under regulations under section 2A [⁴ or 2AA] of the Administration Act (work-focused interviews).]

Alteration of rates of benefit

6. A decision as to the amount of benefit to which a person is entitled, where it appears to the Secretary of State that the amount is determined by—
  (a) the rate of benefit provided for by law; or
  (b) an alteration of a kind referred to in—
      (i) section 159(1)(b) of the Administration Act (income support); [² ...]
     (ii) section 159A(1)(b) of that Act (jobseeker's allowance)[;²
    (iii) section 159B(1)(b) of that Act (state pension credit)]][⁵;
    (iv) section 159C(1)(b) of that Act (employment and support allowance)][⁷; or
     (v) section 159D(1)(b) of that Act (universal credit)].

Increases in income support due to attainment of particular ages

7. A decision as to the amount of benefit to which a person is entitled, where it appears to the Secretary of State that the amount is determined by the recipient's entitlement to an increased amount of income support or income-based jobseeker's allowance in the circumstances referred to in section 160(2) or 160A(2) of the Administration Act.

[⁸ Increases in universal credit due to attainment of particular ages

7A. *A decision as to the amount of benefit to which a person is entitled, where it appears to the Secretary of State that the amount is determined by the recipient's entitlement to an increased amount of universal credit in the circumstances referred to in section 160C(2) of the Administration Act.]*

Reduction in accordance with reduced benefit decision

8. A decision to reduce the amount of a person's benefit in accordance with a reduced benefit decision (within the meaning of section 46 of the Child Support Act).

[⁶ Reduction on application of benefit cap

8A. A decision to apply the benefit cap in accordance with regulations under section 96 of the Welfare Reform Act 2012.]

Power to prescribe other decisions

9. Such other decisions as may be prescribed.

AMENDMENTS

1. Welfare Reform and Pensions Act 1999, s.81 and Sch.11, para.87 (November 11, 1999).
2. State Pension Credit Act 2002, s.11 and Sch.1, para.11 (July 2, 2002 for the purpose of exercising any power to make regulations or orders and October 6, 2003 for all other purposes).

3. Regulatory Reform (Carer's Allowance) Order 2002 (SI 2002/1457), art.2(1) and Sch., para.3(b) September 2002 for the purposes of exercising powers to make subordinate legislation and October 28, 2002 for all other purposes).

4. Employment Act 2002. s.53 and Sch.7, para.51 (July 5, 2003).

5. Welfare Reform Act 2007, Sch.3, para.17(1) and (8) (October 27, 2008).

6. Welfare Reform Act 2012, s.97(6) (April 15, 2013).

7. Welfare Reform Act 2012, s.31, Sch.2, paras 43, 50(1), (2) (April 29, 2013).

8. *Welfare Reform Act 2012, s.31, Sch.2, paras 43, 50(1), (3) (not yet in force).*

DEFINITIONS

"the Administration Act"—see SSA 1998, s.84.
"benefit"—see SSA 1998, s.39(1), and by virtue of SSA 1998, s.39(2), see SSAA 1992, s.191.
"the Child Support Act"—see SSA 1998, s.84.
"the Contributions and Benefits Act"—*ibid.*
"the Jobseekers Act"—*ibid.*
"prescribed"—*ibid.*

Section 12(1)

SCHEDULE 3

DECISIONS AGAINST WHICH AN APPEAL LIES

PART I

BENEFIT DECISIONS

Entitlement to benefit without a claim

1.25   1. In such cases or circumstances as may be prescribed, a decision whether a person is entitled to a relevant benefit for which no claim is required.

2. If so, a decision as to the amount to which he is entitled.

Payability of benefit

3. A decision whether a relevant benefit (or a component of a relevant benefit) to which a person is entitled is not payable by reason of—
(a) any provision of the Contributions and Benefits Act by which the person is disqualified for receiving benefit;
(b) regulations made under section 72(8) of that Act (disability living allowance);
(c) regulations made under section 113(2) of that Act (suspension of payment);
(d) [8 ...]
[5 (da) [8 ...]]
[1 (e) [6 ...] [2 or
(f) section [7 6B,] 7, 8 or 9 of the Social Security Fraud Act 2001][4; [10 ...]
(g) section 18 of the Welfare Reform Act 2007];
[10 (h) regulations made under section 85(1) or 86(1) of the Welfare Reform Act 2012; or
(i) section 87 of that Act].
[9 3A. A decision as to the amount of a relevant benefit that is payable to a person by virtue of regulations under section 6B, 7, 8 or 9 of the Social Security Fraud Act 2001.]

Payments to third parties

4. Except in such cases or circumstances as may be prescribed, a decision whether the whole or part of a benefit to which a person is entitled is, by virtue of regulations, to be paid to a person other than him.

Recovery of benefits

5. A decision whether payment is recoverable under section 71 *or 71A* of the Administration Act.

6. If so, a decision as to the amount of payment recoverable.

[[11]**6A.** *A decision as to whether payment of housing credit (within the meaning of the State Pension Credit Act 2002) is recoverable under section 71ZB of the Administration Act.*]

[10]**6B.** A decision as to the amount of payment recoverable under section 71ZB, 71ZG or 71ZH of the Administration Act.]

Industrial injuries benefit

7. A decision whether an accident was an industrial accident for the purposes of industrial injuries benefit.

Jobseekers' agreements

8. A decision in relation to a jobseeker's agreement as proposed to be made under section 9 of the Jobseekers Act, or as proposed to be varied under section 10 of that Act.

[[5]*State Pension Credit*

8A. A decision whether to specify a period as an assessed income period under section 6 of the State Pension Credit Act 2002.

8B. If so, a decision as to the period to be so specified.

8C. A decision whether an assessed income period comes to an end by virtue of section 9(4) or (5) of that Act.

8D. If so, a decision as to when the assessed income period so ends.]

Power to prescribe other decisions

9. Such other decisions relating to a relevant benefit as may be prescribed.

PART II

CONTRIBUTIONS DECISIONS

10.–15. *[Omitted].*

Responsibilities at home

16. A decision whether a person was (within the meaning of regulations) precluded from regular employment by responsibilities at home.

1.26

Earnings and contributions credits

17. A decision whether a person is entitled to be credited with earnings or contributions in accordance with regulations made under section 22(5) of the Contributions and Benefits Act.

18.–29. *[Omitted].*

AMENDMENTS

1. Child Support, Pensions and Social Security Act 2000, s.66 and Sch.9, Pt V (October 15, 2001).
2. Social Security Fraud Act 2001, s.12(2) (April 1 2002).
3. State Pension Credit Act 2002, Sch.1, para.12 (July 2, 2002 for the purpose of exercising any power to make regulations or orders and October 6, 2003 for other purposes).
4. Welfare Reform Act 2007, Sch.3, para.17(1) and (9) (October 27, 2008).
5. Welfare Reform Act 2009, s.1(4) and Sch.3, para.4 (November 12, 2009).
6. Welfare Reform Act 2009, Sch.7 (March 22, 2010).
7. Welfare Reform Act 2009, Sch.4, para.10 (April 1, 2010).
8. Welfare Reform Act 2012, s.46(4) (October 22, 2012).
9. Welfare Reform Act 2012, s.31 and Sch.2, paras 43 and 51 (April 1, 2013).
10. Welfare Reform Act 2012, s.91 and Sch.9, paras 37 and 43 (April 8, 2013).
11. Welfare Reform Act 2012, s.105(7) (April 29, 2013).
12. Welfare Reform Act 2012, s.105(7) (not yet in force).

Definitions

"the Administration Act"—see SSA 1998, s.84.
"benefit"—see SSA 1998, s.39(1), and by virtue of SSA 1998, s.39(2), see SSAA 1992, s.191.
"claim"—*ibid.*
"the Child Support Act"—see SSA 1998, s.84.
"the Contributions and Benefits Act"—*ibid.*
"industrial injuries benefit"—see SSA 1998, s.39(1), and by virtue of SSA 1998, s.39(2), see SSAA 1992, s.191.
"the Jobseekers Act"—see SSA 1998, s.84.
"prescribed"—*ibid.*
"relevant benefit"—see SSA 1998, s.8(3).

Welfare Reform Act 2012

(2012 c.5)

Arrangement of Sections

Part 1

Universal Credit

Chapter 1

Entitlement and Awards

Introductory

Entitlement

Awards

Elements of an award

CHAPTER 3

SUPPLEMENTARY AND GENERAL

Supplementary and consequential

1.28

Universal credit and other benefits

PART 5

SOCIAL SECURITY: GENERAL

Benefit cap

PART 7

FINAL

SCHEDULES

An Act to make provision for universal credit and personal independence payment; to make other provision about social security and tax credits; to make provision about the functions of the registration service, child support maintenance and the use of jobcentres; to establish the Social Mobility and Child Poverty Commission and otherwise amend the Child Poverty Act 2010; and for connected purposes.

[8th March 2012]

PART 1

UNIVERSAL CREDIT

CHAPTER 1

ENTITLEMENT AND AWARDS

Introductory

Universal credit

1.31

1.—(1) A benefit known as universal credit is payable in accordance with this Part.

(2) Universal credit may, subject as follows, be awarded to—

(a) an individual who is not a member of a couple (a "single person"), or

(b) members of a couple jointly.

(3) An award of universal credit is, subject as follows, calculated by reference to—

(a) a standard allowance;

(b) an amount for responsibility for children or young persons;

(c) an amount for housing; and

(d) amounts for other particular needs or circumstances.

DEFINITIONS

"child"—see s.40.
"couple"—see ss.39 and 40.

GENERAL NOTE

Part 1 of the Welfare Reform Act 2012 ("WRA 2012") contains the provisions and confers regulation-making powers in relation to universal credit. Universal credit is to be the new means-tested, non-contributory benefit for people of working age. It will replace income support, income-based jobseeker's allowance (JSA), income-related employment and support allowance (ESA), housing benefit, working tax credit and child tax credit. Thus it will be paid to people both in and out of work. State pension credit will continue for people who are over the qualifying age for state pension credit (this is gradually rising in line with the staged increase in pensionable age for women until it reaches 65 in November 2018 and will increase to 66 by October 2020)—see s.4(4), which applies the definition of "the qualifying

1.32

41

age" for state pension credit in s.1(6) of the State Pension Credit Act 2002 (see Vol. II in this series) for the purposes of universal credit. ESA and JSA will also continue but as contributory benefits only.

Note that "a person who is subject to immigration control" is not entitled to universal credit (Immigration and Asylum Act 1999, s.115, as amended by WRA 2012, Sch.2, para.54 with effect from April 29, 2013).

Initially universal credit is being introduced only for people in the "pathfinder group" and only on an extremely limited geographical basis—see the Universal Credit (Transitional Provisions) Regulations 2013 (SI 2013/386) and the various Commencement Orders in relation to universal credit in Part IV of this Volume.

As usual, Part 1 creates the legislative framework and the detail is to be found in the Universal Credit Regulations 2013 (SI 2013/376)—on which see Pt III of this Volume.

Subs. (2)

1.33   This provides that in the case of a couple awards are to be made to the couple jointly. Note the definition of "claimant" in reg.40, which states that "claimant" in Pt 1 of the Act means "a single claimant or each of joint claimants".

Subs. (3)

1.34   Depending on the claimant's (or claimants') circumstances, an award of universal credit will include a standard allowance (see s.9 and reg.36 of the Universal Credit Regulations), an amount for children and young persons for whom the claimant is responsible (see s.10 and regs 24 and 36 of the Universal Credit Regulations), housing costs (see s.11 and regs 25–26 of, and Schs 1–5 to, the Universal Credit Regulations) and an amount for "other particular needs or circumstances" (see s.12 and regs 23(2) and 27–35 of, and Schs 6-9 to, the Universal Credit Regulations). Note that although subs.(3)(b) refers to an amount for children and young persons, in the case of the latter, s.10 restricts this to "qualifying young persons". For who counts as a "qualifying young person" see s.40 and reg.5 of the Universal Credit Regulations.

Claims

1.35   **2.**—(1) A claim may be made for universal credit by—

(a) a single person; or

(b) members of a couple jointly.

(2) Regulations may specify circumstances in which a member of a couple may make a claim as a single person.

DEFINITIONS

"claim"—see s.40.
"couple"—see ss.39 and 40.
"single person"—see s.40.

GENERAL NOTE

1.36   In the case of a couple, claims for universal credit are to be made jointly. This does not apply in prescribed circumstances (subs.(2)). On subs.(2), see reg.3(3) of the Universal Credit Regulations.

For the rules for claims for universal credit see the Universal Credit, Personal Independence Payment, Jobseeker's Allowance and Employment and Support Allowance (Claims and Payments) Regulations 2013 (SI 2013/380) in Part V of this Volume. Generally a claim for universal credit has to be made online. Note reg.6 (claims not required for entitlement to universal credit in certain cases).

Entitlement

Entitlement

3.—(1) A single claimant is entitled to universal credit if the claimant meets—   1.37

(a) the basic conditions; and

(b) the financial conditions for a single claimant.

(2) Joint claimants are jointly entitled to universal credit if—

(a) each of them meets the basic conditions; and

(b) they meet the financial conditions for joint claimants.

DEFINITIONS

"claim"—see s.40.
"claimant"—*ibid.*
"joint claimants"—*ibid.*
"single claimant"—*ibid.*

GENERAL NOTE

This sets out the general conditions of entitlement to universal credit. A single   1.38
claimant has to meet all of the basic conditions (see s.4) and the financial conditions
(i.e., the means-test) (see s.5). In the case of joint claimants, both of them have to
meet all of the basic and the financial conditions. Note, however, s.4(2) which allows
for regulations to provide for exceptions from any of these conditions, either in the
case of a single claimant, or one or both joint claimants.

Basic conditions

4.—(1) For the purposes of section 3, a person meets the basic conditions   1.39
who—

(a) is at least 18 years old;

(b) has not reached the qualifying age for state pension credit;

(c) is in Great Britain;

(d) is not receiving education; and

(e) has accepted a claimant commitment.

(2) Regulations may provide for exceptions to the requirement to meet
any of the basic conditions (and, for joint claimants, may provide for an
exception for one or both).

(3) For the basic condition in subsection (1)(a) regulations may specify a
different minimum age for prescribed cases.

(4) For the basic condition in subsection (1)(b), the qualifying age for
state pension credit is that referred to in section 1(6) of the State Pension
Credit Act 2002.

(5) For the basic condition in subsection (1)(c) regulations may—

(a) specify circumstances in which a person is to be treated as being or
not being in Great Britain;

(b) specify circumstances in which temporary absence from Great
Britain is disregarded.

(c) modify the application of this Part in relation to a person not in
Great Britain who is by virtue of paragraph (b) entitled to universal
credit.

(6) For the basic condition in subsection (1)(d) regulations may—

    (a) specify what "receiving education" means;

    (b) specify circumstances in which a person is to be treated as receiving or not receiving education.

(7) For the basic condition in subsection (1)(e) regulations may specify circumstances in which a person is to be treated as having accepted or not accepted a claimant commitment.

DEFINITIONS

    "claim"—see s.40.
    "claimant"—*ibid.*
    "joint claimants"—*ibid.*

GENERAL NOTE

1.40   Subsection (1) lists the basic conditions that have to be satisfied for entitlement to universal credit. Subs.(2) allows for regulations to provide for exceptions from any of these conditions, either in the case of a single claimant, or one or both joint claimants.

Subs.(1)(a)

1.41   The minimum age for entitlement to universal credit is generally 18. However, under subs.(3) regulations can provide for a lower age in certain cases. See reg.8 of the Universal Credit Regulations for the cases where the minimum age is 16.

Subs.(1)(b)

1.42   This subsection excludes the possibility that a person could be entitled to both state pension credit and universal credit by providing that no person who has reached "the qualifying age for state pension credit" will meet the basic conditions for universal credit. But note subs.(2) and see reg.3(2) of the Universal Credit Regulations. The effect of reg.3(2) is that a couple may still be entitled to universal credit even if one member is over the qualifying age for state pension credit, provided that the other member of the couple is under that age.

    Subsection (4) applies the definition of "the qualifying age" for state pension credit in s.1(6) of the State Pension Credit Act 2002 (see Vol.II in this series) for the purposes of universal credit. The effect of that definition is that the qualifying age for state pension credit for both men and women is the pensionable age for women (this was 60 but since April 2010 has been gradually rising and will reach 65 in November 2018).

Subs.(1)(c)

1.43   It is a basic condition of entitlement to universal credit that the person is in Great Britain. Note subs.(5) under which regulations may treat a person as being or not being in Great Britain (see reg.9 of the Universal Credit Regulations for when a person is treated as not being in Great Britain, and reg.10 on Crown servants and armed forces) and provide for the circumstances in which temporary absence from Great Britain is ignored (see reg.11).

Subs.(1)(d)

1.44   A person must not be "receiving education" to be eligible for universal credit. For the regulations made under subs.(6) see regs 12–14 of the Universal Credit Regulations.

Subs.(1)(e)

1.45   The concept of a claimant commitment as a condition of receiving benefit is an important part of the underlying policy behind the Government's welfare benefit reforms. Under subs.(7) regulations may specify the circumstances in which a person can be treated as having accepted or not accepted a claimant commitment—see regs 15–16 of the Universal Credit Regulations.

Financial conditions

5.—(1) For the purposes of section 3, the financial conditions for a single claimant are that—   **1.46**

  (a) the claimant's capital, or a prescribed part of it, is not greater than a prescribed amount, and

  (b) the claimant's income is such that, if the claimant were entitled to universal credit, the amount payable would not be less than any prescribed minimum.

(2) For those purposes, the financial conditions for joint claimants are that—

  (a) their combined capital, or a prescribed part of it, is not greater than a prescribed amount, and

  (b) their combined income is such that, if they were entitled to universal credit, the amount payable would not be less than any prescribed minimum.

DEFINITIONS

  "claim"—see s.40.
  "claimant"—*ibid.*
  "joint claimants"—*ibid.*
  "prescribed"—*ibid.*
  "single claimant"—*ibid.*

GENERAL NOTE

This section contains the means-test for universal credit. Both the capital and the income condition have to be met. For joint claimants it is their combined capital and their combined income that counts (subs.(2)).   **1.47**

Capital

The capital limit for universal credit for both a single claimant and joint claimants is £16,000 (see reg.18(1) of the Universal Credit Regulations). Note that where a claimant who is a member of a couple makes a claim as a single person (see reg.3(3) of the Universal Credit Regulations for the circumstances in which this may occur) the capital of the other member of the couple counts as the claimant's (reg.18(2)).   **1.48**

Thus the capital limit for universal credit is the same as for income support, income-based JSA, income-related ESA and housing benefit. There is no capital limit for working tax credit and child tax credit. See further the notes to s.134(1) SSCBA 1992 in Vol. II of this series.

For the rules on calculating capital see regs 45–50 and 75–77 of, and Sch 10 to, the Universal Credit Regulations.

Income

The effect of subs.(1)(b) in the case of a single claimant and subs.(2)(b) in the case of joint claimants is that there will be no entitlement to universal credit if the amount payable is less than the minimum amount. The minimum amount is 1p (see reg.17 of the Universal Credit Regulations and note reg.6(1) on rounding). Thus it is possible for a person to be entitled to universal credit of 1p.   **1.49**

Note that where a claimant who is a member of a couple makes a claim as a single person (see reg.3(3) of the Universal Credit Regulations for the circumstances in which this may occur) the combined income of the couple is taken into account when calculating an award (reg.22(3)(a)).

Any income of a child is not taken into account.

See also the regulation-making powers as regards the calculation of capital and income in para.4 of Sch.1.

Restrictions on entitlement

1.50
6.—(1) Entitlement to universal credit does not arise—

(a) in prescribed circumstances (even though the requirements in section 3 are met);

(b) if the requirements in section 3 are met for a period shorter than a prescribed period.

(c) for a prescribed period at the beginning of a period during which those requirements are met.

(2) A period prescribed under subsection (1)(b) or (c) may not exceed seven days.

(3) Regulations may provide for exceptions to subsection (1)(b) or (c).

DEFINITION

"prescribed"—see s.40.

GENERAL NOTE

1.51
This enables regulations to be made which provide that a person will not be entitled to universal credit: (i) even though s/he meets the basic and financial conditions (subs.(1)(a)); (ii) if s/he meets those conditions for seven days or less (subs.(1)(b) and subs.(2)); or (iii) for a period of seven days or less at the beginning of a period during which those conditions are met (subs.(1)(c) and subs.(2)).

On subs.(1)(a) see reg.19 of the Universal Credit Regulations. No regulations have been made under subs.1(b) and (c).

Awards

Basis of awards

1.52
7.—(1) Universal credit is payable in respect of each complete assessment period within a period of entitlement.

(2) In this Part an "assessment period" is a period of a prescribed duration.

(3) Regulations may make provision—

(a) about when an assessment period is to start;

(b) for universal credit to be payable in respect of a period shorter than an assessment period;

(c) about the amount payable in respect of a period shorter than an assessment period.

(4) In subsection (1) "period of entitlement" means a period during which entitlement to universal credit subsists.

GENERAL NOTE

1.53
See the commentary to reg.21 of the Universal Credit Regulations.

Calculation of awards

8.—(1) The amount of an award of universal credit is to be the balance of—   1.54
  (a) the maximum amount (see subsection (2)), less
  (b) the amounts to be deducted (see subsection (3)).
  (2) The maximum amount is the total of—
  (a) any amount included under section 9 (standard allowance);
  (b) any amount included under section 10 (responsibility for children and young persons);
  (c) any amount included under section 11 (housing costs), and
  (d) any amount included under section 12 (other particular needs or circumstances).
  (3) The amounts to be deducted are—
  (a) an amount in respect of earned income calculated in the prescribed manner (which may include multiplying some or all earned income by a prescribed percentage), and
  (b) an amount in respect of unearned income calculated in the pre-scribed manner (which may include multiplying some or all unearned income by a prescribed percentage).
  (4) In subsection (3)(a) and (b) the references to income are—
  (a) in the case of a single claimant, to income of the claimant, and
  (b) in the case of joint claimants, to combined income of the claimants.

DEFINITIONS

  "claim"—see s.40.
  "claimant"—*ibid.*
  "joint claimants"—*ibid.*
  "prescribed"—*ibid.*
  "single claimant"—*ibid.*

GENERAL NOTE

See the commentary to reg.22 of the Universal Credit Regulations.   1.55

Elements of an award

Standard allowance

9.—(1) The calculation of an award of universal credit is to include an   1.56
amount by way of an allowance for—
  (a) a single claimant, or
  (b) joint claimants.
  (2) Regulations are to specify the amount to be included under subsection (1).
  (3) Regulations may provide for exceptions to subsection (1).

DEFINITIONS

  "claim"—see s.40.
  "claimant"—*ibid.*

GENERAL NOTE

1.57   See the commentary to regs 23 and 36 of the Universal Credit Regulations.

Responsibility for children and young persons

1.58   **10.**—(1) The calculation of an award of universal credit is to include an amount for each child or qualifying young person for whom a claimant is responsible.

(2) Regulations may make provision for the inclusion of an additional amount if such a child or qualifying young person is disabled.

(3) Regulations are to specify, or provide for the calculation of, amounts to be included under subsection (1) or (2).

(4) Regulations may provide for exceptions to subsection (1).

(5) In this Part, "qualifying young person" means a person of a prescribed description.

DEFINITIONS

"child"—see s.40.
"disabled"—*ibid*.

GENERAL NOTE

1.59   See the commentary to regs 24 and 36 of the Universal Credit Regulations.

Housing costs

1.60   **11.**—(1) The calculation of an award of universal credit is to include an amount in respect of any liability of a claimant to make payments in respect of the accommodation they occupy as their home.

(2) For the purposes of subsection (1)—

(a) the accommodation must be in Great Britain;

(b) the accommodation must be residential accommodation;

(c) it is immaterial whether the accommodation consists of the whole or part of a building and whether or not it comprises separate and self-contained premises.

(3) Regulations may make provision as to—

(a) what is meant by payments in respect of accommodation for the purposes of this section (and, in particular, the extent to which universal credit payments include mortgage payments);

(b) circumstances in which a claimant is to be treated as liable or not liable to make such payments;

(c) circumstances in which a claimant is to be treated as occupying or not occupying accommodation as their home (and, in particular, for temporary absences to be disregarded);

(d) circumstances in which land used for the purposes of any accommodation is to be treated as included in the accommodation.

(4) Regulations are to provide for the determination or calculation of any amount to be included under this section.

(5) Regulations may—

(a) provide for exceptions to subsection (1);

(b) provide for inclusion of an amount under this section in the calculation of an award of universal credit—

  (i) to end at a prescribed time, or
  (ii) not to start until a prescribed time.

DEFINITIONS

  "claim"—see s.40.
  "claimant"—*ibid.*
  "prescribed"—*ibid.*

GENERAL NOTE

  This provides for an award of universal credit to include an amount in respect of **1.61**
the claimant's (or claimants') liability to make payments in respect of the accommodation they occupy as their home. It will cover payments both by people who are renting their homes and by owner occupiers (as well as service charges).
  Under subs.(2), the accommodation must be residential accommodation and must be in Great Britain. It can be the whole or part of a building and need not comprise separate and self-contained premises.
  For the rules relating to housing costs see regs 25–26 of, and Schs 1–5 to, the Universal Credit Regulations.

Other particular needs or circumstances

  12.—(1) The calculation of an award of universal credit is to include **1.62**
amounts in respect of such particular needs or circumstances of a claimant as may be prescribed.
  (2) The needs or circumstances prescribed under subsection (1) may include—
  (a) the fact that a claimant has limited capability for work;
  (b) the fact that a claimant has limited capability for work and work-related activity;
  (c) the fact that a claimant has regular and substantial caring responsibilities for a severely disabled person.
  (3) Regulations are to specify, or provide for the determination or calculation of, any amount to be included under subsection (1).
  (4) Regulations may—
  (a) provide for inclusion of an amount under this section in the calculation of an award of universal credit—
      (i) to end at a prescribed time, or
      (ii) not to start until a prescribed time;
  (b) provide for the manner in which a claimant's needs or circumstances are to be determined.

DEFINITIONS

  "claim"—see s.40.
  "claimant"—*ibid.*
  "limited capability for work"—*ibid.*
  "prescribed"—*ibid.*
  "work"—*ibid.*

GENERAL NOTE

  See the commentary to regs 27–36 of the Universal Credit Regulations. **1.63**

CHAPTER 2

CLAIMANT RESPONSIBILITIES

Introductory

Work-related requirements: introductory

1.64   **13.**—(1) This Chapter provides for the Secretary of State to impose work-related requirements with which claimants must comply for the purposes of this Part.

(2) In this Part "work-related requirement" means—

(a) a work-focused interview requirement (see section 15);

(b) a work preparation requirement (see section 16);

(c) a work search requirement (see section 17);

(d) a work availability requirement (see section 18).

(3) The work-related requirements which may be imposed on a claimant depend on which of the following groups the claimant falls into—

(a) no work-related requirements (see section 19);

(b) work-focused interview requirement only (see section 20);

(c) work-focused interview and work preparation requirements only (see section 21);

(d) all work-related requirements (see section 22).

GENERAL NOTE

1.65   The remaining sections of this Chapter of the WRA 2012 in the main set out what sort of work-related requirements can be imposed on which universal credit claimants, as well as the system for imposing sanctions (reductions in benefit) on claimants for failure to comply with those requirements. Although s.13(1) refers only to work-related requirements as defined in ss.15–18, s.23 allows the Secretary of State to require a claimant to participate in an interview for various related purposes and to provide information and evidence. A failure to comply with a requirement under s.23 can lead to a sanction under s.27(2)(b) in the same way as can a failure to comply with any work-related requirement. Section 14 contains rules about the "claimant commitment", acceptance of which is a condition of entitlement under s.4(1)(e).

There is a handy summary of the sanctions framework in Chapter 52.4 of CPAG's *Welfare Benefits and Tax Credits Handbook* (2013/14 edn.).

Claimant commitment

1.66   **14.**—(1) A claimant commitment is a record of a claimant's responsibilities in relation to an award of universal credit.

(2) A claimant commitment is to be prepared by the Secretary of State an may be reviewed and updated as the Secretary of State thinks fit.

(3) A claimant commitment is to be in such form as the Secretary of State thinks fit.

(4) A claimant commitment is to include—

(a) a record of the requirements that the claimant must comply with under this Part (or such of them as the Secretary of State considers it appropriate to include),

(b) any prescribed information, and

(c) any other information the Secretary of State considers it appropriate to include.

(5) For the purposes of this Part a claimant accepts a claimant commitment if, and only if, the claimant accepts the most up-to-date version of it in such manner as may be prescribed.

DEFINITIONS

"claimant"—see s.40.
"prescribed"—*ibid.*

GENERAL NOTE

Under s.4(1)(e) the final basic condition of entitlement is that the claimant has accepted a claimant commitment. Section 14 defines the nature of a claimant commitment and there are further provisions in regs 15 and 16 of the Universal Credit Regulations. Where a claim has to be made jointly by both members of a couple, both are claimants and subject to this condition.   **1.67**

Subsections (1) and (2) define a claimant commitment as a record prepared by the Secretary of State (in such form as he thinks fit: subs.(3)) of a claimant's responsibilities in relation to an award of universal credit. In particular, by subs. (4)(a), the record is to include the requirements that the particular claimant must comply with under the WRA 2012, in the main work-related requirements (see ss.15–25). Subsection (4)(b) requires the record to contain any prescribed information. Regulations have not as yet prescribed any such information. Subsection (4)(c) allows the record to contain any other information (note, information, not a further requirement) that the Secretary of State considers appropriate. For the claimant commitment to serve the basic purpose discussed below, that information must at least include information about the potential consequences under the Act of receiving a sanction for failure to carry out a requirement.

Exceptions from the application of the basic condition in s.4(1)(e) are set out in reg.16 of the Universal Credit Regulations. The WRA 2012 does not seek to define what is meant by acceptance of a claimant commitment beyond the provision in subs.(5) that it must be the most up-to-date version that has been accepted in such manner as prescribed in regulations. Regulation 15 of the Universal Credit Regulations provides for the time within which and the manner in which the claimant commitment must be accepted, but says nothing about what accepting the commitment entails in substance.

Since the commitment is the record of the particular claimant's responsibilities as imposed by or under the legislation itself it does not seem that acceptance can mean much more than an acknowledgement of its receipt or possibly also that the claimant understands the implications of the requirements set out. There can be no question of a claimant having to express any agreement with the justice or reasonableness of the requirements, let alone of the policy behind universal credit. Nor does acceptance seem to involve any personal commitment to carrying out the stated requirements. A failure to comply with any requirement imposed by the Secretary of State is a matter for a potential sanction under ss.26 or 27, not for a conclusion that the basic condition of entitlement in s.4(1)(e) is no longer met. There is no direct sanction for a failure to comply with a requirement just because it is included in the claimant commitment, nor does such a failure show that the claimant commitment has ceased to be accepted in the sense suggested above.   **1.68**

The notion of the claimant commitment is in many ways at the heart of what "conditionality" is meant to achieve under universal credit. It looks on its face to be an expression of what Charles Reich in his classic essay *The New Property* (1964) 73 Yale Law Journal 733 called "the New Feudalism". The universal credit claimant not only has, as the price of securing entitlement to the benefit, to accept a defined status that involves the giving up of some rights normally enjoyed by ordinary citizens, but appears to have to undertake some kind of oath of fealty by accepting a commitment to the feudal duties of that status. However, in reality the claimant commitment is a much more prosaic, and more sensible, thing. In its interesting paper *Universal Credit and Conditionality* (Social Security Advisory Committee Occasional Paper No. 9, 2012) the SSAC reported research findings that many claimants of current benefits subject to a sanctions regime did not understand what conduct could lead to a sanction, how the sanctions system worked (some not even realising that they had been sanctioned) and in particular what the consequences of a sanction would be on current and future entitlement. Paragraph 3.12 of the paper states:

"The lessons to be learned from the research ought to be relatively straightforward to implement, although providing the appropriate training for a large number of Personal Advisers may present a considerable challenge:

- claimants need to have the link between conditionality and the application of sanctions fully explained at the start of any claim
- clear and unambiguous communication about the sanctions regime between advisers and claimants is vital at the start of any claim and must form a key element in the Claimant Commitment
- claimants need to know when they are in danger of receiving a sanction and to be told when a sanction has been imposed, the amount and the duration
- claimants need to know what actions they have to take to reverse a sanction— the process and consequences of re-compliance."

If one of the main aims of conditionality, of encouraging claimants to avoid behaviour that would impede a possible return to or entry into work and thus reducing the incidence of the imposition of sanctions or of more severe sanctions, is to be furthered, it therefore makes sense to build into the system a requirement to set out each claimant's responsibilities and the consequences of not meeting them in understandable terms. However, as the SSAC suggests, the nature of the personal interaction between personal advisers and claimants may be much more important than a formal written document in getting over the realities of the situation and in encouraging claimants to take steps to avoid or reduce dependence on benefit.

1.69 A similar line of thought seems to be behind what was set out in paras 65 and 66 of the joint judgment of Lords Neuberger and Toulson in *R (on the application of Reilly and Wilson) v Secretary of State for Work and Pensions* [2013] UKSC 68; [2013] 3 W.L.R. 1276, in relation to the JSA regime, after noting the serious consequence of imposing a requirement to engage in unpaid work on a claimant on pain of discontinuance of benefits:

"65.   Fairness therefore requires that a claimant should have access to such information about the scheme as he or she may need in order to make informed and meaningful representations to the decision-maker before a decision is made. Such claimants are likely to vary considerably in their levels of education and ability to express themselves in an interview at a Jobcentre at a time when they may be under considerable stress. The principle does not depend on the categorisation of the Secretary of State's decision to introduce a particular scheme under statutory powers as a policy: it arises as a matter of fairness from the Secretary of State's proposal to invoke a statutory power in a way which will or may involve a requirement to perform work and which may have serious consequences on a claimant's ability to meet his or her living needs.

66.   Properly informed claimants, with knowledge not merely of the schemes available, but also of the criteria for being placed on such schemes, should be able to explain what would, in their view, be the most reasonable and appropriate scheme for them, in a way which would be unlikely to be possible without such information. Some claimants may have access to information downloadable from a government website, if they knew what to look for, but many will not. For

many of those dependent on benefits, voluntary agencies such as Citizens Advice Bureaus play an important role in informing and assisting them in relation to benefits to which they may be entitled, how they should apply, and what matters they should draw to the attention of their Jobcentre adviser."

However, how such principles might impact on the universal credit scheme will have to be worked out in particular legislative contexts.

A sample claimant commitment has been produced by the DWP in response to a freedom of information request (available at *https://www.gov.uk/government/publications/foi-query-universal-credit-claimant-commitment-example* (accessed January 27, 2014), or through a link in the universal credit part of the discussion forum on the Rightsnet website. The document puts things in terms of what the claimant says he or she will do. It is suggested above that that is not quite what the legislation requires, but there is obviously a tension with an attempt to use everyday and simple language. Nevertheless, the document is long and complicated. In the sample, there is no attempt to specify the precise length of the sanction that would be imposed for a failure for no good reason (the document says "without good reason") to comply with a requirement, but the maximum possible duration is included, plus the words "up to". It is arguable that this information is insufficiently precise.

There is some difficulty in working out what remedies a claimant would have who disagrees with the imposition of a requirement included in the claimant commitment. If the claimant declines to accept the Secretary of State's form of the record, at the outset of the claim or as later reviewed and up-dated, then any initial disallowance of the claim or subsequent supersession of an awarding decision would be appealable. However, it is not clear whether such an appeal could succeed on the basis that a requirement in fact included in the claimant commitment should not have been imposed under the conditions in ss.19–24. A claimant who accepts a claimant commitment under protest about some requirement may no doubt request the Secretary of State not to impose the challenged requirement and in consequence to review the claimant commitment. However, it appears that the claimant cannot appeal directly either against the imposition of the requirement or the content of the claimant commitment or against a refusal by the Secretary of State to remove a requirement and to review the claimant commitment. See the discussion in the note to s.24 below, which would apply equally to any of the kinds of decision mentioned. None of them are "outcome" decisions.

Work-related requirements

Work-focused interview requirement

15.—(1) In this Part a "work-focused interview requirement" is a requirement that a claimant participate in one or more work-focused interviews as specified by the Secretary of State.   1.70

(2) A work-focused interview is an interview for prescribed purposes relating to work or work preparation.

(3) The purposes which may be prescribed under subsection (2) include in particular that of making it more likely in the opinion of the Secretary of State that the claimant will obtain paid work (or more paid work or better-paid work).

(4) The Secretary of State may specify how, when and where a work-focused interview is to take place.

DEFINITION

"claimant"—see s.40.

1.71   This section defines what a "work-focused interview" is and makes the related requirement "participation" in the interview. This is for the purposes of ss.20–22, and in particular s.20, which applies the requirement to participate in such an interview to the great majority of claimants.

Under subss.(2) and (3) regulations must prescribe the purposes, relating to work or work preparation, for which an interview may be required. The prescription, in wide terms, is in reg.93 of the Universal Credit Regulations. "Paid work" is not defined in the Act, but when that phrase is used in reg.93 the definition in reg.2 will apply (see the note to reg.93). There is no further provision about what participating in a work-focused interview entails. The Secretary of State is allowed under subss.(1) and (4) to specify how, when and where the interview is to take place, so that the requirement must at least entail turning up at the place and time specified. The requirement to participate must also extend to making some meaningful contribution to the interview, but the limits will probably not be established until there have been some sanctions appeals. A failure for no good reason to comply with any work-related requirement is sanctionable under s.27(2)(a). That is the context in which what amounts to a failure to comply will be identified, as well as what might amount to a good reason for non-compliance. For instance, there appear to be no provisions prescribing the length of notice of an interview to be given or how far a claimant can be required to travel, but there could plainly be a good reason for failing to comply with unreasonable requirements, especially if the claimant had attempted in advance to draw any problem with attendance to the Secretary of State's attention.

Note that under s.23(1) the Secretary of State is empowered to require a claimant to attend an interview relating to the imposition of a work-related requirement on the claimant or assisting the claimant to comply with a requirement.

Work preparation requirement

1.72   **16.**—(1) In this Part a "work preparation requirement" is a requirement that a claimant take particular action specified by the Secretary of State for the purpose of making it more likely in the opinion of the Secretary of State that the claimant will obtain paid work (or more paid work or better-paid work).

(2) The Secretary of State may under subsection (1) specify the time to be devoted to any particular action.

(3) Action which may be specified under subsection (1) includes in particular—

(a) attending a skills assessment;
(b) improving personal presentation;
(c) participating in training;
(d) participating in an employment programme;
(e) undertaking work experience or a work placement;
(f) developing a business plan;
(g) any action prescribed for the purpose in subsection (1).

(4) In the case of a person with limited capability for work, the action which may be specified under subsection (1) includes taking part in a work-focused health-related assessment.

(5) In subsection (4) "work-focused health-related assessment" means an assessment by a health care professional approved by the Secretary of State which is carried out for the purpose of assessing—

(a) the extent to which the person's capability for work may be improved by taking steps in relation to their physical or mental condition, and

(b) such other matters relating to their physical or mental condition and the likelihood of their obtaining or remaining in work or being able to do so as may be prescribed.

(6) In subsection (5) "health care professional" means—

(a) a registered medical practitioner,

(b) a registered nurse,

(c) an occupational therapist or physiotherapist registered with a regulatory body established by an Order in Council under section 60 of the Health Act 1999, or

(d) a member of such other profession regulated by a body mentioned in section 25(3) of the National Health Service Reform and Health Care Professions Act 2002 as may be prescribed.

DEFINITIONS

"claimant"—see s.40.
"limited capability for work"—*ibid.*

GENERAL NOTE

This section defines "work preparation requirement" for the particular purposes of ss.21 and 22. The requirement is to take particular action specified by the Secretary of State for the purpose of making it more likely that the claimant will obtain paid work or obtain more or better-paid such work. Subsection (3) gives a non-exhaustive list of actions that may be specified, including under para.(g) any action prescribed in regulations. No regulations have as yet been made under para. (g). The list is in fairly broad terms, not further defined in the legislation, even "employment programme". The Secretary of State may under subs.(2) specify the time to be devoted to any particular action, but in practice this is likely to be less controversial than the similar power in s.17(2) in relation to a work search requirement. Subsections (4)–(6) allow the application of a particular requirement to take part in a work-focused health-related assessment to claimants with limited capability for work. Paragraph 15 of *JS v SSWP (ESA)*; [2013] UKUT 635 (AAC) suggests that if a claimant is patently not going to be able to obtain work at any stage or is already in a suitable apprenticeship or placement no action could make it more likely that work or more work would be obtained, so that no action could be legitimately specified.

A failure for no good reason by a claimant subject to all work-related requirements to comply with a requirement under this heading to undertake a work placement of a prescribed description is sanctionable under s.26(2)(a) (higher-level sanctions). Outside that limited category, failure for no good reason to comply with any work-related requirement is sanctionable under s.27(2)(a). That is the context in which there will be exploration of what action can be said to make it more likely that the claimant will obtain paid work or more or better-paid work, since the addition of the Secretary of State's opinion in subs.(1) will not be allowed to take away the power of tribunals to reach their own conclusions on that matter. What amounts to a failure to comply will also be identified, as well as what might amount to a good reason for non-compliance.

Note that under s.23(1) the Secretary of State is empowered to require a claimant to attend an interview relating to the imposition of a work-related requirement on the claimant or assisting the claimant to comply with a requirement. Under s.23(3) he can require the provision of information and evidence for the purpose of verifying compliance and that the claimant confirm compliance in any manner.

1.73

Work search requirement

1.74   **17.**—(1) In this Part a "work search requirement" is a requirement that a claimant take—

(a) all reasonable action, and

(b) any particular action specified by the Secretary of State,

for the purpose of obtaining paid work (or more paid work or better-paid work).

(2) The Secretary of State may under subsection (1)(b) specify the time to be devoted to any particular action.

(3) Action which may be specified under subsection (1)(b) includes in particular—

(a) carrying out work searches;

(b) making applications;

(c) creating and maintaining an online profile;

(d) registering with an employment agency;

(e) seeking references;

(f) any action prescribed for the purpose in subsection (1).

(4) Regulations may impose limitations on a work search requirement by reference to the work to which it relates; and the Secretary of State may in any particular case specify further such limitations on such a requirement.

(5) A limitation under subsection (4) may in particular be by reference to—

(a) work of a particular nature,

(b) work with a particular level of remuneration,

(c) work in particular locations, or

(d) work available for a certain number of hours per week or at particular times,

and may be indefinite or for a particular period.

DEFINITION

"claimant"—see s.40.

GENERAL NOTE

1.75   This section defines "work search requirement" for the particular purpose of s.22. It is a requirement that a claimant take both all reasonable action (subs.(1) (a)) and any particular action specified by the Secretary of State (subs.(1)(b)) for the purpose of obtaining paid work or more or better-paid work. "Paid work" is not defined in the Act, nor is it defined in regulations for the specific purpose of ss.17 and 22. However, under the power in s.25, regs 94 and 95 of the Universal Credit Regulations deem the work search requirement not to have been complied with in certain circumstances and make references to "paid work". For those purposes, the definition in reg.2 will apply, i.e. work done for payment or in expectation of payment, excluding work for a charity or voluntary organisation, or as a volunteer, in return for expenses only. Regulation 87 adds nothing to the terms of s.17 itself. Thus it appears that both self-employment and employment can be considered both under the reg.2 definition and under the ordinary meaning of the phrase "paid work".

Subsections (4) and (5) allow regulations to impose limitations on the kind of work search which can be required and also allow the Secretary of State to specify further limitations. Regulation 97 contains the prescribed limitations, in terms of hours of work for carers and those with a disability, of the maximum time for travel to and from work and of the type of work recently undertaken. See the notes to reg.97. There appears to be no limitation on the number of hours a week that work could involve while still falling for consideration, apart from in the cases of the particular categories of claimant identified in reg.97(2).

What is "all reasonable action" under subs.(1)(a) for the purpose of obtaining paid work within any applicable limitations is obviously in general a matter of judgment. That includes a judgment about what counts as "action". The actions mentioned in subs.(3) might be a starting point, but other things could plainly count, such as carrying out research into the job market or potential for self-employment. No doubt just sitting and thinking falls the other side of the line, but can often form an essential element of the hours devoted to some more active action. But reg.95 of the Universal Credit Regulations deems a claimant not to have complied with that requirement unless quite stringent conditions about the weekly hours devoted to work search are satisfied. See the notes to reg.95 and remember that the sanctions in s.26(4)(a), in relation to having, before claiming universal credit, failed to take up an offer of paid work, and s.27(2)(a) can only be imposed when there was no good reason for the failure to comply. Paragraph 15 of *JS v SSWP (ESA)* [2013] UKUT 635 (AAC) suggests that if a claimant is patently not going to be able to obtain work at any stage or is already in a suitable apprenticeship or placement no action could make it more likely that work or more work would be obtained, so that no action could be legitimately specified.

The particular action that can be specified by Secretary of State under subs.(1) **1.76** (b) can, by subs.(3), include a number of actions, including those prescribed in regulations. No relevant regulation has yet been made. Where a claimant has been required to apply for a particular vacancy (which it seems can only fall under subs. (1)(b) rather than (1)(a)), reg.94 of the Universal Credit Regulations deems the work search requirement not to have been complied with where the claimant fails to participate in an interview offered in connection with the vacancy. The specific sanction in s.26(2)(b) for failing to comply with a requirement to apply for a particular vacancy can only be applied when there was no good reason for the failure to comply.

Note that under s.23(1) the Secretary of State is empowered to require a claimant to attend an interview relating to the imposition of a work-related requirement on the claimant or assisting the claimant to comply with a requirement. Under s.23(3) he can require the provision of information and evidence for the purpose of verifying compliance and that the claimant confirm compliance in any manner.

Work availability requirement

18.—(1) In this Part a "work availability requirement" is a requirement **1.77** that a claimant be available for work.

(2) For the purposes of this section "available for work" means able and willing immediately to take up paid work (or more paid work or better-paid work).

(3) Regulations may impose limitations on a work availability requirement by reference to the work to which it relates; and the Secretary of State may in any particular case specify further such limitations on such a requirement.

(4) A limitation under subsection (3) may in particular be by reference to—

(a) work of a particular nature,
(b) work with a particular level of remuneration,
(c) work in particular locations, or
(d) work available for a certain number of hours per week or at particular times,
and may be indefinite or for a particular period.

(5) Regulations may for the purposes of subsection (2) define what is meant by a person being able and willing immediately to take up work.

DEFINITION

"claimant"—see s.40.

GENERAL NOTE

1.78   This section defines "work availability requirement" for the particular purpose of s.22. It requires in general that a claimant be able and willing immediately to take up paid work, or more or better-paid work. "Paid work" is not defined in the Act, nor is it defined in regulations for the specific purpose of ss.18 and 22. However, under the power in s.25, reg.96 of the Universal Credit Regulations deems the work availability requirement not to have been complied with in certain circumstances and to have been satisfied in other circumstances and makes references to "paid work". For those purposes, the definition in reg.2 will apply, i.e. work done for payment or in expectation of payment, excluding work for a charity or voluntary organisation, or as a volunteer, in return for expenses only. Regulation 87 adds nothing to the terms of s.18 itself. Thus it appears that willingness to take up both self-employment and employment can be considered.

Subsections (3) and (4) allow regulations to impose limitations on the kind of work for which a claimant can be required to be available and also allow the Secretary of State to specify further limitations. Regulation 97 contains the prescribed limitations, in terms of hours of work for carers and those with a disability, of the maximum time for travel to and from work and of the type of work recently undertaken. See the notes to reg.97. There appears to be no limitation on the number of hours a week that work could involve while still falling for consideration, apart from in the cases of the particular categories of claimant identified in reg.97(2).

Subsection (5) allows regulations to define what is meant in subs.(1) by being able and willing immediately to take up work. Regulation 99(1)(b) of the Universal Credit Regulations uses this power to provide that claimants in any of the circumstances set out in reg.99(3), (4) or (5) are regarded as being available for work if able and willing to take up paid work immediately after the relevant circumstance ceases to apply. Regulation 96(1) deems the work availability requirement not to be complied with if the claimant is not able and willing immediately to attend an interview in connection with finding paid work. Regulation 96(2) to (5) defines circumstances in which carers, those doing voluntary work and those in paid employment are to be treated as having complied with the requirement, where it is accepted that some longer notice than "immediately" is needed.

1.79   It is notable, by contrast with the position that will be familiar to many readers from jobseeker's allowance and, before it, unemployment benefit, that being available for work is not a condition of entitlement to universal credit, failure to satisfy which means that there can be no entitlement to benefit at all. Instead, a failure to comply with the work availability requirement, if imposed on a claimant, is merely a potential basis for a sanction under ss.26 or 27. Under s.26(2)(c) a higher-level sanction can be imposed if a claimant fails for no good reason to comply by not taking up an offer of paid work. Section 27(2)(a) allows the imposition of a medium-level sanction for a failure for no good reason to comply with any work-related requirement.

Note that under s.23(1) the Secretary of State is empowered to require a claimant to attend an interview relating to the imposition of a work-related requirement on the claimant or assisting the claimant to comply with a requirement. Under s.23(3) he can require the provision of information and evidence for the purpose of verifying compliance and that the claimant confirm compliance in any manner.

Application of work-related requirements

Claimants subject to no work-related requirements

1.80   **19.**—(1) The Secretary of State may not impose any work-related requirement on a claimant falling within this section.

(2) A claimant falls within this section if—
(a) the claimant has limited capability for work and work-related activity,
(b) the claimant has regular and substantial caring responsibilities for a severely disabled person,
(c) the claimant is the responsible carer for a child under the age of 1, or
(d) the claimant is of a prescribed description.
(3) Regulations under subsection (2)(d) may in particular make provision by reference to one or more of the following—
(a) hours worked;
(b) earnings or income;
(c) the amount of universal credit payable.
(4) Regulations under subsection (3) may—
(a) in the case of a claimant who is a member of the couple, make provision by reference to the claimant alone or by reference to the members of the couple together;
(b) make provision for estimating or calculating any matter for the purpose of the regulations.
(5) Where a claimant falls within this section, any work-related requirement previously applying to the claimant ceases to have effect.
(6) In this Part "responsible carer", in relation to a child means—
(a) a single person who is responsible for the child, or
(b) a person who is a member of a couple where—
(i) the person or the other member of the couple is responsible for the child, and
(ii) the person has been nominated by the couple jointly as responsible for the child.

DEFINITIONS

"claimant"—see s.40.
"limited capability for work"—*ibid.*
"limited capability for work-related activity"—*ibid.*
"regular and substantial caring responsibilities"—*ibid.*
"severely disabled"—*ibid.*
"work-related requirement"—see ss.40 and 13(2).

GENERAL NOTE

The default position in s.22 is that a claimant is, unless falling within ss.19—21, to **1.81** be subject to all work-related requirements, i.e. the work search and work availability requirements, with the optional additions of a work-focused interview and/or a work preparation requirement. Section 19 defines the circumstances in which no work-related requirement at all may be imposed. Under reg.98 of the Universal Credit Regulations, made under s.24(5) below, recent victims of domestic violence must be free of any work-related requirement, or a connected requirement under s.23, for a period of 13 weeks. Where a claim has to be made jointly by both members of a couple, both are claimants and it must be asked separately whether work-related requirements can be imposed on each. Section 19 cannot apply where the conditions of reg.92 of the Universal Credit Regulations (claimants with a right to reside in the UK as EEA jobseekers or as a member of the family of such a person) are met, although see the notes to reg.92 for doubts about the validity of that provision in EU law.

Subsection (2)
Three categories are specifically identified in subs.(2)(a)—(c). Others can, and **1.82** have been, prescribed in regulations (subss.(2)(d) and (3)–(4)):

(a) Claimants who have limited capability for work and for work-related activity cannot have any work-related requirement imposed. Once claimants who currently qualify for employment and support allowance (ESA) fall within the ambit of universal credit, limited capability will be tested in essentially the same way as for ESA.

(b) Claimants who have regular and substantial caring responsibilities for a severely disabled person cannot have any work-related requirement imposed. Although s.40 allows the meaning of "regular and substantial caring responsibilities" and "severely disabled person" to be prescribed separately in regulations, reg.30 of the universal credit Regulations defines the two phrases in combination in terms of meeting the conditions of entitlement to carer's allowance, disregarding the earnings conditions. There seems no reason why that should not be valid. The test is therefore, in brief, that the person cared for is entitled to attendance allowance, at least the middle rate of the care component of disability living allowance, the standard or enhanced rate of the daily living component of personal independence payment or armed forces independence payment and that the carer devotes at least 35 hours per week to caring for such a person. But note that by virtue of reg.30(3) anyone who derives any earnings from the caring is excluded from the definition. See the extension in reg.89(1)(b) of the Universal Credit Regulations, under para.(d) below.

(c) Claimants who are the responsible carer for a child under the age of one cannot have any work-related requirement imposed. By subs.(6) a responsible carer is a person who is responsible for a child or a member of a couple where the other member is responsible. Regulation 4 of the Universal Credit Regulations, made under para.5 of Sch.1 to the WRA 2012, sets out how responsibility is to be determined. See the notes to reg.4.

(d) Regulations 89 and 90 of the Universal Credit Regulations set out the additional categories of claimant who cannot have any work-related requirement imposed. Regulation 90 covers the special rules needed by virtue of the special characteristic of universal credit as both an in-work and an out-of-work benefit. Regulation 89 covers more general categories. See the notes to those regulations for the details. Regulation 89(1)(b) allows in some claimants who do not quite meet the conditions of subs.(2)(b). Regulation 89(1)(d) and (f) allow in some claimants who do not quite meet the conditions of subs.(2)(c). Regulation 89(1)(a) applies to claimants who have reached the qualifying age for state pension credit, i.e. state pension age. Regulation 89(1)(c) brings in women for shortish periods before and after confinement. Regulation 89(1)(e) brings in some claimants in education. Regulation 90 secures that no work-related requirements can be imposed on claimants whose earnings equal or exceed their individual threshold, defined in complicated ways according to the circumstances.

Claimants subject to work-focused interview requirement only

1.83   **20.**—(1) A claimant falls within this section if—
(a) the claimant is the responsible carer for a child who is aged at least 1 and is under a prescribed age (which may not be less than 3), or
(b) the claimant is of a prescribed description.

(2) The Secretary of State may, subject to this Part, impose a work-focused interview requirement on a claimant falling within this section.

(3) The Secretary of State may not impose any other work-related requirement on a claimant falling within this section (and, where a claimant falls within this section, any other work-related requirement previously applying to the claimant ceases to have effect).

DEFINITIONS

"claimant"—see s.40.
"responsible carer"—see ss.40 and 19(6).
"work-focused interview requirement"—see ss.40 and 15(1).
"work-related requirement"—see ss.40 and 13(2).

GENERAL NOTE

The default position in s.22 is that a claimant is, unless falling within ss.19–21,   **1.84**
to be subject to all work-related requirements, i.e. the work search and work availability requirements, with the optional additions of a work-focused interview and/
or a work preparation requirement. Section 20 defines the circumstances in which
a claimant who does not fall within s.19 (no work-related requirements) can have
a work-focused interview requirement, but not any other requirement, imposed.
Under s.23(1) the Secretary of State is empowered to require a claimant to attend
an interview relating to the imposition of a work-related requirement or assisting
the claimant to comply with a requirement. Where a claim has to be made jointly
by both members of a couple, both are claimants and it must be asked separately
whether work-related requirements can be imposed on each. Section 19 cannot
apply where the conditions of reg.92 of the Universal Credit Regulations (claimants
with a right to reside in the UK as EEA jobseekers or as a member of the family of
such a person) are met, although see the notes to reg.92 for doubts about the validity of that provision in EU law.

See s.24 for the process of imposing a requirement. Note that there is a discretion
("may") to impose the requirement if the conditions are met.

A claimant who is the responsible carer of a child under the age of five (but who
does not fall within s.19(2)(c) because the child is over one) can be subject to this
requirement (subss.(1)(a) and (2) and Universal Credit Regulations, reg.91(1)).
Under subs.(1)(b), reg.91(2) extends the requirement to a number of foster parents
and carers of children in the category of friends and family. See the notes to reg.91.
The nature of the requirement and the purposes of the interview are defined in s.15
and reg.93 of the Universal Credit Regulations.

Claimants subject to work preparation requirement

21.—(1) A claimant falls within this section if the claimant does not fall   **1.85**
within section 19 or 20 and—

(a) the claimant has limited capability for work, or

(b) the claimant is of a prescribed description.

(2) The Secretary of State may, subject to this Part, impose a work preparation requirement on a claimant falling within this section.

(3) The Secretary of State may also, subject to this Part, impose a work-
focused interview requirement on a claimant falling within this section.

(4) The Secretary of State may not impose any other work-related
requirement on a claimant falling within this section (and, where a claimant falls within this section, any other work-related requirement previously
applying to the claimant ceases to have effect).

(5) Regulations under subsection (1)(b) must prescribe a claimant who
is the responsible carer for a child aged 3 or 4 if the claimant does not fall
within section 20.

DEFINITIONS

"claimant"—see s.40.
"limited capability for work"—see ss.40 and 37(1).
"prescribed"—see s.40.

"work preparation requirement"—see ss.40 and 16(1).
"work-focused interview requirement"—see ss.40 and 15(1).
"work-related requirement"—see ss.40 and 13(2).

GENERAL NOTE

1.86   The default position in s.22 is that a claimant is, unless falling within ss.19–21, to be subject to all work-related requirements, i.e. the work search and work availability requirements, with the optional additions of a work-focused interview and/or a work preparation requirement. Section 21 defines the circumstances in which a claimant who does not fall within ss.19 or 20 (no work-related requirements or work-focused interview requirement only) can have a work preparation requirement and, under subs.(3), a work-focused interview requirement, but not any other requirement, imposed. Under s.23(1) the Secretary of State is empowered to require a claimant to attend an interview relating to the imposition of a work-related requirement or assisting the claimant to comply with a requirement. Where a claim has to be made jointly by both members of a couple, both are claimants and it must be asked separately whether work-related requirements can be imposed on each. Section 19 cannot apply where the conditions of reg.92 of the Universal Credit Regulations (claimants with a right to reside in the UK as EEA jobseekers or as a member of the family of such a person) are met, although see the notes to reg.92 for doubts about the validity of that provision in EU law.

See s.24 for the process of imposing a requirement. Note that there is a discretion ("may") to impose the requirement if the conditions are met.

The only category of claimants currently covered by s.21 is those with limited capability for work (subs.(1)(a)). No regulations have as yet been made under subs.(1)(b), no doubt because reg.91(1) of the Universal Credit Regulations brings responsible carers of children up to the age of five within the scope of s.20, so that the requirement in subs.(5) does not in practice arise. The nature of the requirement is defined in s.16.

Claimants subject to all work-related requirements

1.87   **22.**—(1) A claimant not falling within any of sections 19 to 21 falls within this section.

(2) The Secretary of State must, except in prescribed circumstances, impose on a claimant falling within this section—

(a) a work search requirement, and

(b) a work availability requirement.

(3) The Secretary of State may, subject to this Part, impose either or both of the following on a claimant falling within this section—

(a) a work-focused interview requirement;

(b) a work preparation requirement.

DEFINITIONS

"claimant"—see s.40.
"prescribed"—*ibid.*
"work availability requirement"—see ss.40 and 18(1).
"work preparation requirement"—see ss.40 and 16(1).
"work search requirement"—see ss.40 and 17(1).
"work-focused interview requirement"—see ss.40 and 15(1).

GENERAL NOTE

1.88   This section sets out the default position that a claimant of universal credit is, unless falling within ss.19–21, to be subject to all work-related requirements, i.e. the work search and work availability requirements, with the optional additions of a work-focused interview and/or a work preparation requirement. Under s.23(1) the Secretary of State is empowered to require a claimant to attend an interview relating to the imposition of a work-related requirement or assisting the claimant to comply with a requirement. By contrast with other provisions, where this section applies the work search and work availability requirements *must* be imposed (subs.(2)), but there is a discretion about the other requirements (subs.(3)). See the notes to ss.19–21 for the circumstances in which either no or only some work-related requirements may be imposed. The content of the requirements is set out in ss.15–18 and associated regulations. Where a claim has to be made jointly by both members of a couple, and both are claimants it must be asked separately whether work-related requirements can be imposed on each. See s.24 for the process of imposing a requirement.

Work-related requirements: supplementary

Connected requirements

23.—(1) The Secretary of State may require a claimant to participate in 1.89
an interview for any purpose relating to—
    (a) the imposition of a work-related requirement on the claimant;
    (b) verifying the claimant's compliance with a work-related requirement;
    (c) assisting the claimant to comply with a work-related requirement.
  (2) The Secretary of State may specify how, when and where such an interview is to take place.
  (3) The Secretary of State may, for the purpose of verifying the claimant's compliance with a work-related requirement, require a claimant to—
    (a) provide to the Secretary of State information and evidence specified by the Secretary of State in a manner so specified;
    (b) confirm compliance in a manner so specified.
  (4) The Secretary of State may require a claimant to report to the Secretary of State any specified changes in their circumstances which are relevant to—
    (a) the imposition of work-related requirements on the claimant;
    (b) the claimant's compliance with a work-related requirement.

DEFINITIONS

  "claimant"—see s.40.
  "work-related requirement"—see ss.40 and 13(2).

GENERAL NOTE

  This section gives the Secretary of State power to require a claimant to do various 1.90
things related to the imposition of work-related requirements, verifying compliance and assisting claimants to comply: to participate in an interview (subss.(1) and (2)); for the purpose of verifying compliance, to provide specified information and evidence or to confirm compliance (subs.(3)); or to report specified changes in a claimant's circumstances relevant to the imposition of or compliance with requirements. Such requirements do not fall within the meaning of "work-related requirement", but there is a separate ground of sanction under s.27(2)(b) for failing for no good reason to comply with them, but only for claimants subject to all work-related requirements or to the work preparation requirement (see reg.104(1) of the Universal Credit Regulations). The Secretary of State is allowed under subs.(2) to specify how, when and where any interview under subs.(1) is to take place, so that

the requirement to participate must at least entail turning up at the place and time specified. The requirement to participate must also extend to making some meaningful contribution to the interview, but the limits will probably not be established until some sanctions appeals have reached the Upper Tribunal. The compulsory imposition of a sanction for failure for no good reason to report specified changes in circumstances, to provide specified information and evidence or to confirm compliance with a work-related requirement is a new departure.

See s.24 for the process of imposing a requirement.

Imposition of requirements

1.91

24.—(1) Regulations may make provision—

(a) where the Secretary of State may impose a requirement under this Part, as to when the requirement must or must not be imposed;

(b) where the Secretary of State may specify any action to be taken in relation to a requirement under this Part, as to what action must or must not be specified;

(c) where the Secretary of State may specify any other matter in relation to a requirement under this Part, as to what must or must not be specified in respect of that matter.

(2) Where the Secretary of State may impose a work-focused interview requirement, or specify a particular action under section 16(1) or 17(1)(b), the Secretary of State must have regard to such matters as may be prescribed.

(3) Where the Secretary of State may impose a requirement under this Part, or specify any action to be taken in relation to such a requirement, the Secretary of State may revoke or change what has been imposed or specified.

(4) Notification of a requirement imposed under this Part (or any change to or revocation of such a requirement) is, if not included in the claimant commitment, to be in such manner as the Secretary of State may determine.

(5) Regulations must make provision to secure that, in prescribed circumstances, where a claimant has recently been a victim of domestic violence—

(a) a requirement imposed on that claimant under this Part ceases to have effect for a period of 13 weeks, and

(b) the Secretary of State may not impose any other requirement under this Part on that claimant during that period.

(6) For the purposes of subsection (5)—

(a) "domestic violence" has such meaning as may be prescribed;

(b) "victim of domestic violence" means a person on or against whom domestic violence is inflicted or threatened (and regulations under subsection (5) may prescribe circumstances in which a person is to be treated as being or not being a victim of domestic violence);

(c) a person has recently been a victim of domestic violence if a prescribed period has not expired since the violence was inflicted or threatened.

DEFINITIONS

"claimant"—see s.40.
"work-focused interview requirement"—see ss.40 and 15(1).

GENERAL NOTE

1.92

This section contains a variety of powers and duties in relation to the imposition by the Secretary of State of either a work-related requirement or a connected requirement under s.23. It makes the imposition of a requirement and the notification to the claimant a moderately formal process, which raises the question of whether the decision of the Secretary of State to impose a requirement is a decision that is appealable to a First-tier Tribunal under s.12(1) of the SSA 1998, either as a decision on a claim or award or one which falls to be made under the WRA 2012 as a "relevant enactment" (s.8(1)(a) and (c) of the SSA 1998). However, if it is a decision not made on a claim or award, it is not covered in Sch.3 to the 1998 Act (or in Sch.2 to the Decisions and Appeals Regulations 2013 (see above and below and in Vol.III)), so could not be appealable under that heading. The discussion in the note to s.12(1) of the 1998 Act in Vol.III would indicate that, since the imposition of a requirement is not an "outcome" decision determining entitlement or payability of universal credit or the amount payable, it is not appealable under s.12(1)(a) as a decision on a claim or award or as a decision on another basis.

Thus, it appears that a direct challenge to the imposition of any particular require-ment, including any element specified by the Secretary of State, and/or its inclusion in a claimant commitment under s.14 of this Act, can only be made by way of judi-cial review in the High Court, with the possibility of a discretionary transfer to the Upper Tribunal. Otherwise, a challenge by way of appeal appears not be possible unless and until a reduction of benefit for a sanctionable failure is imposed on the claimant for a failure to comply with a requirement. It must therefore be arguable that in any such appeal the claimant can challenge whether the conditions for the imposition of the requirement in question were met, with the result that, if that challenge is successful, the sanction must be removed. That appears to have been the assumption of the Supreme Court in *R (on the application of Reilly and Wilson) v Secretary of State for Work and Pensions* [2013] UKSC 68; [2013] 3 W.L.R. 1276. In para.29 of their judgment, Lords Neuberger and Toulson mentioned without any adverse comment Foskett J.'s holding at first instance that a consequence of a breach of a regulation requiring a claimant to be given notice of a requirement to participate in a scheme was that no sanctions could lawfully be imposed on the claimants for failure to participate in the scheme.

Subsection (1)

Regulation 99 of the Universal Credit Regulations is made under para.(a), reg.98   **1.93**
on domestic violence falling more specifically under subss.(5) and (6). No regula-tions appear to have been made under paras (b) and (c).

Subsection (2)

No regulations appear to have been made under this provision.   **1.94**

Subsection (3)

The inclusion of this express power to revoke or change any requirement, or any   **1.95**
specification of action, is an indication of the formality entailed in the imposition of a requirement. However, there appears to be no restriction on the circumstances in which the Secretary of State may carry out such a revocation or change, subject of course to the legislative conditions being met for whatever the new position is. A mere change of mind without any change in circumstances or mistake or error as to the existing circumstances will do.

Subsection (4)

This provision allows the Secretary of State to notify the claimant of the imposi-   **1.96**
tion of any requirement, if not included in a claimant commitment under s.14, in any manner. Thus, it may be done orally (or presumably even through the medium of mime), but it is a necessary implication that a requirement must be notified to the claimant. That in turn implies that, whatever the manner of notification, the content must be such as is reasonably capable of being understood by the particular claimant with the characteristics known to the officer of the Secretary of State (so perhaps the medium of mime will not do after all). Less flippantly, this principle may be important for claimants with sensory problems, e.g. hearing or vision dif-ficulties. The expectation of course is that the requirements imposed under the Act

will be included in the claimant commitment, one of whose aims is to ensure that claimants know and understand what is being required of them and the potential consequences of failing to comply. However, it is clear in law that the validity of a requirement is not dependent on inclusion in the claimant commitment. There is no such express condition and under s.14(4)(a) the Secretary of State is only under a duty to record in the claimant commitment such of the requirements under the Act as he considers it appropriate to include. It may be that the fact that a requirement is not recorded in the claimant commitment could be put forward as part of an argument for there having been a good reason for failing to comply with the requirement.

Subsections (5) and (6)

1.97
The duty to make regulations providing that no work-related requirement or connected requirement under s.23 may be imposed for a period of 13 weeks on a claimant who has recently been a victim of domestic violence is carried out in reg.98 of the Universal Credit Regulations. Most of the meat is in the regulation, including the definition of "domestic violence", which in the event merely refers on the specification of abuse in a Department of Health handbook. See the note to reg.98 for the details. However, subs.(6)(b) does define "victim" to include not just those on whom domestic violence is inflicted but also those against whom it is threatened.

Compliance with requirements

1.98
25. Regulations may make provision as to circumstances in which a claimant is to be treated as having—

(a) complied with or not complied with any requirement imposed under this Part or any aspect of such a requirement, or

(b) taken or not taken any particular action specified by the Secretary of State in relation to such a requirement.

GENERAL NOTE

1.99
Under subs.(a) regulations may deem a claimant either to have or not to have complied with any work-related requirement or connected requirement under s.23 in particular circumstances. Regulations 94–97 of the Universal Credit Regulations make use of this power, mainly in treating claimants as not having complied. No regulations appear to have been made as yet under subs.(b).

Reduction of benefit

Higher-level sanctions

1.100
26.—(1) The amount of an award of universal credit is to be reduced in accordance with this section in the event of a failure by a claimant which is sanctionable under this section.

(2) It is a failure sanctionable under this section if a claimant falling within section 22—

(a) fails for no good reason to comply with a requirement imposed by the Secretary of State under a work preparation requirement to undertake a work placement of a prescribed description;

(b) fails for no good reason to comply with a requirement imposed by the Secretary of State under a work search requirement to apply for a particular vacancy for paid work;

(c) fails for no good reason to comply with a work availability requirement by not taking up an offer of paid work;

(d) by reason of misconduct, or voluntarily and for no good reason, ceases paid work or loses pay.

(3) It is a failure sanctionable under this section if by reason of misconduct, or voluntarily and for no good reason, a claimant falling within section 19 by virtue of subsection (3) of that section ceases paid work or loses pay so as to cease to fall within that section and to fall within section 22 instead.

(4) It is a failure sanctionable under this section if, at any time before making the claim by reference to which the award is made, the claimant—

(a) for no good reason failed to take up an offer of paid work, or

(b) by reason of misconduct, or voluntarily and for no good reason, ceased paid work or lost pay,

and at the time the award is made the claimant falls within section 22.

(5) For the purposes of subsections (2) to (4) regulations may provide—

(a) for circumstances in which ceasing to work or losing pay is to be treated as occurring or not occurring by reason of misconduct or voluntarily;

(b) for loss of pay below a prescribed level to be disregarded.

(6) Regulations are to provide for—

(a) the amount of a reduction under this section;

(b) the period for which such a reduction has effect, not exceeding three years in relation to any failure sanctionable under this section.

(7) Regulations under subsection (6)(b) may in particular provide for the period of a reduction to depend on either or both of the following—

(a) the number of failures by the claimant sanctionable under this section;

(b) the period between such failures.

(8) Regulations may provide—

(a) for cases in which no reduction is to be made under this section;

(b) for a reduction under this section made in relation to an award that is terminated to be applied to any new award made within a prescribed period of the termination;

(c) for the termination or suspension of a reduction under this section.

DEFINITIONS

"claimant"—see s.40.
"prescribed"—*ibid.*
"work availability requirement"—see ss.40 and 18(1).
"work preparation requirement"—see ss.40 and 16(1).
"work search requirement"—see ss.40 and 17(1).

GENERAL NOTE

Sections 26–28 set up a very similar structure of sanctions leading to reductions in the amount of universal credit to that already imposed in the new ss.19–20 of the Jobseekers Act 1995 substituted by the WRA 2012 and in operation from October 22, 2012 (see the 2013/14 edition of Vol.II). The similarity is in the creation of higher-level sanctions, here under s.26, and of medium, low and lowest-level sanctions, here under s.27, and in the stringency of the periods and the amount of reductions to be imposed, in particular for higher-level sanctions. See the discussion in the notes to s.19 of the Jobseekers Act 1995 in Vol.II. There are, however, some differences in the wording of otherwise similar provisions, which will be noted below, and a wider scope to the universal credit sanctions to reflect the scope of the benefit as extending beyond jobseekers to include those who are in work as well as out of work for various reasons.

The central concept under these provisions is of a "sanctionable failure", which

1.101

under s.26(1), and s.27(1), is to lead to a reduction in the amount of an award of universal credit. For higher-level sanctions under s.26, the reduction for most adult claimants is in brief of 100 per cent of the claimant's individual standard universal credit allowance for about 13 weeks for a first higher-level failure, 26 weeks for second such failure within a year and 156 weeks for a third or subsequent such failure within a year. As noted below, regulations set out the amount and period of the reduction. There is no discretion under either ss.26 or 27 as to whether or not to apply a reduction if the conditions are met and no discretion under the regulations as to the amount and period of the reduction as calculated under the complicated formulae there. Regulation 113 of the Universal Credit Regulations, made under ss.26(8)(a) and 27(9)(a), sets out circumstances in which no reduction is to be made for a sanctionable failure. There is also provision for hardship payments under s.28.

As a matter of principle, a claimant has to be able, in any appeal against a reduction in benefit on the imposition of a sanction, to challenge whether the conditions for the imposition of sanction were met. See the note to s.24.

Another important concept is that of a "good reason" for the conduct or failure to comply with a requirement under the WRA 2012. Most of the definitions of sanctionable failures in ss.26 and 27 incorporate the condition that the failure was "for no good reason". Paragraph 8 of Sch.1 to the Act allows regulations to prescribe circumstances in which a claimant is to be treated as having or as not having a good reason for an act or omission and to prescribe matters that are or are not to be taken into account in determining whether a claimant has a good reason. No regulations have been made under this power. There is no equivalent to reg.72 of the Jobseeker's Allowance Regulations (although there must be some doubt about whether there was power to make that provision under the JSA legislation).

1.102

Thus, the concept remains a fairly open-ended one, no doubt requiring consideration of all relevant circumstances but also containing a large element of judgment according to the individual facts of particular cases. The amount and quality of information provided to the claimant in the claimant commitment or otherwise about responsibilities under the WRA 2012 and the consequences of a failure to comply will no doubt be relevant, especially in the light of the approach of the Supreme Court in paras 65 and 66 of *R (on the application of Reilly and Wilson) v Secretary of State for Work and Pensions* [2013] UKSC 68; [2013] 3 W.L.R. 1276 (see the notes to s.14 above). Probably, in addition, as in the previously familiar concept of "just cause", a balancing is required between the interests of the claimant and those of the community of those whose contributions and taxes finance the benefit in question. See the discussion under the heading of "Without a good reason" in the note to s.19 of the Jobseekers Act 1995 in Vol.II.

However, there is a potentially significant difference in wording. In ss.26 and 27 the condition is that the claimant fails "for no good reason", not that the claimant acts or omits to act "without a good reason". It may eventually be established that these two phrases have the same meaning, but in the ordinary use of language the phrase "for no good reason" carries a suggestion that something has been done or not done capriciously or arbitrarily, without any real thought or application of reason. It could therefore be argued that it is easier for a claimant to show that s/he did not act for no good reason and on that basis that the balancing of interests mentioned above could not be applicable. It would be enough that the claimant acted or failed to act rationally in the light of his or her own interests. It can of course be objected that such an argument fails to give the proper weight to the identification of what is a good reason and that it would seem contrary to the overall policy of the legislation if it was much easier to escape a universal credit sanction than a JSA sanction. On the other hand, it can be asked why Parliament chose to use a different phrase for the purposes of universal credit sanctions than "without a good reason" when the latter phrase could have fitted happily into ss.26 and 27. It is to be hoped that the ambiguity will be resolved in early decisions of the Upper Tribunal.

Subsections (2)–(4) set out what can be a sanctionable failure for the purposes of s.26 and higher-level sanctions. All are restricted to claimants who are at the time of the imposition of the sanction subject to all work-related requirements under s.22. Thus, claimants excused from all work-related requirements under s.19 (e.g. those with limited capability for work and work-related activity or with specified caring responsibilities) or from some element of such requirements under s.20 or 21 cannot be subject to higher level sanctions. They can be subject to s.27 sanctions. Subsections (5)–(8) give regulation-making powers.

Subsection (2)

(a) It is a higher-level sanctionable failure for a claimant subject to all work-related requirements to fail for no good reason (on which see the note above) to comply with a work preparation requirement under s.16 to undertake a work placement of a description prescribed in regulations. Regulation 114(1) of the Universal Credit Regulations prescribes Mandatory Work Activity as a work placement for the purposes of this provision and reg.114(2) provides a short description of the nature of that scheme with the aim of fulfilling the requirement to give a description and not just a label (the problem identified by the Court of Appeal in relation to the then state of the JSA legislation in *R (on the application of Reilly and Wilson) v Secretary of State for Work and Pensions* [2013] EWCA Civ 66; [2013] 1 WLR 2239). The approach of the Court of Appeal was approved by the Supreme Court [2013] UKSC 68. It could be said that in reg.114(2) there is slightly more description than in the provision in issue in *Reilly and Wilson*, in that something is added to the terms of s.26(2)(a), but scarcely anything is added to the meaning of "work preparation requirement" in s.16(1). There is certainly nothing like the degree of detail that is in reg.3 of the Jobseeker's Allowance (Schemes for Assisting Persons to Obtain Employment) Regulations 2013 (see Vol.II), discussed by the Supreme Court at para.49 of the judgment. The validity of the prescription in reg.114 is therefore in doubt. If it is not valid, there is nothing for subs.(2)(a) to bite on.

1.103

Before undertaking a Mandatory Work Activity scheme can have become a work preparation requirement under s.16 (if reg.114 is validly made) it must have been specified for the claimant in question by the Secretary of State and meet the condition of improving the particular claimant's work prospects (see *JS v SSWP (ESA)* [2013] UKUT 635 (AAC)). The requirement is to take the action specified by the Secretary of State, so that the detail of the specification will be important in determining what amounts to a failure to comply with the requirement. There will be familiar issues, e.g. whether turning up to a scheme and then declining to co-operate or doing so only grudgingly amounts to a failure to comply.

(b) It is a higher-level sanctionable failure for a claimant subject to all work-related requirements to fail for no good reason (on which see the note above) to comply with a work search requirement under s.17 to apply for a particular vacancy for paid work. It would seem that for there to have been a requirement to apply for a particular vacancy the taking of that action must have been specified by the Secretary of State under s.17(1)(b). See the note to s.17 for discussion of the meaning of "paid work". It appears in the nature of the word "vacancy" that it is for employment as an employed earner, or possibly some form of self-employment that is closely analogous to such employment, e.g. through an agency. Regulation 94 of the Universal Credit Regulations deems a claimant not to have complied with a requirement to apply for a particular vacancy for paid work where the claimant fails to participate in an interview offered in connection with the vacancy. Participation must at least entail turning up at the place and time for the interview and extend to making some meaningful contribution to the interview, but the limits will probably not be established until there have been some sanctions appeals to the Upper Tribunal. That is the context in which what amounts to a failure to comply will be identified, as well as what might amount to a good reason for non-compliance. For instance, there appear to be no provisions prescribing the length of notice of an interview to be given or how far a claimant can be required to travel, but there could plainly be a good reason for failing to comply with unreasonable requirements, especially if the claimant had attempted in advance to draw any problem with attendance to the attention of the Secretary of State or the potential employer. See the discussion in the note to s.19(2)(c) of the Jobseekers Act 1995 in Vol.II for what might amount to refusing to apply. See also reg.113(1)(a) of the Universal Credit Regulations excluding reductions in benefit on consideration of vacancies due to strikes arising from trade disputes.

1.104   (c) It is a higher-level sanctionable failure for a claimant subject to all work-related requirements to fail for no good reason (on which see the note above) to comply with a work availability requirement under s.18 by not taking up an offer of paid work. See the note to s.17 for discussion of the meaning of "paid work". Since the requirement under s.18 is in the very general terms of being able and willing immediately to take up paid work, the relevance of not taking up an offer can only be in revealing an absence of such ability or willingness. Therefore, both any limitations under reg.97 of the Universal Credit Regulations on the kinds of paid work that a claimant must be able and willing to take up immediately and the provisions of reg.96(2)–(5) on when a claimant is deemed to have complied with the requirement despite not being able to satisfy the "immediately" condition must be taken into account in determining whether a claimant has failed to comply with the requirement. See the discussion in the note to s.19(2)(c) of the Jobseekers Act 1995 in Vol.II for what might amount to refusing or failing without a good reason to accept a situation, if offered, in any employment, but note that there may be differences between failing to accept a situation in employment and failing to accept an offer of paid work. See also reg.113(1)(a) of the Universal Credit Regulations excluding reductions in benefit on consideration of vacancies due to strikes arising from trade disputes.

    (d) It is a higher-level sanctionable failure for a claimant subject to all work-related requirements to cease paid work or lose pay by reason of misconduct or voluntarily and for no good reason (on which see the note above). Since by definition the claimant must, if already subject to s.22, have an award of universal credit, this sanction can only apply to those claimants who are entitled to the benefit while in work. See the note to s.17 for discussion of the meaning of "paid work". See the note to subs.(4) below for discussion of the meanings of "misconduct" and "voluntarily and for no good reason", as well as of the implications of fixed and severe sanctions for losing pay apparently no matter what the amount of loss, subject to the exception from reductions in benefit in reg.113(1)(g) of the Universal Credit Regulations. See the further exceptions in reg.113(1)(b) (trial periods in work where the claimant attempts hours additional to a limitation under ss.17(4) or 18(3)); (c) (voluntarily ceasing paid work or losing pay because of a strike); (d) (voluntarily ceasing paid work or losing pay as a member of the regular or reserve forces); and (f) (volunteering for redundancy or lay-off or short-time).

Subsection (3)

1.105   This provision applies to claimants with an award of universal credit who are subject to no work-related requirements under s.19(2)(d) because reg.90 of the Universal Credit Regulations, made under the specific powers in s.19(3), applies s.19 where the claimant's earnings equal or exceed the individual threshold. If the claimant ceases the paid work from which those earnings are derived or loses pay so that the earnings are then below the individual threshold, either by reason of misconduct or voluntarily and for no good reason (on which see the note above), and does not fall within either ss.20 or 21, a higher-level sanction is to be imposed. See the note to subs.(4) below for discussion of the meanings of "misconduct" and "voluntarily and for no good reason". The exception in reg.113(1)(g) of the Universal Credit Regulations cannot by definition apply if this provision applies. If the Secretary of State considers under reg.99(6) that the level of the claimant's earnings (or the earnings of a couple) are at a sufficient level that a work search requirement or a work availability requirement should not be imposed, the relevant requirement(s) cannot be imposed and the claimant cannot be subject to all work-related requirements under s.22. A very slight decrease in earnings could, in a marginal case, have the effect identified in subs.(3), yet (no regulations having been made under subs.(5)(b)) the full force of the higher-level sanction must be imposed. It may be that in such circumstances it will be correspondingly easier for a claimant to show that a voluntary loss of pay was not "for no good reason". See also the further exceptions in reg.113(1)(c) (voluntarily ceasing paid work or losing pay because of a strike); (d) (voluntarily ceasing paid work or losing pay as a member of the regular or reserve forces); and (f) (volunteering for redundancy or applying for a redundancy payment after lay-off or short-time).

Subsection (4)

Where a claimant has an award of universal credit and is subject to all work-related requirements under s.22 it is a higher-level sanctionable failure if before making the claim relevant to the award the claimant for no good reason failed to take up an offer of paid work (para.(a)) or by reason of misconduct or voluntarily and for no good reason ceased paid work or lost pay (para.(b)). A practical limit to how far back before the date of claim such action or inaction can be to lead to a reduction of benefit is set by regs 102(4) and 113(1)(e) of the Universal Credit Regulations. If the gap between the action or inaction and the date of claim is longer than or equal to the period of the reduction that would otherwise be imposed, there is to be no reduction. Thus a lot depends on whether it is a first, second or subsequent "offence" within a year. These two grounds of sanction are the most similar to the familiar JSA grounds now in s.19(2)(a), (b) and (c) of the Jobseekers Act 1995.

Under para.(a), see the discussion in the note to subs.(2)(c), but note that this sanction applies to any offer of paid work. Therefore, all questions of whether the work is suitable for the claimant and whether or not it was reasonable for the claimant not to take it up will have to be considered under the "no good reason" condition. See the introductory part of the note to this section for the meaning of that phrase as compared with "without a good reason".

Under para.(b), it would appear that misconduct and voluntarily ceasing work will have the same general meaning as misconduct and leaving employment voluntarily for the purposes of JSA and, before it, unemployment benefit. See the extensive discussion in the notes to s.19(2)(a) and (b) of the Jobseekers Act 1995 in Vol.II, which will not even be summarised here. The scope of the sanction has to be wider to take account of the nature of universal credit. Ceasing paid work certainly has a significantly wider meaning than losing employment as an employed earner if it encompasses self-employment in addition, as suggested in the note to s.17. The notion of ceasing paid work seems in itself wider than that of losing employment and to avoid difficulties over whether suspension from work without dismissal and particular ways of bringing a contract of employment to an end are covered. But remember that under reg.113(1)(f) of the Universal Credit Regulations a reduction cannot be applied on the ground of voluntarily ceasing work where the claimant has volunteered for redundancy or has claimed a redundancy payment after being subject to lay-off or short-time working, although the action remains a sanctionable failure. See also the exceptions for voluntarily ceasing paid work or losing pay because of a strike arising from a trade dispute or as a member of the regular or reserve forces (reg.113(1)(c) and (d)).

The other particularly significant widening of the scope of the sanction as compared with those in JSA is in the application of this and the similar sanctions under previous subsections to losing pay as well as to ceasing paid work. This is necessary, both in relation to circumstances before the date of claim and later, because it is possible for a claimant to be entitled to universal credit while still in paid work. If the earnings from the work are below the amount of the claimant's work allowance (varied according to circumstances) they are disregarded in the calculation of any award. If they exceed that amount, 65 per cent of the excess is taken into account as income to be set against the maximum amount of universal credit. There are also

1.106

1.107

the rules, under s.19(2)(d) and (3), in reg.90 of the Universal Credit Regulations making a claimant subject to no work-related conditions if earnings are at least equal to an individual threshold (in the standard case the National Minimum Wage for 35 hours per week, with lesser hours used in defined circumstances). The sanction regime under s.26 can only apply when at the time of the award in question the claimant is subject to all work-related requirements under s.22 and so cannot be receiving earnings at or above that individual threshold. Subsection (3) above deals with the situation where during the course of an award of universal credit a claimant moves from having earnings at least equal to the individual threshold to a situation where the earnings are lower than that threshold. For loss of pay, short of the ceasing of work, prior to the date of claim to trigger the application of the sanction under subs.(3) it must be within a fairly narrow limit. To bring the claimant within the scope of s.22 the loss of pay must leave earnings below the individual threshold.

Subsection (5)

1.108   Regulations may deem ceasing work or losing pay not to be by reason of misconduct or voluntarily in certain circumstances and may provide that loss of pay below a prescribed level is to be disregarded. No such regulations have been made. Regulation 113 of the Universal Credit Regulations is made under the powers in subs.(8)(a) and only affects whether a reduction in benefit is to be imposed, not whether there is or is not a sanctionable failure.

Subsections (6) and (7)

1.109   See regs 101 and 106—111 of the Universal Credit Regulations for the amount and period of the reduction in benefit under a higher-level sanction. The three-year limit is imposed in subs.(6)(b) and cannot be extended in regulations.

Subsection (8)

1.110   Under para.(a), see reg.113 of the Universal Credit Regulations. Under para.(b), see reg.107. Under para.(c), see regs 108 and 109.

Other sanctions

1.111   **27.**—(1) The amount of an award of universal credit is to be reduced in accordance with this section in the event of a failure by a claimant which is sanctionable under this section.

(2) It is a failure sanctionable under this section if a claimant—

(a) fails for no good reason to comply with a work-related requirement;

(b) fails for no good reason to comply with a requirement under section 23.

(3) But a failure by a claimant is not sanctionable under this section if it is also a failure sanctionable under section 26.

(4) Regulations are to provide for—

(a) the amount of a reduction under this section, and

(b) the period for which such a reduction has effect.

(5) Regulations under subsection (4)(b) may provide that a reduction under this section in relation to any failure is to have effect for—

(a) a period continuing until the claimant meets a compliance condition specified by the Secretary of State,

(b) a fixed period not exceeding 26 weeks which is—

(i) specified in the regulations, or

(ii) determined in any case by the Secretary of State, or

(c) a combination of both.

(6) In subsection (5)(a) "compliance condition" means—

(a) a condition that the failure ceases, or

(b) a condition relating to future compliance with a work-related requirement or a requirement under section 23.

(7) A compliance condition specified under subsection (5)(a) may be—

(a) revoked or varied by the Secretary of State;

(b) notified to the claimant in such manner as the Secretary of State may determine.

(8) A period fixed under subsection (5)(b) may in particular depend on either or both the following—

(a) the number of failures by the claimant sanctionable under this section;

(b) the period between such failures.

(9) Regulations may provide—

(a) for cases in which no reduction is to be made under this section;

(b) for a reduction under this section made in relation to an award that is terminated to be applied to any new award made within a prescribed period of the termination;

(c) for the termination or suspension of a reduction under this section.

DEFINITIONS

"claimant"—see s.40.
"work-related requirement"—see ss.40 and 13(2).

GENERAL NOTE

See the introductory part of the note to s.26 for the general nature of the universal credit sanctions regime under ss.26 and 27 and for discussion of the meaning of "for no good reason". Section 27(1) and (2) requires there to be a reduction, of the amount and period set out in regulations, wherever the claimant has failed for no good reason to comply with any work-related requirement or a connected requirement under s.23. There is no general discretion whether or not to apply the prescribed deduction, but that is subject first to the rule in subs.(3) that if a failure is sanctionable under s.26 (and therefore potentially subject to the higher-level regime) it is not to be sanctionable under s.27 and to the rules in reg.113 of the Universal Credit Regulations about when a reduction is not to be applied although there is a sanctionable failure. While the power and duty under subs.(4) for regulations to provide for the amount and period of the reduction to be imposed is in fact more open-ended than that in s.26(6), because it does not have the three-year limit, subss. (5)–(7) introduce the specific power (that does not of course have to be used) for regulations to provide for the period of the reduction for a particular sanctionable failure to continue until the claimant meets a "compliance condition" (subs.(6)) or for a fixed period not exceeding 26 weeks specified in regulations or determined by the Secretary of State or a combination of both. The 26-week limit in subs.(5)(b) appears not to have any decisive effect because a longer period could always be pre-scribed under subs.(4)(b), unless "may" is to be construed as meaning "may only".

In practice, the powers have been used in the Universal Credit Regulations to set up a structure of medium-level (reg.103), low-level (reg.104) and lowest-level (reg.105) sanctions. See the notes to those regulations for the details.

The medium-level sanction applies only to failures to comply with a work search requirement under s.17(1)(a) to take all reasonable action to obtain paid work etc. or to comply with a work availability requirement under s.18(1). A failure to comply with a work search requirement under s.17(1)(b) to apply for a particular vacancy attracts a higher-level sanction under s.26(2)(b) if the claimant is subject to all work-related requirements. The reduction period under reg.103 is 28 days for a first "offence" and 91 days for a second "offence" or subsequent offence within a year of the previous failure (7 and 14 days for under-18s).

The low-level sanction under reg.104 applies where the claimant is subject either

1.112

1.113

to all work-related requirements under s.22 or to the work preparation requirement under s.21 and fails to comply with a work-focused interview requirement under s.15(1), a work preparation requirement under s.16(1), a work search requirement under s.17(1)(b) to take any action specified by the Secretary of State or a connected requirement in s.23(1), (3) or (4). Note that this is the sanction that applies to a failure for no good reason to report specified changes in circumstances (s.23(4)) or to provide specified information and evidence (s.23(3)) as well as to failure to attend an interview. The reduction period under reg.104 lasts until the claimant complies with the requirement in question, comes within s.19 (no work-related requirements), a work preparation requirement to take particular action is no longer imposed or the award terminates, plus seven days for a first "offence", 14 days for a second "offence" within a year of the previous failure and 28 days for a third or subsequent "offence" within a year (plus seven days in all those circumstances for under-18s).

The lowest-level sanction under reg.105 applies where a claimant is subject to s.20 and fails to comply with a work-focused interview requirement. The reduction period under reg.105 lasts until the claimant complies with the requirement, comes within s.19 (no work-related requirements), a work preparation requirement to take particular action is no longer imposed or the award terminates.

For the purposes of regs 104 and 105, "compliance condition" is defined in subs. (6) to mean either a condition that the failure to comply ceases or a condition relating to future compliance. A compliance condition may be revoked or varied by the Secretary of State, apparently at will, and may be (not must be) notified to the claimant in such manner as the Secretary of State might determine (subs.(7)). But under regs 104 and 105 a compliance condition has to be "specified" by the Secretary of State. On the one hand, it is difficult to envisage it being decided that the Secretary of State can specify such a condition to himself, rather than to the claimant. On the other hand, it is difficult to envisage it being decided that a claimant who has in fact complied with a requirement has not met a compliance condition merely because the Secretary of State failed to give proper notice of the condition.

1.114   Regulation 113 of the Universal Credit Regulations, made in part under subs.(9)(a), prescribes circumstances in which no reduction is to be made for a sanctionable failure under s.27, but none of the circumstances covered seem relevant to s.27.

Under para.(b) of subs.(9), see reg.107. Under para.(c), see regs 108 and 109.

Hardship payments

1.115   **28.**—(1) Regulations may make provision for the making of additional payments by way of universal credit to a claimant ("hardship payments") where—

(a) the amount of the claimant's award is reduced under section 26 or 27, and

(b) the claimant is or will be in hardship.

(2) Regulations under this section may in particular make provision as to—

(a) circumstances in which a claimant is to be treated as being or not being in hardship;

(b) matters to be taken into account in determining whether a claimant is or will be in hardship;

(c) requirements or conditions to be met by a claimant in order to receive hardship payments;

(d) the amount or rate of hardship payments;

(e) the period for which hardship payments may be made;

(f) whether hardship payments are recoverable.

DEFINITION

"claimant"—see s.40.

GENERAL NOTE

The provision of hardship payments is an important part of the sanctions regime 1.116
for universal credit. The payments are to be made by way of universal credit.
However, it will be seen that s.28, first, does not require the making of provision
for hardship payments in regulations and, second, gives almost complete freedom
in how any regulations define the conditions for and amounts of payments. The
provisions made are in regs 115–119 of the Universal Credit Regulations, which
contain stringent conditions and a restricted definition of "hardship", which nevertheless retains a number of subjective elements. Payments are generally recoverable,
subject to exceptions. See the notes to those regulations for the details and the relevant parts of Ch.55 of CPAG's *Welfare benefits and tax credits handbook 2013/2014*
for helpful explanations and examples. There seems to be no reason why a decision
of the Secretary of State to make or not to make hardship payments on an application under reg.116(1)(c) should not be appealable to a First-tier Tribunal.

Administration

Delegation and contracting out

29.—(1) The functions of the Secretary of State under sections 13 to 25 1.117
may be exercised by, or by the employees of, such persons as the Secretary
of State may authorise for the purpose (an "authorised person").

(2) An authorisation given by virtue of this section may authorise the
exercise of a function—

(a) wholly or to a limited extent;
(b) generally or in particular cases or areas;
(c) unconditionally or subject to conditions.

(3) An authorisation under this section—

(a) may specify its duration;
(b) may be varied or revoked at any time by the Secretary of State;
(c) does not prevent the Secretary of State or another person from exercising the function to which the authorisation related.

(4) Anything done or omitted to be done by or in relation to an authorised person (or an employee of that person) in, or in connection with, the
exercise or purported exercise of the function concerned is to be treated for
all purposes as done or omitted to be done by or in relation to the Secretary
of State or (as the case may be) an officer of the Secretary of State.

(5) Subsection (4) does not apply—

(a) for the purposes of so much of any contract made between the
authorised person and the Secretary of State as relates to the exercise
of the function, or
(b) for the purposes of any criminal proceedings brought in respect of
anything done or omitted to be done by the authorised person (or an
employee of that person).

(6) Where—

(a) the authorisation of an authorised person is revoked, and
(b) at the time of the revocation so much of any contract made between
the authorised person and the Secretary of State as relates to the
exercise of the function is subsisting,

the authorised person is entitled to treat the contract as repudiated by
the Secretary of State (and not as frustrated by reason of that revocation).

DEFINITION

"person"—see Interpretation Act 1978, Sch.1.

GENERAL NOTE

1.118   This section allows the Secretary of State to authorise other persons (which word in accordance with the Interpretation Act 1978 includes corporate and unincorporated associations, such as companies) and their employees to carry out any of his functions under ss.13–25. Any such authorisation will not in practice cover the making of regulations, but may well (depending on the extent of the authorisations given) extend to specifying various matters under those sections. The involvement of private sector organisations, operating for profit, in running various schemes within the scope of the benefit system is something that claimants sometimes object to. Such a generalised objection, even if on principled grounds, is unlikely to amount in itself to a good reason for failing to engage with a scheme in question (although see the discussion in the note to s.26 on whether "for no good reason" has a restricted meaning). An objection based on previous experience with the organisation concerned or the nature of the course may raise more difficult issues. See also the discussion in *R(JSA) 7/03* plus *CSJSA/495/2007* and *CSJSA/505/2007*.

CHAPTER 3

SUPPLEMENTARY AND GENERAL

Supplementary and consequential

Supplementary regulation-making powers

1.119   30. Schedule 1 contains supplementary regulation-making powers.

Supplementary and consequential amendments

1.120   31. Schedule 2 contains supplementary and consequential amendments.

Power to make supplementary and consequential provision etc.

1.121   32.—(1) The appropriate authority may by regulations make such consequential, supplementary, incidental or transitional provision in relation to any provision of this Part as the authority considers appropriate.

(2) The appropriate authority is the Secretary of State, subject to subsection (3).

(3) The appropriate authority is the Welsh Ministers for—
  (a) provision which would be within the legislative competence of the National Assembly for Wales were it contained in an Act of the Assembly;
  (b) provision which could be made by the Welsh Ministers under any other power conferred on them.

(4) Regulations under this section may amend, repeal or revoke any primary or secondary legislation (whenever passed or made).

Universal credit and other benefits

Abolition of benefits

1.122   33.—(1) The following benefits are abolished—
  (a) income-based jobseeker's allowance under the Jobseekers Act 1995;
  (b) income-related employment and support allowance under Part 1 of the Welfare Reform Act 2007;

(c) income support under section 124 of the Social Security Contributions and Benefits Act 1992;

(d) housing benefit under section 130 of that Act;

(e) council tax benefit under section 131 of that Act;

(f) child tax credit and working tax credit under the Tax Credits Act 2002.

(2) In subsection (1)—

(a) "income-based jobseeker's allowance" has the same meaning as in the Jobseekers Act 1995;

(b) "income-related employment and support allowance" means an employment and support allowance entitlement to which is based on section 1(2)(b) of the Welfare Reform Act 2007.

(3) Schedule 3 contains consequential amendments.

DEFINITIONS

"income-related employment and support allowance"—see subs(2)(b).

"income-based jobseeker's allowance"—see subs.(2)(a).

GENERAL NOTE

Subs. (1)

The purpose of this provision is simple enough. Sub-section (1) provides for the abolition of income-based JSA, income-related ESA, income support, housing benefit, council tax benefit, child tax credit and working tax credit. The implementation of this section is much less straightforward. Council tax benefit was abolished in favour of localised schemes from April 2013. As a general rule abolition of the other benefits will only happen when all claimants have been transferred to universal credit. The exception to this rule is that when a claimant in the Pathfinder Group claims JSA, ESA or universal credit, this action of itself triggers the abolition at that point (and for that individual) of income-based JSA and income-related ESA (see Commencement Order No.9, art.4).   1.123

This sub-section is modelled on the drafting of s.1(3) of the Tax Credits Act (TCA) 2002, which provided for the abolition of e.g. the personal allowances for children in the income support and income-based JSA schemes. Section 1(3) of the TCA 2002 has never been fully implemented. The fate of subs.(1) here remains to be seen.

Subs. (3)

This introduces Sch.3, which makes consequential amendments relating to the abolition of these benefits. Those changes remove references in other legislation to contributory ESA or JSA, as these will be unnecessary once ESA and JSA are contributory benefits only, and update references to other legislation which has been amended.   1.124

Universal credit and state pension credit

34. Schedule 4 provides for a housing element of state pension credit in consequence of the abolition of housing benefit by section 33.   1.125

GENERAL NOTE

This section provides for a new housing credit element of state pension credit to replace housing benefit for claimants above the qualifying age for state pension credit. In its original form under the SPCA 2002, state pension credit was made up of two elements: the guarantee credit (performing the same function as income support used to) and the savings credit (providing a small top-up for those claimants with modest savings). Schedule 4 amends the SPCA 2002 to create a new third credit to cover housing costs. This will provide support for people who have reached the qualifying age for state pension credit (or for couples where both members have   1.126

reached the qualifying age) once housing benefit is no longer available following the introduction of universal credit.

Universal credit and working-age benefits

1.127   **35.** Schedule 5 makes further provision relating to universal credit, job-seeker's allowance and employment and support allowance.

GENERAL NOTE

1.128   This section (and Sch.5) deals with the inter-relationship between universal credit, JSA and ESA. After the introduction of universal credit, ESA and JSA will continue to be available but only as contributory benefits.

Migration to universal credit

1.129   **36.** Schedule 6 contains provision about the replacement of benefits by universal credit.

GENERAL NOTE

1.130   This section gives effect to Sch.6, which makes provision relating to the replacement of the benefits that will be abolished under s.33, as well as any other prescribed benefits, and the consequential migration (or transfer) of claimants to universal credit.

General

Capability for work or work-related activity

1.131   **37.**—(1) For the purposes of this Part a claimant has limited capability for work if—

    (a) the claimant's capability for work is limited by their physical or mental condition, and

    (b) the limitation is such that it is not reasonable to require the claimant to work.

(2) For the purposes of this Part a claimant has limited capability for work-related activity if—

    (a) the claimant's capability for work-related activity is limited by their physical or mental condition, and

    (b) the limitation is such that it is not reasonable to require the claimant to undertake work-related activity.

(3) The question whether a claimant has limited capability for work or work-related activity for the purposes of this Part is to be determined in accordance with regulations.

(4) Regulations under this section must, subject as follows, provide for determination of that question on the basis of an assessment (or repeated assessments) of the claimant.

(5) Regulations under this section may for the purposes of an assessment—

    (a) require a claimant to provide information or evidence (and may require it to be provided in a prescribed manner or form);

    (b) require a claimant to attend and submit to a medical examination at a place, date and time determined under the regulations.

(6) Regulations under this section may make provision for a claimant to be treated as having or not having limited capability for work or work-related activity.

(7) Regulations under subsection (6) may provide for a claimant who fails to comply with a requirement imposed under subsection (5) without a good reason to be treated as not having limited capability for work or work-related activity.

(8) Regulations under subsection (6) may provide for a claimant to be treated as having limited capability for work until—

(a) it has been determined whether or not that is the case, or

(b) the claimant is under any other provision of regulations under sub-section (6) treated as not having it.

(9) Regulations under this section may provide for determination of the question of whether a claimant has limited capability for work or work-related activity even where the claimant is for the time being treated under regulations under subsection (6) as having limited capability for work or work-related activity.

DEFINITIONS

"claim"—see s.40.
"claimant"—*ibid.*
"limited capability for work"—*ibid.*
"prescribed"—*ibid.*
"work search requirement"—*ibid.*

GENERAL NOTE

If a person has limited capability for work or limited capability for work and work-related activity, this is relevant to universal credit in three ways. Firstly, it affects the amount of the award of universal credit (see ss.1(3)(d) and 12(2)(a) and (b) and regs 27–28 and 36 of the Universal Credit Regulations). Secondly, it determines the work-related requirements that can be imposed. Under s.19(2)(a) no work-related requirements can be imposed on a claimant who has limited capability for work and work-related activity and under s.21(1)(a) a claimant who has limited capability for work is only subject to the work preparation requirement. Thirdly, it determines which level of the lower or higher work allowance applies (see s. 8(3)(a) and reg. 22 of the Universal Credit Regulations).   1.132

This section contains provisions that are broadly equivalent to those in ss.1(4), 2(5), 8 and 9 of the Welfare Reform Act 2007. Thus the question of whether a person has limited capability for work or limited capability for work and work-related activity, will be determined in the same way as for ESA.

In relation to subs.(7), note also the regulation-making power in para.8 of Sch.1.

Information

38. Information supplied under Chapter 2 of this Part or section 37 is to be taken for all purposes to be information relating to social security.   1.133

Couples

39.—(1) In this Part "couple" means—   1.134

(a) a man and woman who are married to each other and are members of the same household;

(b) a man and woman who are not married to each other but are living together as husband and wife;

(c) two people of the same sex who are civil partners of each other and are members of the same household;

(d) two people of the same sex who are not civil partners of each other but are living together as civil partners.

(2) For the purposes of this section, two people of the same sex are to be

treated as living together as if they were civil partners if, and only if, they would be treated as living together as husband and wife were they of opposite sexes.

(3) For the purposes of this section regulations may prescribe—

(a) circumstances in which the fact that two persons are husband and wife or are civil partners is to be disregarded;

(b) circumstances in which a man and a woman are to be treated as living together as husband and wife;

(c) circumstances in which people are to be treated as being or not being members of the same household.

GENERAL NOTE

1.135   See the commentary to reg.3 of the Universal Credit Regulations.

Interpretation of Part 1

1.136   **40.** In this Part—

"assessment period" has the meaning given by section 7(2);

"child" means a person under the age of 16;

"claim" means claim for universal credit;

"claimant" means a single claimant or each of joint claimants;

"couple" has the meaning given by section 39;

"disabled" has such meaning as may be prescribed;

"joint claimants" means members of a couple who jointly make a claim or in relation to whom an award of universal credit is made;

"limited capability for work" and "limited capability for work-related activity" are to be construed in accordance with section 37(1) and (2);

"prescribed" means specified or provided for in regulations;

"primary legislation" means an Act, Act of the Scottish Parliament or Act or Measure of the National Assembly for Wales;

"qualifying young person" has the meaning given in section 10(5);

"regular and substantial caring responsibilities" has such meaning as may be prescribed;

"responsible carer", in relation to a child, has the meaning given in section 19(6);

"secondary legislation" means an instrument made under primary legislation";

"severely disabled" has such meaning as may be prescribed;

"single claimant" means a single person who makes a claim for universal credit or in relation to whom an award of universal credit is made as a single person;

"single person" is to be construed in accordance with section 1(2)(a);

"work" has such meaning as may be prescribed;

"work availability requirement" has the meaning given by section 18(1);

"work preparation requirement" has the meaning given by section 16(1);

"work search requirement" has the meaning given by section 17(1);

" work-focused interview requirement" has the meaning given by section 15(1);

"work-related activity", in relation to a person, means activity which makes it more likely that the person will obtain or remain in work or be able to do so;

"work-related requirement" has the meaning given by section 13(2).

Regulations

Pilot schemes

41.—(1) Any power to make—   1.137

(a) regulations under this Part,

(b) regulations under the Social Security Administration Act 1992 relating to universal credit, or

(c) regulations under the Social Security Act 1998 relating to universal credit, may be exercised so as to make provision for piloting purposes.

(2) In subsection (1), "piloting purposes", in relation to any provision, means the purposes of testing—

(a) the extent to which the provision is likely to make universal credit simpler to understand or to administer,

(b) the extent to which the provision is likely to promote—

    (i) people remaining in work, or

    (ii) people obtaining or being able to obtain work (or more work or better-paid work), or

(c) the extent to which, and how, the provision is likely to affect the conduct of claimants or other people in any other way.

(3) Regulations made by virtue of this section are in the remainder of this section referred to as a "pilot scheme".

(4) A pilot scheme may be limited in its application to—

(a) one or more areas;

(b) one or more classes of person;

(c) persons selected—

    (i) by reference to prescribed criteria, or

    (ii) on a sampling basis.

(5) A pilot scheme may not have effect for a period exceeding three years, but—

(a) the Secretary of State may by order made by statutory instrument provide that the pilot scheme is to continue to have effect after the time when it would otherwise expire for a period not exceeding twelve months (and may make more than one such order);

(b) a pilot scheme may be replaced by a further pilot scheme making the same or similar provision.

(6) A pilot scheme may include consequential or transitional provision in relation to its expiry.

GENERAL NOTE

This important provision is similar to that in s.29 of the Jobseekers Act 1995. It   1.138 contains the power to pilot changes in regulations across particular geographical areas and/or specified categories of claimants for up to three years, although this period can be extended, or the pilot scheme can be replaced by a different pilot scheme making the same or similar provision (subs.(5)). The power can only be exercised in relation to the types of regulation listed in subs.(1) and with a view to assessing whether the proposed changes are likely to make universal credit simpler to understand or administer, to encourage people to find or remain in work (or more or better-paid work) or "to affect the conduct of claimants or other people in any other way" (subs.(2)). Regulations made under this section are subject to the affirmative resolution procedure (s.43(4)). On past experience in relation to JSA, it seems likely that this power will be exercised on a fairly regular basis.

Regulations: general

1.139   **42.**—(1) Regulations under this Part are to be made by the Secretary of State, unless otherwise provided.

(2) A power to make regulations under this Part may be exercised—

(a) so as to make different provision for different cases or purposes;

(b) in relation to all or only some of the cases or purposes for which it may be exercised.

(3) Such a power includes—

(a) power to make incidental, supplementary, consequential or transitional provision or savings;

(b) power to provide for a person to exercise a discretion in dealing with any matter.

(4) Each power conferred by this Part is without prejudice to the others.

(5) Where regulations under this Part provide for an amount, the amount may be zero.

(6) Where regulations under this Part provide for an amount for the purposes of an award (or a reduction from an award), the amount may be different in relation to different descriptions of person, and in particular may depend on—

(a) whether the person is a single person or a member of couple.

(b) the age of the person.

(7) Regulations under section 11(4) or 12(3) which provide for the determination or calculation of an amount may make different provision for different areas.

Definitions

> "couple"—see ss.39 and 40.
> "single person"—see s.40.
> "work"—*ibid.*

Regulations: procedure

1.140   **43.**—(1) Regulations under this Part are to be made by statutory instrument.

(2) A statutory instrument containing regulations made by the Secretary of State under this Part is subject to the negative resolution procedure, subject as follows.

(3) A statutory instrument containing the first regulations made by the Secretary of State under any of the following, alone or with other regulations, is subject to the affirmative resolution procedure—

(a) section 4(7) (acceptance of claimant commitment);

(b) section 5(1)(a) and (2)(a) (capital limits);

(c) section 8(3) (income to be deducted in award calculation);

(d) section 9(2) and (3) (standard allowance);

(e) section 10(3) and (4) (children and young persons element);

(f) section 11 (housing costs element);

(g) section 12 (other needs and circumstances element);

(h) section 18(3) and (5) (work availability requirement);

(i) section 19(2)(d) (claimants subject to no work-related requirements);

(j) sections 26 and 27 (sanctions);

(k) section 28 (hardship payments);
(l) paragraph 4 of Schedule 1 (calculation of capital and income);
(m) paragraph 1(1) of Schedule 6 (migration), where making provision under paragraphs 4, 5 and 6 of that Schedule.

(4) A statutory instrument containing regulations made by the Secretary of State by virtue of section 41 (pilot schemes), alone or with other regulations, is subject to the affirmative resolution procedure.

(5) A statutory instrument containing regulations made by the Secretary of State under this Part is subject to the affirmative resolution procedure if—

(a) it also contains regulations under another enactment, and
(b) an instrument containing those regulations would apart from this section be subject to the affirmative resolution procedure.

(6) For the purposes of subsections (2) to (5)—

(a) a statutory instrument subject to the "negative resolution procedure" is subject to annulment in pursuance of a resolution of either House of Parliament;
(b) a statutory instrument subject to the "affirmative resolution procedure" may not be made unless a draft of the instrument has been laid before, and approved by resolution of, each House of Parliament.

(7) A statutory instrument containing regulations made by the Welsh Ministers under section 32 may not be made unless a draft of the instrument has been laid before, and approved by resolution of, the National Assembly for Wales.

DEFINITIONS

"child"—see s.40.
"claim"—*ibid.*
"claimant"—*ibid.*
"work"—*ibid.*
"work availability requirement"—*ibid.*

PART 5

SOCIAL SECURITY: GENERAL

Benefit cap

Benefit cap

96.—(1) Regulations may provide for a benefit cap to be applied to the welfare benefits to which a single person or couple is entitled.   1.141

(2) For the purposes of this section, applying a benefit cap to welfare benefits means securing that, where a single person's or couple's total entitlement to welfare benefits in respect of the reference period exceeds the relevant amount, their entitlement to welfare benefits in respect of any period of the same duration as the reference period is reduced by an amount up to or equalling the excess.

(3) In subsection (2) the "reference period" means a period of a prescribed duration.

(4) Regulations under this section may in particular—

(a) make provision as to the manner in which total entitlement to welfare benefits for any period, or the amount of any reduction, is to be determined;

(b) make provision as to the welfare benefit or benefits from which a reduction is to be made;

(c) provide for exceptions to the application of the benefit cap;

(d) make provision as to the intervals at which the benefit cap is to be applied;

(e) make provision as to the relationship between application of the benefit cap and any other reduction in respect of a welfare benefit;

(f) provide that where in consequence of a change in the relevant amount, entitlement to a welfare benefit increases or decreases, that increase or decrease has effect without any further decision of the Secretary of State;

(g) make supplementary and consequential provision.

(5) In this section the "relevant amount" is an amount specified in regulations.

(6) The amount specified under subsection (5) is to be determined by reference to estimated average earnings.

(7) In this section "estimated average earnings" means the amount which, in the opinion of the Secretary of State, represents at any time the average weekly earnings of a working household in Great Britain after deductions in respect of tax and national insurance contributions.

(8) The Secretary of State may estimate such earnings in such manner as the Secretary of State thinks fit.

(9) Regulations under this section may not provide for any reduction to be made from a welfare benefit—

(a) provision for which is within the legislative competence of the Scottish Parliament;

(b) provision for which is within the legislative competence of the National Assembly for Wales;

(c) provision for which is made by the Welsh Ministers, the First Minister for Wales or the Counsel General to the Welsh Assembly Government.

(10) In this section—

"couple" means two persons of a prescribed description;

"prescribed" means prescribed in regulations;

"regulations" means regulations made by the Secretary of State;

"single person" means a person who is not a member of a couple;

"welfare benefit" means any prescribed benefit, allowance, payment or credit.

(11) Regulations under subsection (10) may not prescribe as welfare benefits—

(a) state pension credit under the State Pension Credit Act 2002, or

(b) retirement pensions under Part 2 or 3 of the Social Security Contributions and Benefits Act 1992.

GENERAL NOTE

See the commentary to regs 78–83 of the Universal Credit Regulations.   1.142

Benefit cap: supplementary

97.—(1) Regulations under section 96 may make different provision for   1.143
different purposes or cases.

(2) Regulations under section 96 must be made by statutory instrument.

(3) A statutory instrument containing the first regulations under section
96 may not be made unless a draft of the instrument has been laid before,
and approved by resolution of, each House of Parliament.

(4) A statutory instrument containing other regulations under section
96 is subject to annulment in pursuance of a resolution of either House of
Parliament.

(5) In section 150 of the Social Security Administration Act 1992 (annual
up-rating of benefits) after subsection (7) there is inserted—

"(7A) The Secretary of State—

(a) shall in each tax year review the amount specified under subsection
(5) of section 96 of the Welfare Reform Act 2012 (benefit cap) to
determine whether its relationship with estimated average earnings
(within the meaning of that section) has changed, and

(b) after that review may, if the Secretary of State considers it appropriate, include in the draft of an up-rating order provision increasing or
decreasing that amount."

(6) In Schedule 2 to the Social Security Act 1998 (decisions against
which no appeal lies) after paragraph 8 there is inserted—

"Reduction on application of benefit cap

8A A decision to apply the benefit cap in accordance with regulations
under section 96 of the Welfare Reform Act 2012."

GENERAL NOTE

See the commentary to regs 78–83 of the Universal Credit Regulations.   1.144

PART 7

FINAL

Repeals

147. *[Omitted]*   1.145

Financial provision

148. There shall be paid out of money provided by Parliament—   1.146

(a) sums paid by the Secretary of State by way of universal credit or
personal independence payment;

(b) any other expenditure incurred in consequence of this Act by a
Minister of the Crown or the Commissioners for Her Majesty's
Revenue and Customs;

(c) any increase attributable to this Act in the sums payable under any other Act out of money so provided.

Extent

1.147   **149.**—(1) This Act extends to England and Wales and Scotland only, subject as follows.

(2) The following provisions extend to England and Wales, Scotland and Northern Ireland—

    (a) section 32 (power to make consequential and supplementary provision: universal credit);

    (b) section 33 (abolition of benefits);

(c)–(f) *[Omitted]*

    (g) this Part, excluding Schedule 14 (repeals).

(3) *[Omitted]*

(4) Any amendment or repeal made by this Act has the same extent as the enactment to which it relates.

Commencement

1.148   **150.**—(1) The following provisions of this Act come into force on the day on which it is passed—

(a)–(e) *[Omitted]*

    (f) this Part, excluding Schedule 14 (repeals).

(2) *[Omitted]*

(3) The remaining provisions of this Act come into force on such day as the Secretary of State may by order made by statutory instrument appoint.

(4) An order under subsection (3) may—

    (a) appoint different days for different purposes;

    (b) appoint different days for different areas in relation to—

        (i) any provision of Part 1 (universal credit) or of Part 1 of Schedule 14;

    (ii)–(iii) *[Omitted]*

        (iv) section 102 (consideration of revision before appeal);

    (c) make such transitory or transitional provision, or savings, as the Secretary of State considers necessary or expedient.

Short title

151. This Act may be cited as the Welfare Reform Act 2012.

SCHEDULES

Section 30

SCHEDULE 1

UNIVERSAL CREDIT: SUPPLEMENTARY REGULATION-MAKING POWERS

Entitlement of joint claimants

1. Regulations may provide for circumstances in which joint claimants may be entitled to universal credit without each of them meeting all the basic conditions referred to in section 4.

Linking periods

2. Regulations may provide for periods of entitlement to universal credit which are separated by no more than a prescribed number of days to be treated as a single period.

Couples

3.—(1) Regulations may provide—
   (a) for a claim made by members of a couple jointly to be treated as a claim made by one member of the couple as a single person (or as claims made by both members as single persons);
   (b) for claims made by members of a couple as single persons to be treated as a claim made jointly by the couple.

(2) Regulations may provide—
   (a) where an award is made to joint claimants who cease to be entitled to universal credit as such by ceasing to be a couple, for the making of an award (without a claim) to either or each one of them—
       (i) as a single person, or
       (ii) jointly with another person;
   (b) where an award is made to a single claimant who ceases to be entitled to universal credit as such by becoming a member of a couple, for the making of an award (without a claim) to the members of the couple jointly;
   (c) for the procedure to be followed, and information or evidence to be supplied, in relation to the making of an award under this paragraph.

Calculation of capital and income

4.—(1) Regulations may for any purpose of this Part provide for the calculation or estimation of—   **1.149**
   (a) a person's capital,
   (b) a person's earned and unearned income, and
   (c) a person's earned and unearned income in respect of an assessment period.

(2) Regulations under sub-paragraph (1)(c) may include provision for the calculation to be made by reference to an average over a period, which need not include the assessment period concerned.

(3) Regulations under sub-paragraph (1) may—
   (a) specify circumstances in which a person is to be treated as having or not having capital or earned or unearned income;
   (b) specify circumstances in which income is to be treated as capital or capital as earned income or unearned income;
   (c) specify circumstances in which unearned income is to be treated as earned, or earned income as unearned;
   (d) provide that a person's capital is to be treated as yielding income at a prescribed rate;
   (e) provide that the capital or income of one member of a couple is to be treated as that of the other member.

(4) Regulations under sub-paragraph (3)(a) may in particular provide that persons of a prescribed description are to be treated as having a prescribed minimum level of earned income.

(5) In the case of joint claimants the income and capital of the joint claimants includes (subject to sub-paragraph (6)) the separate income and capital of each of them.

(6) Regulations may specify circumstances in which capital and income of either of joint claimants is to be disregarded in calculating their joint capital and income.

Responsibility for children etc

5.—(1) Regulations may for any purpose of this Part specify circumstances in which a   **1.150**
person is or is not responsible for a child or qualifying young person.

(2) Regulations may for any purpose of this Part make provision about nominations of the responsible carer for a child (see section 19(6)(b)(ii)).

Vouchers

6.—(1) This paragraph applies in relation to an award of universal credit where the calcula-   **1.151**
tion of the amount of the award includes, by virtue of any provision of this Part, an amount in respect of particular costs which a claimant may incur.

(2) Regulations may provide for liability to pay all or part of the award to be discharged by means of provision of a voucher.

(3) But the amount paid by means of a voucher may not in any case exceed the total of the

amounts referred to in sub-paragraph (1) which are included in the calculation of the amount of the award.

(4) For these purposes a voucher is a means other than cash by which a claimant may to any extent meet costs referred to in sub-paragraph (1) of a particular description.

(5) A voucher may for these purposes—

    (a) be limited as regards the person or persons who will accept it;

    (b) be valid only for a limited time.

Work-related requirements

1.152   **7.**—Regulations may provide that a claimant who—

    (a) has a right to reside in the United Kingdom under the EU Treaties, and

    (b) would otherwise fall within section 19, 20 or 21,is to be treated as not falling within that section.

Good reason

1.153   **8.**—Regulations may for any purpose of this Part provide for—

    (a) circumstances in which a person is to be treated as having or not having a good reason for an act or omission;

    (b) matters which are or are not to be taken into account in determining whether a person has a good reason for an act or omission.

DEFINITIONS

"assessment period"—see s.40 and s.7(2).

"child"—see s.40.

"claim"—*ibid.*

"claimant"—*ibid.*

"couple"—see ss.39 and 40.

"joint claimants"—see s.40.

"prescribed"—*ibid.*

"single claimant"—*ibid.*

"single person"—*ibid.*

Section 31

SCHEDULE 2

UNIVERSAL CREDIT: AMENDMENTS

[Omitted]

SCHEDULE 3

ABOLITION OF BENEFITS: CONSEQUENTIAL AMENDMENTS

Social Security Contributions and Benefits Act 1992 (c.4)

1.154   1. The Social Security Contributions and Benefits Act 1992 is amended as follows.

2. In section 22 (earnings factors), in subsections (2)(a) and (5), for "a contributory" there is substituted "an".

3. In section 150 (interpretation of Part 10), in subsection (2), in the definition of "qualifying employment and support allowance", for "a contributory allowance" there is substituted "an employment and support allowance".

Social Security Administration Act 1992 (c.5)

1.155   4. The Social Security Administration Act 1992 is amended as follows.

5. In section 7 (relationship between benefits), in subsection (3), for "subsections (1) and (2)" there is substituted "subsection (1)".

6. In section 73 (overlapping benefits), in subsections (1) and (4)(c), for "a contributory" there is substituted "an".

7. In section 159B (effect of alterations affecting state pension credit), for "a contributory", wherever occurring, there is substituted "an".

8. In section 159D (as inserted by Schedule 2 to this Act) (effect of alterations affecting universal credit), for "a contributory", wherever occurring, there is substituted "an".

Immigration and Asylum Act 1999 (c.33)

9. In the Immigration and Asylum Act 1999, in section 115 (exclusion from benefits of persons subject to immigration control)— **1.156**
  (a) in subsection (1), after paragraph (ha) there is inserted "or";
  (b) in subsection (2)(b) for "(a) to (j)" substitute "(a) to (i)".

Child Support, Pensions and Social Security Act 2000 (c.19)

10. The Child Support, Pensions and Social Security Act 2000 is amended as follows. **1.157**

11. (1) Section 69 (discretionary financial assistance with housing) is amended as follows.
  (2) In subsection (1)—
  (a) for "relevant authorities" there is substituted "local authorities";
  (b) in paragraph (a), the words from "housing benefit" to "both," are repealed.
  (3) In subsection (2)—
  (a) in paragraph (b), for "relevant authority" there is substituted "local authority";
  (b) in paragraph (e), for "relevant authorities" there is substituted "local authorities";
  (c) in paragraphs (f), (g) and (h), for "relevant authority" there is substituted "local authority".
  (4) In subsection (5), for "relevant authorities" there is substituted "local authorities".
  (5) In subsection (7), for the definition of "relevant authority" there is substituted—
""local authority" has the meaning given by section 191 of the Social Security Administration Act 1992."

12.(1) Section 70 (grants towards cost of discretionary housing payments) is amended as follows.
  (2) In subsection (1), after "payments" there is inserted "("grants")".
  (3) For subsection (2) there is substituted—
"(2)The amount of a grant under this section shall be determined in accordance with an order made by the Secretary of State with the consent of the Treasury."
  (4) In subsection (8)—
  (a) for the definition of "relevant authority" there is substituted—
""local authority" has the same meaning as in section 69;";
  (b) the definition of "subsidy" is repealed.

13. After section 70 there is inserted—

"70A. Payment of grant
  (1) A grant under section 70 shall be made by the Secretary of State in such instalments, at **1.158** such times, in such manner and subject to such conditions as to claims, records, certificates, audit or otherwise as may be provided by order of the Secretary of State with the consent of the Treasury.
  (2) The order may provide that if a local authority has not complied with the conditions specified in it within such period as may be specified in it, the Secretary of State may estimate the amount of grant under section 70 payable to the authority and employ for that purpose such criteria as he considers relevant.
  (3) Where a grant under section 70 has been paid to a local authority and it appears to the Secretary of State that—
  (a) the grant has been overpaid, or
  (b) there has been a breach of any condition specified in an order under this section, he may recover from the authority the whole or such part of the payment as he may determine.
  (4) Without prejudice to the other methods of recovery, a sum recoverable under this section may be recovered by withholding or reducing subsidy.
  (5) An order under this section may be made before, during or after the end of the period to which it relates.
  (6) In this section "local authority" has the same meaning as in section 69.
  (7) Section 70(5) to (7) applies to orders under this section."

Welfare Reform Act 2012

Capital Allowances Act 2001 (c.2)

1.159   14. In Schedule A1 to the Capital Allowances Act 2001 (first-year tax credits), in paragraph 17(1)(b) after "sick pay," there is inserted "or".

Social Security Fraud Act 2001 (c.11)

1.160   15. The Social Security Fraud Act 2001 is amended as follows.
16. In section 6B (loss of benefit for conviction etc), in subsection (5), for "to (10)" there is substituted "and (8)".
17. In section 7 (loss of benefit for repeated conviction etc), in subsection (2), for "to (5)" there is substituted "and (4A)".
18. In section 11 (regulations), in subsection (3)(c), for the words from "section" to the end there is substituted "section 6B(5A) or (8), 7(2A) or (4A) or 9(2A) or (4A)".

Commissioners for Revenue and Customs Act 2005 (c.11)

1.161   19. The Commissioners for Revenue and Customs Act 2005 is amended as follows.
20. In section 5 (initial functions), in subsection (1), after paragraph (a) there is inserted "and".
21. In section 44 (payment into Consolidated Fund), in subsection (3), after paragraph (b) there is inserted "and".

Welfare Reform Act 2007 (c. 5)

1.162   22. The Welfare Reform Act 2007 is amended as follows.
23. In section 1 (employment and support allowance), in subsection (3)(d), at the end there is inserted "and".
24. In section 2 (amount of contributory allowance), in subsection (1), for "In the case of a contributory allowance, the amount payable" there is substituted "The amount payable by way of an employment and support allowance".
25.(1) Section 27 (financial provisions) is amended as follows.
(2) In subsection (1), for the words from "so much of" to the end there is substituted "any sums payable by way of employment and support allowance".
(3) In subsection (3), for "contributory" there is substituted "employment and support".
26. In each of the following provisions, for "a contributory allowance" there is substituted "an employment and support allowance"
(a) section 1A(1), (3), (4), (5) and (6) (as inserted by section 51 of this Act);
(b) section 1B(1) (as inserted by section 52 of this Act);
(c) section 3(2)(d);
(d) section 18(4);
(e) section 20(2), (3)(a), (b) and (c), (4), (5)(a), (b) and (c), (6), (7)(a), (b) and (c);
(f) in Schedule 1, paragraphs 1(5)(d) and 3(2)(a);
(g) in Schedule 2, paragraphs 6 and 7(2)(d).

Corporation Tax Act 2009 (c. 4)

1.163   27. The Corporation Tax Act 2009 is amended as follows.
28. In section 1059 (relief relating to SME R&D: total amount of company's PAYE and NICs liabilities), in subsection (5) after "sick pay" there is inserted "or".
29. In section 1108 (relief relating to vaccine research etc: total amount of company's PAYE and NICs liabilities), in subsection (5) after "sick pay" there is inserted "or".

GENERAL NOTE

1.164   The amendments contained in this Schedule to other primary legislation fall into two main categories.
First, and for the most part, the amendments are consequential upon the abolition of income support, housing benefit, council tax benefit, child tax credit, working tax credit and the income-based forms of ESA and JSA. So, for example, references in other Acts to "a contributory employment and support allowance" are changed to "an employment and support allowance". This is because, after the full implementation of universal credit, the only form of ESA which will be available will be a contributory allowance.

The second category of amendments concerns those made to the Child Support, Pensions and Social Security Act 2000. These amend the provisions relating to discretionary housing payments and are consequential on the abolition of council tax benefit and housing benefit.

SCHEDULE 4

HOUSING CREDIT ELEMENT OF STATE PENSION CREDIT

PART 1

AMENDMENTS TO STATE PENSION CREDIT ACT 2002

State Pension Credit Act 2002 (c.16)

1. The State Pension Credit Act 2002 is amended as follows.　　　　　　　　　**1.165**
2. In section 1 (entitlement), in subsection (2)(c), at the end there is inserted "or (iii) the conditions in section 3A(1) and (2) (housing credit)."
3. In that section, in subsection (3)—
   (a)　after paragraph (b)　　there is inserted "or
   (c)　to a housing credit, calculated in accordance with section 3A, if he satisfies the conditions in subsections (1) and (2) of that section,";
   (b)　for the words from "(or to both)" to the end there is substituted "(or to more than one of them, if he satisfies the relevant conditions)".
4. After section 3 there is inserted—

"3A. Housing credit
(1) The first of the conditions mentioned in section 1(2)(c)(iii) is that the claimant is liable　　**1.166**
to make payments in respect of the accommodation he occupies as his home.
(2) The second of the conditions mentioned in section 1(2)(c)(iii) is that the claimant's capital and income are such that the amount of the housing credit payable (if he were entitled to it) would not be less than a prescribed amount.
(3) Where the claimant is entitled to a housing credit, the amount of the housing credit shall be an amount calculated in or determined under regulations (which may be zero).
(4) For the purposes of subsection (1)—
   (a)　the accommodation must be in Great Britain;
   (b)　the accommodation must be residential accommodation;
   (c)　it is immaterial whether the accommodation consists of the whole or part of a building and whether or not it comprises separate and self-contained premises.
(5) Regulations may make provision as to—
   (a)　the meaning of "payments in respect of accommodation" for the purposes of this section (and, in particular, as to the extent to which such payments include mortgage payments);
   (b)　circumstances in which a claimant is to be treated as liable or not liable to make such payments;
   (c)　circumstances in which a claimant is to be treated as occupying or not occupying accommodation as his home (and, in particular, for temporary absences to be disregarded);
   (d)　circumstances in which land used for the purposes of any accommodation is to be treated as included in the accommodation.
(6) Regulations under this section may make different provision for different areas."
5. In section 7 (fixing of retirement provision for assessed income period), at the end there is inserted—
"(10) Regulations may prescribe circumstances in which subsection (3) does not apply for the purposes of determining the amount of a housing credit to which the claimant is entitled."
6. In section 12 (polygamous marriages), in subsection (2)(b), after "savings credit" there is inserted "or housing credit".
7. In section 17 (interpretation), in subsection (1), after the definition of "guarantee credit" there is inserted—""housing credit" shall be construed in accordance with sections 1 and 3A;".
8. In Schedule 2 (consequential amendments etc), paragraph 9(5)(a) is repealed.

PART 2

AMENDMENTS TO OTHER ACTS

Social Security Administration Act 1992 (c.5)

1.167   9. The Social Security Administration Act 1992 is amended as follows.

10. In section 5 (regulations about claims and payments) in subsection (6), before "subsection" there is inserted "or housing credit (within the meaning of the State Pension Credit Act 2002)".

11. In section 15A (mortgage interest)—

   (a) in subsection (1A)—

      (i) in paragraph (b), for "the appropriate minimum guarantee for the purposes of" there is substituted "entitlement to";

      (ii) in the closing words, for "appropriate minimum guarantee for the purposes of" there is substituted "entitlement to";

   (b) in subsection (4), the definition of "appropriate minimum guarantee" is repealed.

12.(1) Section 122F (supply by rent officers of information) is amended as follows.

(2) In subsection (3)(a) at the end of the words in brackets there is inserted "or housing credit".

(3) In subsection (4) at the end there is inserted "or housing credit".

(4) After that subsection there is inserted—

"(5) In this section "housing credit" has the same meaning as in the State Pension Credit Act 2002".

Housing Act 1996 (c.52)

1.168   13.(1) Section 122 of the Housing Act 1996 (rent officers) is amended as follows.

(2) In the heading, at the end there is inserted "and housing credit".

(3) In subsection (1), at the end there is inserted "or housing credit (within the meaning of the State Pension Credit Act 2002)".

Child Support, Pensions and Social Security Act 2000 (c.19)

1.169   14. In section 69 of the Child Support, Pensions and Social Security Act 2000 (discretionary financial assistance with housing), in subsection (1)(a), after "universal credit" there is inserted "or housing credit (within the meaning of the State Pension Credit Act 2002)".

GENERAL NOTE

1.170   Schedule 4 amends the State Pension Credit Act 2002 to create a new type of credit within state pension credit to cover housing costs. This will provide support for people who qualify for state pension credit once housing benefit is no longer available. The key provision is para.4, which inserts a new s.3A into the SPCA 2002. This provision sets out the conditions of entitlement to the housing credit (subss. (1) and (2)); it also provides the power to set out the manner in which the housing credit is to be calculated or determined in regulations (subs.(3)). The policy intention is that claimants will be entitled to broadly the same amount of support under the housing credit as they would previously have been entitled to by way of housing benefit. Subsection (5) of new s.3A simply adds detail to the power in subs.(3) by listing a number of specific matters in respect of which regulations may be made. Subsection (6) provides that regulations may make different provision for different areas. The underlying aim is to ensure that persons in different but abutting areas may be treated in a different manner depending on the circumstances obtaining in that area (e.g. to reflect different local taxation applied by different local authorities).

The other provision of note is para.5, which inserts a new s.7(10) into the SPCA 2002. Section 7 provides for assessed income periods in state pension credit, during which a person's retirement provision as assessed at the start of the period is taken to be the same throughout the period. The power exists in s.6(2)(b) to prescribe circumstances in which an assessed income period may not be set. The new s.7(10) provides that regulations may prescribe circumstances in which a person's retirement provision is not taken to be the same throughout the assessed income period for the purposes of determining the amount of housing credit to which a person is entitled. This power is inserted in order to replicate the current position in respect of housing benefit, which does not operate a system based on assessed income periods.

SCHEDULE 5

UNIVERSAL CREDIT AND OTHER WORKING-AGE BENEFITS

General

1.(1) In this Schedule "relevant benefit" means—   **1.171**
  (a) jobseeker's allowance, or
  (b) employment and support allowance.
(2) In this Schedule "work-related requirement" means—
  (a) a work-related requirement within the meaning of this Part,
  (b) a work-related requirement within the meaning of the Jobseekers Act 1995, or
  (c) a work-related requirement within the meaning of Part 1 of the Welfare Reform Act 2007.
(3) In this Schedule "sanction" means a reduction of benefit under—
  (a) section 26 or 27,
  (b) section 6J or 6K of the Jobseekers Act 1995, or
  (c) section 11J of the Welfare Reform Act 2007.

Dual entitlement

2. (1) Regulations may make provision as to the amount payable by way of a relevant benefit   **1.172**
where a person is entitled to that benefit and universal credit.
  (2) Regulations under sub-paragraph (1) may in particular provide for no amount to be payable by way of a relevant benefit.
  (3) Regulations may, where a person is entitled to a relevant benefit and universal credit—
  (a) make provision as to the application of work-related requirements;
  (b) make provision as to the application of sanctions.
  (4) Provision under sub-paragraph (3)(a) includes in particular—
  (a) provision securing that compliance with a work-related requirement for a relevant benefit is to be treated as compliance with a work-related requirement for universal credit;
  (b) provision disapplying any requirement on the Secretary of State to impose, or a person to comply with, a work-related requirement for a relevant benefit or universal credit.
  (5) Provision under sub-paragraph (3)(b) includes in particular—
  (a) provision for the order in which sanctions are to be applied to awards of relevant benefit and universal credit;
  (b) provision to secure that the application of a sanction to an award of a relevant benefit does not result in an increase of the amount of an award of universal credit.

Movement between working-age benefits

3. Regulations may provide—   **1.173**
  (a) in a case where a person ceases to be entitled to universal credit and becomes entitled to a relevant benefit, for a sanction relating to the award of universal credit to be applied to the award of the relevant benefit;
  (b) in a case where a person ceases to be entitled to a relevant benefit and becomes entitled to universal credit, for a sanction relating to the award of the relevant benefit to be applied to the award of universal credit;
  (c) in a case where a person ceases to be entitled to one relevant benefit and becomes entitled to the other, for a sanction relating to the award of the former to apply to the award of the latter.

Hardship payments

4. Regulations under section 28 (hardship payments) may be made in relation to a person   **1.174**
whose award of universal credit is reduced by virtue of regulations under paragraph 2(3)(b) or 3(b) as in relation to a person whose award is reduced under section 26 or 27.

Earnings tapers

1.175   5. In section 4 of the Jobseekers Act 1995 (amount payable by way of a jobseeker's allowance), in subsection (1)(b)—
        (a) after "making" there is inserted—
"(i) deductions in respect of earnings calculated in the prescribed manner (which may
include multiplying some or all earnings by a prescribed percentage), and
        (b) "earnings," (before "pension payments") is repealed.
        6. (1) Section 2 of the Welfare Reform Act 2007 (amount of contributory allowance) is
amended as follows.
        (2) In subsection (1)(c), after "making" there is inserted—
"(i) deductions in respect of earnings calculated in the prescribed manner (which may
include multiplying some or all earnings by a prescribed percentage), and
        (3) At the end there is inserted—
        "(6) In subsection (1)(c)(i) the reference to earnings is to be construed in accordance with
sections 3, 4 and 112 of the Social Security Contributions and Benefits Act 1992."

DEFINITIONS

        "relevant benefit"—para.1(1)
        "sanction"—para.1(3)
        "work-related requirement"—para.1(2)

GENERAL NOTE

1.176   Schedule 5 makes provision to allow the Secretary of State to prescribe details of
the relationship between universal credit on the one hand and ESA and JSA on the
other.

Para. (2)
1.177   In certain circumstances claimants may meet the conditions of entitlement to
both universal credit and JSA or ESA (as contributory benefits only). Paragraph 2
enables the Secretary of State to make provision as to the amount of contributory
benefit payable where a person is entitled to both a contributory benefit and universal credit. According to the Department, Memorandum from the Department for
Work and Pensions, *Welfare Reform Bill, as brought from the House of Commons on 16
June 2011*, House of Lords Select Committee on Delegated Powers and Regulatory
Reform (at para.166):

        "It is intended that the power will in particular be used to:
        a) specify whether, in cases where the claimant might be entitled to both universal
        credit and either ESA or JSA, the claimant will be paid to only universal credit, or
        only the contributory benefit, or to both.
        b) make provision in relation to cases where a claimant might be able to
        choose which benefit to claim, in the event of them being potentially entitled
        to both.
        c) provide for exceptions, if appropriate, from the general rule.
        d) prescribe how work-related requirements are to apply in such cases.
        e) set out, if sanctions are applicable, which benefit is to be reduced first (in a case
        where a claimant is receiving both), what limitations any reductions are subject
        to, and to provide, if appropriate, that the application of a sanction to one benefit
        does not increase payment of the other."

Para. (3)
1.178   Paragraph 3(a) and (b) allows for regulations to provide that where a person is
entitled to universal credit and has their award reduced by a sanction, and then
becomes entitled to JSA or ESA, the sanction can be applied to the new JSA or ESA
award. This is obviously designed to ensure that claimants cannot avoid a sanction
simply because they move between universal credit and JSA or ESA. Paragraph
3(c) makes similar provision for regulations to provide that sanctions imposed on

claimants entitled to JSA or ESA can be applied to a subsequent award of the other benefit.

Para. (4)

This allows for regulations made under s.28 (hardship payments) to apply to a person whose universal credit award is reduced by virtue of either para.2(3)(b) or 3(b) above. Section 28 only allows for universal credit hardship payments to be made to claimants who have their universal credit award reduced under ss.26 or 27, and so para.4 allows for claimants whose awards are reduced under other provisions to also be eligible for universal credit hardship payments.

1.179

Para. (5)

This amendment to s.4 of the Jobseekers Act 1995 creates a power which allows the Secretary of State to deduct earnings which have been calculated in a prescribed manner, which may include multiplying some or all of the earnings by a prescribed percentage. The intention is to make provision for the amount of benefit payable to be tapered as earnings increase and to allow for some earnings to be disregarded before the taper is applied.

1.180

Para. (6)

This amends s.2 of the Welfare Reform Act 2007, and has similar effect on provision for the calculation of earnings in ESA as does para.(5) in relation to JSA.

1.181

SCHEDULE 6

MIGRATION TO UNIVERSAL CREDIT

General

1.(1) Regulations may make provision for the purposes of, or in connection with, replacing existing benefits with universal credit.

1.182

(2) In this Schedule "existing benefit" means—
(a) a benefit abolished under section 33(1);
(b) any other prescribed benefit.
(3) In this Schedule "appointed day" means the day appointed for the coming into force of section 1.

Claims before the appointed day

2. (1) The provision referred to in paragraph 1(1) includes—

1.183

(a) provision for a claim for universal credit to be made before the appointed day for a period beginning on or after that day;
(b) provision for a claim for universal credit made before the appointed day to be treated to any extent as a claim for an existing benefit;
(c) provision for a claim for an existing benefit made before the appointed day to be treated to any extent as a claim for universal credit.

(2) The provision referred to in paragraph 1(1) includes provision, where a claim for universal credit is made (or is treated as made) before the appointed day, for an award on the claim to be made in respect of a period before the appointed day (including provision as to the conditions of entitlement for, and amount of, such an award).

Claims after the appointed day

3. (1) The provision referred to in paragraph 1(1) includes—

1.184

(a) provision permanently or temporarily excluding the making of a claim for universal credit after the appointed day by—
(i) a person to whom an existing benefit is awarded, or
(ii) a person who would be entitled to an existing benefit on making a claim for it;
(b) provision temporarily excluding the making of a claim for universal credit after the appointed day by any other person;
(c) provision excluding entitlement to universal credit temporarily or for a particular period;

    (d) provision for a claim for universal credit made after the appointed day to be treated to any extent as a claim for an existing benefit;

    (e) provision for a claim for an existing benefit made after the appointed day to be treated to any extent as a claim for universal credit.

(2) The provision referred to in paragraph 1(1) includes provision, where a claim for universal credit is made (or is treated as made) after the appointed day, for an award on the claim to be made in respect of a period before the appointed day (including provision as to the conditions of entitlement for, and amount of, such an award).

Awards

1.185   4.(1) The provision referred to in paragraph 1(1) includes—

    (a) provision for terminating an award of an existing benefit;

    (b) provision for making an award of universal credit, with or without application, to a person whose award of existing benefit is terminated.

(2) The provision referred to in sub-paragraph (1)(b) includes—

    (a) provision imposing requirements as to the procedure to be followed, information to be supplied or assessments to be undergone in relation to an award by virtue of that sub-paragraph or an application for such an award;

    (b) provision as to the consequences of failure to comply with any such requirement;

    (c) provision as to the terms on which, and conditions subject to which, such an award is made, including—

        (i) provision temporarily or permanently disapplying, or otherwise modifying, conditions of entitlement to universal credit in relation to the award;

        (ii) provision temporarily or permanently disapplying, or otherwise modifying, any requirement under this Part for a person to be assessed in respect of capability for work or work-related activity;

    (d) provision as to the amount of such an award;

    (e) provision that fulfilment of any condition relevant to entitlement to an award of an existing benefit, or relevant to the amount of such an award, is to be treated as fulfilment of an equivalent condition in relation to universal credit.

(3) Provision under sub-paragraph (2)(d) may secure that where an award of universal credit is made by virtue of sub-paragraph (1)(b)—

    (a) the amount of the award is not less than the amount to which the person would have been entitled under the terminated award, or is not less than that amount by more than a prescribed amount;

    (b) if the person to whom it is made ceases to be entitled to universal credit for not more than a prescribed period, the gap in entitlement is disregarded in calculating the amount of any new award of universal credit.

Work-related requirements and sanctions

1.186   5.(1) The provision referred to in paragraph 1(1) includes—

    (a) provision relating to the application of work-related requirements for relevant benefits;

    (b) provision relating to the application of sanctions.

(2) The provision referred to in sub-paragraph (1)(a) includes—

    (a) provision that a claimant commitment for a relevant benefit is to be treated as a claimant commitment for universal credit;

    (b) provision that a work-related requirement for a relevant benefit is treated as a work-related requirement for universal credit;

    (c) provision for anything done which is relevant to compliance with a work-related requirement for a relevant benefit to be treated as done for the purposes of compliance with a work-related requirement for universal credit;

    (d) provision temporarily disapplying any provision of this Part in relation to work-related requirements for universal credit.

(3) The provision referred to in sub-paragraph (1)(b) includes—

    (a) provision for a sanction relevant to an award of a relevant benefit to be applied to an award of universal credit;

    (b) provision for anything done which is relevant to the application of a sanction for a relevant benefit to be treated as done for the purposes of the application of a sanction for universal credit;

    (c) provision temporarily disapplying any provision of this Part in relation to the application of sanctions.

(4) In this paragraph—

"relevant benefit" means—
 (a) jobseeker's allowance,
 (b) employment and support allowance, and
 (c) income support;
"work-related requirement" means—
 (a) for universal credit, a work-related requirement within the meaning of this Part;
 (b) for jobseeker's allowance, a requirement imposed—
  (i) by virtue of regulations under section 8 or 17A of the Jobseekers Act 1995,
  (ii) by a jobseeker's direction (within the meaning of section 19A of that Act),
  (iii) by virtue of regulations under section 2A, 2AA or 2D of the Social Security Administration Act 1992, or
  (iv) by a direction under section 2F of that Act;
 (c) for employment and support allowance, a requirement imposed—
  (i) by virtue of regulations under section 8, 9, 11, 12 or 13 of the Welfare Reform Act 2007,
  (ii) by a direction under section 15 of that Act,
  (iii) by virtue of regulations under section 2A, 2AA or 2D of the Social Security Administration Act 1992, or
  (iv) by a direction under section 2F of that Act;
 (d) for income support, a requirement imposed—
  (i) by virtue of regulations under section 2A, 2AA or 2D of the Social Security Administration Act 1992, or
  (ii) by a direction under section 2F of that Act;
"sanction" means a reduction of benefit under—
 (a) section 26 or 27 above,
 (b) section 19, 19A or 19B of the Jobseekers Act 1995,
 (c) section 11, 12 or 13 of the Welfare Reform Act 2007, or
 (d) section 2A, 2AA or 2D of the Social Security Administration Act 1992.

Tax credits

6. In relation to the replacement of working tax credit and child tax credit with universal credit, the provision referred to in paragraph 1(1) includes— **1.187**
 (a) provision modifying the application of the Tax Credits Act 2002 (or of any provision made under it);
 (b) provision for the purposes of recovery of overpayments of working tax credit or child tax credit (including in particular provision for treating overpayments of working tax credit or child tax credit as if they were overpayments of universal credit).

Supplementary

7. Regulations under paragraph 1(1) may secure the result that any gap in entitlement to an existing benefit (or what would, but for the provisions of this Part, be a gap in entitlement to an existing benefit) is to be disregarded for the purposes of provision under such regulations. **1.188**

DEFINITIONS

"appointed day"—see para.1(3).
"existing benefit"—see para.1(2).
"relevant benefit"—see para.5(4).
"sanction"—*ibid.*
"work-related requirement"—*ibid.*

GENERAL NOTE

Schedule 6 contains regulation-making powers to make provision in connection with replacing the existing means-tested-benefits system with universal credit, and more particularly with the "migration" of claimants from one benefit to the other. Regulations made under this Schedule were subject to the affirmative resolution procedure where the power in para.1(1) was used in a way described in paras.4, 5 or 6 for the first time. **1.189**

Para. (1)

1.190   The principal such regulations are the Transitional Provisions Regulations 2013.

Para. (2)

1.191   Regulations may specify when a claim can be treated as a claim for an existing benefit and when a claim can be treated as a claim for universal credit. For example, regulations may provide that a claim for an existing benefit made before the day that universal credit comes into effect, but for a period beginning after universal credit is introduced, (i.e. people making advance claims), can be treated as a claim for universal credit.

Para. (3)

1.192   Regulations may provide that after the appointed day (i.e. the day universal credit is introduced), existing benefits cannot be claimed (see Transitional Provisions Regulations 2013, reg.15). Regulations can also provide for a claim to universal credit to be treated as a claim for existing benefit. This might be used where e.g. a claimant's benefit is backdated to a period before universal credit was introduced. Regulations may also provide that these cases may be awarded universal credit on terms, which match wholly or partly, the existing benefit.

Para. (4)

1.193   Regulations will be able to make provision for the "migration" of existing claimants onto universal credit. Such migration may be voluntary or mandatory. Regulations can prescribe the timing, conditions, kind and amount of any such entitlement to universal credit which was previously an award for an existing benefit. As regards para.4(1), see further the Transitional Provisions Regulations 2013, and especially regs 3 (entitlement to claim universal credit), 14 (awards of universal credit without a claim) and 16 (termination of awards of existing benefits).

Para. (5)

1.194   This makes provision for the continuity of both work-related requirements and sanctions; see further especially regs 30–35 of the Transitional Provisions Regulations 2013 as regards sanctions.

Para. (6)

1.195   This provides that the Secretary of State may, through regulations, modify any provision of the Tax Credits Act 2002 (or regulations) as necessary for the purposes of transferring people from working tax credit and child tax credit to universal credit. This power may be used to align certain tax credit rules more closely with universal credit to facilitate the transition process (para.(a)). Paragraph 6 also makes it clear that for overpayments of tax credits could, through the transitional regulations, be treated as overpayments of universal credit (para.(b)). See further regs 8 and 17 of, and the Schedule to, the Transitional Provisions Regulations 2013.

PART III

UNIVERSAL CREDIT: REGULATIONS

Universal Credit Regulations 2013

(SI 2013/376)

Made on February 25, 2013 by the Secretary of State for Work and Pensions in exercise of the powers conferred by sections 2(2), 4(2), (3), (5), (6) and (7), 5, 6(1)(a) and (3), 7(2) and (3), 8(3), 9(2) and (3), 10(2) to (5), 11(3) to (5), 12(1), (3) and (4), 14(5), 15(2), 17(3) and (4), 18(3) and (5), 19(2)(d), (3) and (4), 20(1), 22(2), 24(1), (5) and (6), 25, 26(2)(a), (6) and (8), 27(4), (5), (9), 28, 32(1), 37(3) to (7), 39(3)(a), 40, 96 and 97 of, and paragraphs 1, 4, 5 and 7 of Schedule 1 and paragraphs 2 and 3 of Schedule 5 to, the Welfare Reform Act 2012; a draft having been laid before Parliament in accordance with section 43(3) of the Welfare Reform Act 2012 and approved by a resolution of each House of Parliament; and without the instrument having been referred to the Social Security Advisory Committee because it contains only regulations made by virtue of or consequential on Part 1 and sections 96 and 97 of, and Schedules 1 and 5 to, the Welfare Reform Act 2012 and is made before the end of the period of 6 months beginning with the coming into force of those provisions.
[In force April 2013 but see Pt IV]

2.1

ARRANGEMENT OF REGULATIONS

PART 1

INTRODUCTION

2.2

PART 2

ENTITLEMENT

PART 3

AWARDS

PART 4

ELEMENTS OF AN AWARD

PART 5

CAPABILITY FOR WORK OR WORK-RELATED ACTIVITY

PART 6

CALCULATION OF CAPITAL AND INCOME

CHAPTER 1

CAPITAL

PART 7

THE BENEFIT CAP

PART 8

CLAIMANT RESPONSIBILITIES

CHAPTER 1

WORK-RELATED REQUIREMENTS

CHAPTER 2

SANCTIONS

PART 1

INTRODUCTION

Citation and commencement

2.4   **1.**—These Regulations may be cited as the Universal Credit Regulations 2013 and come into force on 29th April 2013.

GENERAL NOTE

2.5   Although the Regulations come into force on April 29, 2013, they do not apply to all claimants, or in all parts of the country. See further the Universal Credit (Transitional Provisions) Regulations 2013 and the commencement orders in Pt IV of this Volume.

Interpretation

2.6   **2.**—In these Regulations—

"the Act" means the Welfare Reform Act 2012;

"additional statutory paternity pay" means additional statutory paternity pay under Part 12ZA of the Contributions and Benefits Act;

[² "adopter" has the meaning in regulation 89(3)(a);]

"attendance allowance" means—

(a) an attendance allowance under section 64 of the Contributions and Benefits Act;

(b) an increase of disablement pension under section 104 or 105 of that Act (increases where constant attendance needed and for exceptionally severe disablement);

(c) [³ . . .]

(d) a payment by virtue of article 14, 15, 16, 43 or 44 of the Personal Injuries (Civilians) Scheme 1983 or any analogous payment;

(e) any payment based on the need for attendance which is paid as an addition to a war disablement pension;

[¹(f) armed forces independence payment under the Armed Forces and Reserve Forces (Compensation Scheme) Order 2011;]

"bereavement allowance" means an allowance under section 39B of the Contributions and Benefits Act;

"care leaver" has the meaning in regulation 8;

"carer's allowance" means a carer's allowance under section 70 of the Contributions and Benefits Act;

"carer element" has the meaning in regulation 29;

"childcare costs element" has the meaning in regulation 31;

"child element" has the meaning in regulation 24;

"close relative", in relation to a person, means—

(a) a parent, parent-in-law, son, son-in-law, daughter, daughter-in-law, step-parent, step-son, step-daughter, brother or sister; and

(b) if any of the above is a member of a couple, the other member of the couple;

"confinement" has the meaning in regulation 8;

"Contributions and Benefits Act" means the Social Security Contributions and Benefits Act 1992;

"course of advanced education" has the meaning in regulation 12;

"disability living allowance" means an allowance under section 71 of the Contributions and Benefits Act;

"earned income" has the meaning in Chapter 2 of Part 6;

"EEA Regulations" means the Immigration (European Economic Area) Regulations 2006;

"employment and support allowance" means an allowance under Part 1 of the Welfare Reform Act 2007 as amended by Schedule 3 and Part 1 of Schedule 14 to the Welfare Reform Act 2012 (removing references to an income-related allowance);

"ESA Regulations" means the Employment and Support Allowance Regulations 2013;

"expected number of hours per week" has the meaning in regulation 88;

"foster parent" means—

(a) in relation to England, a person with whom a child is placed under the Fostering Services Regulations 2011;

(b) in relation to Wales, a person with whom a child is placed under the Fostering Services (Wales) Regulations 2003;

(c) in relation to Scotland, a foster carer or kinship carer with whom a child is placed under the Looked After Children (Scotland) Regulations 2009;

"grant" has the meaning in regulation 68;

"health care professional" means (except in regulation 98)—

(a) a registered medical practitioner;

(b) a registered nurse; or

(c) an occupational therapist or physiotherapist registered with a regulatory body established by Order in Council under section 60 of the Health Act 1999;

"housing costs element" has the meaning in regulation 25;

"individual threshold" has the meaning in regulation 90(2);

"industrial injuries benefit" means a benefit under Part 5 of the Contributions and Benefits Act;

"ITEPA" means the Income Tax (Earnings and Pensions) Act 2003;

"jobseeker's allowance" means an allowance under the Jobseekers Act 1995 as amended by Part 1 of Schedule 14 to the Act (removing references to an income-based allowance);

"local authority" means—

(a) in relation to England, a county council, a district council, a parish council, a London borough council, the Common Council of the City of London or the Council of the Isles of Scilly;

(b) in relation to Wales, a county council, a county borough council or a community council;

(c) in relation to Scotland, a council constituted under section 2 of the Local Government etc. (Scotland) Act 1994;

"LCW element" and "LCWRA element" have the meaning in regulation 27;

"looked after by a local authority" in relation to a child or young person means a child or young person who is looked after by a local authority within the meaning of section 22 of the Children Act 1989 or section 17(6) of the Children (Scotland) Act 1995;

"maternity allowance" means a maternity allowance under section 35 of the Contributions and Benefits Act;

"Medical Evidence Regulations" means the Social Security (Medical Evidence) Regulations 1976;

"national insurance contribution" means a contribution under Part 1 of the Contributions and Benefits Act;

"ordinary statutory paternity pay" means ordinary statutory paternity pay under Part 12ZA of the Contributions and Benefits Act;

"paid work" means work done for payment or in expectation of payment and does not include being engaged by a charitable or voluntary organisation, or as a volunteer, in circumstances in which the payment received by or due to be paid to the person is in respect of expenses;

"partner" means (except in regulation 77) the other member of a couple;

"personal independence payment" means an allowance under Part 4 of the Welfare Reform Act 2012;

"prisoner" means—

(a) a person who is detained in custody pending trial or sentence upon conviction or under a sentence imposed by a court; or

(b) is on temporary release in accordance with the provisions of the Prison Act 1952 or the Prisons (Scotland) Act 1989,

other than a person who is detained in hospital under the provisions of the Mental Health Act 1983 or, in Scotland, under the provisions of the Mental Health (Care and Treatment) (Scotland) Act 2003 or the Criminal Procedure (Scotland) Act 1995;

"qualifying young person" has the meaning in regulation 5;

"redundancy" has the meaning in section 139(1) of the Employment Rights Act 1996;

"registered as blind" means registered as blind—

(a) in a register compiled by a local authority under section 29 of the National Assistance Act 1948; or

(b) in a register maintained by or on behalf of a council constituted under section 2 of the Local Government etc. (Scotland) Act 1994 in consequence of having been certified as blind;

"regular and substantial caring responsibilities for a severely disabled person" has the meaning in regulation 30;

"relevant childcare" has the meaning in regulation 35;

"responsible for a child or qualifying young person" has the meaning in regulation 4;

"statutory adoption pay" means a payment under Part 12ZB of the Contributions Benefits Act;

"statutory maternity pay" means a payment under Part 12 of the Contributions and Benefits Act;

"statutory sick pay" means a payment under Part 11 of the Contributions and Benefits Act;

"student loan" has the meaning in regulation 68;

"terminally ill" means suffering from a progressive disease where death in consequence of that disease can reasonably be expected within 6 months;

"total outstanding reduction period" has the meaning in regulation 101(5);

"trade dispute" has the meaning in section 244 of the Trade Union and Labour Relations (Consolidation) Act 1992;

"unearned income" has the meaning in Chapter 3 of Part 6;

"war disablement pension" means any retired pay, pension or allowance payable in respect of disablement under an instrument specified in section 639(2) of ITEPA;

"weekly earnings" has the meaning in regulation 90(6);

"widowed mother's allowance" means an allowance under section 37 of the Contributions and Benefits Act;

"widowed parent's allowance" means an allowance under section 39A of the Contributions and Benefits Act;

"widow's pension" means a pension under section 39 of the Contributions and Benefits Act.

DEFINITIONS

"child"—see WRA 2012, s.40.
"couple"—see WRA 2012, ss.39 and 40.
"disabled"—see WRA 2012, s.40.
"qualifying young person"—see WRA 2012, ss.40 and 10(5).
"work"—see WRA 2012, s.40.

AMENDMENTS

1. Armed Forces and Reserve Forces Compensation Scheme (Consequential Provisions: Subordinate Legislation) Order 2013 (SI 2013/591) art.7 and Sch., para.54 (April 8, 2013).

2. Universal Credit (Miscellaneous Amendments) Regulations 2013 (SI 2013/803) reg.2(1) and (2) (April 29, 2013).

3. Social Security (Miscellaneous Amendments) (No.2) Regulations 2013 (SI 2013/1508) reg.3(1) and (2) (October 29, 2013).

GENERAL NOTE

Most of these definitions are either self-explanatory, or references to definitions in other regulations, or discussed in the commentary to the regulations where the defined terms are used. A number are similar to terms defined for the purposes of IS, JSA and ESA: see further the commentary to reg.2(1) of the ESA Regulations 2008 in Vol.I of this series and to reg.2(1) of the IS Regulations and reg.1(2) of the JSA Regulations 1996 in Vol.II.

2.7

The Benefit Unit

Couples

3.—(1) This regulation makes provision in relation to couples, including cases where both members of a couple may be entitled to universal credit jointly without each of them meeting all the basic conditions referred to in section 4 of the Act (see paragraph (2)) and cases where a person whose partner does not meet all the basic conditions [¹ or is otherwise excluded from entitlement to universal credit] may make a claim as a single person (see paragraph (3)).

(2) A couple may be entitled to universal credit as joint claimants where—

2.8

    (a) one member does not meet the basic condition in section 4(1)
    (b) (under the qualifying age for state pension credit) if the other
         member does meet that condition; or

    (b) one member does not meet the basic condition in section 4(1)(d)
         (not receiving education) and is not excepted from that condition if
         the other member does meet that condition or is excepted from it.

(3) A person who is a member of a couple may make a claim as a single person if the other member of the couple—

    (a) does not meet the basic condition in section 4(1)(a) (at least 18 years old) and is not a person in respect of whom the minimum age specified in regulation 8 applies;

    (b) does not meet the basic condition in section 4(1)(c) (in Great Britain);

    (c) is a prisoner; [[1] ...]

    (d) is a person other than a prisoner in respect of whom entitlement does not arise by virtue of regulation 19 (restrictions on entitlement) [; or

    (e) is a person to whom section 115 of the Immigration and Asylum Act 1999 (exclusion from benefits) applies,]

and regulations 18 (capital limit), 36 (amount of elements) and 22 (deduction of income and work allowance) provide for the calculation of the award in such cases.

(4) Where two people are parties to a polygamous marriage, the fact that they are husband and wife is to be disregarded if—

    (a) one of them is a party to an earlier marriage that still subsists; and

    (b) the other party to that earlier marriage is living in the same household,

and, accordingly, the person who is not a party to the earlier marriage may make a claim for universal credit as a single person.

(5) In paragraph (4) "polygamous marriage" means a marriage during which a party to it is married to more than one person and which took place under the laws of a country which permits polygamy.

(6) Where the claimant is a member of a couple, and the other member is temporarily absent from the claimant's household, they cease to be treated as a couple if that absence is expected to exceed, or does exceed, 6 months.

DEFINITIONS

"claim"—see WRA 2012, s.40.
"claimant"—*ibid.*
"prisoner"—see reg.2.
"single person"—see WRA 2012, ss.40 and 1(2)(a).
"couple"—see WRA 2012, ss.39 and 40.

AMENDMENT

1. Universal Credit (Consequential, Supplementary, Incidental and Miscellaneous Provisions) Regulations 2013 (SI 2013/630) reg.8(1) and (2) (April 29, 2013).

GENERAL NOTE

2.9   This regulation is the first of four under the sub-heading, "The Benefit Unit". That phrase is used extensively in departmental guidance (e.g., Chapter E2 of ADM) but is not defined anywhere in WRA 2012 or these Regulations. The Department intends the phrase to mean all the people in a given household who may, or must, be included in a claim for universal credit. That is consistent with these Regulations because identifying those people is also the subject-matter of regs 3–5 inclusive, which appear under the sub-heading.

It is not generally possible for a person who is a member of a couple to claim, or be awarded, universal credit as a single person. By s.2(1) WRA 2012, members of a couple must claim jointly and by s.1(2) any award of benefit is made jointly to both members of the couple. Further, under s.3(2)(a), the basic conditions of entitlement must be met by both members of the couple and, by ss.3(2)(b) and 5(2), whether or not they satisfy the financial conditions is assessed by reference to their combined income and capital.

It is therefore important for claimants to know whether or not they are members of a couple. The word is defined by s.39(1) and (2) WRA 2012 in terms which follow the standard definition for income-related benefits (e.g., in s.137 SSCBA 1992). It therefore covers married couples and civil partners who are members of the same household, a man and woman who are living together as husband and wife and two people of the same sex who are living together as if they were civil partners: see further the commentary to reg.2(1) of the IS Regulations in Vol.II. Note also the commentary to para.(6) below as regards temporary absence.

Para. (2)

Under s.4(2) WRA 2012, the Secretary of State has a general power to make regulations which provide for exceptions to the requirement to meet any of the basic conditions for universal credit. In the case of joint claimants, that power can be used to make an exception for one or both of them. Similarly, WRA 2012 Sch.1, para.1 empowers the Secretary of State to make regulations providing for circumstances in which joint claimants may be entitled to universal credit without each of them meeting all the basic conditions referred to in s.4. Those powers have been exercised to make para.(2) (among other regulations). **2.10**

Under s.4(1)(b) it is a basic condition for universal credit that a person should not have reached the qualifying age for SPC (as defined in s.4(4) and s.1(6) SPCA 2002). However, under para.2(a) a couple may be jointly entitled to universal credit if one member is over that age, as long as the other member is under it. In those circumstances, the couple may be better off if the older member claims SPC. That will depend on a number of circumstances, the most important of which are likely to be whether either member of the couple has earned income and, if so, whether the couple has housing costs. The work allowance for universal credit (see reg.22) is considerably more generous than the disregards for earned income in SPC and universal credit is withdrawn at the rate of 65 pence for every pound of earned income as opposed to the pound for pound reduction applied when calculating the guarantee credit element of SPC. However, for universal credit, owner occupiers who have earned income get a higher work allowance but do not get any amount for housing costs as part of universal credit (see para.4 of Sch.5), whereas, under SPC housing costs are paid. A couple where one member is over SPC age and the other is not should therefore seek advice about which benefit to claim.

Under s.4(1)(b) it is a basic condition for universal credit that a person should not be "receiving education". For the definition of that phrase, see regs 12 and 13. Note also that by s.4(2) and reg.14 some people are exempt from the condition imposed by s.4(1)(b). The effect of para.(2)(b) is that a couple may be jointly entitled to universal credit even though one member is receiving education (and does not fall within reg.14) as long as the other member is not receiving education (or does fall within reg.14).

Note that couples who fall within para.(2) must still claim universal credit jointly. The exceptions are from the requirement that both should meet the basic conditions, not the requirement for a joint claim.

Para. (3)

By contrast, a member of a couple who falls within para.(3) may claim universal credit as a single person. **2.11**

The paragraph is made under s.3(2) WRA 2012 which empowers the Secretary of State to make regulations that "specify circumstances in which a member of a couple may make a claim as a single person". There is no express power to make regulations which disapply the requirement in s.1(2) that universal credit must be awarded jointly where the claimants are members of a couple. However, it is implicit that a member of a couple who may lawfully *claim* universal credit as a single person may also lawfully be *awarded* benefit in that capacity.

Under para.(3) a member of a couple may claim universal credit as a single person if the other member:

- is aged less than 18 (and is not a person who is entitled to claim universal credit from the age of 16 under reg.8): para.(3)(a);

- is not in Great Britain for the purposes of s.4(1)(c) WRA 2012 (see reg.9): para.(3)(b);

- is a prisoner (as defined in reg.2): para.(3)(c).

  (Note that, under reg.19(2), certain prisoners retain entitlement to the housing costs element of universal credit during the first six months of their sentence. However, para.(3)(c) applies whenever the other member of the couple is a prisoner. There is no additional requirement, there is under para. (3)(d)—which also covers people who fall within reg.19—that the other member of the couple should be excluded from entitlement by that regulation. The implication is that the member of the couple who is not in prison can immediately make a claim as a single person.)

- is a member of a religious order or serving a sentence of imprisonment detained in hospital and excluded from entitlement to universal credit by reg.19: para.(3)(d); or

- is a person subject to immigration control who is excluded from entitlement to benefit under s.115 Immigration and Asylum Act 1999 (see in particular s.115(3) and (9) and the commentary to the 1999 Act in Vol.II): para.(3)(e)

There are special rules for calculating entitlement under claims made by virtue of para.(3). Under reg.36(3) the claimant's maximum amount is calculated using the standard allowance for a single claimant. However, under reg.22(3) the couple's combined income is taken into account when calculating the income to be deducted from that amount. and, under reg.18(2), the claimant's capital is treated as including the capital of the other member of the couple.

Note that the restricted standard allowance under reg.36(3) only applies to a member of a couple who claims as a single person under para.(3). It does *not* affect claims by those who are able to make a joint claim by virtue of para.(2).

Under reg.9(1) of the Claims and Payments Regulations 2013, if a person who is a member of a couple but is entitled to claim as a single person under para.(3), instead makes a joint claim, that claim is treated as made by that person as a single person.

Paras (4) and (5)

Paragraphs (4) and (5) apply to those in a polygamous marriage. "Polygamous marriage" is defined by para.(5) as "a marriage during which a party to it is married to more than one person and which took place under the laws of a country which permits polygamy". That definition could clearer. A possible interpretation is that once a party to the marriage has been married to more than one person, the marriage is to be treated as polygamous for as long as it lasts (i.e., because it is a marriage "during which" there were, at least for a period, more than two members). However, it is suggested that in the context of the regulation of the whole, that interpretation is not correct. The use of the present tense ("is married") and the provisions made by para.(4)—which can only apply if the marriage has more than two members—indicate that the head (a) of the definition is to be read as meaning that a marriage is polygamous *during any period in which* a party to it is married to more than one person. In other words, the definition preserves the distinction, which applies elsewhere in social security law, between a marriage that is actually polygamous and one that is only potentially polygamous, so that where neither party is actually married to more than one person, the marriage is not polygamous for universal credit purposes.

For the definition to apply, the party who is married to more than one person 2.12 must be legally married to them under the law of England and Wales or the law of Scotland (as the case may be). This can raise complex issues of the private international law: see further the commentary to the Social Security and Family Allowances Regulations 1975 (SI 1975/561) in Vol.I and s.4 of Ch.17 of Dicey, Morris & Collins *The Conflict of Laws* 15th edn (Sweet & Maxwell, London, 2012).

The effect of para.(4) is that where a marriage is actually polygamous, and at least three members of that marriage live in the same household, the parties to the earlier or earliest marriage are treated as a couple and all other members of the marriage may make a claim for universal credit as a single person.

Para. (6)

At first sight, the drafting of para.6 is puzzling. It seems to draw a distinction 2.13 between the member of the couple who is "the claimant" who, it is implied, is the head of "the claimant's household" and that person's partner who is "the other member", when, as noted above, the structure of universal credit is that if a claim is to be made by a member of a couple, *both* parties must normally be *joint* claimants. However, WRA 2012, s.40, defines "claimant" as including "each of joint claimants". Therefore, the effect of para.(6) is that when either member of the couple is temporarily absent from the household, they cease to be treated as a couple if the absence is expected to last, or actually lasts, for more than six months.

Relationship formation and breakdown

TCA 2002, s.3, which requires couples to make a joint claim for tax credits, con- 2.14 tains an express provision (s.3(4)), that entitlement to tax credits ceases if the claim was made by a couple and the members of that couple split up ("could no longer make a joint claim") or if, in the case of a single claim, the claimant becomes a member of a couple ("could no longer make a single claim"). By contrast, WRA 2012 does not include any such provision relating to universal credit. Various provisions in these Regulations and of the Claims and Payments Regulations 2013 *assume* that a joint award comes to an end when a couple separate and that an award to a single claimant ends if the claimant becomes a member of a couple. However, it is not permissible to interpret primary legislation on the basis of assumptions made in the secondary legislation made under it. It is more persuasive that the same assumption is made by WRA 2012, Sch.1, para.3(2) but even that paragraph empowers the Secretary of State to make regulations about what happens if an award of universal credit comes to an end because of a relationship change, rather than saying that is automatically the case.

It is not hard to imagine circumstances where it will be to a claimant's advantage to argue that the change in his or her relationship status did not bring an earlier award of universal credit to an end. It is therefore likely that this issue will be raised before tribunals. One can argue that it is inherent in the concept of a joint award to a couple, that it should come to an end if that couple no longer exists. But if that is the case, why was it felt necessary to make express provision for the situation in TCA 2002? And, when one thinks about it further, it becomes less and less clear why-in the absence of any provision equivalent to s.3(4) TCA 2002, ceasing to be a couple, or becoming one, should not be treated like any other change of circumstances, like a change of address, or a change in the amount of income or capital, rather than as a change which brings the award of benefit to an end irrespective of the circumstances of the claimants after that change.

When a person is responsible for a child or qualifying young person

2.15   **4.**—(1) Whether a person is responsible for a child or qualifying young person for the purposes of Pt 1 of the Act and these Regulations is determined as follows.

(2) A person is responsible for a child or qualifying young person who normally lives with them.

(3) But a person is not responsible for a qualifying young person if the two of them are living as a couple.

(4) Where a child or qualifying young person normally lives with two or more persons who are not a couple, only one of them is to be treated as responsible and that is the person who has the main responsibility.

(5) The persons mentioned in paragraph (4) may jointly nominate which of them has the main responsibility but the Secretary of State may determine that question—

(a) in default of agreement; or

(b) if a nomination or change of nomination does not, in the opinion of the Secretary of State, reflect the arrangements between those persons.

(6) [¹ Subject to regulation 4A,] a child or qualifying young person is to be treated as not being the responsibility of any person during any period when the child or qualifying young person is—

(a) looked after by a local authority; or

(b) a prisoner,

[¹ . . .]

(7) Where a child or qualifying young person is temporarily absent from a person's household the person ceases to be responsible for the child or qualifying young person if—

(a) the absence is expected to exceed, or does exceed, 6 months; or

(b) the absence is from Great Britain and is expected to exceed, or does exceed, one month unless it is in circumstances where an absence of a person for longer than one month would be disregarded for the purposes of regulation 11(2) or (3) (medical treatment or convalescence or death of close relative etc.).

DEFINITIONS

"the Act"—see reg.2.
"child"—see WRA 2012, s.40.
"couple"—see WRA 2012, ss.39 and 40.
"looked after by a local authority"—see reg.2.
"qualifying young person"—see WRA 2012, s.40 and 10(5) and regs 2 and 5.

AMENDMENT

1. Social Security (Miscellaneous Amendments) (No.2) Regulations 2013 (SI 2013/1508), reg.3(1) and (3) (July 29, 2013).

GENERAL NOTE

2.16   Whether or not a claimant is responsible for a child or qualifying young person is relevant to their maximum amount under Pt. 4, to the level of any work allowance under reg.22 and to the imposition of work-related requirements under Pt.8.

Paras (1)–(5)

The general rule is that a person is responsible for a child or qualifying young   **2.17**
person who normally lives with them (para.(2)) unless (in the case of a qualifying
young person) the two of them are living together as a couple (para.(3)).

Where a child or qualifying young person normally lives with two people who are
a couple, both members of the couple are responsible for him or her (because that
is the effect of para.(2) and no other rule applies).

However, where he or she lives with two or more persons who are not a couple,
only one of them is to be treated as responsible and that is the person who has the
main responsibility for him or her (para.(4)). In those circumstances. the people
with whom the child or qualifying young person lives may agree which of them
has the main responsibility. However, the Secretary of State may overrule that
agreement, if in his opinion, it does not reflect the arrangements those people have
made (i.e., for the care of the child or qualifying young person) (para.(5)(b)). The
Secretary of State may also decide who has main responsibility if the people with
whom the child or qualifying young person lives do not agree who has the main
responsibility (para.(5)(a)).

Para.(6)

Children or qualifying young persons who are being looked after by a local   **2.18**
authority or are prisoners (as defined in reg.2) are treated as not being the responsibility of any person. The effect is that the child or qualifying young person is disregarded for the purposes of reg.22, Pt.4 and Pt.8 even if he or she normally lives
with the claimant or claimants.

However, para.(6) is subject to reg.4A, so that the child or qualifying young
person is not treated as not being the responsibility of any person during any period
in which he or she is being looked after by a local authority and either:

- his or her absence is "in the nature of a planned short term break, or is one
  of a series of such breaks, for the purpose of providing respite for the person
  who normally cares for" him or her; or

- (though being formally looked after by a local authority) the child or qualifying young person is placed with, or continues to live with, their parent or a
  person who has parental responsibility for them. For the definition of parental responsibility, see reg.4A(2).

Para.(7)

Paragraph 7 deals with the temporary absence of a child or qualifying young   **2.19**
person from a claimant's (or the claimants') household. In those circumstances,
the person who was previously responsible for the child or qualifying young person
ceases to be so as soon as the absence is expected to exceed six months or if, unex-
pectedly, it actually exceeds six months (para.7(a)). That period is reduced to one
month if the child or qualifying young person is also absent from Great Britain unless
that absence would be disregarded under reg.11(1) by virtue of reg.11(2) or (3).

[¹ Responsibility for children looked after by a local authority

4A.—(1) There is excluded from regulation 4(6)(a)—   **2.20**
  (a) any period;
  (b) any period during which the child or qualifying young person.
  (2) For the purposes of this regulation, a person has parental responsibility if they are not a foster parent and—
  (a) in England and Wales, they have parental responsibility within the
      meaning of section 3 of the Children Act 1989; or
  (b) in Scotland, they have any or all of the legal responsibilities or rights
      described in sections 1 or 2 of the Children (Scotland) Act 1995.]

Definitions

"child"—see WRA 2012, s.40.
"qualifying young person"—see WRA 2012, ss.40 and 10(5) and regs 2 and 5.
"looked after by a local authority"—see reg.2.
"local authority"—*ibid.*

Amendment

1. Social Security (Miscellaneous Amendments) (No.2) Regulations 2013 (SI 2013/1508) reg.3(1) and (4) (July 29, 2013).

Meaning of "qualifying young person"

2.21   **5.**—(1) A person who has reached the age of 16 but not the age of 20 is a qualifying young person for the purposes of Part 1 of the Act and these Regulations—

(a) up to, but not including, the 1st September following their 16th birthday; and

(b) up to, but not including, the 1st September following their 19th birthday, if they are enrolled on, or accepted for, approved training or a course of education—

(i) which is not a course of advanced education,

(ii) which is provided at a school or college or provided elsewhere but approved by the Secretary of State, and

(iii) where the average time spent during term time in receiving tuition, engaging in practical work or supervised study or taking examinations exceeds 12 hours per week.

(2) Where the young person is aged 19, they must have started the education or training or been enrolled on or accepted for it before reaching that age.

(3) The education or training referred to in paragraph (1) does not include education or training provided by means of a contract of employment.

(4) "Approved training" means training in pursuance of arrangements made under section 2(1) of the Employment and Training Act 1973 or section 2(3) of the Enterprise and New Towns (Scotland) Act 1990 which is approved by the Secretary of State for the purposes of this regulation.

(5) A person who is receiving universal credit, an employment and support allowance or a jobseeker's allowance is not a qualifying young person.

Definitions

"employment and support allowance"—see reg.2.
"jobseeker's allowance"—*ibid.*

General Note

2.22   Under s.8(2)(b) and s.10(1) WRA 2012 the calculation of an award of universal credit includes an amount for a qualifying young person for whom the claimant is responsible. Regulation 5 defines who is a qualifying young person. The definition is similar to that which applies for the purposes of child benefit (see by way of comparison regs 3, 7 and 8 of the Child Benefit (General) Regulations 2006 in Vol.IV of this series) but not quite. In particular, the concept of "terminal date" has gone.

Under reg.5, a person who is aged 16 or over but under 20 counts as a qualifying young person:

   (i) up to (but not including) the 1st September following his/her 16th birthday if s/he is aged 16; or

  (ii) up to (but not including) the 1st September following his/her 19th birthday if s/he is aged 16–19 and has been accepted for (or has enrolled on) approved training (defined in para.(4)) or non-advanced education at a school or college (or elsewhere as approved by the Secretary of State). In the case of a course of education at least 12 hours on average a week must be spent on tuition, practical work, supervised study and examinations. Meal breaks and unsupervised study are not included. *R(F) 1/93* held that "supervised study" (in reg.5 of the Child Benefit Regulations 1976) "would normally be understood to import the presence or close proximity of a teacher or tutor". If the person is aged 19, s/he must have started (or been accepted for or enrolled on) the education or training before reaching 19. The education or training must not be provided as part of a contract of employment.

But note that if a person is receiving universal credit, new style ESA or new style JSA in his/her own right, s/he cannot be a qualifying young person (para.(5)).

See also reg.12(1) which provides that if a person is a qualifying young person s/he is regarded as receiving education and so will not meet the basic condition in s.4(1)(d) WRA 2012 (unless s/he comes within one of the exceptions to this requirement in reg.14).

Rounding

6.—(1) Where the calculation of an amount for the purposes of these Regulations results in a fraction of a penny, that fraction is to be disregarded if it is less than half a penny and otherwise it is to be treated as a penny.

    (2) This regulation does not apply to the calculation in regulation 111 (daily rate for a reduction under section 26 or 27 of the Act).

2.23

DEFINITION

"the Act"—see reg.2.

PART 2

ENTITLEMENT

Introduction

7. This Part contains provisions about—

  (a) the requirement to meet the basic conditions in section 4 of the Act, including exceptions from that requirement;

  (b) the maximum amount of capital and the minimum amount of universal credit for the financial conditions in section 5 of the Act; and

2.24

(c) cases where no entitlement to universal credit arises even if the basic conditions and the financial conditions are met.

DEFINITION

"the Act"—see reg.2.

Minimum age

Cases where the minimum age is 16

2.25   **8.**—(1) For the basic condition in section 4(1)(a) of the Act (at least 18 years old), the minimum age is 16 years old where a person—
   (a) has limited capability for work;
   (b) is awaiting an assessment under Part 5 to determine whether the person has limited capability for work and has a statement given by a registered medical practitioner in accordance with the Medical Evidence Regulations which provides that the person is not fit for work;
   (c) has regular and substantial caring responsibilities for a severely disabled person;
   (d) is responsible for a child;
   (e) is a member of a couple the other member of which is responsible for a child or a qualifying young person (but only where the other member meets the basic conditions in section 4 of the Act);
   (f) is pregnant, and it is 11 weeks or less before her expected week of confinement, or was pregnant and it is 15 weeks or less since the date of her confinement; or
   (g) is without parental support (see paragraph (3)).
   (2) Sub-paragraphs (c), (f) and (g) of paragraph (1) do not include any person who is a care leaver.
   (3) For the purposes of paragraph (1)(g) a young person is without parental support where that person is not being looked after by a local authority and—
   (a) has no parent;
   (b) cannot live with their parents because—
      (i) the person is estranged from them, or
      (ii) there is a serious risk to the person's physical or mental health, or that the person would suffer significant harm if the person lived with them; or
   (c) is living away from their parents, and neither parent is able to support the person financially because that parent—
      (i) has a physical or mental impairment,
      (ii) is detained in custody pending trial or sentence upon conviction or under a sentence imposed by a court, or
      (iii) is prohibited from entering or re-entering Great Britain.
   (4) In this regulation—
"parent" includes any person acting in the place of a parent;
"care leaver" means—
   (a) in relation to England and Wales, an eligible child for the purposes of

118

paragraph 19B of Schedule 2 to the Children Act 1989 or a relevant child for the purposes of section 23A of that Act;

(b) in relation to Scotland, a person under the age of 18 to whom a local authority in Scotland is obliged to provide advice and assistance in terms of section 29(1) of the Children (Scotland) Act 1995 and who, since reaching the age of 14, has been looked after by a local authority for a period of or periods totalling 13 weeks or more (excluding any period where the person has been placed with a member of their family); and

"confinement" means—

(a) labour resulting in the birth of a living child; or

(b) labour after 24 weeks of pregnancy resulting in the birth of a child whether alive or dead,

and where a woman's labour begun on one day results in the birth of a child on another day she is to be taken to be confined on the date of the birth.

DEFINITIONS

"the Act"—see reg.2.
"child"—see WRA 2012, s.40.
"limited capability for work"—see WRA 2012, ss.40 and 37(1).
"local authority"—see reg.2.
"looked after by a local authority"—*ibid.*
"Medical Evidence Regulations"— *ibid.*
"qualifying young person"—see regs 2 and 5.
"regular and substantial caring responsibilities"—see WRA 2012, s.40 and reg.30.
"responsible for a child or qualifying young person"—see reg.4.

GENERAL NOTE

One of the basic conditions for entitlement to universal credit is that the claimant   2.26
must be at least 18 years old (s.4(1)(a) WRA 2012). Regulation 8 provides for the exceptions to that rule.

Under para.(1) a person aged 16 or 17 (who satisfies the other basic conditions) can qualify for universal credit if s/he:

(a) has limited capability for work;

(b) is waiting for a work capability assessment and has submitted a medical certificate stating that s/he is not fit for work;

(c) has "regular and substantial caring responsibilities for a severely disabled person" (see reg.30), but not if s/he is a "care leaver" (defined in para. (4));

(d) is responsible for a child (see reg.4 for when a person is responsible for a child);

(e) is a member of a couple and the other member satisfies the basic conditions and is responsible for a child or a qualifying young person (see reg.5 for who counts as a qualifying young person);

(f) is pregnant and it is 11 weeks or less before her expected week of confinement (defined in para.(4)), or was pregnant and it is 15 weeks or less since the date of confinement, but not if s/he is a care leaver;

(g) is "without parental support" (defined in para.(3)), but not if s/he is a care leaver.

On "care leaver", see the notes to the Children (Leaving Care) Act 2000 and to the Children (Leaving Care) Social Security Benefits Regulations 2001 and the Children (Leaving Care) Social Security Benefits (Scotland) Regulations 2004 in Vol.II of this series.

2.27   A person is "without parental support" if s/he is not being looked after by a local authority and comes within one of the categories listed in para.(3). These categories are similar to those in reg.13(2)(c), (d) and (e) of the Income Support Regulations (see the notes to those provisions in Vol.II of this series). Note the definition of "parent" in para.(4). On para.(3)(b)(ii), para.E1055 of ADM gives examples of "serious risk" as: (i) having a brother or sister who is a drug addict, which poses a risk to the young person who is exposed to the drugs at the parental home; (ii) having a history of mental illness which is made worse by the parent's attitude; or (iii) suffering from chronic bronchitis, which is made worse by the damp conditions of the parent's home.

 Note that under reg.3(3)(a) a person who is a member of a couple (and is either 18 or over or falls within para.(1)) but whose partner is under 18 and does not fall within para.(1) can claim universal credit as a single person.

 A person is not normally eligible for universal credit if s/he is receiving education (see s.4(1)(d) WRA 2012). However, see reg.14 for the exceptions.

In Great Britain

Persons treated as not being in Great Britain

2.28   **9.**—(1) For the purposes of determining whether a person meets the basic condition to be in Great Britain, except where a person falls within paragraph (4), a person is to be treated as not being in Great Britain if the person is not habitually resident in the United Kingdom, the Channel Islands, the Isle of Man or the Republic of Ireland.

 (2) A person must not be treated as habitually resident in the United Kingdom, the Channel Islands, the Isle of Man or the Republic of Ireland unless the person has a right to reside in one of those places.

 (3) For the purposes of paragraph (2), a right to reside does not include a right which exists by virtue of, or in accordance with—

 (a) regulation 13 of the EEA Regulations or Article 6 of Council Directive No.2004/38/EC; or

 (b) regulation 15A(1) of the EEA Regulations, but only in cases where the right exists under that regulation because the claimant satisfies the criteria in regulation 15A(4A) of those Regulations or article 20 of the Treaty on the Functioning of the European Union (in a case where the right to reside arises because a British citizen would otherwise be deprived of the genuine enjoyment of their rights as a European citizen).

 (4) A person falls within this paragraph if the person is—

 (a) a qualified person for the purposes of regulation 6 of the EEA Regulations as a worker or a self-employed person;

 (b) a family member of a person referred to in sub-paragraph (a) within the meaning of regulation 7(1)(a), (b) or (c) of the EEA Regulations;

 (c) a person who has a right to reside permanently in the United Kingdom by virtue of regulation 15(1)(c), (d) or (e) of the EEA Regulations;

 (d) a refugee within the definition in Article 1 of the Convention relating to the Status of Refugees done at Geneva on 28th July 1951, as extended by Article 1(2) of the Protocol relating to the Status of Refugees done at New York on 31st January 1967;

[¹(e) a person who has been granted, or who is deemed to have been granted, leave outside the rules made under section 3(2) of the Immigration Act 1971 where that leave is—

  (i) discretionary leave to enter or remain in the United Kingdom,

  (ii) leave to remain under the Destitution Domestic Violence concession, or

  (iii) leave deemed to have been granted by virtue of regulation 3 of the Displaced Persons (Temporary Protection) Regulations 2005;]

(f) a person who has humanitarian protection granted under those rules; or

(g) a person who is not a person subject to immigration control within the meaning of section 115(9) of the Immigration and Asylum Act 1999 and who is in the United Kingdom as a result of their deportation, expulsion or other removal by compulsion of law from another country to the United Kingdom.

DEFINITION

"EEA Regulations"—see reg.2.

AMENDMENT

1. Social Security (Miscellaneous Amendments) (No.2) Regulations 2013 (SI 2013/1508) reg.3(1) and (5) (October 29, 2013).

GENERAL NOTE

Under s.4(1)(c) WRA 2012, it is a basic condition of entitlement to universal credit that the claimant is "in Great Britain" and s.4(5)(a) empowers the Secretary of State to make regulations specifying "circumstances in which a person is to be treated as being, or not being, in Great Britain". Regulation 9 is made under that power. The general rule (para.(1)) is that to be "in Great Britain" a person must be habitually resident in the United Kingdom, the Channel Islands, the Isle of Man or the Republic of Ireland. Apart from people who fall within para.(4), everyone who is not so habitually resident is treated as not being in Great Britain.   2.29

The habitual residence test in para.(1) is supplemented by para.(2) which establishes an ancillary right to reside test: no-one may treated as habitually resident in the United Kingdom, the Channel Islands, the Isle of Man or the Republic of Ireland for universal credit purposes unless the person has a right to reside in one of those places, other than a right to reside specified in para.(3).

For a detailed analysis of the habitual residence and right to reside tests, see the commentary to reg.21AA of the IS Regulations in Vol.II and the provisions of EU law in Pt III of Vol.III and in the Supplement to those volumes.

Crown servants and members of Her Majesty's forces posted overseas

10.—(1) The following persons do not have to meet the basic condition to be in Great Britain—   2.30

    (a) a Crown servant or member of Her Majesty's forces posted over-
        seas;

    (b) in the case of joint claimants, the partner of a person mentioned in
        sub-paragraph (a) while they are accompanying the person on that
        posting.

(2) A person mentioned in paragraph (1)(a) is posted overseas if
the person is performing overseas the duties of a Crown servant or
member of Her Majesty's forces and was, immediately before their
posting or the first of consecutive postings, habitually resident in the
United Kingdom.

(3) In this regulation—

"Crown servant" means a person holding an office or employment under
    the Crown; and

"Her Majesty's forces" has the meaning in the Armed Forces Act
    2006.

DEFINITIONS

"joint claimants"—see WRA 2012, s.40.
"partner"—see reg.2.

GENERAL NOTE

2.31   Under s.4(1)(c) WRA 2012, it is a basic condition of entitlement to universal credit that the claimant is "in Great Britain". However s.4(2) empowers the
Secretary of State to make regulations that "provide for exceptions to the requirement to meet any of the basic conditions". Regulation 10 is made under that power.

Crown Servants and members of Her Majesty's forces who are posted overseas (as
defined in para.(2)) do not have to meet the basic condition to be in Great Britain.

Neither does the partner of such a Crown Servant or member of Her Majesty's
forces, if a joint claim for universal credit is made. However, as it seems probable
that a Crown Servant or member of Her Majesty's forces who has been posted overseas will be in full-time work, many such joint claims seem likely to fail on the basis
that the financial conditions are not met.

By para.(3), the phrase "Her Majesty's forces" has the meaning in the Armed
Forces Act 2006. However, that phrase is not defined in that Act except to the extent
that ""Her Majesty's forces" . . . do not include any Commonwealth force" (see
s.374). "Commonwealth force" is defined by the same section as meaning "a force
of a Commonwealth country".

Temporary absence from Great Britain

2.32   **11.**—(1) A person's temporary absence from Great Britain is disregarded
in determining whether they meet the basic condition to be in Great Britain
if—

    (a) the person is entitled to universal credit immediately before the
        beginning of the period of temporary absence; and

    (b) either—

        (i) the absence is not expected to exceed, and does not exceed, one
            month, or

        (ii) paragraph (3) or (4) applies.

(2) The period of one month in paragraph (1)(b) may be extended by
up to a further month if the temporary absence is in connection with the
death of—

(a) the person's partner or a child or qualifying young person for whom the person was responsible; or

(b) a close relative of the person, or of their partner or of a child or qualifying young person for whom the person or their partner was responsible,

and the Secretary of State considers that it would be unreasonable to expect the person to return to Great Britain within the first month.

(3) This paragraph applies where the absence is not expected to exceed, and does not exceed, 6 months and is solely in connection with—

(a) the person undergoing—

    (i) treatment for an illness or physical or mental impairment by, or under the supervision of, a qualified practitioner, or

    (ii) medically approved convalescence or care as a result of treatment for an illness or physical or mental impairment, where the person had that illness or impairment before leaving Great Britain; or

(b) the person accompanying their partner or a child or qualifying young person for whom they are responsible for treatment or convalescence or care as mentioned in sub-paragraph (a).

(4) This paragraph applies where the absence is not expected to exceed, and does not exceed, 6 months and the person is—

(a) a mariner; or

(b) a continental shelf worker who is in a designated area or a prescribed area.

(5) In this regulation—

"continental shelf worker" means a person who is employed, whether under a contract of service or not, in a designated area or a prescribed area in connection with any activity mentioned in section 11(2) of the Petroleum Act 1998;

"designated area" means any area which may from time to time be designated by Order in Council under the Continental Shelf Act 1964 as an area within which the rights of the United Kingdom with respect to the seabed and subsoil and their natural resources may be exercised;

"mariner" means a person who is employed under a contract of service either as a master or member of the crew of any ship or vessel, or in any other capacity on board any ship or vessel where—

(a) the employment in that other capacity is for the purposes of that ship or vessel or its crew or any passengers or cargo or mails carried by the ship or vessel; and

(b) the contract is entered into in the United Kingdom with a view to its performance (in whole or in part) while the ship or vessel is on its voyage;

"medically approved" means certified by a registered medical practitioner;

"prescribed area" means any area over which Norway or any member State (other than the United Kingdom) exercises sovereign rights for the purpose of exploring the seabed and subsoil and exploiting their natural resources, being an area outside the territorial seas of Norway or such member State, or any other area which is from time to time specified under section 10(8) of the Petroleum Act 1998;

"qualified practitioner" means a person qualified to provide medical treatment, physiotherapy or a form of treatment which is similar to, or related to, either of those forms of treatment.

DEFINITIONS

"child"—see WRA 2012, s.40.
"close relative"—see reg.2.
"partner"—*ibid.*
"prescribed"—see WRA 2012, s.40.
"responsible for a child or qualifying young person"—see regs 2, 4 and 4A.
"qualifying young person"—see WRA 2012, s.40 and 10(5) and regs 2 and 5.

GENERAL NOTE

2.33   Under s.4(1)(c) WRA 2012, it is a basic condition of entitlement to universal credit that the claimant is "in Great Britain". However s.4(5)(b) and (c) empowers the Secretary of State to make regulations that specify circumstances in which temporary absence from Great Britain is disregarded (subs.(5)(b)) and modify the application of WRA 2012 in relation to a person who is not in Great Britain but who is entitled to universal credit by virtue of subs.(5)(b) (subs.(5)(c)). Regulation 11 is made under the former power.

Paras (1) and (2)

The general rule is that a person who is entitled to universal credit retains that entitlement during a temporary absence—for whatever reason—that is not expected to exceed one month and does not in fact exceed that period (para.(1)(b)(i)). By para.(1)(a), there must be an existing entitlement to universal credit for the rule to apply. It is not possible to claim universal credit for the first time while temporarily absent abroad.

The one-month period in para.(1)(b)(i) can be extended by up to a further month in the circumstances set out in para.(2)(a) and (b) if the Secretary of State considers it would be unreasonable to expect the person to return home during the first month.

Paras (3) and (4)

2.34   The one-month period in para.(1)(b)(i) is also extended to six months if either para.(3) or para.(4) applies. Those paragraphs are not subject to the condition that the Secretary of State should consider that it would be unreasonable to expect the person to return home sooner.

Paragraph (3) permits an extended temporary absence for medical treatment, physiotherapy, or a treatment that is similar to either of those forms of treatment, or medically approved convalescence in the circumstances set out in para.(3)(a) and (b). Note the definitions of "medically approved" and "qualified practitioner" in para.(5). The phrase, "registered medical practitioner" is further defined by para.1 of Sch.1 Interpretation Act 1978 as meaning "a fully registered person within the meaning of the Medical Act 1983 who holds a licence to practise under that Act."

Paragraph (4) permits an extended temporary absence for a "mariner" and a "continental shelf worker" who is in a "designated area" or a "prescribed area". All four of those terms are defined in para.(5). The definition of "mariner" is self-explanatory. The definition of "continental shelf worker" is more technical but, to summarise, it means a person working on an oil or gas rig in a specified area. Readers are referred to the Continental Shelf Act 1964, the Petroleum Act 1998 and the Orders in Council made under those Acts for further details of the areas concerned.

2.35   Note that paras (2) and (3) are also relevant to the question whether a person remains responsible for a child or qualifying young person during the temporary absence of that child or qualifying young person: see the commentary to reg.4(7) above.

Receiving education

Meaning of "receiving education"

12.—(1) For the basic condition in section 4(1)(d) of the Act (not receiving education) a qualifying young person is to be treated as receiving education.

(2) In any other case "receiving education" means—

(a) undertaking a full-time course of advanced education; or

(b) undertaking any other full-time course of study or training at an educational establishment for which a student loan or grant is provided for the person's maintenance.

(3) In paragraph (2)(a) "course of advanced education" means—

(a) a course of study leading to—

   (i) a postgraduate degree or comparable qualification,

   (ii) a first degree or comparable qualification,

   (iii) a diploma of higher education,

   (iv) a higher national diploma; or

(b) any other course of study which is of a standard above advanced GNVQ or equivalent, including a course which is of a standard above a general certificate of education (advanced level), or above a Scottish national qualification (higher or advanced higher).

(4) A claimant who is not a qualifying young person and is not undertaking a course described in paragraph (2) is nevertheless to be treated as receiving education if the claimant is undertaking a course of study or training that is not compatible with any work-related requirement imposed on the claimant by the Secretary of State.

2.36

DEFINITIONS

"claimant"—see WRA 2012, s.40.
"qualifying young person"—see WRA 2012, ss.40 and 10(5) and regs 2 and 5.

GENERAL NOTE

It is a condition of entitlement to universal credit that the person is not receiving education (s.4(1)(d) WRA 2012) (but see reg.14 for the exceptions to this rule).

Note that a couple may be entitled to universal credit as joint claimants even where one member of the couple is receiving education (and does not come within reg.14), provided that the other member is not receiving education, or comes within reg.14 (reg.3(2)(b)).

Regulation 12 defines who counts as receiving education. Firstly, a qualifying young person is deemed to be receiving education (para.(1)) (see reg.5 for who is a qualifying young person). Otherwise, receiving education means being on a full-time course of advanced education (defined in para.(3)) or on another full-time course of study or training at an educational establishment for which a student loan or grant is provided for the person's maintenance (para.(2)). But in addition a claimant will also be treated as receiving education if s/he is on a course of study or training that is not compatible with the work-related requirements imposed on him/her (para.(4)).

The definition of "course of advanced education" in reg.12(3) is the same as the definition in reg.61(1) of the Income Support Regulations (see Vol.II in this series). "Full-time" is not defined.

See reg.13 for when a person is regarded as being on a course.

2.37

Meaning of "undertaking a course"

2.38   **13.**—(1) For the purposes of these Regulations a person is to be regarded as undertaking a course of education [¹, study] or training—

   (a) throughout the period beginning on the date on which the person starts undertaking the course and ending on the last day of the course or on such earlier date (if any) as the person finally abandons it or is dismissed from it; or

   (b) where a person is undertaking a part of a modular course, for the period beginning on the day on which that part of the course starts and ending—

      (i) on the last day on which the person is registered as undertaking that part, or

      (ii) on such earlier date (if any) as the person finally abandons the course or is dismissed from it.

   (2) The period referred to in paragraph (1)(b) includes—

   (a) where a person has failed examinations or has failed to complete successfully a module relating to a period when the person was undertaking a part of the course, any period in respect of which the person undertakes the course for the purpose of retaking those examinations or completing that module; and

   (b) any period of vacation within the period specified in paragraph (1)(b) or immediately following that period except where the person has registered to attend or undertake the final module in the course and the vacation immediately follows the last day on which the person is to attend or undertake the course.

   (3) In this regulation "modular course" means a course which consists of two or more modules, the successful completion of a specified number of which is required before a person is considered by the educational establishment to have completed the course.

   (4) A person is not to be regarded as undertaking a course for any part of the period mentioned in paragraph (1) during which the following conditions are met—

   (a) the person has, with the consent of the relevant educational establishment, ceased to attend or undertake the course because they are ill or caring for another person;

   (b) the person has recovered from that illness or ceased caring for that person within the past year, but not yet resumed the course; and

   (c) the person is not eligible for a grant or student loan.

AMENDMENT

   1. Universal Credit (Consequential, Supplementary, Incidental and Miscellaneous Provisions) Regulations 2013 (SI 2013/630) reg.38(3) (April 29, 2013).

DEFINITIONS

   "grant"—see regs 2 and 68(7).
   "student loan"—*ibid.*

GENERAL NOTE

2.39   Paragraphs (1) to (3) of reg.13 reproduce the rules in reg.61(2) to (4) of the Income Support Regulations. See the notes to reg.61 in Vol.II of this series.

Paragraph (4) is similar to the provision in reg.1(3D) and (3E) of the JSA Regulations 1996 (see Vol.II in this series). The person must have recovered from the illness or his/her caring responsibilities must have ended within the past year for para.(4) to apply (see para.(4)(b)).

Exceptions to the requirement not to be receiving education

14. A person does not have to meet the basic condition in s.4(1)(d) of the Act (not receiving education) if— **2.40**
  (a) the person—
    (i) is undertaking a full-time course of study or training which is not a course of advanced education,
    (ii) is under the age of 21, or is 21 and reached that age whilst undertaking the course, and
    (iii) is without parental support (as defined in regulation 8(3));
  (b) the person is entitled to attendance allowance, disability living allowance or personal independence payment and has limited capability for work;
  (c) the person is responsible for a child or a qualifying young person;
  (d) the person is a single person and a foster parent with whom a child is placed;
  (e) the person is a member of a couple, both of whom are receiving education, and the other member is—
    (i) responsible for a child or qualifying young person, or
    (ii) a foster parent with whom a child is placed; or
  (f) the person—
    (i) has reached the qualifying age for state pension credit, and
    (ii) is a member of a couple the other member of which has not reached that age.

DEFINITIONS

  "the Act"—see reg.2.
  "attendance allowance"—*ibid.*
  "child"—see WRA 2012, s.40.
  "couple"—see WRA 2012, ss.39 and 40.
  "course of advanced education"—see reg.12(3).
  "disability living allowance"—see reg.2.
  "foster parent"—*ibid.*
  "personal independence payment"—*ibid.*
  "qualifying young person"—see WRA 2012, ss.40 and 10(5) and regs 2 and 5.
  "qualifying age for state pension credit"—see WRA 2012, s.4(4), SPCA 2002, s.1(6).

GENERAL NOTE

This regulation sets out the exceptions to the rule in s.4(1)(d) WRA 2012 that **2.41**
a person must not be receiving education. Note that most student funding will count as income—see regs 68–71. If a person who comes within reg.14 has student income in relation to the course that s/he is undertaking which is taken into account in the calculation of his/her universal credit award, s/he will not have any work requirements (see reg.89(1)(e)(ii)).
The following are exempt from the condition in s.4(1)(d):

  • a person who is on a course which is not a course of advanced education (see reg.12(3) for what counts as a course of advanced education) and who is under 21 (or is 21 and reached that age while on the course) and who is "without parental support" (see reg.8(3) for who counts as without parental support) (para (a)). Such a person will have no work requirements (see reg.89(1)(e)(i));

- a person who has limited capability for work (see reg.39(1)) and who is entitled to disability living allowance, personal independence payment, attendance allowance or armed forces independence payment (see the definition of "attendance allowance" in reg.2 which includes armed forces independence payment) para.(b);

- a person who is responsible for a child or qualifying young person (para.(c));

- a single person who is a foster parent with whom a child is placed (para.(d));

- a member of a couple, both of whom are receiving education, whose partner is responsible for a child or qualifying young person or is a foster parent with whom a child is placed (para.(e)); or

- a member of a couple who has reached the qualifying age for state pension credit but whose partner is below that age (para.(f)).

Note that a person who falls within reg.13(4) is not regarded as undertaking a course and so is not treated as receiving education (see reg.12(2)).

Note also that a couple may be entitled to universal credit as joint claimants even where one member of the couple is receiving education (and does not come within this regulation), provided that the other member is not receiving education, or comes within this regulation (reg.3(2)(b)).

Accepting a claimant commitment

Claimant commitment—date and method of acceptance

2.42   **15.**—(1) For the basic condition in section 4(1)(e) of the Act, a person who has accepted a claimant commitment within such period after making a claim as the Secretary of State specifies is to be treated as having accepted that claimant commitment on the first day of the period in respect of which the claim is made.

(2) In a case where an award may be made without a claim, a person who accepts a claimant commitment within such period as the Secretary of State specifies is to be treated as having accepted a claimant commitment on the day that would be the first day of the first assessment period in relation to the award in accordance with regulation 21(3).

(3) The Secretary of State may extend the period within which a person is required to accept a claimant commitment or an updated claimant commitment where the person requests that the Secretary of State review—

(a) any action proposed as a work search requirement or a work availability requirement; or

(b) whether any limitation should apply to those requirements,

and the Secretary of State considers that the request is reasonable.

(4) A person must accept a claimant commitment by one of the following methods, as specified by the Secretary of State—

(a) electronically;

(b) by telephone; or

(c) in writing.

DEFINITIONS

"claimant commitment"—see WRA 2012, s.14(1)
"work availability requirement"—see WRA 2012, ss.40 and 18(1)
"work search requirement"—see WRA 2012, ss.40 and 17(1)

GENERAL NOTE

By virtue of s.4(1)(e) of the WRA 2012 it is one of the basic conditions for making   2.43
an award of universal credit that a claimant, including each of joint claimants, has
accepted a claimant commitment. See the notes to that part of s.4 for the nature
of a claimant commitment (i.e. a record of the claimant's responsibilities under the
WRA 2012) and what is entailed in accepting such a record. There are exceptions
from the basic condition in reg.16 below. Regulation 15 deals with the time within
which and the method by which a claimant commitment must be accepted. The
relevant regulation-making powers are in s.14(5) of the WRA 2012, which requires
the most up-to-date version of a claimant commitment to be accepted "in such
manner as may be prescribed", and in s.4(7), which allows regulations to specify
circumstances in which a person is to be treated as having or as not having accepted
a claimant commitment.

Para. (1)
On a new claim, if the claimant commitment is accepted within the time speci-   2.44
fied by the Secretary of State (as extended under para.(3) if applicable), and by a
method prescribed in para.(4), the basic condition is deemed to be satisfied from
the first day of the period claimed for. Otherwise, the condition would only be
met from the date on which the acceptance by a prescribed method actually took
place. Paragraph (1) must therefore be made under s.4(7) of the WRA 2012. Under
s.14(2) of the WRA 2012, the Secretary of State may review and up-date a claimant commitment as he thinks fit and under s.14(5) a claimant has to accept the
most-up-date version. Such circumstances do not seem to fall within either paras
(1) or (2), although para.(3) refers to a period within which a claimant is required
to accept an up-dated claimant commitment and its possible extension. There is
doubt whether an acceptance under such circumstances strictly takes effect only
from its actual date or from the date of the preparation of the up-dated version, but
no-one is likely to complain if the Secretary of State gives retrospective effect to an
acceptance of an up-dated version within a specified time, as consistency would
suggest is fair.

Para. (2)
Where no claim is required to be made (see reg.6 of the Claims and Payments   2.45
Regulations 2013), effectively the same rule is applied as in para.(1) with effect from
the first day of the award.

Para. (3)
This paragraph allows the Secretary of State, in defined circumstances, to extend   2.46
the period within which a person is required (which is only in the sense of required
in order to take advantage of giving a retrospective effect to the acceptance) to
accept a claimant commitment or an up-dated version. It is arguable that no such
authorisation is needed to allow the Secretary of State to extend any period as first
specified under paras (1) or (2), so that the form of the restrictions in sub-paras (a)
and (b) may not matter too much. Those provisions purport to apply when a claimant has requested that the Secretary of State review any action proposed as a work
search or work availability requirement (see ss.17(1)(b) and 18 of the WRA 2012)
or whether any limitation should apply to those requirements (see reg.97 below).
The main difficulty with them, apart from the fact that s.18 contains no power for
the Secretary of State to specify particular action in relation to a work availability

requirement, is that the legislation contains no formal process of review of the "proposals" mentioned. The reference must presumably be to the power under s.24(3) of the WRA 2012 for the Secretary of State to revoke or change any requirement imposed under the Act or any specification of action to be taken and to a request to exercise that power in relation to action specified under ss.17 or 18. Those difficulties perhaps reinforce the argument for the Secretary of State being able to extend the period for acceptance of the claimant whenever it appears reasonable to do so, although that would involve giving no effective force to para.(3).

Para. (4)

2.47   This paragraph, as allowed by s.14(5) of the WRA 2012, requires that any acceptance of a claimant commitment that can count for the purposes of s.4(1)(e) be done electronically, by telephone or in writing, with the Secretary of State able to specify which in any particular case. "Electronically" will no doubt cover a range of methods. It seems bizarre that acceptance orally or otherwise face-to-face is not allowed, although the telephone is covered. Both methods are capable of being recorded in some permanent form. In so far as no account is taken of the circumstances of claimants with disabilities and the problem cannot be taken care of under reg.16 this provision must be vulnerable to a challenge under the Human Rights Act 1998 for discrimination contrary to art.14 of the European Convention on Human Rights.

Claimant commitment—exceptions

2.48   **16.** A person does not have to meet the basic condition to have accepted a claimant commitment if the Secretary of State considers that—

    (a) the person cannot accept a claimant commitment because they lack the capacity to do so; or

    (b) there are exceptional circumstances in which it would be unreasonable to expect the person to accept a claimant commitment.

DEFINITION

    "claimant commitment"—see WRA 2012, s.14(1)

GENERAL NOTE

2.49   The basic condition in s.4(1)(e) of the WRA 2012 does not have to be met where the claimant either lacks the capacity to accept a claimant commitment (para. (a)) or there are exceptional circumstances in which it would be unreasonable to expect the claimant to accept a claimant commitment (para.(b)). Both provisions, but especially para.(b), contain elements of judgment. If "accepting" a claimant commitment has the restricted meaning suggested in the notes to s.14 of the WRA 2012, that will affect when it might be unreasonable to expect a claimant to do so. If a claimant would be unable or experience undue difficulty in accepting a claimant commitment by one of the methods required by reg.15(4).

Financial conditions

Minimum amount

2.50   **17.** For the purposes of section 5(1)(b) and (2)(b) of the Act (financial conditions: amount payable not less than any prescribed minimum) the minimum is one penny.

DEFINITION

"the Act"—see reg.2.

Capital limit

18.—(1) For the purposes of section 5(1)(a) and (2)(a) of the Act (finan-   2.51
cial conditions: capital limit)—
   (a) the prescribed amount for a single claimant is £16,000; and
   (b) the prescribed amount for joint claimants is £16,000.
   (2) In a case where the claimant is a member of a couple, but makes a
claim as a single person, the claimant's capital is to be treated as including
the capital of the other member of the couple.

DEFINITIONS

"claimant"—see WRA 2012, s.40.
"couple"—see WRA 2012, ss.39 and 40.
"joint claimants"—see WRA 2012, s. 40.
"prescribed"—*ibid.*
"single claimant"—*ibid.*
"single person"—see WRA 2012, ss.40 and 1(2)(a).

GENERAL NOTE

This provides that the capital limit for universal credit for both a single claimant   2.52
and joint claimants is £16,000. Thus the capital limit for universal credit is the same
as for income support, income-based JSA, income-related ESA and housing benefit
(there is no capital limit for working tax credit and child tax credit). See further the
notes to s.134(1) SSCBA 1992 in Vol.II of this series.
   Under para.(2), where a claimant who is a member of a couple makes a claim
as a single person (see reg.3(3) for the circumstances in which this may occur) the
capital of the other member of the couple counts as the claimant's.
   For the rules on calculating capital see regs 45–50 and 75–77 and Sch.10.

Restrictions on entitlement

Restrictions on entitlement—prisoners etc.

19.—(1) Entitlement to universal credit does not arise where a person   2.53
is—
   (a) a member of a religious order who is fully maintained by their order;
   (b) a prisoner; or
   (c) serving a sentence of imprisonment detained in hospital.
   (2) Paragraph (1)(b) does not apply during the first 6 months when the
person is a prisoner where—
   (a) the person was entitled to universal credit immediately before
        becoming a prisoner, and the calculation of their award included an
        amount for the housing costs element; and
   (b) the person has not been sentenced to a term in custody that is
        expected to extend beyond that 6 months.
   (3) In the case of a prisoner to whom paragraph (2) applies, an award of
universal credit is not to include any element other than the housing costs
element.

(4) In paragraph (1)(c) a person serving a sentence of imprisonment detained in hospital is a person who is—

    (a) being detained—

        (i) under section 45A or 47 of the Mental Health Act 1983 (power of higher courts to direct hospital admission; removal to hospital of persons serving sentence of imprisonment etc), and

        (ii) before the day which the Secretary of State certifies to be that person's release date within the meaning of section 50(3) of that Act (in any case where there is such a release date); or

    (b) being detained under—

        (i) section 59A of the Criminal Procedure (Scotland) Act 1995 (hospital direction), or

        (ii) section 136 of the Mental Health (Care and Treatment) (Scotland) Act 2003 (transfer of prisoners for treatment of mental disorder).

DEFINITIONS

    "housing costs element"—see regs 2 and 25.
    "prisoner"—see reg.2.

GENERAL NOTE

2.54   WRA 2012, s.6(1)(a) provides that "entitlement to universal credit does not arise . . . in prescribed circumstances even though the requirements of section 3 [i.e., the requirements to satisfy the basic conditions and the financial conditions] are met". Regulation 19 is made under that power. Its effect is that, where a person's circumstances fall within para.(1), entitlement to universal credit "does not arise" even though that person otherwise meets all the conditions of entitlement. Those circumstances as that the claimant is a fully maintained member of a religious order, a prisoner (subject to para.(2)), or serving a sentence of imprisonment in a hospital (as defined in para.(4)).

    The wording "entitlement . . . does not arise" in both s.6 and reg.19 creates problems. It would have been more natural to say that a person whose circumstances fall within para.(1) "is not entitled to Universal Credit" even if he or she satisfies s.3.

    One possibility is that the wording may have been chosen to forestall any suggestion that the rules in reg.19 amount to conditions of disentitlement or disqualification (in which case, subject to the principles enunciated by the House of Lords in *Kerr v Department of Social Development*, [2004] UKHL 23 (also reported as *R 1/04 (SF)*), the burden would be on the Secretary of State to show that affected claimants were not entitled to universal credit, rather than for the claimants to prove that they were). However, this seems unlikely. Whether or not a person is a fully maintained member of a religious order, a prisoner, or serving a sentence of imprisonment in a hospital are not questions that would normally raise difficult issues of proof. And if this was the intention, it is not entirely clear that s.6 and reg.19 achieve it.

2.55   Whatever the reason for the wording, the problem it creates is that (to use prisoners as an example) although departmental policy is that prisoners should generally have no entitlement to universal credit other than under reg.19(2) (see ADM E3030 and E3040), that is not what s.6 and reg.19 say. They only say that entitlement does not arise where a person is a prisoner. But that does not cover the position in which entitlement has already arisen but the claimant subsequently becomes a prisoner. If s.6 and reg.19 contained a clear statement that a person who is a prisoner "is not entitled" to universal credit (except where reg.19(2) applies), then imprisonment would be a relevant change of circumstances and a ground for superseding the decision awarding universal credit. As it is, the effect of reg.19 appears to be limited to cases in which a new claim is made by a person who is already a prisoner because it is only in such cases that there is any issue about whether entitlement has "arisen". This view is reinforced by s.6(1)(b) and (c) and (2) which provide that entitlement to universal credit does not arise if the basic conditions or the financial conditions are met for a period shorter than a prescribed period or for up to seven days at the beginning of a period during which those conditions are met. In those provisions the "entitlement . . . does not arise" wording is being applied to circumstances where there is no existing entitlement, as is apt.

Paras (2) and (3)

The above analysis, creates some difficulties in the interpretation of para.(2).   2.56
This says that para.(1)(b) "does not apply" during the first six months when the person is a prisoner where that person was entitled to universal credit immediately before becoming a prisoner, and certain other circumstances exist. If what is said above is correct, then para.(1)(b) does not apply at all in such a case, irrespective of the other circumstances. (That is not an objection to the analysis. The "entitlement . . . does not arise" wording is in primary legislation and the way in which the Secretary of State has interpreted that wording when making secondary legislation is not a guide to what it actually means).

The policy which para.(2) seeks to implement is that where someone with an existing award of universal credit that includes the housing costs element is sentenced to a term in custody that is not expected to extend beyond that 6 months, entitlement to universal credit is retained but the award may not include any element other than the housing costs element.

See also the commentary under the headings *Members of religious orders* and *Person serving a sentence of imprisonment in hospital* in the General Note to reg.21 of the IS Regulations in Vol.II.

Part 3

Awards

Introduction

20. This Part contains provisions for the purposes of sections 7 and 8 of   2.57
the Act about assessment periods and about the calculation of the amount of an award of universal credit.

Definitions

"the Act"—see reg.2.
"assessment period"—see WRA 2012, ss.40 and 7(2).

General Note

Part 3 is made under powers conferred by ss.7 to 12 WRA 2012 and is concerned   2.58
with the calculation of an award of universal credit. There are two underlying principles. The first is that an award is made by reference to an "assessment period" (s.7 and reg.21). The second is that the amount of the award is calculated by ascertaining the claimant's (or claimants') "maximum amount" and then deducting "the amounts to be deducted", namely all unearned income and some earned income (s.8 and reg.22).

Assessment periods

2.59   **21.**—(1) An assessment period is, subject to paragraph (5), a period of one month beginning with the first date of entitlement and each subsequent period of one month during which entitlement subsists.

(2) Each assessment period begins on the same day of each month except as follows—

(a) if the first date of entitlement falls on the 31st day of a month, each assessment period begins on the last day of the month; and

(b) if the first date of entitlement falls on the 29th or 30th day of a month, each assessment period begins on the 29th or 30th day of the month (as above) except in February when it begins on the 27th day or, in a leap year, the 28th day.

(3) Where an award of universal credit has terminated and a further award is made without a claim by virtue of regulation 6 or 9 of the Universal Credit, Personal Independence Payment, Jobseeker's Allowance and Employment and Support Allowance (Claims and Payments) Regulations 2013 ("the Claims and Payments Regulations"), each assessment period in relation to the new award begins on the same day of each month as the assessment period in relation to the old award.

(4) Where the further award is to a couple jointly in a case where each of them had an award that terminated when they became a couple, the old award for the purposes of paragraph (3) is the one they nominate or, if they fail to nominate one, the one which the Secretary of State determines.

(5) Where, because the time for making a claim for universal credit is extended by virtue of regulation 26(2) of the Claims and Payments Regulations, the first date of entitlement falls before the date on which the claim is made—

(a) the first assessment period is the period beginning with the first date of entitlement and ending with the day before the date on which the claim is made; and

(b) paragraphs (1) and (2) apply to the second and subsequent assessment periods as if the date on which the claim is made were the first date of entitlement.

(6) The amount payable in respect of that first assessment period is to be calculated as follows—

$$N \times \frac{(A \times 12)}{(365)}$$

where N is the number of days in the period and A is the amount calculated in relation to that period as if it were an assessment period of one month.

DEFINITIONS

"assessment period"—see WRA 2012, ss.40 and 7(2).
"claim"—see WRA 2012, s.40.
"couple"—see WRA 2012, ss.39 and 40.
"jobseeker's allowance"—see reg.2.
"personal independence payment"—*ibid.*

GENERAL NOTE

WRA 2012, s.7(1) provides that universal credit "is payable in respect of each complete assessment period within a period of entitlement". "Assessment period" is defined by s.7(2) as a "period of prescribed duration" and "period of entitlement" is defined by s.7(4) as a "period during which entitlement to universal credit subsists". Selection 7(3) empowers the Secretary of State to make regulations about when an assessment period is to start, for universal credit to be payable in respect of a period shorter than an assessment period and for the amount payable in respect of a period shorter than an assessment period. Regulation 21 is made under the powers conferred by s.7(2) and (3). **2.60**

Para. (1)

The general rule in para.(1) is that an assessment period is a period of one month beginning with the first date of entitlement and each subsequent period of one month during which entitlement subsists. That rule is subject to the exception in para.(5) which applies in cases where the time for claiming universal credit has been extended so that entitlement begins before the date of claim (i.e., under reg.26(2) of the Claims and Payments Regulations 2013). **2.61**

Para. (2)

Paragraph 2 makes provision to avoid the administrative problems that would otherwise occur in shorter months. The general rule is that each assessment period begins on the same day of each month. But that is not always possible when the first assessment period began on the 29th, 30th or 31st of a month because not all months have more than 28 days. Therefore: **2.62**

- if the first date of entitlement falls on the 31st day of a month, each subsequent assessment period begins on the last day of the month (para.(2)(a)); or

- if the first date of entitlement falls on the 29th or 30th day of a month, each subsequent assessment period begins on the 29th or 30th day of the month except in February when it begins on the 27th day or, in a leap year, the 28th day.

Paras (3) and (4)

Regulations 6 and 9(6) and (7) of the Claims and Payments Regulations 2013 specify circumstances in which it is possible to become entitled to universal credit without making a claim for it. Further details are given in the General Notes to those regulations. For present purposes, it is sufficient to note that all of those circumstances involve there having been a previous award of universal credit. Paragraph (3) provides that in those circumstances each assessment period in relation to the new award begins on the same day of each month as the assessment period in relation to the old award. **2.63**

However, that will not always be possible. Under reg.9(7) of the Claims and Payments Regulations 2013, the members of a couple do not have to make a fresh claim if they had previous awards as single persons that were terminated because they became a couple (see however the commentary under the heading, *Relationship formation and breakdown* in the General Note to reg.3). In such a case the dates on which the assessment periods began under the previous awards will not necessarily be the same. In those circumstances, the assessment period for the joint award must begin on the same day of the month as the assessment period for one of the previous awards, but the couple may nominate which previous award. If they do not do so, the Secretary of State may decide. Under reg.50(2) and Sch.3, para.3 of the Decisions and Appeals Regulations 2013, that decision does not attract a right of appeal.

Paras (5) and (6)

Where the time for making a claim for universal credit is extended under reg.26(2) of the Claims and Payments Regulations 2013, the *second* assessment period begins **2.64** on the date of the claim and subsequent assessment periods begin on the same day of the month (subject to the administrative rules in para.(2)). Entitlement in respect of the period before the claim was made is calculated by reference to an assessment period which begins with the first date of entitlement and ending with the day before the date on which the claim is made. This is necessary because issues of backdating will often not be resolved until after a prospective award of universal credit has been made and a pattern of assessment periods established. It is therefore easier administratively to treat the period of backdated entitlement as a separate, discrete period.

Entitlement for that period is calculated using the formula in para.(6). First the amount 'A' is calculated. This is the amount of universal credit to which the claimant(s) would have been entitled had the assessment period been a full month. That sum is then converted to a daily rate by multiplying it by 12 and dividing it by 365. The award of universal credit for the first assessment period is that daily rate multiplied by 'N', the number of days in that period.

Deduction of income and work allowance

2.65 **22.**—(1) The amounts to be deducted from the maximum amount in accordance with section 8(3) of the Act to determine the amount of an award of universal credit are—

(a) all of the claimant's unearned income (or in the case of joint claimants all of their combined unearned income) in respect of the assessment period; and

(b) 65% of the amount by which the claimant's earned income (or, in the case of joint claimants, their combined earned income) in respect of the assessment period exceeds the work allowance.

(2) The amount of the work allowance is—

(a) if the award contains no amount for the housing costs element, the applicable amount of the higher work allowance specified in the table below; and

(b) if the award does contain an amount for the housing costs element, the applicable amount of the lower work allowance specified in that table.

(3) In the case of an award where the claimant is a member of a couple, but makes a claim as a single person, the amount to be deducted from the maximum amount in accordance with section 8(3) of the Act is—

(a) all of the couple's combined unearned income in respect of the assessment period; and

(b) 65% of the amount by which the couple's combined earned income in respect of the assessment period exceeds the work allowance,

and the applicable amount of the work allowance is the same amount as for joint claimants.

Higher work allowance (taking the highest of whichever of the following amounts is applicable)—	
Single claimant—	
not responsible for a child or qualifying young person	£111
responsible for one or more children or qualifying young persons	£734
has limited capability for work	£647

Joint claimants—	
neither responsible for a child or qualifying young person	£111
responsible for one or more children or qualifying young persons	£536
one or both have limited capability for work	£647
Lower work allowance (taking the highest of whichever of the following amounts is applicable)—	
Single claimant—	
not responsible for a child or qualifying young person	£111
responsible for one or more children or qualifying young persons	£263
has limited capability for work	£192
Joint claimants—	
neither responsible for a child or qualifying young person	£111
responsible for one or more children or qualifying young persons	£222
one or both have limited capability for work	£192

DEFINITIONS

"the Act"—see reg.2.
"assessment period"—see WRA 2012, ss.40 and 7(2).
"child"—see WRA 2012, s.40.
"claimant"—*ibid.*
"couple"—see WRA 2012, ss.39 and 40.
"earned income"—see reg.2.
"housing costs element"—see regs 2 and 25.
"joint claimants"—see WRA 2012, s.40.
"limited capability for work"—see WRA 2012, ss.40 and 37(1).
"qualifying young person"—see WRA 2012, ss.40 and 10(5) and regs 2 and 5.
"responsible for a child or qualifying young person"—see regs 2, 4 and 4A.
"single claimant"—see WRA 2012, s.40.
"unearned income"—see reg.2.
"work"—see WRA 2012, s.40.

GENERAL NOTE

Under s.8(1) WRA 2012, the amount of an award of universal credit is the balance of the maximum amount less the amounts to be deducted which, by s.8(3), are to be two prescribed amounts, one in respect of earned income and the other in respect of unearned income. Regulation 22 is made under s.8(3) and specifies how those prescribed amounts are to be determined.   **2.66**

Paras (1) and (3)

Paragraph (1) contains the two general principles. The first (para.(1)(a)) is that the claimant (or the claimants' combined) unearned income (i.e., as calculated in accordance with regs 65–74) is deducted in full. The second (para.(1)(b)) is that the deduction for earned income is 65 per cent of the amount by which the claimant's (or the claimant's combined) earned income (i.e., as calculated in accordance with regs 51–64) exceeds the "work allowance". Paragraph(3) modifies those principles where a member of a couple is claiming as a single claimant under reg.3(3): the couple's combined income is take into account when calculation earned and unearned income, even though the circumstances of the other member of the couple will be excluded when calculating his or her maximum amount (see reg.36(3)).   **2.67**

Paragraph (1)(b) is the main mechanism by which the policy that, under universal credit, claimants should be better off in work is achieved. The "work allowance" is what would previously have been described as an earnings disregard: an amount deducted from a claimant's earnings before any means-test is carried out. But, even at the lowest rate, it is a much more generous disregard than applied for the purposes of IS, income-based JSA and income-related ESA. Further, the 65 per cent "taper" means that the claimants keep 35 pence in every additional pound they earn, whereas under IS, income-based JSA and income-related ESA, benefit was reduced pound for pound so that, once a claimant's earnings exceeded the earnings disregard (and ignoring any potential entitlement to WTC), there was no financial incentive to work unless he or she could earn enough to come off income-related benefits altogether.

Para. (2)

2.68 The amount of the work allowance to be deducted from earned income is specified in para.(2) and set out in the table at the end of the regulation. The higher work allowance is applicable when the award of universal credit does not contain the housing costs element and the lower work allowance when it does. Very few universal credit claimants will not have to pay anything towards housing costs. The most likely recipients of the higher work allowance are, those living as non-dependants in another person's household, owner-occupiers whose earnings exclude them from entitlement to housing costs under Sch.5, para.4 and those renters treated as not liable to make payments under Sch.2, paras 5 to 10.

PART 4

ELEMENTS OF AN AWARD

Introduction

2.69 **23.**—(1) This Part contains provisions about the amounts ("the elements") under—

 (a) section 9 (the standard allowance);
 (b) section 10 (responsibility for children and young persons);
 (c) section 11 (housing costs); and
 (d) section 12 (particular needs and circumstances),

of the Act that make up the maximum amount of an award of universal credit, as provided in section 8(2) of the Act.

 (2) The elements to be included in an award under section 12 of the Act in respect of particular needs or circumstances are—

 (a) the LCW element and the LCWRA element (see regulations 27 and 28);
 (b) the carer element (see regulations 29 and 30); and
 (c) the childcare costs element (see regulations 31 to 35).

DEFINITION

"the Act"—see reg.2.

GENERAL NOTE

2.70 The maximum amount for the purposes of s.8 WRA is the total of:

- the standard allowance: WRA 2012, s.9 and reg.36;

- an amount for each child or young person for whom a claimant is responsible ("the child element") WRA 2012, s.10 and reg.24;

- any amount included in respect of any liability of the claimant to make payments in respect of the accommodation they occupy as their home ("the housing costs element"): WRA 2012, s.11 and regs 25 and 26; or

- any amount included in respect of "other particular needs and circumstances": WRA 2012, s.12 and regs.27 to 35.

The amounts to be included in respect of other particular needs and circumstances are the LCW element and the LCWRA element (regs 27 and 28), the carer element (see regs 29 and 30) and the childcare costs element (regs 31–35).

Responsibility for children or young persons

The child element

24.—(1) The amount to be included in an award of universal credit for each child or qualifying young person for whom a claimant is responsible ("the child element") is given in the table in regulation 36.

(2) An additional amount as shown in that table is to be included in respect of each child or qualifying young person who is disabled and that amount is—

   (a) the lower rate, where the child or qualifying young person is entitled to disability living allowance or personal independence payment (unless sub-paragraph (b) applies); or

   (b) the higher rate where the child or qualifying young person is—

   (i) entitled to the care component of disability living allowance at the highest rate or the daily living component of personal independence payment at the enhanced rate, or

   (ii) registered as blind.

2.71

DEFINITIONS

"child"—see WRA 2012, s.40.
"child element"—see reg.2.
"disability living allowance"—*ibid.*
"disabled"—see WRA 2012, s.40.
"personal independence payment"—see reg.2.
"responsible for a child or qualifying young person"—see regs 2, 4 and 4A.
"qualifying young person"—see WRA 2012, s.40 and 10(5) and regs 2 and 5.
"registered as blind"—see reg.2.

GENERAL NOTE

The child element includes two amounts, which are specified in reg.36. The first, which is included for each child or qualifying young person for whom a claimant is responsible, is £272.08 per assessment period for the first child or qualifying young person and £226.67 for each subsequent child or qualifying young person. An additional amount is included for each child or qualifying young person who is entitled to disability living allowance or personal independence payment or is registered as blind. The higher amount of £352.92 per assessment period is included where the child or qualifying young person is registered as blind or entitled to the highest rate of the care component of disability living allowance or the enhanced rate of personal independence payment; the lower amount of £123.62 is included in any other case.

2.72

Housing costs

The housing costs element

2.73   **25.**—(1) Paragraphs (2) to (4) specify for the purposes of section 11 of the Act (award of universal credit to include an amount in respect of any liability of a claimant to make payments in respect of the accommodation they occupy as their home)—

(a)   what is meant by payments in respect of accommodation (see paragraph (2));

(b)   the circumstances in which a claimant is to be treated as liable or not liable to make such payments (see paragraph (3));

(c)   the circumstances in which a claimant is to be treated as occupying or not occupying accommodation and in which land used for the purposes of any accommodation is to be treated as included in the accommodation (see paragraph (4)).

(2) The payments in respect of accommodation must be—

(a)   payments within the meaning of paragraph 2 of Schedule 1 ("rent payments");

(b)   payments within the meaning of paragraph 4 of that Schedule ("owner-occupier payments");

(c)   payments within the meaning of paragraph 7 of that Schedule ("service charge payments").

(3) The circumstances of the liability to make the payments must be such that—

(a)   the claimant (or either joint claimant)—

(i)   has a liability to make the payments which is on a commercial basis, or

(ii)   is treated under Part 1 of Schedule 2 as having a liability to make the payments; and

(b)   none of the provisions in Part 2 of that Schedule applies to treat the claimant (or either joint claimant) as not being liable to make the payments.

(4) The circumstances in which the accommodation is occupied must be such that—

(a)   the claimant is treated under Part 1 of Schedule 3 as occupying the accommodation as their home (including any land used for the purposes of the accommodation which is treated under that Part as included in the accommodation); and

(b)   none of the provisions in Part 2 of that Schedule applies to treat the claimant as not occupying that accommodation.

(5) References in these Regulations—

(a)   to the housing costs element are to the amount to be included in a claimant's award under section 11 of the Act;

(b)   to a claimant who meets the payment condition, the liability condition or the occupation condition are, respectively, to any claimant in whose case the requirements of paragraph (2), (3) or (4) are met (and any reference to a claimant who meets all of the conditions specified in this regulation is to be read accordingly).

DEFINITIONS

"the Act"—see reg.2.
"claimant"—see WRA 2012, s.40.

GENERAL NOTE

Since universal credit replaces benefits which can include an amount for house   2.74
purchase costs (income support, income-based JSA and income-related ESA) and
housing benefit, the housing costs element of universal credit covers payments both
by people who are renting their homes and by owner-occupiers (as well as service
charges).

Section 11 WRA 2012 allows for universal credit to include "an amount in
respect of any liability of a claimant to make payments in respect of the accommodation they occupy as their home". It also provides that the accommodation must be
residential accommodation and must be in Great Britain, and that the accommodation can be the whole or part of a building and need not comprise separate and self-
contained premises. All the other detailed rules relating to the housing costs element
are in this regulation and reg.26 and in Schs 1–5 to these Regulations (made under
the powers in s.11).

Paragraphs (2) to (4) contain the three basic conditions for the payment of a
housing costs element: the payment condition (para.(2)), the liability condition
(para.(3)) and the occupation condition (para.(4)).

Under para.(2) and Sch.1 the payments in respect of the accommodation   2.75
must be "rent payments", "owner-occupier payments" or "service charges"
(referred to hereafter as "eligible payments"). See the notes to Sch.1 for further
discussion.

Under para.(3) and Sch.2 the claimant (or either joint claimant) must be liable
to make the eligible payments on a commercial basis, or be treated as liable to
make them, and must not be treated as not liable to make them. See the notes to
Sch.2.

Under para.(4) and Sch.3 the claimant (or each claimant in the case of joint
claimants: s.40 WRA 2012) must be treated as occupying the accommodation as
his/her home, and not be treated as not occupying it. See the notes to Sch.3.

Note:

- Paragraph 4 of Sch. 4 which excludes any 16 or 17 year old who is a care
  leaver (defined in reg.8(4)) from entitlement to a housing costs element.

- If the claimant (and/or other member of the couple, in the case of couples)
  who is an owner-occupier has *any* earned income during an assessment
  period (i.e. month), no housing costs element will be payable (Sch.5, para.4,
  although in the case of a shared-ownership tenancy (see reg.26(6)), rent payments and service charges can still be met).

- The lower work allowance applies if an award includes a housing costs
  element (reg.22(2)(b)). This will only affect people in rented accommodation
  because owner-occupiers cannot get a housing costs element if they have any
  earned income (see above).

- People who live in "exempt accommodation" (defined in para.1 of Sch.1)
  do not receive help with housing costs through universal credit but for
  the time being at least this will continue to be provided by way of housing
  benefit.

- There are no deductions for non-dependants (referred to as a housing cost
  contribution) in the case of owner-occupiers.

Amount of the housing costs element—renters and owner-occupiers

2.76   **26.**—(1) This regulation provides for the amount to be included in an award in respect of an assessment period in which the claimant meets all the conditions specified in regulation 25.

(2) Schedule 4 has effect in relation to any claimant where—

(a) the claimant meets all of those conditions; and

(b) the payments for which the claimant is liable are rent payments (whether or not service charge payments are also payable).

(3) Schedule 5 has effect in relation to any claimant where—

(a) the claimant meets all of those conditions; and

(b) the payments for which the claimant is liable are—

(i) owner-occupier payments (whether or not service charge payments are also payable), or

(ii) service charge payments only.

(4) Where both paragraphs (2) and (3) apply in relation to a claimant who occupies accommodation under a shared ownership tenancy—

(a) an amount is to be calculated under each of Schedules 4 and 5; and

(b) the amount of the claimant's housing cost element is the aggregate of those amounts.

(5) But where, in a case to which paragraph (4) applies, there is a liability for service charge payments, the amount in respect of those payments is to be calculated under Schedule 4.

(6) "Shared ownership tenancy" means—

(a) in England and Wales, a lease granted on payment of a premium calculated by reference to a percentage of the value of accommodation or the cost of providing it;

(b) in Scotland, an agreement by virtue of which the tenant of accommodation of which the tenant and landlord are joint owners is the tenant in respect of the landlord's interest in the accommodation or by virtue of which the tenant has the right to purchase the accommodation or the whole or part of the landlord's interest in it.

DEFINITION

"claimant"—see WRA 2012, s.40.

GENERAL NOTE

2.77   This provides that the amount of the housing costs element for renters (whether or not service charges are also payable) is to be calculated in accordance with Sch.4 (para.(2)). The amount for owner-occupiers (whether or not service charges are also payable) is calculated in accordance with Sch.5 (para.(3)(a) and (b)(i)). Schedule 5 also applies if only service charges are payable (para.(3)(b)(ii)). If the claimant occupies the accommodation under a shared ownership tenancy (defined in para.(6)), the amount of the claimant's (or claimants') housing costs element is the aggregate of the amount calculated under Schs 4 and 5 (para.(4)); in the case of shared ownership any amount for service charges is calculated under Sch.4 (para.(5)).

Note reg.39(4) of the Decisions and Appeals Regulations 2013 which provides that if the Secretary of State considers that he does not have all the relevant information or evidence to decide what housing costs element to award, the decision will be made on the basis of the housing costs element that can immediately be awarded.

Particular needs or circumstances—capability for work

Award to include LCW and LCWRA elements

27.—(1) An award of universal credit is to include an amount—   2.78

(a) in respect of the fact that a claimant has limited capability for work ("the LCW element"); or

(b) in respect of the fact that a claimant has limited capability for work and work-related activity ("the LCWRA element").

(2) The amounts of those elements are given in the table in regulation 36.

(3) Whether a claimant has limited capability for work or for work and work-related activity is determined in accordance with Part 5.

(4) In the case of joint claimants, where each of them has limited capability for work or for work and work-related activity, the award is only to include one element and that is the LCWRA element if one of them has limited capability for work and work-related activity, but otherwise it is the LCW element.

Definitions

"claimant"—see WRA 2012, s.40.
"limited capability for work"—see WRA 2012, ss.40 and 37(1).
"limited capability for work-related activity"—see WRA 2012, ss.40 and 37(2).
"work-related activity"— see WRA 2012, s.40.

General Note

Section 12(2)(a) and (b) WRA 2012 allows for an award of universal credit to   2.79
include an additional element if the claimant (or each claimant in the case of joint claimants: s.40 WRA 2012) has limited capability for work ("LCW"), or limited capability for work and work-related activity ("LCWRA"). Under para.(1) an additional element will be included for either LCW or LCWRA (but not both). See reg.29(4) where the claimant also qualifies for the carer element (note if it is the other member of the couple that qualifies for the carer element reg.29(4) will not apply).

If both joint claimants have LCW, or LCWRA, only one additional element will be included. If either of them has LCWRA, it will be the LCWRA element that is included (para.(4)).

See reg.36 for the amounts of these elements and reg.28 for when a LCW, or LCWRA, element will be included.

LCW and LCWRA is assessed in accordance with Part 5 of these Regulations.   2.80
Under reg.39(1) a claimant will have LCW if it has been decided on the basis of an assessment under these Regulations or Part 4 of the ESA Regulations 2013 that s/he has LCW, or if s/he is treated as having LCW because any of the circumstances in Sch.8 apply (see reg.39(6)). Similarly, under reg.40(1), a claimant will have LCWRA if it has been decided on the basis of an assessment under these Regulations that s/he has LCW and LCWRA or under Part 5 of the ESA Regulations 2013 that s/he has LCWRA, or if s/he is treated as having LCW and LCWRA because any of the circumstances in Sch.9 apply (see reg.40(5)).

See reg.41 as to when an assessment may be carried out.

In relation to the effect of a determination of LCW (or not), see reg.40(1) and (2) of the Decisions and Appeals Regulations 2013 which is the equivalent of reg.10 of the Social Security and Child Support (Decisions and Appeals) Regulations 1999. See the notes to reg.10 in Vol.III of this series.

Period for which the LCW or LCWRA element is not to be included

2.81   **28.**—(1) An award of universal credit is not to include the LCW or LCWRA element until the beginning of the assessment period that follows the assessment period in which the relevant period ends.

(2) The relevant period is the period of three months beginning with—

    (a) if regulation 41(2) applies (claimant with weekly earnings equal to or above the relevant threshold) the date on which the award of universal credit commences or, if later, the date on which the claimant applies for the LCW or LCWRA element to be included in the award; or

    (b) in any other case, the first day on which the claimant provides evidence of their having limited capability for work in accordance with the Medical Evidence Regulations.

(3) But where, in the circumstances referred to in paragraph (4), there has been a previous award of universal credit—

    (a) if the previous award included the LCW or LCWRA element, paragraph (1) does not apply; and

    (b) if the relevant period in relation to that award has begun but not ended, the relevant period ends on the date it would have ended in relation to the previous award.

(4) The circumstances are where—

    (a) immediately before the award commences, the previous award has ceased because the claimant ceased to be a member of a couple or became a member of a couple; or

    (b) within the six months before the award commences, the previous award has ceased because the financial condition in section 5(1)(b) (or, if it was a joint claim, section 5(2)(b)) of the Act was not met.

(5) Paragraph (1) also does not apply if—

    (a) the claimant is terminally ill; or

    (b) the claimant—

        (i) is entitled to an employment and support allowance that includes the support component or the work-related activity component, or

        (ii) was so entitled on the day before the award of universal credit commenced and has ceased to be so entitled by virtue of section 1A of the Welfare Reform Act 2007 (duration of contributory allowance).

(6) Paragraph (1) does not apply where an award includes the LCW element and it is subsequently determined that the claimant has limited capability for work and work-related activity.

(7) Where, by virtue of this regulation, the condition in section 5(1)(b) or 5(2)(b) of the Act is not met, the amount of the claimant's income (or, in the case of joint claimants, their combined income) is to be treated during the relevant period as such that the amount payable is the prescribed minimum (see regulation 17).

DEFINITIONS

"the Act"—see reg.2.
"assessment period"—see WRA 2012, ss.40 and 7(2) and reg.21.
"claim"—see WRA 2012, s.40.
"claimant"—*ibid.*
"couple"—see WRA 2012, ss.39 and 40.
"employment and support allowance"—see reg.2.
"joint claimants"—see WRA 2012, s.40.
"LCW element"—see regs.2 and 27.
"LCWRA element"—*ibid.*
"limited capability for work"—see WRA 2012, ss.40 and 37(1).
"limited capability for work-related activity"—see WRA 2012, ss.40 and 37(2).
"Medical Evidence Regulations"—see reg.2.
"work-related activity"—see WRA 2012, s.40.

GENERAL NOTE

A LCW or LCWRA element will not normally be included until the beginning   2.83
of the assessment period following the assessment period in which the "relevant
period" ends (para.(1)), but see the exceptions below.

The "relevant period" is a three months waiting period, starting on the first
day on which the claimant submits a medical certificate, or if reg.41(2) applies
because the claimant has earnings equal to or above the "relevant threshold" (16
× the national minimum national wage, which is £6.31 per hour from October 1,
2013), the date on which the claimant's universal credit award starts, or the date
the claimant applies for the LCW or LCWRA element to be included, if later (para.
(2)).

A claimant does not have to serve the three months waiting period if s/he:

- was previously entitled to universal credit including a LCW or LCWRA
  element, or the three months waiting period for a LCW or LCWRA element
  in relation to the previous award had started but not ended, and the previous award ended immediately before the current award started because the
  claimant had stopped being or become a couple, or ended in the six months
  before the current award started because the income condition was not met
  (and note para.(7)). If the three month waiting period in the previous award
  had not been completed, the claimant will have to serve the remainder of it
  (paras.(3) and (4));

- is terminally ill (para.(5)(a)); or

- is entitled to ESA that includes the work-related activity or support component, or was so entitled on the day before the universal credit award started
  but the ESA ended because of the 52 week limit on entitlement to contributory ESA (para.(5)(b)).

If the claimant's universal credit already includes the LCW element and it is subsequently decided that s/he has LCWRA, the claimant will not have serve a further
waiting period (para.(6)).

Particular needs or circumstances–carers

Award to include the carer element

29.—(1) An award of universal credit is to include an amount ("the   2.84
carer element") specified in the table in regulation 36 where a claimant has

regular and substantial caring responsibilities for a severely disabled person, but subject to paragraphs (2) to (4).

(2) In the case of joint claimants, an award is to include the carer element for both joint claimants if they both qualify for it, but only if they are not caring for the same severely disabled person.

(3) Where two or more persons have regular and substantial caring responsibilities for the same severely disabled person, an award of universal credit may only include the carer element in respect of one them and that is the one they jointly elect or, in default of election, the one the Secretary of State determines.

(4) Where an amount would, apart from this paragraph, be included in an award in relation to a claimant by virtue of paragraphs (1) to (3), and the claimant has limited capability for work or for work and work-related activity, only one out of the carer element, the LCW element and the LCWRA element may be included in respect of the claimant and that element is—

(a) if the claimant has limited capability for work and work-related activity (and, in the case of joint claimants, the LCWRA element has not been included in respect of the other claimant), the LCWRA element; or

(b) in any other case, the carer element.

DEFINITIONS

> "carer element"—see reg.2.
> "claimant"—see WRA 2012, s.40.
> "disabled"—*ibid.*
> "joint claimants"—see WRA 2012, s.40.
> "LCW element"—see regs 2 and 27.
> "LCWRA element"—*ibid.*
> "limited capability for work"—see WRA 2012, ss.40 and 37(1).
> "limited capability for work-related activity"—see WRA 2012, ss.40 and 37(2).
> "regular and substantial caring responsibilities for a severely disabled person"—
> > see regs 2 and 30.
> "severely disabled"—*ibid.*
> "work"—*ibid.*
> "work-related activity"—*ibid.*

GENERAL NOTE

2.85   The carer element (£144.70 per assessment period: see reg.36) is included in the maximum amount if a claimant has "regular and substantial caring responsibilities for a severely disabled person" (as defined in reg.30): para.(1). Where there is a joint claim, and both parties have regular and substantial caring responsibilities for a severely disabled person, the amount is included twice, as long as they are caring for different severely disabled people: para.(2). However, if awards would also include the LCW element or the LCWRA element (see regs 27 and 28) as well as the carer element, then only one of the three elements is to be included. That element is the carer element unless:

● the claimant has limited capability for work and work-related activity; and

● (in the case of a joint claim), the LCWRA element has not been included in respect of the other member of the couple (see reg.27(4)), in which case the LCWRA element is included. This reflects the fact that, at £144.70 per assessment period, the carer element is higher than the LCW element at £123.62 but not as high as the LCWRA element at £303.66.

Paragraph (3) governs the situation where two or more people have regular and substantial caring responsibilities for the same person. Only one of those carers can have the carer element included in an award of universal credit. They can agree between them which it is to be but, if they do not do so, the Secretary of State will decide. Under reg.50(2) and Sch.3, para.4 of the Decisions and Appeals Regulations 2013, there is no right of appeal against the Secretary of State's decision on that point.

Meaning of "regular and substantial caring responsibilities for a severely disabled person"

30.—(1) For the purposes of Part 1 of the Act and these Regulations,   2.86
a person has regular and substantial caring responsibilities for a severely disabled person if they satisfy the conditions for entitlement to a carer's allowance or would do so but for the fact that their earnings have exceeded the limit prescribed for the purposes of that allowance.

(2) Paragraph (1) applies whether or not the person has made a claim for a carer's allowance.

(3) But a person does not have regular and substantial caring responsibilities for a severely disabled person if the person derives earned income from those caring responsibilities.

DEFINITIONS

"carer's allowance"—see reg.2.
"disabled"—see WRA 2012, s.40.
"prescribed"—see WRA 2012, s.40.
"severely disabled"—see WRA 2012, s.40.

GENERAL NOTE

A claimant has regular and substantial caring responsibilities for a severely   2.87
disabled person if he or she satisfies the conditions of entitlement to carer's allow-ance (see Vol.I) as long as he or she does not have earned income from those responsibilities. It is not necessary for the claimant to have claimed carer's allow-ance (para.(2)): it is enough that they would meet the conditions of entitlement if they did.

Particular needs or circumstances—childcare costs

Award to include childcare costs element

31. An award of universal credit is to include an amount in respect of   2.88
childcare costs ("the childcare costs element") in respect of an assessment period in which the claimant meets both—
(a) the work condition (see regulation 32); and
(b) the childcare costs condition (see regulation 33).

Definition

"childcare costs element"—see reg.2.

General Note

2.89   The childcare costs element is included in the maximum amount if a claimant satisfies both the work condition (reg.32) and the childcare costs condition (reg.33). By reg.34, the amount of the element is 70 per cent of the charges incurred by the claimant for "relevant childcare" up to a maximum of £532.29 per assessment period for a single child or £912.50 for two or more children (reg.36). The childcare costs element is not reduced under the benefit cap: see reg.81(1) and (2).

The work condition

2.90   **32.**—(1) The work condition is met in respect of an assessment period if—
    (a) the claimant is in paid work or has an offer of paid work that is due to start before the end of the next assessment period; and
    (b) if the claimant is a member of a couple (whether claiming jointly or as a single person), the other member is either in paid work or is unable to provide childcare because that person—
        (i) has limited capability for work,
        (ii) has regular and substantial caring responsibilities for a severely disabled person, or
        (iii) is temporarily absent from the claimant's household.
    (2) For the purposes of meeting the work condition in relation to an assessment period a claimant is to be treated as being in paid work if—
    (a) the claimant has ceased paid work—
        (i) in that assessment period,
        (ii) in the previous assessment period, or
        (iii) if the assessment period in question is the first or second assessment period in relation to an award, in that assessment period or in the month immediately preceding the commencement of the award; or
    (b) the claimant is receiving statutory sick pay, statutory maternity pay, ordinary statutory paternity pay, additional statutory paternity pay, statutory adoption pay or a maternity allowance.

Definitions

"additional statutory paternity pay"—see reg.2.
"assessment period"—see WRA 2012, ss.40 and 7(2).
"claimant"—see WRA 2012, s.40.
"maternity allowance"—see reg.2.
"ordinary statutory paternity pay"—*ibid*.
"paid work"—*ibid*.
"single person"—see WRA 2012, ss.40 and 1(2)(a).
"work"—see WRA 2012, s.40.

GENERAL NOTE

A claimant satisfies the work condition if she or he is in paid work or has an offer of paid work that is due to start before the end of the next assessment period: para. (1)(a). For joint claims (or in cases where by a member of a couple claims as a single person under reg.3(3)) there is an additional condition that the other member is either in paid work or is unable to provide childcare for one of the reasons set out in heads (i)–(iii). Claimants are treated as if they were still in paid work if they have stopped work within the periods set out in para.(2)(a) or if they are receiving statutory sick pay, statutory maternity pay, ordinary statutory paternity pay, additional statutory paternity pay, statutory adoption pay (see Vol.IV) or a maternity allowance (see Vol.I). **2.91**

The childcare costs condition

33.—(1) The childcare costs condition is met in respect of an assessment period if— **2.92**
    (a) the claimant pays charges in that period for relevant childcare in respect of—
        (i) a child, or
        (ii) a qualifying young person who has not reached the 1st September following their 16th birthday,
for whom the claimant is responsible; and
    (b) the charges are for childcare arrangements—
        (i) that are to enable the claimant to take up paid work or to continue in paid work, or
        (ii) where the claimant is treated as being in paid work by virtue of regulation 32(2), that are to enable the claimant to maintain childcare arrangements that were in place when the claimant ceased paid work or began to receive those benefits.
    (2) The childcare costs condition is only met in respect of an assessment period if those charges are reported to the Secretary of State before the end of the assessment period following the assessment period in which they are paid.

DEFINITIONS

"assessment period"—see WRA 2012, ss.40 and 7(2).
"claimant"—see WRA 2012, s.40.
"paid work"—see reg.2.
"relevant childcare"—see reg.35.
"responsible for a child or qualifying young person"—see regs 2, 4 and 4A.

GENERAL NOTE

A claimant satisfies the childcare costs condition in the circumstances set out in para.(1)(a) and (b). Those paragraphs are cumulative. Both must apply before the childcare costs condition is satisfied. **2.93**

Para. (1)(a) applies if a claimant pays charges for relevant childcare (as defined in reg.35) in respect of a child or a qualifying young person for whom she or he is responsible. A qualifying young person ceases to count for these purposes on September 1st following his or her 16th birthday. **2.94**

2.95   *Para.(1)(b)* applies if the charges are for childcare arrangements to enable the claimant to work or to maintain childcare arrangements that were in place before a period when she or he is not in paid work but is treated by reg.32(2) as if she or he were.

Amount of childcare costs element

2.96   **34.**—(1) The amount of the childcare costs element for an assessment period is the lesser of—

(a) 70% of the amount paid as charges for relevant childcare; or

(b) the maximum amount specified in the table in regulation 36.

(2) In determining the amount of charges paid for relevant childcare, there is to be left out of account any amount—

(a) that the Secretary of State considers excessive having regard to the extent to which the claimant (or, if the claimant is a member of a couple, the other member) is engaged in paid work; or

(b) that is met or reimbursed by an employer or some other person or is covered by other relevant support.

(3) "Other relevant support" means payments out of funds provided by the Secretary of State or by Scottish or Welsh Ministers in connection with the claimant's participation in work-related activity or training.

DEFINITIONS

"childcare costs element"—see reg.2.
"claimant"—see WRA 2012, s.40.
"couple"—see WRA 2012, ss.39 and 40.
"relevant childcare"—see reg.2.
"work"—see WRA 2012, s.40.

GENERAL NOTE

2.97   *Para.(1)*: See the note to reg.31.

2.98   *Paras (2) and (3)*: Charges for relevant childcare are not taken into account to the extent that the Secretary of State considers them excessive; if they are reimbursed by the claimant's employer or some other person; or if they are covered by "other relevant support" (as defined in para.(3)) paid to claimants participating in work-related activity or training.

Meaning of "relevant childcare"

2.99   **35.**—(1) "Relevant childcare" means any of the care described in paragraphs (2) to (5) other than care excluded by paragraph (7) or (8).

(2) Care provided in England for a child—

(a) by a person registered under Part 3 of the Childcare Act 2006; or

[¹(b) by or under the direction of the proprietor of a school as part of the school's activities—

(i) out of school hours, where a child has reached compulsory school age, or

150

  (ii) at any time, where a child has not yet reached compulsory school age; or]

[¹(c) by a domiciliary care provider registered with the Care Quality Commission in accordance with the requirements of the Health and Social Care Act 2008.]

(3) Care provided in Scotland for a child—

(a) by a person in circumstances in which the care service provided by the person consists of child minding or of day care of children within the meaning of [¹ schedule 12 to the Public Services Reform (Scotland) Act 2010 and is registered under Part 5 of that Act; or]

(b) by a childcare agency where the care service consists of or includes supplying, or introducing to persons who use the service, childcarers within the meaning of [¹ paragraph 5 of schedule 12 to the Public Services Reform (Scotland) Act 2010; or]

(c) by a local authority in circumstances in which the care service provided by the local authority consists of child minding or of day care of children within the meaning of [¹ schedule 12 to the Public Services Reform (Scotland) Act 2010 and is registered under Part 5 of that Act].

(4) Care provided in Wales for a child—

(a) by a person registered under Part 2 of the Children and Families (Wales) Measure 2010;

(b) in circumstances in which, but for articles 11, 12 or 14 of the Child Minding and Day Care Exceptions (Wales) Order 2010, the care would be day care for the purposes of Part 2 of the Children and Families (Wales) Measure 2010;

(c) by a childcare provider approved in accordance with a scheme made by the National Assembly for Wales under section 12(5) of the Tax Credits Act 2002;

[¹(d) out of school hours, by a school on school premises or by a local authority;]

(e) by a domiciliary care worker under the Domiciliary Care Agencies (Wales) Regulations 2004; or

(f) by a foster parent in relation to the child (other than one whom the foster parent is fostering) in circumstances in which the care would be child minding or day care for the purposes of Part 2 of the Children and Families (Wales) Measure 2010 but for the fact that the child is over the age of the children to whom that Measure applies.

(5) Care provided anywhere outside Great Britain by a childcare provider approved by an organisation accredited by the Secretary of State.

[¹ (5A) In paragraph (2)(b), "school" means a school that Her Majesty's Chief Inspector of Education, Children's Services and Skills is, or may be, required to inspect.]

(6) In paragraphs (2)(b) and (4)(d)—

(a) "proprietor", in relation to a school, means—

  (i) the governing body incorporated under section 19 of the Education Act 2002, or

  (ii) if there is no such governing body, the person or body of persons responsible for the management of the school; and

(b) "school premises" means premises that may be inspected as part of an inspection of the school.

(7) The following are not relevant childcare—

(a) care provided for a child by a close relative of the child, wholly or mainly in the child's home; and

(b) care provided by a person who is a foster parent of the child.

(8) Care is not within paragraph (2)(a) if it is provided in breach of a requirement to register under Part 3 of the Childcare Act 2006.

(9) In this regulation "child" includes a qualifying young person mentioned in regulation 33(1)(a)(ii).

DEFINITIONS

"child"—see WRA 2012, s.40 and para.(9).
"foster parent"—see reg.2.
"local authority"—*ibid.*
"qualifying young person"—see WRA 2012, s.40 and 10(5) and regs 2 and 5.

AMENDMENT

1. Social Security (Miscellaneous Amendments) (No.2) Regulations 2013 (SI 2013/1508) reg.3(1) and (6) (July 29, 2013).

GENERAL NOTE

2.100   Under reg.33(1)(a), charges only count for the purposes of the childcare costs condition if they are paid for "relevant childcare". Regulation 35 defines that phrase. By para.(1) care is "relevant childcare" if it falls within paras (2) to (5) unless it is excluded by paras (7) or (8).

2.101   *Paras (2)–(5)*: The details differ as between England, Scotland and Wales but the rule may be summarised as being that to qualify as relevant childcare, the care must be provided by a person authorised or approved by an organ of the state to do so. In England and Wales, it can also be provided by the "proprietor" of a "school" on "school premises". The words and phrase in quotation marks are defined in paras (5A) and (6).

2.102   *Paras (7) and (8)*: Care is not relevant childcare if it is provided by an unregistered childminder (para.(8)), by a foster parent (para.(7)(b) or by a close relative of the child (or qualifying young person: see para.(9)) wholly or mainly in the child's own home (para.(7)(a)).

General

Table showing amounts of elements

36.—(1) The amounts of the standard allowance, the child element, the LCW and LCWRA elements and the carer element (which are all fixed amounts) and the maximum amounts of the childcare costs element are given in the following table.

(2) The amount of the housing costs element is dealt with in regulation 26.

(3) In the case of an award where the claimant is a member of a couple,

but claims as a single person, the amounts are those shown in the table for a single claimant.

Element	Amount for each assessment period
Standard allowance—	
single claimant aged under 25	£246.81
single claimant aged 25 or over	£311.55
joint claimants both aged under 25	£387.42
joint claimants where either is aged 25 or over	£489.06
Child element—	
first child or qualifying young person	£272.08
second and each subsequent child or qualifying young person	£226.67
Additional amount for disabled child or qualifying young person—	
lower rate	£123.62
higher rate	£352.92
LCW and LCWRA elements—	
limited capability for work	£123.62
limited capability for work and work-related activity	£303.66
Carer element	£144.70
Childcare costs element—	
maximum amount for one child	£532.29
maximum amount for two or more children	£912.50

DEFINITIONS

"assessment period"—see WRA 2012, ss.40 and 7(2).
"carer element"—see reg.2.
"child element"—*ibid.*
"childcare costs element"—see reg.2.
"claimant"—see WRA 2012, s.40.
"disabled"—*ibid.*
"housing costs element"—see regs 2 and 25.
"joint claimants"—see WRA 2012, s.40.
"LCWRA element"—see regs 2 and 27.
"limited capability for work"—see WRA 2012, ss.40 and 37(1).
"limited capability for work-related activity"—see WRA 2012, ss.40 and 37(2).
"qualifying young person"—see WRA 2012, s.40 and 10(5) and regs 2 and 5.
"single claimant"—see WRA 2012, s.40.

GENERAL NOTE

See the notes to the individual regulations in Pt. 4.

2.103

Run-on after a death

2.104   **37.** In calculating the maximum amount of an award where any of the following persons has died—

    (a) in the case of a joint award, one member of the couple;

    (b) a child or qualifying young person for whom a claimant was responsible; or

    (c) in the case of a claimant who had regular and substantial caring responsibilities for a severely disabled person, that person,

the award is to continue to be calculated as if the person had not died for the assessment period in which the death occurs and the following two assessment periods.

DEFINITIONS

    "assessment period"—see WRA 2012, ss.40 and 7(2).

    "claimant"—see WRA 2012, s.40.

    "couple"—see WRA 2012, ss.39 and 40.

    "regular and substantial caring responsibilities for a severely disabled person"— see regs 2 and 30.

    "responsible for a child or qualifying young person"—see regs 2, 4 and 4A.

    "severely disabled"—see WRA 2012, s.40.

GENERAL NOTE

2.105   Where a joint claimant, a child or qualifying young person for whom a claimant is responsible, or a severely disabled person for whom a claimant had regular and substantial caring responsibilities dies, the award of universal credit runs-on (i.e., it continues as if that person had not died) for the assessment period in which the death occurred and the following two assessment periods.

PART 5

CAPABILITY FOR WORK OR WORK-RELATED ACTIVITY

Introduction

2.106   **38.** The question whether a claimant has limited capability for work, or for work and work-related activity, is to be determined for the purposes of the Act and these Regulations in accordance with this Part.

DEFINITIONS

    "the Act"—see reg.2.

    "work-related activity"—see WRA 2012, s.40.

GENERAL NOTE

2.107   The question of whether a person has limited capability for work ("LCW") or limited capability for work and work-related activity ("LCWRA") is relevant for three reasons. Firstly, if a person has LCW or LCWRA, it affects the work requirements that can or cannot be imposed on him/her (see ss.19(2)(a) and 21(1)(a) WRA 2012). Secondly, it will entitle him/her to an additional element as part of his/her universal credit (see regs 27–28), although note reg.29(4) where the claimant is also eligible for the carer element. Thirdly, it determines which level of the lower or higher work allowance applies (see reg. 22).

Note also that the minimum age for claiming universal credit is 16 (not 18) if a person has LCW or is waiting for a work capability assessment and has submitted a medical certificate stating that s/he is not fit for work (see reg.8(1)(a) and (b)). In addition, if a claimant's universal credit award includes the LCWRA element, or the claimant (or either or both joint claimants) is receiving new style ESA that includes the support component, the benefit cap does not apply (see reg.83(1)(a)).

Limited capability for work

39.—(1) A claimant has limited capability for work if— 2.108

(a) it has been determined that the claimant has limited capability for work on the basis of an assessment under this Part or under Part 4 of the ESA Regulations; or

(b) the claimant is to be treated as having limited capability for work (see paragraph (6)).

(2) An assessment under this Part is an assessment as to the extent to which a claimant who has some specific disease or bodily or mental disablement is capable of performing the activities prescribed in Schedule 6 or is incapable by reason of such disease or bodily or mental disablement of performing those activities.

(3) A claimant has limited capability for work on the basis of an assessment under this Part if, by adding the points listed in column (3) of Schedule 6 against each descriptor listed in column (2) of that Schedule that applies in the claimant's case, the claimant obtains a total score of at least—

(a) 15 points whether singly or by a combination of descriptors specified in Part 1 of that Schedule;

(b) 15 points whether singly or by a combination of descriptors specified in Part 2 of that Schedule; or

(c) 15 points by a combination of descriptors specified in Parts 1 and 2 of that Schedule.

(4) In assessing the extent of a claimant's capability to perform any activity listed in Schedule 6, it is a condition that the claimant's incapability to perform the activity arises—

(a) in respect of any descriptor listed in Part 1 of Schedule 6, from a specific bodily disease or disablement;

(b) in respect of any descriptor listed in Part 2 of Schedule 6, from a specific mental illness or disablement; or

(c) in respect of any descriptor or descriptors listed in—

(i) Part 1 of Schedule 6, as a direct result of treatment provided by a registered medical practitioner for a specific physical disease or disablement, or

(ii) Part 2 of Schedule 6, as a direct result of treatment provided by a registered medical practitioner for a specific mental illness or disablement.

(5) Where more than one descriptor specified for an activity applies to a claimant, only the descriptor with the highest score in respect of each activity which applies is to be counted.

(6) A claimant is to be treated as having limited capability for work if any of the circumstances set out in Schedule 8 applies.

DEFINITIONS

"the Act"—see reg.2.
"claimant"—see WRA 2012, s.40.
"ESA Regulations"—see reg.2.
"limited capability for work"—see WRA 2012, ss.40 and 37(1).

GENERAL NOTE

2.109   A claimant will have LCW if it has been decided on the basis of an assessment under these Regulations or Part 4 of the ESA Regulations 2013 that s/he has LCW, or if s/he is treated as having LCW because any of the circumstances in Sch.8 apply (paras (1) and (6)). Note that if a claimant has reached the qualifying age for state pension credit (the qualifying age for state pension credit for both men and women is the pensionable age for women—since April 2010 this has been increasing from 60 and will reach 65 in November 2018: s.4(4) WRA 2012 and s.1(6) State Pension Credit Act 2002) and is entitled to disability living allowance or personal independence payment, s/he is treated as having LCW (para.6 of Sch.8).

See Sch.6 for the activities and descriptors for assessing LCW.

Limited capability for work and work-related activity

2.110   **40.**—(1) A claimant has limited capability for work and work-related activity if—
   (a) it has been determined that—
      (i) the claimant has limited capability for work and work-related activity on the basis of an assessment under this Part, or
      (ii) the claimant has limited capability for work related activity on the basis of an assessment under Part 5 of ESA Regulations; or
   (b) the claimant is to be treated as having limited capability for work and work-related activity (see paragraph (5)).

(2) A claimant has limited capability for work and work-related activity on the basis of an assessment under this Part if, by reason of the claimant's physical or mental condition—
   (a) at least one of the descriptors set out in Schedule 7 applies to the claimant;
   (b) the claimant's capability for work and work-related activity is limited; and
   (c) the limitation is such that it is not reasonable to require that claimant to undertake such activity.

(3) In assessing the extent of a claimant's capability to perform any activity listed in Schedule 7, it is a condition that the claimant's incapability to perform the activity arises—
   (a) in respect of descriptors 1 to 8, 15(a), 15(b), 16(a) and 16(b)—
      (i) from a specific bodily disease or disablement; or
      (ii) as a direct result of treatment provided by a registered medical practitioner for a specific physical disease or disablement; or
   (b) in respect of descriptors 9 to 14, 15(c), 15(d), 16(c) and 16(d)—
      (i) from a specific mental illness or disablement; or
      (ii) as a direct result of treatment provided by a registered medical practitioner for a specific mental illness or disablement.

(4) A descriptor applies to a claimant if that descriptor applies to the claimant for the majority of the time or, as the case may be, on the majority

of the occasions on which the claimant undertakes or attempts to undertake the activity described by that descriptor.

(5) A claimant is to be treated as having limited capability for work and work-related activity if any of the circumstances set out in Schedule 9 applies.

DEFINITIONS

"the Act"—see reg.2.
"claimant"—see WRA 2012, s.40.
"ESA Regulations"—see reg.2.
"limited capability for work"—see WRA 2012, ss.40 and 37(1).
"limited capability for work-related activity"—see WRA 2012, ss.40 and 37(2).

GENERAL NOTE

A claimant will have LCWRA if it has been decided on the basis of an assess-   **2.111**
ment under these Regulations that s/he has LCW and LCWRA or under Part 5 of the ESA Regulations 2013 that s/he has LCWRA, or if s/he is treated as having LCW and LCWRA because any of the circumstances in Sch.9 apply (see paras (1) and (5)). Note that if a claimant has reached the qualifying age for state pension credit (the qualifying age for state pension credit for both men and women is the pensionable age for women—since April 2010 this has been increasing from 60 and will reach 65 in November 2018: s.4(4) WRA 2012 and s.1(6) State Pension Credit Act 2002) and is entitled to the highest rate of the care component of disability living allowance, the enhanced rate of the daily living component of personal independence payment, attendance allowance or armed forces inde-pendence payment (see the definition of "attendance allowance" in reg.2 which includes armed forces independence payment) s/he is treated as having LCWRA (para.5 of Sch.9).

See Sch.7 for the activities and descriptors for assessing LCWRA.

Work Capability Assessment

When an assessment may be carried out

41.—(1) The Secretary of State may carry out an assessment under this   **2.112**
Part where—

(a) it falls to be determined for the first time whether a claimant has limited capability for work or for work and work-related activity; or

(b) there has been a previous determination and the Secretary of State wishes to determine whether there has been a relevant change of circumstances in relation to the claimant's physical or mental condi-tion or whether that determination was made in ignorance of, or was based on a mistake as to, some material fact,

but subject to paragraphs (2) to (4).

(2) If the claimant has weekly earnings that are equal to or exceed the relevant threshold, the Secretary of State may not carry out an assessment under this Part unless—

(a) the claimant is entitled to attendance allowance, disability living allowance or personal independence payment; or

(b) the assessment is for the purposes of reviewing a previous deter-mination that a claimant has limited capability for work or for

> work and work-related activity that was made on the basis of an assessment under this Part or under Part 4 or 5 of the ESA Regulations,

and, in a case where no assessment may be carried out by virtue of this paragraph, the claimant is to be treated as not having limited capability for work unless they are treated as having limited capability for work or for work and work-related activity by virtue of regulation 39(6) or 40(5).

(3) The relevant threshold for the purposes of paragraph (2) is the amount that a person would be paid at the hourly rate set out in regulation 11 of the National Minimum Wage Regulations 1999 for 16 hours a week.

(4) If it has previously been determined on the basis of an assessment under this Part or under Part 4 or 5 of the ESA Regulations that the claimant does not have limited capability for work, no further assessment is to be carried out unless there is evidence to suggest that—

> (a) the determination was made in ignorance of, or was based on a mistake as to, some material fact; or
>
> (b) there has been a relevant change of circumstances in relation to the claimant's physical or mental condition.

DEFINITIONS

"attendance allowance"—see reg.2.
"claimant"—see WRA 2012, s.40.
"disability living allowance"—see reg.2.
"ESA Regulations"—*ibid.*
"limited capability for work"—see WRA 2012, ss.40 and 37(1).
"limited capability for work-related activity"—see WRA 2012, ss.40 and 37(2).
"personal independence payment"— see reg.2.
"weekly earnings"—see regs 2 and 90(6).
"work-related activity"—see WRA 2012, s.40.

GENERAL NOTE

2.113   *Para.(1)*
This provides when a work capability assessment can be carried out but it is subject to paras (2)–(4).

Paras (2) and (3)
The effect of these two paragraphs is that a claimant who has weekly earnings that are equal to or above the "relevant threshold" (16 × the national minimum national wage, which is £6.31 per hour from October 1, 2013) is treated as not having LCW and no assessment may be carried out, unless s/he is deemed to have LCW under reg.39(6) and Sch.8 or LCW and LCWRA under reg.40(5) and Sch. 9. But this rule does not apply if the claimant:

* is entitled to disability living allowance, personal independence payment, attendance allowance or armed forces independence payment (see the definition of "attendance allowance" in reg.2 which includes armed forces independence payment); or

* has already been assessed as having LCW or LCW and LCWRA under these Regulations or Pt 4 or 5 of the ESA Regulations 2013 and the purpose of the assessment is to review that determination.

Paragraphs (2) and (3) thus contain what could be viewed as a rump of a "permitted work rule" (somewhat oddly placed in a regulation that is also concerned with when an assessment may be carried out). But the effect of para.(2)(b) is that a claimant will only be treated as not having LCW under para.(2) if his/her weekly earnings are equal to or above the relevant threshold (see para.(3)) *and* s/he has not yet been assessed under the work capability assessment. If the claimant has already been assessed as having LCW or LCW and LCWRA, para.(2) will not apply, although the work capability assessment may well be re-applied in these circumstances. Until that is carried out, the claimant's universal credit award will continue to include the LCW or LCWRA element (as appropriate) (confirmed in para.G1035 ADM).

Note reg.40(1) and (2) of the Decisions and Appeals Regulations 2013 which provides that a determination that a person has, or does not have, LCW, or is to treated as having, or not having, LCW, that has been made for the purposes of new style ESA or UC is conclusive for the purpose of any further decision relating to that benefit.

Para. (4)

If it has been decided that the claimant does not have LCW either under these Regulations or the ESA Regulations 2013, no further assessment will be carried out for the purposes of universal credit unless the evidence suggests that the decision was made in ignorance of or mistake as to a material fact or that there has been a relevant change in the claimant's physical or mental condition (para.(4)). Note that this provision applies without time limit.

Assessment—supplementary

42.—(1) The following provisions apply to an assessment under this Part.   2.114

(2) The claimant is to be assessed as if the claimant were fitted with or wearing any prosthesis with which the claimant is normally fitted or normally wears or, as the case may be, wearing or using any aid or appliance which is normally, or could reasonably be expected to be, worn or used.

(3) If a descriptor applies in the case of the claimant as a direct result of treatment provided by a registered medical practitioner for a specific disease, illness or disablement, it is to be treated as applying by reason of the disease, illness or disablement.

DEFINITION

"claimant"—see WRA 2012, s.40.

Information requirement

43.—(1) The information required to determine whether a claimant has   2.115
limited capability for work or for work and work-related activity is—

   (a) any information relating to the descriptors specified in Schedule 6 or 7 requested by the Secretary of State in the form of a questionnaire; and

   (b) any additional information that may be requested by the Secretary of State.

(2) But where the Secretary of State is satisfied that there is enough information to make the determination without the information mentioned in paragraph (1)(a), that information is not required.

(3) Where a claimant fails without a good reason to comply with a request under paragraph (1), the claimant is to be treated as not having

limited capability for work or, as the case may be, for work and work-related activity.

(4) But paragraph (3) does not apply unless the claimant was sent a further request to provide the information at least 3 weeks after the date of the first request and at least 1 week has passed since the further request was sent.

DEFINITIONS

"claimant"—see WRA 2012, s.40.
"limited capability for work"—see WRA 2012, ss.40 and 37(1).
"limited capability for work-related activity"—see WRA 2012, ss.40 and 37(2).
"work-related activity"—see WRA 2012, s.40.

GENERAL NOTE

2.116   On paras (3) and (4), see regs 22 and 37 of the ESA Regulations 2008 and the notes to those regulations in Vol.I of this series.

Medical examinations

2.117   **44.**—(1) Where it falls to be determined whether a claimant has limited capability for work or for work and work-related activity, the claimant may be called by or on behalf of a health care professional approved by the Secretary of State to attend a medical examination.

(2) Where a claimant who is called by or on behalf of such a health care professional to attend a medical examination fails without a good reason to attend or submit to the examination, the claimant is to be treated as not having limited capability for work or, as the case may be, for work and work-related activity.

(3) But paragraph (2) does not apply unless—
(a) notice of the date, time and place of the examination was given to the claimant at least 7 days in advance; or
(b) notice was given less than 7 days in advance and the claimant agreed to accept it.

DEFINITIONS

"claimant"—see WRA 2012, s.40.
"health care professional"—see reg.2.
"limited capability for work"—see WRA 2012, ss.40 and 37(1).
"limited capability for work-related activity"—see WRA 2012, ss.40 and 37(2).
"work-related activity"—see WRA 2012, s.40.

GENERAL NOTE

2.118   See regs 23 and 38 of the ESA Regulations 2008 and the notes to those regulations in Vol.I of this series. But note that unlike regs 23 and 38, the notice under reg.44 does not have to be in writing (see para.(3)).

PART 6

CALCULATION OF CAPITAL AND INCOME

CHAPTER 1

CAPITAL

Introduction

45. This Chapter provides for the calculation of a person's capital for the purpose of section 5 of the Act (financial conditions) and section 8 of the Act (calculation of awards).

2.119

DEFINITION

"the Act"—see reg. 2.

GENERAL NOTE

A claimant's resources are either capital or income. There is nothing in between. On the distinction between capital and income, see the notes to reg. 23 of the Income Support Regulations in Vol. II of this series.

Compared with income support, income-based JSA, income-related ESA and housing benefit, the rules for the treatment of capital under universal credit are refreshingly concise. For example, there are only 19 paragraphs in Sch. 10 (capital to be disregarded), whereas Sch. 10 to the Income Support Regulations has 70 (although a few have been omitted over the years).

2.120

The capital limit for universal credit for both a single claimant and joint claimants is £16,000 (see reg. 18(1)). Note that where a claimant who is a member of a couple makes a claim as a single person (see reg. 3(3) for the circumstances in which this may occur) the capital of the other member of the couple counts as the claimant's (reg. 18(2)).

What is included in capital?

46.—(1) The whole of a person's capital is to be taken into account unless—

2.121

(a) it is to be treated as income (see paragraphs (3) and (4)); or

(b) it is to be disregarded (see regulation 48).

(2) A person's personal possessions are not to be treated as capital.

(3) Subject to paragraph (4), any sums that are paid regularly and by reference to a period, for example payments under an annuity, are to be treated as income even if they would, apart from this provision, be regarded as capital or as having a capital element.

(4) Where capital is payable by instalments, each payment of an instalment is to be treated as income if the amount outstanding, combined with any other capital of the person (and, if the person is a member of a couple, the other member), exceeds £16,000, but otherwise such payments are to be treated as capital.

2.122   The whole of a claimant's capital, both actual and notional (see reg.50), counts towards the £16,000 limit, except if it is treated as income under paras (3) and (4), or is ignored under Sch.10 and regs 75 and 76 (para.(1)). In the case of joint claimants, it is their combined capital that counts towards the £16,000 limit (s.5(2)(a) WRA 2012). A child's capital is not taken into account.

Note reg.49 which maintains the rule that applies for income support, JSA, ESA and housing benefit that it is only if a debt is secured on a capital asset that it can be deducted.

The capital must of course be the claimant's, that is, s/he must be the beneficial owner of it. See the notes to reg.46 of the Income Support Regulations in Vol.II of this series on beneficial ownership and what can constitute capital.

2.123   Note that personal possessions are not treated as capital (para.(2)). There is no equivalent to the rule for income support, JSA, ESA and housing benefit that personal possessions are taken into account if they have been acquired for the purpose of reducing capital in order to secure, or increase, entitlement to benefit (see, e.g., para.10 of Sch.10 to the Income Support Regulations in Vol.II of this series).

Under paras (3) and (4), certain payments that might otherwise be capital are treated as income (and therefore do not count as capital).

Paragraph (4) deals with capital payable by instalments. If the amount outstanding plus the claimant's (including, in the case of couples, the other member of the couple's) other capital is more than £16,000, each instalment when paid is treated as income. Otherwise the payment counts as capital. See the notes to reg.41(1) of the Income Support Regulations in Vol.II of this series.

2.124   Paragraph (3) applies to sums (other than capital payable by instalments) that are paid regularly and by reference to a period, such as payments under an annuity, that may otherwise be capital or have a capital element. They are treated as income. This is wider than the existing rule in, e.g., reg.41(2) of the Income Support Regulations (which only applies to payments under an annuity) and would seem to be an attempt to draw more of a line between capital and income. See the notes to reg.23 of the Income Support Regulations in Vol.II of this series on the distinction between capital and income.

Capital that is treated as income under paras (3) or (4) is included in a person's unearned income (see reg.66(1)(l)).

Note the "assumed yield from capital" rule in reg.72 (the equivalent to the "tariff income rule" for income support, JSA, ESA and housing benefit). Actual income from capital (unless the capital is disregarded or the income is taken into account under reg.66(1)(i) or (j)) is treated as capital from the day it is due to be paid.

Jointly held capital

2.125   **47.** Where a person and one or more other persons have a beneficial interest in a capital asset, those persons are to be treated, in the absence of evidence to the contrary, as if they were each entitled to an equal share of the whole of that beneficial interest.

2.126   The important words in this provision are "in the absence of evidence to the contrary". Although this regulation deems joint owners to have equal shares in the beneficial ownership of a capital asset, this will not apply if there is evidence to show that this is not the case.

See the notes to reg.52 of the Income Support Regulations in Vol.II of this series for the complexities caused by the wording of the rule for jointly held capital in the past.

Capital disregarded

48.—(1) Any capital specified in Schedule 10 is to be disregarded from the calculation of a person's capital (see also regulations 75 to 77).

2.127

(2) Where a period of 6 months is specified in that Schedule, that period may be extended by the Secretary of State where it is reasonable to do so in the circumstances of the case.

GENERAL NOTE

The number of disregards in Sch.10 is considerably reduced from those that apply for income support, JSA, ESA and housing benefit but they cover many of the same items, such as premises, business assets, rights in pension schemes, earmarked assets, etc. But note that some of the disregards that are in Schedules for the purposes of income support, JSA, ESA and housing benefit are to be found elsewhere in these Regulations, e.g., in regs 46(2), 49(3), 75 and 76. See also reg.77 in relation to companies in which the person is like a sole trader or partner.

2.128

Note the general extension on the grounds of reasonableness that can be applied to the six months' period in any of the provisions in Sch.10 (para.(2)).

Valuation of capital

49.—(1) Capital is to be calculated at its current market value or surrender value less—

2.129

  (a) where there would be expenses attributable to sale, 10 per cent; and
  (b) the amount of any encumbrances secured on it.

(2) The market value of a capital asset possessed by a person in a country outside the United Kingdom is—

  (a) if there is no prohibition in that country against the transfer of an amount equal to the value of that asset to the United Kingdom, the market value in that country; or
  (b) if there is such a prohibition, the amount it would raise if sold in the United Kingdom to a willing buyer.

(3) Where capital is held in currency other than sterling, it is to be calculated after the deduction of any banking charge or commission payable in converting that capital into sterling.

GENERAL NOTE

The rules for the valuation of capital are the same as those for income support, JSA, ESA and housing benefit. See the notes to regs 49 and 50 of the Income Support Regulations in Vol. II of this series.

2.130

The provision in para.(3) previously took the form of a disregard—see, e.g., para.21 of Sch.10 to the Income Support Regulations.

Notional capital

50.—(1) A person is to be treated as possessing capital of which the person has deprived themselves for the purpose of securing entitlement to universal credit or to an increased amount of universal credit.

2.131

(2) A person is not to be treated as depriving themselves of capital if the person disposes of it for the purposes of—

  (a) reducing or paying a debt owed by the person; or
  (b) purchasing goods or services if the expenditure was reasonable in the circumstances of the person's case.

(3) Where a person is treated as possessing capital in accordance with this

regulation, then for each subsequent assessment period (or, in a case where the award has terminated, each subsequent month) the amount of capital the person is treated as possessing ("the notional capital") reduces—

    (a) in a case where the notional capital exceeds £16,000, by the amount which the Secretary of State considers would be the amount of an award of universal credit that would be made to the person (assuming they met the conditions in section 4 and 5 of the Act) if it were not for the notional capital; or

    (b) in a case where the notional capital exceeds £6,000 but not £16,000 (including where the notional capital has reduced to an amount equal to or less than £16,000 in accordance with sub-paragraph (a)) by the amount of unearned income that the notional capital is treated as yielding under regulation 72.

DEFINITION

    "unearned income"—see reg.2.

GENERAL NOTE

Paras (1) and (2)

2.132   Under universal credit the only circumstance in which a person will be treated as having notional capital is where s/he has deprived him/herself of it for the purpose of securing, or increasing, entitlement to universal credit (although note also reg.77(2) in relation to companies in which the person is like a sole trader or partner).

There is a considerable amount of case law on the "deprivation rule"—see the notes to reg.51(1) of the Income Support Regulations in Vol.II of this series. But note that some of the case law will need to be read in the light of para.(2).

Paragraph (2)(a) provides that a person will not be treated as having deprived him/herself of capital if s/he has used it to repay or reduce a debt. This provision seems reasonably wide, for example, there is no requirement that the debt is legally enforceable or even that it is due to be repaid, or any limitation as to the type of debt. It would therefore seem to cover, for instance, repayment of loans from friends or family as well as more formal loans such as a mortgage or credit card debts.

2.133   In addition, if the person has used the capital to purchase goods or services and the expenditure was reasonable in his/her circumstances, the deprivation rule will not apply (para.(2)(b)).

Note that if neither of the two situations in para.(2) apply, it remains necessary to consider whether the person did deprive him/herself of the capital with the intention of securing, or increasing, entitlement to universal credit.

There is no longer any specific exclusion from the notional capital rule for trusts that have been set up as a result of personal injury or funds administered by a court that relate to personal injury but it would seem that the intention of the extensive disregard in reg.75 is that the notional capital rule does not apply.

Para. (3)

2.134   This paragraph contains the diminishing notional capital rule for universal credit. If the notional capital is more than £16,000, it is reduced in each subsequent assessment period, or each subsequent month if the universal credit award has ceased, by the amount of universal credit that the person would have received but for the notional capital. In the case of a person who has notional capital of between £6,000 and £16,000, the notional capital reduces by the amount of income deemed to be generated by that amount of capital under the "assumed yield from capital" rule in reg.72.

Presumably a person's notional capital will be calculated in the same way as if it were actual capital, that is, by applying any relevant disregard, although reg.50 does not specifically state this. This is assumed in para.H1885 ADM.

CHAPTER 2

EARNED INCOME

Introduction

51. This Chapter provides for the calculation or estimation of a person's   **2.135**
earned income for the purposes of section 8 of the Act (calculation of
awards).

DEFINITION

"the Act"—see reg.2.

GENERAL NOTE

In the case of joint claimants their income is aggregated (see s.8(4) WRA 2012).   **2.136**
If a member of a couple is claiming as a single person (see reg.3(3) for the circumstances in which this can happen) the income of the other member of the couple
is taken into account when calculating the universal credit award (see reg.22(3)).
   Any income of a child is ignored.
   In calculating universal credit, 65 per cent of the amount by which the claimant's,
or the claimants' combined, earned income exceeds the applicable work allowance
is taken into account (see s.8(3) WRA 2012 and reg.22).
   Regulations 51–64 deal with the calculation of earned income and regs 65–74
with unearned income. Regulations 75–77 contain a number of additional rules in
relation to treatment of a person's capital and income.

Meaning of "earned income"

52. "Earned income" means—   **2.137**
  (a) the remuneration or profits derived from—
     (i) employment under a contract of service or in an office, includ-
       ing elective office,
     (ii) a trade, profession or vocation, or
     (iii) any other paid work; or
  (b) any income treated as earned income in accordance with this
     Chapter.

DEFINITION

"paid work"—see reg.2.

GENERAL NOTE

Paragraph (a) spells out what counts as earned income. It comprises earnings as   **2.138**
an employee, as an office-holder, including a holder of elective office, such as a local
councillor, self-employed earnings, and any other paid work (for the definition of
"paid work" see reg.2).
   On para.(b), see reg.55(4). Note also reg.60 on notional earned income.

Meaning of other terms relating to earned income

53.—(1) In this Chapter—
   "car" has the meaning in section 268A of the Capital Allowances Act   **2.139**
    2001;

"employed earnings" has the meaning in regulation 55;

"gainful self-employment" has the meaning in regulation 64;

"HMRC" means Her Majesty's Revenue and Customs;

"motor cycle" has the meaning in section 268A of the Capital Allowances Act 2001;

"PAYE Regulations" means the Income Tax (Pay As You Earn) Regulations 2003;

"relievable pension contributions" has the meaning in section 188 of the Finance Act 2004;

"self-employed earnings" has the meaning in regulation 57; and

"start-up period" has the meaning in regulation 63.

(2) References in this Chapter to a person participating as a service user are to—

(a) a person who is being consulted by or on behalf of—

    (i) a body which has a statutory duty to provide services in the field of health, social care or social housing; or

    (ii) a body which conducts research or undertakes monitoring for the purpose of planning or improving such services,

in their capacity as a user, potential user, carer of a user or person otherwise affected by the provision of those services; or

(b) the carer of a person consulted under sub-paragraph (a).

Calculation of earned income—general principles

2.140
    54.—(1) The calculation of a person's earned income in respect of an assessment period is, unless otherwise provided in this Chapter, to be based on the actual amounts received in that period.

(2) Where the Secretary of State—

(a) makes a determination as to whether the financial conditions in section 5 of the Act are met before the expiry of the first assessment period in relation to a claim for universal credit; or

(b) makes a determination as to the amount of a person's earned income in relation to an assessment period where a person has failed to report information in relation to that earned income,

that determination may be based on an estimate of the amounts received or expected to be received in that assessment period.

DEFINITIONS

"the Act"—see reg.2.

"assessment period"—see WRA 2012, ss.40 and 7(2) and reg.21.

"claim"—see WRA 2012, s.40.

GENERAL NOTE

Under para.(1), the normal rule is that a person's earned income (both employed and self-employed earnings) is to be based on the actual amount received during an assessment period.

However, para.(2) allows an estimate to be made (i) where the calculation is made before the expiry of the first assessment period or (ii) where there has been a failure to report information about earned income in an assessment period.

An assessment period is normally a period of one month beginning with the first day of entitlement to universal credit and each subsequent month while entitlement continues (see reg.21(1)).

Employed earnings

55.—(1) This regulation applies for the purposes of calculating earned income from employment under a contract of service or in an office, including elective office ("employed earnings").

(2) Employed earnings comprise any amounts that are general earnings, as defined in section 7(3) of ITEPA, but excluding—

(a) amounts that are treated as earnings under Chapters 2 to 11 of Part 3 of ITEPA (the benefits code); and

(b) amounts that are exempt from income tax under Part 4 of ITEPA.

(3) In the calculation of employed earnings the following are to be disregarded—

(a) expenses that are allowed to be deducted under Chapter 2 of Part 5 of ITEPA; and

(b) expenses arising from participation as a service user (see regulation 53(2)).

(4) The following benefits are to be treated as employed earnings—

(a) statutory sick pay;

(b) statutory maternity pay;

(c) ordinary statutory paternity pay;

(d) additional statutory paternity pay; and

(e) statutory adoption pay.

(5) In calculating the amount of a person's employed earnings in respect of an assessment period, there are to be deducted from the amount of general earnings or benefits specified in paragraphs (2) to (4)—

(a) any relievable pension contributions made by the person in that period;

(b) any amounts paid by the person in that period in respect of the employment by way of income tax or primary Class 1 contributions under section 6(1) of the Contributions and Benefits Act; and

(c) any sums withheld as donations to an approved scheme under Part 12 of ITEPA (payroll giving) by a person required to make deductions or repayments of income tax under the PAYE Regulations.

DEFINITIONS

"Contributions and Benefits Act"—see reg.2.
"ITEPA"—*ibid.*
"relievable pension contributions" —see reg.53(1).
"PAYE Regulations" —*ibid.*
"statutory adoption pay"—see reg.2.
"statutory maternity pay"—*ibid.*
"statutory sick pay"—*ibid.*

GENERAL NOTE

This regulation applies to employed earnings (i.e., under a contract of service or as an office holder) (para.(1)). See reg.57 for the calculation of self-employed earnings.

Unlike income support, JSA, ESA and housing benefit, what counts as employed earnings for the purposes of universal credit is defined in terms of the income tax rules (paras (2) and (3)(a)). However, not all amounts that HMRC treats as earnings count for universal credit purposes (see para.(2)(a)). Under para.(2)) (a) benefits in kind, for example living accommodation provided by reason of the employment, are excluded.

2.141

2.142

Under para.(3)(a) expenses that are deductible under ITEPA, Pt 5, Ch.2, are disregarded in calculating employed earnings—this includes, for example, expenses that are "wholly, exclusively and necessarily" incurred in the course of the claimant's employment (see s.336(1) ITEPA). In addition, expenses from participation as a service user (defined in reg.53(2)) are ignored (para.(3)(b)), although payments for attendance at meetings, etc., will count as earnings.

Note that employed earnings also include statutory sick pay, statutory maternity pay, ordinary statutory paternity pay, additional statutory paternity pay and statutory adoption pay (para.(4)).

In calculating a person's employed earnings in an assessment period the following are deducted: any income tax and Class 1 contributions paid in that assessment period, together with any contributions to a registered pension scheme and any charity payments under a payroll giving scheme made in that period (para.(5)).

Information on a person's employed earnings and deductions made will normally be taken from what is recorded on PAYE records. See further the note to reg.61.

Earnings on cessation of employment

There are no special provisions for the treatment of final earnings under universal credit. A claimant's final earnings will be taken into account in the assessment period in which they are paid under the general rule in reg.54(1). Termination payments (e.g., payments in lieu of notice and holiday pay) are "general earnings" under ss.7(3)(a) and 62 ITEPA (see HMRC, *Employment Income Manual*, para.12850) and so will be taken into account for the purposes of universal credit. However, employment tribunal awards for unfair dismissal, damages for breach of contract and redundancy payments (statutory and contractual) will not count as they are only taxable under s.401 ITEPA and so do not come within s.7(3) (see *Employment Income Manual*, paras 12960, 12970, 12978, 13005 and 13750). For other employment tribunal awards which do count as earnings see para.02550 of the *Employment Income Manual*.

Employee involved in trade dispute

2.143 **56.** A person who has had employed earnings and has withdrawn their labour in furtherance of a trade dispute is, unless their contract of service has been terminated, to be assumed to have employed earnings at the same level as they would have had were it not for the trade dispute.

DEFINITIONS

"employed earnings"—see regs 53(1) and 55.
"trade dispute"—see reg.2.

GENERAL NOTE

A person who is involved in a trade dispute but still employed is treated as having the same level of earnings as s/he would have had but for the trade dispute. "Trade dispute" has the same meaning as in s.244 of the Trade Union and Labour Relations (Consolidation) Act 1992 (reg.2).

Self-employed earnings

2.144 **57.**—(1) This regulation applies for the purpose of calculating earned income that is not employed earnings and is derived from carrying on a trade, profession or vocation ("self-employed earnings").

(2) A person's self-employed earnings in respect of an assessment period are to be calculated by taking the amount of the gross profits (or, in the case

of a partnership, the person's share of those profits) of the trade, profession or vocation and deducting from that amount—

    (a) any payment made to HMRC in the assessment period in respect of the trade, profession or vocation by way of—

        (i) Class 2 contributions payable under section 11(1) or (3) of the Contributions and Benefits Act or any Class 4 contributions payable under section 15 of that Act, or

        (ii) income tax; and

    (b) any relievable pension contributions made by the person in the assessment period (unless a deduction has been made in respect of those contributions in calculating a person's employed earnings).

(3) The gross profits of the trade, profession or vocation in respect of an assessment period are the actual receipts in that period less any deductions for expenses allowed under regulation 58 or 59.

(4) The receipts referred to in paragraph (3) include receipts in kind and any refund or repayment of income tax, value added tax or national insurance contributions relating to the trade, profession or vocation.

DEFINITIONS

    "assessment period"—see WRA 2012, ss.40 and 7(2) and reg.21.
    "Contributions and Benefits Act"—see reg.2.
    "employed earnings"—see regs 53(1) and 55.
    "relievable pension contributions"—see reg.53(1).

GENERAL NOTE

This regulation applies for the purpose of calculating self-employed earnings. As with employed earnings, it is the actual amount received during the assessment period that is taken into account. Thus a person who is self-employed will need to report his or her earnings every month.

Self-employed earnings are earnings that are not employed earnings and are derived from carrying on a trade, profession or vocation (para.(1)). On the tests for deciding whether a person is an employed earner or in self-employment, see, for example, *CJSA/4721/2001*. Whether particular earnings are self-employed earnings for the purposes of universal credit is not determined by how they have been treated for other purposes, e.g. contribution purposes (see *CIS/14409/1996* and para.H4017 ADM).

Thus the first question is whether the person is engaged in self-employment. The issue will have to be determined according to the facts. Paragraph H4013 ADM quotes as examples a person who sells his two classic cars after losing his job because he can no longer afford their upkeep (who is not engaged in a trade) and a person who buys 10,000 toilet rolls from a wholesaler with the intention of selling them for a profit (who is so engaged). If it is decided that the person is engaged in self-employment, the question of whether s/he is in "gainful self-employment" will also need to be considered for the purpose of applying the minimum income floor rule (see the note to reg.62). If the person is not in gainful self-employment, no minimum income floor will apply and the person's actual self-employed earnings will be taken into account for the purposes of calculating his/her universal credit award.

There are no specific rules excluding certain payments from being self-employed earnings (contrast, for example, reg.37(2) of the Income Support Regulations in Vol.II of this series).

The starting point for assessing the earnings of the self-employed is the amount of gross profits in an assessment period (i.e. month), from which the following are deducted: any income tax, Class 2 and Class 4 contributions paid in that assessment period, together with any contributions to a registered pension scheme made in that period (unless such pension contributions have already been deducted from the person's employed earnings) (para.(2)). Many self-employed people do not pay tax and NI contributions regularly but they can arrange with HMRC to make such payments monthly and for most people it will be to their advantage to do so for the purposes of universal credit.

The gross profits are the actual receipts from the self-employment in the assessment period (regardless of when they were earned), less amounts for any allowable expenses (see regs 58 and 59) paid in the assessment period (para.(3)). Under para.(4) receipts include receipts in kind and any refund or repayment of income tax, value added tax or national insurance contributions for the self-employment. This method of calculating self-employed earnings on the basis of receipts actually received and expenses actually paid is based on HMRC's "cash basis and simplified expenses accounting system" (the cash basis model, or "cash in/cash out"). According to para.H4141 ADM, self-employed claimants will be asked to report monthly between seven days before and 14 days after the end date of each assessment period details of actual income receipts and actual expenditure on allowable expenses during the assessment period that has just come to an end.

Capital receipts, such as funds introduced by the self-employed person or loans from third parties for financing purposes, do not count (see *R(FC) 1/97* and the other cases discussed in the note to reg.37(1) of the Income Support Regulations in Vol.II of this series and para.H4190 ADM).

But note reg.62 for the level of earned income a self-employed person will be assumed to have if s/he is in "gainful employment" (see reg.64) and his/her earned income is less than the minimum income floor (see the note to reg.62).

See also reg.77 for the special rules that apply if a person's control of a company is such that s/he is like a sole trader or a partner.

Permitted expenses

2.145   **58.**—(1) The deductions allowed in the calculation of self-employed earnings are amounts paid in the assessment period in respect of—

(a) expenses that have been wholly and exclusively incurred for purposes of the trade, profession or vocation; or

(b) in the case of expenses that have been incurred for more than one purpose, an identifiable part or proportion that has been wholly and exclusively incurred for the purposes of the trade, profession or vocation,

excluding any expenses that were incurred unreasonably.

(2) Payments deducted under paragraph (1) may include value added tax.

(3) No deduction may be made for payments in respect of—

(a) expenditure on non-depreciating assets (including property, shares or other assets held for investment purposes);

(b) any loss incurred in respect of a previous assessment period;

(c) repayment of capital [¹ ...] in relation to a loan taken out for the purposes of the trade, profession or vocation;

(d) expenses for business entertainment.

[¹(3A) A deduction for a payment of interest in relation to a loan taken out for the purposes of the trade, profession or vocation may not exceed £41.]

(4) This regulation is subject to regulation 59.

AMENDMENT

1. Social Security (Miscellaneous Amendments) (No.2) Regulations 2013 (SI 2013/1508) reg.3(7) (July 29, 2013).

DEFINITION

"assessment period"—see WRA 2012, ss.40 and 7(2) and reg.21.

GENERAL NOTE

This regulation, and reg.59, provide for the deductions that can be made from self-employed earnings. Only these deductions can be made.

The amount of the deduction will normally be the actual amount of the permitted expenses paid in the assessment period, but note para.(4). The effect of para.(4) is that the alternative deductions under reg.59 in respect of the expenses referred to in paras (2)–(4) of that regulation may be made instead. However, note that in the case of a car, the actual costs involved in acquiring or using it are not allowable and the only deduction that can be made is a flat rate deduction for mileage under reg.59(2).

To be deductible, the expenses must have been paid in the assessment period, be reasonable and have been "wholly and exclusively" incurred for the purposes of the self-employment (para.(1)), but note para.(1)(b). See para.H4214 ADM for examples of allowable expenses. Permitted expenses include value added tax (para.(2)).

Paragraph (1)(b) specifically provides for the apportionment of expenses that have been incurred for more than one purpose (e.g., for business and private purposes). In such a case, a deduction will be made for the proportion of the expenses that can be identified as wholly and exclusively incurred for the purposes of the self-employment. See *R(FC) 1/91* and *R(IS) 13/91* which holds that any apportionment already agreed by HMRC should normally be accepted. But note the alternative flat-rate deductions for expenses if a person uses his/her home for business purposes in reg.59(3). See also reg.59(4) which provides for flat-rate reductions from expenses if business premises are also used for personal use.

No deduction can be made for the payments listed in para.(3). Note the rule in para.(3)(b) which provides that payments in respect of a loss in a previous assessment period cannot be deducted. In addition, a loss in one employment cannot be set off against a profit or earnings in another separate employment (see *R(FC) 1/93* and the other cases discussed in the note to reg.38(11) of the Income Support Regulations in Vol.II of this series).

Repayments of capital on a loan taken out for the purposes of the self-employment are not deductible (para.(3)(c)) but deductions can be made for interest paid on such a loan up to a limit of £41 per assessment period (para.(3A)). Paragraph (3A) was introduced to bring universal credit into line with the tax rules which now allow a deduction of up to £500 annually for interest payments made on loans taken out for the purposes of a business. This will include interest on credit cards and overdraft charges if the original expense related to the business. According to para.H4217 ADM only £41 can be deducted in any assessment period, regardless of the number of relevant loans a person has (although para.(3A) does not expressly excludes the normal rule that singular includes plural (Interpretation Act 1978, s.6(c)).

Flat rate deductions for mileage and use of home and adjustment for personal use of business premises

59.—(1) This regulation provides for alternatives to the deductions that would otherwise be allowed under regulation 58.   **2.146**

(2) Instead of a deduction in respect of the actual expenses incurred in relation to the acquisition or use of a motor vehicle, the following deductions are allowed according to the mileage covered on journeys undertaken in the assessment period for the purposes of the trade, profession or vocation—

(a) in a car, van or other motor vehicle (apart from a motorcycle), 45 pence per mile for the first 833 miles and 25 pence per mile thereafter; and

(b) on a motorcycle, 24 pence per mile,

and, if the motor vehicle is a car [¹ . . .], the only deduction allowed for the acquisition or use of that vehicle is a deduction under this paragraph.

(3) Where a person carrying on a trade, profession or vocation incurs expenses in relation to the use of accommodation occupied as their home, instead of a deduction in respect of the actual expenses, a deduction is allowed according to the number of hours spent in the assessment period on income generating activities related to the trade, profession or vocation as follows—

(a) at least 25 hours but no more than 50 hours, £10;

(b) more than 50 hours but no more than 100 hours, £18;

(c) more than 100 hours, £26.

(4) Where premises which are used by a person mainly for the purposes of a trade, profession or vocation are also occupied by that person for their personal use, whether alone or with other persons, the deduction allowed for expenses in relation to those premises is the amount that would be allowed under regulation 58(1) if the premises were used wholly and exclusively for purposes of the trade, profession or vocation, but reduced by the following amount according to the number of persons occupying the premises for their personal use—

(a) £350 for one person;

(b) £500 for two persons;

(c) £650 for three or more persons.

AMENDMENT

1. Social Security (Miscellaneous Amendments) (No.2) Regulations 2013 (SI 2013/1508) reg.3(8) (July 29, 2013).

DEFINITIONS

"the Act"—see reg.2.
"assessment period"—see WRA 2012, ss.40 and 7(2) and reg.21.
"car"—see reg.53(1).
"motor cycle"—*ibid.*

GENERAL NOTE

This regulation provides for alternatives deductions to those that would otherwise be permitted under reg.58 (para.(1)). However, note that in the case of a car, there is no choice: only a flat rate deduction for mileage is allowed and no deduction can be made for the actual cost of buying or using the car (para.(2)). This does not apply to other motor vehicles.

Under para.(2), a deduction for mileage on journeys undertaken for the purposes of the business in the assessment period:

• on a motorcycle, of 24 pence per mile; or

• in a car, van or other motor vehicle (other than a motorcycle), of 45 pence per mile for the first 833 miles and 25 pence per mile after that,

can be made instead of the actual cost of buying or using the motor vehicle (except in the case of a car).

If a person uses his/her own home for the purposes of his/her self-employment, a flat-rate deduction of:

- £10 for at least 25 hours but no more than 50 hours;

- £18 for more than 50 hours but no more than 100 hours; or

- £26 for more than 100 hours,

of "income generating activities" related to the self-employment in an assessment period can be made instead of the actual expenses incurred in the use of the home (para.(3)). The guidance in paras H4241–H4242 ADM suggests that "income generating activities" include providing services to customers, general administration of the business (e.g., filing and record-keeping) and action to secure business (e.g., sales and marketing) but do not include being on call (e.g., a taxi driver waiting for customers to ring), the use of the home for storage or time spent on completing tax returns (presumably on this basis the DWP would also discount time spent collating evidence of actual receipts and expenses for the purposes of the person's universal credit claim).

For the alternative provision for apportionment of expenses, see reg.58(1)(b).

Paragraph (4) provides that if the person lives in premises that are mainly used for business purposes, the expenses that would be allowed if the premises were used wholly and exclusively for the purposes of the person's self-employment are to be reduced by a set amount depending on the number of people living in the premises. The reduction is £350 for one person, £500 for two and £650 for three or more people in each assessment period. It is not entirely clear but the reduction under this paragraph appears to be a set rule, rather than an alternative to an apportionment under reg.58(1)(b).

Notional earned income

60.—(1) A person who has deprived themselves of earned income, or whose employer has arranged for them to be so deprived, for the purpose of securing entitlement to universal credit or to an increased amount of universal credit is to be treated as possessing that earned income.   2.147

(2) Such a purpose is to be treated as existing if, in fact, entitlement or higher entitlement to universal credit did result and, in the opinion of the Secretary of State, this was a foreseeable and intended consequence of the deprivation.

(3) If a person provides services for another person and—
(a) the other person makes no payment for those services or pays less than would be paid for comparable services in the same location; and
(b) the means of the other person were sufficient to pay for, or pay more for, those services,
the person who provides the services is to be treated as having received the remuneration that would be reasonable for the provision of those services.

(4) Paragraph (3) does not apply where—
(a) the person is engaged to provide the services by a charitable or voluntary organisation and the Secretary of State is satisfied that it is reasonable to provide the services free of charge or at less than the rate that would be paid for comparable services in the same location;
(b) the services are provided by a person who is participating as a service user (see regulation 53(2)); or
(c) the services are provided under or in connection with a person's participation in an employment or training programme approved by the Secretary of State.

GENERAL NOTE

This regulation treats a person as having employed or self-employed earnings in two situations. For the rules relating to notional unearned income, see reg.74.

Paras (1)–(2)

This contains the deprivation of earnings rule for universal credit. It applies if a person has deprived himself/herself of earned income, for the purpose of securing entitlement to, or increasing the amount of, universal credit. It also applies if the person's employer has "arranged for" the deprivation. Presumably this will only apply if the person's intention was to secure, or increase, entitlement to universal credit by way of the arrangement.

See the notes to regs 42(1) and 51(1) of the Income Support Regulations in Vol. II of this series on the deprivation rule.

Note, however, para.(2). The effect of para.(2) is that the person will be deemed to have the necessary purpose if s/he did obtain universal credit, or more universal credit, and in the opinion of the Secretary of State, this was "a foreseeable and intended consequence" of the deprivation. To some extent para.(2) represents a codification of the case law on the "purpose" part of the deprivation rule. However, it seems likely that much will continue to depend on the view taken by the Secretary of State (and on appeal a tribunal) of the person's intention.

Paras (3)–(4)

This is similar but not identical to the notional earnings rule for income support, JSA, ESA and housing benefit. For example, the exception in para.(4)(a) only applies if the person is engaged to provide the services by a charitable or voluntary organisation and does not also include the situation where the person is a volunteer (on the meaning of "volunteer" see *R(IS) 12/92*).

See the notes to reg.41(6) and (6A) of the Income Support Regulations in Vol.II of this series.

Information for calculating earned income

2.148
61.—(1) Where—
   (a) a person has employed earnings in respect of which deductions or repayments of income tax are required to be made under the PAYE Regulations; and
   (b) the person required to make those deductions or repayments is a Real Time Information employer,

the information on which the calculation of those earnings is to be based for the purposes of determining the person's earned income is the information about those earnings reported to HMRC in accordance with the PAYE Regulations.

(2) Where paragraph (1) does not apply or where a Real Time Information employer fails to report information to HMRC, the person must provide such information for the purposes of calculating the person's earned income at such times as the Secretary of State may require.

(3) Where, by virtue of paragraph (1), the calculation of employed earnings is to be based on information reported under the PAYE Regulations, those employed earnings are to be treated as if they had been received by the person in the assessment period in which the Secretary of State receives that information, unless the Secretary of State has made a determination in accordance with regulation 54(2)(b) (estimate where information not reported) in relation to a previous assessment period.

(4) In this regulation "Real Time Information employer" has the meaning in regulation 2A(1) of the PAYE Regulations.

DEFINITIONS

"assessment period"—see WRA 2012, ss.40 and 7(2) and reg.21.
"employed earnings"—see regs 53(1) and 55.
"HMRC"—see reg.53(1).
"PAYE Regulations"—*ibid.*

GENERAL NOTE

This regulation is concerned with the collection of information in relation to employed earnings. One of the new features of universal credit is that normally PAYE information is to be used to calculate a person's employed earnings (and thus his/her entitlement to universal credit) and that direct reporting of employed earnings by a claimant (or "self-reporting") is only to be the fall-back position. It is mainly for this reason that universal credit is assessed on a monthly basis and paid in arrears after the end of the assessment period.

The general rule is in para.(1). This provides that if the claimant's employer is a "Real Time Information employer", the information on which the calculation of the claimant's employed earnings is to be based is the information reported by the employer to HMRC through the PAYE system. Since October 6, 2013 most employers have been Real Time Information employers (see reg.2A(1)(d) of the Income Tax (Pay As You Earn) Regulations 2003 (SI 2003/2682) ("the PAYE Regulations"). Under reg.67B of the PAYE Regulations a Real Time Information employer is required to deliver specified information to HMRC before or at the time of making payments to an employee. During the period October 6, 2013 to April 5, 2014 this requirement is relaxed for Real Time Information employers with less than 49 employees in that they only have to provide the information by the last day of the tax month, i.e. by the 5th of the following calendar month. In December 2013 HMRC announced a further relaxation of this rule that will apply until April 2016 but only to existing employers with nine or less employees. They will be required to provide the information on or before the last pay day of the month.)

The employed earnings used in the calculation of the person's universal credit in an assessment period are those in respect of which the DWP received information in that assessment period (para.(3)). But if the DWP had estimated employed earnings for a previous assessment period because they had not been reported (see reg.54(2)(b)), those earnings will be treated as received in the assessment period for which the estimate was made.

If para.(1) does not apply, or a Real Time Information employer fails to report information to HMRC, the DWP can require the claimant to provide the information needed to calculate his/her employed earnings (para.(2)).

If the claimant does not comply, presumably the Secretary of State will estimate the claimant's earnings under reg.54(2)(b).

See also para.22 of Sch.1 to the Decisions and Appeals Regulations 2013 for the date that a supersession decision takes effect where a person's employed earnings have reduced and s/he has provided the information required by the Secretary of State for calculating those earnings.

Note that under s.159D (Effect of alterations affecting universal credit) SSAA 1992, inserted by s.31 of, and para.23 of Sch.2 to, WRA 2012, and reg.41 of the Decisions and Appeals Regulations 2013, an alteration (i.e., an increase or decrease) in the amount of a person's employed earnings as a result of information provided to the Secretary of State by HMRC takes effect without any further decision by the Secretary of State. However, if the person disputes the figure used in accordance with reg.55 to calculate his/her employed earnings in any assessment period, s/he can ask the Secretary of State to give a decision in relation to that assessment period (which must be given within 14 days of the request, or as soon as practicable thereafter). The person will then be able to appeal against that decision.

Gainful self-employment

Minimum income floor

2.149   **62.**—(1) Where, in any assessment period, a claimant is in gainful self-employment (see regulation 64) and the claimant's earned income in respect of that assessment period is less than the minimum income floor, the claimant is to be treated as having earned income equal to the minimum income floor.

(2) The "minimum income floor" is, subject to paragraph (3)—

(a)   the amount of the claimant's individual threshold (see regulation 90(2)(b)) multiplied by 52 and divided by 12; minus

(b)   an amount that the Secretary of State considers appropriate to take account of any income tax or national insurance contributions for which the person would be liable in respect of the assessment period if they had earned income of that amount.

(3) But if the claimant is a member of a couple and, by virtue of paragraph (1), the amount of the couple's earned income would exceed the maximum for a couple—

(a)   in a case where the couple's combined earned income (before the application of paragraph (1)) is equal to or exceeds the maximum for a couple, paragraph (1) does not apply; and

(b)   in any other case, the minimum income floor is to be reduced so that the amount of the couple's earned income does not exceed the maximum for a couple.

(4) In paragraph (3) the "maximum for a couple" is—

(a)   the amount applicable in regulation 90(3) (earnings threshold for a couple) multiplied by 52 and divided by 12; minus

(b)   an amount that the Secretary of State considers appropriate to take account of any income tax or national insurance contributions for which the couple would be liable in respect of the assessment period if they had earned income of that amount.

(5) Paragraph (1) does not apply where—

(a)   the assessment period falls within a start-up period or is the assessment period in which a start-up period begins or ends; or

(b)   the claimant falls within any of the following sections of the Act—

(i)   section 19 (claimants subject to no work-related requirements), except by virtue of regulation 90,

(ii)   section 20 (claimants subject to a work-focused interview requirement only), or

(iii)   section 21 (claimants subject to a work preparation requirement only).

DEFINITIONS

"assessment period"—see WRA 2012, ss.40 and 7(2) and reg.21.
"claimant"—see WRA 2012, s.40.
"couple"—see WRA 2012, ss.39 and 40.
"gainful self-employment"—see regs 53(1) and 64.
"national insurance contribution"—see reg.2.
"start-up period"—see regs 53(1) and 63.
"work-related requirement"—see WRA 2012, ss.40 and 13(2).

GENERAL NOTE

This regulation provides for the "minimum income floor" which applies to certain   **2.150**
self-employed claimants. It is an anti-abuse provision which has presumably been
introduced because of the difficulties of checking the hours of work of self-employed
people.

If the conditions for the application of the minimum income floor apply, the
claimant is treated as having earned income equal to the minimum income floor that
is applicable to him/her for the purpose of assessing entitlement to universal credit,
even if his/her actual earned income is lower (para.(1)).

The minimum income floor only applies if in any assessment period a claimant

• is in "gainful self-employment" (as defined in reg.64) (para.(1));

• is not in a "start-up period" (see reg.63) (para.(5)(a));

• is subject to all work-related requirements (para.(5)(b)). Note that if a claimant only falls within the no work-related requirements group by virtue of
  reg.90, the application of the minimum income floor is not excluded (see
  para.(5)(b)(i)). However, it is difficult to see how the minimum income floor
  will ever apply to a claimant who is subject to no work-related requirements
  by virtue of reg.90. This is because reg.90 applies if the claimant's weekly
  earnings equal or exceed his/her individual threshold. The minimum income
  floor is the claimant's individual threshold *minus* notional tax and NI contributions (see para.(2)), i.e. a claimant's minimum income floor will usually
  be *less* than his/her individual threshold (because of the deduction of tax and
  NI contributions). But even if no deductions for tax and NI contributions
  are applicable, the claimant's minimum income floor will still equal his/her
  individual threshold and so the rule in para.(1) will not apply; and

• has self-employed earnings, which together with any employed earnings, are
  below the minimum income floor (para.(1)).

Note that if the minimum income floor does apply and a claimant is treated in
an assessment period as having earned income under para.(1), the effect will be
that s/he is not subject to work-related requirements in that assessment period (see
reg.90(5)).

In the case of a single claimant, the minimum income floor is the claimant's individual threshold multiplied by 52 and divided by 12 (to make it monthly), less an
amount for income tax and national insurance contributions that would be payable
if the claimant's actual earned income was at that level (para.(2)). If the claimant's earned income equals or exceeds this minimum income floor, para.(1) does
not apply and his/her actual earnings (including the amount above the minimum
income floor) will be taken into account in the normal way.

For a claimant's individual threshold see reg.90(2). It is the hourly rate of the
national minimum wage for a claimant of that age multiplied by, in the case of a
claimant who would otherwise be subject to all work-related requirements under
s.22 WRA 2012, the expected number of hours per week (usually 35, see reg.88).
In the case of a claimant who would otherwise fall within ss.20 or 21, the multiplier
is 16.

In the case of a couple, the position is more complicated. If the couple's actual
combined earned income in an assessment period equals or exceeds their individual
thresholds added together, multiplied by 52 and divided by 12, less an appropriate
amount for income tax and national insurance contributions (this is referred to as
the "maximum for a couple"—see para.(4)), the minimum income floor does not
apply (para.(3)(a)). (See reg.90(3)(b) for how the threshold is calculated in the case
of a claimant who is a member of a couple but claims as a single person by virtue
of reg.3(3)).

If the couple's actual combined earned income is less than the maximum for
a couple, but applying the minimum income floor would result in the couple's

combined earned income (actual and deemed) exceeding the maximum for a couple, the minimum income floor is reduced to the extent that this is necessary for the couple's combined earned income (actual and deemed) not to exceed the maximum for a couple (para.(3)(b)).

Example 1

Michael is single, aged 25 and is a self-employed plumber. He declares earnings of £580 (£700 less permitted expenses of £120) for the current assessment period. He also has employed earnings of £200 a month as he works in a hardware store on Saturday mornings. His minimum income floor is £914.33 a month (£6.31 (the national minimum wage hourly rate for a person aged 21 or over) x 35 hours a week = £220.85, multiplied by 52 and divided by 12 = £957.02, minus £42.69 for notional income tax and national insurance contributions). As his self-employed earnings and employed earnings added together amount to £780, this is less than his minimum income floor and so he is treated as having earnings of £914.33 and his universal credit is assessed on that basis.

Example 2

Rafiq and Maggie are a couple and they have one child, Charlie, who is aged 2. Rafiq has a photography business and Maggie works in a pub on Friday and Saturday evenings. Maggie's earnings are £450 and Rafiq's are £600 in the current assessment period.

Maggie has been accepted as the "responsible carer" for Charlie and so falls within s.20 WRA 2012. Her individual threshold is therefore £437.49 a month (£6.31 x 16 hours a week = £100.96, multiplied by 52 and divided by 12 = £437.49; no tax or NI contributions will be deducted at this level of earnings).

Rafiq's individual threshold is £957.02 (£6.31 x 35 hours a week = £220.85, multiplied by 52 and divided by 12 = £957.02) and his minimum income floor is £914.33 (£957.02 after deducting £42.69 for notional income tax and NI contributions).

Rafiq and Maggie's actual combined earnings are £1,050 (£600 plus £450).

This is below the sum of their individual thresholds (£957.02 plus £437.49 = £1394.51) minus an appropriate amount for income tax and NI contributions (£42.69) = £1351.82 (the "maximum for a couple" in their case).

However, adding Rafiq's minimum income floor to Maggie's actual earnings gives £1364.33 (£914.33 plus £450), which is above the maximum for a couple in their case (£1351.82).

Rafiq's minimum income floor is therefore reduced by £12.51 (£1364.33 - £1351.82) and their universal credit award is assessed on the basis of earned income of £1351.82.

Note that income a claimant is deemed as having by virtue of the minimum income floor does not count as earned income for the purposes of the benefit cap (see reg.82(4)).

Start-up period

2.151   **63.**—(1) A "start-up period" is a period of 12 months and applies from the beginning of the assessment period in which the Secretary of State determines that a claimant is in gainful self-employment where—

    (a) the claimant has begun to carry on the trade, profession or vocation which is their main employment in the 12 months preceding the beginning of that assessment period; and

    (b) the claimant is taking active steps to increase their earnings from that employment to the level of the claimant's individual threshold (see regulation 90).

(2) But no start-up period may apply in relation to a claimant where a start-up period has previously applied in relation to that claimant, whether in relation to the current award or any previous award of universal credit, unless that previous start-up period—

(a) began more than 5 years before the beginning of assessment period referred to in paragraph (1); and

(b) applied in relation to a different trade, profession or vocation which the claimant has ceased to carry on.

(3) The Secretary of State may terminate a start-up period at any time if the person is no longer in gainful self-employment or is no longer taking the steps referred to in paragraph (1)(b).

DEFINITIONS

"assessment period"—see WRA 2012, ss.40 and 7(2) and reg.21.
"claimant"—see WRA 2012, s.40.
"gainful self-employment"—see regs 53(1) and 64.
"individual threshold"—see regs 2 and 90(2).

GENERAL NOTE

If the claimant is in a "start-up period", the minimum income floor does not apply even if s/he is in gainful self-employment (as defined in reg.64) (see reg.62(5)(a)).

A start-up period is a period of up to 12 months starting from the beginning of the assessment period in which the Secretary of State decides that the claimant is in gainful self-employment, provided that the claimant (i) started his/her trade, profession or vocation which is his/her main employment in the 12 months before the beginning of that assessment period and (ii) is taking active steps to increase his/her earnings from that self-employment to the level of his/her individual threshold under reg.90, i.e., the level at which s/he will no longer have to meet work-related requirements (para.(1)).

If the claimant is no longer in gainful self-employment, or is not taking active steps to increase his/her earnings as required by para.(1)(b), the Secretary of State can end the start-up period (para.(3)).

A claimant can only have one start-up period in relation to the same trade, profession or vocation. In addition, a claimant who has had a previous start-up period can only have a further start-up period in relation to a different trade, profession or vocation if the previous start-up period began more than five years before the start of the assessment period in which the new one begins (para.(2)).

Meaning of "gainful self-employment"

64. A claimant is in gainful self-employment for the purposes of regulations 62 and 63 where the Secretary of State has determined that—

(a) the claimant is carrying on a trade, profession or vocation as their main employment;

(b) their earnings from that trade, profession or vocation are self-employed earnings; and

(c) the trade, profession or vocation is organised, developed, regular and carried on in expectation of profit.

2.152

DEFINITIONS

"claimant"—see WRA 2012, s.40.
"self-employed earnings"—see regs 53(1) and 57.

GENERAL NOTE

This defines when a claimant is in "gainful self-employment". This is important because it determines whether the "minimum income floor" (see reg.62) applies to the claimant's earned income.

A claimant is in gainful self-employment if s/he is undertaking a trade, profession or vocation as his/her main employment, the earnings from which are self-employed earnings, and the trade, profession or vocation is "organised, developed, regular and carried on in expectation of profit". If any of these conditions are not met, the claimant will not be in gainful self-employment.

In order to decide whether a claimant is in gainful self-employment, s/he will be asked to attend a Gateway interview soon after making a claim for universal credit or after declaring that s/he is in self-employment.

There is lengthy guidance on the gainful self-employment test at paras H4020–4058 ADM. This suggests that the question of whether the self-employment is the claimant's main employment will depend on a number of factors, such as the hours spent undertaking it each week, whether this is a significant proportion of the claimant's expected hours per week, how many hours (if any) the claimant spends on employed activity, the amount of income received, whether the claimant receives a greater proportion of his/her income from self-employed or employed activity, and whether self-employment is the claimant's main aim.

In order to decide whether the self-employment is "organised, developed, regular and carried on in expectation of profit", the guidance suggests that factors such as whether the work is undertaken for financial gain, the number of hours worked each week, whether there is a business plan, the steps being taken to increase the income from the work, whether the business is being actively marketed or advertised, how much work is in the pipeline and whether HMRC regard the activity as self-employment may be relevant.

Clearly if the claimant's business is an established one that has been operating for some time and is still receiving income, it may be relatively straightforward to decide that the claimant is in gainful self-employment. If, however, the business is receiving little or no income, it may be that the self-employment is no longer "organised", "regular" or "carried on in expectation of profit". All the circumstances will need to be considered, including future prospects and whether this is part of the normal pattern of the claimant's work. A claimant may still be in gainful employment while unable to work through illness but in that situation should consider submitting medical certificates with a view to no longer being subject to all work-related requirements and thus the minimum income floor not applying.

If the claimant is not in gainful self-employment, the minimum income floor will not apply and the claimant's actual self-employed earnings will be taken into account.

CHAPTER 3

UNEARNED INCOME

Introduction

2.153   **65.** This Chapter provides for the calculation of a person's unearned income for the purposes of section 8 of the Act (calculation of awards).

DEFINITION

"the Act"—see reg.2.

What is included in unearned income?

66.—(1) A person's unearned income is any of their income, including   2.154
income the person is treated as having by virtue of regulation 74 (notional
unearned income), falling within the following descriptions—
  (a) retirement pension income (see regulation 67);
  (b) any of the following benefits to which the person is entitled, subject
      to any adjustment to the amount payable in accordance with regu-
      lations under section 73 of the Social Security Administration Act
      1992 (overlapping benefits)—
       (i) jobseeker's allowance,
      (ii) employment and support allowance,
     (iii) carer's allowance,
      (iv) bereavement allowance,
       (v) widowed mother's allowance,
      (vi) widowed parent's allowance,
     (vii) widow's pension,
    (viii) maternity allowance, or
      (ix) industrial injuries benefit, excluding any increase in that benefit
           under section 104 or 105 of the Contributions and Benefits Act
           (increases where constant attendance needed and for excep-
           tionally severe disablement);
  (c) any benefit, allowance, or other payment which is paid under the
      law of a country outside the United Kingdom and is analogous to a
      benefit mentioned in sub-paragraph (b);
  (d) payments made towards the maintenance of the person by their
      spouse, civil partner, former spouse or former civil partner under a
      court order or an agreement for maintenance;
  (e) student income (see regulation 68);
  (f) a payment made under section 2 of the Employment and Training
      Act 1973 or section 2 of the Enterprise and New Towns (Scotland)
      Act 1990 which is a substitute for universal credit or is for a person's
      living expenses;
  (g) a payment made by one of the Sports Councils named in section
      23(2) of the National Lottery etc. Act 1993 out of sums allocated
      to it for distribution where the payment is for the person's living
      expenses;
  (h) a payment received under an insurance policy to insure against—
       (i) the risk of losing income due to illness, accident or redundancy,
           or
      (ii) the risk of being unable to maintain payments on a loan, but
           only to the extent that the payment is in respect of owner-
           occupier payments within the meaning of paragraph 4 of
           Schedule 1 in respect of which an amount is included in an
           award for the housing costs element;
  (i) income from an annuity (other than retirement pension income),
      unless disregarded under regulation 75 (compensation for personal
      injury);
  (j) income from a trust, unless disregarded under regulation 75 (com-
      pensation for personal injury) or 76 (special schemes for compensa-
      tion);

   (k) income that is treated as the yield from a person's capital by virtue of regulation 72;

   (l) capital that is treated as income by virtue of regulation 46(3) or (4);

  (m) income that does not fall within sub-paragraphs (a) to (l) and is taxable under Part 5 of the Income Tax (Trading and Other Income) Act 2005(miscellaneous income).

(2) In paragraph (1)(f) and (g) a person's living expenses are the cost of—

   (a) food;

   (b) ordinary clothing or footwear;

   (c) household fuel, rent or other housing costs (including council tax), for the person, their partner and any child or qualifying young person for whom the person is responsible.

DEFINITIONS

"bereavement allowance"—see reg.2.
"carer's allowance" —*ibid.*
"child" —see WRA 2012 , s.40
"employment and support allowance" —see reg.2.
"industrial injuries benefit" —*ibid.*
"jobseeker's allowance" —*ibid.*
"maternity allowance" —*ibid.*
"partner"—*ibid.*
"qualifying young person" —see WRA 2012, ss.40 and 10(5) and regs 2 and 5.
"widowed mother's allowance" —*ibid.*
"widowed parent's allowance" —*ibid.*
"widow's pension"—*ibid.*

2.155   GENERAL NOTE

Para. (1)

Universal credit adopts the approach taken in state pension credit of specifying what is to be included as unearned income. If a type of income is not listed as included, it is ignored and does not affect the claimant's (or claimants') award.

In calculating universal credit, all of the claimant's, or the claimants' combined, unearned income that counts is taken into account in full (see s.8(3) WRA 2012 and reg.22).

Unearned income also includes notional unearned income (see reg.74).

On para.(1)(a) (retirement pension income), see the note to reg.67 and on para.(1)(e) (student income), see the note to reg.68.

Not all benefit income is taken into account—see para.(1)(b) for the benefits that do count. Thus, for example, child benefit is ignored, as is disability living allowance, attendance allowance and personal independence payment. War disablement pension and war widows', widowers' or surviving civil partners' pensions are also ignored (for income support, JSA, ESA and housing benefit there is only a £10 disregard). Bereavement allowance is taken into account but not bereavement payment (although this will count as capital).

Under para.(1)(d) payments "towards the maintenance of a person" from a spouse, or former spouse, or civil partner, or former civil partner, under a court order or maintenance agreement count. Thus maintenance payments that are not made pursuant to an agreement (e.g., ad hoc voluntary payments) will be ignored. There is also no provision for treating such payments as unearned income if they are made directly to a third party. Maintenance for a child is ignored.

The list in reg.66 does not include charitable or voluntary payments and so these will be ignored. On the meaning of charitable and voluntary payments, see the notes to para.15 of Sch.9 to the Income Support Regulations in Vol.II of this series.

Payments from employment and training programmes under s.2 of the Employment and Training Act 1973 or s.2 of the Enterprise and New Towns (Scotland) Act 1990 are only taken into account in so far as they are a substitute for universal credit (e.g., a training allowance) or for a person's living expenses (para. (1)(f)). See para.(2) for what counts as "living expenses".

Under para.(1)(h) payments under an insurance policy count but only if the policy was to insure against the contingencies in heads (i) and (ii). Under head (ii) payments under a mortgage (or other loan) protection policy will only be taken into account if the payment is to pay interest on a mortgage or loan secured on the person's home or to meet "alternative finance payments" (see the notes to paras 4–6 of Sch.1) *and* if the person's universal credit award includes a housing costs element. Thus insurance policy payments to meet, e.g., capital repayments or policy premiums, will be ignored.

Income from an annuity (other than retirement pension income) counts unless it was purchased with personal injury compensation—see reg.75, as does income from a trust (unless it is disregarded under regs 75 or 76) (para.(1)(i) and (j)).

On para.(1)(k), "assumed yield from capital" (the equivalent to the "tariff income rule" for income support, JSA, ESA and housing benefit), see the note to reg.72.

Paragraph (1)(l) includes as income capital that is treated as income under reg.46(3) or (4)—see the note to reg.46.

Paragraph (1)(m) covers income that does not fall within paras (1)(a)–(l) but which is taxable under Pt 5 of the Income Tax (Trading and Other Income) Act 2005. The types of income that are taxable under Pt 5 include royalty payments, income from films and sound recordings, and income from estates in administration.

See also reg.28 of the Universal Credit (Transitional Provisions) Regulations 2013 if an award of universal credit is made to a person who is entitled to incapacity benefit or severe disablement allowance.

Unearned income is calculated monthly in accordance with reg.73, except in the case of student income which is calculated in accordance with reg.71.

Meaning of "retirement pension income"

67.—(1) Subject to paragraph (2), in regulation 66(1)(a) "retirement pension income" has the same meaning as in section 16 of the State Pension Credit Act 2002 as extended by regulation 16 of the State Pension Credit Regulations 2002.

2.156

(2) Retirement pension income includes any increase in a Category A or Category B retirement pension mentioned in section 16(1)(a) of the State Pension Credit Act 2002 which is payable under Part 4 of the Contributions and Benefits Act in respect of a person's partner.

DEFINITIONS

"Contributions and Benefits Act"—see reg.2.
"partner"—*ibid.*

GENERAL NOTE

"Retirement pension income" has the same meaning for the purposes of universal credit as it does for state pension credit. See the notes to s.16 of the State Pension Credit Act 2002 and reg.16 of the State Pension Credit Regulations 2002 in Vol.II of this series. Presumably para.(2) is felt to be necessary because s.16(1)(a) of the 2002 Act does not refer to such increases (although in the case of a couple it is their combined income that counts (s.8(4)(b) WRA 2012)).

Person treated as having student income

2.157 **68.**—(1) A person who is undertaking a course [¹ of education, study or training] (see regulation 13) and has a student loan or a grant in respect of that course, is to be treated as having student income in respect of—

(a) an assessment period in which the course begins;

(b) in the case of a course which lasts for two or more years, an assessment period in which the second or subsequent year begins;

(c) any other assessment period in which, or in any part of which, the person is undertaking the course, excluding—

(i) an assessment period in which the long vacation begins or which falls within the long vacation, or

(ii) an assessment period in which the course ends.

(2) Where a person has a student loan, their student income for any assessment period referred to in paragraph (1) is to be based on the amount of that loan.

(3) Where paragraph (2) applies, any grant in relation to the period to which the loan applies is to be disregarded except for—

(a) any specific amount included in the grant to cover payments which are rent payments in respect of which an amount is included in an award of universal credit for the housing costs element;

(b) any amount intended for the maintenance of another person in respect of whom an amount is included in the award.

(4) Where paragraph (2) does not apply, the person's student income for any assessment period in which they are treated as having that income is to be based on the amount of their grant.

(5) A person is to be treated as having a student loan where the person could acquire such a loan by taking reasonable steps to do so.

(6) Student income does not include any payment referred to in regulation 66(1)(f) (training allowances).

(7) In this regulation and regulations 69 to 71—

"grant" means any kind of educational grant or award, excluding a student loan or a payment made under a scheme to enable persons under the age of 21 to complete courses of education or training that are not advanced education;

"the long vacation" is a period of no less than one month which, in the opinion of the Secretary of State, is the longest vacation during a course which is intended to last for two or more years;

"student loan" means a loan towards a student's maintenance pursuant to any regulations made under section 22 of the Teaching and Higher Education Act 1998, section 73 of the Education (Scotland) Act 1980 or Article 3 of the Education (Student Support) (Northern Ireland) Order 1998 and includes, in Scotland, a young student's bursary paid under regulation 4(1)(c) of the Students' Allowances (Scotland) Regulation 2007.

AMENDMENT

1. Universal Credit (Consequential, Supplementary, Incidental and Miscellaneous Provisions) Regulations 2013 (SI 2013/630) reg. 38(5) (April 29, 2013).

DEFINITIONS

"assessment period"—see WRA 2012, ss.40 and 7(2) and reg.21.
"housing costs element"—see regs 2 and 25.

GENERAL NOTE

See the notes to reg.13 for when a person is regarded as undertaking a course of education, study or training. If a person who is exempt from the requirement not to be receiving education under reg.14 has student income that is taken into account in calculating his/her universal credit award, s/he will not have any work requirements (see reg.89(1)(e)(ii)). If the person leaves his/her course, student income is taken into account up to the end of the assessment period before the one in which s/he leaves the course. This is because the person is no longer undertaking the course and so para.(1) of this regulation does not apply (the change of circumstance will take effect from the first day of the assessment period in which it occurs—para.20 of Sch.1 to the Decisions and Appeals Regulations 2013). As any student income that is left over at the end of a course or when a person finally abandons or is dismissed from it does not fall within any other paragraph in reg.66(1), it will be ignored.

Para.(1)

This provides for the assessment periods (i.e. months) in which student income will be taken into account. These are any assessment periods during which, or during part of which, the person is undertaking the course of education, study or training, including the assessment period in which the course begins, or any subsequent year of the course begins. But student income will be ignored in the assessment period in which the course ends, in the assessment period in which the long vacation (defined in para.(7)) starts and in any assessment periods that fall wholly within the long vacation.

Paras (2)–(7)

These paragraphs define what counts as student income. It does not include training allowances and payment for living expenses taken into account under reg.66(1)(f) (para.(6)).

If a person has a student loan (defined in para.(7)), or is treated as having a student loan under para.(5), the amount of that loan counts as income and any grant (defined in para.(7)) paid for the same period as the loan is ignored. But any specific amount included in the grant for rent payments which are being met by universal credit, or any amount intended for the maintenance of another person included in the person's universal credit award will count as income (paras (2) and (3)).

If the person does not have, and is not treated under para.(5) as having, a student loan, grant income is taken into account (para.4)).

Note the exclusion from the definition of "grant" of payments made to enable people under 21 to complete courses of non-advanced education or training. This means that payments from the "16–19 Bursary Fund" and educational maintenance allowances (in so far as they still exist) do not count as student income (they are fully disregarded for the purposes of income support, JSA, ESA and housing benefit). Paragraph H6008 ADM also states that grant income does not include any payment derived from Access Funds (although the basis for this is not clear).

"Student loan" for the purposes of regs 68–71 only includes a loan towards the student's maintenance (see para.(7)). In Scotland it also includes a young student's bursary. Any loan for tuition fees will be ignored.

See regs 69–71 for the calculation of student income. There is a disregard for student income of £110 per assessment period (reg.71).

Calculation of student income—student loans

2.158   **69.**—(1) Where, in accordance with regulation 68(2), a person's student income is to be based on the amount of a student loan for a year, the amount to be taken into account is the maximum student loan (including any increases for additional weeks) that the person would be able to acquire in respect of that year by taking reasonable steps to do so.

(2) For the purposes of calculating the maximum student loan in paragraph (1) it is to be assumed no reduction has been made on account of—

(a) the person's means or the means of their partner, parent or any other person; or

(b) any grant made to the person.

DEFINITIONS

"partner"—see reg.2.
"student loan"—see regs 2 and 68(7).

GENERAL NOTE

The amount of a student loan that is taken into account is the maximum amount (including any increases for additional weeks) that a person could obtain for that year if s/he took reasonable steps to do so (para.(1)). No reduction is made for any assessed contribution from a parent or partner (or any other person) or for any grant which may have reduced the loan.

See reg.71 for how the amount of student income to be taken into account in an assessment period is calculated (note the disregard of £110).

Calculation of student income—grants

2.159   **70.** Where, in accordance with regulation 68(4), a person's student income is to be based on the amount of a grant, the amount to be taken into account is the whole of the grant excluding any payment—

(a) intended to meet tuition fees or examination fees;

(b) in respect of the person's disability;

(c) intended to meet additional expenditure connected with term time residential study away from the person's educational establishment;

(d) intended to meet the cost of the person maintaining a home at a place other than that at which they reside during their course, except where an award of universal credit includes an amount for the housing costs element in respect of those costs;

(e) intended for the maintenance of another person, but only if an award of universal credit does not include any amount in respect of that person;

(f) intended to meet the cost of books and equipment;

(g) intended to meet travel expenses incurred as a result of the person's attendance on the course; or

(h) intended to meet childcare costs.

DEFINITION

"grant"—see regs 2 and 68(7).

GENERAL NOTE

If a grant counts as student income (on which see reg.68 and the note to that regulation), the whole of the grant is taken into account, subject to the disregards in paras (a)–(h). The disregards in paras (d) and (e) do not apply if the person's universal credit award includes these amounts (see also reg.68(3)).

See reg.71 for how the amount of student income to be taken into account in an assessment period is calculated (note the disregard of £110).

Calculation of student income—amount for an assessment period

71. The amount of a person's student income in relation to each assess-   **2.160**
ment period in which the person is to be treated as having student income
in accordance with regulation 68(1) is calculated as follows.

Step 1

Determine whichever of the following amounts is applicable—   **2.161**
   (a) if regulation 68(2) applies (person with a student loan) the amount
      of the loan (and, if applicable, the amount of any grant) in relation to
      the year of the course in which the assessment period falls; or
   (b) if regulation 68(4) applies (person with a grant but no student loan)
      the amount of the grant in relation to the year of the course in which
      the assessment period falls.
But if the period of the course is less than a year determine the amount of
the grant or loan in relation to the course.

Step 2

Determine in relation to—   **2.162**
   (a) the year of the course in which the assessment period falls; or
   (b) if the period of the course is less than a year, the period of the course,
the number of assessment periods for which the person is to be treated as
having student income under regulation 68(1).

Step 3

Divide the amount produced by step 1 by the number of assessment   **2.163**
periods produced by step 2.

Step 4

Deduct £110.   **2.164**

DEFINITIONS

   "grant"—see regs 2 and 68(7).
   "student loan"—*ibid.*

GENERAL NOTE

The amount of a person's student income that is to be taken into account in each
assessment period (i.e. month) is worked out as follows:

Step 1:
   (a)   if the person has, or is treated as having, a student loan, calculate the annual
       amount of the loan, plus, if applicable, the annual amount of any grant that is
       to be taken into account (see regs 68 and 70), for that year of the course; or

(b) if the person has a grant but does not have, and is not treated as having, a student loan, calculate the amount of the grant for that year of the course; or

(c) if the course lasts for less than a year, calculate the amount of the loan and/or grant for the course.

Step 2: calculate the number of assessment periods for which the person is to be treated as having student income in that year of the course, or if the course lasts for less than a year, during the course, in accordance with reg.68(1). Note that this will include assessment periods during which the person was undertaking the course and which count under reg.68(1), even if the person had not made a claim for universal credit at that time. See H6140-6144 ADM (example 2).

Step 3: divide the amount in Step 1 by the number of assessments periods in Step 2.

Step 4: deduct £110, as £110 of student income is ignored in each assessment period.

General

Assumed yield from capital

2.165   **72.**—(1) A person's capital is to be treated as yielding a monthly income of £4.35 for each £250 in excess of £6,000 and £4.35 for any excess which is not a complete £250.

(2) Paragraph (1) does not apply where the capital is disregarded or the actual income from that capital is taken into account under regulation 66(1)(i) (income from an annuity) or (j) (income from a trust).

(3) Where a person's capital is treated as yielding income, any actual income derived from that capital, for example rental, interest or dividends, is to be treated as part of the person's capital from the day it is due to be paid to the person.

GENERAL NOTE

2.166   This contains the universal credit equivalent of the tariff income rule that applies for income support, JSA, ESA and housing benefit. Under universal credit it is referred to as "assumed yield from capital".

If a person has capital above £6,000 but below £16,000, it is treated as producing £4.35 per month for each complete £250 above £6,000 and £4.35 per month for any odd amount left over (para.(1)). But this does not apply if the capital is disregarded (see Sch.10 and regs 75 and 76), or if the actual income is taken into account under reg.66(1)(i) (income from an annuity) or (j) (income from a trust) (para.(2)).

If the assumed yield from capital rule does apply, actual income from the capital counts as part of the person's capital from the day it is due to be paid (para. (3)).

Unearned income calculated monthly

2.167   **73.**—(1) A person's unearned income is to be calculated as a monthly amount.

(2) Where the period in respect of which a payment of income is made is not a month, an amount is to be calculated as the monthly equivalent, so for example—

(a) weekly payments are multiplied by 52 and divided by 12;

(b) four weekly payments are multiplied by 13 and divided 12;

(c) three monthly payments are multiplied by 4 and divided by 12; and

(d) annual payments are divided by 12.

(3) Where the amount of a person's unearned income fluctuates, the monthly equivalent is to be calculated—

(a) where there is an identifiable cycle, over the duration of one such cycle; or

(b) where there is no identifiable cycle, over three months or such other period as may, in the particular case, enable the monthly equivalent of the person's income to be determined more accurately.

(4) This regulation does not apply to student income.

DEFINITION

"student income"—see reg. 68.

GENERAL NOTE

Para. (1)

Unearned income is calculated as a monthly amount (paras (1) and (2)). But unlike earned income the amount taken into account in an assessment period (i.e. month) is not necessarily the amount actually received in that month. If the amount of the unearned income varies, the monthly equivalent is calculated in accordance with para.(3)).

Para. (3)

This provides that if there is an identifiable cycle, the amount of unearned income received during that cycle is converted into a monthly amount (para.(3)(a)). If there is no cycle, the amount taken into account is averaged over three months, or over another period if this produces a more accurate monthly equivalent (para.(3)(b)).

Para. (4)

This regulation does not apply to the calculation of student income. See reg.71 for the amount of a person's student income that is to be taken into account in each assessment period.

Notional unearned income

74.—(1) If unearned income would be available to a person upon the making of an application for it, the person is to be treated as having that unearned income.

(2) Paragraph (1) does not apply to the benefits listed in regulation 66(1)(b).

(3) A person who has reached the qualifying age for state pension credit is to be treated as possessing the amount of any retirement pension income for which no application has been made and to which the person might expect to be entitled if a claim were made.

(4) The circumstances in which a person is to be treated as possessing retirement pension income for the purposes of universal credit are the same as the circumstances set out in regulation 18 of the State Pension Credit Regulations 2002 in which a person is treated as receiving retirement pension income for the purposes of state pension credit.

2.168

DEFINITION

"retirement pension income"—see reg.67.

GENERAL NOTE

Paras (1) and (2)

A person is treated as having unearned income if "it would be available [to him or her] upon the making of an application for it". But this does not apply to the benefits listed in reg.66(1)(b).

A person should only be treated as having unearned income under para.(1) if it is clear that it would be paid if an application for it was made. Thus, for example, para.(1) would not apply to payments from a trust that are within the discretion of the trustees.

Paras (3) and (4)

If a person has reached the qualifying age for state pension credit, he or she will be treated as having retirement pension income (defined in reg.67) in the same circumstances as he or she would be so treated for the purposes of state pension credit under reg.18 of the State Pension Credit Regulations 2002. See the notes to reg.18 in Vol.II of this series. The qualifying age for state pension credit was 60 but since April 2010 it has been gradually rising in line with the staged increase in pensionable age for women and will reach 65 in November 2018; thereafter state pension age for both men and women is set to rise from 65 in December 2018 until it reaches 66 by October 2020. Although it is a condition of entitlement to universal credit that a person is below the qualifying age for state pension credit (see s.4(1)(b) WRA 2012), a couple may still be entitled if one member of the couple is under that age (see reg.3(2)).

If a person below the qualifying age for state pension credit chooses not to apply for retirement pension income, he or she will not be caught by this rule.

For the rules relating to notional earned income, see reg.60.

CHAPTER 4

MISCELLANEOUS

Compensation for personal injury

2.169   **75.**—(1) This regulation applies where a sum has been awarded to a person, or has been agreed by or behalf of a person, in consequence of a personal injury to that person.

(2) If, in accordance with an order of the court or an agreement, the person receives all or part of that sum by way of regular payments, those payments are to be disregarded in the calculation of the person's unearned income.

(3) If the sum has been used to purchase an annuity, payments under the annuity are to be disregarded in the calculation of the person's unearned income.

(4) If the sum is held in trust, any capital of the trust derived from that sum is to be disregarded in the calculation of the person's capital and any income from the trust is to be disregarded in the calculation of the person's unearned income.

(5) If the sum is administered by the court on behalf of the person or can only be disposed of by direction of the court, it is to be disregarded in the calculation of the person's capital and any regular payments from that amount are to be disregarded in the calculation of the person's unearned income.

(6) If the sum is not held in trust or has not been used to purchase an annuity or otherwise disposed of, but has been paid to the person within the past 12 months, that sum is to be disregarded in the calculation of the person's capital.

GENERAL NOTE

This regulation provides for an extensive disregard of compensation for personal injury, both as capital and income. 2.170

Firstly, the compensation is ignored for 12 months from the date it is paid to the person (para.(6)). Thus if it is spent during that 12 months or reduces to £6,000 or less, it will not have any effect on universal credit. Secondly, if the compensation is put in trust, it will be disregarded as capital indefinitely and any income from the trust will be disregarded in the calculation of the person's unearned income (para. (4)). Similarly, if the compensation payment is administered by a court, or can only be disposed of by direction of a court, its capital value is ignored and any regular payments from it are ignored in the calculation of the person's unearned income (para.(5)). Thirdly, if the compensation is used to purchase an annuity, payments under the annuity are disregarded as unearned income (para.(3)). Fourthly, if, in accordance with a court order or agreement, the person receives all or part of the compensation by way of regular payments, these are ignored as unearned income (see para.(2)).

See the notes to para.12 of Sch.10 to the Income Support Regulations in Vol.II of this series, as to what constitutes personal injury.

Special schemes for compensation etc.

76.—(1) This regulation applies where a person receives a payment from a scheme established or approved by the Secretary of State or from a trust established with funds provided by the Secretary of State for the purpose of— 2.171

    (a) providing compensation in respect of—
        (i) a person having been diagnosed with variant Creutzfeldt-Jacob disease or infected from contaminated blood products,
        (ii) the bombings in London on 7th July 2005,
        (iii) persons who have been interned or suffered forced labour, injury, property loss or loss of a child during the Second World War; or
    (b) supporting persons with a disability to live independently in their accommodation.

(2) Any such payment, if it is capital, is to be disregarded in the calculation of the person's capital and, if it is income, is to be disregarded in the calculation of the person's income.

(3) In relation to a claim for universal credit made by the partner, parent, son or daughter of a diagnosed or infected person referred to in paragraph (1)(a)(i) a payment received from the scheme or trust, or from the diagnosed or infected person or from their estate is to be disregarded if it would be disregarded in relation to an award of state pension credit by virtue of paragraph 13 or 15 of Schedule 5 to the State Pension Credit Regulations 2002.

DEFINITION

"claim"—see WRA 2012, s.40.

GENERAL NOTE

2.172   This regulation disregards payments from various compensation schemes and schemes to support people with a disability to live independently set up or approved by the Government. Any payment from these schemes or trusts is ignored as capital if it is capital, and as income if it is income (para.(2)). Payments of capital under para.(3) that are made to a parent of a person diagnosed with variant Creutzfeldt-Jacob disease are disregarded for two years; in the case of a payment to a parent of a person infected from contaminated blood products they are ignored until two years after the date of the person's death.

Company analogous to a partnership or one person business

2.173   **77.**—(1) Where a person stands in a position analogous to that of a sole owner or partner in relation to a company which is carrying on a trade or a property business, the person is to be treated, for the purposes of this Part, as the sole owner or partner.

(2) Where paragraph (1) applies, the person is to be treated, subject to paragraph (3)(a), as possessing an amount of capital equal to the value, or the person's share of the value, of the capital of the company and the value of the person's holding in the company is to be disregarded.

(3) Where paragraph (1) applies in relation to a company which is carrying on a trade—

    (a) any assets of the company that are used wholly and exclusively for the purposes of the trade are to be disregarded from the person's capital while they are engaged in activities in the course of that trade;

    (b) the income of the company or the person's share of that income is to be treated as the person's income and calculated in the manner set out in regulation 57 as if it were self-employed earnings; and

    (c) where the person's activities in the course of the trade are their main employment, the person is to be treated as if they were in gainful self-employment and, accordingly, regulation 62 (minimum income floor) applies in relation to any assessment period where the amount of the person's earned income is below the minimum income floor specified in paragraph (2) of that regulation.

(4) Any self-employed earnings which the person is treated as having by virtue of paragraph (3)(b) are in addition to any employed earnings the person receives as a director or employee of the company.

(5) This regulation does not apply where the person derives income from the company that is employed earnings by virtue of Chapter 8 (workers under arrangements made by intermediaries) or Chapter 9 (managed service companies) of Part 2 of ITEPA.

(6) In paragraph (1) "property business" has the meaning in section 204 of the Corporation Tax Act 2009.

GENERAL NOTE

2.174   If a person's control of a company, which is carrying on a trade or a property business (defined in para.(6)), is such that s/he is like a sole trader or a partner, the value of the person's shareholding is disregarded and s/he is treated as having a proportionate share of the capital of the company (para.(2)). However, as long as the person undertakes activities in the course of the business of the company, this capital is ignored (para.(3)(a)). See the notes to reg.51(4) and (5) of the Income Support Regulations in Vol. II of this series.

The income of the company, or the person's share of it, is regarded as self-employed earnings (para.(3)(b)). If this is the person's main employment, the person counts as in gainful self-employment and so can be treated as having earnings equal to the minimum income floor under reg.62 (para.(3)(c)). This is in addition to any employed earnings the person may receive as a director or employee of the company (para.(4)). Note para.(5) as to when this regulation does not apply.

PART 7

THE BENEFIT CAP

GENERAL NOTE

Introduction

Regulations 78–83 are made under ss.96–97 WRA 2012. They establish a "benefit cap" under which affected claimants can receive no more in social security benefits than £2,167 per assessment period (for joint claimants or those responsible for a child or qualifying young person), or £1,517 per assessment period (for single claimants who are not responsible a child or a qualifying young person). Those amounts are equivalent to £500 per week and £350 per week respectively. The higher rate applies irrespective of how many people are in the benefit unit: families consisting of a couple with six children are capped at the same rate as a single parent with one. Both rates apply irrespective of where the claimant(s) live, and hence of the level of housing costs included in the universal credit award.   **2.175**

How the benefit cap works

Under reg.79, the benefit cap applies where the total amount of the "welfare benefits"—by which is meant the "social security benefits"—listed in reg.79(4) exceed whichever "relevant amount"—£2,167 or £1,517, as above—applies to the award: reg.79(3). The amount of universal credit that the claimant would otherwise be awarded for the assessment period is reduced by the amount of the excess: reg.81.   **2.176**

Calculation of entitlement to welfare benefits

Regulation 80 deals with how the amount of the claimant's (or claimants') entitlement to "welfare benefits" is calculated. The rule is that the total entitlement to all specified benefits during the assessment period is taken into account except where that entitlement is not payable because of the overlapping benefit rules: reg.80(1). Under reg.66, all the benefits listed in reg.79(4) (apart from child benefit, guardian's allowance, and universal credit itself) are taken into account as unearned income when calculating entitlement to universal credit. Regulation 80(4) provides that they are to be taken into account for benefit cap purposes at the same rate as they are taken into account under reg.66. Universal credit itself is (obviously) taken into account at the rate to which the claimant(s) would be entitled if the benefit cap did not apply: reg.80(2). Regulation 80(3) provides (presumably for the avoidance of doubt) that where a claimant is disqualified from receiving (new-style) ESA by virtue of reg.93 ESA Regulations 2013, that benefit is not taken into account. Finally, reg.80(5) provides that where a "welfare benefit" is awarded in respect of a period other than a month (which will always be the case, except for universal credit itself) the monthly equivalent is to be calculated in the same way as for other unearned income under reg.73.   **2.177**

Exceptions

There are a number of exceptions, where the benefit cap does not apply, or the reduction is less than the full amount of the excess. The benefit cap does not apply in any assessment period:

- where the award of universal credit includes the LCWRA element, or a claimant (including one or more joint claimants) is receiving "new-style" ESA at a rate that includes the support component: reg.83(1)(a);

- a claimant is receiving industrial injuries benefit, attendance allowance, disability living allowance or personal independence payment: reg.83(1)(b), (c), (f) and (g) and note that—for obvious reasons—those benefits are not "welfare benefits" as defined in reg.79(4);

- a child or qualifying young person for whom a claimant is responsible is receiving disability living allowance or personal independence payment: reg.83(1)(f) and (g); and

- a claimant is receiving a war pension (as defined in reg.83(2))or certain payments under the Armed Forces and Reserve Forces Compensation Scheme: reg.83(1)(d) and (e)

Where a claimant (or a child or qualifying young person) is entitled to attendance allowance, disability living allowance, personal independence payment—or a war pension or a relevant payment under the Armed Forces Compensation Scheme— but is not receiving it because he or she is in a hospital or a care home, the benefit cap does not apply by virtue of reg.83(1)(h).

Under reg.82(1), the benefit cap does not apply if the claimant's earned income (or the claimants' combined earned income) in the assessment exceeds £430 (roughly equivalent to £99.25 per week) or during the nine month "grace period" as defined in reg.82(2). The rules on the "minimum income floor" in reg.62 (which, in this instance, would be advantageous for the claimant(s)) do not apply to the calculation of earned income in this context.

Finally, where the award of universal credit includes the childcare costs element, the amount of that element is deducted from the amount of the reduction under reg.81. If that amount exceeds the excess of the total entitlement to welfare benefits over the relevant amount, then no reduction is made: reg.81(1) and (2).

Introduction

78.—(1) This Part makes provision for a benefit cap under section 96 of the Act which, if applicable, reduces the amount of an award of universal credit.

(2) In this Part "couple" means—

(a) joint claimants; or

(b) a single claimant who is a member of a couple within the meaning of section 39 of the Act and the other member of that couple,

and references to a couple include each member of that couple individually.

DEFINITION

"the Act"—see reg.2.

Circumstances where the benefit cap applies

79.—(1) Unless regulation 82 or 83 applies, the benefit cap applies where the welfare benefits to which a single person or couple is entitled during the reference period exceed the relevant amount.

(2) The reference period for the purposes of the benefit cap is the assessment period for an award of universal credit.

(3) The "relevant amount" is—

(a) £2167 for joint claimants or a single claimant who is responsible for a child or qualifying young person; or

(b) £1517 for a single claimant who is not responsible for a child or qualifying young person.

(4) The welfare benefits referred to in paragraph (1) are—

(a) bereavement allowance;

(b) carer's allowance;

(c) child benefit under section 141 of the Contributions and Benefits Act;

(d) employment and support allowance;

(e) guardian's allowance under section 77 of the Contributions and Benefits Act;

(f) jobseeker's allowance;

(g) maternity allowance;

(h) universal credit;

(i) widowed mother's allowance;

(j) widowed parent's allowance;

(k) widow's pension.

DEFINITIONS

"assessment period"—see WRA 2012, ss.40 and 7(2).
"bereavement allowance"—see reg.2.
"carer's allowance"—*ibid.*
"child"—see WRA 2012, s.40.
"claimant"—*ibid.*
"Contributions and Benefits Act"—see reg.2.
"couple"—see reg.78(2).
"employment and support allowance"—see reg.2.
"jobseeker's allowance"—*ibid.*
"joint claimants"—see WRA 2012, s.40.
"maternity allowance"—see reg.2.
"qualifying young person"—see WRA 2012, s.40 and 10(5) and regs 2 and 5.
"responsible for a child or qualifying young person"—see regs 2, 4 and 4A.
"single claimant"—see WRA 2012, s.40.
"single person"—see WRA 2012, ss.40 and 1(2)(a).
"widowed mother's allowance"—see reg.2.
"widowed parent's allowance"—*ibid.*
"widow's pension"—*ibid.*

GENERAL NOTE

Although "couple" is defined by reg.78(2) as including a member of a couple who is permitted to claim as a single person under reg.3(3), the higher "relevant amount" in reg.79(3)(a) is only available to "joint claimants" and those responsible for a child or a qualifying young person. A member of a couple claiming as a single person who is not responsible for a child or a qualifying young person, will therefore be capped at the lower rate.

2.181

Manner of determining total entitlement to welfare benefits

80.—(1) Subject to the following provisions of this regulation, the amount of a welfare benefit to be used when determining total entitlement

2.182

to welfare benefits is the amount to which the single person or couple is entitled during the reference period subject to any adjustment to the amount payable in accordance with regulations under section 73 of the Social Security Administration Act 1992 (overlapping benefits).

(2) Where the welfare benefit is universal credit, the amount to be used is the amount to which the claimant is entitled before any reduction under regulation 81 or under section 26 or 27 of the Act.

(3) Where a person is disqualified for receiving an employment and support allowance by virtue of section 18 of the Welfare Reform Act 2007, it is disregarded as a welfare benefit.

(4) Where an amount of a welfare benefit is taken into account in assessing a single person's or a couple's unearned income for the purposes of an award of universal credit the amount to be used is the amount taken into account as unearned income in accordance with regulation 66.

(5) Where a welfare benefit is awarded in respect of a period that is not a month, the amount is to be calculated as the monthly equivalent as set out in regulation 73 (unearned income calculated monthly).

DEFINITIONS

"couple"—see reg.78(2).
"earned income"—see reg.2.
"single person"—see WRA 2012, ss.40 and 1(2)(a).
"unearned income"—see reg.2.

Reduction of universal credit

2.183   **81.**—(1) Where the benefit cap applies in relation to an assessment period for an award of universal credit, the amount of the award for that period is to be reduced by—

(a) the excess; minus
(b) any amount included in the award for the childcare costs element in relation to that assessment period.

(2) But no reduction is to be applied where the amount of the childcare costs element is greater than the excess.

(3) The excess is the total amount of welfare benefits that the single person or the couple are entitled to in the reference period, minus the relevant amount applicable under regulation 79(3).

DEFINITIONS

"childcare costs element"—see reg.2.
"assessment period"—see WRA 2012, ss.40 and 7(2).

Exceptions—earnings

2.184   **82.**—(1) The benefit cap does not apply to an award of universal credit in relation to an assessment period where—

(a) the claimant's earned income or, if the claimant is a member of a couple, the couple's combined earned income, is equal to or exceeds £430; or
(b) the assessment period falls within a grace period or is an assessment period in which a grace period begins or ends.

(2) A grace period is a period of 9 consecutive months that begins on the most recent of the following days in respect of which the condition in paragraph (3) is met—

   (a) a day falling within the current period of entitlement to universal credit which is the first day of an assessment period in which the claimant's earned income (or, if the claimant is a member of a couple, the couple's combined earned income) is less than the amount mentioned in paragraph (1)(a);

   (b) a day falling before the current period of entitlement to universal credit which is the day after a day on which the claimant has ceased paid work.

(3) The condition is that, in each of the 12 months immediately preceding that day, the claimant's earned income or, if the claimant was a member of a couple, the couple's combined earned income was equal to or exceeded the amount mentioned in paragraph (1)(a).

(4) "Earned income" for the purposes of this regulation does not include income a person is treated as having by virtue of regulation 62 (minimum income floor).

DEFINITIONS

   "assessment period"—see WRA 2012, ss.40 and 7(2).
   "claimant"—see WRA 2012, s.40.
   "couple"—see reg.78(2).
   "earned income"—see reg.2 and para.(4).

Exceptions—entitlement or receipt of certain benefits

83.—(1) The benefit cap does not apply in relation to any assessment period where—

   (a) the LCWRA element is included in the award of universal credit or the claimant is receiving an employment and support allowance that includes the support component;

   (b) a claimant is receiving industrial injuries benefit;

   (c) a claimant is receiving attendance allowance;

   (d) a claimant is receiving a war pension;

   (e) a claimant is receiving a payment under article 15(1)(c) or article 29(1)(a) of the Armed Forces and Reserve Forces (Compensation Scheme) Order 2011;

   (f) a claimant, or a child or qualifying young person for whom a claimant is responsible, is receiving disability living allowance;

   (g) a claimant, or a qualifying young person for whom a claimant is responsible, is receiving personal independence payment;

   (h) a claimant, or a child or qualifying young person for whom a claimant is responsible, is entitled to a payment listed in [¹ sub-paragraphs (b) to (g)] but—

      (i) is not receiving it by virtue of regulation 6 (hospitalisation) or regulation 7 (persons in care homes) of the Social Security (Attendance Allowance) Regulations 1991,

     (ii) it is being withheld by virtue of article 53 of the Naval, Military and Air Forces etc (Disablement and Death) Service Pensions Order 2006 (maintenance in hospital or an institution),

2.185

> (iii) is not receiving it by virtue of regulation 8 (hospitalisation) or regulation 9 (persons in care homes) of the Social Security (Disability Living Allowance) Regulations 1991, or
>
> (iv) in the case of personal independence payment, is not receiving it by virtue of regulations under section 85 (care home residents) or 86 (hospital in-patients) of the Act.

(2) For the purposes of this regulation, "war pension" means—

(a) any pension or allowance payable under any of the instruments listed in section 639(2) of ITEPA—

> (i) to a widow, widower or a surviving civil partner, or
>
> (ii) in respect of disablement;

(b) a pension payable to a person as a widow, widower or surviving civil partner under any power of Her Majesty otherwise than under an enactment to make provision about pensions for or in respect of persons who have been disabled or have died in consequence of service as members of the armed forces of the Crown;

(c) a payment which is made under any of—

> (i) the Order in Council of 19th December 1881,
>
> (ii) the Royal Warrant of 27th October 1884, or
>
> (iii) the Order by His Majesty of 14th January 1922,

to a widow, widower or surviving civil partner of a person whose death was attributable to service in a capacity analogous to service as a member of the armed forces of the Crown and whose service in such capacity terminated before 31st March 1973;

(d) a pension paid by the government of a country outside the United Kingdom which is analogous to any of the pensions, allowances or payments mentioned in paragraphs (a) to (c).

DEFINITIONS

"the Act"—see reg.2.
"attendance allowance"—see reg.2.
"child"—see WRA 2012, s.40.
"claimant"—*ibid.*
"disability living allowance"—see reg.2.
"employment and support allowance"—*ibid.*
"industrial injuries benefit"—*ibid.*
"ITEPA"—*ibid.*
"partner"—see reg.2.
"personal independence payment"—see reg.2.
"responsible for a child or qualifying young person"—see regs 2, 4 and 4A.
"qualifying young person"—see WRA 2012, s.40 and 10(5) and regs 2 and 5.

AMENDMENT

1. Universal Credit (Consequential, Supplementary, Incidental and Miscellaneous Provisions) Regulations 2013 (SI 2013/630) reg.38(1) and (6) (April 29, 2013).

PART 8

CLAIMANT RESPONSIBILITIES

CHAPTER 1

WORK-RELATED REQUIREMENTS

Introductory

Introduction

84. This Chapter contains provisions about the work-related require- 2.186
ments under sections 15 to 25 of the Act, including the persons to whom
they are to be applied, the limitations on those requirements and other
related matters.

DEFINITION

"work-related requirement"—see WRA 2012, ss.40 and 13(2)

Meaning of terms relating to carers

85. In this Chapter— 2.187
"relevant carer" means—
(a) a parent of a child who is not the responsible carer, but has caring
    responsibilities for the child; or
(b) a person who has caring responsibilities for a person who has a physi-
    cal or mental impairment; and
"responsible foster parent" in relation to a child means a person who is the
only foster parent in relation to that child or, in the case of a couple both
members of which are foster parents in relation to that child, the member
who is nominated by them in accordance with regulation 86.

DEFINITIONS

"child"—see WRA 2012, s.40
"couple"—see WRA 2012, ss.40 and 39
"foster parent"—see reg.2
"responsible carer"—see WRA 2012, ss.40 and 19(6)

GENERAL NOTE

The definitions of "relevant carer" and "responsible foster parent" are relevant for 2.188
the purposes of regs 86, 88, 89(1)(f), 91(2), 96(3) and 97(2). A child is a person
under the age of 16. Responsibility for a child is to be determined in accordance
with the rules in reg.4, under which the basic test is whether the child normally lives
with the person in question. The definition of "relevant carer" allows the inclusion
into that category of people who do not count as responsible under the reg.4 rules
but nevertheless have caring responsibilities (not further defined) for the child in

question or have caring responsibilities for a person of any age who has a physical or mental impairment (not further defined). If a child has only one foster parent, that person is the "responsible foster parent". If both members of a couple are foster parents of the child, there must be a nomination of one of them under reg.86.

Nomination of responsible carer and responsible foster parent

2.189   **86.**—(1) This regulation makes provision for the nomination of the responsible carer or the responsible foster parent in relation to a child.

(2) Only one of joint claimants may be nominated as a responsible carer or a responsible foster parent.

(3) The nomination applies to all the children, where there is more than one, for whom either of the joint claimants is responsible.

(4) Joint claimants may change which member is nominated—

(a) once in a 12 month period, starting from the date of the previous nomination; or

(b) on any occasion where the Secretary of State considers that there has been a change of circumstances which is relevant to the nomination.

DEFINITIONS

"child"—see WRA 2012, s.40
"joint claimant"—*ibid.*
"responsible carer"—see WRA 2012, ss.40 and 19(6)
"responsible foster parent"—see reg.85

GENERAL NOTE

2.190   This regulation provides, for the purposes of s.19(6) of the WRA 2012 and reg.85, for the nomination by a couple of which one of them is to be the "responsible carer" or "responsible foster parent". Under s.19(6) the nomination has to be made jointly. Presumably that is implied where the nomination is of the responsible foster parent under reg.85. Where more than one child is involved, the same nomination must cover all of them. The nomination can be changed once within 12 months from the date of the previous nomination or when there has been a relevant change of circumstances

References to paid work

2.191   **87.** References in this Chapter to obtaining paid work include obtaining more paid work or better paid work.

DEFINITION

"paid work"—see reg.2

GENERAL NOTE

2.192   References to obtaining paid work, which appears to include self-employment as well as employment, includes obtaining more or better paid work. This provision does not appear to add anything to the conditions of most of the provisions to which obtaining paid work is relevant.

Expected hours

2.193   **88.**—(1) The "expected number of hours per week" in relation to a claimant for the purposes of determining their individual threshold in regulation 90 or for the purposes of regulation 95 or 97 is 35 unless some lesser number of hours applies under paragraph (2).

(2) The lesser number of hours is—

(a) where—
  (i) the claimant is a relevant carer, a responsible carer or a responsible foster parent, and
  (ii) the Secretary of State is satisfied that the claimant has reasonable prospects of obtaining paid work,
  the number of hours that the Secretary of State considers is compatible with those caring responsibilities;

(b) where the claimant is a responsible carer for a child under the age of 13, the number of hours that the Secretary of State considers is compatible with the child's normal school hours (including the normal time it takes the child to travel to and from school); or

(c) where the claimant has a physical or mental impairment, the number of hours that the Secretary of State considers is reasonable in light of the impairment.

DEFINITIONS

"child"—see WRA 2012, s.40.
"claimant"—*ibid.*
"relevant carer"—see reg.85.
"responsible carer"—see WRA 2012, ss.40 and 19(6).
"responsible foster parent"—see reg.85.

GENERAL NOTE

Regulation 90 calculates the amount of earnings that will take a claimant out of being subject to all work-related requirements under s.22 of the WRA 2012 by reference to the "expected number of hours per week" and the National Minimum Wage. Regulation 95 uses the same number as one of the tests for the time that a claimant has to spend in action aimed at obtaining paid work to avoid being deemed not to have complied with the work search requirement under s.17 of the WRA 2012. Regulation 97(2) allows certain claimants to limit the work for which they must be available and for which they must search to work for the expected number of hours per week. Regulation 88 defines the expected number of hours for all these purposes.   2.194

The number under para.(1) is 35, unless some lesser number is applicable under para.(2). There are three alternative categories in para.(2). Sub-paragraph (a) applies where the claimant is a relevant carer, a responsible carer or a responsible foster parent, and so has some substantial caring responsibility. Then, if the claimant nonetheless has reasonable prospects of obtaining paid work (including obtaining more or better paid work), the expected hours are what is compatible with those caring responsibilities. Sub-paragraph (b) applies where the claimant is a responsible carer (as defined in s.19(6) of the WRA 2012) for a child under the age of 13, when the expected hours are those compatible with the child's normal school and travel hours. Sub-paragraph (c) applies where the claimant has physical or mental disablement (not further defined), when the expected hours are those reasonable in the light of the impairment.

Work-related groups

Claimants subject to no work-related requirements

89.—(1) A claimant falls within section 19 of the Act (claimants subject to no work-related requirements) if—   2.195

(a) the claimant has reached the qualifying age for state pension credit;

(b) the claimant has caring responsibilities for one or more severely disabled persons for at least 35 hours a week but does not meet the conditions for entitlement to a carer's allowance and the Secretary of State is satisfied that it would be unreasonable to require the claimant to comply with a work search requirement and a work availability requirement, including if such a requirement were limited in accordance with section 17(4) or 18(3) of the Act;

(c) the claimant is pregnant and it is 11 weeks or less before her expected week of confinement, or was pregnant and it is 15 weeks or less since the date of her confinement;

(d) the claimant is an adopter and it is 12 months or less since—

    (i) the date that the child was placed with the claimant, or

    (ii) if the claimant requested that the 12 months should run from a date within 14 days before the child was expected to be placed, that date;

(e) the claimant does not have to meet the condition in section 4(1)(d) of the Act (not receiving education) by virtue of regulation 14 and—

    (i) is a person referred to in paragraph (a) of that regulation (under 21, in non-advanced education and without parental support), or

    (ii) has student income in relation to the course they are undertaking which is taken into account in the calculation of the award; or

(f) the claimant is the responsible foster parent of a child under the age of 1.

(2) In paragraph (1)(b) "severely disabled" has the meaning in section 70 of the Contributions and Benefits Act.

(3) In paragraph (1)(d)—

(a) "adopter" means a person who has been matched with a child for adoption and who is, or is intended to be, the responsible carer for the child, but excluding a person who is a foster parent or close relative of the child; and

(b) a person is matched with a child for adoption when it is decided by an adoption agency that the person would be a suitable adoptive parent for the child.

DEFINITIONS

"child"—see WRA 2012, s.40.
"claimant"—*ibid.*
"close relative"—see reg.2.
"Contributions and Benefits Act"—*ibid.*
"responsible carer"—see WRA 2012, ss.40 and 19(6).
"responsible foster parent"—see reg.85.

GENERAL NOTE

2.196   Section 19(2) of the WRA 2012 sets out in paras (a), (b) and (c) three categories of claimants who can be subject to no work-related requirements: (a) those who have limited capability for work and work-related activity; (b) those who meet the definition of having regular and substantial caring responsibilities for a severely disabled person (i.e. satisfy the conditions, apart from level of earnings and claiming, for carer's allowance, but gain no earned income from the caring: reg.30); and (c) those who are the responsible carer for a child under the age of one. Paragraph (d) of s.19(2) includes claimants of a description prescribed in regulations. Regulation 89(1) sets out categories prescribed for this purpose, as noted below. Regulation 90 prescribes another category, dependent on earnings. See also reg.98 on recent victims of domestic violence.

(a) Claimants who have reached the qualifying age for state pension credit. The qualifying age for men is the same as for a woman born on the same day and for women depends on the date of birth in accordance with a complicated formula. See p.102 of and Appendix 5 to CPAG's *Welfare benefits and tax credits handbook* (2013/2014 edition) for the details. For anyone born before April 6, 1950 the age is 60. For those born on or after that date there is a sliding scale currently up to 65, a maximum that will increase in the future.

(b) Claimants who do not meet the conditions of entitlement for carer's allowance, but have caring responsibilities for at least 35 hours per week for a severely disabled person (defined in the same way as for carer's allowance: para.(2)), where it would be unreasonable to expect the claimant to comply with a work search and a work availability requirement, even with limitations. Some claimants who fall within this category will already be covered by s.19(2)(b) and it is not easy to work out who could benefit from the extension. Perhaps the main category would be those who are paid for the caring, who are expressly excluded from the scope of s.19(2)(b) by the definition in reg.30 above.

(c) Claimants who are pregnant in the period from 11 weeks before the expected date of confinement and 15 weeks after the date of confinement.

(d) Claimants who are "adopters" (i.e. who have been matched with a particular child for adoption under the complicated conditions in para.(3)) within 12 months or so of placement. It does not matter how old the child is, so long as below the age of 16. Any person who is actually the responsible carer of a child under the age of one is already covered by s.19(2)(c). It appears that para.(d) can continue to apply after the child has actually been adopted, for the 12 months following placement. See para.(f) for foster parents.

(e) Claimants who, by virtue of reg.14(1)(a), do not have to meet the basic condition in s.4(1)(d) of the WRA 2012 of not receiving education or who have student income (see regs 68–71) that is taken into account in the award of universal credit.

(f) Claimants who are the responsible foster parent (there can only be one under reg.85) of a child under the age of one. It appears that such a person cannot get within s.19(2)(c) because reg.4(6)(a) prevents their being treated as responsible for the child while the child is "looked after" by a local authority under s.22 of the Children Act 1989 or s.17(6) of the Children (Scotland) Act 1995.

Claimants subject to no work-related requirements—the earnings thresholds

90.—(1) A claimant falls within section 19 of the Act (claimants subject to no work-related requirements) if the claimant's weekly earnings are equal to or exceed the claimant's individual threshold.

    2.197

(2) A claimant's individual threshold is the amount that a person of the same age as the claimant would be paid at the hourly rate applicable under regulation 11 or regulation 13(1) or (2) of the National Minimum Wage Regulations for—

    (a) 16 hours per week, in the case of a claimant who would otherwise fall within section 20 (claimants subject to work-focused interview requirement only) or section 21 (claimants subject to work-preparation requirement) of the Act; or

    (b) the expected number of hours per week in the case of a claimant who would otherwise fall within section 22 of the Act (claimants subject to all work-related requirements).

(3) A claimant who is a member of a couple falls within section 19 of the Act if the couple's combined weekly earnings are equal to or exceed whichever of the following amounts is applicable—

    (a) in the case of joint claimants, the sum of their individual thresholds; or

    (b) in the case of a claimant who claims universal credit as a single person by virtue of regulation 3(3), the sum of—

        (i) the claimant's individual threshold, and

        (ii) the amount a person would be paid for 35 hours per week at the hourly rate specified in regulation 11 of the National Minimum Wage Regulations.

(4) A claimant falls within section 19 of the Act if the claimant is employed under a contract of apprenticeship and has weekly earnings that are equal to or exceed the amount they would be paid for—

    (a) 30 hours a week; or

    (b) if less, the expected number of hours per week for that claimant,

at the rate specified in regulation 13(3) of the National Minimum Wage Regulations.

(5) A claimant who is treated as having earned income in accordance with regulation 62 (minimum income floor) in respect of an assessment period is to be taken to have weekly earnings equal to their individual threshold in respect of any week falling within that assessment period.

(6) A person's weekly earnings are the person's earned income taken as a weekly average by reference to—

    (a) the amount of that earned income calculated or estimated in relation to the current assessment period before any deduction for income tax, national insurance contributions or relievable pension contributions; or

    (b) in a case where the person's earned income fluctuates (or is likely to fluctuate) the amount of that income—

        (i) where there is an identifiable cycle, over the duration of one such cycle, or

        (ii) where there is no identifiable cycle, over three months or such other period as may, in the particular case, enable the weekly average to be determined more accurately.

(7) In this regulation "the National Minimum Wage Regulations" means the National Minimum Wage Regulations 1999.

DEFINITIONS

"the Act"—see reg.2.
"assessment period"—see WRA 2012, ss.40 and 7(2), and reg.21.
"claimant"—see WRA 2012, s.40(1).
"couple"—see WRA 2012, ss.40 and 39.
"earned income"—see regs 2 and 52.
"joint claimants"—see WRA 2012, s.40.
"single person"—see WRA 2012, ss.40 and 1(2)(a).

GENERAL NOTE

2.198   Regulation 90 prescribes additional circumstances, beyond those prescribed by reg.89, in which a claimant falls within s.19(2)(d) of the WRA 2012 and therefore can be subject to no work-related requirements. The basic test under para.(1) is that the claimant's weekly earnings are at least equal to his or her "individual threshold".

This provision is necessary because universal credit, in contrast to the terms of pre-existing benefits, can be payable while a claimant is in work. The policy is that if a claimant is already earning above a minimum level there is no need to require them to do anything to seek further paid work. Entitlement then depends on the income calculation under s.8 of the WRA 2012.

Paragraph (3) applies the para.(1) test to couples. For joint claimants their individual thresholds are added together, as are their weekly earnings. The threshold is calculated under para.(2) by multiplying the hourly rate of National Minimum Wage by, in the case of a claimant who would otherwise be subject to all work-related requirements under s.22 of the WRA 2012, the expected number of hours per week (see reg.88, usually 35). In the case of a claimant who would otherwise fall within s.20 or 21, the multiplier is 16.

Under para.(6) weekly earnings are earned income as calculated under Chapter 2 of Part 6 of the Universal Credit Regulations (i.e. regs 51–64) averaged out within each monthly assessment period but without deductions for income tax, national insurance contributions or pension contributions, subject to an averaging provision in sub-para.(b) where earned income fluctuates or is likely to fluctuate. The ordinary calculation in regs 51–64 involves the use of "real time" information. In the case of both employment and self-employment the calculation of earned income in respect of any assessment period (i.e. month) is to be based on amounts received in that assessment period (regs 54, 55 and 57). There will be obvious difficulties in carrying out that process, on which see the notes to those regulations. If the process does work, it may be proper for the amount of universal credit to fluctuate month by month or for the claimant to fall in and out of entitlement on the means test. However, if entitlement continues there are plainly arguments against a claimant drifting in and out of exemption from all work-related requirements on the basis of the amount of earned income. That is presumably the thinking behind para.(6)(b). The reference to fluctuation of earned income must be to fluctuation over more than one assessment period, because fluctuation within each assessment period is dealt with by the introductory averaging process. Under sub-para.(i) it is not clear whether the identifiable cycle refers merely to the pattern of receipts or to the pattern of the employment or self-employment or other paid work that produces the income. It would appear that there cannot be an identifiable cycle until it has started and come to an end, which is by definition the start of the next cycle, at least once. Given the difficulties that the notion of a recognisable cycle has given in other contexts it may be that most cases will be dealt with by sub-para.(ii), which requires the taking of an average over the previous three months or such other period as in the particular case enables the weekly average to be determined more accurately. That gives a very wide discretion.

Claimants subject to work-focused interview requirement only

91.—(1) For the purposes of section 20(1)(a) of the Act (claimant is the responsible carer for a child aged at least 1 and under a prescribed age) the prescribed age is 5.   2.199

(2) A claimant falls within section 20 of the Act if—

(a) the claimant is the responsible foster parent in relation to a child aged at least 1;

(b) the claimant is the responsible foster parent in relation to a qualifying young person, and the Secretary of State is satisfied that the qualifying young person has care needs which would make it unreasonable to require the claimant to comply with a work search requirement or a work availability requirement, including if such a requirement were limited in accordance with section 17(4) or 18(3) of the Act;

(c) the claimant is a foster parent, but not the responsible foster parent, in relation to a child or qualifying young person, and the Secretary of State is satisfied that the child or qualifying young person has care needs which would make it unreasonable to require the claimant to comply with a work search requirement or a work availability requirement, including if such a requirement were limited in accordance with section 17(4) or 18(3) of the Act;

(d) the claimant has fallen within paragraph (a), (b) or (c) within the past 8 weeks and has no child or qualifying young person currently placed with them, but expects to resume being a foster parent; or

(e) the claimant has become a friend or family carer in relation to a child within the past 12 months and is also the responsible carer in relation to that child.

(3) In paragraph (2)(e) "friend or family carer" means a person who is responsible for a child, but is not the child's parent or step-parent, and has undertaken the care of the child in the following circumstances—

(a) the child has no parent or has parents who are unable to care for the child; or

(b) it is likely that the child would otherwise be looked after by a local authority because of concerns in relation to the child's welfare.

DEFINITIONS

"the Act"—see reg.2.
"child"—see WRA 2012, s.40.
"claimant"—*ibid.*
"foster parent"—see reg.2.
"qualifying young person"—see regs 2 and 5.
"responsible carer"—see WRA 2012, ss.40 and 19(6).
"responsible foster parent"—see reg.85.
"work availability requirement"—see WRA 2012, ss.40 and 18(1).
"work search requirement"—see WRA 2012, ss.40 and 17(1).

GENERAL NOTE

Para. (1)

2.200 See the notes to s.20 of the WRA 2012. Subsection (1)(a) in combination with para.(1) exempts a responsible carer of a child over the age of one and below the age of five from all work-related requirements apart from the work-focused interview requirement and any connected requirements under s.23. A responsible carer of a child under the age of one is exempted from all work-related requirements under s.19(1)(c).

Para. (2)

2.201 This provision prescribes the categories of claimant who are subject only to the work-focused interview requirement under s.20(1)(b) and any connected requirements under s.23. They cover mainly foster parents.

Under sub-para.(a) responsible foster parents of children of any age from one to 15 are covered. Responsible foster parents of children under one are exempted from all work-related requirements under reg.89(1)(f).

That is extended to young persons in education up to the age of 19 if it would be unreasonable to subject the claimant to other work-related requirements (sub-para. (b)).

Sub-paragraph (c) extends the scope of sub-paras (a) and (b) to foster parents who do not meet the condition of being "responsible" if the child or qualifying young person has care needs that make it unreasonable to subject the claimant to other work-related requirements.

Sub-paragraph (d) allows the effect of sub-paras (a)–(c) to continue for eight weeks after the claimant ceases to have any child or qualifying young person placed with them, if a new placement is expected.

Sub-paragraph (e) applies to claimants who are responsible carers of a child of any age up to 15 if they fall within the meaning of "friend or family carer" in para.(3).

Claimants subject to all work-related requirements—EEA jobseekers

92.—(1) A claimant who is—   2.202

(a) a person mentioned in regulation 6(1)(a) of the EEA Regulations;

(b) a person who is treated as a worker for the purposes of regulation 6(1)(b) of the EEA Regulations by reason of satisfying the conditions set out in regulation 6(2)(b) of those Regulations; or

(c) a person who has a right to reside by virtue of article 45 of the Treaty on the Functioning of the European Union (in a case where the person is seeking work in the United Kingdom, Channel Islands, Isle of Man or the Republic of Ireland),

and who would otherwise fall within section 19, 20 or 21 of the Act, is to be treated as not falling within any of those sections.

(2) A claimant who is a family member of person mentioned in paragraph (1)(a) or (c) and who would otherwise fall within section 19, 20 or 21 of the Act, is to be treated as not falling within any of those sections.

(3) In this regulation "family member" has the same meaning as in regulation 7(1)(a), (b) or (c) of the EEA Regulations.

DEFINITIONS

"the Act"—see reg.2
"claimant"—see WRA 2012, s.40
"EEA Regulations"—see reg.2

GENERAL NOTE

This provision, made under para.7 of Sch.1 to the WRA 2012, purports to impose   2.203
all work-related requirements on any claimant who has a right to reside in the United Kingdom by virtue of any of the specified provisions of the Immigration (European Economic Area) Regulations 2006 (EEA jobseekers) or art.45 of the Treaty on the Functioning of the European Union (TFEU) who would otherwise fall within s.19, 20 or 21 of the WRA 2012. Claimants who are family members of persons covered by para.(1)(a) or (c) are made subject to the same rule by para.(2).

Under para.(1)(a) the category mentioned in reg.6(1)(a) of the EEA Regulations is "jobseeker". Under para.(1)(b), the category mentioned in reg.6(1)(b) is a person who has not ceased to be a worker by reason of being, and being duly recorded as, involuntarily unemployed. Both these categories are "qualified persons" who have a right to reside in the UK under reg.14(1) of the EEA Regulations. See the notes to reg.21AA of the Income Support Regulations in Vol.II for very extensive discussion of rights to reside. Under para.(1)(c), "workers" who have a right to remain under art.45 of the TFEU can include those whose work in the UK has come to an end and workseekers. See the notes to art.45 in Vol.III.

Since the purported effect is to subject EEA nationals to more onerous conditions than would be imposed on British nationals in the same circumstances, the regulation will be bound to come under challenge as incompatible with EU law and will require far more detailed examination in future editions than can be given below. In so far as the claimants identified fall within the meaning of "worker" in art.7 of Council Regulation (EU) No.492/2011 (the consolidation of the rules previously contained in Council Regulation No.1612/68) (see Vol.III), as some will, there appears to be a clear breach of the right to enjoy the same social and tax advantages as national workers. In so far as the claimants mentioned do not fall within that meaning, the position is not clear. The view of the government (Social Security Advisory Committee, Report on the draft Universal Credit Regulations etc., statement by the Secretary of State for Work and Pensions, para.21) is that universal credit does not fall within the scope of Council Regulation (EC) No.883/2004 (see Vol.III) at all. Accordingly, the benefit has not been listed as a special non-contributory benefit in Annex X to the Regulation. It therefore cannot be subject to the special non-contributory benefit regime even if, objectively, all the other conditions in art.7(2) are met. It could clearly be argued that universal credit cannot come within the scope of the Regulation as a social security benefit under art.3 because it is a general means-tested benefit not specifically within any of the art.3 categories, e.g. a sickness benefit or invalidity benefit or an unemployment benefit. On the other hand, the approach of the ECJ in *European Commission v European Parliament and Council* (Case C-299/05) [2007] E.C.R. I–8695 and in *Bartlett and others v SSWP* (Case C-537/09) [2012] P.T.S.R. 535 in dealing with the care component and the mobility component of disability living allowance as separate benefits in substance could support an argument that universal credit provides an umbrella structure for a number of benefits within the scope of art.3. If that were right, there would then be the basis for an argument for breach of art.4 of Regulation No.883/2004 requiring persons to whom the Regulation applies to enjoy the same benefits as UK nationals. That argument might be strengthened if the actual future rollout of universal credit results in its being limited to particular categories of claimant, such as jobseekers.

Since there appears to be no right of appeal against the imposition of a work-related requirement as such, the challenge would have to come by way of judicial review or by appeal against a sanction imposed for non-compliance with a requirement.

The work-related requirements

Purposes of a work-focused interview

2.204   **93.** The purposes of a work-focused interview are any or all of the following—

  (a) assessing the claimant's prospects for remaining in or obtaining paid work;
  (b) assisting or encouraging the claimant to remain in or obtain paid work;
  (c) identifying activities that the claimant may undertake that will make remaining in or obtaining paid work more likely;
  (d) identifying training, educational or rehabilitation opportunities for the claimant which may make it more likely that the claimant will remain in or obtain paid work or be able to do so;
  (e) identifying current or future work opportunities for the claimant that are relevant to the claimant's needs and abilities;
  (f) ascertaining whether a claimant is in gainful self-employment or meets the conditions in regulation 63 (start-up period).

DEFINITIONS

  "claimant"—see WRA 2012, s.40.
  "obtaining paid work"—see reg.87.
  "paid work"—see reg.2.

This provision prescribes the purposes of a work-focused interview under the definition in s.15(2) of the WRA 2012. The purposes could probably not be set out more widely, especially given that obtaining paid work includes obtaining more or better paid work. Arguably, even if there is no realistic prospect of a claimant obtaining any kind of paid work, the purpose of assessing those prospects or lack of prospects in an interview could still be fulfilled.

2.205

Work search requirement—interviews

94. A claimant is to be treated as not having complied with a work search requirement to apply for a particular vacancy for paid work where the claimant fails to participate in an interview offered to the claimant in connection with the vacancy.

2.206

DEFINITIONS

"claimant"—see WRA 2012, s.40.
"paid work"—see reg.2.
"work search requirement"—see WRA 2012, ss.40 and 17(1).

GENERAL NOTE

This provision, made under s.25(a) of the WRA 2012, applies when the Secretary of State has required under s.17(1)(b) that the claimant take the particular action of applying for a specified vacancy for paid work. If the claimant fails to participate in an interview offered in connection with the vacancy the work search requirement is deemed not to have been complied with. See the notes to s.17, and the notes to s.15 for "participation" in an interview.

2.207

Work search requirement—all reasonable action

95.—(1) A claimant is to be treated as not having complied with a work search requirement to take all reasonable action for the purpose of obtaining paid work in any week unless—
(a) either—
   (i) the time which the claimant spends taking action for the purpose of obtaining paid work is at least the claimant's expected number of hours per week minus any relevant deductions, or
   (ii) the Secretary of State is satisfied that the claimant has taken all reasonable action for the purpose of obtaining paid work despite the number of hours that the claimant spends taking such action being lower than the expected number of hours per week; and
(b) that action gives the claimant the best prospects of obtaining work.
(2) In this regulation "relevant deductions" means the total of any time agreed by the Secretary of State—
(a) for the claimant to carry out paid work, voluntary work, a work preparation requirement, or voluntary work preparation in that week; or
(b) for the claimant to deal with temporary childcare responsibilities, a domestic emergency, funeral arrangements or other temporary circumstances.
(3) For the purpose of paragraph (2)(a) the time agreed by the Secretary of State for the claimant to carry out voluntary work must not exceed 50% of the claimant's expected number of hours per week.

2.208

(4) "Voluntary work preparation" means particular action taken by a claimant and agreed by the Secretary of State for the purpose of making it more likely that the claimant will obtain paid work, but which is not specified by the Secretary of State as a work preparation requirement under section 16 of the Act.

DEFINITIONS

"claimant"—see WRA 2012, s.40.
"expected number of hours"—see regs 2 and 88.
"obtaining paid work"—see reg.87.
"paid work"—see reg.2.
"work preparation requirement"—see WRA 2012, ss.40 and 16(1).
"work search requirement"—see WRA 2012, ss.40 and 17(1).

GENERAL NOTE

2.209   This regulation, made under s.25(a) of the WRA 2012, deems certain claimants not to have complied with a work search requirement under s.17(1)(a) of the WRA 2012 to take all reasonable action for the purpose of obtaining paid work (including more or better paid work). See the notes to s.17 and see reg.97 for limitations on the kind of work that needs to be searched for. A failure for no good reason to comply with the requirement under s.17(1)(a) can lead to a medium-level sanction under s.27(2)(a) of the WRA 2012 and reg.103(1)(a).

To avoid the deeming a claimant must get within both sub-paras.(a) and (b) of para.(1). Under (a), the primary rule is that the claimant must spend at least the "expected number of hours per week" (reg.88), less deductions for work or work-related activities or various emergency, urgent or other temporary difficulties (para.(2), subject to the further rules in paras (3) and (4)), in taking action for the purpose of obtaining paid work. However, if the claimant cannot meet the expected hours condition, which for most claimants will be for 35 hours per week, sub-para.(a) can nevertheless be satisfied if the claimant has taken all reasonable action for the purpose of obtaining paid work. Under (b), the action under (a) must give the claimant the best prospects of obtaining work. Taken at face value that condition imposes an almost impossibly high standard, because there will nearly always be something extra that the claimant could do to improve prospects of obtaining work. The condition must therefore be interpreted in a way that leaves some work for condition (a) to do and with some degree of common sense. There will of course be considerable difficulty in checking on the precise number of hours spent in taking relevant action, depending on what might count as action, and in what might be required from claimants in the way of record keeping. It may be that it will be much easier to define non-compliance with the requirement in s.17(1)(b) of the WRA 2012 to take particular action specified by the Secretary of State, although such a failure will only attract a low-level sanction under s.27(2)(a) and reg.104(1)(b)(iii).

Work availability requirement—able and willing immediately to take up paid work

2.210   **96.**—(1) Subject to paragraph (2) a claimant is to be treated as not having complied with a work availability requirement if the claimant is not able and willing immediately to attend an interview offered to the claimant in connection with obtaining paid work.

(2) But a claimant is to be treated as having complied with a work availability requirement despite not being able immediately to take up paid work, if paragraph (3), (4) or (5) applies.

(3) This paragraph applies where—

(a) a claimant is a responsible carer or a relevant carer;
(b) the Secretary of State is satisfied that, as a consequence the claimant needs a longer period of up to 1 month to take up paid work, or up to 48 hours to attend an interview in connection with obtaining work, taking into account alternative care arrangements; and
(c) the claimant is able and willing to take up paid work, or attend an interview, on being given notice for that period.

(4) This paragraph applies where—
(a) a claimant is carrying out voluntary work;
(b) the Secretary of State is satisfied that, as a consequence, the claimant needs a longer period of up to 1 week to take up paid work, or up to 48 hours to attend an interview in connection with obtaining work; and
(c) the claimant is able and willing to take up paid work, or attend an interview, on being given notice for that period.

(5) This paragraph applies where a claimant—
(a) is employed under a contract of service;
(b) is required by section 86 of the Employment Rights Act 1996, or by the contract of service, to give notice to terminate the contract;
(c) is able and willing to take up paid work once the notice period has expired; and
(d) is able and willing to attend an interview on being given 48 hours notice.

DEFINITIONS

"claimant"—see WRA 2012, s.40.
"obtaining paid work"—see reg.87.
"paid work"—see reg.2.
"relevant carer"—see reg.85.
"responsible carer"—see WRA 2012, ss.40 and 19(6).
"work availability requirement"—see WRA 2012, ss.40 and 18(1).

GENERAL NOTE

This regulation is made under s.25 of the WRA 2012 and relates to the work availability requirement under s.18(1) and (2) of being able and willing immediately to take up paid work or more or better paid work. See reg.97 for limitations on the kind of work for which a claimant must be available and reg.99, and in particular para. (5), for other situations in which the ordinary test of being able and willing immediately to take up work or attend an interview is modified.   2.211

Para. (1)

Paragraph (1) simply confirms that the requirement of being able and willing immediately to take up paid work extends to being able and willing immediately to attend an interview in connection with obtaining paid work.   2.212

Paras (2) to (5)

A claimant who falls within paras (3), (4) or (5) is to be treated as complying with the work availability required, including as extended by para.(1). Paragraph (3) applies to those with child-care responsibilities who would need to take up to one month to take up paid work or up to 48 hours to attend an interview and are able and willing to do so if given that length of notice. Paragraph (4) applies to claimants doing voluntary work (not further defined), subject to the same conditions. Paragraph (5) applies to claimants in employment who are required to give notice to   2.213

terminate their contract of employment and who are able and willing to take up paid work once that notice has expired and to attend an interview on 48 hours' notice.

Work search requirement and work availability requirement—limitations

2.214   **97.**—(1) Paragraphs (2) to (5) set out the limitations on a work search requirement and a work availability requirement.

(2) In the case of a claimant who is a relevant carer or a responsible carer or who has a physical or mental impairment, a work search and work availability requirement must be limited to the number of hours that is determined to be the claimant's expected number of hours per week in accordance with regulation 88.

(3) A work search and work availability requirement must be limited to work that is in a location which would normally take the claimant—

(a) a maximum of 90 minutes to travel from home to the location; and

(b) a maximum of 90 minutes to travel from the location to home.

(4) Where a claimant has previously carried out work of a particular nature, or at a particular level of remuneration, a work search requirement and a work availability requirement must be limited to work of a similar nature, or level of remuneration, for such period as the Secretary of State considers appropriate, but only if the Secretary of State is satisfied that the claimant will have reasonable prospects of obtaining paid work in spite of such limitation.

(5) The limitation in paragraph (4) is to apply for no more than 3 months beginning with—

(a) the date of claim; or

(b) if later, the date on which the claimant ceases paid work after falling within section 19 of the Act by virtue of regulation 90 (claimants subject to no work-related requirements- the earnings thresholds).

(6) Where a claimant has a physical or mental impairment that has a substantial adverse effect on the claimant's ability to carry out work of a particular nature, or in particular locations, a work search or work availability requirement must not relate to work of such a nature or in such locations.

DEFINITIONS

"claimant"—see WRA 2012, s.40.
"expected number of hours per week"—see regs 2 and 88.
"relevant carer"—see reg.85.
"responsible carer"—see WRA 2012, ss.40 and 19(6).
"work availability requirement"—see WRA 2012, ss.40 and 18(1).
"work search requirement"—see WRA 2012, ss.40 and 17(1).

GENERAL NOTE

2.215   This regulation is made under ss.17(4) and (5) (work search requirement) and 18(3) and (4) (work availability requirement) of the WRA 2012. It sets out limitations on the kind of work that a claimant can be required to search for or be able and willing immediately to take up. See reg.99 for other situations in which the ordinary tests for those requirements is modified.

Para. (2)

2.216   This paragraph establishes an important limitation on the kind of work that can be considered, but only for the particular categories of claimant identified: those with child care responsibilities and the disabled. Those categories of claimant can only be required to search for or be able and willing to take up work for no more than the number of hours per week compatible with those circumstances, as worked out under reg.88. So, as far as the work search requirement is concerned, this limitation appears to apply as much to the sort of work in relation to which the Secretary of State may specify particular action under s.17(1)(b) of the WRA 2012 as to the requirement under s.17(1)(a) to take all reasonable action for the purpose of obtaining paid work or more or better paid work. Although the drafting of para.(2) appears to limit the hours for which either requirement is applicable, it can only, in view of the terms of the regulation-making powers in ss.17(4) and 18(3), relate to the hours of work to which the relevant requirement can be attached.

Para. (3)

A work search or availability requirement cannot relate to work in a location where the claimant's normal travel time either from home to work or from work to home would exceed 90 minutes, subject to the further limitation in para.(6) for some disabled claimants. Travel times below that limit could be relevant in relation to a sanction for non-compliance with a requirement, on the question of whether the claimant had no good reason for the failure to comply. On that question all circumstances could be considered, including the effect of any physical or mental impairment not serious enough to count under para.(6), whereas under this provision time is the conclusive factor unless the location is completely excluded under para.(6).   **2.217**

Paras (4) and (5)

A claimant who has previously carried out work of a particular nature or at a particular level of remuneration is to have the kind of work to be considered limited to similar conditions for so long as considered appropriate up to three months from the date of claim or ceasing to fall within s.19 of the WRA 2012 by virtue of the level of earnings (para.(5)). But the rule only applies if and so long as the claimant will have reasonable prospects of work subject to that limitation.   **2.218**

Para. (6)

A claimant who has a physical or mental impairment which has a substantial adverse effect on their ability to carry out work of a particular nature or in particular locations (a significant additional condition over and above that of impairment or disability on its own) is to have the kind of work to be considered under the work search and work availability requirements limited to avoid such work.

Victims of domestic violence

98.—(1) Where a claimant has recently been a victim of domestic violence, and the circumstances set out in paragraph (3) apply—   **2.219**

- (a) a work-related requirement imposed on that claimant ceases to have effect for a period of 13 consecutive weeks starting on the date of the notification referred to in paragraph (3)(a); and
- (b) the Secretary of State must not impose any other work-related requirement on that claimant during that period.

(2) A person has recently been a victim of domestic violence if a period of 6 months has not expired since the violence was inflicted or threatened.

(3) The circumstances are that—

- (a) the claimant notifies the Secretary of State, in such manner as the Secretary of State specifies, that domestic violence has been inflicted on or threatened against the claimant by the claimant's partner or former partner or by a family member during the period of 6 months ending on the date of the notification;

    (b) this regulation has not applied to the claimant for a period of 12 months before the date of the notification;

    (c) on the date of the notification the claimant is not living at the same address as the person who inflicted or threatened the domestic violence; and

    (d) as soon as possible, and no later than 1 month, after the date of the notification the claimant provides evidence from a person acting in an official capacity which demonstrates that—

        (i) the claimant's circumstances are consistent with those of a person who has had domestic violence inflicted or threatened against them during the period of 6 months ending on the date of the notification, and

        (ii) the claimant has made contact with the person acting in an official capacity in relation to such an incident, which occurred during that period.

(4) In this regulation—

"domestic violence" means abuse of a kind specified on page 11, of section 2.2. of 'Responding to domestic abuse: a handbook for health professionals' published by the Department of Health in December 2005;

"family member", in relation to a claimant, means the claimant's grandparent, grandchild, parent, step-parent, parent-in-law, son, step-son, son-in-law, daughter, step-daughter, daughter-in-law, brother, step-brother, brother-in-law, sister, step-sister, sister-in law and, if any of those persons is member of a couple, the other member of the couple;

"health care professional" means a person who is a member of a profession regulated by a body mentioned in section 25(3) of the National Health Service Reform and Health Care Professions Act 2002;

"person acting in an official capacity" means a health care professional, a police officer, a registered social worker, the claimant's employer, a representative of the claimant's trade union, or any public, voluntary or charitable body which has had direct contact with the claimant in connection with domestic violence;

"registered social worker" means a person registered as a social worker in a register maintained by—

(a)   The General Social Care Council;

(b)   The Care Council for Wales;

(c)   The Scottish Social Services Council; or

(d)   The Northern Ireland Social Care Council.

DEFINITIONS

"claimant"—see WRA 2012, s.40.

"partner"—see reg.2.

"victim of domestic violence"—see WRA 2012, s.24(6)(b).

"work-related requirement"—see WRA 2012, ss.40 and 13(2).

GENERAL NOTE

2.220   This regulation, made as required by s.24(5) and (6) of the WRA 2012, exempts recent victims of domestic violence from the imposition of any work-related requirements for a period of 13 weeks from the date of notification to the Secretary of State under para.(3)(a) and lifts the effect of any existing imposition for the same period.

For these purposes para.(4) requires the meaning of "domestic violence" to be in terms of abuse which is specified on the particular page of the December 2005 Department of Health document *Responding to domestic abuse: a handbook for health professionals*. The document is very difficult to find through the website reference given in the footnote in the printed version of these Regulations (*www.dh.gov. uk* accessed December 11, 2013.) following the amalgamation of departmental websites into one gov.uk site. Page 11 of section 2.2 of the document sets out the following examples of domestic abuse, a term used there in preference to "domestic violence" to avoid any suggestion that only physical violence counts:

"Physical
Shaking, smacking, punching, kicking, presence of finger or bite marks, starving, tying up, stabbing, suffocation, throwing things, using objects as weapons, female genital mutilation, 'honour violence'.
Physical effects are often in areas of the body that are covered and hidden (i.e. breasts and abdomen).
Sexual
Forced sex, forced prostitution, ignoring religious prohibitions about sex, refusal to practise safe sex, sexual insults, sexually transmitted diseases, preventing breastfeeding.
Psychological
Intimidation, insulting, isolating a woman from friends and family, criticizing, denying the abuse, treating her as an inferior, threatening to harm children or take them away, forced marriage.
Financial
Not letting a woman work, undermining efforts to find work or study, refusing to give money, asking for an explanation of how every penny is spent, making her beg for money, gambling, not paying bills.
Emotional
Swearing, undermining confidence, making racist remarks, making a woman feel unattractive, calling her stupid or useless, eroding her independence."

That is obviously a very wide definition, perfectly understandable in the context of the December 2005 document, but not as helpful in the legislative context. That makes the specification in para.(3) of the circumstances in which reg.98 applies more important.

Section 24(6)(b) of the WRA 2012 defines a victim of domestic violence as a person on or against whom domestic violence (as defined above) is inflicted or threatened. Under s.24(6)(c) and para.(2) a person is to be treated as having recently been a victim of domestic violence if no more than six months has expired since the infliction or threat.

Para.(3)
This paragraph lays down four quite restrictive conditions that must all be satis- 2.221
fied for reg.98 to apply. Under sub-para.(a) the claimant must have notified the Secretary of State of the infliction or threatening of domestic violence by a partner, former partner of family member (as defined in para.(4)) within the previous six months. Under sub-para.(b), reg.98 must not have applied within the 12 months before the notification. Under sub-para.(c), the claimant must not on the date of the notification have been living at the same address as the person named as the assailant. Under sub-para.(d), the claimant must also provide, as soon as possible and no more than one month after the notification, evidence from person acting in an official capacity (defined quite widely in para.(4)) both that the claimant's circumstances are consistent with having had domestic violence inflicted or threatened in the six months before notification and that the claimant had made contact (apparently not necessarily within the six months) with the person in relation to

an incident of infliction or threat of domestic violence that occurred during the six months before notification.

Circumstances in which requirements must not be imposed

2.222   **99.**—(1) Where paragraph (3), (4), (5) or (6) applies—
    (a) the Secretary of State must not impose a work search requirement on a claimant; and
    (b) "able and willing immediately to take up work" under a work availability requirement means able and willing to take up paid work, or attend an interview, immediately once the circumstances set out in paragraph (3), (4), (5) or (6) no longer apply.

(2) A work search requirement previously applying to the claimant ceases to have effect from the date on which the circumstances set out in paragraph (3), (4), (5) or (6) begin to apply.

(3) This paragraph applies where—
    (a) the claimant is attending a court or tribunal as a party to any proceedings or as a witness;
    (b) the claimant is a prisoner;
    (c) regulation 11(3) (temporary absence from Great Britain for treatment or convalescence) applies to the claimant;
    (d) any of the following persons has died within the past 6 months—
        (i) where the claimant was a member of a couple, the other member,
        (ii) a child or qualifying young person for whom the claimant or, where the claimant is a member of a couple, the other member, was responsible, or
        (iii) a child, where the claimant was the child's parent;
    (e) the claimant is, and has been for no more than 6 months, receiving and participating in a structured recovery-orientated course of alcohol or drug dependency treatment;
    (f) the claimant is, and has been for no more than 3 months, a person for whom arrangements have been made by a protection provider under section 82 of the Serious Organised Crime and Police Act 2005; or
    (g) the claimant is engaged in an activity of a kind approved by the Secretary of State as being in the nature of a public duty.

(4) This paragraph applies where the claimant—
    (a) is unfit for work—
        (i) for a period of no more than 14 consecutive days after the date that the evidence referred to in sub-paragraph (b) is provided, and
        (ii) for no more than 2 such periods in any period of 12 months; and
    (b) provides to the Secretary of State the following evidence—
        (i) for the first 7 days when they are unfit for work, a declaration made by the claimant in such manner and form as the Secretary of State approves that the claimant is unfit for work, and
        (ii) for any further days when they are unfit for work, if requested by the Secretary of State, a statement given by a doctor in accordance with the rules set out in Part 1 of Schedule 1 to the Medical Evidence Regulations which provides that the person is not fit for work.

(5) This paragraph applies where the Secretary of State is satisfied that it would be unreasonable to require the claimant to comply with a work search requirement or a work availability requirement, including if such a requirement were limited in accordance with section 17(4) or 18(3) of the Act, because the claimant—

(a) is carrying out a work preparation requirement or voluntary work preparation (as defined in regulation 95(4));

(b) has temporary child care responsibilities or is dealing with a domestic emergency, funeral arrangements or other temporary circumstances; or

(c) is unfit for work for longer than the period of 14 days specified in paragraph (4)(a) or for more than 2 such periods in any period of 12 months and, where requested by the Secretary of State, provides the evidence mentioned in paragraph (4)(b)(ii).

(6) This paragraph applies where the claimant's weekly earnings or, if the claimant is a member of a couple, the couple's combined weekly earnings are at a level where the Secretary of State is satisfied that a work search requirement or work availability requirement should not be imposed at the present time.

(7) In this regulation "tribunal" means any tribunal listed in Schedule 1 to the Tribunals and Inquiries Act 1992.

DEFINITIONS

"child"—see WRA 2012, s.40.
"claimant"—*ibid.*
"couple"—see WRA 2012, ss.40 and 39.
"Medical Evidence Regulations"—see reg.2.
"prisoner"—*ibid.*
"qualifying young person"—see WRA 2012, ss.40 and 10(5).
"voluntary work preparation"—see reg.95(4).
"work availability requirement"—see WRA 2012, ss.40 and 18(1).
"work preparation requirement"—see WRA 2012, ss.40 and 16(1).
"work search requirement"—see WRA 2012, ss.40 and 17(1).

GENERAL NOTE

This regulation is made under s.24(1)(a) of the WRA 2012 in respect of the work search requirement and under s.18(5) in respect of the work availability requirement. Any claimant falling under paras (3)–(6) cannot have a work search requirement imposed (para.(1)(a)) and any existing such requirement ceases to have effect (para.(2)). And the requirement in s.18(2) to be able and willing immediately to take up work means able to take up work, or attend an interview immediately the relevant circumstance under paras (3)–(6) ceases to exist.

Para.(3)

Paragraph (3) lists a number of categories of claimant where the circumstances mean that the claimant could not be expected to look for or take up work or attend an interview, generally of a temporary nature:

(a) Attending a court or tribunal (defined in para.(7)) as a party to proceedings or as a witness, apparently so long as the hearing continues for a party and so long as attendance is required for a witness.

(b) A prisoner, under the reg.2 definition covering those detained in custody pending trial or sentence on conviction or under sentence or on temporary release, but excluding anyone detained in hospital under mental health legislation.

2.223

2.224

(c) Temporary absence from Great Britain in connection with medical treatment for illness etc or convalescence, or accompanying a partner or child or qualifying young person undergoing such treatment or convalescence, under the conditions in reg.11(3). See the notes to that provision.

(d) The claimant's then partner, a child or qualifying young person for whom the claimant or partner was responsible or a child of the claimant has died within the previous six months.

(e) Attending a structured recovery-oriented course of alcohol or drug dependency treatment, for no more than six months.

(f) Having protection arrangements made under s.82 of the Serious Organised Crime and Police Act 2005 (protection of persons involved in investigations or proceedings whose safety is considered to be at risk), for no more than three months.

(g) Any other activity of a kind approved by the Secretary of State as being in the nature of a public duty, apparently for as long as the activity and approval lasts. It is therefore unclear whether on any appeal against a sanction where the application of this paragraph is in issue a First-tier Tribunal is required to accept non-approval of an activity by the Secretary of State or can substitute its own judgment.

Para.(4)

2.225   A claimant who is unfit for work (not further defined) and provides a self-certificate for the first seven days and, if requested, a statement from a doctor under the Medical Evidence Regulations (see Vol.I) for any further days falls within the basic rules in this regulation. But the benefit of para.(4) is limited to a period of no more than 14 days after the evidence is provided and to no more than two such periods in any 12 months. There is a possible extension of those restrictions under para.(5)(c).

Para.(5)

2.226   In three sorts of circumstances the imposition of a work search requirement or the satisfaction of a work availability requirement, even as limited under reg.97, can be further restricted where it would be unreasonable for the claimant to comply. Sub-para.(a) applies if the claimant is carrying out a work preparation requirement (s.16(1) of the WRA 2012) or a voluntary work preparation requirement (reg.95(4)). Sub-para.(b) applies if the claimant has temporary child care responsibilities (for any child) or is dealing with a domestic emergency, funeral arrangements (for a claimant who is already covered by para.(3)(d)) or with other temporary circumstances. Sub-paragraph (c) applies where the claimant is unfit for work and the restrictions in para.(4) have been exceeded.

Para.(6)

2.227   Where a claimant or joint claimants are not already free of all work-related requirements by having earnings of at least the individual earnings threshold or the combined thresholds (reg.90), the work search requirement cannot be imposed and the work availability requirement is complied with if the level of earnings is such that those requirements "should not" be imposed. That gives a very open-ended discretion. It is plain on general principle that the reference to the Secretary of State being satisfied does not prevent a First-tier Tribunal substituting its own judgment in any appeal against a sanction for failing to comply with either requirement where this provision is in issue.

CHAPTER 2

SANCTIONS

Introduction

100.—(1) This Chapter contains provisions about the reduction in the amount of an award of universal credit in the event of a failure by a claimant which is sanctionable under section 26 or 27 of the Act ("a sanctionable failure").

(2) How the period of the reduction for each sanctionable failure is to be determined is dealt with in regulations 101 to 105.

(3) When the reduction begins or ceases to have effect is dealt with in regulations 106 to 109.

(4) How the amount of a reduction is calculated for an assessment period in which the reduction has effect is set out in regulations 110 and 111.

(5) Regulations 112 to 114 provide for some miscellaneous matters (movement of sanctions from a jobseeker's allowance or an employment and support allowance, cases in which no reduction is made for a sanctionable failure and prescription of work placement scheme for the purposes of section 26(2)(a) of the Act).

2.228

DEFINITIONS

"the Act"—see reg.2.
"assessment period"—see WRA 2012, ss.40 and 7(2) and reg.21.
"claimant"—see WRA 2012, s.40.
"employment and support allowance"—see reg.2.
"jobseeker's allowance"—*ibid.*

Reduction periods

General principles for calculating reduction periods

101.—(1) The number of days for which a reduction in the amount of an award is to have effect ("the reduction period") is to be determined in relation to each sanctionable failure in accordance with regulations 102 to 105, but subject to paragraphs (3) and (4).

2.229

(2) Reduction periods are to run consecutively.

(3) If the reduction period calculated in relation to a sanctionable failure in accordance with regulations 102 to 105 would result in the total outstanding reduction period exceeding 1095 days, the reduction period in relation to that failure is to be adjusted so that the total outstanding reduction period does not exceed 1095 days.

(4) In determining the reduction period in relation to a sanctionable failure, a previous sanctionable failure is disregarded if it occurred in the 14 days immediately preceding the failure in question.

(5) In paragraph (3) "the total outstanding reduction period" is the total number of days for which no reduction in an award under section 26 or 27 of the Act has yet been applied.

DEFINITIONS

"the Act"—see reg.2.
"sanctionable failure"—see reg.100(1).

GENERAL NOTE

2.230   Under reg.100 and this provision the way in which a sanction bites is through a reduction in the amount of an award of universal credit for a period determined under regs 101–105 (the "reduction period": para.(1)) for each sanctionable failure. A sanctionable failure is a failure which is sanctionable under s.26 or 27 of the WRA 2012. This regulation contains some general rules on sanctions.

Under para.(2) reduction periods for separate reduction periods run consecutively. That is subject to the general overall three-year limit in paras (3) and (5). The drafting is fairly impenetrable, but the upshot seems to be that if adding a new reduction period to the end of an existing period or, more likely, chain of reduction periods would take the total days in the periods over 1095 days the new reduction period is to be adjusted to make the total 1095 days exactly. Paragraph (4) applies in the main to situations in regs 102–104 where the length of a reduction period depends on whether there have been any previous sanctionable failures. A sanctionable failure within the 14 days immediately preceding the sanctionable failure in question is to be disregarded for this purpose. What is not so clear is whether para. (4) also qualifies para.(3) to allow a total outstanding reduction period to exceed 1095 days.

Note also the circumstances prescribed in reg.109 (earnings over the individual threshold for 26 weeks) in which a reduction is to be terminated and the circumstances prescribed in reg.113 where there is to be no reduction despite the existence of a sanctionable failure. Under reg.111(3) the amount of the reduction is nil in an assessment period at the end of which the claimant is subject to no work-related requirements because of having limited capability for work and work-related activity under s.19 of the WRA 2012.

Higher-level sanction

2.231   **102.**—(1) This regulation specifies the reduction period for a sanctionable failure under section 26 of the Act ("higher level sanction").

(2) Where the sanctionable failure is not a pre-claim failure the reduction period is—

(a) where the claimant is aged 18 or over on the date of the sanctionable failure—

  (i) 91 days, if paragraphs (ii) and (iii) do not apply,

  (ii) 182 days, if there was another sanctionable failure giving rise to a higher-level sanction in the 365 days preceding the failure in question for which a 91 day reduction period applies, or

  (iii) 1095 days, if there was another sanctionable failure giving rise to a higher-level sanction in that period of 365 days for which a 182 day or 1095 day reduction period applies; or

(b) where the claimant is aged 16 or 17 on the date of the sanctionable failure—

  (i) 14 days, if paragraph (ii) does not apply, or

  (ii) 28 days, if there was another sanctionable failure giving rise to a higher-level sanction in the 365 days preceding the failure in question for which a 14 day or 28 day reduction period applies.

(3) But where the other sanctionable failure referred to in paragraph (2)

220

was a pre-claim failure it is disregarded in determining the reduction period in accordance with that paragraph.

(4) Where the sanctionable failure for which a reduction period is to be determined is a pre-claim failure, the period is the lesser of—

(a) the period that would be applicable to the claimant under paragraph (2) if it were not a pre-claim failure; or

(b) where the sanctionable failure relates to paid work that was due to last for a limited period, the period beginning with the day after the date of the sanctionable failure and ending with the date on which the limited period would have ended,

minus the number of days beginning with the day after the date of the sanctionable failure and ending on the day before the date of claim.

(5) In this regulation "pre-claim failure" means a failure sanctionable under section 26(4) of the Act.

DEFINITIONS

"the Act"—see reg.2.
"claimant"—see WRA 2012, s.40.
"reduction period"—see reg.101(1).
"sanctionable failure"—see reg.100(1).

GENERAL NOTE

Higher-level sanctions are applicable to failures under s.26 of the WRA 2012. **2.232** Such failures fall outside the scope of regs 103–105 and no failures under s.27 can come within the present regulation. There is a distinction between "pre-claim failures", i.e. a failure under s.26(4) (before the relevant claim failing for no good reason to take up an offer of paid work or ceasing paid work or losing pay by reason of misconduct or voluntarily and for no good reason), and other failures.

The general rule in para.(2)(a) for non-pre-claim failures is that the reduction period is 91 days if there have been no other higher-level sanctionable failures (or equivalent ESA or JSA failures if the claimant moved to universal credit with some days of an ESA or JSA reduction period outstanding: Sch.11, para.3) in the previous 365 days. The reduction period is 182 days if there has been one other such failure in the previous 365 days and 1095 days if there have been two or more such failures. That is subject first to the rule in para.(3) that pre-claim failures are disregarded for this purpose. It is also subject to the limit in reg.101(3) and (5) and to the disregard in reg.101(4) of sanctionable failures in the 14 days before the sanctionable failure in question. For claimants aged under 18, shorter reduction periods are prescribed in para.(2)(b), of 14 days if there have been no other higher-level non-pre-claim sanctionable failures in the previous 365 days and 28 days if there has been one or more.

For pre-claim sanctionable failures, under para.(4) the number of days between the date of the failure and the date of the relevant claim is deducted from the number of days in the reduction period calculated as under para.(2). That is subject to the further rule that if the sanctionable failure relates to paid work that was due to last only for a limited period, the period down to the date when the work was due to end is substituted for the para.(2) period in the calculation. Presumably that is to give an incentive to people to take such work. See also reg.113(1)(e).

Medium-level sanction

103.—(1) This regulation specifies the reduction period for a sanction- **2.233** able failure under section 27 of the Act (other sanctions) where it is a failure by the claimant to comply with—

(a) a work search requirement under section 17(1)(a) (to take all reasonable action to obtain paid work etc.); or
(b) a work availability requirement under section 18(1).
(2) The reduction period is—
(a) where the claimant is aged 18 or over on the date of the sanctionable failure—
  (i) 28 days, if paragraph (ii) does not apply, or
  (ii) 91 days, if there was another sanctionable failure of a kind mentioned in paragraph (1) in the 365 days preceding the failure in question for which a 28 day or 91 day reduction period applies; or
(b) where the claimant is aged 16 or 17 years on the date of the sanctionable failure—
  (i) 7 days, if paragraph (ii) does not apply, or
  (ii) 14 days, if there was another sanctionable failure of a kind mentioned in paragraph (1) in the 365 days preceding the failure in question, for which a 7 day or 14 day reduction period applies.

DEFINITIONS

"the Act"—see reg.2.
"claimant"—see WRA 2012, s.40.
"reduction period"—see reg.101(1).
"sanctionable failure"—see reg.100(1).

GENERAL NOTE

2.234   This regulation applies to failures for no good reason to comply with two particular work-related requirements to which the claimant in question is subject: the requirement under s.17(1)(a) of the WRA 2012 to take all reasonable action to obtain paid work (but note, not the requirement under s.17(1)(b) to take particular action specified by the Secretary of State, where only some failures to comply fall under s.26 and the higher-level sanctions regime) and the work availability requirement in s.18(1).
The reduction period under para.(2)(a) is 28 days if there have been no other medium-level sanctionable failures (or equivalent ESA or JSA failures if the claimant moved to universal credit with some days of an ESA or JSA reduction period outstanding: Sch.11, para.3) in the previous 365 days and 91 days if there have been one or more such failures in that period. That is subject to the disregard in reg.101(4) of sanctionable failures in the 14 days before the sanctionable failure in question. For claimants aged under 18, shorter reduction periods are prescribed in para.(2)(b), of seven days if there have been no other medium-level sanctionable failures in the previous 365 days and 14 days if there has been one or more.

Low-level sanction

2.235   **104.**—(1) This regulation specifies the reduction period for a sanctionable failure under section 27 of the Act (other sanctions) where—
(a) the claimant falls within section 21 (claimants subject to work preparation requirement) or 22 (claimants subject to all work-related requirements) of the Act on the date of that failure; and
(b) it is a failure to comply with—
  (i) a work-focused interview requirement under section 15(1),
  (ii) a work preparation requirement under section 16(1),
  (iii) a work search requirement under section 17(1)(b) (to take any particular action specified by the Secretary of State to obtain work etc.), or

    (iv) a requirement under section 23(1), (3) or (4) (connected requirements: interviews and verification of compliance).

(2) Where the claimant is aged 18 or over on the date of the sanctionable failure, the reduction period is the total of—

(a) the number of days beginning with the date of the sanctionable failure and ending with—

    (i) the day before the date on which the claimant meets a compliance condition specified by the Secretary of State,

    (ii) the day before the date on which the claimant falls within section 19 of the Act (claimant subject to no work-related requirements),

    (iii) the day before the date on which the claimant is no longer required to take a particular action specified as a work preparation requirement by the Secretary of State under section 16, or

    (iv) the date on which the award terminates (other than by reason of the claimant ceasing to be, or becoming, a member of a couple),

whichever is soonest; and

(b) whichever of the following number of days is applicable in the claimant's case—

    (i) 7 days, if paragraphs (ii) and (iii) do not apply,

    (ii) 14 days, if there was another sanctionable failure of a kind mentioned in paragraph (1) in the 365 days preceding the failure in question for which a 7 day reduction period applies, or

    (iii) 28 days, if there was another sanctionable failure of a kind mentioned in paragraph (1) in the 365 days preceding the failure in question for which a 14 day or 28 day reduction period applies.

(3) Where the claimant is aged 16 or 17 years on the date of the sanctionable failure, the reduction period is—

(a) the number of days beginning with the date of the sanctionable failure and ending with—

    (i) the day before the date on which the claimant meets a compliance condition specified by the Secretary of State,

    (ii) the day before the date on which the claimant falls within section 19 of the Act (claimant subject to no work-related requirements),

    (iii) the day before the date on which the claimant is no longer required to take a particular action specified as a work preparation requirement by the Secretary of State under section 16, or

    (iv) date on which the award terminates (other than by reason of the claimant ceasing to be, or becoming, a member of a couple),

whichever is soonest; and

(b) if there was another sanctionable failure giving rise to a low level sanction in the 365 days preceding the failure in question, the number of days in sub-paragraph (a) plus 7 days.

DEFINITIONS

"the Act"—see reg.2.
"claimant"—see WRA 2012, s.40.
"compliance condition"—see WRA 2012, s.27(6).
"reduction period"—see reg.101(1).
"sanctionable failure"—see reg.100(1).

2.236   This regulation applies only to claimants who are subject to all work-related requirements under s.22 of the WRA 2012 or to the work preparation requirement under s.21 at the time of the sanctionable failure. Then a low-level sanction is attracted by a failure for no good reason to comply with a work-focused interview requirement under s.15(1), a work preparation requirement under s.16(1), a work search requirement under s.17(1)(b) to take particular action specified by the Secretary of State (see reg.103—medium-level sanction—for failures to comply with the requirement to take all reasonable action to obtain paid work under s.17(1)(a)) or one of the extensive connected requirements under s.23.

The calculation of the reduction period under para.(2) is more complicated than that for higher and medium-level sanctions. It is made up of a period of flexible length depending on the ongoing circumstances under sub-para.(a) plus a fixed period of days under sub-para.(b) to be added to the sub-para.(a) period.

The basic rule in sub-para.(a) is that the period runs until any compliance condition specified by the Secretary of State is met. See the notes to s.27(5) of the WRA 2012 for the authorisation for this provision. A compliance condition is of the failure to comply ceasing to exist (e.g. attending a work-focused interview) or as to future compliance. The condition must in accordance with s.27(5)(a) and sub-para.(a)(i) be specified by the Secretary of State. Although s.27(7) allows the Secretary of State to notify a claimant of a compliance condition in such manner as he determines, the approach of the Supreme Court in *R (on the application of Reilly and Wilson) v Secretary of State for Work and Pensions* [2013] UKSC 68; [2013] 3 W.L.R. 1276 might possibly be relevant to the substance of what must be specified, as discussed further in the notes to s.27(5). The sub-para.(a) period will also end if the claimant becomes subject to no work-related requirements for any reason under s.19 of the WRA 2012, is no longer required to take a specific action as a work preparation requirement or the award of universal credit terminates.

Under sub-para.(b) the additional number of days is seven if there have been no other low-level sanctionable failures (or equivalent ESA or JSA failures if the claimant moved to universal credit with some days of an ESA or JSA reduction period outstanding: Sch.11, para.3) in the previous 365 days, 14 if there has been one such failure in that period and 28 if there have been two or more such failures in that period. That is subject to the disregard in reg.101(4) of sanctionable failures in the 14 days before the sanctionable failure in question.

Under para.(3) for claimants aged under 18, the same rules as in para.(2)(a) apply, plus an additional seven days if there has been one or more low-level sanctionable failures in the previous 365 days.

Lowest-level sanction

2.237   **105.**—(1) This regulation specifies the reduction period for a sanctionable failure under section 27 of the Act (other sanctions) where it is a failure by a claimant who falls within section 20 of the Act (claimants subject to work-focused interview requirement only) to comply with a requirement under that section.

(2) The reduction period is the number of days beginning with the date of the sanctionable failure and ending with—

(a) the day before the date on which the claimant meets a compliance condition specified by the Secretary of State;

(b) the day before the date on which the claimant falls within section 19 of the Act (claimant subject to no work-related requirements); or

(c) the day on which the award terminates (other than by reason of the claimant ceasing to be, or becoming, a member of a couple),

whichever is soonest.

DEFINITIONS

"the Act"—see reg.2.
"claimant"—see WRA 2012, s.40.
"compliance condition"—see WRA 2012, s.27(6).
"reduction period"—see reg.101(1).
"sanctionable failure"—see reg.100(1).

GENERAL NOTE

This regulation applies only to claimants who are subject only to the work-focused   **2.238**
interview requirement under s.20 of the WRA 2012. The reduction period for a
sanctionable failure to comply with that requirement runs until the claimant meets
a compliance condition specified by the Secretary of State (see notes to reg.104),
becomes subject to no work-related requirements for any reason under s.19 or the
award of universal credit terminates.

When reduction to have effect

Start of the reduction

106. A reduction period determined in relation to a sanctionable failure   **2.239**
takes effect from—
  (a) the first day of the assessment period in which the Secretary of State
      determines that the amount of the award is to be reduced under
      section 26 or 27 of the Act (but see also regulation 107(2));
  (b) if the amount of the award of universal credit for the assessment
      period referred to in paragraph (a) is not reduced in that period, the
      first day of the next assessment period; or
  (c) if the amount of the award for the assessment period referred to
      in paragraph (a) or (b) is already subject to a reduction because
      of a previous sanctionable failure, the first day in respect of
      which the amount of the award is no longer subject to that reduc-
      tion.

DEFINITIONS

"the Act"—see reg.2.
"assessment period"—see WRA 2012, ss.40 and 7(2) and reg.21.
"claimant"—see WRA 2012, s.40.
"reduction period"—see reg.101(1).
"sanctionable failure"—see reg.100(1).

GENERAL NOTE

These rules for the start of the reduction period follow fairly logically from the   **2.240**
structure of the sanctions regime. Where no other reduction period is running the
reduction period starts either in the assessment period (month) in which the decision to make the reduction is made or in the following assessment period (paras.
(a) and (b)). If there is already a reduction applied in that assessment period, then,
unless affected by the overall limit in reg.101(3) and (5), the new period starts on
the expiry of the existing one.

Reduction period to continue where award terminates

2.241   **107.**—(1) If an award of universal credit terminates while there is an outstanding reduction period, the period continues to run as if a daily reduction were being applied and if the claimant becomes entitled to a new award (whether as single or joint claimant) before that period expires, that award is subject to a reduction for the remainder of the total outstanding reduction period.

(2) If an award of universal credit terminates before the Secretary of State determines that the amount of the award is to be reduced under section 26 or 27 of the Act in relation to a sanctionable failure and that determination is made after the claimant becomes entitled to a new award the reduction period in relation to that failure is to have effect for the purposes of paragraph (1) as if that determination had been made on the day before the previous award terminated.

DEFINITIONS

"the Act"—see reg.2.
"claimant"—see WRA 2012, s.40.
"joint claimants"—*ibid.*
"reduction period"—see reg.101(1).
"sanctionable failure"—see reg.100(1).
"single claimant"—see WRA 2012, s.40.

GENERAL NOTE

2.242   If an award of universal credit terminates while there is an outstanding reduction period, subsequent days count as if an actual reduction of benefit were being applied, so that on any further claim for universal credit the claimant is subject to the reduction only for the remainder of the period (para.(1)). If an award of universal credit terminates before the Secretary of State has made a decision about a reduction for a sanctionable failure, but a new award is in place by the time the decision is made (so that under reg.106 the reduction period would otherwise take effect in the current assessment period), the reduction period starts as if the decision had been made on the day before the previous award terminated.

Suspension of a reduction where fraud penalty applies

2.243   **108.**—(1) A reduction in the amount of an award under section 26 or 27 of the Act is to be suspended for any period during which the provisions of section 6B, 7 or 9 of the Social Security Fraud Act 2001 apply to the award.

(2) The reduction ceases to have effect on the day on which that period begins and begins again on the day after that period ends.

DEFINITION

"the Act"—see reg.2.

When a reduction is to be terminated

2.244   **109.**—(1) A reduction in the amount of an award under section 26 or 27 of the Act is to be terminated where—

   (a) since the date of the most recent sanctionable failure which gave rise to a reduction, the claimant has been in paid work for a period of, or for periods amounting in total to, at least 26 weeks; and

(b) the claimant's weekly earnings during that period or those periods were equal to or exceeded—
    (i) the claimant's individual threshold, or
    (ii) if paragraph (4) of regulation 90 applies (threshold for an apprentice) the amount applicable under that paragraph.

(2) The termination of the reduction has effect—
(a) where the date on which paragraph (1) is satisfied falls within a period of entitlement to universal credit, from the beginning of the assessment period in which that date falls; or
(b) where that date falls outside a period of entitlement to universal credit, from the beginning of the first assessment period in relation to any subsequent award.

(3) A claimant who is treated as having earned income in accordance with regulation 62 (minimum income floor) in respect of an assessment period is to be taken to have weekly earnings equal to their individual threshold in respect of any week falling within that assessment period.

DEFINITIONS

"the Act"—see reg.2.
"assessment period"—see WRA 2012, ss.40 and 7(2) and reg.21.
"claimant"—see WRA 2012, s.40.
"individual threshold"—see regs 2 and 90(2).
"sanctionable failure"—see reg.100(1).

GENERAL NOTE

Any reduction for any level of sanction or sanctions terminates where since the date of the most recent sanctionable failure the claimant has been in paid work with earnings at least equal to the appropriate individual threshold for at least 26 weeks, not necessarily consecutive. It does not matter what the total outstanding reduction period is. The claimant could have had a reduction period of 1095 days imposed, yet after 26 weeks' work (which will have reduced the outstanding period accordingly) the basis for the entire reduction disappears, just as much as if the outstanding period was much shorter. Paragraph (2) confirms that the termination takes effect immediately if the condition in para.(1) is met while the claimant is entitled to universal credit. If the claimant is not then entitled to universal credit the termination takes effect from the beginning of the first assessment period under any new award. Note that this regulation does not take away the status of any sanctionable failure(s) on which the terminated reduction period was based. Thus for the purpose of asking in the future whether there have been other sanctionable failures within 365 days of a new sanctionable failure all such sanctionable failures must be counted.

2.245

Amount of reduction

Amount of reduction for each assessment period

110. Where it has been determined that an award of universal credit is to be reduced under section 26 or 27 of the Act, the amount of the reduction for each assessment period in respect of which a reduction has effect is to be calculated as follows.

2.246

Step 1

2.247   Take the number of days—
    (a) in the assessment period; or
    (b) if lower, the total outstanding reduction period,
and deduct any days in that assessment period for which the reduction is
suspended in accordance with regulation 108.

Step 2

2.248   Multiply the number of days produced by step 1 by the daily reduction rate
(see regulation 111).

Step 3

2.249   If necessary, adjust the amount produced by step 2 so that it does not
exceed—
    (a) the amount of the standard allowance applicable to the award; or
    (b) in the case of a joint claim where a determination under section 26 or
        27 of the Act applies only in relation to one claimant, half the amount
        of that standard allowance.

Step 4

2.250   Deduct the amount produced by steps 2 and 3 from the amount of the
award for the assessment period after any deduction has been made in
accordance with Part 7 (the benefit cap).

DEFINITIONS

    "the Act"—see reg.2.
    "assessment period"—see WRA 2012 ss.40 and 7(2) and reg.21.
    "claimant"—see WRA 2012, s.40.
    "standard allowance"—see WRA 2012, s.9.

GENERAL NOTE

2.251   This apparently complex calculation will work out easily enough in practice. Its
main point is to translate the daily rate of reduction under reg.111 into the appropriate amount for an assessment period, depending on the number of days in the
period affected by a reduction. There is a rule of substance concealed in step 3, in
that the reduction can never exceed the amount of the claimant's standard allowance, or half of a couple's standard allowance.

Daily reduction rate

2.252   **111.**—(1) The daily reduction rate for the purposes of regulation 110 is,
unless paragraph (2), or (3) applies, an amount equal to the amount of the
standard allowance that is applicable to the award multiplied by 12 and
divided by 365.
    (2) The daily reduction rate is 40 per cent of the rate set out in paragraph
(1) if, at the end of the assessment period—
    (a) the claimant is aged 16 or 17;
    (b) the claimant falls within section 19 of the Act (claimant subject to no
        work-related requirements) by virtue of—

      (i) subsection (2)(c) of that section (responsible carer for a child under the age of 1), or

      (ii) regulation 89(1)(c),(d) or (f) (adopter, claimant within 11 weeks before or 15 weeks after confinement or responsible foster parent of a child under the age of 1); or

  (c) the claimant falls within section 20 (claimant subject to work-focused interview only).

(3) The daily reduction rate is nil if, at the end of the assessment period, the claimant falls within section 19 of the Act by virtue of having limited capability for work and work-related activity.

(4) The amount of the rate in paragraphs (1) to (3) is to be rounded down to the nearest 10 pence.

(5) In the case of joint claimants—

  (a) each joint claimant is considered individually for the purpose of determining the rate applicable under paragraphs (1) to (3); and

  (b) half of any applicable rate is applied to each joint claimant accordingly.

DEFINITIONS

"the Act"—see reg.2.
"assessment period"—see WRA 2012 ss.40 and 7(2) and reg.21.
"claimant"—see WRA 2012, s.40.
"joint claimants"—*ibid.*
"limited capability for work and work-related activity"—see WRA 2012, ss.40 and 37(1) and (2).
"single claimant"—see WRA 2012, s.40.
"standard allowance"—see WRA 2012, s.9.

GENERAL NOTE

    The basic rule under para.(1) is that the reduction for the purposes of the calculation in reg.110 is by the whole amount of the claimant's standard allowance under s.9 of the WRA 2012. There is no reduction to the elements that can make up the maximum amount of universal credit for responsibility for children and young persons (s.10), housing costs (s.11) or particular needs and circumstances (s.12). In the case of joint claimants, under para.(5) each claimant is considered separately for the purposes of calculating the reduction and treated as having half of the standard allowance applicable to them as joint claimants.

2.253

    Under para.(2) the reduction is by 40 per cent of the standard allowance, rather than 100 per cent, for claimants under 18, claimants subject to no work-related requirements under s.19 of the WRA 2012 by virtue of s.19(2)(c) (responsible carer of a child under one) or reg.89(1)(c), (d) or (f) and claimants subject to the work-focused interview requirement only under s.20.

    Under para.(3) a nil reduction is to be applied, apparently for a whole assessment period, if at the end of that period the claimant is subject to no work-related requirements under s.19 by virtue of having limited capability for work and work-related activity.

    See reg.113 for other circumstances in which no reduction is to be applied despite the existence of a sanctionable failure that would otherwise trigger a reduction.

Miscellaneous

Application of ESA or JSA sanctions to universal credit

2.254   **112.** Schedule 11 has effect in relation to persons who are, or have been, entitled to an employment and support allowance or a jobseeker's allowance and who are, or become, entitled to universal credit.

DEFINITIONS

"employment and support allowance"—see reg.2.
"jobseeker's allowance"—*ibid.*

GENERAL NOTE

2.255   The general effect of Sch.11 is that if a claimant moves from ESA or JSA to universal credit with some days of an ESA or JSA reduction period outstanding, the reduction for those days translates to the universal credit awards. The failures giving rise to those reductions count as previous sanctionable failures at the equivalent level for the purpose of calculating the length of the reduction period for higher, medium and low-level sanctions under regs 102–104.

Failures for which no reduction is applied

2.256   **113.**—(1) No reduction is to be made under section 26 or 27 of the Act for a sanctionable failure where—

(a) the sanctionable failure is listed in section 26(2)(b) or (c) (failure to apply for a particular vacancy for paid work, or failure to take up an offer of paid work) and the vacancy is because of a strike arising from a trade dispute;

(b) the sanctionable failure is listed in section 26(2)(d) (claimant ceases paid work or loses pay), and the following circumstances apply—

(i) the claimant's work search and work availability requirements are subject to limitations imposed under section 17(4) and 18(3) in respect of work available for a certain number of hours,

(ii) the claimant takes up paid work, or is in paid work and takes up more paid work that is for a greater number of hours, and

(iii) the claimant voluntarily ceases that paid work, or more paid work, or loses pay,

within a trial period;

(c) the sanctionable failure is that the claimant voluntarily ceases paid work, or loses pay, because of a strike arising from a trade dispute;

(d) the sanctionable failure is that the claimant voluntarily ceases paid work as a member of the regular or reserve forces, or loses pay in that capacity;

(e) the sanctionable failure is listed in section 26(4) (failure to take up an offer of paid work, or to cease paid work or lose pay before making a claim), and the period of the reduction that would otherwise apply under regulation 102(4) is the same as, or shorter than, the number of days beginning with the day after the date of the sanctionable failure and ending with the date of claim;

(f) the sanctionable failure is that the claimant voluntarily ceases paid work in one of the following circumstances—

230

    (i)   the claimant has been dismissed because of redundancy after volunteering or agreeing to be dismissed,

    (ii) the claimant has ceased work on an agreed date without being dismissed in pursuance of an agreement relating to voluntary redundancy, or

    (iii) the claimant has been laid-off or kept on short-time to the extent specified in section 148 of the Employment Rights Act 1996, and has complied with the requirements of that section; or

(g) the sanctionable failure is that the claimant by reason of misconduct, or voluntarily and for no good reason, ceases paid work or loses pay, but the claimant's weekly earnings (or, if the claimant is a member of a couple, their joint weekly earnings) have not fallen below the level which the Secretary of State considers sufficient for the purposes of regulation 99(6) (circumstances in which requirements must not be imposed).

(2) In this regulation "regular or reserve forces" has the same meaning as in section 374 of the Armed Forces Act 2006.

DEFINITIONS

"the Act"—see reg.2.
"claimant"—see WRA 2012, s.40.
"couple"—see WRA 2012, ss.40 and 39.
"paid work"—see reg.2.
"redundancy"—*ibid.*
"sanctionable failure"—see reg.100(1).
"trade dispute"—see reg.2.
"work availability requirement"—see WRA 2012, ss.40 and 18(1).
"work search requirement"—see WRA 2012, ss.40 and 17(1).

GENERAL NOTE

    This is an important provision in prescribing, under ss.26(8)(a) and 27(9)(a) of the WRA 2012, cases of sanctionable failure for which no reduction of benefit can be imposed. Note that if case comes within this regulation that does not affect the status of the sanctionable failure in question. It can still count if in relation to a future sanctionable failure it has to be asked whether there have been any sanctionable failures at the equivalent level in the previous 365 days. In view of the issues, including issues of principle, involved in the cases below, it does not seem satisfactory that the protection offered should be restricted in this way. There remains scope for argument that in some of the circumstances listed there is a good reason for the particular claimant's failure to comply with the requirement in question, so that there is not in fact a sanctionable failure. 2.257

    The cases are as follows:

(a) Where the sanctionable failure is failing for no good reason to apply for a particular vacancy for paid work or to take up an offer of paid work (WRA 2012, s.26(2)(b) or (c)), no reduction is to be imposed if the vacancy arose because of a strike arising from a trade dispute. "Trade dispute" is defined in reg.2 by adopting the rather long definition in s.244 of the Trade Union and Labour Relations (Consolidation) Act 1992:

    "(1) In this Part a "trade dispute" means a dispute between workers and their employer which relates wholly or mainly to one or more of the following—

    (a) terms and conditions of employment, or the physical conditions in which any workers are required to work;

(b) engagement or non-engagement, or termination or suspension of employment or the duties of employment, of one or more workers;

(c) allocation of work or the duties of employment between workers or groups of workers;

(d) matters of discipline;

(e) a worker's membership or non-membership of a trade union;

(f) facilities for officials of trade unions; and

(g) machinery for negotiation or consultation, and other procedures, relating to any of the above matters, including the recognition by employers or employers' associations of the right of a trade union to represent workers in such negotiation or consultation or in the carrying out of such procedures.

(2) A dispute between a Minister of the Crown and any workers shall, notwithstanding that he is not the employer of those workers, be treated as a dispute between those workers and their employer if the dispute relates to matters which—

(a) have been referred for consideration by a joint body on which, by virtue of provision made by or under any enactment, he is represented, or

(b) cannot be settled without him exercising a power conferred on him by or under an enactment.

(3) There is a trade dispute even though it relates to matters occurring outside the United Kingdom, so long as the person or persons whose actions in the United Kingdom are said to be in contemplation or furtherance of a trade dispute relating to matters occurring outside the United Kingdom are likely to be affected in respect of one or more of the matters specified in subsection (1) by the outcome of the dispute.

(4) An act, threat or demand done or made by one person or organisation against another which, if resisted, would have led to a trade dispute with that other, shall be treated as being done or made in contemplation of a trade dispute with that other, notwithstanding that because that other submits to the act or threat or accedes to the demand no dispute arises.

(5) In this section—
"employment" includes any relationship whereby one person personally does work or performs services for another; and
"worker", in relation to a dispute with an employer, means—

(a) a worker employed by that employer; or

(b) a person who has ceased to be so employed if his employment was terminated in connection with the dispute or if the termination of his employment was one of the circumstances giving rise to the dispute."

That is a fairly comprehensive definition, although as compared with s.35(1) of the Jobseekers Act 1995 it does not cover disputes between employees and employees. "Strike" is not defined. It is possible that vacancies could arise because of industrial action short of a strike. There seems no good reason why claimants who on principle are not prepared to apply for such vacancies or accept offers should not also be protected. Perhaps it is arguable that in any event they have a good reason for failing to comply with the requirement in question, so that there is no sanctionable failure.

(c) This provision protects claimants who take up work for a trial period, but only current universal credit claimants who are required only to search for and be available for work subject to limitations as to hours of work under reg.97, made under ss.17(4) and 18(3) of the WRA 2012. Then if such a claimant takes up work, or more work, for more than the hours of limitation for a trial period, but then voluntarily gives up that work or extra work or loses pay within the trial period, there is to be no reduction. As above, it would be arguable there was good reason for such action, so no sanctionable failure.

(d) This provision provides the same protection as under sub-para.(a) for voluntarily ceasing paid work or losing pay because of a strike arising from a trade dispute.

(e) Members of the armed forces, both regular and reserve forces, who voluntarily cease paid work as such or lose pay, cannot suffer a reduction on that ground, whatever the circumstances.

(f) Where there is a pre-claim sanctionable failure and the reduction period normally applicable would expire on or before the date of the relevant universal credit claim, there is to be no reduction. It may be that the same result is achieved by reg.102(4).

(g) This provides protection in the same circumstances as prescribed in reg.71 of the Jobseeker's Allowance Regulations 1996 for JSA purposes (see the notes to reg.71 in Vol II), except that there the claimant is deemed not to have left employment voluntarily and so not subject to any sanction. Here the claimant is merely protected from having a reduction of benefit imposed, subject to any argument that there was a good reason under general principles for voluntarily ceasing work, so no sanctionable failure.

(h) Under reg.99(6) the Secretary of State may decide that a claimant's or joint claimants' earnings are at a level where a work search or work availability requirement should not be imposed, although the earnings are below the individual threshold or combined individual thresholds that has to be reached to make the claimant(s) subject to no work-related requirements under s.19 of the WRA 2012 and reg.90. If that decision is made after a claimant by reason of misconduct or voluntarily and for no good reasons ceases paid work or loses pay, no reduction of benefit is to be imposed.

Sanctionable failures under section 26—work placements

114.—(1) Mandatory Work Activity is prescribed as a work placement for the purpose of section 26(2)(a) of the Act (failure to undertake a work placement of a prescribed description).   2.258

(2) "Mandatory Work Activity" is a scheme designed to provide work or work-related activity with a view to assisting claimants to improve their prospects of obtaining paid work.

DEFINITIONS

"the Act"—see reg.2.
"claimant"—see WRA 2012, s.40.
"paid work"—see reg.2.
"work-related activity"—see WRA 2012, s.40.

GENERAL NOTE

See the note to s.26(2)(a) of the WRA 2012 for doubts about the validity of this regulation under the power in that provision   2.259

CHAPTER 3

HARDSHIP

Introduction

115. This Chapter contains provisions under section 28 of the Act for the making of hardship payments where the amount of an award is reduced under section 26 or 27 of the Act.   2.260

"the Act"—see reg.2.

Conditions for hardship payments

2.261

116.—(1) The Secretary of State must make a hardship payment to a single claimant or to joint claimants only where—

(a) the claimant in respect of whose sanctionable failure the award has been reduced under section 26 or 27 of the Act is aged 18 or over;

(b) the single claimant or each joint claimant has met any compliance condition specified by the Secretary of State under regulation 104(2)(a)(i);

(c) the single claimant or either joint claimant completes and submits an application—

(i) approved for the purpose by the Secretary of State, or in such other form as the Secretary of State accepts as sufficient, and

(ii) in such manner as the Secretary of State determines;

(d) the single claimant or either joint claimant furnishes such information or evidence as the Secretary of State may require, in such manner as the Secretary of State determines:

(e) the single claimant or each joint claimant accepts that any hardship payments that are paid are recoverable;

(f) the Secretary of State is satisfied that the single claimant or each joint claimant has complied with all the work-related requirements that they were required to comply with in the 7 days proceeding the day on which the claimant or joint claimants submitted an application in accordance with sub-paragraph (c); and

(g) the Secretary of State is satisfied that the single claimant or each joint claimant is in hardship.

(2) For the purposes of paragraph (1)(g) a single claimant or joint claimants must be considered as being in hardship only where—

(a) they cannot meet their immediate and most basic and essential needs, specified in paragraph (3), or the immediate and most basic and essential needs of a child or qualifying young person for whom the single claimant or either of joint claimants is responsible, only because the amount of their award has been reduced—

(i) under section 26 or 27 of the Act, by the daily reduction rate set out in regulation 111, or

(ii) by the daily reduction rate prescribed in regulations made under section 6B(5A), 7(2A) or 9(2A) of the Social Security Fraud Act 2001 which is equivalent to the rate referred to in paragraph (i);

(b) they have made every effort to access alternative sources of support to meet, or partially meet, such needs; and

(c) they have made every effort to cease to incur any expenditure which does not relate to such needs.

(3) The needs referred to in paragraph (2) are—

(a) accommodation;

(b) heating;

(c) food;

(d) hygiene.

"the Act"—see reg.2.
"claimant"—see WRA 2012, s.40.
"joint claimants"—*ibid.*
"sanctionable failure"—see reg.100(1).
"single claimant"—see WRA 2012, s.40.
"work-related requirement"—see WRA 2012, ss.40 and 13(2).

GENERAL NOTE

This regulation is made under s.28 of the WRA 2012 and sets out the very strin- **2.262**
gent conditions for the making of hardship payments to claimants to whom a sanction has been applied under s.26 or 27, that limitation being imposed by reg.115
and s.28(1)(a). The amount and period of any payment is dealt with in regs 117 and
118. Paragraph (1) of reg.116 lays down seven conditions, all of which must be satisfied. Paragraphs (2) and (3) provide further exhaustive definition of when claimants
can be considered to be in hardship for the purpose of condition (g).

Para. (1)
The seven conditions are as follows: **2.263**
(a)   The claimant to whom the sanction has been applied must be aged at least 18.
      Under-18s can be sanctioned, but will not have the amount of benefit reduced
      to nil, as for most over-18s (see reg.111(1) and (2)).
(b)   Under reg.104(2)(a) reduction periods for low-level sanctions last unless and
      until the claimant satisfies a compliance condition specified by the Secretary
      of State, i.e. the failure to comply with the work-related requirement in ques-
      tion has come to an end or a condition about future compliance is met (WRA
      2012, s.27(6)), plus a fixed period on top. If such a compliance condition has
      been specified, a hardship payment can only be made after it has been met. The
      result is that in these cases a hardship payment can only be made during the
      final fixed period.
(c)   The claimant or one of joint claimants must make an application for a hardship
      payment. The Secretary of State may accept an application in any sufficient
      form, but it is not clear what could also be required by the additional condition
      of the submission of the application being in such manner as determined by
      the Secretary of State. Condition (f) below can make the timing of an applica-
      tion important, but there seems nothing to stop multiple applications being
      made day by day. A payment cannot be made for a period prior to the date of
      issue of the application (reg.117), which presumably must mean the issue of an
      approved form. But since no payment can be made for any period prior to the
      date on which all the conditions in reg.116(1) are met, the crucial date appears
      to be the date of lodging of the application, if later than the date of issue.
(d)   The claimant must have supplied any information or evidence required by the
      Secretary of State.
(e)   The claimant or both joint claimants must accept that any hardship payments
      are recoverable. Since the recoverability is imposed by reg.119 and s.71ZH of
      the Administration Act, independent of any advance agreement by the claim-
      ant, it is not clear quite what level or manner of acceptance will satisfy this
      condition. The claimant in a sense has no option but to submit to what the law
      requires, no matter how vehemently dislike of the result is expressed.
(f)   The claimant or both joint claimants must have complied with all work-related
      requirements imposed in the seven days preceding, presumably immediately
      preceding, the day of submission of the application under condition (c).
(g)   The most fundamental condition is that the claimant or both joint claimants
      are in hardship, presumably as at the date of making the payment or possibly
      as at the date of the application in question. Because of the use of the present
      tense, it is arguable that it is not a necessary condition that the claimant

or claimants are expected to be in hardship for the duration of the period covered by the payment. Paragraphs (2) and (3) define when a claimant can be accepted as in hardship.

Paras (2) and (3)

2.264   The use of the word "only" means that claimants can only be accepted as in hardship if they meet all three of the following conditions:

(a)   The claimant or both joint claimants must be unable to meet their most immediate and basic and essential needs, or those of children or young person for whom they are responsible, only by reason of the reduction in benefit due to a sanction or of a reduction for a benefit offence under the Social Security Fraud Act 2001. The only needs to be considered are accommodation, heating, food and hygiene (para.(3)) and then this condition limits consideration to immediate, basic and essential needs of those kinds. That plainly involves a large element of judgment, but the highly restrictive intention is made clear. There is no specific category of need relating to children no matter how young, e.g. for bedding, clothing or education.

(b)   The claimant or both joint claimants must have made every effort to access alternative sources of support to at least go towards meeting needs within condition (a). Some limitations must necessarily be implied either in terms of what efforts can be required or in terms of what alternative sources of support can be considered. The alternative source must at least be lawful. But presumably claimants are not to be required to beg on the streets. Are they to be required to go to back street or payday lenders? How far are they required to explore sources from which there is no practical possibility of support?

(c)   The claimant or both joint claimants must have made every effort to cease to incur expenditure not related to condition (a) needs. Given the restrictive scope of those needs, the range of expenditure to be considered is wide. But again some notions of reasonableness and practicability must necessarily be implied, especially if avoiding immediate expenditure in the short term might lead to disproportionate financial penalties or burdens in the longer term.

The period of hardship payments

2.265   **117.** A hardship payment is made in respect of—

(a) a period which—

(i)   begins with the date of issue of the application under regulation 116(1)(c), or, if later, the date on which all the conditions in regulation 116(1) are met, and

(ii) ends with the day before the date on which the single claimant's, or the joint claimants', next full payment of universal credit for an assessment period is due to be made (or would be made but for a reduction under section 26 or 27); or

(b) where the period calculated in accordance with paragraph (a) is 7 days or less, that period plus a further period ending with the day referred to in sub-paragraph (a)(ii) or, if sooner, the last day in respect of which their award is reduced pursuant to regulation 111.

DEFINITIONS

"assessment period"—see WRA 2012, ss.40 and 7(2) and reg.21.
"joint claimants"—see WRA 2012, s.40.
"single claimant"—*ibid.*

Each hardship payment is made for a limited period. Once each period expires   2.266
a new application must be made. The period starts with the date of the issue of
the application under reg.116(1)(c), or, if later, the date when all the conditions
in reg.116(1) are met. See the note to reg.116(1)(c). It ends with the date the next
payment of universal credit for an assessment period is due to be paid, or would
have been if it were not for the sanction (para.(a)(ii)). If that period is less than eight
days, the period can extend to the next due date or the end of the period subject to
sanction (para.(b)).

The amount of hardship payments

118. The amount of a hardship payment for each day in respect of which   2.267
such a payment is to be made is to be determined in accordance with the
formula—

$$60\% \ of \left(\frac{(A \times 2)}{365} \right)$$

where A is equal to the amount of the reduction in the single claimant's or
joint claimants' award calculated under regulation 110 for the assessment
period preceding the assessment period in which an application is submitted under regulation 116(1)(c).

DEFINITIONS

"assessment period"—see WRA 2012, ss.40 and 7(2), and reg.21.
"joint claimants"—see WRA 2012, s.40.
"single claimant"—*ibid.*

GENERAL NOTE

The amount of any hardship payment payable per day is effectively 60 per cent   2.268
of the reduction in the amount of benefit in the assessment period before that in
which the application is made. See reg.111 for the daily reduction rate for different
categories of claimant.

Recoverability of hardship payments

119.—(1) Subject to paragraphs (2) and (3), hardship payments are   2.269
recoverable in accordance with section 71ZH of the Social Security
Administration Act 1992.

(2) Paragraph (1) does not apply in relation to any assessment period
in which the single claimant, or each joint claimant, falls within section 19
of the Act by virtue of regulation 90 (claimant subject to no work-related
requirements - the earnings thresholds).

(3) Hardship payments cease to be recoverable where, since the last
day on which the claimant's or the joint claimants' award was subject to a
reduction under section 26 or 27 of the Act—

(a) a single claimant has had weekly earnings that are equal to or exceed
their individual threshold; or

(b) joint claimants have had combined weekly earnings that are equal to
or exceed the sum of their individual thresholds,

for a period of, or more than one period where the total of those periods
amounts to, at least 26 weeks.

DEFINITIONS

"the Act"—see reg.2.
"claimant"—see WRA 2012, s.40.
"individual threshold"—see regs2 and 90(2).
"joint claimants"—see WRA 2012, s.40.
"single claimant"—*ibid.*

GENERAL NOTE

2.270   The basic rule is that any hardship payment is recoverable from the person to whom it was paid (Administration Act, s.71ZH(2)(a)), by the means provided in ss.71ZC to 71ZF. A payment made to one of joint claimants is treated as also paid to the other (s.71ZH(4)). The amount is not recoverable during any assessment period in which the claimant or both joint claimants are subject to no work-related requirements by reason of having earnings of at least the individual threshold(s) under reg.90 (para.(2)). It appears from the contrast with the terms of para.(3) that once the reason for freedom from any work-related requirements ceases, the payment becomes recoverable again. Under para.(3) recoverability ceases if since the end of the sanction period the claimant or both joint claimants have had earnings of at least the individual threshold(s) for a period or periods amounting to 26 weeks.

SCHEDULE 1

MEANING OF PAYMENTS IN RESPECT OF ACCOMMODATION

General

Interpretation

1. In this Schedule—   2.271

"approved premises" means premises approved by the Secretary of State under section 13 of the Offender Management Act 2007 (which contains provision for the approval etc. of premises providing accommodation for persons granted bail in criminal proceedings or for or in connection with the supervision or rehabilitation of persons convicted of offences);

"care home"—

   (a) in England and Wales, means a care home within the meaning of section 3 of the Care Standards Act 2000;

   (b) in Scotland, means a care home service within the meaning of paragraph 2 of Schedule 12 to the Public Services Reform (Scotland) Act 2010; and

   (c) in either case, includes an independent hospital;

"exempt accommodation" means—

   (a) accommodation which is a resettlement place within the meaning of section 30 of the Jobseekers Act 1995 (grants for resettlement places) and which is provided by persons to whom the Secretary of State has given assistance by way of grant pursuant to that section;

   (b) accommodation provided to a claimant by any of the following bodies, where the body providing the accommodation, or a person acting on its behalf, also provides the claimant with care, support or supervision—

      (i)   an upper-tier county council,

      (ii) a housing association,

      (iii) a registered charity, or

      (iv) a voluntary organisation;

"housing association" has the meaning given by section 1(1) of the Housing Associations Act 1985;

"independent hospital"—

   (a) in England, means a hospital as defined by section 275 of the National Health Service Act 2006 that is not a health service hospital as defined by that section;

   (b) in Wales, has the meaning assigned to it by section 2 of the Care Standards Act 2000;

   (c) in Scotland, means an independent health care service as defined in section 10F(1)(a) and (b) of the National Health Service (Scotland) Act 1978;

"registered charity" means a charity entered in the register of charities maintained under Part 4 of the Charities Act 2011 or a body entered on the register of charities maintained under the Charities and Trustee Investment (Scotland) Act 2005;

"shared ownership tenancy" has the meaning given in regulation 26(6);

"tent" means a moveable structure that is designed or adapted (solely or mainly) for the purpose of sleeping in a place for any period and that is not a caravan, a mobile home or a houseboat;

"upper-tier county council" means a council for a county in England for each part of whose area there is a district council;

"voluntary organisation" means a body (other than a public or local authority) whose activities are carried on otherwise than for profit.

Rent payments

Rent payments

2. "Rent payments" are such of the following as are not excluded by paragraph 3—   2.272

   (a) payments of rent;

   (b) payments for a licence or other permission to occupy accommodation;

   (c) mooring charges payable for a houseboat;

   (d) in relation to accommodation which is a caravan or mobile home, payments in respect of the site on which the accommodation stands;

   (e) contributions by residents towards maintaining almshouses (and essential services in them) provided by a housing association which is—

      (i) a registered charity, or

     (ii) an exempt charity within Schedule 3 to the Charities Act 2011.

Payments excluded from being rent payments

2.273   **3.** The following are excluded from being "rent payments"—

  (a) payments of ground rent;

  (b) payments in respect of a tent or the site on which a tent stands;

  (c) payments in respect of approved premises;

  (d) payments in respect of a care home;

  (e) payments in respect of exempt accommodation;

  (f) payments which are owner-occupier payments within the meaning of paragraph 4;

  (g) payments which are service charge payments within the meaning of paragraph 7.

Owner-occupier payments

Owner-occupier payments

2.274   **4.**—(1) "Owner-occupier payments" are—

  (a) loan interest payments within the meaning of paragraph 5;

  (b) alternative finance payments within the meaning of paragraph 6.

(2) Payments are excluded from sub-paragraph (1) if they are service charge payments within the meaning of paragraph 7.

Meaning of "loan interest payments"

2.275   **5.** "Loan interest payments" means payments of interest on a loan which is secured on the accommodation in respect of which the claimant meets the occupation condition.

Meaning of "alternative finance payments"

2.276   **6.**—(1) "Alternative finance payments" means payments that are made under alternative finance arrangements which were entered into to enable a person to acquire an interest in the accommodation in respect of which the claimant meets the occupation condition.

(2) "Alternative finance arrangements" has the same meaning as in Part 10A of the Income Tax Act 2007.

Service charge payments

Service charge payments

2.277   **7.**—(1) "Service charge payments" are payments which—

  (a) fall within sub-paragraph (2);

  (b) are not excluded by sub-paragraph (3); and

  (c) in any case to which paragraph 8 applies, meet all of the conditions set out in that paragraph.

(2) The payments falling within this sub-paragraph are payments of amounts which are, in whole or in part—

  (a) payments of, or towards, the costs of or charges for providing services or facilities for the use or benefit of persons occupying accommodation; or

  (b) fairly attributable to the costs of or charges for providing such services or facilities connected with accommodation as are available for the use or benefit of persons occupying accommodation.

(3) Payments are excluded by this sub-paragraph where—

  (a) a loan that falls within paragraph 5 was taken out for the purposes of making the payments; or

  (b) the services or facilities to which the payments relate are provided for the use or benefit of any person occupying—

      (i) a tent,

     (ii) approved premises,

    (iii) a care home, or

    (iv) exempt accommodation.

(4) It is irrelevant for the purposes of sub-paragraph (2)—

  (a) whether or not the payments are separately identified as relating to the costs or charges referred to in sub-paragraph (2);

  (b) whether they are made in addition to or as part of any other payment (including a payment that would otherwise be regarded as a rent payment within the meaning of paragraph 2);

  (c) whether they are made under the same or a different agreement as that under which the accommodation is occupied.

Additional conditions: social rented sector renters and owner-occupiers

8.—(1) This paragraph applies for the purposes of calculating the amount of housing costs element to be included in a claimant's award of universal credit but only as regards calculations made under—

    (a) Part 5 of Schedule 4 (social rented sector other than temporary accommodation); or

    (b) Schedule 5 (housing costs element for owner-occupiers).

(2) The following are the conditions referred to in paragraph 7(1)(c).

(3) The first condition is that making the payments is a condition on which the right to occupy the accommodation depends.

(4) The second condition is that the payments fall within one or more of the following categories:

Category A—Payments to maintain the general standard of the accommodation

Payments within this category are for—

    (a) the external cleaning of windows, but only in relation to upper floors of a multi-storey building;

    (b) other internal or external maintenance or repair of the accommodation, but only where the payments are separately identifiable as relating to such maintenance or repair and payable by—

        (i) a claimant who occupies accommodation under a shared ownership tenancy, or

        (ii) a claimant in whose case any amount of housing costs element to be included in their award in respect of those payments would fall to be calculated under Schedule 5.

Category B—Payments for the general upkeep of areas of communal use

Payments within this category are for ongoing maintenance or cleaning of, and the supply of water, fuel or any other commodity relating to the common use of, internal or external areas, including areas for reasonable facilities (such as laundry rooms or children's play areas).

Category C—Payments in respect of basic communal services

Payments within this category are for provision, ongoing maintenance, cleaning or repair in connection with basic services generally available to all persons living in the accommodation (such as refuse collection, communal lifts, secure building access or wireless or television aerials to receive a service free of charge).

Category D—Accommodation-specific charges

Payments within this category are specific to the particular accommodation occupied by a claimant but are limited to payments for the use of essential items contained in it (such as furniture or domestic appliances).

(5) The third condition is that the costs and charges to which the payments relate are of a reasonable amount and relate to services or facilities of such description as it is reasonable to provide.

(6) The fourth condition is that the payments are none of the following—

    (a) payments to the extent that they relate to the costs of or charges for providing services or facilities in respect of which payments out of public funds might otherwise be made (irrespective of whether the claimant has any entitlement to payments so made);

    (b) payments in connection with the use of an asset which result in the transfer of the asset or any interest in it;

    (c) payments to the extent that they relate to the costs of or charges for providing food, medical services or personal services (including personal care) of any description.

(7) Payments that are not service charge payments within the meaning of paragraph 7 by reason only that they fail to meet any of the conditions set out in sub-paragraphs (3) to (6) are nevertheless to be treated as if they were such service charge payments for the purposes of paragraphs 3(g) and 4(2).

DEFINITION

"claimant"—see WRA 2012, s.40.

2.278

2.279

2.280

2.281

2.282

2.283   In order to be eligible for a housing costs element, the claimant (or claimants) must meet the three basic conditions in reg.25(2) to (4): the payment condition, the liability condition, and the occupation condition. This Schedule is concerned with the payment condition.

Under reg.25(2) there are three types of payments that can be met: rent payments, owner-occupier payments and service charge payments.

Paras 2 and 3

2.284   Paragraph 2 lists the payments that are eligible as rent payments and para.3 the payments that are not eligible. Note that the amount of the housing costs element may be restricted under Sch.4 if the rent is higher than allowed (private tenants and temporary accommodation) or the accommodation is larger than allowed (social rented sector).

The payments listed in para.2 include most of the payments that can be met by housing benefit but not all, e.g. payments by way of mesne profits (or, in Scotland, violent profits) are not included.

Under para.3 payments in respect of ground rent and in respect of a tent and the site on which it stands are excluded (para.3(a) and (b)). These qualify as "other housing costs" for income support, JSA and ESA but there seems to be no provision for such payments under universal credit.

Payments by Crown tenants no longer seem to be excluded (as they are for housing benefit).

Paras 4–6

2.285   The owner-occupier payments that can be met are "loan interest payments" and "alternative finance payments". They do not include service charge payments that came within para.7.

Note the £200,000 limit on loans in step 3 of para.10(2) of Sch.5 (except for loans for adaptations for disablement needs: see para.10(3) of Sch.5) and on the purchase price of the accommodation in the case of alternative finance payments in step 2 of para.11(2) of Sch.5. Note also that any increase, or decrease, in the amount of a loan during the currency of an award is only taken into account from the anniversary date (see para.10(4) and (5) of Sch.5).

"Loan interest payments" are defined in para.5 as "payments of interest on a loan which is secured on the accommodation in respect of which the claimant meets the occupation condition".

Thus payments of interest will be eligible (as calculated under Sch.5), provided only that the loan is secured on the accommodation that the claimant (or claimants: s.40 WRA 2012) is occupying, or is treated as occupying, as his/her home. Note that there is no requirement as to the purpose for which the loan (or loans) was taken out. Compare the income support, JSA and ESA provisions under which the loan has to be taken out to acquire an interest in the home or for the purpose of repairs or improvements (but does not have to be secured on the home, although it normally will be). Thus this could include a loan taken out, for example, to pay service charges (payments on loans secured on a claimant's home which were taken out to meet service charges are not eligible as service charge payments (see para.7(1)(b) and (3)(a)), or for repairs. But it could also include a loan taken out for any other purpose, for example, to buy a car, as long as the loan is secured on the claimant's home. This does seem surprising but is acknowledged in the examples given in para.F4082 ADM. Furthermore, a remortgage to roll up arrears of interest would also be covered. Thus a claimant may receive a housing costs element in respect of interest payments on loans that include arrears of interest (provided that they are secured on the home), which is a significant change from the position under the income support, JSA and ESA housing costs rules.

"Alternative finance payments" are defined in para.6. This will cover home financing schemes designed to be compliant with Shari'a principles. Such schemes are not eligible for income support (or JSA or ESA) housing costs (see the notes to para.15 of Sch.3 to the Income Support Regulations in Vol.II of this series).

Note that there is a three month qualifying (i.e. waiting) period for owner-occupier payments (see Pt 3 of Sch.5) and that if the claimant (or other member of the couple, in the case of couples) has *any* earned income during an assessment period (i.e. month), no owner-occupier payments will be payable (Sch.5, para.4).

Unlike income support, JSA and ESA, there is no rule that a housing costs element cannot be paid if the loan was taken out while the claimant (or either joint claimant) was in receipt of universal credit.

Paras 7 and 8

Service charge payments are eligible payments if they fall within para.7(2) and are not excluded under para.7(3). They do not have to be separately identified, nor does it matter if they are paid in addition to, or as part of, any other payment (including a rent payment within the meaning of para.2), or if they are paid under the same or a different agreement than that under which the accommodation is occupied (para.7(4)). **2.286**

Note the additional conditions in para.8 that have to be met in the case of service charge payments by social sector renters (other those in temporary accommodation) and owner-occupiers. This does not apply to private renters.

Regulation 25(3)

SCHEDULE 2

CLAIMANT TREATED AS LIABLE OR NOT LIABLE TO MAKE PAYMENTS

PART I

TREATED AS LIABLE TO MAKE PAYMENTS

Certain other persons liable to make payments

1.—(1) A claimant is to be treated as liable to make payments where the person who is liable to make the payments is— **2.287**

(a) any child or qualifying young person for whom the claimant (or if the claimant is a member of a couple, either member) is responsible; or

(b) in the case of a claimant who is a member of a couple claiming as a single person, the other member of the couple.

(2) Sub-paragraph (1)(b) does not apply to a person who is claiming as a single person by virtue of regulation 3(4).

Failure to pay by the person who is liable

2.—(1) A claimant is to be treated as liable to make payments where all of the conditions specified in sub-paragraph (2) are met. **2.288**

(2) These are the conditions—

(a) the person who is liable to make the payments is not doing so;

(b) the claimant has to make the payments in order to continue occupation of the accommodation;

(c) the claimant's circumstances are such that it would be unreasonable to expect them to make other arrangements;

(d) it is otherwise reasonable in all the circumstances to treat the claimant as liable to make the payments.

(3) In determining what is reasonable for the purposes of sub-paragraph (2)(d) in the case of owner-occupier payments, regard may be had to the fact that continuing to make the payments may benefit the person with the liability to make the payments.

Payments waived in return for repair work

3. A claimant is to be treated as liable to make payments where— **2.289**

(a) the liability to make payments is waived by the person ("P") to whom the liability is owed; and

(b) the waiver of that liability is by way of reasonable compensation for reasonable repair or re-decoration works carried out by the claimant to the accommodation which P would otherwise have carried out or been required to carry out.

Rent free periods

2.290   **4.**—(1) Where the arrangements under which the claimant occupies the accommodation provide for rent free periods, the claimant is to be treated as liable to make rent payments and service charge payments in respect of accommodation for the whole of any rent free period.

(2) In paragraph (1), "rent free period" has the meaning given in paragraph 7(4) of Schedule 4.

Part 2

Treated as Not Liable to Make Payments

Liability to make rent and other payments to close relative

2.291   **5.**—(1) A claimant is to be treated as not liable to make rent payments where the liability to make them is owed to a person who lives in the accommodation and who is—

(a) if the claimant is a member of a couple, the other member; or

(b) a child or qualifying young person for whom—

(i) the claimant is responsible, or

(ii) if the claimant is a member of a couple, the other member is responsible; or

(c) a close relative of—

(i) the claimant, or

(ii) if the claimant is a member of a couple, the other member, or

(iii) any child or qualifying young person who falls within paragraph (b).

(2) A claimant who is treated under sub-paragraph (1) as not liable to make rent payments to any person is also to be treated as not liable to make service charge payments where the liability to make the service charge payments is to the same person.

Liability to make rent and other payments to company

2.292   **6.**—(1) A claimant is to be treated as not liable to make rent payments where the liability to make them is owed to a company and the owners or directors of the company include—

(a) the claimant;

(b) if the claimant is a member of a couple, the other member;

(c) a qualifying young person for whom a person who falls within paragraph (a) or (b) is responsible; or

(d) a close relative of any of the above who lives in the accommodation with the claimant.

(2) A claimant who is treated under sub-paragraph (1) as not liable to make rent payments to the company is also to be treated as not liable to make service charge payments where the liability to make the service charge payments is to—

(a) the same company; or

(b) another company of which the owners or directors include any of the persons listed in sub-paragraph (1)(a) to (d).

(3) In this paragraph, "owner", in relation to a company ("C"), means a person ("A") who has a material interest in C.

(4) For the purposes of sub-paragraph (3), A has a material interest in C if A—

(a) holds at least 10% of the shares in C; or

(b) is able to exercise a significant influence over the management of C by virtue of A's shareholding in C; or

(c) holds at least 10% of the shares in a parent undertaking ("P") of C; or

(d) is able to exercise a significant influence over the management of P by virtue of A's shareholding in P; or

(e) is entitled to exercise, or control the exercise of, voting power in C which, if it consists of voting rights, constitutes at least 10% of the voting rights in C; or

(f) is able to exercise a significant influence over the management of C by virtue of A's entitlement to exercise, or control the exercise of, voting rights in C; or

(g) is entitled to exercise, or control the exercise of, voting power in P which, if it consists of voting rights, constitutes at least 10% of the voting rights in P; or

(h) is able to exercise a significant influence over the management of P by virtue of A's entitlement to exercise, or control the exercise of, voting rights in P.

(5) For the purposes of sub-paragraph (4), references to "A" are to—

(a) the person; or

(b) any of the person's associates; or

(c) the person and any of the person's associates taken together.

(6) For the purposes of sub-paragraph (5), "associate", in relation to a person ("A") holding shares in an undertaking ("X") or entitled to exercise or control the exercise of voting power in relation to another undertaking ("Y"), means—

(a) the spouse or civil partner of A;

(b) a child or step-child of A (if under 18);

(c) the trustee of any settlement under which A has a life interest in possession (in Scotland a life interest);

(d) an undertaking of which A is a director;

(e) a person who is an employee or partner of A;

(f) if A has with any other person an agreement or arrangement with respect to the acquisition, holding or disposal of shares or other interests in X or Y, that other person;

(g) if A has with any other person an agreement or arrangement under which they undertake to act together in exercising their voting power in relation to X or Y, that other person.

(7) In sub-paragraph (6)(c), "settlement" means any disposition or arrangement under which property is held on trust (or subject to comparable obligations).

(8) For the purposes of this paragraph—

"parent undertaking" has the same meaning as in the Financial Services and Markets Act 2000 (see section 420 of that Act);

"shares" means—

(a) in relation to an undertaking with shares, allotted shares (within the meaning of Part 17 of the Companies Act 2006);

(b) in relation to an undertaking with capital but no share capital, rights to share in the capital of the body;

(c) in relation to an undertaking without capital, interests—

(i) conferring any right to share in the profits, or liability to contribute to the losses, of the body, or

(ii) giving rise to an obligation to contribute to the debts or expenses of the undertaking in the event of a winding up;

"voting power", in relation to an undertaking which does not have general meetings at which matters are decided by the exercise of voting rights, means the rights under the constitution of the undertaking to direct the overall policy of the undertaking or alter the terms of its constitution.

Liability to make rent and other payments to a trust

7.—(1) A claimant is to be treated as not liable to make rent payments where the liability to make them is owed to a trustee of a trust and the trustees or beneficiaries of the trust include—

    2.293

(a) the claimant;

(b) if the claimant is a member of a couple, the other member;

(c) a child or qualifying young person for whom a person who falls within paragraph (a) or (b) is responsible; or

(d) a close relative of any of the above who lives in the accommodation with the claimant.

(2) A claimant who is treated under sub-paragraph (1) as not liable to make rent payments to the trustee of a trust is also to be treated as not liable to make service charge payments where the liability to make the service charge payments is to—

(a) a trustee of the same trust; or

(b) a trustee of another trust of which the trustees or beneficiaries include any of the persons listed in sub-paragraph (1)(a) to (d).

Liability to make owner-occupier and other payments to member of same household

8.—(1) A claimant is to be treated as not liable to make owner-occupier payments where the liability to make the payments is owed to a person who lives in the claimant's household.

    2.294

(2) A claimant who is treated under sub-paragraph (1) as not liable to make owner-occupier payments to any person is also to be treated as not liable to make service charge payments where the liability to make the service charge payments is to the same person.

(3) A claimant is to be treated as not liable to make service charge payments where—

(a) there is no liability to make rent payments or owner-occupier payments; but

(b) the liability to make service charge payments is to a person who lives in the claimant's household.

Arrears of payments

9.—(1) A claimant is to be treated as not liable to make payments in respect of any amount which—

    2.295

(a) represents an increase in the sum that would be otherwise payable; and

(b) is the result of—

    (i) outstanding arrears of any payment or charge in respect of the accommodation,

    (ii) outstanding arrears of any payment or charge in respect of other accommodation, previously occupied by the claimant, or

    (iii) any other unpaid liability to make a payment or charge.

(2) Sub-paragraph (1) does not apply if the claimant is treated as not liable to make the payments under any of the preceding provisions of this Part of this Schedule.

Contrived liability

2.296   **10.**—(1) A claimant is to be treated as not liable to make payments where the Secretary of State is satisfied that the liability to make the payments was contrived in order to secure the inclusion of the housing costs element in an award of universal credit or to increase the amount of that element.

(2) Sub-paragraph (1) does not apply if the claimant is treated as not liable to make the payments under any of the preceding provisions of this Part of this Schedule.

DEFINITIONS

"child"—see WRA 2012, s.40.

"claimant"—*ibid.*

"close relative"—see reg.2.

"couple"—see WRA 2012, ss.39 and 40.

"partner"—see reg.2.

"qualifying young person"—see WRA 2012, ss.40 and 10(5) and regs 2 and 5.

"rent free period"—see Sch.4, para.7(4).

"single person"—see WRA 2012, ss.40 and 1(2)(a).

GENERAL NOTE

2.297   In order to be eligible for a housing costs element, the claimant (or claimants) must meet the three basic conditions in reg.25(2) to (4): the payment condition, the liability condition, and the occupation condition. This Schedule is concerned with the liability condition.

Under reg.25(3) the claimant (or either joint claimant) must be liable to make rent payments, owner-occupier payments or service charge payments on a commercial basis, or be treated as liable to make them, and must not be treated as not liable to make them.

For the meaning of "on a commercial basis", see the notes to "*Board and lodging accommodation*" in reg.2 of the Income Support Regulations in Vol.II of this series and the notes to reg.9(1)(a) of the Housing Benefit Regulations in *CPAG's Housing Benefit and Council Tax Benefit Legislation*.

Paras 1–4

2.298   A claimant is treated as liable to make payments if the person who is liable is (i) a child or qualifying young person for whom the claimant (or the other member of the couple in the case of a couple) is responsible (sub-para.(1)(a)); or (ii) the other member of the couple, if the claimant is a member of a couple but claiming as a single person (see reg.3(3) for the circumstances in which this can apply) (sub-para. (1)(b); note that sub-para.(1)(b) does not apply in the case of polygamous marriages (sub-para.(2)).

A claimant is also treated as liable to make payments if the payments have been waived by the person to whom they were due in order to compensate the claimant for carrying out repair or redecoration works (para.3), or during rent free periods (para.4).

Paragraph 2 applies where the person who is liable to make the payments is not doing so. The claimant will be treated as liable if the claimant has to make the payments in order to continue to occupy the accommodation, it would be unreasonable to expect the claimant to make other arrangements and it is reasonable to treat the claimant as liable. These conditions are similar to those in, e.g., reg.8(1)(c) of the

Housing Benefit Regulations and para.2(1)(b) of Sch.3 to the Income Support Regulations (see the notes to para.2 of Sch.3 in Vol.II of this series), except for the added condition that it would be unreasonable to expect the claimant to make other arrangements.

Note para.2(3) which provides that in the case of owner-occupier payments, in deciding whether it would be reasonable to treat the claimant as liable, account may be taken of the fact that the payments continuing to be made may benefit the person who is liable to make the payments. Paragraph F2090 ADM gives the following example of where this might apply. A couple split up and C, the member in whose name the mortgage is, moves out and refuses to pay the mortgage. The other member, P, remains in the property. A decision-maker decides not to include a housing costs element in P's universal credit award as C could still pay the mortgage.

Paras 5–10

These paragraphs deal with when the claimant will be treated as not liable to make payments in respect of his/her home. Note that some of the exclusions only apply to some types of eligible payments. The situations in which this rule applies to rent payments are reduced compared with housing benefit (see reg.9 of the Housing Benefit Regulations 2006). Note that the "on a commercial basis" requirement applies to any liability to make payments in respect of accommodation under universal credit (see reg.25(3)(a)(i)).

2.299

Paras 5–7

A claimant is treated as not liable to make rent payments and service charges payments if the liability is to the following:

2.300

- Someone who also lives in the accommodation, and who is (i) the other member of the couple if the claimant is a member of a couple, (ii) a child or qualifying young person for whom the claimant or other member of the couple is responsible (see reg.4), or (iii) a close relative (defined in reg.2) of the claimant, the other member of the couple or child or qualifying person (para.5).

  "Lives in the accommodation" probably means the same as "resides in the dwelling" in reg.9(1)(b) of the Housing Benefit Regulations (see the notes to reg.9(1)(b) in *CPAG's Housing Benefit and Council Tax Benefit Legislation*).

- A company, and the owners or directors of the company include (i) the claimant, (ii) the other member of the couple if the claimant is a member of a couple, (iii) a qualifying young person for whom the claimant or other member of the couple is responsible, or (iv) a close relative of the claimant, other member of the couple or qualifying young person (in the case of a close relative, s/he must live in the accommodation with the claimant) (para.6(1) and (2)).

  Note that the claimant will also be treated as not liable to pay the service charges if the liability for them is to another company whose owners or directors include any of the people listed in para.6(1) (para.6(2)(b)).

  An owner of a company for the purposes of para.6 is a person who has a "material interest" in it (para.6(3)). See para.6(4)–(8) for the detail.

- A trustee of a trust, and the trustees or beneficiaries of the trust include (i) the claimant, (ii) the other member of the couple if the claimant is a member of a couple, (iii) a child or qualifying young person for whom the claimant or other member of the couple is responsible, or (iv) a close relative of the claimant, other member of the couple or child or qualifying young person (in the case of a close relative, s/he must live in the accommodation with the claimant) (para.7(1) and (2)).

Note that the claimant will also be treated as not liable to pay the service charges if the liability for them is to a trustee of another trust whose trustees or beneficiaries include any of the people listed in para.7(1) (para.7(2) (b)).

See the notes to reg.9(1)(e) and (f) of the Housing Benefit Regulations in CPAG's Housing Benefit and Council Tax Benefit Legislation.

Para. 8

2.301   Paragraph 8(1) and (2) are concerned with owner-occupier payments and service charges payments. They treat a claimant as not liable to make owner-occupier payments and service charges payments if the liability is to a person who is lives in the claimant's household. Clearly this is different from "lives in the accommodation" under paras 5 to 8. On the meaning of "household", see the notes to *"couple"* (under the heading *"Spouses and civil partners"*) in reg.2 of the Income Support Regulations in Vol.II of this series.

Under para.8(3) a claimant is treated as not liable to make service charges payments if s/he is not liable for rent payments or owner-occupier payments and the liability for the service charges is to someone who is a member of the claimant's household.

Para. 9

2.302   This paragraph only applies if paras 5–8 do not apply (sub-para.(2)). It applies to all types of eligible payments.

It treats a claimant as not liable to pay any increase in the amount that s/he would otherwise be liable to pay, if that increase is the result of outstanding arrears of any payment or charge in respect of his/her current or previous accommodation. This also applies in respect of "any other unpaid liability to make a payment or charge" (see sub-para.(1)(b)(iii)) but only if that results in an increase in the amount the claimant is liable to pay.

What does "an increase in the sum that would otherwise be payable" mean? According to para.F2143 ADM, in relation to owner-occupier payments, because any loan secured on the claimant's home is eligible for inclusion in the calculation of the housing costs element (see para.5 of Sch.1) (subject to the £200,000 limit on loans in step 3 of para.10(2) of Sch.5), any increase in the loan (or loans) does not "represent an increase in the sum that would otherwise be payable" and so is not caught by para.9. According to the ADM, this will include the situation when the loan is a remortgage to roll up arrears of interest. Thus a claimant may receive a housing costs element in respect of interest payments on loans that include arrears of interest (provided that they are secured on the home), which is a significant change from the position under the income support, JSA and ESA housing costs rules.

An example of a payment that would come within para.9 is where a tenant has agreed to pay off arrears of rent by paying an increased amount of rent each month. S/he would be treated under para.9 as not liable to pay the extra amount above the rent that was originally agreed.

Para. 10

2.303   This paragraph only applies if paras 5–8 do not apply (sub-para.(2)). It applies to all types of eligible payments.

It contains a similar rule to the contrived tenancy provision in housing benefit (see reg.9(1)(l) of the Housing Benefit Regulations). See the notes to reg.9(1)(l) in *CPAG's Housing Benefit and Council Tax Benefit Legislation.* But note that reg.9(1)(l) refers to the liability being "created to take advantage of the housing benefit scheme", whereas the test under para.10 is the liability "was contrived in order to secure the inclusion of the housing costs element". There may be a distinction between "created" and "contrived".

Schedule 3

Claimant Treated as Occupying or not Occupying Accommodation

Part I

Treated as Occupying Accommodation

The occupation condition: the general rule

1.—(1) The general rule is that a claimant is to be treated as occupying as their home the accommodation which the claimant normally occupies as their home.

(2) Subject to the following provisions of this Part, no claimant is to be treated as occupying accommodation which comprises more than one dwelling.

(3) Where none of those provisions applies and the claimant occupies more than one dwelling, regard is to be had to all the circumstances in determining which dwelling the claimant normally occupies as their home, including (among other things) any persons with whom the claimant occupies each dwelling.

(4) "Dwelling"—

    (a) in England and Wales, means a dwelling within the meaning of Part 1 of the Local Government Finance Act 1992;

    (b) in Scotland, means a dwelling within the meaning of Part 2 of that Act.

2.304

Croft land included in accommodation

2.—(1) Where accommodation which a claimant normally occupies as their home is situated on or pertains to a croft, croft land used for the purposes of the accommodation is to be treated as included in the accommodation.

(2) "Croft" means a croft within the meaning of section 3(1) of the Crofters (Scotland) Act 1993.

2.305

Claimant living in other accommodation during essential repairs

3.—(1) Where a claimant—

    (a) is required to move into accommodation ("the other accommodation") on account of essential repairs being carried out to the accommodation the claimant normally occupies as their home;

    (b) intends to return to the accommodation which is under repair; and

    (c) meets the payment condition and the liability condition in respect of either the other accommodation or the accommodation which they normally occupy as their home (but not both),

the claimant is to be treated as normally occupying as their home the accommodation in respect of which those conditions are met.

(2) A claimant is subject to the general rule in paragraph 1 where—

    (a) sub-paragraph (1)(a) and (b) apply to the claimant; but

    (b) the claimant meets the payment condition and the liability condition in respect of both the other accommodation and the accommodation which they normally occupy as their home.

2.306

Claimant housed in two dwellings by provider of social housing

4.—(1) In sub-paragraph (2), "relevant claimant" means a claimant who meets all of the following conditions—

    (a) the first condition is that the claimant has been housed in two dwellings ("accommodation A" and "accommodation B") by a provider of social housing on account of the number of children and qualifying young persons living with the claimant;

    (b) the second condition is that the claimant normally occupies both accommodation A and accommodation B with children or qualifying young persons for whom the claimant is responsible;

    (c) the third condition is that the claimant meets the payment condition and the liability condition in respect of both accommodation A and accommodation B (and for these purposes it is irrelevant whether the claimant's liability is to the same or a different person).

(2) In the case of a relevant claimant, both accommodation A and accommodation B are to be treated as the single accommodation which the relevant claimant normally occupies as their home.

2.307

(3) In sub-paragraph (1), "provider of social housing" has the meaning given in paragraph 2 of Schedule 4.

Moving home: adaptations to new home for disabled person

2.308   **5.**—(1) Sub-paragraph (2) applies where—

(a) the claimant has moved into accommodation ("the new accommodation") and, immediately before the move, met the payment condition and liability condition in respect of the new accommodation; and

(b) there was a delay in moving in that was necessary to enable the new accommodation to be adapted to meet the disablement needs of a person specified in sub-paragraph (3).

(2) The claimant is to be treated as occupying both the new accommodation and the accommodation from which the move was made ("the old accommodation") if—

(a) immediately before the move, the claimant was entitled to the inclusion of the housing costs element in an award of universal credit in respect of the old accommodation; and

(b) the delay in moving into the new accommodation was reasonable.

(3) A person is specified in this sub-paragraph if the person is—

(a) a claimant or any child or qualifying young person for whom a claimant is responsible; and

(b) in receipt of—

(i) the care component of disability living allowance at the middle or highest rate,

(ii) attendance allowance, or

(iii) the daily living component of personal independence payment.

(4) No claimant may be treated as occupying both the old accommodation and the new accommodation under this paragraph for more than one month.

Claimant living in other accommodation because of reasonable fear of violence

2.309   **6.**—(1) This paragraph applies where—

(a) a claimant is occupying accommodation ("the other accommodation") other than the accommodation which they normally occupy as their home ("the home accommodation"); and

(b) it is unreasonable to expect the claimant to return to the home accommodation on account of the claimant's reasonable fear of violence in the home, or by a former partner, against the claimant or any child or qualifying young person for whom the claimant is responsible; but

(c) the claimant intends to return to the home accommodation.

(2) The claimant is to be treated as normally occupying both the home accommodation and the other accommodation as their home if—

(a) the claimant meets the payment condition and the liability condition in respect of both the home accommodation and other accommodation; and

(b) it is reasonable to include an amount in the housing costs element for the payments in respect of both the home accommodation and the other accommodation.

(3) Where the claimant meets the payment condition and the liability condition in respect of one accommodation only, the claimant is to be treated as normally occupying that accommodation as their home but only if it is reasonable to include an amount in the housing costs element for the payments in respect of that accommodation.

(4) No claimant may be treated as occupying both the home accommodation and the other accommodation under sub-paragraph (2) for more than 12 months.

Moving in delayed by adaptations to accommodation to meet disablement needs

2.310   **7.**—(1) The claimant is to be treated as having occupied accommodation before they moved into it where—

(a) the claimant has since moved in and, immediately before the move, met the payment condition and the liability condition in respect of the accommodation;

(b) there was a delay in moving in that was necessary to enable the accommodation to be adapted to meet the disablement needs of a relevant person; and

(c) it was reasonable to delay moving in.

(2) "Relevant person" means a person specified in paragraph 5(3).

(3) No claimant may be treated as occupying accommodation under this paragraph for more than one month.

Moving into accommodation following stay in hospital or care home

2.311   **8.**—(1) The claimant is to be treated as having occupied accommodation before they moved into it where—

(a) the claimant has since moved in and, immediately before the move, met the payment condition and the liability condition in respect of that accommodation; and

(b) the liability to make the payments arose while the claimant was a patient or accommodated in a care home (or, in the case of a joint claim, while both joint claimants were patients or were accommodated in a care home).

(2) No claimant may be treated as occupying the accommodation under this paragraph for more than one month.

(3) In this paragraph—

"care home" has the meaning given in paragraph 1 of Schedule 1;

"patient" means a person who is undergoing medical or other treatment as an in-patient in any hospital or similar institution.

PART 2

TREATED AS NOT OCCUPYING ACCOMMODATION

Periods of temporary absence exceeding 6 months

9.—(1) Subject to sub-paragraphs (2) and (3), a claimant is to be treated as no longer occupying accommodation from which they are temporarily absent where the absence exceeds, or is expected to exceed, 6 months.

(2) Sub-paragraph (1) does not apply to a claimant who falls within paragraph 3.

(3) Where a claimant who falls within paragraph 6 is temporarily absent from the accommodation which they normally occupy as their home, the claimant is to be treated as no longer occupying that accommodation where the absence exceeds, or is expected to exceed, 12 months.

2.312

DEFINITIONS

"attendance allowance"—see reg.2.
"care home"—see Sch.1, para.1.
"child"—see WRA 2012, s.40.
"claimant"—*ibid.*
"disability living allowance"—see reg.2.
"partner"—*ibid.*
"personal independence payment"—*ibid.*
"provider of social housing"—see Sch.4, para.2.
"qualifying young person"—see WRA 2012, ss.40 and 10(5) and regs 2 and 5.

GENERAL NOTE

In order to be eligible for a housing costs element, the claimant (or claimants) must meet the three basic conditions in reg.25(2) to (4): the payment condition, the liability condition, and the occupation condition. This Schedule is concerned with the occupation condition.

2.313

Under reg.25(4) the claimant (or each claimant in the case of joint claimants: s.40 WRA 2012) must be treated as occupying the accommodation as his/her home and not be treated as not occupying it. Croft land is included (see para.2).

Para.1

This contains the general rule that the claimant must be normally occupying the accommodation as his/her home (sub-para.(1)). In addition, the claimant cannot usually be treated as occupying accommodation which comprises more than one dwelling (sub-para.(2)). However, there are exceptions to these rules (see below). Where these exceptions do not apply, and the claimant (or claimants: s.40 WRA 2012) occupies more than one dwelling, to decide which is the dwelling normally occupied as the home, all the circumstances, including the people who live with the claimant (or claimants) in each dwelling, are to be taken into account (sub-para. (3)).

2.314

See also the notes to "dwelling occupied as the home" in reg.2 of the Income Support Regulations in Vol.II of this series.

Para.3

2.315   If the claimant has to move into temporary accommodation because essential repairs (see *R(SB) 10/81)* are being carried out to his/her normal home, intends to return to that home, and satisfies the payment and liability conditions for either the temporary accommodation or his/her normal home (but not both), s/he is treated as occupying as his/her home the accommodation in respect of which the payment and liability conditions are met (sub-para.(1)). If the claimant satisfies the payment and liability conditions for both the temporary accommodation and his/her normal home, s/he is treated as occupying the accommodation that s/he normally occupies as his/her home (sub-para.(2)). This may not necessarily be the accommodation that was his/her normal home.

There is no time limit in para.3 itself as to how long it can apply.

Para.4

2.316   This allows a housing costs element to be paid for two dwellings in the following circumstances. If the claimant (or claimants: s.40 WRA 2012) has been housed in two dwellings by a "provider of social housing" (defined in para.2 of Sch.4) due to the number of children and qualifying young persons living with him/her, the claimant normally occupies both dwellings with children or qualifying young persons for whom s/he is responsible (see reg.4) and the claimant meets the payment and liability conditions in respect of both dwellings, the claimant will be treated as normally occupying both dwellings as his/her home.

This paragraph can apply without time limit.

See para.17 of Sch.4 as to how the housing costs element is calculated under para.4. A single calculation is made for both dwellings together. This will be carried out under Pt 5 of Sch.4 if the rent is paid to a social sector landlord for both dwellings and neither is temporary accommodation (see para.21 of Sch.4 for the meaning of "temporary accommodation"). Otherwise, the calculation is made under Pt 4 of Sch.4, including applying the four bedroom limit. Note that under para.25(3)–(4) of Sch.4, if the cap rent for the two dwellings is different (e.g. because they are in different areas), the cap rent that is lower at the time the housing costs element is first calculated is the cap rent that applies. The calculation of the renter's housing costs element will continue to be based on that cap rent for as long as the renter is housed in those two homes.

Paras 5 and 7

2.317   Under para.5 a claimant (or claimants) can be treated as occupying two homes for up to one month if the claimant;

   (i)   has moved into his/her new home;

  (ii)   met the payment and liability conditions for that home immediately before s/he moved in,

 (iii)   was entitled to a housing costs element in respect of his/her old home immediately before the move; and

 (iv)   the delay in moving in was reasonable and was necessary to enable the new home to be adapted to the disablement needs (not defined) of the claimant (or claimants: s.40 WRA 2012) or any child or qualifying young person for whom the claimant (or claimants) is responsible. The person with the disablement needs must be in receipt of the middle or highest rate of the care component of disability living allowance, the daily living component of personal independence payment (either rate), attendance allowance or armed forces independence payment (note that the definition of "attendance allowance" in reg.2 includes armed forces independence payment).

If the above circumstances apply but the claimant was not receiving a housing costs element in respect of his/her old home immediately before s/he moved in, para.7 will apply to treat the claimant as occupying his/her home for up to one month before s/he moves in.

On the meaning of "moving in" see *R(H) 9/05* and on "adapting the accommodation to meet disablement needs" see the notes to para.3(7)(c)(i) of Sch.3 to the Income Support Regulations in Vol.II of this series.

See para.18 of Sch.4 as to how the housing costs element is calculated under para.5. Note that any housing cost contributions for non-dependants are only deducted from the housing costs element for the old home.

Para. 6

If the claimant is living in accommodation other than the accommodation s/he normally occupies as his/her home because of a reasonable fear of violence in the home, or from a former partner against him/her or any child or qualifying young person for whom s/he is responsible (see reg.4), and s/he intends to return to the accommodation s/he normally occupies as his/her home, she can be treated as occupying both for up to 12 months. This applies if s/he meets the payment and liability conditions in respect of both the accommodation s/he normally occupies as his/her home and the other accommodation, provided that it is reasonable to pay a housing costs element for both. If the claimant only satisfies the payment and liability conditions in respect of one accommodation, s/he will be treated as occupying that accommodation as his/her home but only if it is reasonable to pay a housing costs element for that accommodation.

Note that if a claimant in these circumstances is living in a refuge, s/he may not meet the payment condition for that accommodation (see para.3(e) of Sch.1 under which payments in respect of exempt accommodation (defined in para.1 of Sch.1) do not count as rent payments).

See para.19 of Sch.4 as to how the housing costs element is calculated under para.6 where the claimant is entitled to a housing costs element for both homes. This will be calculated for each home under Pt 4 of Sch.4 or under Pt 5 of Sch.4, as the case may be. Note that any housing cost contributions for non-dependants are only deducted from the housing costs element for the home that the claimant is normally occupying.

2.318

Para. 8

Under this paragraph a claimant can be treated as occupying his/her home for up to one month before s/he moves in if s/he met the payment and liability conditions immediately before moving in and s/he became liable to make the payments while s/he was a patient (defined in sub-para.(3)) or in a care home, or in the case of joint claimants, while both of them were patients or in a care home.

2.319

Para. 9

Unless the absence is due to essential repairs (see para.3) or domestic violence (see para.6), if a claimant is temporarily absent from the accommodation, s/he will be treated as no longer occupying it if the absence has lasted, or is expected to last, more than six months.

This is a considerably simplified provision compared with the rules for temporary absence that apply for the purposes of housing benefit and income support, JSA and ESA housing costs.

If at any time during the six months it becomes clear that the absence is likely to exceed six months, the claimant will be treated as no longer occupying the accommodation from that point (this could apply from the start if the absence was expected to last more than six months from the beginning). However, if the claimant returns to the accommodation for a period, even a very short period (24 hours?), the six months should restart (see *R v Penrith DC Housing Benefit Review Board ex p. Burt* (1990) 22 H.L.R. 292). See further the notes to para.3(8) to (12) of Sch.3 to the Income Support Regulations in Vol. II of this series.

Note that if a person was entitled to universal credit which included a housing costs element immediately before becoming a prisoner (defined in reg.2), and his/her term in custody is not expected to last more than six months, s/he will be

2.320

entitled to universal credit consisting of a housing costs element only during that absence (see reg.19(2) and (3)).

Regulation 26(2)

SCHEDULE 4

HOUSING COSTS ELEMENT FOR RENTERS

PART I

GENERAL

Introduction

2.321   **1.**—(1) This Schedule contains provisions about claimants to whom regulation 26(2) applies.

(2) Claimants who fall within sub-paragraph (1) are referred to in this Schedule as "renters" (and references to "joint renters" are to joint claimants to whom regulation 26(2) applies).

(3) Part 2 of this Schedule sets out an exception to section 11(1) of the Act for certain renters in whose case an award of universal credit is not to include an amount of housing costs element calculated under this Schedule.

(4) The following Parts of this Schedule provide for the calculation of the amount of housing costs element to be included under regulation 26(2) in a renter's award of universal credit—

    (a) Part 3 contains general provisions that apply to all calculations, whether under Part 4 or Part 5;

    (b) Part 4 applies in relation to renters who occupy accommodation in the private rented sector or who occupy temporary accommodation; and

    (c) Part 5 applies in relation to renters who occupy accommodation in the social rented sector other than temporary accommodation.

Interpretation

2.322   **2.** In this Schedule—

"exempt accommodation" has the meaning given in paragraph 1 of Schedule 1;

"extended benefit unit" has the meaning given in paragraph 9;

"Housing Act functions" means functions under section 122 of the Housing Act 1996 (functions of rent officers in connection with universal credit, housing benefit and rent allowance subsidy and housing credit);

"housing cost contribution" has the meaning given in paragraph 13;

"joint renter" has the meaning given in paragraph 1(2);

"listed persons", in relation to a renter, means—

    (a) the renter;

    (b) where the renter is a member of a couple, the other member of the couple; and

    (c) any child or qualifying young person for whom the renter (or either joint renter) is responsible;

[1 "member of the armed forces" means a member of the regular forces or the reserve forces within the meaning of section 374 of the Armed Forces Act 2006;]

"non-dependant" has the meaning given in paragraph 9(2);

"provider of social housing" means—

    (a) a local authority;

    (b) a non-profit registered provider of social housing;

    (c) in relation to accommodation which is social housing, a profit-making registered provider of social housing;

    (d) a registered social landlord;

"registered social landlord" means—

    (a) a body which is registered in the register maintained by the Welsh Ministers under Chapter 1 of Part 1 of the Housing Act 1996;

    (b) a body which is registered in the register maintained by the Scottish Housing Regulator under section 20(1) of the Housing (Scotland) Act 2010;

"relevant payments" has the meaning given in paragraph 3;

"the Rent Officers Order 2013" means the Rent Officers (Universal Credit Functions) Order 2013;

"renter" means a single renter within the meaning of paragraph 1(2) or each of joint renters;

"renter who requires overnight care" is to be understood in accordance with paragraph 12(3) to (5);

"shared accommodation" has the meaning given in paragraph 27;

"social housing" has the meaning given in sections 68 to 77 of the Housing and Regeneration Act 2008.

"Relevant payments" for purposes of this Schedule

3.—(1) "Relevant payments" means one or more payments of any of the following descriptions— 2.323

    (a) rent payments;

    (b) service charge payments.

(2) "Rent payments", in relation to any calculation under Part 4 or 5 of this Schedule, has the meaning given in paragraph 2 of Schedule 1.

(3) "Service charge payments"—

    (a) for the purposes of calculations under Part 4 of this Schedule, has the meaning given in paragraph 7 of Schedule 1;

    (b) for the purposes of calculations under Part 5 of this Schedule, is to be understood in accordance with paragraphs 7 and 8 of Schedule 1.

PART 2

EXCEPTION TO INCLUSION OF HOUSING COSTS ELEMENT

No housing costs element for 16 or 17 year old care leavers

4. Section 11(1) of the Act (housing costs) does not apply to any renter who is 16 or 17 years old and is a care leaver. 2.324

PART 3

GENERAL PROVISIONS ABOUT CALCULATION OF AMOUNT OF
HOUSING COSTS ELEMENT FOR RENTERS

Application of Part 3

5. This Part contains provisions of general application in calculating the amount of a renter's housing costs element under Part 4 or 5 of this Schedule. 2.325

Payments taken into account

Relevant payments to be taken into account

6.—(1) Where a renter meets the payment condition, liability condition and occupation condition in respect of one or more descriptions of relevant payment, each such description is to be taken into account for the purposes of the calculation under Part 4 or 5 of this Schedule. 2.326

(2) No account is to be taken of any amount of a relevant payment to the extent that all of the conditions referred to in sub-paragraph (1) are not met in respect of that amount.

(3) Any particular payment for which a renter is liable is not to be brought into account more than once, whether in relation to the same or a different renter (but this does not prevent different payments of the same description being brought into account in respect of an assessment period).

Relevant payments calculated monthly

7.—(1) Where any relevant payment is to be taken into account under paragraph 6, the amount of that payment is to be calculated as a monthly amount. 2.327

(2) Where the period in respect of which a renter is liable to make a relevant payment is not a month, an amount is to be calculated as the monthly equivalent, so for example—

    (a) weekly payments are multiplied by 52 and divided by 12;

    (b) four-weekly payments are multiplied by 13 and divided by 12;

    (c) three-monthly payments are multiplied by 4 and divided by 12; and

    (d) annual payments are divided by 12.

(3) Where a renter is liable for relevant payments under arrangements that provide for one or more rent free periods, the monthly equivalent is to be calculated over 12 months by reference to the total number of relevant payments which the renter is liable to make in that 12 month period.

(4) "Rent free period" means any period in respect of which the renter has no liability to make one or more of the relevant payments which are to be taken into account under paragraph 6.

Room allocation

Size criteria applicable to the extended benefit unit of all renters

2.328   8.—(1) In calculating the amount of the renter's housing costs element under Part 4 or 5 of this Schedule, a determination is to be made in accordance with the provisions referred to in sub-paragraph (2) as to the category of accommodation which it is reasonable for the renter to occupy, having regard to the number of persons who are members of the renter's extended benefit unit (see paragraph 9).

(2) The provisions referred to in this sub-paragraph are the following provisions of this Schedule—

(a) in respect of a calculation under Part 4, paragraphs 9 to 12 and 26 to 29;

(b) in respect of a calculation under Part 5, paragraphs 9 to 12.

Extended benefit unit of a renter for purposes of this Schedule

2.329   9.—(1) For the purposes of this Schedule, the members of a renter's extended benefit unit are—

(a) the renter (or joint renters);

(b) any child or qualifying young person for whom the renter or either joint renter is responsible; and

(c) any person who is a non-dependant.

(2) A person is a non-dependant if the person [6 normally] lives in the accommodation with the renter (or joint renters) and is none of the following—

(a) a person within sub-paragraph (1)(a) or (b);

(b) where the renter is a member of a couple claiming as a single person, the other member of the couple;

(c) a foster child;

(d) a person who is liable to make payments on a commercial basis in respect of the person's occupation of the accommodation (whether to the renter, joint renters or another person);

(e) a person to whom the liability to make relevant payments is owed or a member of their household;

(f) a person who has already been treated as a non-dependant in relation to a claim for universal credit by another person liable to make relevant payments in respect of the accommodation occupied by the renter.

[6 (g) a child or qualifying young person for whom no-one in the renter's extended benefit unit is responsible.]

(3) "Foster child" means a child in relation to whom the renter (or either joint renter) is a foster parent.

Number of bedrooms to which a renter is entitled

2.330   10.—(1) A renter is entitled to one bedroom for each of the following categories of persons in their extended benefit unit—

(a) the renter (or joint renters);

(b) a qualifying young person for whom the renter or either joint renter is responsible;

(c) a non-dependant who is not a child;

(d) two children who are under 10 years old;

(e) two children of the same sex;

(f) any other child.

(2) A member of the extended benefit unit to whom two or more of the descriptions in sub-paragraph (1) apply is to be allotted to whichever description results in the renter being entitled to the fewest bedrooms.

(3) In determining the number of bedrooms to which a renter is entitled, the following must also be taken into account—

(a) the provisions of paragraph 11 as to treatment of periods of temporary absence of members of the renter's extended benefit unit;

(b) any entitlement to an additional bedroom in accordance with paragraph 12;

(c) for the purpose of any calculation under Part 4 of this Schedule, the additional requirements in paragraphs 26 to 29.

Temporary absence of member of renter's extended benefit unit

2.331   11.—(1) A member of the renter's extended benefit unit who is temporarily absent from the accommodation occupied by the renter is to be included in a determination of the number of bedrooms to which the renter is entitled ("relevant determination") in the circumstances specified in sub-paragraphs (2) to (4).

(2) In the case of a child or qualifying young person, the circumstances specified in this sub-paragraph are that the relevant determination relates to any time—

(a) during the first 6 months of the absence of a child or qualifying young person for whom the renter is treated as not being responsible in accordance with regulation 4(6) (a) (child or qualifying young person looked after by local authority) where, immediately before the local authority started looking after them, the child or qualifying young person was included in the renter's extended benefit unit and the renter's award included the housing costs element;

(b) during the first 6 months of the absence of a child or qualifying young person for whom the renter is treated as not being responsible in accordance with regulation 4(6) (b) (child or qualifying young person is a prisoner) where—
   (i) immediately before becoming a prisoner, the child or qualifying young person was included in the renter's extended benefit unit and the renter's award included the housing costs element, and
   (ii) the child or qualifying young person has not been sentenced to a term in custody that is expected to extend beyond that 6 months; or

(c) before the renter or joint renter ceases to be responsible for a temporarily absent child or qualifying young person in accordance with regulation 4(7) (absence exceeding specified duration).

(3) In the case of a renter, the circumstances specified in this sub-paragraph are that the relevant determination relates to any time when—

(a) the temporary absence from Great Britain of the renter is disregarded in accordance with regulation 11(1) or (2); or

(b) the renter is a prisoner to whom regulation 19(2) (existing award includes housing costs when person becomes a prisoner) applies.

(4) In the case of a non-dependant, the circumstances specified in this sub-paragraph are that—

(a) the relevant determination relates to any time during a period specified in sub-paragraph (5); and

(b) immediately before the start of that period, the non-dependant was included in the renter's extended benefit unit and [², in the circumstances specified in sub-paragraph (5)(a) to (c),] the renter's award included the housing costs element.

(5) The specified periods are—

(a) the first month of the non-dependant's temporary absence from Great Britain and, if the circumstances of the non-dependant are such as would be disregarded for the purposes of regulation 11(2) (death of a close relative), a further one month;

(b) the first 6 months of the non-dependant's temporary absence from Great Britain in the circumstances described in regulation 11(3)(a) (absence solely in connection with treatment for illness or physical or mental impairment);

(c) the first 6 months that the non-dependant is a prisoner where the non-dependant has not been sentenced to a term in custody that is expected to extend beyond that 6 months.

[³ (d) any period during which a non-dependant who is the son, daughter, step-son or step-daughter of a renter or joint renters is a member of the armed forces away on operations.]

(6) Any non-dependant who is temporarily absent from the accommodation occupied by the renter in circumstances other than those specified in sub-paragraphs (4) and (5) is not to be treated as being a member of the renter's extended benefit unit if that absence exceeds, or is expected to exceed, 6 months.

[⁶ Additional room

12.—(1) A renter is entitled to an additional bedroom if they satisfy any of the following conditions—

(a) the overnight care condition (see sub-paragraph (3));

(b) the foster parent condition (see sub-paragraphs (4) and (5)); or

(c) the disabled child condition (see sub-paragraph (6)).

(2) Sub-paragraph (1) applies subject to sub-paragraphs (7) to (9).

(3) A renter satisfies the overnight care condition if—

(a) they are in receipt of—
   (i) the care component of disability living allowance at the middle or highest rate;
   (ii) attendance allowance; or
   (iii) the daily living component of personal independence payment;

(b) one or more persons who do not live in the renter's accommodation are engaged to provide overnight care for the renter and to stay overnight in the accommodation on a regular basis; and

2.333

(c) overnight care is provided under arrangements entered into for that purpose.

(4) A renter satisfies the foster parent condition if the renter is—

(a) a foster parent; or

(b) an adopter with whom a child has been placed for adoption.

(5) For the purposes of sub-paragraph (4) "foster parent" includes a person who would be a foster parent, but for the fact that they do not currently have any child placed with them, provided that any period since the date when their last placement ended (or, if they have not yet had a child placed with them, since the date when they were approved to be a foster parent) does not exceed 12 months.

(6) A renter satisfies the disabled child condition if they or another member of their extended benefit unit are responsible for a child who would (but for the provisions of this paragraph) be expected to share a bedroom and that child is—

(a) in receipt of the care component of disability living allowance at the middle or highest rate; and

(b) by virtue of their disability, not reasonably able to share a room with another child.

(7) Where a renter, or one or both of joint renters, satisfy—

(a) the overnight care condition; or

(b) the foster parent condition,

or both, they are entitled to one additional bedroom by virtue of satisfying each condition.

(8) Where a renter, or one or both of joint renters, satisfy the disabled child condition in relation to one or more children, they are entitled to as many additional bedrooms as are necessary to ensure that each such child has their own bedroom.

(9) Where a renter, or one or both of joint renters, satisfy two or more of—

(a) the overnight care condition;

(b) the foster parent condition; or

(c) the disabled child condition,

the total number of additional bedrooms they are entitled to is determined by adding together the number of additional bedrooms which they are entitled to by virtue of satisfying each of those conditions.]

Housing cost contributions

Housing cost contributions

2.334 **13.**—(1) In calculating the amount of the housing costs element under Part 4 or 5 of this Schedule, a deduction is to be made in respect of each non-dependant who is a member of the renter's extended benefit unit.

(2) Paragraph (1) is subject to paragraphs 15 and 16.

(3) Any amount to be deducted under sub-paragraph (1) is referred to in this Schedule as a "housing cost contribution".

Amount of housing cost contributions

2.335 **14.**—(1) The amount of each housing cost contribution to be deducted under paragraph 13 is £68.

(2) Deductions are not to be made until the amount has been determined which results from all other steps in the calculation required in relation to the renter under Parts 4 and 5 of this Schedule.

(3) Where the sum of all the housing cost contributions to be deducted in the renter's case exceeds the amount referred to in sub-paragraph (2)—

(a) the amount determined under this Schedule is to be reduced to nil; but

(b) no further reduction in respect of housing cost contributions is to be made from the renter's award.

Exempt renters

15.—(1) No deduction is to be made under paragraph 13 in the case of—

(a) any renter who is a single person to whom sub-paragraph (2) applies; or

(b) any joint renter where at least one joint renter is a person to whom sub-paragraph (2) applies.

(2) This sub-paragraph applies to—

(a) a person who is registered as blind;

(b) a person in receipt of the care component of disability living allowance at the middle or highest rate;

(c) a person in receipt of attendance allowance;

(d) a person in receipt of the daily living component of personal independence payment;

(e) a person who is entitled to a payment within paragraph (b), (c) or (d) but is not receiving it under, as the case may be—

    (i) regulation 8 of the Social Security (Disability Living Allowance) Regulations 1991,

    (ii) regulation 6 of the Social Security (Attendance Allowance) Regulations 1991,

    (iii) regulation 21 of the Social Security (General Benefit) Regulations 1982, or

    (iv) regulations under section 86 of the Act (payment of personal independence payment while a person is a hospital in-patient).

No deduction for housing cost contributions in respect of certain non-dependants

16.—(1) No deduction is to be made under paragraph 13 in respect of any non-dependant who is a member of the renter's extended benefit unit to whom sub-paragraph (2) applies.   **2.336**

(2) This sub-paragraph applies to—

  (a) a person who is under 21 years old;

  (b) a person in receipt of state pension credit;

  (c) a person in receipt of the care component of disability living allowance at the middle or highest rate;

  (d) a person in receipt of attendance allowance;

  (e) a person in receipt of the daily living component of personal independence payment;

  (f) a person who is entitled to a payment within paragraph (c), (d) or (e) but is not receiving it under, as the case may be—

    (i) regulation 8 of the Social Security (Disability Living Allowance) Regulations 1991,

    (ii) regulation 6 of the Social Security (Attendance Allowance) Regulations 1991,

    (iii) regulation 21 of the Social Security (General Benefit) Regulations 1982, or

    (iv) regulations under section 86 of the Act (payment of personal independence payment while a person is a hospital in-patient);

  (g) a person in receipt of carer's allowance;

  (h) a person who is a prisoner;

  (i) a person who is responsible for a child under 5 years old.

  [⁴ (j) a person who is a member of the armed forces away on operations who—

    (i) is the son, daughter, step-son or step-daughter of a renter or joint renters, and

    (ii) resided with the renter or joint renters immediately before leaving to go on operations and intends to return to reside with the renter or joint renters at the end of the operations.]

Calculations involving more than one accommodation

Single calculation for renter treated as occupying single accommodation

17.—(1) This paragraph applies to any renter where, under paragraph 4 of Schedule 3 (claimant housed in two dwellings by provider of social housing), two dwellings ("accommodation A" and "accommodation B") occupied by a renter are treated as the single accommodation in respect of which the renter meets the occupation condition.   **2.337**

(2) The amount of the renter's housing costs element is to be determined by a single calculation in respect of accommodation A and accommodation B as if they were one, taking account of—

  (a) all relevant payments in respect of accommodation A and all relevant payments in respect of accommodation B; and

  (b) the total number of bedrooms in accommodation A and accommodation B taken together.

(3) The single calculation is to be made under Part 5 of this Schedule in any case where—

  (a) the renter's liability to make rent payments in respect of accommodation A and accommodation B is to a provider of social housing; and

  (b) neither accommodation A nor accommodation B is temporary accommodation within the meaning of paragraph 21.

(4) In any other case, the single calculation is to be made under Part 4 of this Schedule.

Calculation where move to new accommodation delayed for adaptations for disabled person

18.—(1) Sub-paragraph (2) applies to any renter where, under paragraph 5 of Schedule 3 (moving home: adaptations to new home for disabled person), the renter meets the occupation condition in respect of both the new accommodation and the old accommodation.   **2.338**

(2) The amount of the renter's housing costs element under this Schedule is to be calculated as follows.

Step 1

2.339   Calculate an amount in accordance with Part 4 or Part 5 of this Schedule (as the case may be) in respect of both—
         (a) the new accommodation; and
         (b) the old accommodation.

Step 2

2.340   Add together the amounts determined in step 1.

Step 3

2.341   If a deduction was made for housing cost contributions in respect of both the new accommodation and the old accommodation, take the amount of the housing costs contributions deducted in respect of the new accommodation and add that to the amount resulting from step 2.
     (3) In this paragraph, references to "the new accommodation" and "the old accommodation" are to be understood in accordance with paragraph 5 of Schedule 3.

Calculation where renter moves out because of reasonable fear of violence

2.342   **19.**—(1) Sub-paragraph (2) applies to any renter where, under paragraph 6(2) of Schedule 3 (claimant living in other accommodation because of reasonable fear of violence), the renter meets the occupation condition in respect of both the home accommodation and the other accommodation.
     (2) The amount of the renter's housing costs element under this Schedule is to be calculated as follows:

Step 1

2.343   Calculate an amount in accordance with Part 4 or Part 5 of this Schedule (as the case may be) in respect of—
         (a) the home accommodation; and
         (b) the other accommodation.

Step 2

2.344   Add together the amounts determined in step 1.

Step 3

2.345   If a deduction was made for housing cost contributions in respect of both the home accommodation and the other accommodation—
         (c) determine which accommodation the renter normally occupies as their home; and
         (d) take the amount of the housing costs contributions deducted in respect of the accommodation not so occupied and add that to the amount resulting from step 2.
     (3) In this paragraph, references to "the home accommodation" and "the other accommodation" are to be understood in accordance with paragraph 6 of Schedule 3.

PART 4

PRIVATE RENTED SECTOR AND TEMPORARY ACCOMMODATION

Application of Part 4

2.346   **20.**—(1) This Part applies to—
         (a) renters who are liable to make rent payments to a person other than a provider of social housing; and
         (b) renters who meet the occupation condition in respect of temporary accommodation (see paragraph 21).
     (2) Sub-paragraph (1) applies irrespective of whether renters are also liable to make service charge payments.

Meaning of "temporary accommodation"

2.347   **21.**—(1) Accommodation is temporary accommodation for the purposes of paragraph 20(1)(b) if it falls within Case 1 or Case 2.
     (2) Case 1 is where—
         (a) rent payments are payable to a local authority;

(b) the local authority makes the accommodation available to the renter—
    (i) to discharge any of the local authority's functions under Part 3 of the Housing Act 1985, Part 7 of the Housing Act 1996 or Part 2 of the Housing (Scotland) Act 1987, or
    (ii) to prevent the person being or becoming homeless within the meaning of Part 7 of the Housing Act 1996 or Part 2 of the Housing (Scotland) Act 1987; and
(c) the accommodation is not exempt accommodation.

(3) Case 2 is where—
  (a) rent payments are payable to a provider of social housing other than a local authority;
  (b) that provider makes the accommodation available to the renter in pursuance of arrangements made with it by a local authority—
    (i) to discharge any of the local authority's functions under Part 3 of the Housing Act 1985, Part 7 of the Housing Act 1996 or Part 2 of the Housing (Scotland) Act 1987, or
    (ii) to prevent the renter being or becoming homeless within the meaning of Part 7 of the Housing Act 1996 or Part 2 of the Housing (Scotland) Act 1987; and
  (c) the accommodation is not exempt accommodation.

(4) Sub-paragraph (1) applies irrespective of whether the renter is also liable to make service charge payments.

The calculation of the housing costs element under this Part

The amount of housing costs element under this Part
22. The amount of the renter's housing costs element under this Part is to be calculated as follows:　　　　　　2.348

Step 1

Determine—　　　　　　2.349
  (a) the amount of the renter's core rent; and
  (b) the amount of the renter's cap rent,
and identify which is the lower amount (if both amounts are the same, that is the identified amount).

Step 2

Deduct the sum of the housing cost contributions (if any) under paragraph 13 from the amount identified in step 1.　　　　　　2.350
The result is the amount of the renter's housing costs element calculated under this Part.

Core rent
23. Except where paragraph 24 applies, the renter's core rent is to be determined as follows:　　　　　　2.351

Step 1

Determine the amount of each relevant payment to be taken into account under paragraph 6.　　　　　　2.352

Step 2

Determine the period in respect of which each relevant payment is payable and, in accordance with paragraph 7, determine the amount of the payment in respect of a month.　　　　　　2.353

Step 3

If there is more than one relevant payment, add together the amounts determined in step 2 in relation to all relevant payments.　　　　　　2.354
The result is the renter's core rent.

Core rent for joint tenants
24.—(1) This paragraph applies where, in respect of the accommodation occupied by the renter, one or more persons other than the renter are liable to make relevant payments which are of the same description as those for which the renter is liable and which are to be taken into account under paragraph 6.　　　　　　2.355
(2) The following steps are to be taken in order to determine the renter's core rent.

Step 1

2.356   Determine the total of all relevant payments referred to in sub-paragraph (1) for which the renter and others are liable in respect of the accommodation taken as a whole.

Step 2

2.357   Determine the period in respect of which each relevant payment is payable and, in accordance with paragraph 7, determine the amount of the payment in respect of a month.

Step 3

2.358   Add together all of the amounts determined in step 2 in relation to all relevant payments.

Step 4

2.359   Find the allocated amount in accordance with whichever of sub-paragraphs (3) to (5) applies in the renter's case.
The result is the renter's core rent.

(3) Where the only persons liable to make relevant payments are listed persons, the allocated amount is the amount resulting from step 3 in sub-paragraph (2).

(4) Where the persons liable for the relevant payments are one or more listed persons and one or more other persons, the allocated amount is to be found by the applying the formula—

$$\left(\frac{A}{B}\right) \times C$$

where—
"A" is the amount resulting from step 3 in sub-paragraph (2),
"B" is the total number of all persons (including listed persons) liable to make the relevant payments, and
"C" is the number of listed persons [5 liable to make relevant payments].

(5) If the Secretary of State is satisfied that it would be unreasonable to allocate the amount resulting from step 3 in sub-paragraph (2) in accordance with sub-paragraph (4), that amount is to be allocated in such manner as the Secretary of State considers appropriate in all the circumstances, having regard (among other things) to the number of persons liable and the proportion of the relevant payments for which each of them is liable.

Cap rent

2.360   25.—(1) The renter's cap rent is to be determined as follows.

Step 1

2.361   Determine the category of accommodation to which the renter is entitled under paragraphs 8 to 12 and 26 to 29.

Step 2

2.362   Having regard to the determination at step 1, determine the maximum allowable amount for the renter under sub-paragraph (2) or (4) (as the case may be).
The result is the renter's cap rent.

(2) The maximum allowable amount to be used in relation to the renter is the local housing allowance which applies at the relevant time to—
(a) the broad rental market area in which the renter's accommodation is situated; and
(b) the category of accommodation determined at step 1 as that to which the renter is entitled.

(3) But the maximum allowable amount in relation to the renter is to be determined under sub-paragraph (4) in any case where—
(a) paragraph 4 of Schedule 3 (claimant housed in two dwellings by provider of social housing) applies to the renter; and
(b) the maximum allowable amount determined under sub-paragraph (2) for the renter in relation to accommodation A and the amount so determined in relation to accommodation B are different (references to accommodation A and accommodation B are to be understood in accordance with paragraph 4 of Schedule 3); and

   (c) a single calculation is to be made in relation to the renter under paragraph 17 (renter treated as occupying single accommodation).

(4) In any such case, the maximum allowable amount to be used in making the single calculation required by paragraph 17—

   (a) is to be determined by reference to the accommodation for which the amount referred to in sub-paragraph (3)(b) is lower when the calculation is first made; and

   (b) is to continue to be determined by reference to that accommodation for so long as paragraph 4 of Schedule 3 applies to the renter in respect of the same accommodation A and the same accommodation B; and

   (c) is to be re-determined in accordance with paragraphs (a) and (b) on each occasion when the renter is re-housed in any other accommodation, provided that paragraph 4 of Schedule 3 continues to apply to the renter.

(5) In this paragraph—

"broad rental market area" means the broad rental market area determined under article 3 of the Rent Officers Order 2013;

"local housing allowance", in relation to a broad rental market area, means the amount determined by a rent officer for that area under article 4 of the Rent Officers Order 2013;

"relevant time" means the time at which the amount of the renter's housing costs element is calculated under paragraph 22.

Further provisions about size criteria for cases to which this Part applies

Four bedroom limit

26. In calculating the amount of a renter's housing costs element under paragraph 22, no renter is entitled to more than 4 bedrooms.

2.363

Specified renters entitled to shared accommodation only

27.—(1) In calculating the amount of a renter's housing costs element under paragraph 22, any specified renter (within the meaning of paragraph 28) is entitled to shared accommodation only.

2.364

(2) "Shared accommodation" means the category of accommodation specified in paragraph 1(a) of Schedule 1 to the Rent Officers Order 2013.

Meaning of "specified renters"

28.—(1) For the purposes of paragraph 27, "specified renter" means a renter in respect of whom all of the following conditions are met.

2.365

(2) The first condition is that the renter is a single person (or a member of a couple claiming as a single person) who—

   (a) is under 35 years old; and

   (b) is not an excepted person under paragraph 29.

(3) The second condition is that the renter is not responsible for any children or qualifying young persons.

(4) The third condition is that no person is a non-dependant in relation to the renter.

Renters excepted from shared accommodation

29.—(1) "Excepted person" means any renter ("E") who falls within any of sub-paragraphs (2) to (9).

2.366

(2) In relation to England and Wales, E is at least 18 but under 22 years old and—

   (a) was formerly provided with accommodation under section 20 of the Children Act 1989 (which makes provision for local authorities to provide accommodation for certain children); and

   (b) was living in such accommodation on E's 16th birthday.

(3) In relation to Scotland, E is at least 18 but under 22 years old and—

   (a) was previously provided with accommodation by a local authority under section 25 of the Children (Scotland) Act 1995 (provision of accommodation for children etc); and

   (b) was living in that accommodation on E's 16th birthday.

(4) E is at least 25 but under 35 years old and—

   (a) has, for a total of at least 3 months (whether or not continuously), lived in one or more hostels for homeless people; and

   (b) whilst E was living in such a hostel, was offered and has accepted services which the Secretary of State considers are intended to assist E to be rehabilitated or resettled within the community.

(5) E is under 35 years old and is in receipt of—

   (a) the care component of disability living allowance at the middle or highest rate;

(b) attendance allowance; or

(c) the daily living component of personal independence payment.

(6) In relation to England and Wales, E is under 35 years old and is the subject of active multi-agency management pursuant to arrangements established by a responsible authority under section 325(2) of the Criminal Justice Act 2003 (arrangements for assessing etc. risks posed by certain offenders).

(7) In relation to Scotland, E is under 35 years old and is the subject of active multi-agency risk management pursuant to arrangements established by the responsible authorities under section 10(1) of the 2005 Act (arrangements for assessing and managing risks posed by certain offenders).

(8) In relation to Scotland, E is under 35 years old and—

(a) section 10(1) of the 2005 Act does not apply to E by reason only of the fact that section 10(1)(b) or (d) has not been brought fully into force; and

(b) E is considered by the Secretary of State to be a person who may cause serious harm to the public at large.

(9) In relation to Scotland, E is under 35 years old and—

(a) section 10(1) of the 2005 Act does not apply to E by reason only of the fact that section 10(1)(e) has not been brought fully into force; and

(b) by reason of an offence of which E has been convicted, E is considered by the Secretary of State to be a person who may cause serious harm to the public at large.

(10) In this paragraph—

"the 2005 Act" means the Management of Offenders etc. (Scotland) Act 2005;

"care home", "registered charity" and "voluntary organisation" have the meaning given in Schedule 1;

"hostel" means a building—

(a) in which there is provided, for persons generally or for a class of persons, domestic accommodation, otherwise than in separate and self-contained premises, and either board or facilities for the preparation of food adequate to the needs of those persons, or both; and

(b) which—

(i) is managed or owned by a provider of social housing other than a local authority, or

(ii) is operated other than on a commercial basis and in respect of which funds are provided wholly or in part by a government department or agency or a local authority, or

(iii) is managed by a voluntary organisation or a registered charity and provides care, support or supervision with a view to assisting those persons to be rehabilitated or resettled within the community; and

(c) which is not a care home;

"hostel for homeless people" means a hostel the main purpose of which is to provide accommodation together with care, support or supervision for homeless people with a view to assisting such persons to be rehabilitated or resettled within the community.

PART 5

SOCIAL RENTED SECTOR OTHER THAN TEMPORARY ACCOMMODATION

Application of Part 5

2.367 30.—(1) This Part—

(a) applies to renters who are liable to make rent payments to a provider of social housing; but

(b) does not apply to any renter who falls within paragraph 20(1)(b) (temporary accommodation).

(2) Sub-paragraph (1) applies irrespective of whether renters are also liable to make service charge payments.

Reduction in certain cases of amounts to be taken into account

Deduction from relevant payments of amounts relating to use of particular accommodation

2.368 31. In determining the amount of any relevant payment to be taken into account under paragraph 6, a deduction is to be made for any amount which the Secretary of State is satisfied—

(a) is included in the relevant payment; but

(b) relates to the supply to the accommodation of a commodity (such as water or fuel) for use by any member of the renter's extended benefit unit.

Power to apply to rent officer if relevant payments excessive

32.—(1) Sub-paragraph (2) applies where it appears to the Secretary of State that the amount of any relevant payment for which the renter is liable in respect of accommodation occupied by the renter is greater than it is reasonable to meet by way of the housing costs element under this Part.

(2) The Secretary of State may apply to a rent officer for a determination to be made as to the amount of the relevant payment by the officer in exercise of the officer's Housing Act functions.

(3) Sub-paragraph (4) applies in any case where a rent officer determines that a landlord might, at the time of the application under sub-paragraph (2), reasonably have expected to obtain a lower amount of the description of relevant payment referred to the rent officer.

(4) The lower amount determined by the rent officer is to be used in making the calculation under this Part, instead of the amount of the relevant payment for which the renter is liable, unless the Secretary of State is satisfied that it is not appropriate to use that lower amount.

The calculation of the housing costs element under this Part

The amount of housing costs element

33. The amount of the renter's housing costs element under this Part is to be calculated by reference to the formula—

$$S - HCC$$

where—

"S" is the amount resulting from whichever of paragraph 34 or 35 applies in the renter's case, and

"HCC" is the sum of the housing cost contributions (if any) under paragraph 13.

Determining the amount from which HCC deductions are to be made

34. Except where paragraph 35 applies, amount S referred to in paragraph 33 is to be found as follows:

Step 1

Determine which relevant payments are to be taken into account under paragraph 6 and determine the amount of each of them (applying paragraphs 31 and 32(3) and (4) as necessary).

Step 2

Determine the period in respect of which each relevant payment is payable and, in accordance with paragraph 7, determine the amount of the payment in respect of a month.

Step 3

If there is more than one relevant payment, add together the amounts determined in step 2 in relation to all relevant payments.

Step 4

Determine under paragraph 36(1) whether an under-occupation deduction is to be made and, if one is to be made, determine the amount of the deduction under paragraph 36(2) and deduct it from the amount resulting from step 2 or 3 (as the case may be).

The result is amount S from which the sum of the housing costs contributions are to be deducted under paragraph 33.

Determining the amount from which HCC deductions are to be made: joint tenants

35.—(1) This paragraph applies where, in respect of the accommodation occupied by the renter, one or more persons other than the renter is liable to make relevant payments which are of the same description as those for which the renter is liable and which are to be taken into account under paragraph 6.

(2) Amount S referred to in paragraph 33 is to be found as follows:

2.369

2.370

2.371

2.372

2.373

2.374

2.375

2.376

Step 1

2.377   Determine the total of all relevant payments referred to in sub-paragraph (1) for which the renter and others are liable in respect of the accommodation taken as a whole (applying paragraphs 31 and 32(3) and (4) as necessary).

Step 2

2.378   Determine the period in respect of which each relevant payment is payable and, in accordance with paragraph 7, determine the amount of the payment in respect of a month.

Step 3

2.379   Add together all of the amounts determined in step 2 in relation to all relevant payments.

Step 4

2.380   Find amount S in accordance with whichever of sub-paragraphs (3) to (5) applies in the renter's case.

The result is amount S from which the sum of the housing costs contributions are to be deducted under paragraph 33.

(3) Where the only persons liable to make relevant payments are listed persons, amount S is the amount resulting from step 3 in sub-paragraph (2) less the amount of the under-occupation deduction (if any) required by paragraph 36.

(4) Where the persons liable for the relevant payments are one or more listed persons and one or more other persons, amount S is to be found by the applying the formula—

$$\left(\frac{A}{B}\right) \times C$$

where—

"A" is the amount resulting from step 3 in sub-paragraph (2),

"B" is the total number of all persons (including listed persons) liable to make the relevant payments, and

"C" is the number of listed persons [5 liable to make relevant payments].

(5) If the Secretary of State is satisfied that it would be unreasonable to determine amount S in accordance with sub-paragraph (4), amount S is to be determined in such manner as the Secretary of State considers appropriate in all the circumstances, having regard (among other things) to the number of persons liable and the proportion of the relevant payments for which each of them is liable.

Under-occupancy deduction

2.381   **36.**—(1) A deduction for under-occupancy is to be made under this paragraph where the number of bedrooms in the accommodation exceeds the number of bedrooms to which the renter is entitled under paragraphs 8 to 12.

(2) Where a deduction is to be made, the amount of the deduction is to be determined by the formula—

$$A \times B$$

where—

"A"—

    (a) in relation to any deduction under paragraph 34, is the amount resulting from step 2 or 3 in that paragraph (as the case may be), or

    (b) in relation to any deduction under paragraph 35(3), is the amount resulting from step 3 in paragraph 35(2);

"B" is the relevant percentage.

(3) The relevant percentage is 14% in the case of one excess bedroom.

(4) The relevant percentage is 25% in the case of two or more excess bedrooms.

(5) No deduction for under-occupation is to be made in calculating the amount of the renter's housing costs element under this Part in any case to which regulation 26(4) to (6) (shared ownership) applies.

AMENDMENTS

1. Universal Credit (Miscellaneous Amendments) Regulations 2013 (SI 2013/803), reg.2(3)(a) (April 29, 2013).
2. Universal Credit (Miscellaneous Amendments) Regulations 2013 (SI 2013/803), reg.2(3)(b)(i) (April 29, 2013).
3. Universal Credit (Miscellaneous Amendments) Regulations 2013 (SI 2013/803), reg.2(3)(b)(ii) (April 29, 2013).
4. Universal Credit (Miscellaneous Amendments) Regulations 2013 (SI 2013/803), reg.2(3)(e) (April 29, 2013).
5. Social Security (Miscellaneous Amendments) (No.2) Regulations 2013 (SI 2013/1508), reg.3(10) (July 29, 2013).
6. Housing Benefit and Universal Credit (Size Criteria) (Miscellaneous Amendments) Regulations 2013 (SI 2013/2828), reg.4 (December 4, 2013).

DEFINITIONS

"the Act"—see reg.2.
"assessment period"—see WRA 2012, ss.40 and 7(2) and reg.21.
"attendance allowance"—see reg.2.
"care leaver"—see regs 2 and 8.
"carer's allowance"—see reg.2.
"child"—see WRA 2012, s.40.
"claim"—*ibid.*
"claimant"—see WRA 2012, s.40.
"couple"—see WRA 2012, ss.39 and 40.
"disability living allowance"—see reg.2.
"disabled"—see WRA 2012, s.40.
"foster parent"—see reg.2.
"joint claimants"—see WRA 2012, s.40.
"local authority"—see reg.2.
"personal independence payment"—*ibid.*
"prisoner"—*ibid.*
"qualifying young person"—see WRA 2012, ss.40 and 10(5) and regs 2 and 5.
"registered as blind"—see reg.2.
"single person"—see WRA 2012, ss.40 and 1(2)(a).

GENERAL NOTE

Paras 1–7   2.382
This Schedule concerns the calculation of the housing costs element for "renters" (see para.1(2)). For the definition of "renter" see para.2. References to "joint renters" are to joint claimants who are renters (para.1(2)).

For a renter (or joint renters) to be entitled to a housing costs element under this Schedule, s/he must meet the payment, liability and occupation conditions in respect of one or more "relevant payments" (para.6(1) and (2)).

"Relevant payments" for the purpose of Sch.4 mean rent payments (for the meaning of rent payments see para.2 of Sch.1) and service charges (on which see paras 7 and 8 of Sch.1) (if payable) (para.3)). Relevant payments are calculated as a monthly amount (see para.7).

Note para.4 which excludes any 16 or 17 year old renter who is a care leaver (defined in reg.8(4)) from entitlement to a housing costs element.

Part 3 of this Schedule contains general provisions, which apply to all calculations under the Schedule. The rules in Pt 4 apply to renters in the private sector or who occupy temporary accommodation. Part 5 applies to renters in the social rented sector.

A housing costs element for renters is normally paid to the claimant as part of his/her universal credit award. However, it can be paid to another person (e.g.

the claimant's landlord) if this appears to the Secretary of State to be necessary to protect the interest of the claimant, his/her partner, a child or qualifying young person for whom the claimant or his/her partner is responsible or a severely disabled person in respect of whom the claimant receives a carer element (see reg.58(1) of the Claims and Payments Regulations 2013).

Note also reg.39(4) of the Decisions and Appeals Regulations 2013 which provides that if the Secretary of State considers that he does not have all the relevant information or evidence to decide what housing costs element to award, the decision will be made on the basis of the housing costs element that can immediately be awarded.

Paras 8–12 and 26–29

In order to calculate the amount of a renter's housing costs element, it is first necessary to decide the number of bedrooms that s/he is allowed under "the size criteria" (para.8). This depends on who counts as a member of the renter's "extended benefit unit".

The extended benefit unit comprises the renter, or joint renters, any child or qualifying young person for whom the renter or either joint renter is responsible (see reg.4), and any non-dependant (para.9(1)).

A non-dependant is a person who normally lives in the renter's (or joint renters') accommodation and who is not excluded under para.9(2). There is no definition of "normally lives in the accommodation" but see the notes to reg.3(1) of the Income Support Regulations in Vol.II of this series on the general meaning of "residing with".

See paras 10–12 for the number of bedrooms allowed. Bedroom is not defined.

Note that in the case of renters in the private sector or who occupy temporary accommodation (see para.21 for the meaning of "temporary accommodation") the maximum number of bedrooms allowed is four (see para.26). There is no limit for renters in the social rented sector. In addition, in the case of private sector renters and those in temporary accommodation, the housing costs element for single claimants (including a member of a couple who is claiming as a single person: see reg.3(3)) aged under 35, with no children or qualifying young persons for whom they are responsible and no non-dependants, is restricted to the local housing allowance rate for one bedroom shared accommodation, unless they are exempt from this restriction (see paras 27–29).

Under para.10, a renter is allowed one bedroom for each of the categories of people in his/her extended benefit unit listed in sub-para.(1). If a person falls into more than one category, s/he is treated as in the category that results in the renter being allowed the lowest number of bedrooms (see sub-para.(2)). Paragraph F3112 ADM gives the following example of when sub-para.(2) might apply. A couple have four children, two boys aged 15 and 6 and two girls aged 12 and 8. The two boys could be allocated one room and the two girls one room under sub-para.(1)(e). Alternatively, having allocated the two girls one room under sub-para.(1)(e), the boys could be allocated one room each under sub-para.(1)(f). But as the first alternative results in a fewer number of bedrooms, that will be the number of bedrooms (two) that is allocated.

Note that joint renters (i.e. joint claimants: see para.1(2)) are allowed one bedroom but a non-dependant couple will be allocated one bedroom each (although a housing cost contribution (see paras 13–16) may be made in respect of each of them).

Under para.12, a renter is allowed additional bedrooms for each of the following conditions that s/he meets: (i) the overnight care condition (for the test for this see sub-para.(3)); (ii) the foster parent condition (see sub-paras (4) and (5) for the test); or (iii) the disabled child condition (see sub-para.(6) for the test). If the renter satisfied two or more of the conditions, the number of additional bedrooms allowed will be the total for both or all conditions (sub-para.(9)).

If both joint renters (i.e. joint claimants: see para.1(2)) satisfy the overnight care condition, they will only be allowed one additional bedroom (sub-para.(7)). (Note that the overnight care condition does not apply in the case of a disabled child who needs overnight care.) Similarly, only one additional bedroom will be allowed if both joint renters meet the foster parent condition (sub-para.(7)). However, if one or both of them satisfies both these conditions, one additional bedroom will be allowed in respect of each condition.

Example

Amy and Nick are foster parents to two children. Nick also meets the overnight care condition. They are allowed two additional bedrooms. One for satisfying the overnight care condition and one for satisfying the foster parent condition.

If the disabled child condition is met, one additional bedroom will be allowed for each disabled child (see sub-para.(8)).

Note that the disabled child condition applies if it is the renter (or joint renters) *or* a member of the renter's extended benefit unit who is responsible for the disabled child. The requirement under sub-para.(6)(b) that the child is "not reasonably able to share a room with another child" will be a matter of judgment, depending on the circumstances.

See para.11 for the circumstances in which a renter, a child or qualifying young person or a non-dependant will continue to count for the purpose of deciding the number of bedrooms allowed, despite being temporarily absent. Note also the temporary absence rule for a claimant (or claimants) in para.9 of Sch.3.

See also reg.37 (run-on after a death). Under this provision if the claimant's partner, a child or qualifying young person for whom s/he was responsible, or a severely disabled person for whom s/he was caring dies, the claimant's universal credit award continues to be calculated as if the person had not died for the assessment period in which the death occurred and the following two assessment periods. Thus if such a death affects the number of bedrooms a renter is allowed, it will not do so for that run-on period.

The application of the size criteria has caused considerable controversy, particularly since its extension to tenants in the social rented sector for the purposes of housing benefit on April 1, 2013 and the introduction of the "under-occupation deduction" (see below). A number of challenges have been made to the legality of the size criteria, including *Burnip, Trengove and Gorry v Secretary of State for Work and Pensions* [2012] EWCA Civ 629. This has led to some extension of the criteria—see para.12. However, this extension still does not provide, for example, for couples who are unable to share a bedroom due to disability, claimants who have mental health problems or separated parents who have shared caring responsibilities. A further challenge by a number of claimants with differing circumstances was mounted in *R (on the application of MA & Ors) v Secretary of State for Work and Pensions and Ors* [2013] EWHC 2213. The claimants lost but the matter was pursued to the Court of Appeal and was heard on January 20, 2014. On February 21, 2014, the Court of Appeal dismissed the appeal, ruling that while the under-occupation deduction discriminated against people with disabilities the discriminatory effect of the policy was justified.

Paras 13–16

After the calculation of the renter's (or joint renters') housing costs element has been carried out under Pt 4 or 5 of this Schedule, a deduction (referred to as a "housing cost contribution") is made for non-dependants, unless they, or the renter, or joint renters, are exempt. The deduction is £68 for each non-dependant who is a member of the renter's extended benefit unit.

Paras 17–19

See the notes to paras 4, 5 and 6 of Sch.3.

Paras 20–25

The housing costs element for private sector renters and those in temporary accommodation (as defined in para.21) is calculated by taking the lower of the renter's core rent and his/her cap rent and deducting from that amount any housing cost contributions (para.22).

Core rent

If the renter is solely liable to make the relevant payments, his/her core rent is the total of the monthly equivalents of the rent payments (as defined in para.2 of Sch.1) and service charges (see para.7 of Sch.1) that s/he is liable (or treated as liable) to pay (para.23).

If the renter is jointly liable with another person or persons to make the relevant payments, his/her core rent is worked out by taking the total of the monthly equivalents of the rent payments and service charges for which s/he and the other person(s) are liable for the whole accommodation and applying the following rules. If the only people who are jointly liable are "listed persons" (as defined in para.2) (i.e. the renter, his/her partner and any child or qualifying young person for whom either of them is responsible), the renter's core rent is that total amount. If the liability is with one or more people who are not listed persons, the total amount is divided by the number of people who are liable and multiplied by the number of listed persons who are liable to make the relevant payments. This is the renter's core rent. If, however, the Secretary of State (and on appeal a tribunal) is satisfied that it would be unreasonable to apportion the liability in this way, it is to be apportioned in a way that is appropriate in the circumstances. Paragraph F3197 ADM gives the following example of where such an adjustment might be appropriate. Two brothers are joint tenants of a three bedroom property. One brother has his daughter living with him and pays two thirds of the rent. The decision maker considers that this is reasonable and that the appropriate core rent for that brother is two thirds (not half) of the rent payable.

Cap rent

A renter's cap rent depends on the category of dwelling, i.e. how many bedrooms, s/he is allowed under the size criteria, subject to the four bedroom limit (see paras 8–2 and 26–29). His/her cap rent is the local housing allowance that applies at the time his/her housing costs element is calculated for that category of dwelling in the area in which s/he lives (para.25(1) and (2)). For how the cap rent is calculated if para.4 of Sch.3 (claimant housed in two dwellings by provider of social housing) applies, see the note to para.4 of Sch.3.

Paras 30–36

The housing costs element for social sector renters (other than those in temporary accommodation, as defined in para.21) is calculated as follows. First, a deduction is made from any relevant payments (as defined in para.6) of any amount that is for the supply of a commodity (e.g. water or fuel) to the accommodation for use by the renter or any member of his/her extended benefit unit (para.31). Secondly, if, on the application of the Secretary of State, a rent officer has determined that a landlord might reasonably expect to get a lower amount than the amount of the relevant payment the renter pays, that lower figure will be used in the calculation of the renter's housing costs element, unless the Secretary of State (or on appeal a tribunal) considers that it is not appropriate to use that lower amount (para.32(3) and (4)). An example might be where the rent is higher because it includes payment for modifications made to enable a disabled person to live in the property (see para. F3253 ADM) but the wording of para.32(4) is quite wide and is not restricted to this type of situation. Note, however, that (like housing benefit) there is no right of appeal against "so much of a decision as adopts a decision of a rent officer . . ." (para.6 of Sch.3 to the Decisions and Appeals Regulations 2013).

Thirdly, if the number of bedrooms in the accommodation is more than the number the renter is allowed under paras 8–12, an "under-occupation deduction" will be made. The reduction is 14 per cent in the case of one excess bedroom and 25 per cent in the case of two or more excess bedrooms.

If a renter is solely liable to make the relevant payments, this deduction will be made from the monthly equivalent of the total of the rent payments and service charges that s/he is liable (or treated as liable) to pay, as reduced in accordance with paras 31 and 32(3) and (4), if applicable (para.34, step 4).

If the renter is jointly liable with another person or persons to make the relevant payments, an under-occupancy deduction will only be made if the only people who are jointly liable are "listed persons" (as defined in para.2) (i.e. the renter, his/her partner and any child or qualifying young person for whom either of them is responsible) (para.35(3)). If the joint liability is with one or more people who are not listed persons, no under-occupancy deduction will be made (see para.35(4) and (5))

Note also that no under-occupancy deduction is made in the case of a shared ownership tenancy (see para.36(5)).

The rules for working out the amount of the renter's housing costs element if s/he is jointly liable with another person or persons to make the relevant payments are the same that apply for the purpose of working out a renter's core rent under Part 4 of this Schedule (paras 35(3)–(5)) (see above).

Finally, a deduction will be made for any housing cost contribution (para.33).

Regulation 26(3)

SCHEDULE 5

HOUSING COSTS ELEMENT FOR OWNER-OCCUPIERS

PART I

GENERAL

Introduction
1.—(1) This Schedule contains provisions about claimants to whom regulation 26(3) applies.

(2) Claimants who fall within sub-paragraph (1) are referred to in this Schedule as "owner-occupiers" (and references to "joint owner-occupiers" are to joint claimants to whom regulation 26(3) applies).

(3) Part 2 of this Schedule sets out an exception to section 11(1) of the Act for certain owner-occupiers in whose case an award of universal credit is not to include an amount of housing costs element calculated under this Schedule.

(4) Part 3 of this Schedule provides for a qualifying period that is to elapse before an amount of housing costs element calculated under this Schedule may be included in an owner-occupier's award of universal credit.

(5) Part 4 provides for the calculation of the amount of housing costs element to be included under this Schedule in an owner-occupier's award of universal credit.

2.383

Interpretation
2. In this Schedule—
"alternative finance payments" has the meaning given in paragraph 6 of Schedule 1;
"joint owner-occupier" has the meaning given in paragraph 1;
"loan interest payments" has the meaning given in paragraph 5 of Schedule 1;
"owner-occupier" means a single owner-occupier within the meaning of paragraph 1(2) or each of joint owner-occupiers;
"qualifying period" has the meaning given in paragraph 5;
"relevant payments" has the meaning given in paragraph 3;
"standard rate" has the meaning given in paragraph 12.

2.384

"Relevant payments" for purposes of this Schedule
3.—(1) "Relevant payments" means one or more payments of any of the following descriptions—
    (a) owner-occupier payments;
    (b) service charge payments.

(2) "Owner-occupier payments" has the meaning given in paragraph 4 of Schedule 1.

(3) "Service charge payments" is to be understood in accordance with paragraphs 7 and 8 of that Schedule.

2.385

Part 2

Exception to Inclusion of Housing Costs Element

No housing costs element where owner-occupier has any earned income

2.386   **4.**—(1) Section 11(1) of the Act (housing costs) does not apply to any owner-occupier in relation to an assessment period where—

   (a) the owner-occupier has any earned income; or

   (b) if the owner-occupier is a member of a couple, either member of the couple has any earned income.

(2) Sub-paragraph (1) applies irrespective of the nature of the work engaged in, its duration or the amount of the earned income.

(3) Nothing in this paragraph prevents an amount calculated under Schedule 4 from being included in the award of any claimant who falls within regulation 26(4) to (6) (shared ownership).

Part 3

No Housing Costs Element for Qualifying Period

No housing costs element under this Schedule for qualifying period

2.387   **5.**—(1) An owner-occupier's award of universal credit is not to include any amount of housing costs element calculated under this Schedule until the beginning of the assessment period that follows the assessment period in which the qualifying period ends.

(2) "Qualifying period" means a period of—

   (a) in the case of a new award, 3 consecutive assessment periods in relation to which—

      (i) the owner-occupier has been receiving universal credit, and

      (ii) would otherwise qualify for the inclusion of an amount calculated under this Schedule in their award;

   (b) in any case where an amount calculated under this Schedule has for any reason ceased to be included in the award, 3 consecutive assessment periods in relation to which the owner-occupier would otherwise qualify for the inclusion of an amount calculated under this Schedule in their award.

(3) Where, before the end of a qualifying period, an owner-occupier for any reason ceases to qualify for the inclusion of an amount calculated under this Schedule—

   (a) that qualifying period stops running; and

   (b) a new qualifying period starts only when the owner-occupier again meets the requirements of sub-paragraph (2)(a) or (b).

Application of paragraph 5: receipt of JSA and ESA

2.388   **6.**—(1) This paragraph applies to any owner-occupier who immediately before the commencement of an award of universal credit is entitled to—

   (a) a jobseeker's allowance; or

   (b) an employment and support allowance.

(2) In determining when the qualifying period in paragraph 5 ends in relation to the owner-occupier, any period that comprises only days on which the owner-occupier was receiving a benefit referred to in sub-paragraph (1) may be treated as if it were the whole or part of one or more assessment periods, as determined by the number of days on which any such benefit was received.

Application of paragraph 5: joint owner-occupiers ceasing to be a couple

2.389   **7.**—(1) This paragraph applies where—

   (a) an award of universal credit to joint owner-occupiers is terminated because they cease to be a couple;

   (b) a further award is made to one of them (or to each of them); and

   (c) in relation to the further award (or in relation to each further award), the occupation condition is met in respect of the same accommodation as that occupied by the joint owner-occupiers as their home.

(2) In determining when the qualifying period in paragraph 5 ends in relation to the further award (or each further award), the whole or part of any assessment period which would have counted in relation to the award that is terminated is to be carried forward and taken into account in relation to the further award (or each further award).

(3) But where, immediately before the joint owner-occupiers' award was terminated, an

amount of housing costs element calculated under this Schedule was already included in the award, no qualifying period under paragraph 5 applies to the owner-occupier in relation to the commencement of the further award (or each further award).

(4) For the purposes of sub-paragraph (1)(b), it is irrelevant whether the further award—
- (a) is made on a claim; or
- (b) by virtue of regulation 9(6) of the Universal Credit, Personal Independence Payment, Jobseeker's Allowance and Employment and Support Allowance (Claims and Payments) Regulations 2013 is made without a claim.

PART 4

CALCULATION OF AMOUNT OF HOUSING COSTS ELEMENT FOR OWNER-OCCUPIERS

Payments to be taken into account
8.—(1) Where an owner-occupier meets the payment condition, liability condition and occupation condition in respect of one or more relevant payments and the qualifying period has ended, each of the relevant payments is to be taken into account for the purposes of the calculation under this Part.   2.390

(2) No account is to be taken of any amount of a relevant payment to the extent that the conditions referred to in sub-paragraph (1) are not met in respect of that amount.

(3) Any particular payment for which an owner-occupier is liable is not to be brought into account more than once, whether in relation to the same or a different owner-occupier (but this does not prevent different payments of the same description being brought into account in respect of an assessment period).

The amount of housing costs element
9. The amount of the owner-occupier's housing costs element under this Schedule is the aggregate of the amounts resulting from paragraphs 10, 11 and 13 in respect of all relevant payments which are to be taken into account under paragraph 8.   2.391

Amount in respect of interest on loans
10.—(1) This paragraph provides for the calculation of the amount to be included in the owner-occupier's housing costs element under this Schedule in respect of relevant payments which are loan interest payments.   2.392

(2) Subject to sub-paragraphs (3) to (5), the amount in respect of the loan or loans to which the payments relate is to be calculated as follows.

Step 1

Determine the amount of the capital for the time being owing in connection with each loan.   2.393

Step 2

If there is more than one loan, add together the amounts determined in step 1.   2.394

Step 3

Identify which is the lower of these two amounts—   2.395
- (a) the amount resulting from step 1 or 2 (as the case may be); and
- (b) £200,000,
and, if both amounts are the same, that is the identified amount.

Step 4

Apply the formula—   2.396

$$(A \times SR / 12)$$

where—
"A" is the amount identified in step 3, and
"SR" is the standard rate that applies at the date of the calculation (see paragraph 12).
The result is the amount to be included under this Schedule in respect of loan interest payments.

(3) In the application of sub-paragraph (2) to a loan (or any part of a loan) which was

taken out for the purpose of making necessary adaptations to the accommodation to meet the disablement needs of a person specified in paragraph 5 of Schedule 3—

    (a) the loan (or the part of the loan) is to be disregarded for the purposes of steps 2 and 3; and

    (b) "A" in step 4 is to be read as the amount resulting from step 1 in respect of the loan (or the sum of those amounts if there is more than one loan taken out for the purpose of making such adaptations) plus the amount (if any) resulting from step 3 in relation to any other loan or loans.

(4) Any variation in the amount of capital for the time being owing in connection with a loan is not to be taken into account after the relevant date until such time as the Secretary of State recalculates the amount under this Schedule by reference to the amount of capital owing in connection with the loan—

    (a) on the first anniversary of the relevant date; or

    (b) in respect of any variation after the first anniversary, on the next anniversary which follows the date of the variation.

(5) "Relevant date", in relation to an owner-occupier, means the date on which an amount of housing costs element calculated under this Schedule is first included in the owner-occupier's award.

Amount in respect of alternative finance arrangements

2.397   **11.**—(1) This paragraph provides for the calculation of the amount to be included in the owner-occupier's housing costs element under this Schedule in respect of relevant payments which are alternative finance payments.

(2) The amount in respect of the alternative finance arrangements to which the payments relate is to be calculated as follows.

Step 1

2.398   Determine the purchase price of the accommodation to which the alternative finance payments relate.

Step 2

2.399   Identify which is the lower of these two amounts—

    (a) the amount resulting from Step 1; and

    (b) £200,000,

and, if both amounts are the same, that is the identified amount.

Step 3

2.400   Apply the formula—

$$(A \times SR / 12)$$

where—

"A" is the amount identified in step 2, and

"SR" is the standard rate that applies at the date of the calculation (see paragraph 12).

The result is the amount to be included under this Schedule in respect of alternative finance payments.

(3) "Purchase price" means the price paid by a party to the alternative financial arrangements other than the owner-occupier in order to acquire the interest in the accommodation to which those arrangements relate less the amount of any initial payment made by the owner-occupier in connection with the acquisition of that interest.

Standard rate to be applied under paragraphs 10 and 11

2.401   **12.**—(1) The standard rate is the average mortgage rate published by the Bank of England which, immediately before this Schedule comes into force, has effect for the purposes of paragraph 12 of Schedule 3 to the Income Support (General) Regulations 1987 (which makes provision as to the standard rate to be used in determining amounts applicable to a claimant in respect of income support).

(2) The standard rate is to be varied each time that sub-paragraph (3) applies.

(3) This sub-paragraph applies when, on any reference day, the Bank of England publishes an average mortgage rate which differs by 0.5% or more from the standard rate that applies on that reference day (whether it applies by virtue of sub-paragraph (1) or by virtue of a previous application of this sub-paragraph).

(4) The average mortgage rate published on that reference day then becomes the new standard rate in accordance with sub-paragraph (5).

(5) Any variation in the standard rate by virtue of sub-paragraphs (2) to (4) comes into effect—

(a) for the purposes of sub-paragraph (3), on the day after the reference day referred to in sub-paragraph (4);

(b) for the purpose of calculating the amount of housing costs element to be included under this Schedule in an owner-occupier's award, on the day specified by the Secretary of State for that purpose.

(6) At least 7 days before a variation of the standard rate comes into effect under sub-paragraph (5)(b), the Secretary of State must arrange for notice to be published on a publicly accessible website of—

(a) the new standard rate; and

(b) the day specified in relation to that rate under sub-paragraph (5)(b).

(7) In this paragraph—

"average mortgage rate" means the effective interest rate (non-seasonally adjusted) of United Kingdom resident banks and building societies for loans to households secured on dwellings published by the Bank of England in respect of the most recent period specified for that rate at the time of publication;

"reference day" means any day falling on or after the date on which this Schedule comes into force.

Amount in respect of service charge payments

13.—(1) This paragraph provides for the calculation of the amount to be included in the owner-occupier's housing costs element under this Schedule in respect of relevant payments which are service charge payments.   **2.402**

(2) The amount in respect of the service charge payments is to be calculated as follows.

Step 1

Determine the amount of each service charge payment.   **2.403**

Step 2

Determine the period in respect of which each service charge payment is payable and determine the amount of the payment in respect of a month (see sub-paragraphs (3) and (4)).   **2.404**

Step 3

If there is more than one service charge payment, add together the amounts determined in step 2.   **2.405**

The result is the amount to be included under this Schedule in respect of service charge payments.

(3) Where the period in respect of which an owner-occupier is liable to make a service charge payment is not a month, an amount is to be calculated as the monthly equivalent, so for example—

(a) weekly payments are multiplied by 52 and divided by 12;

(b) four-weekly payments are multiplied by 13 and divided by 12;

(c) three-monthly payments are multiplied by 4 and divided by 12; and

(d) annual payments are divided by 12.

(4) Where an owner-occupier is liable for service charge payments under arrangements that provide for one or more service charge free periods, the monthly equivalent is to be calculated over 12 months by reference to the total number of service charge payments which the owner-occupier is liable to make in that 12 month period.

(5) "Service charge free period" means any period in respect of which the owner-occupier has no liability to make one or more of the service charge payments which are to be taken into account under paragraph 8.

DEFINITIONS

"the Act"—see reg.2.

"assessment period"—see WRA 2012, ss.40 and 7(2) and reg.21.

"claim"—see WRA 2012, s.40.

"claimant"—*ibid.*

"couple"—see WRA 2012, ss.39 and 40.
"earned income"—see reg.2.
"employment and support allowance"—*ibid.*
"jobseeker's allowance"—*ibid.*
"personal independence payment"—*ibid.*

GENERAL NOTE

2.406   *Paras 1–4*
This Schedule concerns the calculation of the housing costs element for "owner-occupiers" (see para.1(2)). For the definition of "owner-occupier" see para.2. References to "joint owner-occupiers" are to joint claimants who are owner-occupiers (para.1(2)).

For an owner-occupier (or joint owner-occupier) to be entitled to a housing costs element under this Schedule, s/he must meet the payment, liability and occupation conditions in respect of one or more "relevant payments" (as defined in para.3) and the qualifying period (see paras 5–7) must have ended.

"Relevant payments" for the purposes of Sch.5 are owner-occupier payments (for the meaning of owner-occupier payments see para.4 of Sch.1) and service charges (on which see paras 7 and 8 of Sch.1). If the claimant (or claimants) is only liable for service charges payments, these will be calculated under this Schedule (see reg.26(3)). But if the claimant has a shared ownership tenancy, any service charges are calculated in accordance with Sch.4 (reg.26(5)).

Note the significant exclusion in para.4 from entitlement to a housing costs element under Sch.5. If an owner-occupier, or if s/he is a member of a couple, either member of the couple, has *any* earned income in an assessment period (i.e. month), s/he will not be entitled to a housing costs element in that assessment period. However, in the case of a shared-ownership tenancy, rent payments and service charges can still be met (para.4(3)).

Paras 5–7
There is a waiting period (referred to as "a qualifying period") for owner-occupier and service charges payments. In the case of a new award of universal credit, a housing costs element cannot be included until there have been three consecutive assessment periods (i.e. months) during which the owner-occupier has been receiving universal credit *and* would otherwise have qualified for a housing costs element under Sch.5 (para.5(2)(a)). A housing costs element is included from the start of the next assessment period. If, once awarded, there is a break in entitlement to a housing costs element under Sch.5 (e.g. because of earnings), the owner-occupier has to serve a further three consecutive months during which s/he would otherwise qualify for a housing costs element before s/he can be awarded a housing costs element under Sch.5 again (para.5(2)(b)). This applies even if the owner-occupier continues to be entitled to universal credit during the break in entitlement to a housing costs element under Sch.5. If during a waiting period an owner-occupier ceases to qualify for a housing costs element under Sch.5, that waiting period ends and a new waiting period will have to be served (para.5(3)).

Paragraphs 6 and 7 contain exceptions to this rule.

If immediately before the owner-occupier's award of universal credit began, s/he was entitled to "new style" JSA or "new style" ESA, the days that s/he was only receiving one of these benefits can count towards the waiting period (para.6).

Under para.7, if a universal credit award made to joint owner-occupiers comes to an end because they have ceased to be a couple, and a further award is made to one of them who continues to occupy the same accommodation as they did when they were a couple, the further award will include a housing costs element under Sch.5 without a waiting period if a housing costs element was included in the joint award. If a housing costs element was not yet included in the joint award, any assessment period, or part of an assessment period, which counted towards the waiting period under the joint award counts towards the waiting period for the new award. If both members of the former couple remain in the same accommodation and both claim and are awarded universal credit again, this provision will apply to both of them.

The waiting period may also be extinguished or reduced under reg.29 of the Transitional Provisions Regulations 2013, which applies where the owner-occupier (or his/her former partner) was previously entitled to income support, JSA or ESA that included help with housing costs or did not yet do so only because a waiting period was being served.

Paras 9–13

There is an upper limit of £200,000 for eligible loans (see para.10(2), step 3) and for the purchase price (defined in para.11(5)) of the accommodation in the case of alternative finance arrangements (see para.11(2), step 2).

However, if a loan (or part of a loan) was taken out to make necessary adaptations to the accommodation to meet the disablement needs of the claimant (or claimants: s.40 WRA 2012) or any child or qualifying young person for whom the claimant (or either joint claimant) is responsible, that loan (or part of the loan) is disregarded in applying the £200,000 limit (para.10(3)). The person with disablement needs must be in receipt of the middle or highest rate of the care component of disability living allowance, the daily living component of personal independence payment (either rate), attendance allowance or armed forces independence payment (see the definition of "attendance allowance" in reg.2 which includes armed forces independence payment).

To calculate the housing costs element for loan interest payments, the amount of the capital outstanding on the eligible loan or loans (subject to the £200,000 limit) is multiplied by the standard rate (currently 3.63 per cent) (para.10(2), steps 3 and 4). If the £200,000 limit applies, the housing costs element will also include loan interest payments on any loan (or part of a loan) for adaptations for disablement needs on top of loan interest payments on the £200,000 (para.10(3)).

In the case of alternative finance arrangements, the housing costs element is the "purchase price" of the accommodation (subject to the £200,000 limit) multiplied by the standard rate (para.11(2)). The "purchase price" of the accommodation is the price paid by a party to the alternative finance arrangements, other than the owner-occupier, to acquire an interest in the accommodation, minus the amount of any initial payment made by the owner-occupier in acquiring that interest (para.11(3)).

The amount for service charges that can be included in an owner-occupier's housing costs element is the monthly equivalent of the actual service charges (see para.13).

Note:

- No "housing cost contribution" for a non-dependant is made in the case of amounts awarded under Sch.5 (this is to be contrasted with the position under income support, JSA and ESA).

- Any increase, or decrease, in the amount of a loan during the currency of an award is only taken into account from the anniversary date (see para.10(4) and (5)). But if a *new* loan is taken out that is secured on the home, that would seem to be a change of circumstances (to be taken into account from the first day of the assessment period in which the loan was taken out: see para.20 of Sch.1 to the Decisions and Appeals Regulations 2013).

- A housing costs element that is awarded in respect of payments of interest on a loan will be paid direct to the lender (see reg.59 of, and Sch.5 to, the Claims and Payments Regulations 2013).

- Under reg.39(4) of the Decisions and Appeals Regulations 2013, if the Secretary of State considers that he does not have all the relevant information or evidence to decide what housing costs element to award, the decision will be made on the basis of the housing costs element that can immediately be awarded.

Regulation 39(2) and(3)

SCHEDULE 6

ASSESSMENT OF WHETHER A CLAIMANT HAS LIMITED CAPABILITY FOR WORK

PART I

2.407

PHYSICAL DISABILITIES

(1)	(2)			(3)
Activity	Descriptors			Points
1. Mobilising unaided by another person with or without a walking stick, manual wheelchair or other aid if such aid is normally or could reasonably be worn or used.	1	(a)	Cannot, unaided by another person, either:	15
		(i)	mobilise more than 50 metres on level ground without stopping in order to avoid significant discomfort or exhaustion; or	
		(ii)	repeatedly mobilise 50 metres within a reasonable timescale because of significant discomfort or exhaustion.	
		(b)	Cannot, unaided by another person, mount or descend two steps even with the support of a handrail.	9
		(c)	Cannot, unaided by another person, either:	9
		(i)	mobilise more than 100 metres on level ground without stopping in order to avoid significant discomfort or exhaustion; or	
		(ii)	repeatedly mobilise 100 metres within a reasonable timescale because of significant discomfort or exhaustion.	
		(d)	Cannot, unaided by another person, either:	6
		(i)	mobilise more than 200 metres on level ground without stopping in order to avoid significant discomfort or exhaustion; or	
		(ii)	repeatedly mobilise 200 metres within a reasonable timescale because of significant discomfort or exhaustion.	
		(e)	None of the above applies.	0
2. Standing and sitting.	2	(a)	Cannot move between one seated position and another seated position which are located next to one another without receiving physical assistance from another person.	15

278

(1)	(2)	(3)
Activity	Descriptors	Points
	(b) Cannot, for the majority of the time, remain at a work station: (i) standing unassisted by another person (even if free to move around); (ii) sitting (even in an adjustable chair); or (iii) a combination of paragraphs (i) and (ii), for more than 30 minutes, before needing to move away in order to avoid significant discomfort or exhaustion.	9
	(c) Cannot, for the majority of the time, remain at a work station: (i) standing unassisted by another person (even if free to move around); (ii) sitting (even in an adjustable chair); or (iii) a combination of paragraphs (i) and (ii), for more than an hour before needing to move away in order to avoid significant discomfort or exhaustion.	6
	(d) None of the above applies.	0
3. Reaching.	3 (a) Cannot raise either arm as if to put something in the top pocket of a coat or jacket.	15
	(b) Cannot raise either arm to top of head as if to put on a hat.	9
	(c) Cannot raise either arm above head height as if to reach for something.	6
	(d) None of the above applies.	0
4. Picking up and moving or transferring by the use of the upper body and arms.	4 (a) Cannot pick up and move a 0.5 litre carton full of liquid.	15
	(b) Cannot pick up and move a one litre carton full of liquid.	9
	(c) Cannot transfer a light but bulky object such as an empty cardboard box.	6
	(d) None of the above applies.	0
5. Manual dexterity.	5 (a) Cannot press a button (such as a telephone keypad) with either hand or cannot turn the pages of a book with either hand.	15
	(b) Cannot pick up a £1 coin or equivalent with either hand.	15
	(c) Cannot use a pen or pencil to make a meaningful mark with either hand.	9
	(d) Cannot single-handedly use a suitable keyboard or mouse.	9
	(e) None of the above applies.	0
6. Making self understood through speaking, writing, typing, or other means which are normally or could reasonably be used, unaided by another person.	6 (a) Cannot convey a simple message, such as the presence of a hazard.	15
	(b) Has significant difficulty conveying a simple message to strangers.	15
	(c) Has some difficulty conveying a simple message to strangers.	6
	(d) None of the above applies.	0

(1)	(2)	(3)
Activity	Descriptors	Points
7. Understanding communication by: (i) verbal means (such as hearing or lip reading) alone; (ii) non-verbal means (such as reading 16 point print or Braille) alone; or (iii) a combination of sub-paragraphs (i) and (ii), using any aid that is normally or could reasonably be used, unaided by another person.	7 (a) Cannot understand a simple message, such as the location of a fire escape, due to sensory impairment.	15
	(b) Has significant difficulty understanding a simple message from a stranger due to sensory impairment.	15
	(c) Has some difficulty understanding a simple message from a stranger due to sensory impairment.	6
	(d) None of the above applies.	0
8. Navigation and maintaining safety using a guide dog or other aid if either or both are normally used or could reasonably be used.	8 (a) Unable to navigate around familiar surroundings, without being accompanied by another person, due to sensory impairment.	15
	(b) Cannot safely complete a potentially hazardous task such as crossing the road, without being accompanied by another person, due to sensory impairment.	5
	(c) Unable to navigate around unfamiliar surroundings, without being accompanied by another person, due to sensory impairment.	9
	(d) None of the above applies.	0
9. Absence or loss of control whilst conscious leading to extensive evacuation of the bowel and/or bladder, other than enuresis (bed-wetting), despite the wearing or use of any aids or adaptations which are normally or could reasonably be worn or used.	9 (a) At least once a month experiences: (i) loss of control leading to extensive evacuation of the bowel and/or voiding of the bladder; or (ii) substantial leakage of the contents of a collecting device, sufficient to require cleaning and a change in clothing.	15
	(b) The majority of the time is at risk of loss of control leading to extensive evacuation of the bowel and/or voiding of the bladder, sufficient to require cleaning and a change in clothing, if not able to reach a toilet quickly.	6
	(c) Neither of the above applies.	0
10. Consciousness during waking moments.	10 (a) At least once a week, has an involuntary episode of lost or altered consciousness resulting in significantly disrupted awareness or concentration.	15
	(b) At least once a month, has an involuntary episode of lost or altered consciousness resulting in significantly disrupted awareness or concentration.	6
	(c) Neither of the above applies.	0

PART II

MENTAL, COGNITIVE AND INTELLECTUAL FUNCTION ASSESSMENT   **2.408**

(1)	(2)			(3)
Activity	Descriptors			Points
11. Learning tasks.	11	(a)	Cannot learn how to complete a simple task, such as setting an alarm clock.	15
		(b)	Cannot learn anything beyond a simple task, such as setting an alarm clock.	9
		(c)	Cannot learn anything beyond a moderately complex task, such as the steps involved in operating a washing machine to clean clothes.	6
		(d)	None of the above applies.	0
12. Awareness of everyday hazards (such as boiling water or sharp objects).	12	(a)	Reduced awareness of everyday hazards leads to a significant risk of:	15
		(i)	injury to self or others; or	
		(ii)	damage to property or possessions, such that the claimant requires supervision for the majority of the time to maintain safety.	
		(b)	Reduced awareness of everyday hazards leads to a significant risk of:	9
		(i)	injury to self or others; or	
		(ii)	damage to property or possessions, such that the claimant frequently requires supervision to maintain safety.	
		(c)	Reduced awareness of everyday hazards leads to a significant risk of:	6
		(i)	injury to self or others; or	
		(ii)	damage to property or possessions, such that the claimant occasionally requires supervision to maintain safety.	
		(d)	None of the above applies.	0
13. Initiating and completing personal action (which means planning, organisation, problem solving, prioritising or switching tasks).	13	(a)	Cannot, due to impaired mental function, reliably initiate or complete at least two sequential personal actions.	15
		(b)	Cannot, due to impaired mental function, reliably initiate or complete at least two sequential personal actions for the majority of the time.	9
		(c)	Frequently cannot, due to impaired mental function, reliably initiate or complete at least two sequential personal actions.	6
		(d)	None of the above applies.	0
14. Coping with change.	14	(a)	Cannot cope with any change to the extent that day to day life cannot be managed.	15
		(b)	Cannot cope with minor planned change (such as a pre-arranged change to the routine time scheduled for a lunch break), to the extent that, overall, day to day life is made significantly more difficult.	9

(1)	(2)		(3)
Activity	Descriptors		Points
	(c) Cannot cope with minor unplanned change (such as the timing of an appointment on the day it is due to occur), to the extent that, overall, day to day life is made significantly more difficult.		6
	(d) None of the above applies.		0
15. Getting about.	15 (a)	Cannot get to any place outside the claimant's home with which the claimant is familiar.	15
	(b)	Is unable to get to a specified place with which the claimant is familiar, without being accompanied by another person.	9
	(c)	Is unable to get to a specified place with which the claimant is unfamiliar without being accompanied by another person.	6
	(d)	None of the above applies.	0
16. Coping with social engagement due to cognitive impairment or mental disorder.	16 (a)	Engagement in social contact is always precluded due to difficulty relating to others or significant distress experienced by the claimant.	15
	(b)	Engagement in social contact with someone unfamiliar to the claimant is always precluded due to difficulty relating to others or significant distress experienced by the claimant.	9
	(c)	Engagement in social contact with someone unfamiliar to the claimant is not possible for the majority of the time due to difficulty relating to others or significant distress experienced by the claimant.	6
	(d)	None of the above applies.	0
17. Appropriateness of behaviour with other people, due to cognitive impairment or mental disorder.	17 (a)	Has, on a daily basis, uncontrollable episodes of aggressive or disinhibited behaviour that would be unreasonable in any workplace.	15
	(b)	Frequently has uncontrollable episodes of aggressive or disinhibited behaviour that would be unreasonable in any workplace.	15
	(c)	Occasionally has uncontrollable episodes of aggressive or disinhibited behaviour that would be unreasonable in any workplace.	9
	(d)	None of the above applies.	0

DEFINITIONS

"claimant"—see WRA 2012, s.40.
"limited capability for work"—see WRA 2012, ss.40 and 37(1).

GENERAL NOTE

2.409   See the notes to Sch.2 to the ESA Regulations 2008 in Vol.I of this series.

SCHEDULE 7

ASSESSMENT OF WHETHER A CLAIMANT HAS LIMITED CAPABILITY FOR
WORK AND WORK-RELATED ACTIVITY

Activity	Descriptors
1. Mobilising unaided by another person with or without a walking stick, manual wheelchair or other aid if such aid is normally or could reasonably be worn or used.	1 Cannot either: (a) mobilise more than 50 metres on level ground without stopping in order to avoid significant discomfort or exhaustion; or (b) repeatedly mobilise 50 metres within a reasonable timescale because of significant discomfort or exhaustion.
2. Transferring from one seated position to another.	2. Cannot move between one seated position and another seated position located next to one another without receiving physical assistance from another person.
3. Reaching.	3 Cannot raise either arm as if to put something in the top pocket of a coat or jacket.
4. Picking up and moving or transferring by the use of the upper body and arms (excluding standing, sitting, bending or kneeling and all other activities specified in this Schedule).	4 Cannot pick up and move a 0.5 litre carton full of liquid.
5. Manual dexterity.	5 Cannot press a button (such as a telephone keypad) with either hand or cannot turn the pages of a book with either hand.
6. Making self understood through speaking, writing, typing, or other means which are normally, or could reasonably be, used unaided by another person.	6 Cannot convey a simple message, such as the presence of a hazard.
7. Understanding communication by: (i) verbal means (such as hearing or lip reading) alone; (ii) non-verbal means (such as reading 16 point print or Braille) alone; or (iii) a combination of sub-paragraphs (i) and (ii), using any aid that is normally, or could reasonably, be used unaided by another person.	7 Cannot understand a simple message, such as the location of a fire escape, due to sensory impairment.
8. Absence or loss of control whilst conscious leading to extensive evacuation of the bowel and/or voiding of the	8 At least once a week experiences: (a) loss of control leading to extensive evacuation of the bowel and/or voiding of the bladder; or

Activity	Descriptors
bladder, other than enuresis (bed-wetting), despite the wearing or use of any aids or adaptations which are normally or could reasonably be worn or used.	(b) substantial leakage of the contents of a collecting device sufficient to require the individual to clean themselves and change clothing.
9. Learning tasks.	9 Cannot learn how to complete a simple task, such as setting an alarm clock, due to cognitive impairment or mental disorder.
10. Awareness of hazard.	10 Reduced awareness of everyday hazards, due to cognitive impairment or mental disorder, leads to a significant risk of: (a) injury to self or others; or (b) damage to property or possessions, such that the claimant requires supervision for the majority of the time to maintain safety.
11. Initiating and completing personal action (which means planning, organisation, problem solving, prioritising or switching tasks).	11 Cannot, due to impaired mental function, reliably initiate or complete at least two sequential personal actions.
12. Coping with change.	12 Cannot cope with any change, due to cognitive impairment or mental disorder, to the extent that day to day life cannot be managed.
13. Coping with social engagement, due to cognitive impairment or mental disorder.	13 Engagement in social contact is always precluded due to difficulty relating to others or significant distress experienced by the claimant.
14. Appropriateness of behaviour with other people, due to cognitive impairment or mental disorder.	14 Has, on a daily basis, uncontrollable episodes of aggressive or disinhibited behaviour that would be unreasonable in any workplace.
15. Conveying food or drink to the mouth.	15 (a) Cannot convey food or drink to the claimant's own mouth without receiving physical assistance from someone else; (b) Cannot convey food or drink to the claimant's own mouth without repeatedly stopping or experiencing breathlessness or severe discomfort; (c) Cannot convey food or drink to the claimant's own mouth without receiving regular prompting given by someone else in the claimant's presence; or (d) Owing to a severe disorder of mood or behaviour, fails to convey food or drink to the claimant's own mouth without receiving: (i) physical assistance from someone else; or (ii) regular prompting given by someone else in the claimant's presence.
16. Chewing or swallowing food or drink.	16 (a) Cannot chew or swallow food or drink; (b) Cannot chew or swallow food or drink without repeatedly stopping or experiencing breathlessness or severe discomfort; (c) Cannot chew or swallow food or drink without repeatedly receiving regular prompting given by someone else in the claimant's presence; or

Activity	Descriptors
	(d) Owing to a severe disorder of mood or behaviour, fails to:
	(i) chew or swallow food or drink; or
	(ii) chew or swallow food or drink without regular prompting given by someone else in the claimant's presence.

DEFINITIONS

"claimant"—see WRA 2012, s.40.
"limited capability for work"—see WRA 2012, ss.40 and 37(1).
"limited capability for work-related activity"—see WRA 2012, ss.40 and 37(2).

GENERAL NOTE

See the notes to Sch.3 to the ESA Regulations 2008 in Vol.I of this series.   2.411

Regulation 39(6)

SCHEDULE 8

CIRCUMSTANCES IN WHICH A CLAIMANT IS TO BE TREATED AS HAVING
LIMITED CAPABILITY FOR WORK

Receiving certain treatments
1. The claimant is receiving—   2.412
    (a) regular weekly treatment by way of haemodialysis for chronic renal failure;
    (b) treatment by way of plasmapheresis; or
    (c) regular weekly treatment by way of total parenteral nutrition for gross impairment of enteric function,
or is recovering from any of those forms of treatment in circumstances in which the Secretary of State is satisfied that the claimant should be treated as having limited capability for work.

In hospital
2.—(1) The claimant is—   2.413
    (a) undergoing medical or other treatment as [¹ a patient] in a hospital or similar institution; or
    (b) recovering from such treatment in circumstances in which the Secretary of State is satisfied that the claimant should be treated as having limited capability for work.
    (2) The circumstances in which a claimant is to be regarded as undergoing treatment falling within sub-paragraph (1)(a) include where the claimant is attending a residential programme of rehabilitation for the treatment of drug or alcohol dependency.
    (3) For the purposes of this paragraph, a claimant is to be regarded as undergoing treatment as a patient in a hospital or similar institution only if that claimant has been advised by a health care professional to stay [² for a period of 24 hours or longer] following medical or other treatment.

Prevented from working by law
3.—(1) The claimant—   2.414
    (a) is excluded or abstains from work pursuant to a request or notice in writing lawfully made or given under an enactment; or
    (b) is otherwise prevented from working pursuant to an enactment,
by reason of it being known or reasonably suspected that the claimant is infected or contaminated by, or has been in contact with a case of, a relevant infection or contamination.
    (2) In sub-paragraph (1) "relevant infection or contamination" means—
    (a) in England and Wales—
        (i) any incidence or spread of infection or contamination, within the meaning of section 45A(3) of the Public Health (Control of Disease) Act 1984 in respect of which regulations are made under Part 2A of that Act (public health protection)

for the purpose of preventing, protecting against, controlling or providing a public health response to, such incidence or spread, or

 (ii) tuberculosis or any infectious disease to which regulation 9 of the Public Health (Aircraft) Regulations 1979 (powers in respect of persons leaving aircraft) applies or to which regulation 10 of the Public Health (Ships) Regulations 1979 (powers in respect of certain persons on ships) applies; and

 (b) in Scotland any—

 (i) infectious disease within the meaning of section 1(5) of the Public Health etc (Scotland) Act 2008, or exposure to an organism causing that disease; or

 (ii) contamination within the meaning of section 1(5) of that Act, or exposure to a contaminant,

to which sections 56 to 58 of that Act (compensation) apply.

Risk to self or others

2.415

4.—(1) The claimant is suffering from a specific illness, disease or disablement by reason of which there would be a substantial risk to the physical or mental health of any person were the claimant found not to have limited capability for work.

(2) This paragraph does not apply where the risk could be reduced by a significant amount by—

 (a) reasonable adjustments being made in the claimant's workplace; or

 (b) the claimant taking medication to manage their condition where such medication has been prescribed for the claimant by a registered medical practitioner treating the claimant.

Life threatening disease

2.416

5. The claimant is suffering from a life threatening disease in relation to which—

 (a) there is medical evidence that the disease is uncontrollable, or uncontrolled, by a recognised therapeutic procedure; and

 (b) in the case of a disease that is uncontrolled, there is a reasonable cause for it not to be controlled by a recognised therapeutic procedure.

Disabled and over the age for state pension credit

2.417

6. The claimant has reached the qualifying age for state pension credit and is entitled to disability living allowance or personal independence payment.

AMENDMENTS

1. Universal Credit (Consequential, Supplementary, Incidental and Miscellaneous Provisions) Regulations 2013 (SI 2013/630), reg.38(10) (April 29, 2013).

2. Social Security (Miscellaneous Amendments) (No.2) Regulations 2013 (SI 2013/1508), reg.3(11) (July 29, 2013).

DEFINITIONS

"claimant"—see WRA 2012, s.40.
"disability living allowance"—see reg.2.
"limited capability for work"—see WRA 2012, ss.40 and 37(1).

Regulation 40(5)

SCHEDULE 9

CIRCUMSTANCES IN WHICH A CLAIMANT IS TO BE TREATED AS HAVING LIMITED CAPABILITY
FOR WORK AND WORK-RELATED ACTIVITY

Terminal illness

2.418

1. The claimant is terminally ill.

Pregnancy

2.419

2. The claimant is a pregnant woman and there is a serious risk of damage to her health or to the health of her unborn child if she does not refrain from work and work-related activity.

Receiving treatment for cancer

    3. The claimant is—   **2.420**

      (a) receiving treatment for cancer by way of chemotherapy or radiotherapy;

      (b) likely to receive such treatment within 6 months after the date of the determination of capability for work and work-related activity; or

      (c) recovering from such treatment,

and the Secretary of State is satisfied that the claimant should be treated as having limited capability for work and work-related activity.

Risk to self or others

    4. The claimant is suffering from a specific illness, disease or disablement by reason of which   **2.421** there would be a substantial risk to the physical or mental health of any person were the claimant found not to have limited capability for work and work-related activity.

Disabled and over the age for state pension credit

    5. The claimant has reached the qualifying age for state pension credit and is entitled to   **2.422** attendance allowance, the care component of disability living allowance at the highest rate or the daily living component of personal independence payment at the enhanced rate.

DEFINITIONS

    "attendance allowance"—see reg.2.

    "child"—see WRA 2012, s.40.

    "claimant"—*ibid.*

    "limited capability for work"—see WRA 2012, ss.40 and 37(1).

    "limited capability for work-related activity"—see WRA 2012, ss.40 and 37(2).

    "personal independence payment"—see reg.2.

Regulation 48

SCHEDULE 10

CAPITAL TO BE DISREGARDED

Premises

    1.—(1) Premises occupied by a person as their home.   **2.423**

    (2) For the purposes of this paragraph and paragraphs 2 to 5, only one set of premises may be treated as a person's home.

    2. Premises occupied by a close relative of a person as their home where that close relative has limited capability for work or has reached the qualifying age for state pension credit.

    3. Premises occupied by a person's former partner as their home where the person and their former partner are not estranged, but living apart by force of circumstances, for example where the person is in residential care.

    4.—(1) Premises that a person intends to occupy as their home where—

      (a) the person has acquired the premises within the past 6 months but not yet taken up occupation;

      (b) the person is taking steps to obtain possession and has commenced those steps within the past 6 months; or

      (c) the person is carrying out essential repairs or alterations required to render the premises fit for occupation and these have been commenced within the past 6 months.

    (2) A person is to be taken to have commenced steps to obtain possession of premises on the date that legal advice is first sought or proceedings are commenced, whichever is earlier.

    5. Premises that a person has ceased to occupy as their home following an estrangement from their former partner where—

      (a) the person has ceased to occupy the premises within the past 6 months; or

      (b) the person's former partner is a lone parent and occupies the premises as their home.

    6. Premises that a person is taking reasonable steps to dispose of where those steps have been commenced within the past 6 months.

Business assets

2.424   7. Assets which are used wholly or mainly for the purposes of a trade, profession or vocation which the person is carrying on.

8. Assets which were used wholly or mainly for a trade, profession or vocation that the person has ceased to carry on within the past 6 months if—

(a) the person is taking reasonable steps to dispose of those assets; or

(b) the person ceased to be engaged in carrying on the trade, profession or vocation because of incapacity and can reasonably expect to be reengaged on recovery.

Rights in pensions schemes etc.

9. The value of any policy of life insurance.

2.425   10.—(1) The value of any right to receive a pension under an occupational or personal pension scheme or any other pension scheme registered under section 153 of the Finance Act 2004.

(2) "Occupational pension scheme" and "personal pension scheme" have the meaning in section 1 of the Pension Schemes Act 1993.

11.—(1) The value of a funeral plan contract.

(2) "Funeral plan contract" means a contract under which the person makes payments to a person to secure the provision of a funeral and where the sole purpose of the plan is the provision of a funeral.

Amounts earmarked for special purposes

2.426   12. An amount deposited with a housing association as a condition of the person occupying premises as their home.

13. An amount received within the past 6 months which is to be used for the purchase of premises that the person intends to occupy as their home where that amount—

(a) is attributable to the proceeds of the sale of premises formerly occupied by the person as their home;

(b) has been deposited with a housing association as mentioned in paragraph 12; or

(c) is a grant made to the person for the sole purpose of the purchase of a home.

14. An amount received under an insurance policy within the past 6 months in connection with the loss or damage to the premises occupied by the person as their home or to their personal possessions.

15. An amount received within the past 6 months that is to be used for making essential repairs or alterations to premises occupied or intended to be occupied as the person's home where that amount has been acquired by the person (whether by grant or loan or otherwise) on condition that it is used for that purpose.

Other payments

2.427   16. A payment made within the past 12 months under Part 8 of the Contributions and Benefits Act (the social fund).

17.—(1) A payment made within the past 12 months by or on behalf of a local authority—

(a) under section 17, 23B, 23C or 24A of the Children Act 1989, section 12 of the Social Work (Scotland) Act 1968 or section 29 or 30 of Children (Scotland) Act 1995; or

(b) under any other enactment in order to meet a person's welfare needs related to old age or disability, other than living expenses.

(2) In sub-paragraph (1) "living expenses" has the meaning in regulation 66(2).

18.—(1) A payment received within the past 12 months by way of arrears of, or compensation for late payment of—

(a) universal credit;

(b) a benefit abolished by section 33 of the Act; or

(c) a social security benefit which is not included as unearned income under regulation 66(1)(a) or (b).

(2) "Social security benefit" means a benefit under any enactment relating to social security in any part of the United Kingdom.

19. A payment to a person by virtue of being a holder of the Victoria Cross or George Cross.

DEFINITIONS

"close relative"—see reg.2.

"grant"—see regs 2 and 68(7).

"partner"—see reg.2.

GENERAL NOTE

The list of capital that is ignored for the purposes of universal credit is greatly reduced compared with that which applies for the purposes of income support, JSA, ESA and housing benefit. Many of the provisions in Sch.10 are similar to those that apply for those benefits but not all. Paragraph 11—the disregard of the value of a funeral plan—is new.

Note that where a period of six months is specified in the provisions in this Schedule, that period can be extended by the Secretary of State (and on appeal a tribunal) if this is reasonable in the circumstances of the case (see reg.48(2)).

Regulation 110

SCHEDULE 11

APPLICATION OF ESA OR JSA SANCTIONS TO UNIVERSAL CREDIT

Moving an ESA sanction to UC

1. (1) This paragraph applies where—   **2.428**
  (a) a person is, or has ceased to be, entitled to an employment and support allowance;
  (b) there is a reduction relating to the award of the employment and support allowance under section 11J of the Welfare Reform Act 2007; and
  (c) the person becomes entitled to universal credit.

(2) Any reduction relating to the award of the employment and support allowance is to be applied to the award of universal credit.

(3) The period for which the reduction is to have effect is the number of days which apply to the person under regulations 52 and 53 of the ESA Regulations minus—
  (a) any days which have already resulted in a reduction to the amount of the employment and support allowance; and
  (b) if the award of the employment and support allowance has terminated, any days falling after the date of that termination and before the date on which the award of universal credits starts, and that period is to be added to the total outstanding reduction period.

(4) The amount of the reduction in the award of universal credit for any assessment period in which the reduction is applied is the amount calculated in accordance with regulation 110.

Moving a JSA sanction to UC

2. (1) This paragraph applies where—   **2.429**
  (a) a person is, or has ceased to be, entitled to a jobseeker's allowance;
  (b) there is a reduction relating to the person's award of a jobseeker's allowance under section 6J or 6K of the Jobseekers Act 1995; and
  (c) the person becomes entitled to universal credit.

(2) Any reduction relating to the award of the jobseeker's allowance is to be applied to the award of universal credit.

(3) The period for which the reduction is to have effect is the number of days which apply to the person under regulations 19 to 21 of the Jobseeker's Allowance Regulations 2013 minus—
  (a) any days which have already resulted in a reduction to the amount of the jobseeker's allowance; and
  (b) if the award of the jobseeker's allowance has terminated, any days falling after the date of that termination and before the date on which the award of universal credits starts, and that period is to be added to the total outstanding reduction period.

(4) The amount of the reduction in the award of universal credit for any assessment period in which the reduction is applied is the amount calculated in accordance with regulation 110.

Effect of ESA or JSA sanction on escalation of UC sanction

3. Where—   **2.430**
  (a) a reduction in relation to an award of an employment and support allowance or an award of a jobseeker's allowance is applied to an award of universal credit by virtue of paragraph 1 or 2;
  (b) there is a subsequent sanctionable failure under section 26 or 27 of the Act; and

    (c) the failure giving rise to the reduction in relation to the award of an employment and support allowance or the award of a jobseeker's allowance ("the previous failure") and the reduction period determined for that failure correspond with a failure specified under section 26 or 27 of the Act to which the same reduction period would apply under Chapter 2 of Part 8 of these Regulations,

for the purposes of determining the reduction period for that subsequent failure, the previous failure is to be treated as if it were the corresponding failure under section 26 or 27 of the Act.

Rent Officers (Universal Credit Functions) Order 2013

(SI 2013/382) (AS AMENDED)

The Secretary of State for Work and Pensions makes the following Order in exercise of the powers conferred by section 122 of the Housing Act 1996.

[*In force April 29, 2013*]

ARRANGEMENT OF REGULATIONS

SCHEDULES

Citation and commencement

2.431   **1.**—This Order may be cited as the Rent Officers (Universal Credit Functions) Order 2013 and comes into force on 29th April 2013.

Interpretation

2.432   **2.**—In this Order—
"Welfare Reform Act" means the Welfare Reform Act 2012;
"the Universal Credit Regulations" means the Universal Credit Regulations 2013;
"accommodation" means any residential accommodation whether or not consisting of the whole or part of a building and whether or not comprising separate and self-contained premises;
[1 . . .]
"assured tenancy"—

(a) in England and Wales, has the same meaning as in Part 1 of the Housing Act 1988, except that it includes—
   (i) a tenancy which would be an assured tenancy but for paragraph 2, 8 or 10 of Schedule 1 (tenancies which cannot be assured tenancies) to that Act; and
   (ii) a licence which would be an assured tenancy (within the extended meaning given in this definition) were it a tenancy; and
(b) in Scotland, has the same meaning as in Part 2 of the Housing (Scotland) Act 1988, except that it includes—
   (i) a tenancy which would be an assured tenancy but for paragraph 7 or 9 of Schedule 4 (tenancies which cannot be assured tenancies) to that Act; and
   (ii) any other form of occupancy which would be an assured tenancy (within the extended meaning given in this definition) were it a tenancy;

"broad rental market area" has the meaning given in article 3;

"housing payment" means a relevant payment within the meaning of paragraph 3 of Schedule 4 (housing costs element for renters) to the Universal Credit Regulations;

"local authority" means—

(a) in relation to England, the council of a district or London borough, the Common Council of the City of London or the Council of the Isles of Scilly;
(b) in relation to Wales, the council of a county or county borough; and
(c) in relation to Scotland, a council constituted under section 2 (constitution of councils) of the Local Government etc. (Scotland) Act 1994;

"provider of social housing" has the meaning given in paragraph 2 of Schedule 4 to the Universal Credit Regulations;

"relevant time" means the time the request for the determination is made or, if earlier, the date the tenancy ends;

"service charge payments" has the meaning given in paragraph 7 of Schedule 1 (meaning of payments in respect of accommodation) to the Universal Credit Regulations;

"tenancy" includes—

(a) in England and Wales, a licence to occupy premises; and
(b) in Scotland, any other right of occupancy,
   and references to rent, a tenant, a landlord or any other expression appropriate to a tenancy are to be construed accordingly;

"tenant" includes, where the tenant is a member of a couple within the meaning of section 39 of the Welfare Reform Act, the other member of the couple;

"working day" means any day other than—

(a) a Saturday or a Sunday;
(b) Christmas Day or Good Friday; or
(c) a day which is a bank holiday under the Banking and Financial Dealings Act 1971 in any part of Great Britain.

AMENDMENT

1. Rent Officers (Housing Benefit and Universal Credit Functions) (Amendment) Order 2013 (SI 2013/1544), art.4(2) (September 1, 2013).

Broad rental market area determinations

2.433 **3.**—(1) Broad rental market area determinations taking effect on 29th April 2013 are determined in accordance with paragraph (7) and all other broad rental market area determinations are determined in accordance with paragraphs (2) to (6).

(2) A rent officer must, at such times as the rent officer considers appropriate and if the Secretary of State agrees—

(a) determine one or more broad rental market areas; and

(b) in respect of that broad rental market area, or those broad rental market areas, give to the Secretary of State a notice which identifies the local authority areas and the postcodes contained within the broad rental market area (or each of them).

(3) A broad rental market area is an area within which a person could reasonably be expected to live having regard to facilities and services for the purposes of health, education, recreation, personal banking and shopping, taking account of the distance of travel, by public and private transport, to and from those facilities and services.

(4) A broad rental market area must contain—

(a) residential premises of a variety of types, including such premises held on a variety of tenures; and

(b) sufficient privately rented residential premises to ensure that, in the rent officer's opinion, the local housing allowance for the categories of accommodation in the area for which the rent officer is required to determine a local housing allowance is representative of the rents that a landlord might reasonably be expected to obtain in that area.

(5) Every part of Great Britain must fall within a broad rental market area and a broad rental market area must not overlap with another broad rental market area.

(6) Any broad rental market area determination made in accordance with paragraph (2) is to take effect—

(a) on the day the determination is made for the purpose of enabling a rent officer to determine a local housing allowance for that area; and

(b) for all other purposes on the next [¹ 7th April] following the day on which the determination is made.

(7) For broad rental market area determinations that take effect on 29th April 2013, a rent officer must use the broad rental market area determinations determined in accordance with article 4B of, and Schedule 3B to, the Rent Officers (Housing Benefit Functions) Order 1997 or the Rent Officers (Housing Benefit Functions) (Scotland) Order 1997 that apply on 29th April 2013.

AMENDMENT

1. Rent Officers (Housing Benefit and Universal Credit Functions) (Local Housing Allowance Amendments) Order 2013 (SI 2013/2978), art.4(2) (January 13, 2014).

Local housing allowance determinations

2.434 **4.**—(1) Local housing allowance determinations taking effect on 29th April 2013 are determined in accordance with paragraph (4) and all other local housing allowance determinations are determined in accordance with paragraphs (2) and (3).

(2) [¹ In 2014 and in each subsequent year, on the date specified in paragraph (2A),] a rent officer must—

(a) for each broad rental market area determine, in accordance with Schedule 1, a local housing allowance for each of the categories of accommodation set out in paragraph 1 of Schedule 1; and

(b) notify the Secretary of State of the local housing allowance determination made in accordance with sub-paragraph (a) for each broad rental market area.

[¹ (2A) The date specified for the purposes of paragraph (2) is—

(a) 15ᵗʰ January where that is a Tuesday; or

(b) where 15ᵗʰ January is not a Tuesday, the first Tuesday following 15ᵗʰ January.]

(3) Any local housing allowance determination made in accordance with paragraph (1) is to take effect on the next [² 7th April] following the day on which the determination is made.

(4) For local housing allowance determinations that take effect on 29th April 2013, a rent officer must use—

(a) the broad rental market area determinations referred to in article 3(7); and

(b) the approximate monthly local housing allowance determinations notified to local authorities in accordance with article 4B(6) of the Rent Officers (Housing Benefit Functions) Order 1997 or the Rent Officers (Housing Benefit Functions) (Scotland) Order 1997 that apply on 29th April 2013.

AMENDMENTS

1. Rent Officers (Housing Benefit and Universal Credit Functions) (Amendment) Order 2013 (SI 2013/1544), art.4(3) (September 1, 2013).

2. Rent Officers (Housing Benefit and Universal Credit Functions) (Local Housing Allowance Amendments) Order 2013 (SI 2013/2978), art.4(2) (January 13, 2014).

DEFINITIONS

"accommodation"—see art.2.
"broad rental market area"—see arts 2 and 3.

Housing payment determination

5.—Where a rent officer receives a request from the Secretary of State for a determination in respect of housing payments for accommodation let by a provider of social housing, the rent officer must—   **2.435**

(a) determine in accordance with Schedule 2 whether each of the housing payments specified by the Secretary of State in that request is reasonable for that accommodation; and

(b) where the rent officer determines that a housing payment is not reasonable, determine in accordance with Schedule 2 the amount that is reasonable for the accommodation and notify the Secretary of State of that amount.

DEFINITIONS

"accommodation"—see art.2.
"housing payment"—see art.2 and Universal Credit Regs, Sch.4, para.3.

Redeterminations

2.436   **6.**—(1) Where a rent officer has made a determination under article 3, 4 or 5 ("the determination") and paragraph (2) applies, a rent officer must make a further determination ("a redetermination") and notify the Secretary of State of the redetermination.

(2) This paragraph applies where—

(a) the determination was made under article 3 or 4 and the rent officer considers that there is an error in relation to that determination; or

(b) the determination was made under article 5 and—

(i) the Secretary of State requests that the rent officer makes a redetermination;

(ii) the Secretary of State informs the rent officer that the information supplied when requesting the determination was incorrect or incomplete; or

(iii) the rent officer considers that there is an error in relation to the determination.

(3) Where a rent officer makes a redetermination the rent officer must do so in accordance with the provisions of this Order that applied to the determination and use the same information that was used for the determination except that, where the information used was incorrect or incomplete, the rent officer must use the correct or complete information.

(4) Where a rent officer makes a redetermination by virtue of paragraph (2)(b)(i), the rent officer must have regard to the advice of at least one other rent officer in relation to that redetermination.

Information

2.437   **7.**—Where a rent officer considers that the information supplied by the Secretary of State or a landlord under regulation 40 (information to be provided to rent officers) of the Universal Credit, Personal Independence Payment, Jobseeker's Allowance and Employment and Support Allowance (Claims and Payments) Regulations 2013 is incomplete or incorrect, the rent officer must—

(a) notify the Secretary of State or the landlord of that fact; and

(b) request that the Secretary of State or the landlord supplies the further information or to confirm whether, in their opinion, the information already supplied is correct and, if they agree that it is not, to supply the correct information.

Means of giving notice

2.438   **8.**—Any notice given by a rent officer under this Order may be given in writing or by electronic means unless the Secretary of State requests that notice is given in writing only.

Article 4

SCHEDULE 1

LOCAL HOUSING ALLOWANCE DETERMINATIONS

Categories of accommodation
2.439   1. The categories of accommodation for which a rent officer is required to determine a local housing allowance in accordance with article 4 are—

   (a) accommodation where the tenant has the exclusive use of only one bedroom and where the tenancy provides for the tenant to share the use of one or more of—
      (i) a kitchen;
     (ii) a bathroom;
    (iii) a toilet; or
    (iv) a room suitable for living in;
   (b) accommodation where the tenant has the exclusive use of only one bedroom and exclusive use of a kitchen, a bathroom, a toilet and a room suitable for living in;
   (c) accommodation where the tenant has the use of only two bedrooms;
   (d) accommodation where the tenant has the use of only three bedrooms;
   (e) accommodation where the tenant has the use of only four bedrooms.

[¹ Local housing allowance for category of accommodation in paragraph 1
   2.—(1) Subject to paragraph 5 (anomalous local housing allowances) the rent officer must determine a local housing allowance for each category of accommodation in paragraph 1 as follows.   **2.440**

   (2) For the broad rental market areas listed in column 1 of the table in paragraph 6 the local housing allowance is—
   (a) for a category of accommodation listed in column 2 in relation to that broad rental market area, either—
      (i) the rate last determined increased by 4 per cent; or
     (ii) the maximum local housing allowance for that category of accommodation listed in column (2) of the table in paragraph 4 (Maximum local housing allowance) where that is lower than or equal to the rate last determined increased by 4 per cent;
   (b) for any category of accommodation not listed in column 2 of the table in paragraph 6 in relation to that broad rental market area, either—
      (i) the rent at the 30th percentile determined in accordance with paragraph 3 (Rent at the 30th percentile); or
     (ii) the rate last determined for that category of accommodation increased by 1 per cent. where that is lower than or equal to the rent at the 30th percentile determined in accordance with paragraph 3.
   (3) For all other broad rental market areas the local housing allowance for a category of accommodation is, either—
   (a) the rent at the 30th percentile determined in accordance with paragraph 3; or
   (b) the rate last determined for that category of accommodation increased by 1 per cent. where that is lower than or equal to the rent at the 30th percentile determined in accordance with paragraph 3.
   (4) Where the local housing allowance would otherwise not be a whole number of pence, it must be rounded to the nearest whole penny by disregarding any amount less than half a penny and treating any amount of half a penny or more as a whole penny.]

Rent at the 30th percentile
   3.—(1) The rent officer must determine the rent at the 30th percentile in accordance with the following sub-paragraphs.   **2.441**

   (2) The rent officer must compile a list of rents.
   [¹ (3) The rent officer must compile a list of rents in ascending order of the monthly rents which, in the rent officer's opinion, are payable—
   (a) for accommodation let under an assured tenancy for each category of accommodation specified in paragraph 1; and
   (b) in the 12 month period ending on the 30th day of the September preceding the date of the determination.]
   (4) The list must include any rents which are of the same amount.
   (5) The criteria for including an assured tenancy on the list of rents in relation to each category of accommodation specified in paragraph 1 are that—
   (a) the accommodation let under the assured tenancy is in the broad rental market area for which the local housing allowance for that category of accommodation is being determined;
   (b) the accommodation is in a reasonable state of repair; and
   (c) the assured tenancy permits the tenant to use exclusively or share the use of, as the case may be, the same number and type of rooms as the category of accommodation in relation to which the list of rents is being compiled.
   [¹ (6) Sub-paragraph (7) applies where the rent officer is not satisfied that the list of rents in respect of any category of accommodation would contain sufficient rents, payable in the 12

month period ending on the 30th day of the September preceding the date of the determination for accommodation in the broad rental market area, to enable a local housing allowance to be determined which is representative of the rents that a landlord might reasonably be expected to obtain in that area.]

(7) In a case where this sub-paragraph applies, the rent officer may add to the list rents for accommodation in the same category in other areas in which a comparable market exists.

(8) Where rent is payable other than monthly the rent officer must use the figure which would be payable if the rent were to be payable monthly by calculating the rent for a year and dividing the total by 12.

(9) When compiling the list of rents for each category of accommodation, the rent officer must—

  (a) assume that no-one had sought or is seeking the tenancy who would have been entitled to housing benefit under Part 7 of the Social Security Contributions and Benefits Act 1992(12) or universal credit under Part 1 of the Welfare Reform Act; and

  (b) exclude the amount of any rent which, in the rent officer's opinion, is fairly attributable to the provision of services performed or facilities (including the use of furniture) provided for, or rights made available to, the tenant and which would not be classed as service charge payments.

(10) The rent at the 30th percentile in the list of rents ("R") is determined as follows—

  (a) where the number of rents on the list is a multiple of 10, the formula is—

$$R = \frac{\text{the amount of the rent at P} + \text{the amount of the rent at P1}}{2}$$

  where—

    (i) P is the position on the list found by multiplying the number of rents on the list by 3 and dividing by 10; and

    (ii) P1 is the following position on the list;

  (b) where the number of rents on the list is not a multiple of 10, the formula is—

$$R = \text{the amount of the rent at P2}$$

  where P2 is the position on the list found by multiplying the number of rents on the list by 3 and dividing by 10 and rounding the result upwards to the nearest whole number.

[¹ **Maximum local housing allowance**

4. The maximum local housing allowance for each category of accommodation specified in the paragraph of this Schedule listed in column (1) is the amount specified for that category of accommodation in column (2).

(1) Paragraph of this Schedule defining the category of accommodation	(2) Maximum local housing allowance for that category of accommodation
paragraph 1(a) (one bedroom, shared accommodation)	£1121.33
paragraph 1(b) (one bedroom, exclusive use)	£1121.33
paragraph 1(c) (two bedrooms)	£1300.70
paragraph 1(d) (three bedrooms)	£1524.96
paragraph 1(e) (four bedrooms)	£1794.11]

Anomalous local housing allowances

2.443   **5.** Where—

  (a) the rent officer has determined the local housing allowance for each of the categories of accommodation in paragraph 1 in accordance with the preceding paragraphs of this Schedule; and

  (b) the local housing allowance for a category of accommodation in paragraph 1(b) to (e) is lower than the local housing allowance for any of the categories of accommodation which precede it,

that local housing allowance is to be the same as the highest local housing allowance which precedes it.

[¹ **6.** The table referred to in paragraph 2(2) of this Schedule is below.

(1) Broad rental market area	*(2) Paragraph of this Schedule defining the category of accommodation*
Aberdeen and Shire	paragraph 1(1)(a) (one bedroom, shared accommodation) paragraph 1(1)(c) (two bedrooms) paragraph 1(1)(d) (three bedrooms) paragraph 1(1)(e) (four bedrooms)
Argyll and Bute	paragraph 1(1)(b) (one bedroom, exclusive use)
Ashford	paragraph 1(1)(a) (one bedroom, shared accommodation)
Aylesbury	paragraph 1(1)(a) (one bedroom, shared accommodation) paragraph 1(1)(d) (three bedrooms)
Barnsley	paragraph 1(1)(b) (one bedroom, exclusive use)
Bath	paragraph 1(1)(b) (one bedroom, exclusive use) paragraph 1(1)(c) (two bedrooms) paragraph 1(1)(d) (three bedrooms)
Bedford	paragraph 1(1)(b) (one bedroom, exclusive use) paragraph 1(1)(e) (four bedrooms)
Blackwater Valley	paragraph 1(1)(a) (one bedroom, shared accommodation)
Blaenau Gwent	paragraph 1(1)(a) (one bedroom, shared accommodation)
Bolton and Bury	paragraph 1(1)(a) (one bedroom, shared accommodation)
Brecon and Radnor	paragraph 1(1)(d) (three bedrooms)
Bridgend	paragraph 1(1)(a) (one bedroom, shared accommodation)
Brighton and Hove	paragraph 1(1)(d) (three bedrooms)
Bristol	paragraph 1(1)(e) (four bedrooms)
Caerphilly	paragraph 1(1)(e) (four bedrooms)
Cambridge	paragraph 1(1)(a) (one bedroom, shared accommodation) paragraph 1(1)(b) (one bedroom, exclusive use) paragraph 1(1)(d) (three bedrooms) paragraph 1(1)(e) (four bedrooms)
Canterbury	paragraph 1(1)(e) (four bedrooms)
Central Lancs	paragraph 1(1)(a) (one bedroom, shared accommodation)
Central London	paragraph 1(1)(a) (one bedroom, shared accommodation)
Ceredigion	paragraph 1(1)(a) (one bedroom, shared accommodation) paragraph 1(1)(b) (one bedroom, exclusive use)
Cheltenham	paragraph 1(1)(a) (one bedroom, shared accommodation)
Cherwell Valley	paragraph 1(1)(b) (one bedroom, exclusive use) paragraph 1(1)(c) (two bedrooms) paragraph 1(1)(e) (four bedrooms)
Chesterfield	paragraph 1(1)(a) (one bedroom, shared accommodation)
Chichester	paragraph 1(1)(a) (one bedroom, shared accommodation)
Coventry	paragraph 1(1)(c) (two bedrooms)
Crawley & Reigate	paragraph 1(1)(e) (four bedrooms)
Derby	paragraph 1(1)(a) (one bedroom, shared accommodation)

(1) Broad rental market area	(2) Paragraph of this Schedule defining the category of accommodation
Durham	paragraph 1(1)(a) (one bedroom, shared accommodation)
East Cheshire	paragraph 1(1)(e) (four bedrooms)
East Thames Valley	paragraph 1(1)(c) (two bedrooms) paragraph 1(1)(d) (three bedrooms)
Exeter	paragraph 1(1)(a) (one bedroom, shared accommodation)
Fife	paragraph 1(1)(a) (one bedroom, shared accommodation)
Forth Valley	paragraph 1(1)(e) (four bedrooms)
Gloucester	paragraph 1(1)(a) (one bedroom, shared accommodation)
Greater Glasgow	paragraph 1(1)(a) (one bedroom, shared accommodation)
High Weald	paragraph 1(1)(d) (three bedrooms)
Hull & East Riding	paragraph 1(1)(a) (one bedroom, shared accommodation)
Inner East London	paragraph 1(1)(a) (one bedroom, shared accommodation) paragraph 1(1)(b) (one bedroom, exclusive use)
Inner North London	paragraph 1(1)(a) (one bedroom, shared accommodation)
Inner South East London	paragraph 1(1)(a) (one bedroom, sharedaccommodation) paragraph 1(1)(b) (one bedroom, exclusive use) paragraph 1(1)(c) (two bedrooms) paragraph 1(1)(d) (three bedrooms) paragraph 1(1)(e) (four bedrooms)
Inner South West London	paragraph 1(1)(a) (one bedroom, shared accommodation) paragraph 1(1)(b) (one bedroom, exclusive use) paragraph 1(1)(c) (two bedrooms)
Inner West London	paragraph 1(1)(a) (one bedroom, shared accommodation) paragraph 1(1)(b) (one bedroom, exclusive use) paragraph 1(1)(c) (two bedrooms)
Lancaster	paragraph 1(1)(a) (one bedroom, shared accommodation)
Leeds	paragraph 1(1)(a) (one bedroom, shared accommodation)
Luton	paragraph 1(1)(a) (one bedroom, shared accommodation) paragraph 1(1)(c) (two bedrooms) paragraph 1(1)(d) (three bedrooms)
Maidstone	paragraph 1(1)(a) (one bedroom, shared accommodation)
Mendip	paragraph 1(1)(e) (four bedrooms)
Merthyr Cynon	paragraph 1(1)(a) (one bedroom, shared accommodation)
Mid & East Devon	paragraph 1(1)(a) (one bedroom, shared accommodation) paragraph 1(1)(b) (one bedroom, exclusive use)
Mid & West Dorset	paragraph 1(1)(a) (one bedroom, shared accommodation)
Mid Staffs	paragraph 1(1)(a) (one bedroom, shared accommodation)
Neath Port Talbot	paragraph 1(1)(a) (one bedroom, shared accommodation)
Newbury	paragraph 1(1)(a) (one bedroom, shared accommodation)
North Cornwall & Devon Borders	paragraph 1(1)(a) (one bedroom, shared accommodation)
North Nottingham	paragraph 1(1)(b) (one bedroom, exclusive use)

(1) Broad rental market area	(2) Paragraph of this Schedule defining the category of accommodation
North West Kent	paragraph 1(1)(a) (one bedroom, shared accommodation)
North West London	paragraph 1(1)(a) (one bedroom, shared accommodation) paragraph 1(1)(b) (one bedroom, exclusive use) paragraph 1(1)(c) (two bedrooms) paragraph 1(1)(d) (three bedrooms) paragraph 1(1)(e) (four bedrooms)
North West Wales	paragraph 1(1)(e) (four bedrooms)
Northampton	paragraph 1(1)(a) (one bedroom, shared accommodation)
Outer East London	paragraph 1(1)(a) (one bedroom, shared accommodation) paragraph 1(1)(b) (one bedroom, exclusive use) paragraph 1(1)(c) (two bedrooms) paragraph 1(1)(d) (three bedrooms) paragraph 1(1)(e) (four bedrooms)
Outer North London	paragraph 1(1)(a) (one bedroom, shared accommodation) paragraph 1(1)(b) (one bedroom, exclusive use) paragraph 1(1)(c) (two bedrooms) paragraph 1(1)(e) (four bedrooms)
Outer South London	paragraph 1(1)(d) (three bedrooms) paragraph 1(1)(e) (four bedrooms)
Outer South West London	paragraph 1(1)(a) (one bedroom, shared accommodation) paragraph 1(1)(c) (two bedrooms) paragraph 1(1)(d) (three bedrooms) paragraph 1(1)(e) (four bedrooms)
Oxford	paragraph 1(1)(d) (three bedrooms)
Rotherham	paragraph 1(1)(c) (two bedrooms)
Scarborough	paragraph 1(1)(a) (one bedroom, shared accommodation)
Scottish Borders	paragraph 1(1)(a) (one bedroom, shared accommodation)
Sheffield	paragraph 1(1)(a) (one bedroom, shared accommodation)
South Cheshire	paragraph 1(1)(b) (one bedroom, exclusive use) paragraph 1(1)(c) (two bedrooms)
South East Herts	paragraph 1(1)(b) (one bedroom, exclusive use)
South Gwynedd	paragraph 1(1)(a) (one bedroom, shared accommodation)
Southampton	paragraph 1(1)(a) (one bedroom, shared accommodation)
Southern Greater Manchester	paragraph 1(1)(d) (three bedrooms)
Staffordshire North	paragraph 1(1)(a) (one bedroom, shared accommodation)
Taff Rhondda	paragraph 1(1)(a) (one bedroom, shared accommodation)
Thanet	paragraph 1(1)(a) (one bedroom, shared accommodation)
Walton	paragraph 1(1)(a) (one bedroom, shared accommodation) paragraph 1(1)(e) (four bedrooms)
Warwickshire South	paragraph 1(1)(d) (three bedrooms)
West Wiltshire	paragraph 1(1)(e) (four bedrooms)
Wolds and Coast	paragraph 1(1)(a) (one bedroom, shared accommodation)
Worcester North	paragraph 1(1)(a) (one bedroom, shared accommodation)

(1) Broad rental market area	(2) Paragraph of this Schedule defining the category of accommodation
Worcester South	paragraph 1(1)(a) (one bedroom, shared accommodation)
Yeovil	paragraph 1(1)(a) (one bedroom, shared accommodation)]

AMENDMENT

1. Rent Officers (Housing Benefit and Universal Credit Functions) (Local Housing Allowance Amendments) Order 2013 (SI 2013/2978), art.4(3) (January 13, 2014).

DEFINITIONS

"accommodation"—see art.2.
"assured tenancy"—*ibid.*
"broad rental market area"—see arts 2 and 3.
"tenancy"—see art.2.
"tenant"—*ibid.*

Article 5

SCHEDULE 2

HOUSING PAYMENT DETERMINATION

2.444
1. The rent officer must determine whether, in the rent officer's opinion, each of the housing payments payable for the tenancy of the accommodation at the relevant time is reasonable.
2. If the rent officer determines under paragraph 1 that a housing payment is not reasonable, the rent officer must also determine the amount of the housing payment which is reasonable.
3. When making a determination under this Schedule, the rent officer must—
  (a) have regard to the level of similar payments under tenancies for accommodation which—
    (i) is let by the same type of landlord;
    (ii) is in the same local authority area or, where paragraph 4 applies, an adjoining local authority area;
    (iii) has the same number of bedrooms; and
    (iv) is in the same reasonable state of repair,
  as the accommodation in respect of which the determination is being made;
  (b) exclude—
    (i) the cost of any care, support or supervision provided to the tenant by the landlord or by someone on the landlord's behalf;
    (ii) any payments for services performed or facilities (including the use of furniture) provided for, or rights made available to, the tenant which are not service charge payments; and
  (c) where the accommodation is let at an Affordable Rent, assume that the rent is reasonable.
4. Where the rent officer is not satisfied that the local authority area contains sufficient accommodation to allow a determination of the housing payments which a landlord might reasonably have been expected to charge, the rent officer may have regard to the level of housing payments in one adjoining local authority area or, if the rent officer considers it necessary, more than one adjoining local authority areas.
5. For the purposes of this Schedule—
  (a) a housing payment is reasonable where it is not higher than the payment which the landlord might reasonably have been expected to obtain for the tenancy at the relevant time;
  (b) accommodation is let by the same type of landlord where—
    (i) in a case where the landlord of the accommodation in respect of which the determination is being made is a local authority, the landlord of the other accommodation is also a local authority; and

(ii) in a case where the landlord of the accommodation in respect of which the determination is being made is a provider of social housing other than a local authority, the landlord of the other accommodation is also a provider of social housing other than a local authority;

(c) accommodation is let at an Affordable Rent where—

    (i) the rent is regulated under a standard by the Regulator of Social Housing under section 194 of the Housing and Regeneration Act 2008(13) ("the 2008 Act") which requires the initial rent to be set at no more than 80% of the local market rent (including service charges); or

    (ii) the accommodation is let by a local authority and, under arrangements between the local authority and the Homes and Communities Agency (as established by section 1 of the 2008 Act), the Greater London Authority or the Secretary of State, the rent payable is set on the same basis as would be the case if the rent were regulated under a standard set by the Regulator of Social Housing under section 194 of the 2008 Act which requires the initial rent to be set at no more than 80% of the local market rent (including service charges).

DEFINITIONS

"accommodation"—see art.2.

"housing payment"—see art.2 and Universal Credit Regs, Sch.4, para.3.

"local authority"—see art.2.

"provider of social housing"—see art.2 and Universal Credit Regs, Sch.4, para.4.

"relevant time"—see art.2.

"service charge payments"—see art.2 and Universal Credit Regs, Sch.1 para.7.

"tenancy"—see art.2.

"tenant"—*ibid.*

PART IV

UNIVERSAL CREDIT: TRANSITIONAL PROVISIONS AND COMMENCEMENT ORDERS

Universal Credit (Transitional Provisions) Regulations 2013

(SI 2013/386) (AS AMENDED)

In accordance with section 43(3) and (6)(b) of the Welfare Reform Act 2012(1) ("the Act"), a draft of this instrument was laid before Parliament and approved by resolution of each House of Parliament.

The Secretary of State for Work and Pensions makes the following Regulations in exercise of the powers conferred by section 42(2) and (3) of and paragraphs 1(1) and (2)(b), 3(1)(a), (b) and (c), 4(1)(a), 5(1), (2)(c) and (d) and (3) (a) and 6 of Schedule 6 to the Act.

This instrument has not been referred to the Social Security Advisory Committee because it contains only regulations made under the Act and is made before the end of the period of 6 months beginning with the coming into force of the Act.

In accordance with section 176(2)(b) of the Social Security Administration Act 1992(3), the Secretary of State has obtained the agreement of organisations appearing to him to be representative of the authorities concerned that proposals in respect of these Regulations should not be referred to them.

ARRANGEMENT OF REGULATIONS

SCHEDULE   Modifications to tax credits legislation

GENERAL NOTE

These Regulations ("the Transitional Provisions Regulations 2013") provide for the first phase of the replacement of certain existing means-tested benefits by universal credit, established under the WRA 2012. Those existing benefits (and tax credits) are income-based jobseeker's allowance (JSA), income-related employment and support allowance (ESA), income support, housing benefit, working tax credit and child tax credit. These Regulations are divided into three Parts.   3.1

Part 1 (regs 1 and 2) simply deal with citation, commencement and interpretation. These Regulations came into force on April 29, 2013 (reg.1(2)).

Part 2 (regs 3–14) concerns "The first stage of transition to universal credit". This Part, in effect, begins the initial (and limited) roll-out of universal credit. Claimants may only claim universal credit if they meet two overarching requirements. First, and by virtue of reg.3, in this initial phase claims for universal credit may only be made by a narrowly-defined group of claimants, known as the "Pathfinder Group". Individuals are in the Pathfinder Group if they meet *all* the various criteria set out in regs 5–12 inclusive (reg.4(1)). Second, a claimant in the Pathfinder Group must also live in the right part of the country, i.e. they must reside in one the designated postcode districts set out in the various associated Commencement Orders. The first such Commencement Order is the Welfare Reform Act 2012 (Commencement No.9 and Transitional and Transitory Provisions and Commencement No.8 and Savings and Transitional Provisions (Amendment)) Order 2013 (SI 2013/983) ("the Commencement No.9 Order"), also in force as from April 29, 2013. Articles 3 and 4 of the Commencement No.9 Order, when read with Schs 1–3 of that Order, enable Pathfinder Group claimants in four postcode districts in the North West of England (see Sch.1 of that Order) to claim universal credit. It follows that, to make any sense, the Transitional Provisions Regulations 2013 have to be read together with the respective Commencement Orders. The geographical scope of further Commencement Orders is summarised in the note to the Commencement No.9 Order.

Part 3 (regs. 15–35) of these Regulations then concerns the "effect of transition to universal credit". Chapter 1 (regs 15–18) deals with entitlement (or rather non-entitlement) to existing benefits. Thus reg.15 provides for the exclusion of entitlement to various existing benefits and reg.16 allows for the termination of awards of existing benefits as part of the process of transition to universal credit. Regulation 17 and the Schedule make detailed provision for the position as regards entitlement to tax credits and the transfer to universal credit. Regulation 18 is concerned with the effect of ongoing benefit appeals. Chapter 2 (regs 19–35) makes provision for the transition from existing benefits to universal credit, including in particular the process of transfer from existing incapacity benefits (regs 23–28) and the continuation of existing benefit sanctions and penalties (regs 30–35).

PART I

INTRODUCTION AND INTERPRETATION

Citation and commencement

1.—(1) These Regulations may be cited as the Universal Credit (Transitional Provisions) Regulations 2013.   3.2

(2) These Regulations come into force on 29th April 2013.

Interpretation

3.3   **2.**—(1) In these Regulations—

"the Act" means the Welfare Reform Act 2012;

"the 2007 Act" means the Welfare Reform Act 2007;

"assessment period" has the same meaning as in the Universal Credit Regulations;

"the Claims and Payments Regulations" means the Universal Credit, Personal Independence Payment, Jobseeker's Allowance and Employment and Support Allowance (Claims and Payments) Regulations 2013;

"contribution-based jobseeker's allowance" has the same meaning as in the Jobseekers Act 1995 as it has effect apart from the amendments made by Part 1 of Schedule 14 to the Act (to remove references to an income-based allowance);

"contributory employment and support allowance" means a contributory allowance under Part 1 of the 2007 Act as it has effect apart from the amendments made by Schedule 3, and Part 1 of Schedule 14, to the Act (to remove references to an income-related allowance);

"employment and support allowance" means an allowance under Part 1 of the 2007 Act as it has effect apart from the amendments made by Schedule 3, and Part 1 of Schedule 14, to the Act (to remove references to an income-related allowance);

[¹ "exempt accommodation" has the same meaning as in paragraph 1 of Schedule 1 to the Universal Credit Regulations;]

"existing benefit" means income-based jobseeker's allowance, income-related employment and support allowance, income support under section 124 of the Social Security Contributions and Benefits Act 1992, housing benefit [¹ ...] and child tax credit and working tax credit under the Tax Credits Act 2002, but see also regulation 28(2);

"First-tier Tribunal" has the same meaning as in the Social Security Act 1998;

[¹ "housing benefit" means housing benefit under section 130 of the Social Security Contributions and Benefits Act 1992;]

"income-based jobseeker's allowance" has the same meaning as in the Jobseekers Act 1995;

"income-related employment and support allowance" means an income-related allowance under Part 1 of the 2007 Act;

"jobseeker's allowance" means an allowance under the Jobseekers Act 1995 as it has effect apart from the amendments made by Part 1 of Schedule 14 to the Act (to remove references to an income-based allowance);

"new claimant partner" has the meaning given in regulation 16;

"new style ESA" means an award of employment and support allowance under Part 1 of the 2007 Act as amended by Schedule 3, and Part 1 of Schedule 14, to the Act (to remove references to an income-related allowance);

"new style JSA" means an award of jobseeker's allowance under the Jobseekers Act 1995 as amended by Part 1 of Schedule 14 to the Act (to remove references to an income-based allowance);

"tax credit", "tax credits" and "tax year" have the same meanings as in the Tax Credits Act 2002;

"the Universal Credit Regulations" means the Universal Credit Regulations 2013;

"Upper Tribunal" has the same meaning as in the Social Security Act 1998.

(2) For the purposes of these Regulations, the date on which a claim for universal credit is made is to be determined in accordance with the Claims and Payments Regulations.

AMENDMENT

1. Universal Credit (Transitional Provisions) and Housing Benefit (Amendment) Regulations 2013 (SI 2013/2070), reg.3(1) (October 28, 2013).

GENERAL NOTE   3.4

Para. (1)

"new claimant partner": where a single universal credit claimant becomes a   3.5
member of a couple, and their award terminates, and the other member of
the couple was not previously entitled to universal credit as a single person, but
an award of universal credit is then made to the couple as joint claimants, then
the other member of the couple is known as a "new claimant partner" (see also
reg.16).

"new style ESA": in effect, this means (new variant) contribution-based ESA,
shorn of its previous income-based element, and as defined in the Pathfinder areas
as from April 29, 2013.

"new style JSA": similarly, this means (new variant) contribution-based JSA, again
shorn of its income-related element, and as defined in the Pathfinder areas as from
April 29, 2013.

Para. (2)

The normal rule is that the date of a universal credit claim is the date the   3.6
claim is received, whether electronically or by telephone or, if later, the first
day for which the claim is made: see Claims and Payments Regulations 2013,
reg.10.

PART II

FIRST STAGE OF TRANSITION TO UNIVERSAL CREDIT

CHAPTER 1

ENTITLEMENT TO CLAIM UNIVERSAL CREDIT

Entitlement to claim universal credit

3.—(1) Unless a claim may be made by virtue of paragraph (2), or   3.7
treated as made by virtue of paragraph (4), a person may not make, or be
treated as making, a claim for universal credit unless—

(a) the claim is in respect of a period which begins on or after the date
on which these Regulations come into force; and

(b) on the date on which the claim is made, or treated as made, the
person falls within the Pathfinder Group.

(2) Subject to paragraph (3), where an award of universal credit to joint claimants terminates because they cease to be a couple, the claimant who is not exempt (by virtue of regulation 9(6) of the Claims and Payments Regulations) from the requirement to make a claim, may make a claim for universal credit during the period of one month starting with the date on which notification is given to the Secretary of State that the claimants have ceased to be a couple, even if the claimant does not fall within the Pathfinder Group on the date on which the claim is made.

(3) No claim may be made by a person by virtue of paragraph (2) at any time when the person or their partner is entitled to—

(a) state pension credit; or

(b) an existing benefit [¹ (but see paragraph (6))].

(4) Subject to paragraph (5), where regulation 9(8) of the Claims and Payments Regulations (Claims for universal credit by members of a couple) applies to a couple, they may be treated as making a claim for universal credit in accordance with that regulation, even though they do not fall within the Pathfinder Group on the date on which the claim is treated as made.

(5) No claim is to be treated as made by a couple by virtue of paragraph (4) at any time when—

(a) the member of the couple who was previously entitled to universal credit as a single claimant is entitled to—

(i) state pension credit; or

(ii) an existing benefit [¹ (but see paragraph (6))];

(b) the member of the couple who did not previously have an award of universal credit as a single person is entitled to state pension credit.

[¹ (6) For the purposes of paragraphs (3)(b) and (5)(a)(ii), "existing benefit" does not include housing benefit in respect of exempt accommodation.]

AMENDMENT

1. Universal Credit (Transitional Provisions) and Housing Benefit (Amendment) Regulations 2013 (SI 2013/2070), reg.3(2) (October 28, 2013).

DEFINITIONS

"Claims and Payments Regulations"—see reg.2(1).
"existing benefit"—*ibid.*, and para.(6).

GENERAL NOTE

Para.(1)

3.8
The general rule is that a person may only make a claim for universal credit if (1) the claim is for a period beginning on or after April 29, 2013; *and* (2) he or she falls within the "Pathfinder Group". In addition, of course, the Commencement No.9 Order provides that the claimant must live in one of four designated postcode districts in the North West of England (all in Tameside). Subsequent Commencement Orders have since "rolled out" universal credit to various other specified postcode districts across the country (see further the note to the Commencement No.9 Order). The terms for membership of the

Pathfinder Group are set out in regs 5–12 below (see reg.4(1)). In outline, claim-ants must:

- be British Citizens who are habitually resident in the United Kingdom;

- be aged between 18 years and 60 years and 6 months;

- be resident in the Pathfinder locations (but not owner-occupiers or in temporary accommodation);

- be single;

- be available for work or in work with low earnings (but not have earnings from self-employment);

- not be receiving specified existing benefits;

- not have capital above £6,000; and

- not have children.

In general, the Pathfinder Group inclusions are tightly defined and the exclusions broadly defined, so as to confine membership to "straightforward" cases without complicating circumstances.

The principle that a person may not make, or be treated as making, a claim for universal credit unless the conditions set out in para.(1), including membership of the Pathfinder Group, is not absolute. There are, inevitably, exceptions to this general principle—these are where a claim is either made by virtue of para.(2) or treated as made by para.(4).

Para. (2)

The first exception to the general principle set out in para.(1) applies to certain cases in which a couple who have a joint award of universal credit sepa-rate. Normally entitlement to universal credit depends on a claim having been made. However, in this situation, the claim requirement does not apply to the member of the former couple who either (a) does not inform the Secretary of State that they have ceased to be a couple (where their ex-partner has already so notified) or (b) is the second of them to inform the Secretary of State of the separation (see reg.9(6) of the Claims and Payments Regulations 2013). In such a scenario, the member of the couple who is *not* exempt from the requirement to make a claim (in other words, the one who either informed the Secretary of State of the separation, or who was first to do so) may claim universal credit even though s/he is not in the Pathfinder Group at the date of claim. However, such a claim must be made within one month of the date on which the notification of separation is given to the Secretary of State. This exception is itself subject to para.(3).

3.9

Para. (3)

This provides for an exception to the exception in para.(2). The special rule in para.(2) does not apply where either member of the separating couple is entitled to state pension credit or to an "existing benefit" (see reg.2(1)), i.e. one of the means-tested benefits or tax credits being replaced by universal credit. Presumably the claimant or their partner would need to relinquish entitlement to state pension credit or the existing benefit in order to qualify for universal credit, if that were advantageous. Official advice suggests that a request to stop receiving benefit should be treated as an application for supersession, and staff are advised to ensure the wish to relinquish benefit is genuine and the consequences have been explained (see ADM paras A4120–A4131).

However, note that, in what amounts to an exception to the exception to the exception, housing benefit in respect of exempt accommodation does not fall within

3.10

para.(2)—see para.(6). Thus, in summary, cases that fall within para.(3) are covered by the general rule in para.(1).

Para. (4)

3.11 This provides for a second exception to the general principle set out in para.(1). It provides for certain claimants to be treated as having made a claim for universal credit even though they do not fall in the Pathfinder Group at the relevant date. This covers couples who are covered by reg.9(9) of the Claims and Payments Regulations 2013. This provides that a couple who are joint claimants are to be treated as making a claim for universal credit where (a) one of them was entitled to universal credit as a single person and ceased to be so entitled on becoming a member of the couple; and (b) their partner did not have an award of universal credit as a single person before they became a couple. This is subject to the exception in para.(5), which is drawn in essentially the same terms as that in para.(3), with necessary adjustments.

Para. (5)

3.12 Note that the second limb of para.(3), the existing benefit exception, does not apply to the member of the couple who did not previously have an award of universal credit as a single person.

Para. (6)

3.13 The effect of para.(6) is that an award of housing benefit in respect of exempt accommodation does not prevent a claim to universal credit being made by a person who was formerly a member of a universal credit joint claim couple, or a joint claim to universal credit being treated as made where one member of the couple previously had an award of universal credit as a single person.

This special provision has to be understood against the policy background. Payments made in respect of exempt accommodation (in effect, supported accommodation) are not taken into account as "rent payments" under the universal credit scheme. This means in turn that the housing element of universal credit is not payable in respect of exempt accommodation. The Government has announced that it is exploring the feasibility of a localised funding system for the additional housing-related costs of those living in supported housing that is "exempt accommodation" for housing benefit purposes. Meanwhile, as an interim measure, the Universal Credit Regulations, as amended, make provision to allow supported exempt accommodation housing costs for universal credit claimants to be met by way housing benefit. Thus, for the time being at least, the prohibition in the original version of the Regulations on a claimant being entitled simultaneously to both universal credit and housing benefit has been removed.

CHAPTER 2

THE PATHFINDER GROUP

The Pathfinder Group

3.14 **4.**—(1) A person falls within the Pathfinder Group if they meet the requirements of regulations 5 to 12.

(2) Any declaration which is required by regulation 6(3)(c), 9(1), or 12(a)

or (b) is to be made by such method as may be required by the Secretary of State in relation to the person.

GENERAL NOTE

It might have been more helpful if the term "Pathfinder Group" itself had appeared in the interpretation provision (reg.2 above) as well. Be that as it may, this makes it clear that a person is in the Pathfinder Group—and so eligible to claim (or be treated as claiming) universal credit (see reg.3(1), but subject to the exceptions in reg.3(2) and (4))—only if they meet *all* of the conditions set out in regs 5–12 inclusive. Presumably, as and when (or possibly if and when) universal credit is "rolled out" to all claimants, then these special Pathfinder Group conditions will be removed. In the meantime, of course, these various requirements can be expanded or contracted as experience in the first affected districts shows is necessary.

3.15

Personal characteristics

5. The person must be—
(a) aged at least 18 years, but under 60 years and six months;
(b) a single person;
(c) a British citizen who—
   (i) has resided in the United Kingdom throughout the period of two years ending with the date on which the claim for universal credit is made; and
   (ii) has not, during that period, left the United Kingdom for a continuous period of four weeks or more.

3.16

DEFINITION

"single person"—WRA 2012, ss.1(2)(a) and 40.

GENERAL NOTE

This regulation defines the essential or core personal characteristics for membership of the Pathfinder Group. In short, these are being of working age (para.(a)), being single (para.(b)) and being a British citizen with two years' residence before the date of claim (para.(c)). A "single person" is "an individual who is not a member of a couple" (WRA 2012, s.1(2)(a))—and for the definition of couple see WRA 2012, s.39. The Government has indicated its intention to expand the Pathfinder Group's category of personal circumstances to include (childless) couples as from summer 2014 and families with children from autumn 2014 (Written Ministerial Statement, *Universal Credit progress*, Thursday December 5, 2013).

3.17

Fitness to work

6.—(1) The person must not—
(a) be pregnant; or
(b) have been pregnant, if the date of her confinement occurred during the period of 15 weeks ending with the date on which the claim for universal credit is made.
(2) In this regulation, "confinement" has the same meaning as in regulation 8(4) of the Universal Credit Regulations.
(3) The person—
(a) must not have obtained from a doctor a statement given in accordance with the rules set out in Part 1 of Schedule 1 to the Social

3.18

Security (Medical Evidence) Regulations 1976 ("a statement of fitness for work") in respect of the day on which the claim for universal credit is made, unless it has been determined, since the statement was given, that the person does not have limited capability for work within the meaning of the 2007 Act;

(b) must not have applied for a statement of fitness for work;

(c) must declare that they do not consider themselves to be unfit for work; and

(d) must not have been the subject of a determination that they have limited capability for work within the meaning of the 2007 Act, unless it has subsequently been determined that they do not have limited capability for work within the meaning of that Act.

DEFINITIONS

"the 2007 Act"—see reg.2(1).
"a statement of fitness for work"—para.(3)(a).
"Universal Credit Regulations"—see reg.2(1).

GENERAL NOTE

3.19   A claimant of universal credit must not be pregnant or recently pregnant (para.(1)) and must not be unfit for work, as (very) broadly defined here (para.(3)).

Paras (1) and (2)

3.20   "Confinement" is defined by reg.8(4) of the Universal Credit Regulations 2013 as "(a) labour resulting in the birth of a living child; or (b) labour after 24 weeks of pregnancy resulting in the birth of a child whether alive or dead, and where a woman's labour begun on one day results in the birth of a child on another day she is to be taken to be confined on the date of the birth."

Para.(3)

3.21   Fitness for work is an essential requirement for membership of the Pathfinder Group. However, perhaps counter-intuitively, fitness for work is not judged by whether or not someone has limited capability for work for the purposes of ESA. For the purposes of universal credit, the following are regarded as being unfit for work (and so ineligible for the Pathfinder Group): (a) those with a doctor's note (unless they have since actually scored less than 15 points); (b) those who have applied for a doctor's note; (c) those who have self-declared themselves as unfit for work (see also reg.4(2)); and (d) those who are subject to a current ruling that they have limited capability for work. The intention, it seems, is to keep out of the Pathfinder Group anyone with as much as a hint of incapacity, whether or not they have scored 15 points under the work capability assessment.

Existing benefits

3.22   7.—(1) The person must not be entitled to—

(a) any existing benefit;

(b) contribution-based jobseeker's allowance;

(c) contributory employment and support allowance;

(d) incapacity benefit or severe disablement allowance, as defined in Schedule 4 to the 2007 Act;

(e) disability living allowance under section 71 of the Social Security Contributions and Benefits Act 1992; or

(f) personal independence payment.

(2) The person must not be treated by regulation 8 as being entitled to a tax credit.

(3) The person must not be awaiting—

(a) a decision on a claim for any benefit mentioned in paragraph (1)(a) to (c); or

(b) the outcome of an application—

    (i) to the Secretary of State to consider whether to revise, under section 9 of the Social Security Act 1998, a decision that the person is not entitled to jobseeker's allowance, employment and support allowance or income support; or

    (ii) to the relevant authority (within the meaning of the Child Support, Pensions and Social Security Act 2000) to consider whether to revise, under Schedule 7 to that Act, a decision that the person is not entitled to housing benefit.

(4) If the person has appealed against a decision that they are not entitled to a benefit mentioned in paragraph (1)(a) to (c), the Secretary of State must be satisfied—

(a) that the appeal to the First-tier Tribunal, and any subsequent appeal to the Upper Tribunal or to a court, is not ongoing; and

(b) where an appeal has been finally determined, that there is no possibility of a further appeal by any party.

(5) If the person was previously entitled to jobseeker's allowance, the award of that benefit must not have terminated during the period of two weeks ending with the date on which the claim for universal credit is made.

(6) If the person was previously entitled to employment and support allowance, the award of that benefit must not have terminated during the period of two weeks ending with the date on which the claim for universal credit is made, unless the award terminated as a result of a decision which incorporated a determination that the person no longer had limited capability for work within the meaning of the 2007 Act.

DEFINITIONS

"the 2007 Act"—see reg.2(1).
"contribution-based jobseeker's allowance"—*ibid.*
"contributory employment and support allowance"—*ibid.*
"employment and support allowance"—*ibid.*
"existing benefit"—*ibid.*
"First-tier Tribunal"—*ibid.*
"jobseeker's allowance"—*ibid.*
"Upper Tribunal"—*ibid.*

GENERAL NOTE   3.23

Paras (1)–(3)

Claimants who have an entitlement to an existing benefit pose significant complications in terms of the operational transfer (or "migration") to universal credit. For that reason, such existing claimants are excluded from membership of the Pathfinder Group (para.(1)) and therefore cannot claim universal credit. The references to contribution-based JSA and contributory ESA mean awards of those benefits made under the legislation as in force before the amendments made by the WA 2012 in 2013. This category of existing claimants includes those treated being entitled to tax credits by reg.8 (para.(2)) and those awaiting either decisions or the   3.24

outcome of applications in respect of certain benefits (para.(3)). It is only receipt of those benefits and tax credits listed in paras (1) and (2), as modified by paras (3)–(6) inclusive which preclude a claim for universal credit. Thus a person with a current award of industrial disablement benefit but no other such benefit or tax credit may be in the Pathfinder Group.

Para. (4)

3.25   Those persons who are subject to ongoing appeals are also excluded from the Pathfinder Group. However, it is not entirely clear that this exclusion sits neatly with the procedural rules governing time limits for appealing. As a general rule the time limit for appealing to the First-tier Tribunal is one month, a time limit which may be extended, but subject to the statutory maximum, being 12 months from the date that the time limit for appealing expired. However, the position is different as regards appeals to the Upper Tribunal. The time limit for applying to the Upper Tribunal for permission to appeal is also one month (e.g. from the date that the First-tier Tribunal refused permission to appeal). That time limit can also be extended. However, unlike the position at the First-tier Tribunal, there is no absolute statutory time limit. That being so, while it may be that the First-tier Tribunal has determined an appeal, and there may not appear to be an appeal to the Upper tribunal ongoing, strictly it may not be possible to say that "there is no possibility of a further appeal by any party" within para.(4)(b).

Paras (5) and (6)

3.26   In the case of jobseeker's allowance, a universal credit claim is not possible where the JSA award ended in the previous fortnight (para.(5)). There is a similar provision for awards of ESA which have recently ended, unless the award terminated because the person has been found fit for work (para.(6)).

Existing benefits: ongoing awards of tax credits

3.27   **8.**—(1) For the purposes of regulations 7(2) and 16(4)—

(a) a person is to be treated as being entitled to working tax credit with effect from the start of the current tax year even though a decision has not been made under section 14 of the Tax Credits Act 2002 ("the 2002 Act") in respect of a claim for that tax credit for that tax year, if the person was entitled to working tax credit for the previous tax year and any of the cases specified in paragraph (2) applies; and

(b) a person is to be treated as being entitled to child tax credit with effect from the start of the current tax year even though a decision has not been made under section 14 of the 2002 Act in respect of a claim for that tax credit for that tax year, if the person was entitled to child tax credit for the previous tax year and any of the cases specified in paragraph (2) applies.

(2) The cases are—

(a) a final notice has not been given to the person under section 17 of the 2002 Act in respect of the previous tax year;

(b) a final notice has been given, which includes provision by virtue of subsection (2) or (4) of section 17, or a combination of those subsections and subsection (6) and—

(i) the date specified in the notice for the purposes of section 17(2) and (4) or, where different dates are specified, the later of them, has not yet passed and no claim for a tax credit for the current year has been made, or treated as made, or

(ii) a claim for a tax credit has been made, or treated as made, on or before the date mentioned in paragraph (i), but no decision has been made in relation to that claim under section 14(1) of the 2002 Act;

(c) a final notice has been given, no claim for a tax credit for the current year has been made, or treated as made, and no decision has been made under section 18(1) of the 2002 Act in respect of entitlement to a tax credit for the previous tax year; or

(d) a final notice has been given and—

    (i) the person did not make a declaration in response to provision included in that notice by virtue of section 17(2)(a), (4)(a) or (6)(a), or any combination of those provisions, by the date specified in the notice;

    (ii) they were given notice that payments of tax credit under section 24(4) of the 2002 Act had ceased due to their failure to make the declaration; and

    (iii) their claim for universal credit is made during the period of 30 days starting with the date on the notice referred to in paragraph (ii) or, where the person is a new claimant partner, notification of formation of a couple with a person who is entitled to universal credit is given to the Secretary of State during that period.

DEFINITIONS

"new claimant partner"—see reg.2(1).
"tax credit"—*ibid.*
"tax year"—*ibid.*

GENERAL NOTE

Regulation 7 provides that those entitled to existing benefits are excluded from the Pathfinder Group. This category includes those who are treated by reg.8 "as being entitled to a tax credit" (reg.7(2)).   3.28

Para. (1)

This gives a fairly broad meaning to the concept of being treated as entitled to tax credits. In particular, it means those claimants who had an award of either working tax credit (para.(1)(a)) or child tax credit (para.1(b)) for the previous tax year but who have not yet had an initial decision under s.14 of the Tax Credits Act 2002 for the current tax year, so long as one of the situations set out in para.(2) applies.   3.29

Para. (2)

This sets out the four circumstances in which a person without an initial award of tax credits in the current tax year is still treated as being entitled to tax credits. The first type of case is where no final notice for the previous tax year has been issued yet under s.17 of the Tax Credits Act 2002 (para.(2)(a)). The other three categories are where a s.17 notice has been issued for the previous year and various other circumstances also apply.   3.30

Income and capital

9.—(1) The person must declare that, during the period of one month starting with the date on which the claim for universal credit is made, their earned income is expected not to exceed—   3.31

(a) £270, if they are aged under 25; or

(b) £330, if they are aged 25 or over.

(2) The person's capital must not exceed £6,000.

(3) For the purposes of this regulation, "earned income" and "capital" have the same meanings as they have in Part 6 of the Universal Credit Regulations.

DEFINITIONS

"capital"—para.(3) and Pt 6 of the Universal Credit Regulations.
"earned income"—para.(3) and Pt 6 of the Universal Credit Regulations.
"Universal Credit Regulations"—see reg.2(1).

GENERAL NOTE

3.32   This is, in effect, the basic means test for membership of the Pathfinder Group. There is both an earned income test and a capital test (both concepts defined by reference to Part 6 of the Universal Credit Regulations (para.(3)). The limit for earned income, as expected to be received in the month after the claim is £330 (or £270 for those aged under 25) (para.(1)). The capital limit is £6,000—there is no lower and upper limit with tariff income on capital in between, as under the existing means-tested benefit systems. On declaring (for the purpose of para.(1), see reg.4(2)).

Housing

3.33   **10.** The person must not—
   (a) be homeless (within the meaning of section 175 of the Housing Act 1996) and must currently reside at their usual address;
   (b) reside in accommodation in which care, supervision, counselling, advice or other support services (other than services connected solely with the provision of adequate accommodation) are made available to them by or on behalf of the person by whom the accommodation is provided, with a view to enabling them to live there;
   [[1](ba) reside in the same household as a person who is a member of the regular forces or the reserve forces (within the meaning of section 374 of the Armed Forces Act 2006) and who is absent from the household in connection with that role;]
   (c) own, or partly own, the property in which they reside.

AMENDMENT

1. Universal Credit (Miscellaneous Amendments) Regulations 2013 (SI 2013/803) reg.3(2) (April 29, 2013).

GENERAL NOTE

3.34   At present the Pathfinder Group is only open to what might be described as "standard" tenants. So the following categories of claimant are excluded: the homeless (para.(a); see further below); those in supported accommodation (para.(b)); persons sharing a household with a member of the armed forces, where the latter is absent on service (para.(ba)); and owner-occupiers (para.(c)). However, note that "standard" tenants in effect also means that a tenant who does not "currently reside at their usual address" is equated with being homeless and so cannot claim universal credit.

Note that para.(ba) is not limited to those claimants with e.g. adult children who are away on operations. It excludes from the Pathfinder Group those with *any* member of their *household* who is away on armed forces duties. The Explanatory Memorandum to the amending regulations states that this approach "ensures that the restrictions can be readily explained so that people can easily determine whether or not they are eligible to claim."

"homeless"

Section 175(1)–(3) of the Housing Act 1996 (subs.(4), not included here, deals with threatened homelessness) defines the term as follows:

"(1) A person is homeless if he has no accommodation available for his occupation, in the United Kingdom or elsewhere, which he—

(a) is entitled to occupy by virtue of an interest in it or by virtue of an order of a court,

(b) has an express or implied licence to occupy, or

(c) occupies as a residence by virtue of any enactment or rule of law giving him the right to remain in occupation or restricting the right of another person to recover possession.

(2) A person is also homeless if he has accommodation but—

(a) he cannot secure entry to it, or

(b) it consists of a moveable structure, vehicle or vessel designed or adapted for human habitation and there is no place where he is entitled or permitted both to place it and to reside in it.

(3) A person shall not be treated as having accommodation unless it is accommodation which it would be reasonable for him to continue to occupy."

Inevitably there is a considerable body of case law on s.175 of the Housing Act 1996. As to s.175(1), "accommodation" means a place that can fairly be described as such and which it is reasonably, having regard to the general housing conditions in the area, for a person to continue to occupy—it need not be permanent accommodation (*R v Brent LBC, ex p. Awua* [1996] AC 55); see also s.176 of the Housing Act 1996. A person may have accommodation but be unable to gain access to it, e.g. if the property has squatters, and so be homeless (s.175(2)). On the issue of reasonableness, in the context of s.175(3), a person who has accommodation anywhere in the world which is both legally and practically available for his occupation is not homeless, unless it is accommodation in which he was living but cannot reasonably continue to live (*Begum (Nipa) v Tower Hamlets LBC* [2000] 1 WLR 306 and *Birmingham CC v Ali & Ors* [2009] UKHL 362009] 1 WLR 1506. See also on reasonableness *Maloba v Waltham Forest LBC* [2007] EWCA Civ 1281; [2008] 1 WLR 2079. Note also that by virtue of s.177(1) it is not reasonable for a person to continue to occupy accommodation if it is probable that this will lead to domestic violence or other violence against him, or against either a person who normally resides with him as a member of his family, or any other person who might reasonably be expected to reside with him.

"household"

This term is not defined by these Regulations. There is, of course, much learning and case law on what is meant by a 'household'; see e.g. the discussion in the note to reg.2 of the Income Support Regulations in Vol.II of this series.

"reside"

The concept of ordinary residence has been defined as referring to "a man's abode in a particular place or country which he has adopted voluntarily and for settled purposes as part of the regular order of his life for the time being, whether of short or of long duration" (*Shah v Barnet LBC* [1983] 2 AC 309 at 343–344 (per Lord Scarman). The question of where someone resides is ultimately an issue of fact.

"usual address"

There is no statutory definition of what is meant by "usual address"; presumably this will also be a question of fact. However, a similar concept appears in the Civil Procedure Rules, which provide that where an individual defendant does not give an address at which they may be served, they may be served at their "*usual* or last known *residence*" (see rule 6.9). The case law on that expression shows that a person may have more than one "usual residence" and that what matters is the person's overall pattern of life and not simply the period of occupation (see e.g. *Varsani v Relfo Ltd (In Liquidation)* [2010] EWCA Civ 560).

Caring responsibilities

3.35   **11.** [[1] (1)] The person must not—

(a) have a child living with them some or all of the time;

(b) have a person ("the young person") living with them some or all of the time if—

    (i) the young person is not a child, but is under the age of 20; and

    (ii) they would be responsible for the young person for the purposes of regulation 4 of the Universal Credit Regulations, if the young person were a qualifying young person within the meaning of regulation 5 of those Regulations;

(c) be an adopter (within the meaning of regulation 89(3) of the Universal Credit Regulations) with whom a child is expected to be placed during the period of two weeks beginning with the date on which the claim for universal credit is made;

[[1](ca) be a foster parent;]

(d) be liable to pay child support maintenance under the Child Support Act 1991;

(e) have any responsibility for providing care to a person who has a physical or mental impairment, other than in the course of paid or voluntary employment.

[[1](2) For the purposes of this regulation—

"foster parent" means—

(a) in relation to England, a person who is approved as a foster parent under the Fostering Services (England) Regulations 2011;

(b) in relation to Wales, a person who is approved as a foster parent under the Fostering Services (Wales) Regulations 2003;

(c) in relation to Scotland, a person who is approved as a kinship carer or a foster carer under the Looked After Children (Scotland) Regulations 2009.]

AMENDMENT

1. Universal Credit (Miscellaneous Amendments) Regulations 2013 (SI 2013/803 reg.3(3) (April 29, 2013).

DEFINITIONS

"foster parent"—para.(2).
"Universal Credit Regulations"—see reg.2(1).
"the young person"—para.(1)(b).

GENERAL NOTE

3.36   A further illustration of the drive for simplicity in the launch of universal credit is that anyone with caring responsibilities is excluded from the Pathfinder Group. However, the notion of having caring responsibilities is not limited to those in receipt of carer's allowance, although some (or probably) all of those will doubtless qualify for exclusion from the Pathfinder Group under the broader definition of carer in para.(e). Rather, "caring responsibilities" includes any claimant falling into any of the following six categories.

Para. (a)

The first is any claimant who has a child living with them "some or all of the time". A "child" is someone under the age of 16 (WRA 2012, s.40). Note that (i) the child need not be the claimant's own child; (ii) the claimant need not be a lone parent; and (iii) the child need only live with the claimant "some . . . of the time". It follows that a non-resident parent with a child who has staying contact will have "caring responsibilities" and so be excluded from the Pathfinder Group, whether or not he is liable to pay child support (see para.(d)).

3.37

Para. (b)

This covers claimants who have 17–19 year olds living with them (again, "some or all of the time"), so long as the young person would be a qualifying young person and the claimant would be responsible for them under the tests in the Universal Credit Regulations 2013. As with para.(a), the young person need not be the claimant's own child and the claimant need not be a lone parent.

3.38

Para. (c)

Regulation 89(3)(a) of the Universal Credit Regulations defines an adopter as "a person who has been matched with a child for adoption and who is, or is intended to be, the responsible carer for the child, but excluding a person who is a foster parent or close relative of the child". Further, "a person is matched with a child for adoption when it is decided by an adoption agency that the person would be a suitable adoptive parent for the child" (reg.89(3)(b)).

3.39

Para. (ca)

"Foster parent" is defined in effect as an "approved foster parent" (para.(2)). Note that the test is whether the person is an approved foster parent, not whether he or she currently has a child placed with them.

3.40

Para. (d)

A claimant who is "liable to pay child support maintenance under the Child Support Act 1991" is a person with "caring responsibilities". So the question is, in effect, whether the claimant is a non-resident parent as defined by that Act (see Child Support Act 1991, ss.1(2) and 3(2)). The question is not whether he is actually paying child support. Presumably—although the point is not entirely free from doubt—a non-resident parent with a nil liability qualifies as having caring responsibilities. He is liable to pay child support, it is just that his liability is the nil rate (Child Support Act 1991, Sch.1, para.5 and Child Support (Maintenance Calculations and Special Cases) Regulations 2000 (SI 2001/155) reg.5).

3.41

Para. (e)

Carers are excluded from the Pathfinder Group so long as they are acting "other than in the course of paid or voluntary employment", but regardless of whether or not they qualify for carer's allowance. So a person who is simultaneously both a paid carer e.g. for a neighbour and a carer at home is outside the Pathfinder Group by virtue of their domestic unpaid care.

3.42

Other requirements

12. The person—

(a) must declare that they do not expect to have any self-employed earnings, as defined in regulation 57 of the Universal Credit Regulations, during the period of one month starting with the date on which the claim for universal credit is made;

3.43

    (b) must not be engaged in education or training of any kind and must declare that they do not intend to engage in education or training of any kind (other than where required to do so by the Secretary of State, or by agreement with the Secretary of State, in connection with an award of universal credit) during the period of one month starting with the date on which the claim for universal credit is made;

    (c) must not have—

        (i) a deputy appointed by the Court of Protection under Part 1 of the Mental Capacity Act 2005 ("the 2005 Act");

        (ii) a receiver appointed under Part 7 of the Mental Health Act 1983 and treated as a deputy by virtue of the 2005 Act; or

        (iii) any other person acting on their behalf in relation to the claim for universal credit;

    (d) must have a national insurance number;

    (e) must have an account with a bank, a building society or the Post Office [¹ or a current account with a Credit Union (within the meaning of the Credit Unions Act 1979)].

AMENDMENT

1. Universal Credit (Transitional Provisions) and Housing Benefit (Amendment) Regulations 2013 (SI 2013/2070) reg.4 (October 28, 2013).

DEFINITIONS

"the 2005 Act"—para.(c).
"Universal Credit Regulations"—see reg.2(1).

GENERAL NOTE

3.44   Regulations 5–11 deal with various common exclusions from the Pathfinder Group which are related to personal status or receipt of benefits or tax credits. This final regulation in Chapter 2 deals with a miscellaneous ragbag of exclusions from, and requirements for, membership of the Pathfinder Group.

Para.(a)
3.45   The self-employed are presumably regarded as too difficult to include in the Pathfinder Group. However, note that this only excludes those expecting self-employed earnings in the month after the claim. "Self-employed earnings" for this purpose is earned income which is "not employed earnings and is derived from carrying on a trade, profession or vocation" (Universal Credit Regulations 2013, reg.57(1)). On declaring, see reg.4(2).

Para.(b)
3.46   Current students or trainees are excluded, as are those expecting to have that status in the next month (unless otherwise required or agreed). Note that the terms "education" and "training" are not defined by these Regulations. Furthermore, the concept of "education" is not qualified by e.g. being "advanced" or "non-advanced", or "full-time" or "part-time". The exclusion applies very liberally to "education or training of any kind". On that basis taking (or soon planning to start) evening classes for two hours a week in a foreign language or in car maintenance is enough to take one outside the Pathfinder Group. Thus the ADM states that education "includes adult education classes, for example in art or computing skills" (para.M1130). On declaring, see reg.4(2).

Para. (c)

Those who have someone else acting for them are excluded from the Pathfinder   **3.47**
Group. For those unable to act for themselves in the context of universal credit, see
Claims and Payments Regulations 2013, reg.57.

Para. (d)

A claimant can only be in the Pathfinder Group if they have a National Insurance   **3.48**
number; having applied for one is not enough.

Para. (e)

Over the years the Department has moved further and further away from paying   **3.49**
benefits by cash or giro. Claimants who do not have a relevant type of account will
be excluded from the Pathfinder Group. Note that *any* bank, building society or Post
Office account will suffice, but only a *current* account with a credit union qualifies.
So other types of account that a credit union may offer are not included. According
to the Explanatory Memorandum with the amending regulations, "current account'
has its usual meaning—i.e. it is a transactional account for day-to-day use that
identifiably belongs to the person concerned, including by means of a six-digit sort
code and individual account number. As such, the amendment continues to ensure
that universal credit claimants have an account into which universal credit payments
can be made by direct transfer while being more consistent with the wider work on
financial inclusion being undertaken by DWP with credit unions" (Explanatory
Memorandum, para.7.13).

CHAPTER 3

TREATMENT OF INVALID CLAIMS FOR UNIVERSAL CREDIT

Incorrect information regarding entitlement to claim

13.—(1) This regulation applies where a claim for universal credit is   **3.50**
made and it is subsequently discovered by the Secretary of State that the
claimant gave incorrect information regarding any of the requirements of
regulations 5 to 12 and did not in fact fall within the Pathfinder Group on
the date on which the claim was made.

(2) Where the discovery is made before the claim for universal credit has
been decided—

(a) the claimant is to be informed that they are not entitled to claim
universal credit;

(b) if the claimant makes a claim for jobseeker's allowance, employment
and support allowance or income support ("the existing benefit") and
the date on which that claim is made (as determined in accordance
with the Social Security (Claims and Payments) Regulations 1987
("the 1987 Regulations")) is after the date on which the claim for
universal credit was made, but no later than one month after the date
on which the information required by sub-paragraph (a) was given—

   (i) the claim for the existing benefit is to be treated as made on the
date on which the claim for universal credit was made; and

   (ii) any provision of the 1987 Regulations under which the claim
for the existing benefit is treated as made on a later date does
not apply;

(c) if the claimant makes a claim for housing benefit and the date of that claim (as determined in accordance with the Housing Benefit Regulations 2006 or, as the case may be, the Housing Benefit (Persons who have attained the qualifying age for state pension credit) Regulations 2006 (together referred to as "the Housing Benefit Regulations")) is after the date on which the claim for universal credit was made, but no later than one month after the date on which the information required by sub-paragraph (a) was given—

    (i) the claim for housing benefit is to be treated as made on the date on which the claim for universal credit was made; and

    (ii) any provision of the Housing Benefit Regulations under which the claim for housing benefit is treated as made on a later date does not apply;

(d) if the claimant makes a claim for a tax credit and that claim is received by a relevant authority at an appropriate office (within the meaning of the Tax Credits (Claims and Notifications) Regulations 2002 ("the 2002 Regulations")) during the period of one month beginning with the date on which the information required by sub-paragraph (a) was given—

    (i) the claim is to be treated as having been so received on the date on which the claim for universal credit was made; and

    (ii) any provision of the 2002 Regulations under which the claim is treated as having been made on a later date does not apply.

(3) Where the discovery is made after a decision has been made that the claimant is entitled to universal credit, but before any payment has been made—

(a) that decision is to cease to have effect immediately, by virtue of this regulation;

(b) the claimant is to be informed that they are not entitled to claim universal credit; and

(c) paragraph (2)(b) to (d) applies.

(4) Where the discovery is made after a decision has been made that the claimant is entitled to universal credit and one or more payments have been made to the claimant—

(a) the claim is to be treated as one which the claimant was entitled to make;

(b) the decision is to be treated as a decision under section 8 of the Social Security Act 1998; and

(c) the award shall continue, if the claimant meets the conditions of entitlement for universal credit.

DEFINITIONS

"the 1987 Regulations"—para.(2)(b).
"the 2002 Regulations"—para.(2)(d).
"Claims and Payments Regulations"—see reg.2(1).
"employment and support allowance"—*ibid.*
"existing benefit"—*ibid.* and para.(2)(b).
"the Housing Benefit Regulations"—para.(2)(c).
"jobseeker's allowance"—see reg.2(1).
"tax credit"—*ibid.*

GENERAL NOTE

Regulations 5–12 make detailed provision for membership of the Pathfinder   3.51
Group. Errors are bound to occur in the information provided by claimants about
such matters. This regulation deals with the treatment of claims which have been
allowed to proceed on the basis of such inaccurate information. The basic rule is that
no entitlement to universal credit will arise in respect of an invalid claim, unless payments have already started. Thus if the error comes to light before a decision is made
on the universal credit claim, the claimant will be so informed and the date of claim
for one of the "old" benefits (or tax credits) will be the date of their universal credit
claim, so long as they claim within a month (para.(2)). If the claim has been decided,
but no payment has been made, they are likewise informed and the same rules apply
as regards the date of claim for an "old" benefit (para.(3)). It is only if universal credit
has actually been paid out that the claim is treated as being a valid universal credit
claim and award, irrespective of the error which has since come to light (para.(4)).

CHAPTER 4

AWARDS OF UNIVERSAL CREDIT WITHOUT A CLAIM

Awards of universal credit without a claim

14.—(1) [² Subject to paragraph (3)], an award of universal credit may be   3.52
made without a claim in accordance with regulation 6 (Claims not required
for entitlement to universal credit in certain cases) or regulation 9(6) or (7)
(Claims for universal credit by members of a couple) of the Claims and
Payments Regulations, even if the person to whom that award is made would
not otherwise be permitted to claim universal credit by these Regulations.

(2) [² . . .]

(3) No award of universal credit may be made to a person under regulation 6 or 9(6) or (7) of the Claims and Payments Regulations at any time
when they or their partner are entitled to—

(a) state pension credit; or

(b) an existing benefit [¹ (other than housing benefit in respect of exempt
accommodation)].

AMENDMENTS

1. Universal Credit (Transitional Provisions) and Housing Benefit (Amendment)
Regulations 2013 (SI 2013/2070) reg.3(3) (October 28, 2013).

2. Universal Credit (Transitional Provisions) and Housing Benefit (Amendment)
Regulations 2013 (SI 2013/2070) reg.5 (October 28, 2013).

DEFINITIONS

"assessment period"—see reg.2(1).
"Claims and Payments Regulations"–*ibid.*
"existing benefit"—*ibid.*

GENERAL NOTE

Para. (1)
This deals with cases in which awards of universal credit may be made without a   3.53
claim, in accordance with the Claims and Payments Regulations 2013. It provides

that, subject to certain exceptions, such awards may be made to persons who would not otherwise be entitled to claim universal credit at the relevant time. In practice this seems to cover two types of case.

The first is that where a person is no longer entitled to universal credit because of their earned income, but becomes entitled again within six months (or is not entitled as at the date of claim but becomes entitled within six months) then a claim for universal credit is not mandatory before an award is made (Claims and Payments Regulations 2013, reg.6).

The second is that where two single universal credit claimants become a couple and they are entitled to universal credit as joint claimant, without the need for a claim, then a fresh joint universal credit award may be made even though they would not fall within the Pathfinder Group (Claims and Payments Regulations 2013, reg.9(6) and (7)).

Para. (3)

3.54   On the exception to the exception specified in para.(3)(b), see the annotation to reg.3(6).

PART III

EFFECT OF TRANSITION TO UNIVERSAL CREDIT

CHAPTER 1

ENTITLEMENT TO EXISTING BENEFITS

Exclusion of entitlement to existing benefits

3.55   **15.**—(1) [¹ Subject to paragraph (2A),] a person is not entitled to any benefit mentioned in paragraph (2) at any time when they are entitled to universal credit.

(2) The benefits are—

(a) income support under section 124 of the Social Security Contributions and Benefits Act 1992;

(b) housing benefit [¹ ...];

(c) tax credits;

(d) state pension credit.

[¹(2A) Entitlement to universal credit does not preclude the claimant from entitlement to housing benefit in respect of exempt accommodation.]

(3) A person who is entitled to universal credit may not make a claim for any benefit mentioned in paragraph (2)(a) to (c), even if, because of any of the provisions mentioned in paragraph (4), the claim is made or treated as made at a time when the person was not entitled to universal credit.

(4) The provisions are—

(a) regulation 6(1A)(b), (1F)(c), (3), (4ZC)(b), (16), (19), (28) or (30) of the Social Security (Claims and Payments) Regulations 1987 ("the 1987 Regulations");

(b) regulation 83(5) or (12) of the Housing Benefit Regulations 2006 ("the 2006 Regulations");

(c) regulation 64(6) of the Housing Benefit (Persons who have attained the qualifying age for state pension credit) Regulations 2006 ("the 2006 (SPC) Regulations");

(d) regulation 7, 8, 11(3) or 12(6) of the Tax Credits (Claims and Notifications) Regulations 2002 ("the 2002 Regulations").

(5) For the purposes of paragraph (3)—

(a) the date on which a claim for income support is made or treated as made is to be determined in accordance with the 1987 Regulations;

(b) the date on which a claim for housing benefit is made or treated as made is to be determined in accordance with the 2006 Regulations or, as the case may be, the 2006 (SPC) Regulations;

(c) the date on which a claim for a tax credit is made or treated as made is to be the date on which the claim is received by a relevant authority at an appropriate office, within the meaning of the 2002 Regulations, or such other date on which it is treated as made under those Regulations.

AMENDMENT

1. Universal Credit (Transitional Provisions) and Housing Benefit (Amendment) Regulations 2013 (SI 2013/2070) reg.3(4) (October 28, 2013).

DEFINITIONS

"the 1987 Regulations—para.(4)(a).
"the 2002 Regulations—para.(4)(d).
"the 2006 Regulations"—para.(4)(b).
"the 2006 (SPC) Regulations"—para.(4)(c).
"Claims and Payments Regulations"—see reg.2(1).
"tax credit"—*ibid.*
"tax credits"—*ibid.*

GENERAL NOTE

The basic rule is that entitlement to universal credit and entitlement to any of the benefits or tax credits in para.(2) are mutually exclusive. Income-based JSA and income-related ESA are not included in the list in para.(2) as they do not need to be—when a claimant in the Pathfinder Group claims JSA, ESA or universal credit, this action of itself triggers the abolition at that point (and for that individual) of those benefits (see Commencement Order No.9, art.4). For the context to the special rule relating to exempt or supported accommodation in para.(2A), see the annotation to reg.3(6). Not only can a person entitled to universal credit not be entitled to one of the specified benefits, such an individual cannot make a claim for income support, housing benefit or tax credits (note that state pension credit is not in this list). This exclusion applies even if a claim for one of these benefits is made (or treated as made) under specified legislation at a time when the person was not entitled to universal credit (subs.(3)). The date on which a claim is made, or treated as made, is determined in accordance with the usual rules (subs.(5)). **3.56**

Termination of awards of existing benefits

16.—(1) This regulation applies where— **3.57**

(a) a person ("A") to whom an award of universal credit was made as a single claimant ceases to be entitled as such by becoming a member of a couple;

(b) the other member of the couple ("B") was not entitled to universal credit as a single claimant immediately before formation of the couple; and

(c) an award of universal credit is made to the members of the couple jointly.

(2) In these Regulations, B is referred to as "the new claimant partner".

(3) [¹ Subject to paragraph (3A),] where this regulation applies, all awards of an existing benefit to which the new claimant partner is entitled which did not terminate on formation of the couple are to terminate, by virtue of this regulation, on the day before the first date on which the joint claimants are entitled to universal credit.

[¹(3A) An award of housing benefit to which the new claimant partner is entitled in respect of exempt accommodation does not terminate by virtue of this regulation.]

(4) Where the new claimant partner was, immediately before forming a couple with A, treated by regulation 8 as being entitled to a tax credit, the new claimant partner is to be treated, for the purposes of the Tax Credits Act 2002, as having made a claim for the tax credit in question for the current tax year.

(5) Any award of a tax credit which is made in respect of a claim which is treated as having been made by virtue of paragraph (4) is to terminate, by virtue of this regulation, on the day before the first date on which the joint claimants are entitled to universal credit.

AMENDMENT

1. Universal Credit (Transitional Provisions) and Housing Benefit (Amendment) Regulations 2013 (SI 2013/2070) reg.3(5) (October 28, 2013).

DEFINITIONS

"A"—para.(1)(a).
"B"—para.(1)(b).
"existing benefit"—see reg.2(1).
"new claimant partner"—para.(2) and see reg.2(1).
"tax credit"—see reg.2(1).
"tax year"—*ibid.*

GENERAL NOTE

3.58   This has the effect of ensuring that, as a general rule, all existing benefit or tax credit awards will terminate when an award of universal credit is made to a newly formed couple, one of whom was previously entitled to universal credit and the other to an existing benefit (or tax credit). The mechanics of this process are different for existing benefit and tax credits awards respectively. Any remaining awards of existing benefits simply terminate on the day before the joint award of universal credit begins (para.(3); for the context to the exception in para.(3A) relating to exempt or supported accommodation, see the annotation to reg.3(6)). The process is more complicated with tax credits—where the new partner is treated as having an ongoing tax credit award by virtue of reg.8, then they are treated as having made a new claim for the current year, whether or not they actually have (para.(4)), and any award made under such a deemed claim likewise terminates on the day before the start of the joint award of universal credit.

Finalisation of tax credits and modification of tax credits legislation

3.59   **17.**—(1) This regulation applies where an award of universal credit is made to a person who was previously entitled to a tax credit and the award of that tax credit terminated at any time during the tax year in which the award of universal credit is made.

(2) Where this regulation applies—

(a) the Tax Credits Act 2002 ("the 2002 Act") is to apply in relation to the person with the modifications made by paragraphs 9, 10, 13 and 14 of the Schedule to these Regulations; and

(b) subject to paragraph (3), the amount of the tax credit to which the person is entitled is to be calculated in accordance with the 2002 Act and regulations made under that Act, as modified by the other provisions of that Schedule ("the legislation as further modified").

(3) Where, in the opinion of the Commissioners of Her Majesty's Revenue and Customs, it is not reasonably practicable to apply the legislation as further modified in relation to any case or category of cases, the 2002 Act is to apply without further modification, and regulations made under that Act are to apply without modification, in that case or category of cases.

DEFINITIONS

"the 2002 Act"—para.(2)(a).
"the legislation as further modified"—para.(2)(b).
"tax credit"—see reg.2(1).
"tax year"—*ibid.*

GENERAL NOTE

This deals with the situation in which an award of universal credit is made to a person who was previously entitled to an award of tax credits which terminated in the same tax year. It provides for the scheme of the Tax Credits Act 2002 to apply to that person with certain modifications (para.(2)(a)). It also provides for the amount of the tax credit to which the person was entitled to be calculated in accordance with a modified version of the Tax Credits Act and regulations made under that Act (para.(2)(b)). The modifications, which are set out in the Schedule to these Regulations, allow for calculation of entitlement to a tax credit before the end of the tax year in which the award terminated. This modified regime applies unless, in the opinion of HMRC, it is not reasonably practicable (para.(3)). 3.60

The thinking behind this regulation, and the modifications made by the Schedule, were set out in some detail in the Explanatory Memorandum to the Transitional Provisions Regulations 2013, paras.7.73–7.76:

"7.73 Where a claimant was previously entitled to tax credits in the same tax year as they are awarded Universal Credit, the Regulations modify the tax credits legislation which will apply to them. Provisions of the Tax Credits Act 2002 are modified to ensure that an overpayment of tax credits can be treated as an overpayment of Universal Credit, enabling recovery of the overpayment from the Universal Credit award. In addition, the provisions that specify the time limits for the imposition of tax credits penalties made under Sections 31 or 32 of the Tax Credits Act are amended to take account of the fact that, as a result of other changes to tax credits legislation made by these Regulations, a tax credits award may be made for a part tax year, rather than the whole tax year.

7.74 Other modifications to the Tax Credits Act, and to regulations made under that Act, allow for tax credits awards to be finalised before the end of the tax year. Finalising tax credits awards in-year will ensure that Universal Credit claimants do not have to wait until the end of the tax year for any earlier entitlement to tax credits to be calculated. This means that any over or underpayments are identified and dealt with much sooner in these cases than by continuing to finalise awards after the end of the tax year.

7.75 The intention is that in-year finalisation of tax credits awards will be the default approach in every case. However, the Regulations allow the Commissioners of Her Majesty's Revenue and Customs to continue to finalise tax credits awards after the end of the tax year, if they are of the opinion that it is not reasonably practicable to apply the modified legislation to any particular case or category of case. This flexibility has been built in as a sensible contingency to guard against unforeseen operational difficulties with the in-year finalisation process.

7.76 Whilst it is inevitably difficult to predict the types of problem that might arise, it is envisaged that the Commissioners' discretion might, for example, be exercised where there is an unforeseen system or process failure. Similarly, it could be exercised in the event that it proved difficult to verify income in a case or class of case where income is particularly complex, such as, for example, those including particular combinations of self-employed and other income."

Ongoing appeals etc.

3.61   **18.**—(1) This regulation applies where—
  (a) a new claimant partner to whom an award of universal credit has been made appealed against a decision relating to entitlement to an existing benefit; and
  (b) the appeal to the First-tier Tribunal, or any subsequent appeal to the Upper Tribunal or a court, was ongoing at the date on which the award of universal credit was made, or a further appeal (by any party) was made after that date.

(2) This regulation also applies where—
  (a) a new claimant partner to whom an award of universal credit has been made applied—
    (i) to the Secretary of State to consider whether to revise, under section 9 of the Social Security Act 1998, or to supersede, under section 10 of that Act, a decision relating to the new claimant partner's entitlement to jobseeker's allowance, employment and support allowance or income support; or
    (ii) to the relevant authority (within the meaning of the Child Support, Pensions and Social Security Act 2000) to consider whether to revise or supersede, under Schedule 7 to that Act, a decision relating to the new claimant partner's entitlement to housing benefit,
    and that application is pending at the date on which the award of universal credit was made; or
  (b) the Secretary of State or, as the case may be, a relevant authority mentioned in sub-paragraph (a)(ii), is considering whether to revise or supersede such a decision on their own initiative.

(3) Where this regulation applies, and the new claimant partner is still entitled to universal credit when the appeal is finally determined or a decision is revised or superseded—
  (a) any entitlement to an existing benefit [¹ (other than housing benefit in respect of exempt accommodation)] arising from the appeal, or from the decision as revised or superseded, is to terminate, by virtue of this regulation, on the day before the first date of entitlement to universal credit;
  (b) the new claimant partner is not entitled to any payment in respect of an existing benefit [¹ (other than a payment of housing benefit to which the new claimant partner is entitled in respect of exempt accommodation)] for any period after the day before the first date of entitlement to universal credit; and

(c) the Secretary of State is to consider whether it is appropriate to revise under section 9 of the 1998 Act the decision in relation to entitlement to universal credit or, if that decision has been superseded under section 10 of that Act, the decision as so superseded (in either case, "the UC decision").

(4) Where it appears to the Secretary of State to be appropriate to revise the UC decision, it is to be revised in such manner as appears to the Secretary of State to be necessary to take account of—

(a) the decision of the First-tier Tribunal, Upper Tribunal, or court or, as the case may be, the decision relating to entitlement to an existing benefit, as revised or superseded by the Secretary of State or relevant authority; and

(b) any finding of fact by the Tribunal, Upper Tribunal, or court.

AMENDMENT

1. Universal Credit (Transitional Provisions) and Housing Benefit (Amendment) Regulations 2013 (SI 2013/2070) reg.3(6) (October 28, 2013).

DEFINITIONS

"employment and support allowance"—see reg.2(1).
"existing benefit"—*ibid*.
"First-tier Tribunal"—*ibid*.
"jobseeker's allowance"—*ibid*.
"new claimant partner"—*ibid*.
"the UC decision"—para.(3)(c).
"Upper Tribunal"—see reg.2(1).

GENERAL NOTE

A new partner may have a pending application for revision or supersession (para.(2)) or an outstanding appeal (para.(1)) against a decision in relation to an existing benefit. This regulation provides that any entitlement to an existing benefit arising from such an appeal, revision or supersession will terminate immediately (para.(2)). A decision made about entitlement to universal credit may be revised to take account of any findings of fact by the appeal body (para.(3)).   3.62

CHAPTER 2

TRANSITION FROM EXISTING BENEFITS TO UNIVERSAL CREDIT

Advance payments of universal credit

19.—(1) This regulation applies where—   3.63

(a) the Secretary of State is deciding a claim for universal credit, other than a claim which is treated as having been made by virtue of regulation 9(8) of the Claims and Payments Regulations;

(b) the claimant was previously entitled to an existing benefit ("the existing award"); and

(c) the claim for universal credit was made during the period of one month starting with the date on which the existing award terminated.

(2) This regulation also applies where—

(a) the Secretary of State is deciding a claim for universal credit which is treated as having been made by virtue of regulation 9(8) of the Claims and Payments Regulations;

(b) one of the claimants is a new claimant partner who was previously entitled to an existing benefit; and

(c) the award of that benefit terminated on formation of the couple, or by virtue of regulation 16.

(3) Where this regulation applies, the claimant may request an advance payment of universal credit at any time during the first assessment period for universal credit and, in the case of joint claimants, such a request may be made by either of them or by them jointly.

(4) Where a request has been made in accordance with this regulation, the Secretary of State may make an advance payment to the claimant, or joint claimants, of such amount in respect of universal credit as the Secretary of State considers appropriate.

(5) After an advance payment has been made under this regulation, payments of any award of universal credit to the claimant, or joint claimants, may be reduced until the amount of the advance payment is repaid.

DEFINITIONS

"assessment period"—see reg.2(1).
"Claims and Payments Regulations"—*ibid.*
"existing benefit"—*ibid.*, and para.(1)(b).
"new claimant partner"—see reg.2(1).

GENERAL NOTE

3.64   As a general rule universal credit is payable monthly in arrears (Claims and Payments Regulations 2013, reg.47(1)). However, where an award of universal credit is made to a person who was entitled to an existing benefit before they became entitled to universal credit (paras (1) and (2)), this provision allows the claimants to apply for an advance payment of universal credit during their first assessment period (para.(3)). The amount of any advance payment is at the discretion of the Secretary of State (para.(4)). Repayment is by reduction of subsequent payments (para.(5)).

[¹ Benefit Cap

3.65   **20.** *Part 7 of the Universal Credit Regulations (The Benefit Cap) does not apply to a person who was permitted to claim universal credit by these Regulations (including a person to whom regulation 13(4)(a) applies), or to a person to whom an award of universal credit has been made without a claim in accordance with these Regulations.*]

AMENDMENT

1. Repealed by Universal Credit (Transitional Provisions) and Housing Benefit (Amendment) Regulations 2013 (SI 2013/2070) reg.6 (October 28, 2013).

GENERAL NOTE

3.66   Regulation 20 provided that the benefit cap will not apply to awards of universal credit during the initial phase of introduction of the new benefit. This provision was revoked by reg.6(1) of the Universal Credit (Transitional Provisions) and Housing Benefit (Amendment) Regulations 2013 (SI 2013/2070) with effect from October 28, 2013. However, by reg.6(2) it continues to have effect in relation to a person who is entitled to universal credit on the date on which those Regulations came into force ("the commencement date") for the duration of the assessment period in relation to the person which includes the commencement date. This saving does not apply where the commencement date is the first day of an assessment period in relation to the person (reg.6(3)). By reg.6(4) "assessment period" has the same meaning as in the Universal Credit Regulations 2013.

Income from existing benefits

21.—(1) This regulation applies where—   **3.67**
(a) an award of universal credit is made to joint claimants;
(b) one of those claimants is a new claimant partner who was previously entitled to income-based jobseeker's allowance, income-related employment and support allowance, or income support under section 124 of the Social Security Contributions and Benefits Act 1992 ("the relevant existing benefit");
(c) the award of the relevant existing benefit terminated on formation of the couple, or by virtue of regulation 16; and
(d) a payment of that benefit is made which includes payment in respect of a period which falls within one or more assessment periods for universal credit ("the overlapping payment").
(2) Where this regulation applies, for the purposes of calculating the amount of the award of universal credit to the joint claimants in respect of an assessment period—
(a) regulation 66 of the Universal Credit Regulations (What is included in unearned income?) applies as if the overlapping payment which was made in respect of that assessment period were added to the descriptions of unearned income in paragraph (1)(b) of that regulation; and
(b) regulation 73 of the Universal Credit Regulations (Unearned income calculated monthly) does not apply to the overlapping payment.

DEFINITIONS

"assessment period"—see reg.2(1).
"income-related employment and support allowance"—*ibid.*
"new claimant partner"—*ibid.*
"the overlapping payment"—para.(1)(d).
"the relevant existing benefit"—para.(1)(b).
"Universal Credit Regulations"—see reg.2(1).

GENERAL NOTE

This deals with a problem of overlap where a new couple is formed. It applies   **3.68**
where a new partner who was previously entitled to certain existing benefits forms a couple with a universal credit claimant. If a payment is made in respect of one of those former benefits for a period which is included in a universal credit assessment period, the payment will be taken into account as unearned income when calculating entitlement to universal credit for the assessment period in question.

Deductions from benefits

22.—(1) This regulation applies where—   **3.69**
(a) an award of universal credit is made to joint claimants;
(b) one of those claimants is a new claimant partner who was previously entitled to income-based jobseeker's allowance, income-related

employment and support allowance or income support ("the earlier award"), or was, immediately before termination of the award, the partner of a person who was so entitled;

(c) the earlier award terminated by virtue of regulation 16; and

(d) at the time at which the earlier award terminated, deductions in respect of fuel costs or water charges were being made under regulation 35 of the Social Security (Claims and Payments) Regulations 1987, in accordance with Schedule 9 to those Regulations.

(2) Where this regulation applies, deductions in respect of fuel costs or, as the case may be, water charges, may be made from the award of universal credit in accordance with Schedule 6 to the Claims and Payments Regulations, without the need for any consent which would otherwise be required under paragraph 3(3) of that Schedule.

DEFINITIONS

"Claims and Payments Regulations"—see reg.2(1).
"earlier award"—para.(1)(b).
"income-related employment and support allowance"—see reg.2(1).
"new claimant partner"—*ibid.*

GENERAL NOTE

3.70   The new partner in a couple may have had deductions for fuel costs or water charges being made from their award of an existing benefit. This provision allows for such deductions to continue to be made from an award of universal credit without the need for the consents which might otherwise be required.

Transition from employment and support allowance

3.71   **23.**—(1) This regulation applies where—

(a) an award of universal credit is made to joint claimants;

(b) one of the claimants is a new claimant partner;

(c) that person was previously entitled to employment and support allowance; and

(d) the award of employment and support allowance—

(i) terminated on formation of the couple or by virtue of regulation 16, in so far as it was an award of income-related employment and support allowance;

(ii) continued in existence as an award of new style ESA, in so far as it was an award of contributory employment and support allowance.

(2) In this regulation, the "relevant date" means—

(a) in relation to an award to which paragraph (1)(d)(i) applies and paragraph (1)(d)(ii) does not apply, the date on which the award terminated; and

(b) in relation to an award to which paragraph (1)(d)(ii) applies, or to which that paragraph and paragraph (1)(d)(i) both apply, the day before the first date of entitlement to universal credit.

(3) Where, on or before the relevant date, it had been determined that the new claimant partner was entitled to the work-related activity component—

(a) regulation 27(3) of the Universal Credit Regulations (Award to include LCW and LCWRA elements) does not apply; and

(b) the new claimant partner is to be treated as having limited capability for work for the purposes of regulation 27(1)(a) of those Regulations and section 21(1)(a) of the Act.

(4) Unless the assessment phase had not ended at the relevant date (7), if a new claimant partner who is treated as having limited capability for work under paragraph (3) is entitled to an award of universal credit as a joint claimant—

(a) regulation 28 of the Universal Credit Regulations (Period for which the LCW or LCWRA element is not to be included) does not apply; and

(b) the LCW element is (subject to the provisions of Part 4 of the Universal Credit Regulations) to be included in the award with effect from the beginning of the first assessment period.

(5) Where, on or before the relevant date, it had been determined that the new claimant partner was entitled to the support component—

(a) regulation 27(3) of the Universal Credit Regulations does not apply; and

(b) the new claimant partner is to be treated as having limited capability for work and work-related activity for the purposes of regulation 27(1)(b) of those Regulations and section 19(2)(a) of the Act.

(6) Unless the assessment phase had not ended at the relevant date, if a new claimant partner who is treated as having limited capability for work and work-related activity under paragraph (5) is entitled to an award of universal credit—

(a) regulation 28 of the Universal Credit Regulations does not apply; and

(b) the LCWRA element is (subject to the provisions of Part 4 of the Universal Credit Regulations) to be included in the award of universal credit with effect from the beginning of the first assessment period.

(7) Where a person is treated, by virtue of this regulation, as having limited capability for work or, as the case may be, limited capability for work and work-related activity, the Secretary of State may at any time make a fresh determination as to these matters, in accordance with the Universal Credit Regulations.

(8) In this regulation and in regulations 24 to 28—

"assessment phase", "support component" and "work-related activity component" have the same meanings as in the 2007 Act;

"incapacity benefit" and "severe disablement allowance" have the same meanings as in Schedule 4 to that Act;

"LCW element" and "LCWRA element" have the same meanings as in the Universal Credit Regulations.

DEFINITIONS

"the Act"—see reg.2(1).
"the 2007 Act"—*ibid.*
"assessment period"—*ibid.*
"assessment phase"—para.(8).
"contributory employment and support allowance"—see reg.2(1).
"employment and support allowance"—*ibid.*
"incapacity benefit"—para.(8).
"income-related employment and support allowance"—see reg.2(1).
"LCW element"—para.(8).

"LCWRA element"—*ibid.*
"new claimant partner"—*ibid.*
"new style ESA"—*ibid.*
"severe disablement allowance"—*ibid.*
"support component"—*ibid.*
"Universal Credit Regulations"—see reg.2(1).
"work-related activity component"—*ibid.*

GENERAL NOTE

3.72   The purpose of this apparently complex provision is relatively simple. It provides
that the new claimant partner in a couple may be treated as having limited capability
for work, or limited capability for work and work-related activity, for the purposes
of an award of universal credit, if they were previously entitled to the work-related
activity component, or the support component, on an ESA award. If the claimant
in question was in the process of assessment of their capability for work in connection with an award of employment and support allowance at the time the award
terminated, the assessment period for universal credit will be adjusted accordingly,
under reg.24.

**Transition from employment and support allowance before the end
of the assessment phase**

3.73   **24.**—(1) This regulation applies where—
(a) an award of universal credit is made to joint claimants;
(b) one of the claimants is a new claimant partner;
(c) that person was previously entitled to employment and support
allowance; and
(d) the award of employment and support allowance—
    (i) terminated on formation of the couple or by virtue of regulation
        16, in so far as it was an award of income-related employment
        and support allowance;
    (ii) continued in existence as an award of new style ESA, in so far as
        it was an award of contributory employment and support allow-
        ance.
(2) In this regulation, the "relevant date" means—
(a) in relation to an award to which paragraph (1)(d)(i) applies and
paragraph (1)(d)(ii) does not apply, the date on which the award
terminated; and
(b) in relation to an award to which paragraph (1)(d)(ii) applies, or to
which that paragraph and paragraph (1)(d)(i) both apply, the day
before the first date of entitlement to universal credit.
(3) Where, on the relevant date, the assessment phase in relation to the
person to whom it was awarded had lasted for less than 13 weeks—
(a) regulation 28(2) of the Universal Credit Regulations (Period for
which the LCW or LCWRA element is not to be included) does not
apply; and
(b) for the purposes of regulation 28 of those Regulations, the relevant
period is the period of 13 weeks starting with the first day of the
assessment phase.
(4) Where, on the relevant date, the assessment phase in relation to the
person to whom it was awarded had not ended and had lasted for more than
13 weeks—
(a) regulation 28 of the Universal Credit Regulations does not apply;

(b) if it is subsequently determined in accordance with Part 5 of those Regulations that the person has limited capability for work—
    (i) the LCW element is (subject to the provisions of Part 4 of those Regulations) to be included in the award of universal credit with effect from the beginning of the first assessment period; and
    (ii) for the purposes of determining the person's entitlement to employment and support allowance prior to the relevant date, the person is to be treated as having been entitled to the work-related activity component from the day after the day on which the period referred to in paragraph (3)(b) ended;

(c) if it is subsequently determined in accordance with Part 5 of the Universal Credit Regulations that the person has limited capability for work and work-related activity—
    (i) the LCWRA element is (subject to the provisions of Part 4 of those Regulations) to be included in the award of universal credit with effect from the beginning of the first assessment period; and
    (ii) for the purposes of determining the person's entitlement to employment and support allowance prior to the relevant date, the person is to be treated as having been entitled to the support component from the day after the day on which the period referred to in paragraph (3)(b) ended.

DEFINITIONS

    "assessment period"—see reg.2(1).
    "contributory employment and support allowance"—*ibid*.
    "employment and support allowance"—*ibid*.
    "income-related employment and support allowance"—*ibid*.
    "new claimant partner"—*ibid*.
    "new style ESA"—*ibid*.
    "relevant date"—para.(2).
    "Universal Credit Regulations"—see reg.2(1).

GENERAL NOTE

This regulation adjusts the assessment period for universal credit where a new   3.74
claimant partner was in the process of assessment of their capability for work in connection with an award of employment and support allowance at the time that the award terminated (see reg.23).

Transition from income support based on incapacity

25.—(1) This regulation applies where—   3.75
(a) an award of universal credit is made to joint claimants;
(b) one member of the couple is a new claimant partner; and
(c) that person was previously entitled to income support based on incapacity and the award of that benefit terminated on formation of the couple or by virtue of regulation 16.
(2) Where this regulation applies—
(a) if it is determined in accordance with Part 5 of the Universal Credit Regulations that the new claimant partner has limited capability for work—
    (i) that person is to be treated as having had limited capability for work for the purposes of regulation 27(1)(a) of the Universal

Credit Regulations (Award to include LCW and LCWRA elements) from the beginning of the first assessment period;

    (ii) regulation 28 of those Regulations (Period for which the LCW or LCWRA element is not to be included) does not apply to the joint award of universal credit; and

    (iii) the LCW element is (subject to the provisions of Part 4 of the Universal Credit Regulations) to be included in the award with effect from the beginning of the first assessment period;

(b) if it is determined in accordance with Part 5 of the Universal Credit Regulations that the new claimant partner has limited capability for work and work-related activity—

    (i) that person is to be treated as having had limited capability for work and work-related activity for the purposes of regulation 27(1)(b) of the Universal Credit Regulations from the beginning of the first assessment period;

    (ii) regulation 28 of those Regulations does not apply to the joint award of universal credit; and

    (iii) the LCWRA element is (subject to the provisions of Part 4 of the Universal Credit Regulations) to be included in the award of universal credit with effect from the beginning of the first assessment period.

(3) In this regulation—

"income support based on incapacity" means an award of income support which is an "existing award" within the meaning of Schedule 4 to the 2007 Act;

DEFINITIONS

"the 2007 Act"—see reg.2(1).
"assessment period"—*ibid*.
"income support based on incapacity"—para.(3).
"new claimant partner"—see reg.2(1).
"Universal Credit Regulations"—*ibid*.

GENERAL NOTE

3.76   This concerns the transition from income support on grounds of incapacity to universal credit in cases where there is a couple with a new claimant partner.

Transition from other incapacity benefits

3.77   **26.**—(1) This regulation applies where—

(a) an award of universal credit is made to joint claimants;

(b) one member of the couple is a new claimant partner;

(c) that person was entitled to incapacity benefit or severe disablement allowance at the time the award of universal credit was made; and

(d) it is subsequently determined in accordance with the Employment and Support Allowance (Transitional Provisions, Housing Benefit and Council Tax Benefit) (Existing Awards) (No.2) Regulations 2010 that the award qualifies for conversion into an award ("the converted award") in accordance with regulation 7 of those Regulations (Qualifying for conversion).

(2) Where this regulation applies, and the converted award includes the work-related activity component—

(a) regulation 27(3) of the Universal Credit Regulations (Award to include LCW and LCWRA elements) does not apply and, where a decision on the award of universal credit incorporates a determination which has already been made in accordance with that regulation, that decision is to be revised in accordance with this regulation;

(b) the new claimant partner is to be treated as having had limited capability for work for the purposes of regulation 27(1)(a) of the Universal Credit Regulations from the beginning of the first assessment period;

(c) regulation 28(1) of the Universal Credit Regulations (Period for which LCW or LCWRA element is not to be included) does not apply;

(d) the LCW element is (subject to the provisions of Part 4 of the Universal Credit Regulations) to be included in the award of universal credit with effect from the beginning of the first assessment period; and

(e) the new claimant partner is to be treated as having limited capability for work for the purposes of section 21(1)(a) of the Act.

(3) Where this regulation applies and the converted award includes the support component—

(a) regulation 27(3) of the Universal Credit Regulations does not apply and, where a decision on the award of universal credit incorporates a determination which has already been made in accordance with that regulation, that decision is to be revised in accordance with this regulation;

(b) the new claimant partner is to be treated as having had limited capability for work and work-related activity for the purposes of regulation 27(1)(b) of the Universal Credit Regulations from the beginning of the first assessment period;

(c) regulation 28(1) of the Universal Credit Regulations does not apply;

(d) the LCWRA element is (subject to the provisions of Part 4 of the Universal Credit Regulations) to be included in the award of universal credit with effect from the beginning of the first assessment period; and

(e) the new claimant partner is to be treated as having limited capability for work and work-related activity for the purposes of section 19(2)(a) of the Act.

DEFINITIONS

"the Act"—see reg.2(1).
"assessment period"—*ibid.*
"new claimant partner"—*ibid.*
"Universal Credit Regulations"—*ibid.*

GENERAL NOTE

This concerns the transition from incapacity benefit or severe disablement allowance to universal credit in cases where there is a couple with a new claimant partner. There is a variant in reg.27 for claimants approaching pensionable age.

3.78

Transition from other incapacity benefits: claimants approaching pensionable age

3.79   **27.**—(1) This paragraph applies where—

(a) an award of universal credit is made to joint claimants;

(b) one member of the couple is a new claimant partner;

(c) that person is entitled to incapacity benefit or severe disablement allowance;

(d) no notice may be issued to the new claimant partner under the Employment and Support Allowance (Transitional Provisions, Housing Benefit and Council Tax Benefit) (Existing Awards) (No.2) Regulations 2010 ("the 2010 Regulations") because they will reach pensionable age (within the meaning of those Regulations) before 6th April 2014; and

(e) the new claimant partner is also entitled to—

    (i) personal independence payment, where neither the daily living component nor the mobility component is payable at the enhanced rate;

    (ii) disability living allowance under section 71 of the Social Security Contributions and Benefits Act 1992 ("the 1992 Act"), where the care component is payable at the middle rate within the meaning of section 72(4) of that Act or the mobility component is payable at the lower rate within the meaning of section 73(11) of that Act (or both components are payable at those rates); or

    (iii) attendance allowance under section 64 of the 1992 Act, where the allowance is payable at the lower rate in accordance with section 65 of that Act.

(2) Where paragraph (1) applies—

(a) regulation 27(3) of the Universal Credit Regulations (Award to include LCW and LCWRA elements) does not apply;

(b) the new claimant partner is to be treated as having limited capability for work for the purposes of regulation 27(1)(a) of the Universal Credit Regulations from the beginning of the first assessment period;

(c) regulation 28(1) of the Universal Credit Regulations (Period for which LCW or LCWRA element is not to be included) does not apply;

(d) the LCW element is (subject to the provisions of Part 4 of the Universal Credit Regulations) to be included in the award of universal credit with effect from the beginning of the first assessment period; and

(e) the new claimant partner is to be treated as having limited capability for work for the purposes of section 21(1)(a) of the Act.

(3) This paragraph applies where—

(a) an award of universal credit is made to joint claimants;

(b) one member of the couple is a new claimant partner;

(c) that person is entitled to incapacity benefit or severe disablement allowance;

(d) no notice may be issued to the new claimant partner under the 2010 Regulations because they will reach pensionable age (within the meaning of those Regulations) before 6th April 2014; and

(e) the new claimant partner is also entitled to—
- (i) personal independence payment, where either the daily living component or the mobility component is (or both components are) payable at the enhanced rate;
- (ii) disability living allowance under section 71 of the 1992 Act, where the care component is payable at the highest rate within the meaning of section 72(4) of that Act or the mobility component is payable at the higher rate within the meaning of section 73(11) of that Act (or both components are payable at those rates); [¹ . . .]
- (iii) attendance allowance under section 64 of the 1992 Act, where the allowance is payable at the higher rate in accordance with section 65 of that Act [¹; or
- (iv) armed forces independence payment under the Armed Forces and Reserve Forces (Compensation Scheme) Order 2011.]

(4) Where paragraph (3) applies—
(a) regulation 27(3) of the Universal Credit Regulations does not apply;
(b) the new claimant partner is to be treated as having limited capability for work and work-related activity for the purposes of regulation 27(1)(b) of the Universal Credit Regulations from the beginning of the first assessment period;
(c) regulation 28(1) of the Universal Credit Regulations does not apply;
(d) the LCWRA element is (subject to the provisions of Part 4 of the Universal Credit Regulations) to be included in the award of universal credit with effect from the beginning of the first assessment period; and
(e) the new claimant partner is to be treated as having limited capability for work and work-related activity for the purposes of section 19(2)(a) of the Act.

<small>AMENDMENT</small>

1. Armed Forces and Reserve Forces Compensation Scheme (Consequential Provisions: Subordinate Legislation) Order 2013 (SI 2013/591), art.7 and Sch., para.53 (April 8, 2013).

<small>DEFINITIONS</small>

"the 1992 Act"—para.(1)(e)(ii).
"the Act"—see reg.2(1).
"assessment period"—*ibid.*
"new claimant partner"—*ibid.*
"Universal Credit Regulations"—*ibid.*

<small>GENERAL NOTE</small>

Regulation 26 concerns the transition from incapacity benefit or severe disablement allowance to universal credit in cases where there is a couple with a new claimant partner. This regulation provides for a variant where the new claimant partner is approaching pensionable age. Depending on the level of disability benefit being received by the new claimant partner, it provides for that person to be treated as having either limited capability for work (para.(1) and (2)) or both limited capability for work and work-related activity (paras (3) and (4)). Paragraph (1)(a)–(c) and para.(3)(a)–(c) are equivalent to reg.26(1)(a)–(c). However, whereas reg.26 is predicated on conversion (see reg.26(1)(d)), this

3.80

provision applies where no conversion notice can be issued because the new claim partner will reach pensionable age before April 6, 2014 (see para.(1)(d) and (3) (d)). In addition, the new claimant partner must be entitled to one of the benefits specified in para.(1)(e) (for the less disabled) or para.(3)(e) (for the more disabled) for this provision to apply.

Transition from other incapacity benefits: supplementary

3.81   **28.**—(1) Where an award of universal credit is made to a person who is entitled to incapacity benefit or severe disablement allowance, regulation 66 of the Universal Credit Regulations (What is included in unearned income?) applies to that person as if incapacity benefit or, as the case may be, severe disablement allowance were added to the descriptions of unearned income in paragraph (1)(b) of that regulation.

(2) For the purposes of regulations 26 and 27 and this regulation only, incapacity benefit and severe disablement allowance are prescribed benefits under paragraph 1(2)(b) of Schedule 6 to the Act.

DEFINITIONS

"the Act"—see reg.2(1).
"Universal Credit Regulations"—*ibid.*

GENERAL NOTE

3.82   In cases covered by either reg.26 or reg.27, incapacity benefit (or, as appropriate, severe disablement allowance) counts as unearned income for the purposes of calculating entitlement to universal credit.

Support for housing costs

3.83   **29.**—(1) Paragraph (2) applies where—
(a) an award of universal credit ("the current award") is made—
    (i) to a person who was previously entitled to income-based jobseeker's allowance, income-related employment and support allowance or income support ("the earlier award"); or
    (ii) to a person who was the partner of a person falling within paragraph (i) immediately before the earlier award terminated, but is no longer their partner;
(b) the earlier award terminated—
    (i) during the period of one month ending with the first date of entitlement to universal credit; or
    (ii) in the case of an award to joint claimants, on formation of the couple or by virtue of regulation 16; and
(c) the earlier award included an amount in respect of housing costs under—
    (i) paragraphs 14 to 16 of Schedule 2 to the Jobseeker's Allowance Regulations 1996 ("the 1996 Regulations");
    (ii) paragraphs 16 to 18 of Schedule 6 to the Employment and Support Allowance Regulations 2008 ("the 2008 Regulations"); or, as the case may be,
    (iii) paragraphs 15 to 17 of Schedule 3 to the Income Support (General) Regulations 1987 ("the 1987 Regulations").

(2) Where this paragraph applies, paragraph 5 of Schedule 5 to the Universal Credit Regulations (No housing costs element under this

Schedule for qualifying period) does not apply to the person in respect of the current award.

(3) Paragraph (4) applies where paragraph (1)(a) and (b) applies, but the earlier award did not include an amount in respect of housing costs because the person's entitlement (or, as the case may be, their partner's entitlement) was nil by virtue of—

(a) paragraph 6(1)(c) or 7(1)(b) of Schedule 2 to the 1996 Regulations;
(b) paragraph 8(1)(c) or 9(1)(b) of Schedule 6 to the 2008 Regulations; or, as the case may be,
(c) paragraph 6(1)(c) or 8(1)(b) of Schedule 3(21) to the 1987 Regulations.

(4) Where this paragraph applies, the "qualifying period" for which paragraph 5 of Schedule 5 to the Universal Credit Regulations provides is to be reduced by—

(a) the length of time during which the person (or, as the case may be, their partner) was continuously entitled to the earlier award, including the length of any period which was treated as a period of continuing entitlement under—
   (i) paragraph 13 of Schedule 2 to the 1996 Regulations(22);
   (ii) paragraph 15 of Schedule 6 to the 2008 Regulations(23); or, as the case may be,
   (iii) paragraph 14 of Schedule 3 to the 1987 Regulations(24); and
(b) the length of time (if any) between the date on which the earlier award terminated and the first date of entitlement to universal credit.

(5) WHERE PARAGRAPH (4) APPLIES, PARAGRAPH 6 OF SCHEDULE 5 TO THE UNIVERSAL CREDIT REGULATIONS (APPLICATION OF PARAGRAPH 5: RECEIPT OF JSA AND ESA) DOES NOT APPLY. DEFINITIONS

"the 1987 Regulations"—para.(1)(c).
"the 1996 Regulations"—para.(1)(a).
"the 2008 Regulations"—para.(1)(b).
"the current award"—para.(1)(a).
"the earlier award"—para.(1)(a)(i).
"income-based jobseeker's allowance"—see reg.2(1).
"income-related employment and support allowance"—*ibid.*
"Universal Credit Regulations"—*ibid.*

GENERAL NOTE

This is a hideously opaque regulation. It is designed to ensure that where a universal credit claimant was previously entitled to jobseeker's allowance, employment and support allowance or income support, then any support for housing costs which was included in that award (paras (1) and (2)), or time spent waiting to qualify for such support (paras (3)–(5)), is to be carried over to the award of universal credit (assuming that the claimant is entitled to the universal credit housing element).   3.84

Sanctions: transition from employment and support allowance

30.—(1) This regulation applies where—   3.85

(a) an award of universal credit is made to a person who was previously entitled to employment and support allowance ("the ESA award"); and
(b) immediately before the relevant date, payments in respect of the

ESA award were reduced under regulation 63 of the Employment and Support Allowance Regulations 2008 ("the 2008 Regulations").

(2) In this regulation, the "relevant date" means—

(a) in relation to an ESA award which terminated otherwise than by virtue of regulation 16, the date on which the ESA award terminated;

(b) in relation to an ESA award which terminated by virtue of regulation 16 (in so far as it was an award of income-related employment and support allowance), or which continued in existence as an award of new style ESA (in so far as it was an award of contributory employment and support allowance), the day before the first date of entitlement to universal credit.

(3) Where this regulation applies—

(a) the failure which led to reduction of the ESA award ("the ESA failure") is to be treated, for the purposes of the Universal Credit Regulations, as a failure which is sanctionable under section 27 of the Act;

(b) the award of universal credit is to be reduced in relation to the ESA failure, in accordance with the provisions of this regulation and Chapter 2 of Part 8 of the Universal Credit Regulations (Sanctions), as modified by this regulation; and

(c) the reduction is to be treated, for the purposes of the Universal Credit Regulations, as a reduction under section 27 of the Act.

(4) The reduction period for the purposes of the Universal Credit Regulations is to be the number of days which is equivalent to the length of the fixed period applicable to the person under regulation 63 of the 2008 Regulations in relation to the ESA failure, minus—

(a) the number of days (if any) in that period in respect of which the amount of employment and support allowance was reduced; and

(b) the number of days (if any) in the period starting with the day after the relevant date and ending with the day before the first date on which the person is entitled to universal credit.

(5) Accordingly, regulation 101 of the Universal Credit Regulations (General principles for calculating reduction periods) applies in relation to the ESA failure as if, in paragraphs (1) and (3), for the words "in accordance with regulations 102 to 105", there were substituted the words "in accordance with regulation 30 of the Universal Credit (Transitional Provisions) Regulations 2013".

DEFINITIONS

"the 2008 Regulations"—para.(1).
"the Act"—see reg.2(1).
"contributory employment and support allowance"—*ibid.*
"employment and support allowance"—*ibid.*
"the ESA award"—para.(1).
"the ESA failure"—para.(3).
"income-related employment and support allowance"—*ibid.*
"new style ESA"—*ibid.*
"the relevant date"—para.(2).
"Universal Credit Regulations"—see reg.2(1).

GENERAL NOTE

This regulation, together with regs 31–34, deals with the treatment of any sanc-   **3.86** tions which have been imposed on awards of jobseeker's allowance and employment and support allowance before the transition to universal credit. The underlying principle is one of equivalence of treatment—thus current sanctions will continue to have effect by way of deductions from the award of universal credit and past sanctions will be taken into account for the purposes of determining the sanction applicable to any future sanctionable failure. However, where there is a period of entitlement to an existing benefit between two periods of entitlement to universal credit, any sanctions arising prior to that intervening period will not be taken into account.

So, for example, where a new universal credit claimant was previously entitled to ESA, and subject to an ESA sanction for failure to take part in a work-focused interview or to undertake a work-related activity, the ESA failure is treated as a sanctionable failure for the purposes of universal credit (paras (1) and (3)). The reduction period is adjusted accordingly (para.(4)).

Escalation of sanctions: transition from employment and support allowance

31.—(1) This regulation applies where an award of universal credit is   **3.87** made to a person who was at any time previously entitled to employment and support allowance.

(2) Where this regulation applies, for the purposes of determining the reduction period under regulation 104 of the Universal Credit Regulations (Low-level sanction) in relation to a sanctionable failure by the person, other than a failure which is treated as sanctionable by virtue of regulation 30—

  (a) a reduction of universal credit in accordance with regulation 30; and

  (b) any reduction of an employment and support allowance under the 2008 Regulations which did not result in a reduction under regulation 30,

is, subject to paragraph (3), to be treated as arising from a sanctionable failure for which the reduction period which applies is the number of days which is equivalent to the length of the fixed period which applied under regulation 63 of the 2008 Regulations.

(3) In determining a reduction period under regulation 104 of the Universal Credit Regulations in accordance with paragraph (2), no account shall be taken of—

  (a) a reduction of universal credit in accordance with regulation 30 if, at any time after that reduction, the person was entitled to an existing benefit;

  (b) a reduction of an employment and support allowance under the 2008 Regulations if, at any time after that reduction, the person was entitled to universal credit, new style ESA or new style JSA, and was subsequently entitled to an existing benefit.

DEFINITIONS

"employment and support allowance"—see reg.2(1).
"existing benefit"—*ibid.*
"new style ESA"—*ibid.*
"Universal Credit Regulations"—*ibid.*

GENERAL NOTE

3.88   This ensures that any previous ESA fixed period reductions are taken into account when deciding the appropriate reduction period for the purposes of a universal credit sanction.

Sanctions: transition from jobseeker's allowance

3.89   **32.**—(1) This regulation applies where—

(a) an award of universal credit is made to a person who was previously entitled to jobseeker's allowance ("the JSA award");

(b) immediately before the relevant date, payments in respect of the JSA award were reduced under section 19 (as it applied either before or after substitution by the Act or section 19A of the Jobseekers Act 1995 ("the 1995 Act"), or under regulation 69B of the Jobseeker's Allowance Regulations 1996 ("the 1996 Regulations"); and

(c) if the JSA award was made to a joint-claim couple within the meaning of the 1995 Act and the reduction related to—

(i) in the case of a reduction under section 19 as it applied before substitution by the Act, circumstances relating to only one member of the couple; or,

(ii) in the case of a reduction under section 19 as it applied after substitution by the Act, a sanctionable failure by only one member of the couple,

the award of universal credit was made to that person.

(2) In this regulation, the "relevant date" means—

(a) in relation to a JSA award which terminated otherwise than by virtue of regulation 16, the date on which the JSA award terminated;

(b) in relation to a JSA award which terminated by virtue of regulation 16 (in so far as it was an award of income-based jobseeker's allowance), or which continued in existence as an award of new style JSA (in so far as it was an award of contribution-based jobseeker's allowance), the day before the first date of entitlement to universal credit.

(3) Where this regulation applies—

(a) the circumstances or failure which led to reduction of the JSA award (in either case, "the JSA failure") is to be treated, for the purposes of the Universal Credit Regulations, as—

(i) a failure which is sanctionable under section 26 of the Act, where the reduction was under section 19 of the 1995 Act; or

(ii) a failure which is sanctionable under section 27 of the Act, where the reduction was under section 19A of the 1995 Act or regulation 69B of the 1996 Regulations;

(b) the award of universal credit is to be reduced in relation to the JSA failure, in accordance with the provisions of this regulation and Chapter 2 of Part 8 of the Universal Credit Regulations (Sanctions), as modified by this regulation; and

(c) the reduction is to be treated, for the purposes of the Universal Credit Regulations, as a reduction under section 26 or, as the case may be, section 27 of the Act.

(4) The reduction period for the purposes of the Universal Credit Regulations is to be the number of days which is equivalent to the length of the period of reduction of jobseeker's allowance which is applicable to the person under regulation 69, 69A or 69B of the 1996 Regulations, minus—

(a) the number of days (if any) in that period in respect of which the amount of jobseeker's allowance was reduced; and

(b) the number of days (if any) in the period starting with the day after the relevant date and ending with the day before the first date on which the person is entitled to universal credit.

(5) Accordingly, regulation 101 of the Universal Credit Regulations (General principles for calculating reduction periods) applies in relation to the JSA failure as if, in paragraphs (1) and (3), for the words "in accordance with regulations 102 to 105", there were substituted the words "in accordance with regulation 32 of the Universal Credit (Transitional Provisions) Regulations 2013".

(6) Where the JSA award was made to a joint-claim couple within the meaning of the 1995 Act and the JSA failure related to only one member of the couple, the daily reduction rate for the purposes of the Universal Credit Regulations is the amount calculated in accordance with regulation 74B(3) of the 1996 Regulations in respect of the JSA award, divided by seven and rounded down to the nearest 10 pence, unless regulation 111(2) or (3) of the Universal Credit Regulations (Daily Reduction Rate) applies.

(7) Where the daily reduction rate is to be determined in accordance with paragraph (6), regulation 111(1) of the Universal Credit Regulations applies in relation to the JSA failure as if, for the words from "an amount equal to" to the end there were substituted the words "an amount determined in accordance with regulation 32 of the Universal Credit (Transitional Provisions) Regulations 2013".

DEFINITIONS

"the 1995 Act"—para.(1)(b).
"the 1996 Regulations"—*ibid.*
"the Act"—see reg.2(1).
"contribution-based jobseeker's allowance"—*ibid.*
"income-based jobseeker's allowance"—*ibid.*
"the JSA award"—para.(1)(a).
"the JSA failure"—para.(3)(a).
"jobseeker's allowance"—see reg.2(1).
"new style JSA"—*ibid.*
"relevant date"—para.(2).
"Universal Credit Regulations"—see reg.2(1).

GENERAL NOTE

This has similar effect for JSA as reg.30 does for ESA. It is designed to ensure that current JSA sanctions carry forward into the universal credit scheme.

3.90

Escalation of sanctions: transition from jobseeker's allowance

33.—(1) This regulation applies where an award of universal credit is made to a person who was at any time previously entitled to jobseeker's allowance.

3.91

(2) Where this regulation applies, for the purposes of determining the applicable reduction period under regulation 102 (Higher-level sanction), 103 (Medium-level sanction) or 104 (Low-level sanction) of the Universal Credit Regulations in relation to a sanctionable failure by the person, other than a failure which is treated as sanctionable by virtue of regulation 32—

(a) a reduction of universal credit in accordance with regulation 32; and

   (b) any reduction of a jobseeker's allowance under section 19 or 19A of the 1995 Act, or under regulation 69B of the 1996 Regulations which did not result in a reduction under regulation 32,

is, subject to paragraph (3), to be treated as arising from a sanctionable failure for which the reduction period is the number of days which is equivalent to the length of the period which applied under regulation 69, 69A or 69B of the 1996 Regulations.

(3) In determining a reduction period under regulation 102, 103 or 104 of the Universal Credit Regulations in accordance with paragraph (2), no account shall be taken of—

   (a) a reduction of universal credit in accordance with regulation 32 if, at any time after that reduction, the person was entitled to an existing benefit;

   (b) a reduction of a jobseeker's allowance under section 19 or 19A of the 1995 Act, or under regulation 69B of the 1996 Regulations if, at any time after that reduction, the person was entitled to universal credit, new style ESA or new style JSA, and was subsequently entitled to an existing benefit.

DEFINITIONS

   "existing benefit"—see reg.2(1).
   "jobseeker's allowance"—*ibid.*
   "new style ESA"—*ibid.*
   "new style JSA"—*ibid.*
   "Universal Credit Regulations"—*ibid.*

GENERAL NOTE

3.92   This is the JSA equivalent of reg.31, which applies to ESA.

Sanctions: temporary return to existing benefits

3.93   **34.** If an award of universal credit terminates while there is an outstanding reduction period (within the meaning of regulation 107 of the Universal Credit Regulations) and the claimant becomes entitled to an existing benefit during that period—

   (a) regulation 107 of the Universal Credit Regulations (Reduction period to continue where award terminates) shall cease to apply; and

   (b) the reduction period shall terminate on the first date of entitlement to the existing benefit.

DEFINITIONS

   "existing benefit"—see reg.2(1).
   "Universal Credit Regulations"—*ibid.*

GENERAL NOTE

3.94   This has the effect that where a claimant comes off universal credit and claims one of the former benefits (e.g. JSA, because he is no longer in a Pathfinder area), then if he subsequently becomes entitled again to universal credit (e.g. by forming a couple with a universal credit claimant) then the universal credit sanction does not bite, even if it had on the face of it not expired. This is because the reduction period is deemed as having terminated on the first day of the award of the existing benefit such as JSA.

Loss of benefit penalties

35.—(1) This regulation applies where—   3.95

(a) an award of universal credit is made to a person who was previously entitled to an existing benefit other than a tax credit ("the earlier award");

(b) the person is an offender, within the meaning of the Social Security Fraud Act 2001(31) ("the 2001 Act");

(c) at the time the earlier award terminated, payments were subject to a restriction under section 6B (Loss of benefit in case of conviction, penalty or caution for benefit offence), 7 (Repeated benefit fraud) or 8 (Effect of offence on joint-claim jobseeker's allowance) of the 2001 Act; and

(d) the first date of entitlement to universal credit is during the period of one month beginning with the date on which the earlier award terminated.

(2) This regulation also applies where—

(a) an award of universal credit is made to a person who is an offender, within the meaning of the 2001 Act;

(b) another person who was the offender's family member within the meaning of the 2001 Act was previously entitled to an existing benefit other than a tax credit ("the earlier award");

(c) at the time the earlier award terminated, payments were subject to a restriction under section 9 (effect of offence on benefits for members of offender's family) of the 2001 Act; and

(d) the first date of entitlement to universal credit is during the period of one month beginning with the date on which the earlier award terminated.

(3) Where this regulation applies—

(a) payments of universal credit to the person are to be reduced by an amount determined in accordance with paragraphs (4) and (5) in respect of each day which is included in the remainder of the disqualification period applicable to the offender under the Social Security (Loss of Benefit) Regulations 2001 ("the 2001 Regulations"); and

(b) any provision in regulations made under section 6B(5A)(a) or 7(2A) (a) of the 2001 Act, under which payments of universal credit would otherwise be reduced by a different amount, does not apply.

(4) The payment of universal credit is to be reduced by—

(a) an amount which is equal to the amount by which payments in respect of the earlier award were reduced in accordance with the 2001 Act and the 2001 Regulations immediately before termination of that award, multiplied by the relevant multiplication factor and divided by the number of days in the year; or

(b) such lesser amount as reduces a payment of universal credit to nil.

(5) The relevant multiplication factor is—

(a) where payments in respect of the existing benefit were made weekly, 52;

(b) where payments in respect of the existing benefit were made fortnightly, 26;

(c) where payments in respect of the existing benefit were made every four weeks, 13; and

(d) where payments in respect of the existing benefit were made monthly, 12.

DEFINITIONS

"the 2001 Act"—para.(1)(b).
"the 2001 Regulations"—para.(3)(a).
"the earlier award"—paras (1)(a) and (2)(b).
"existing benefit"—see reg.2(1).
"jobseeker's allowance"—*ibid.*
"tax credit"—*ibid.*

GENERAL NOTE

3.96   This provides that where a claimant moves to universal credit within one month of the end of an award of an existing benefit and is subject to a loss of benefit penalty, the penalty will continue at the same rate. Any award of universal credit will be reduced by an amount equivalent to the reduction of the existing benefit for the remainder of the disqualification period.

Regulation 17(2)

SCHEDULE

MODIFICATIONS TO TAX CREDITS LEGISLATION

Modifications to the Tax Credits Act 2002

3.97   (1) Paragraphs 2 to 14 prescribe modifications to the application of the Tax Credits Act 2002 where regulation 17 applies.

(2) In section 7—

(a) in subsection (3), before "current year income" in each place where it occurs, insert "notional";

(b) in subsection (4)—

(i) for "current year" substitute "current part year";

(ii) in paragraphs (a) and (b), before "tax year" insert "part";

(c) after subsection (4), insert—

"(4A) In this section "the notional current year income" means—

(a) in relation to persons by whom a joint claim for a tax credit is made, the aggregate income of the persons for the part tax year to which the claim relates, divided by the number of days in that part tax year, multiplied by the number of days in the tax year in which the part tax year is included and rounded down to the next whole number of pence, and

(b) in relation to a person by whom a single claim for a tax credit is made, the income of the person for that part tax year, divided by the number of days in that part tax year, multiplied by the number of days in the tax year in which the part tax year is included and rounded down to the next whole number of pence.".

(3) In section 17—

(a) in subsection (1)(a), before "tax year" insert "part";

(b) in subsection (3), before "tax year" insert "part";

(c) in subsections (4)(a) and (4)(b), for "current year" in both places where it occurs, substitute "current part year";

(d) in subsection (5)(a) for "current year" in both places where it occurs, substitute "current part year";

(e) omit subsection (8).

(4) In section 18—

(a) in subsection (1), before "tax year" insert "part";

(b) omit subsections (6) to (9);

(c) in subsection (10), for "subsection (1), (5), (6) or (9)" substitute "subsection (1) or (5)";

(d) in subsection (11)—

(i) after "subsection (5)" omit "or (9)";

      (ii) omit paragraph (a);

      (iii) in paragraph (b) omit "in any other case,";

      (iv) before "tax year" in each place where it occurs, insert "part".

(5) In section 19—

  (a) in subsection (1)(a) and (b), before "tax year" insert "part";

  (b) in subsection (3), before "tax year" insert "part";

  (c) for subsection (5) substitute—

"(5) "The relevant section 18 decision" means the decision under subsection (1) of section 18 in relation to the person or persons and the part tax year.";

  (d) for subsection (6) substitute—

"(6) "The relevant section 17 date" means the date specified for the purposes of subsection (4) of section 17 in the notice given to a person or persons under that section in relation to the part tax year.";

  (e) in subsection (11), before "tax year" insert "part";

  (f) in subsection (12), before "tax year" in each place where it occurs, insert "part".

(6) In section 20—

  (a) in subsection (1), before "tax year" insert "part";

  (b) in subsection (4)(a), before "tax year" insert "part";

  (c) in subsection (5)(b), before "tax year" insert "part";

  (d) in subsection (6)—

      (i) before "tax year" insert "part";

      (ii) in paragraph (a), for "section 18(1), (5), (6) or (9)" substitute "section 18(1) or (5)";

  (e) in subsection (7), before "tax year" in each place where it occurs, insert "part".

(7) In section 21, for "18(1), (5), (6) or (9)" substitute "18(1) or (5)".

(8) In section 23—

  (a) in subsection (1), for "18(1), (5), (6) or (9)" substitute "18(1) or (5)";

  (b) in subsection (3)—

      (i) after "18(1)" omit "or (6)";

      (ii) for paragraph (b) substitute—

"(b) the notice of the decision under subsection (1) of section 18,".

(9) In section 28—

  (a) in subsection (1)—

      (i) after "tax year" in both places where it occurs, insert "or part tax year";

      (ii) at the end, insert "or treated as an overpayment of universal credit";

  (b) in subsections (3) and (4), after "repaid" insert "to the Board or, as the case may be, to the Secretary of State";

  (c) omit subsection (5);

  (d) in subsection (6) omit "(apart from subsection (5))".

(10) In section 29(4), for "any tax credit" substitute "universal credit".

(11) In section 30(1), before "tax year" in each place where it occurs, insert "part".

(12) In section 38—

  (a) in subsection (1)(b), before "tax year" insert "part";

  (b) for subsection (2), substitute—

"(2) "The relevant section 18 decision" means the decision under subsection (1) of section 18 in relation to the person or persons and the tax credit for the part tax year."

(13) In section 48, after the definition of "overpayment", insert-

""part tax year" means a period of less than a year beginning with 6th April and ending with the date on which the award of a tax credit terminated,".

(14) In Schedule 2, in paragraph 6(1)(a) and (c) and (2)(a), after the words "for the tax year", insert "or part tax year".

Modifications to the Tax Credits (Definition and Calculation of Income) Regulations 2002

(15) Paragraphs 16 to 28 prescribe modifications to the application of the Tax Credits (Definition and Calculation of Income) Regulations 2002 where regulation 17 applies.   **3.98**

(16) In regulation 2(2), after the definition of "the Macfarlane Trusts" insert-

""part tax year" means a period of less than a year beginning with 6th April and ending with the date on which the award of a tax credit terminated,".

(17) In regulation 3—

  (a) in paragraph (1)—

      (i) before "tax year" insert "part";

      (ii) in Steps 1 and 2, after "of the claimant, or in the case of a joint claim, of the claimants" insert "received in or relating to the part tax year";

  (iii) for the first sentence of Step 4, substitute "Where a claimant was entitled to a tax credit and an award of universal credit is made to that person, calculate the trading income (as defined in regulation 6) of the claimant, or in the case of a joint claim, of the claimants, in accordance with regulations 6A and 6B.";

  (iv) in the second and third sentences of Step 4, before "year" insert "part";

 (b) in paragraph (6A), for the words from "ending on 31st March" to the end, substitute "ending on the last day of the month immediately preceding the month in which the claimant's award of a tax credit terminated";

 (c) in paragraph (8)(b), before "year" insert "part".

(18) In regulation 4—

 (a) in paragraph (1)(a), before "tax year" insert "part";

 (b) in paragraph (1)(b), (c), (d), (e), (g) and (k), before "year" insert "part";

 (c) in paragraph (1)(f), after "ITEPA" insert "which is treated as received in the part tax year and in respect of which the charge arises in the part tax year";

 (d) in paragraph (1)(h), after "week" insert "in the part tax year";

 (e) in paragraph (1)(i), after "ITEPA" insert "which is treated as received in the part tax year";

 (f) in paragraph (1)(j), after "applies" insert "received in the part tax year";

 (g) in paragraph (1)(l), after "ITEPA" insert "in respect of which the charge arises in the part tax year";

 (h) in paragraph (1)(m), after "paid" insert "in the part tax year";

 (i) in paragraph (4), after "employment income" in both places where it occurs, insert "received in the part tax year";

 (j) in paragraph (5), after "calculating earnings" insert "received in the part tax year".

(19) In regulation 5—

 (a) in paragraph (1)(o), after "applies" insert "received in or relating to the part tax year";

 (b) in paragraph (2) after "pension income" in both places where it occurs, insert "received in or relating to the part tax year";

 (c) in paragraph (3), after "income tax purposes", insert "in relation to the part tax year".

(20) In regulation 6—

 (a) after "claimant's trading income is" insert ", subject to regulations 6A and 6B";

 (b) in paragraph (a), before "tax year" insert "part";

 (c) in paragraph (b), before "year" insert "part".

(21) After regulation 6 insert-

"Trading Income: in-year finalisation

3.99 (6A) This regulation applies where—

 (a) an award of universal credit is made to a person who was previously entitled to a tax credit;

 (b) the award of that tax credit has terminated;

 (c) the date on which the award terminated falls in the tax year to which that award relates ("the relevant tax year"); and

 (d) the claimant carried on a trade, vocation or profession during the part tax year.

(6B)—(1) Where regulation 6A applies, a claimant's trading income for the purposes of the first paragraph in Step 4 in regulation 3(1) is the claimant's actual or estimated taxable profits attributable to the part tax year ("the relevant trading income").

(2) The relevant trading income is to be calculated by reference to the basis period ending during the relevant tax year.

(3) The basis period is to be determined by reference to the rules in Chapter 15 of Part 2 of ITTOIA.

(4) The relevant trading income is calculated by—

 (a) taking the figure for the actual or estimated taxable income earned in the basis period;

 (b) dividing that figure by the number of days in the basis period to give the daily figure; and

 (c) multiplying the daily figure by the number of days in the part tax year on which the trade, profession or vocation was carried on.".

(22) In regulation 7—

 (a) in paragraph (1), after "social security income" insert "received in the part tax year";

 (b) in paragraph (3), after "social security income" in both places where it occurs, insert "received in the part tax year".

(23) In regulation 8, after "in relation to a student" insert ", any of the following which is received in the part tax year".

(24) In regulation 10—

 (a) in paragraph (1), after "gross amount" insert "received in the part tax year";

(b) in paragraph (1)(e), before "year" insert "part";

(c) in paragraph (2), after "investment income" in both places where it occurs, insert "received in the part tax year".

(25) In regulation 11(1)—

(a) omit "annual";

(b) after "taxable profits" insert "for the part tax year".

(26) In regulation 12(1), before "year" insert "part tax".

(27) In regulation 13, after "means income" insert "received in the part tax year".

(28) In regulation 18, after "means income" insert "received in the part tax year".

Modifications to the Tax Credits (Income Thresholds and Determination of Rates) Regulations 2002

(29) Paragraphs 30 to 32 prescribe modifications to the application of the Tax Credits (Income Thresholds and Determination of Rates) Regulations 2002 where regulation 17 applies.

3.100

(30) In regulation 2 (interpretation)—

(a) after the definition of "the income threshold" insert—

"part tax year" means a period of less than a year beginning with 6th April and ending with the date on which the award of a tax credit terminated,";

(b) in the definition of "the relevant income" insert "as modified by the Universal Credit (Transitional Provisions) Regulations 2013" at the end.

(31) In regulation 7(3)—

(a) in Step 1, in the definition of "MR", after "maximum rate" insert "(determined in the manner prescribed at the date on which the award of the tax credit terminated)";

(b) in Step 3—

(i) in the definition of "I", before "tax year" insert "part";

(ii) in the definition of "N1", before "tax year" insert "part".

(32) In regulation 8(3)—

(a) in Step 1, in the definition of "MR", after "maximum rate" insert "(determined in the manner prescribed at the date on which the award of the tax credit terminated)";

(b) in Step 3—

(i) in the definition of "I", before "tax year" insert "part";

(ii) in the definition of "N1", before "tax year" insert "part".

Modifications to the Tax Credits (Claims and Notifications) Regulations 2002

(33) Paragraphs 34 to 42 prescribe modifications to the application of the Tax Credits (Claims and Notifications) Regulations 2002 where regulation 17 applies.

3.101

(34) In regulation 4, omit paragraph (b).

(35) Omit regulation 10.

(36) Omit regulation 11.

(37) Omit regulation 12.

(38) In regulation 13—

(a) in paragraph (1), after "prescribed by paragraph" omit "(2) or";

(b) omit paragraph (2).

(39) In regulation 15(1)(c), for "section 18(1), (5), (6) or (9)" substitute "section 18(1) or (5)".

(40) In regulation 21(1A), for "regulation 27(2), (2A) or (3)" substitute "regulation 27(2A) or (3)".

(41) In regulation 27—

(a) in paragraph (1), after "prescribed by paragraphs" omit "(2),";

(b) omit paragraph (2).

(42) In regulation 33—

(a) in paragraph (a), for the words from "not later than 31st July" to "if later", substitute "not less than 28 days after the date on which the notice is given";

(b) omit paragraph (b) and the "and" which precedes it.

Modification to the Tax Credits (Payment by the Commissioners) Regulations 2002

(43) Paragraph 44 prescribes a modification to the application of the Tax Credits (Payment by the Commissioners) Regulations 2002 where regulation 17 applies.

3.102

(44) Omit regulation 7.

Modification to the Tax Credits (Residence) Regulations 2003

(45) Paragraph 46 prescribes a modification to the application of the Tax Credits (Residence) Regulations 2003 where regulation 17 applies.

GENERAL NOTE

3.103   See note to reg.17.

Welfare Reform Act 2012 (Commencement No. 9 and Transitional and Transitory Provisions and Commencement No. 8 and Savings and Transitional Provisions (Amendment)) Order 2013

(SI 2013/983) (c.41)

3.104   *The Secretary of State, in exercise of the powers conferred by section 150(3) and (4)(a), (b)(i) and (c) of the Welfare Reform Act 2012, makes the following Order:*

ARRANGEMENT OF ARTICLES

GENERAL NOTE

This Commencement Order ("the Commencement No.9 Order") was the first   3.105
to "roll out" the new universal credit scheme. It has to be read together with the
Transitional Provisions Regulations 2013. This Order accordingly brings into force
provisions of the WRA 2012 that relate to both the introduction of universal credit
and the abolition of income-related ESA and income-based JSA. This is achieved
by reference to the specific categories of cases set out in arts 3 and 4. However,
these provisions apply only to four postcode districts in Manchester, Oldham and
Stockport (or "the relevant districts"; see Sch.1) as from April 29, 2013 (also the
date on which the Transitional Provisions Regulations 2013 come into force). In
addition, of course, a claimant who lives in one of the four specified postcode districts must also be a member of the Pathfinder Group, i.e. be a person who meets
the requirements of regs 5–12 of the Transitional Provisions Regulations 2013. The
justification for the limited "roll out" was that it "will facilitate an evaluation of the
Universal Credit business processes and information technology functionality in a
live environment before it is rolled out nationally from October 2013" (*Explanatory
Memorandum to the Transitional Provisions Regulations 2013*, para.7.64).

This Order was followed by the Commencement No.11 Order (certain postcodes
in Wigan ("the No.2 relevant districts") and Manchester, Oldham and Warrington
("the No.3 relevant districts") as from July 1, 2013), the Commencement No.13
Order (certain postcodes in West London, Manchester and Wigan ("the No.4 relevant districts") as from October 28, 2013) and the Commencement No.14 Order
(certain postcodes in Rugby, Inverness and Perth ("the No.5 relevant districts") as
from November 25, 2013).

In this Order and its following companions, an award of ESA under Pt 1 of the
Welfare Reform Act 2007, in a case where income-related ESA has been abolished
(i.e. in a Pathfinder area), is referred to as a "new style ESA award". Likewise an
award of JSA under the Jobseekers Act 1995, in a case where income-based JSA has
been abolished, is referred to as a "new style JSA award". Conversely an award of
ESA under Pt 1 of the Welfare Reform Act 2007, in a case where income-related
ESA has not been abolished, is referred to as an "old style ESA award". Similarly an
award of JSA under the Jobseekers Act 1995, in a case where income-based JSA has
not been abolished, is referred to as an "old style JSA award".

Citation

1. This Order may be cited as the Welfare Reform Act 2012 (Commencement   3.106
No.9 and Transitional and Transitory Provisions and Commencement No.8
and Savings and Transitional Provisions (Amendment)) Order 2013.

Interpretation

2.—(1) In this Order—   3.107
"the Act" means the Welfare Reform Act 2012 (apart from in Schedule
   4);
"the 1995 Act" means the Jobseekers Act 1995;
"the 2007 Act" means the Welfare Reform Act 2007;
"the amending provisions" means the provisions referred to in article
   4(1)(a) to (c);

"appointed day" means the day appointed for the coming into force of the amending provisions in accordance with article 4(3);

"the Claims and Payments Regulations 1987" means the Social Security (Claims and Payments) Regulations 1987;

"the Claims and Payments Regulations 2013" means the Universal Credit, Personal Independence Payment, Jobseeker's Allowance and Employment and Support Allowance (Claims and Payments) Regulations 2013;

"contribution-based jobseeker's allowance" means a contribution-based allowance under the 1995 Act as it has effect apart from the amendments made by Part 1 of Schedule 14 to the Act that remove references to an income-based allowance;

"contributory employment and support allowance" means a contributory allowance under Part 1 of the 2007 Act as it has effect apart from the amendments made by Schedule 3, and Part 1 of Schedule 14, to the Act that remove references to an income-related allowance;

"the Decisions and Appeals Regulations 2013" means the Universal Credit, Personal Independence Payment, Jobseeker's Allowance and Employment and Support Allowance (Decisions and Appeals) Regulations 2013;

"employment and support allowance" means an employment and support allowance under Part 1 of the 2007 Act;

"the ESA Regulations 2008" means the Employment and Support Allowance Regulations 2008;

"the ESA Regulations 2013" means the Employment and Support Allowance Regulations 2013;

"income-based jobseeker's allowance" means an income-based jobseeker's allowance under the 1995 Act;

"income-related employment and support allowance" means an income-related allowance under Part 1 of the 2007 Act;

"jobseeker's allowance" means an allowance under the 1995 Act;

"the JSA Regulations 1996" means the Jobseeker's Allowance Regulations 1996;

"the JSA Regulations 2013" means the Jobseeker's Allowance Regulations 2013;

"new style ESA award" means an award of an employment and support allowance under Part 1 of the 2007 Act as amended by the provisions of Schedule 3, and Part 1 of Schedule 14, to the Act that remove references to an income-related allowance;

"new style JSA award" means an award of a jobseeker's allowance under the 1995 Act as amended by the provisions of Part 1 of Schedule 14 to the Act that remove references to an income-based jobseeker's allowance;

"old style ESA award" means an award of an employment and support allowance under Part 1 of the 2007 Act as it has effect apart from the amendments made by Schedule 3, and Part 1 of Schedule 14, to the Act that remove references to an income-related allowance;

"old style JSA award" means a jobseeker's allowance under the 1995 Act as it has effect apart from the amendments made by Part 1 of Schedule 14 to the Act that remove references to an income-based jobseeker's allowance;

"relevant districts" means the postcode districts specified in Schedule 1;

"the Transitional Regulations" means the Universal Credit (Transitional Provisions) Regulations 2013;

"the 2010 Transitional Regulations" means the Employment and Support Allowance (Transitional Provisions, Housing Benefit and Council Tax Benefit)(Existing Awards)(No.2) Regulations 2010.

(2) For the purposes of this Order, a reference to a person falling within the Pathfinder Group is a reference to a person who meets the requirements of regulations 5 to 12 of the Transitional Regulations.

GENERAL NOTE

Para. (2)

On membership of the Pathfinder Group, see also the notes to regs 3 and 4 of the Transitional Provisions Regulations 2013.   **3.108**

Day appointed for commencement of the universal credit provisions in Part 1 of the Act

3.—(1) 29th April 2013 is the day appointed for the coming into force of—   **3.109**

(a) sections 29 (delegation and contracting out), 37(1), (2), (8) and (9) (capability for work or work-related activity), 38 (information) and 39(1), (2), (3)(b) and (c) (couples) of the Act;

(b) the following paragraphs of Schedule 2 to the Act (universal credit: amendments) and section 31 of the Act (supplementary and consequential amendments) in so far as it relates to those paragraphs, in so far as they are not already in force—

(i) paragraphs 1, 2, 32 to 35, 37 to 42, 52 to 55 and 65;

(ii) paragraphs 4, 8, 10 to 23, 25 and 27 to 31 and paragraph 3 in so far as it relates to those paragraphs; and

(iii) paragraphs 44, 45, 47, 49, 50(2) and 50(1) in so far as it relates to 50(2), and paragraph 43 in so far as it relates to those paragraphs and sub-paragraphs; and

(c) paragraph 1 of Schedule 5 to the Act (universal credit and other working-age benefits) and section 35 of the Act in so far as it relates to that paragraph.

(2) The day appointed for the coming into force of the provisions of the Act listed in Schedule 2, in so far as they are not already in force, in relation to the case of a claim referred to in paragraph (3)(a) to (d) and any award that is made in respect of such a claim, and in relation to the case of an award referred to in paragraph (3)(e) or (f), is the day appointed in accordance with paragraph (4).

(3) The claims and awards referred to are—

(a) a claim for universal credit that is made or treated as made in respect of a period that begins on or after 29th April 2013 by a person who, on the day on which the claim is made or treated as made, resides in one of the relevant districts;

(b) a claim for universal credit that is made or treated as made by a person in respect of a period that begins on or after 29th April 2013 where—

(i) the person does not reside in one of the relevant districts on the day on which the claim is made or treated as made;

(ii) in connection with the claim, the person gives incorrect information regarding their residence in such a district; and

     (iii) after a decision is made that the person is entitled to universal credit and one or more payments have been made in respect of the person, the Secretary of State discovers that the person gave that incorrect information;

    (c) a claim for universal credit that is treated as made by a couple in the circumstances referred to in regulation 3(4) of the Transitional Regulations (entitlement to claim universal credit);

    (d) a claim for universal credit by a former member of a couple that is made or treated as made in the circumstances referred to in regulation 3(2) of the Transitional Regulations (entitlement to claim universal credit), within the period of one month referred to in that provision;

    (e) an award of universal credit that is made without a claim in the circumstances referred to in regulation 6(1) or (2) of the Claims and Payments Regulations 2013 (claims not required for entitlement to universal credit in some cases); and

    (f) an award of universal credit that is made without a claim in the circumstances referred to in regulation 9(6), (7) or (10) the Claims and Payments Regulations 2013 (claims for universal credit by members of a couple).

(4) The day appointed in relation to the cases of the claims and awards referred to in paragraph (2) is—

    (a) in the case of a claim referred to in paragraph (3)(a) to (d), the first day of the period in respect of which the claim is made or treated as made;

    (b) in the case of an award referred to in paragraph (3)(e) or (f), the first day on which a person is entitled to universal credit under that award.

(5) For the purposes of paragraph (3)(a) to (d), the Claims and Payments Regulations 2013 apply for the purpose of deciding—

    (a) whether a claim for universal credit is made or is to be treated as made; and

    (b) the day on which the claim is made or is to be treated as made.

(6) For the purposes of paragraph (4)(a), where the time for making a claim for universal credit is extended under regulation 26(2) of the Claims and Payments Regulations 2013, the reference to the first day of the period in respect of which the claim is made or treated as made is a reference to the first day of the period in respect of which the claim is, by reason of the operation of that provision, timeously made or treated as made.

DEFINITIONS

    "the Act"—art.2(1).
    "the Claims and Payments Regulations 2013"—*ibid.*
    "relevant districts"—*ibid.*
    "the Transitional Regulations"—*ibid.*

3.110   GENERAL NOTE

Para. (1)

3.111   This brings into force various provisions relating to universal credit (including some supplementary and consequential provisions set out in Sch.2 to the 2012 Act) on April 29, 2013.

Para. (2)

This tortuously worded provision has the effect of bringing into force those provisions relating to universal credit in Pt 1 of the WRA 2012, as set out in Sch.2, where one of six different categories of case referred to in art.3(3) applies. These relate to claims for universal credit and any resulting award as well as to awards of universal credit without a claim.

3.112

Para. (3)

This specifies the six situations in which para.(2) has the effect of applying the new universal credit rules.

3.113

Sub-para. (3) (a)

This covers the situation where a person makes a claim for universal credit in respect of a period that begins on or after April 29, 2013 where that individual resides in a "relevant district" at the time that the claim is made (the "relevant districts" are defined by postcode in Sch.1). The other conditions (known as "Pathfinder Group conditions") for making a claim for universal credit are set out in the Transitional Provisions Regulations 2013.

3.114

Sub-para. (3) (b)

Where a person claims universal credit and incorrectly states that they live in a relevant district, but this is only discovered once payments of the new benefit have been made, that person remains subject to the new regime.

3.115

Sub-para. (3) (c)

This covers the case of a single person who becomes a member of a couple where the other member is already entitled to universal credit.

3.116

Sub-para. (3) (d)

Where a couple separate, and the member of the couple who is not exempt from making a claim for universal credit makes a claim within a period of one month, the new rules apply.

Sub-para. (3) (e)

A person may be awarded universal credit without making a claim as a result of changes in their income within six months of their income being such that they were not previously entitled to universal credit.

3.117

Sub-para. (3) (f)

Again, a person may be awarded universal credit without making a claim where a couple cease to be a couple and an award is made to the member of the couple who is exempt from making a claim. Similarly, an award of universal credit may be made without a claim to a couple where the members of the couple were previously entitled to the new benefit as single claimants. In addition, the new regime applies where an award of universal credit is made without a claim to a member of a couple where the other member of the couple has died.

3.118

Paras (4)–(6)

These make supplementary provision dealing with the effective date of universal credit claims and awards under the preceding rules.

3.119

Day appointed for the abolition of income-related employment and support allowance and income-based jobseeker's allowance

4.—(1) The day appointed for the coming into force of—
  (a) section 33(1)(a) and (b) and (2) of the Act (abolition of benefits);

3.120

(b) paragraphs 22 to 26 of Schedule 3 to the Act (abolition of benefits: consequential amendments) and section 33(3) of the Act in so far as it relates to those paragraphs; and

(c) the repeals in Part 1 of Schedule 14 to the Act (abolition of benefits superseded by universal credit) that are referred to in Schedule 3,

in relation to the case of a claim referred to in paragraph (2)(a) to (d) and any award that is made in respect of such a claim, and in relation to the case of an award referred to in paragraph (2)(e) and (f), is the day appointed in accordance with paragraph (3).

(2) The claims and awards referred to are—

(a) a claim for universal credit, an employment and support allowance or a jobseeker's allowance that is made or treated as made in respect of a period that begins on or after 29th April 2013 by a person who, on the day on which the claim is made or treated as made, resides in one of the relevant districts and falls within the Pathfinder Group;

(b) a claim for universal credit that is made or treated as made by a person in respect of a period that begins on or after 29th April 2013 where—

   (i) the person does not reside in one of the relevant districts or does not fall within the Pathfinder Group on the day on which the claim is made or treated as made;

  (ii) in connection with the claim, the person gives incorrect information regarding their residence in such a district or their falling within the Pathfinder Group; and

 (iii) after a decision is made that the person is entitled to universal credit and one or more payments have been made in respect of the person, the Secretary of State discovers that the person gave that incorrect information;

(c) a claim for universal credit that is treated as made by a couple in the circumstances referred to in regulation 3(4) of the Transitional Regulations (entitlement to claim universal credit);

(d) a claim for universal credit by a former member of a couple that is made or treated as made in the circumstances referred to in regulation 3(2) of the Transitional Regulations (entitlement to claim universal credit), within the period of one month referred to in that provision;

(e) an award of universal credit that is made in the circumstances referred to in regulation 6(1) or (2) of the Claims and Payments Regulations 2013 (claims not required for entitlement to universal credit in some cases); and

(f) an award of universal credit that is made without a claim in the circumstances referred to in regulation 9(6), (7) or (10) of the Claims and Payments Regulations 2013 (claims for universal credit by members of a couple).

(3) The day appointed in relation to the cases of the claims and awards referred to in paragraph (1) is—

(a) in the case of a claim referred to in paragraph (2)(a) to (d), the first day of the period in respect of which the claim is made or treated as made; and

(b) in the case of an award referred to in paragraph (2)(e) or (f), the first day on which a person is entitled to universal credit under that award.

(4) The references in paragraph (1) to an award of universal credit include a reference to any claim for an employment and support allowance or a jobseeker's allowance that does not fall within paragraph (2)(a) and that is made or treated as made during the period of the award by any person to whom the award is made and to any notice under regulation 4 of the 2010 Transitional Regulations that is issued to such a person within that period, and to any—

    (a) award of an employment and support allowance or of a jobseeker's allowance that is made in respect of the claim; or

    (b) award of an employment and support allowance that is made in respect of the award of incapacity benefit or severe disablement allowance to which the notice relates,

where, in relation to a claim, the claim meets the condition referred to in paragraph (5).

(5) The condition referred to is that the claim is made or treated as made in respect of a period that begins on or after the day appointed in relation to—

    (a) where the award of universal credit is made with respect to a claim referred to in paragraph (2)(a) to (d), the case of that claim and the award;

    (b) where the award of universal credit is an award referred to in paragraph (2)(e) or (f), the case of the award.

DEFINITIONS

    "the Act"—art.2(1).
    "the Claims and Payments Regulations 2013"—*ibid.*
    "employment and support allowance"—*ibid.*
    "income-based jobseeker's allowance"—*ibid.*
    "income-related employment and support allowance"—*ibid.*
    "jobseeker's allowance"—*ibid.*
    "relevant districts"—*ibid.*
    "the Transitional Regulations"—*ibid.*
    "the 2010 Transitional Regulations"—*ibid.*

GENERAL NOTE   **3.121**

Para. (1)

This brings into force provisions relating to the abolition of both income-related   **3.122** employment and support allowance and income-based jobseeker's allowance. This includes the repeal of various provisions relating to the abolished allowances as set out in Sch.3. However, these provisions are only brought into force where one of the six different categories of case set out in para.(2) applies.

Para. (2)

This sets out the six categories of case affected by the amendments made by   **3.123** para.(1).

Para. (2) (a)

Where a person (i) resides in a relevant district (see Sch.1); (ii) meets the   **3.124** Pathfinder Group conditions; and (iii) makes a claim for universal credit, employment and support allowance or jobseeker's allowance, which is (iv) in respect of a period that begins on or after April 29, 2013, then the amendments made by para.(1) above govern both the claim and any award made in respect of that claim.

In this context, in deciding whether a person falls within the Pathfinder Group for the purposes of point (ii), the requirements of regs 5 to 12 of the Transitional Regulations are to be read as though any reference to making a claim for universal credit included a reference to making a claim for an employment and support allowance or a jobseeker's allowance (see art.5(2)).

As regards point (iii), the Claims and Payments Regulations 1987 govern both whether and when a claim for an employment and support allowance or a jobseeker's allowance is made or is to be treated as made (see art.5(1)), while the Claims and Payments Regulations 2013 determine the same issues as regards universal credit (see art.5(3)).

Para. (2) (b)

3.125   This covers the situation where a person claims universal credit and incorrectly states that they live in a relevant district, or provides incorrect information as to their meeting the Pathfinder Group conditions, but the error is only discovered once payments of the new benefit have been made. Such a claim remains within the universal credit regime despite the error. As to claims, see art.5(3).

Para. (2) (c)

3.126   This is analogous to art.3(3)(c). As to claims, see art.5(3).

Para. (2) (d)

3.127   This is analogous to art.3(3)(d). As to claims, see art.5(3).

Para. (2) (e)

3.128   This is analogous to art.3(3)(e).

Para. (2) (f)

3.129   This is analogous to art.3(3)(f).

Para. (3)

3.130   See further art.5(4).

Para. (4)

3.131   This provides that a reference in para.(1) to an award of universal credit includes a reference to any claim for either ESA or JSA, and any award that is made in respect of that claim, where the claim is made within the period of the universal credit award by a person to whom the award is made and with respect to a period that commences on or after the first day of entitlement to universal credit. It also includes a reference to any notice under the Transitional Provisions Regulations 2010 that is issued to such a person. Such notices deal with the conversion of existing awards of incapacity benefit and severe disablement allowance to employment and support allowance, and to any award of the latter benefit that is made as a result of a conversion decision, where the notice is issued within the period of the universal credit award.

Provisions that apply in connection with the abolition of income-related employment and support allowance and income-based jobseeker's allowance under article 4

3.132   **5.**—(1) For the purposes of article 4(2)(a), the Claims and Payments Regulations 1987 apply for the purposes of deciding—

(a) whether a claim for an employment and support allowance or a jobseeker's allowance is made or is to be treated as made; and

(b) the day on which the claim is made or is to be treated as made.

(2) For the purposes of article 4(2)(a), in determining whether a person falls within the Pathfinder Group, the requirements of regulations 5 to 12

of the Transitional Regulations are to be read as though any reference to making a claim for universal credit included a reference to making a claim for an employment and support allowance or for a jobseeker's allowance as the case may be.

(3) For the purposes of article 4(2)(a) to (d), the Claims and Payments Regulations 2013 apply for the purpose of deciding—

(a) whether a claim for universal credit is made or is to be treated as made; and

(b) the day on which the claim is made or is to be treated as made.

(4) For the purposes of article 4(3)(a)—

(a) in the case of a claim for universal credit, where the time for making a claim is extended under regulation 26(2) of the Claims and Payments Regulations 2013 (time within which a claim for universal credit is to be made), the reference to the first day of the period in respect of which the claim is made or treated as made is a reference to the first day of the period in respect of which the claim is, by reason of the operation of that provision, timeously made or treated as made;

(b) in the case of a claim for an employment and support allowance or a jobseeker's allowance, where the time for making a claim is extended under regulation 19 of, and Schedule 4 to, the Claims and Payments Regulations 1987, the reference to the first day of the period in respect of which the claim is made or treated as made is a reference to the first day of the period in respect of which the claim is, by reason of the operation of those provisions, timeously made or treated as made.

DEFINITIONS

"the Claims and Payments Regulations 1987"—art.2(1).
"the Claims and Payments Regulations 2013"—*ibid.*
"income-based jobseeker's allowance"—*ibid.*
"income-related employment and support allowance"—*ibid.*
"jobseeker's allowance"—*ibid.*
"the Transitional Regulations"—*ibid.*

GENERAL NOTE

These provisions supplement and further define the provisions of art.4.   **3.133**

Transitional provision: where the abolition of income-related employment and support allowance and income-based jobseeker's allowance is treated as not applying

6.—(1) Paragraph (2) applies where—   **3.134**

(a) a person has or had a new style ESA award or a new style JSA award ("the award");

(b) in respect of all or part of the period to which the award relates, the person—

(i) makes a claim, or is treated as making a claim, for universal credit; or

(ii) makes an application to the Secretary of State for supersession of the decision to make the award, on the basis of a relevant change of circumstances that would relate to the grounds for

363

entitlement to an income-related employment and support allowance or an income-based jobseeker's allowance if the amending provisions had not come into force under article 4(1);

(c) if the amending provisions had not come into force under article 4(1) and, in the case of a claim for universal credit, an application for supersession of the decision to make the award had been made, the person would be entitled to an income-related employment and support allowance or an income-based jobseeker's allowance, as the case may be, with respect to the period for which the claim for universal credit or application for supersession is made;

(d) where the person makes an application for supersession of the decision to make the award, the period in respect of which the application is made does not include any period in respect of which the person has been awarded universal credit;

(e) where the person makes a claim, or is treated as making a claim, for universal credit, the claim does not fall within a case referred to in article 4(2)(b), (c) or (d); and

(f) on the day on which the claim for universal credit is made or treated as made, or the application for supersession is received, as the case may be, the person—

  (i) does not reside in one of the relevant districts; or
  (ii) does not fall within the Pathfinder Group.

(2) Where this paragraph applies, then, in relation to the award and with effect from the first day of the period in respect of which the claim is made or treated as made, or the application for supersession is made, the 1995 Act or Part 1 of the 2007 Act, as the case may be, is to apply as though the amending provisions had not come into force under article 4(1).

(3) For the purposes of paragraph (1)(f)—

(a) the Claims and Payments Regulations 2013 apply for the purpose of deciding—

  (i) whether a claim for universal credit is made or is to be treated as made; and
  (ii) the day on which the claim is made or is to be treated as made; and

(b) in determining whether a person falls within the Pathfinder Group, the requirements of regulations 5 to 12 of the Transitional Regulations are to be read as though any reference to making a claim for universal credit included a reference to making an application for supersession of a decision to make an award of an employment and support allowance or of a jobseeker's allowance, as the case may be.

(4) For the purposes of paragraph (2), the reference to the period in respect of which the application for supersession is made is a reference to the period beginning with the day from which the superseding decision takes effect in accordance with section 10(5) of the Social Security Act 1998 and regulation 35 of, and Schedule 1 to, the Decisions and Appeals Regulations 2013 (effectives dates: Secretary of State decisions).

(5) For the purposes of paragraph (2), the reference to the first day of the period in respect of which the claim for universal credit is made or treated as made, in a case where the time for making a claim for universal credit is extended under regulation 26(2) of the Claims and Payments Regulations 2013, is a reference to the first day of the period in respect of which the

claim is, by reason of the operation of that provision, timeously made or treated as made.

DEFINITIONS

"the 1995 Act"—art.2(1).
"the 2007 Act"—*ibid.*
"the amending provisions"—*ibid.*
"the award"—para.1(a)
"the Claims and Payments Regulations 2013"—art.2(1).
"employment and support allowance"—*ibid.*
"the Decisions and Appeals Regulations 2013"—*ibid.*
"income-based jobseeker's allowance"—*ibid.*
"income-related employment and support allowance"—*ibid.*
"jobseeker's allowance"—*ibid.*
"new style ESA award"—*ibid.*
"new style JSA award"—*ibid.*
"relevant districts"—*ibid.*
"the Transitional Regulations"—*ibid.*

GENERAL NOTE

This makes transitional provision for cases where the six conditions in para.(1) **3.135**
are met. These all concern cases where the claimant either moves out of a relevant district or is not in the Pathfinder Group. In these cases, the award is treated as though the provisions in art.4(1)(a)–(c) above had not come into force (para.(2); see further art.9(2)). In consequence the person concerned will be able to claim an existing benefit, i.e. income-related ESA or income-based JSA, once again. The six conditions set out in para.(1) are (in summary) that:
  (a) the claimant has a new style ESA award or new style JSA award;
  (b) s/he makes a claim for universal credit or applies for supersession of the decision to make the award;
  (c) she would otherwise be entitled to income-related employment and support allowance or income-based jobseeker's allowance;
  (d) any award of universal credit has come to an end;
  (e) any claim for universal credit does not fall within the cases in art.4(2)(b) to (d); and
  (f) the person neither resides in a relevant district nor meets the Pathfinder Group conditions at the time that the application is received or the claim is made.
Paragraphs (3)–(5) make supplementary provision for paras (1)(f) and (2).

Day appointed for commencement of provisions relating to claimant responsibilities with respect to employment and support allowance and jobseeker's allowance, and transitional provisions

7.—(1) The day appointed for the coming into force of— **3.136**
  (a) section 44(2) of the Act and section 44(1) of the Act in so far as it relates to section 44(2) (claimant commitment for jobseeker's allowance);
  (b) section 49(2) and (3) to (5) of the Act (and section 49(1) of the Act in so far as it relates to those provisions) (claimant responsibilities for jobseeker's allowance);
  (c) section 54(2) of the Act (and section 54(1) of the Act in so far as it relates to that provision) (claimant commitment for employment and support allowance);
  (d) section 57(2), (4), (5) and (9) of the Act (and section 57(1) of the

Act in so far as it relates to those provisions) (claimant responsibilities for employment and support allowance);

(e) the repeals in Part 4 of Schedule 14 to the Act (jobseeker's allowance: responsibilities after introduction of universal credit); and

(f) the repeals in Part 5 of Schedule 14 to the Act (employment and support allowance: responsibilities after introduction of universal credit),

in so far as they are not already in force, is, in relation to a particular case, the day on which the amending provisions come into force, under any secondary legislation, in relation to that case.

(2) Where, under any secondary legislation, in relation to a new style JSA award, the 1995 Act applies as though the amending provisions had not come into force, the 1995 Act is to apply in relation to that award as though the provisions referred to in paragraph (1)(a), (b) and (e) had not come into force.

(3) Where, under any secondary legislation, in relation to a new style ESA award, Part 1 of the 2007 Act applies as though the amending provisions had not come into force, that Part is to apply in relation that award as though the provisions referred to in paragraph (1)(c), (d) and (f) had not come into force.

(4) For the purposes of paragraphs (1) to (3), "secondary legislation" means an instrument made under an Act.

DEFINITIONS

"the Act"—art.2(1).
"the 1995 Act"—*ibid.*
"the 2007 Act"—*ibid.*
"the amending provisions"—*ibid.*
"employment and support allowance"—*ibid.*
"jobseeker's allowance"—*ibid.*
"new style ESA award"—*ibid.*
"new style JSA award"—*ibid.*
"secondary legislation"—para.(4).

GENERAL NOTE

3.137   This provides for the appointed day and transitional provisions for the measures in the WRA 2012 that relate to claimant responsibilities in relation to a new style ESA award or a new style JSA award. Those new provisions are effective in relation to any case with respect to which the provisions of art.4(1)(a)–(c) come into force.

Note, however, that art.6 of the No.11 Commencement Order amends and modifies this provision with respect to certain cases that are to occur after that Order is made.

Day appointed for commencement of provisions concerning consideration of revision before appeal

3.138   **8.** 29th April 2013 is the day appointed for the coming into force of paragraphs 1 to 11 and 15 to 18 of Schedule 11 to the Act (power to require consideration of revision before appeal) and section 102(6) of the Act in so far as it relates to those paragraphs, to the extent that those provisions are not already in force.

DEFINITION

"the Act"—art.2(1).

GENERAL NOTE

This simply brings into force those provisions of Sch.11 to the Act concerning consideration of revision before appeal.

3.139

Transitional provision: conversion of incapacity benefits

9.—(1) Subject to paragraph (2), where the amending provisions come into force under article 4(1) in relation to the case of a claim referred to in article 4(2)(a) to (d) and any award made in respect of the claim, or the case of an award referred to in article 4(2)(e) or (f), the 2010 Transitional Regulations are to apply in relation to that case as if the modifications set out in Schedule 4 were made.

3.140

(2) Where article 6(2) applies in relation to a new style ESA award (such that the award continues as an old style ESA award), the 2010 Transitional Regulations are to apply in relation to the award, in its continuation as an old style ESA award, as if those modifications had not been made.

DEFINITIONS

"the amending provisions"—art.2(1).
"new style ESA award"—*ibid*.
"old style ESA award"—*ibid*.
"the 2010 Transitional Regulations"—*ibid*.

GENERAL NOTE

The introduction of universal credit was always going to be complicated. That complexity has been made worse by the fact that many existing awards of employment and support allowance have not been assessed for conversion, sometimes described as "reassessment", to ESA, even though that process began on October 11 2010. This regulation allows for transitional provisions whereby, in relation to cases with respect to which art.4(1)(a)–(c) have come into force, the Transitional Provisions Regulations 2010 are to be read as if the amendments set out in Sch.4 were made. Those amendments substitute references to provisions that apply to new style ESA awards, including the ESA Regulations 2013.

3.141

Limited capability for work or work-related activity: transition from old style ESA

10.—(1) This article applies where—
(a) a person is entitled to a new style ESA award and they were previously entitled to an old style ESA award that was not in existence immediately before the first day on which the person in question is entitled to the new style ESA award; or
(b) (i) the amending provisions have come into force under article 4(1) in relation to the case of a claim for universal credit referred to in article 4(2)(b) to (d) (and any award that is made in respect of the claim) or an award of universal credit referred to in article 4(2)(e) or (f); and
(ii) the person in question had an old style ESA award immediately before the appointed day, which consisted of or included a contributory employment and support allowance (which allowance therefore continues as a new style ESA award).

3.142

(2) Where this article applies, the ESA Regulations 2013 are to be read as if—

   (a) (i) in the definitions of "period of limited capability for work" in regulations 2 (interpretation) and 3 (further interpretation), the reference to a period throughout which a person has, or is treated as having, limited capability for work included a reference to a period throughout which the person in question had, or was treated as having, limited capability for work under the ESA Regulations 2008; and

       (ii) the reference, in the definition in regulation 2, to regulation 28 of the Claims and Payments Regulations 2013 (time within which a claim for employment and support allowance is to be made) included a reference to regulation 19 of, and Schedule 4 to, the Claims and Payments Regulations 1987 (prescribed times for claiming benefit);

   (b) in regulation 6 (the assessment phase–previous claimants)—

       (i) any reference to an employment and support allowance included a reference to an old style ESA award; and

       (ii) in paragraph (2)(b)(v) and (c)(iii), the reference to regulation 26 (conditions for treating a claimant as having limited capability for work until a determination about limited capability for work has been made) included a reference to regulation 30 of the ESA Regulations 2008 (conditions for treating a claimant as having limited capability for work until a determination about limited capability for work has been made);

   (c) in regulation 7 (circumstances where the condition that the assessment phase has ended before entitlement to the support component or the work-related activity component arises does not apply)—

       (i) any reference to an employment and support allowance included a reference to an old style ESA award; and

       (ii) in paragraph (3)(b)(iv), (c)(iii), (c)(iv) and (d)(iii), the reference to regulation 26 included a reference to regulation 30 of the ESA Regulations 2008;

   (d) in regulation 11 (condition relating to youth–previous claimants), any reference to an employment and support allowance included a reference to an old style ESA award;

   (e) in regulation 15 (determination of limited capability for work)—

       (i) the reference in paragraph (7)(a) to a claimant having been determined to have limited capability for work included a reference to such a determination made under Part 5 of the ESA Regulations 2008; and

       (ii) the reference in paragraph (7)(b) to a person being treated as having limited capability for work included a reference to a person being so treated under regulation 20 (certain claimants to be treated as having limited capability for work), 25 (hospital patients), 26 (claimants receiving certain regular treatment) or 29 (exceptional circumstances) of the ESA Regulations 2008;

   (f) in regulation 26 (conditions for treating a claimant as having limited capability for work until a determination about limited capability for work has been made)—

       (i) in paragraph (2)(b), the reference to regulation 18 (failure to provide information in relation to limited capability for work) and 19 (claimant may be called for a medical examination to determine whether the claimant has limited capability for work) included a reference to regulation 22 (failure to provide information in relation to limited capability for work) and 23 (claimant may be called for a medical examination to determine whether the claimant has limited capability for work) of the ESA Regulations 2008; and

    (ii) in paragraph (4)(c), the reference to regulation 18 included a reference to regulation 22 of the ESA Regulations 2008;

(g) in regulation 30(4) (determination of limited capability for work-related activity), the reference to a determination about whether a claimant has, or is to be treated as having or not having, limited capability for work-related activity included such a determination that was made under Part 6 of the ESA Regulations 2008; and

(h) in regulation 87(1) (claimants appealing a decision), the reference to a determination that the claimant does not have limited capability for work under the ESA Regulations 2013 included a reference to such a determination under the ESA Regulations 2008.

DEFINITIONS

"the amending provisions"—art.2(1)
"appointed day"—*ibid.*
"the Claims and Payments Regulations 1987"—*ibid.*
"the Claims and Payments Regulations 2013"—*ibid.*
"contributory employment and support allowance"—*ibid.*
"employment and support allowance"—*ibid.*
"the ESA Regulations 2008"—*ibid.*
"the ESA Regulations 2013"—*ibid.*
"new style ESA award"—*ibid.*
"old style ESA award"—*ibid.*

GENERAL NOTE

This makes transitional provisions for assessments of limited capability for work   **3.143** or for work and work-related activity where a person has a new style ESA award and previously had an old style ESA award. Article 11 deals with the converse position.

So, for example, under the new style ESA award the definition of a period of limited capability for work includes a period throughout which the claimant had, or was treated as having, limited capability for work for the purposes of old style ESA (para.(2)(a)). Similarly, where the old style and new style awards link, then days of entitlement to old styled ESA in the linked award are included in calculating the end of the assessment phase (para.(2)(b)). To the same end, any earlier period of limited capability for work under the old style ESA award is counted in working out whether the work related activity component or support component is payable from the first day of entitlement (para.(2)(c)). Likewise, the six months rule for the purposes of treating a claimant as having limited capability for work until a further determination is made includes having limited capability for work (or being treated as such) under an old style ESA award (subs.(2)(f)).

Note, however, that art.8 of the No.11 Commencement Order amends and modifies this provision with respect to certain cases that are to occur after that Order is made.

Limited capability for work or work-related activity: transition from new style ESA

11.—(1) This article applies where—   **3.144**

(a) a person is entitled to an old style ESA award and they were previously entitled to a new style ESA award that was not in existence immediately before the first day on which the person in question is entitled to the old style ESA award; or

(b) article 6(2) applies in relation to a new style ESA award (such that it continues as an old style ESA award).

(2) Where this article applies, the ESA Regulations 2008 are to be read as if—

(a) (i) in the definitions of "period of limited capability for work" in regulation 2(1) and (5) (interpretation), the reference to a period throughout which a person has, or is treated as having, limited capability for work included a reference to a period throughout which the person in question had, or was treated as having, limited capability for work under the ESA Regulations 2013; and

(ii) the reference, in the definition in regulation 2(1), to regulation 19 of the Claims and Payments Regulations 1987 (time for claiming benefit) included a reference to regulation 28 of the Claims and Payments Regulations 2013 (time within which a claim for an employment and support allowance is to be made);

(b) in regulation 5 (the assessment phase–previous claimants)—

(i) any reference to an employment and support allowance included a reference to a new style ESA award; and

(ii) in paragraph (2)(b)(v) and (c)(iii), the reference to regulation 30 (conditions for treating a claimant as having limited capability for work until a determination about limited capability for work has been made) included a reference to regulation 26 of the ESA Regulations 2013 (conditions for treating a claimant as having limited capability for work until a determination about limited capability for work has been made);

(c) in regulation 7 (circumstances where the condition that the assessment phase has ended before entitlement to the support component or the work-related activity component arises does not apply)—

(i) any reference to an employment and support allowance included a reference to a new style ESA award; and

(ii) in paragraph (1B)(b)(iv), (c)(iii), (c)(iv) and (d)(iii), the reference to regulation 30 included a reference to regulation 26 of the ESA Regulations 2013;

(d) in regulation 10 (condition relating to youth – previous claimants), any reference to an employment and support allowance included a reference to a new style ESA award;

(e) in regulation 19 (determination of limited capability for work)—

(i) the reference in paragraph (7)(a) to a claimant having been determined to have limited capability for work included a reference to such a determination made under Part 4 of the ESA Regulations 2013; and

(ii) the reference in paragraph (7)(b) to a person being treated as having limited capability for work included a reference to a person being so treated under regulation 16 (certain claimants to be treated as having limited capability for work), 21 (hospital patients), 22 (claimants receiving certain treatment) or 25 (exceptional circumstances) of the ESA Regulations 2013;

(f) in regulation 30 (conditions for treating a claimant as having limited capability for work until a determination about limited capability for work has been made)—

(i) in the initial words of paragraph (2)(b), the reference to regulation 22 (failure to provide information in relation to limited capability for work) and 23 (claimant may be called for a medical examination to determine whether the claimant has limited capability for work) included a reference to regulation 18 (failure to provide information in relation to limited capability for work) and 19 (claimant may be called for a medical examination to determine whether the claimant has limited capability for work) of the ESA Regulations 2013; and
(ii) in [¹ paragraph (4)(c)], the reference to regulation 22 included a reference to regulation 18 of the ESA Regulations 2013;
(g) in regulation 34(4) (determination of limited capability for work-related activity), the reference to a determination about whether a claimant has, or is to be treated as having or not having, limited capability for work-related activity included such a determination that was made under Part 5 of the ESA Regulations 2013; and
(h) in regulation 147A(1) (claimants appealing a decision), the reference to a determination that the claimant does not have limited capability for work included a reference to such a determination under the ESA Regulations 2013.

AMENDMENT

1. Welfare Reform Act 2012 (Commencement No.13 and Transitional and Transitory Provisions) Order 2013 (SI 2013/2657), art.5(a) (October 29, 2013).

DEFINITIONS

"the Claims and Payments Regulations 1987"—art.2(1)
"the Claims and Payments Regulations 2013"—*ibid.*
"employment and support allowance"—*ibid.*
"the ESA Regulations 2008"—*ibid.*
"the ESA Regulations 2013"—*ibid.*
"new style ESA award"—*ibid.*
"old style ESA award"—*ibid.*

GENERAL NOTE

This makes transitional provisions for assessments of limited capability for work   **3.145**
or for work and work-related activity where a person has an old style ESA award and previously had a new style ESA award. Article 10 deals with the converse position. The modifications are to similar effect as in art.10.

Note, however, that art.9 of the No.11 Commencement Order amends and modifies this provision with respect to certain cases that are to occur after that Order is made.

Continuity of jobseeking period in the case of transition from old style JSA

12.—(1) Paragraph (2) applies where—   **3.146**
(a) a person is entitled to a new style JSA award and they were previously entitled to an old style JSA award that was not in existence immediately before the first day on which the person in question is entitled to the new style JSA award; or
(b) (i) the amending provisions have come into force under article 4(1) in relation to the case of a claim for universal credit referred to in article 4(2)(b) to (d) (and any award that is made in respect of the

claim) or an award of universal credit referred to in article 4(2)(e) or (f); and

(ii) the person in question had an old style JSA award immediately before the appointed day, which consisted of or included a contribution-based jobseeker's allowance (which allowance therefore continues in existence as a new style JSA award).

(2) Where this paragraph applies, regulation 37 of the JSA Regulations 2013 (jobseeking period) is to be read as if—

(a) any reference in the regulation to the jobseeking period in relation to a claimant included a reference to any period that, under regulation 47 of the JSA Regulations 1996 (jobseeking period), forms part of such a jobseeking period; and

(b) in paragraph (3) of the regulation, the reference to a day that is to be treated as a day in respect of which the claimant was entitled to a jobseeker's allowance included a reference to any day that, under regulation 47(4) of the JSA Regulations 1996, is to be treated as a day in respect of which the claimant was entitled to a contribution-based jobseeker's allowance.

DEFINITIONS

"the amending provisions"—art.2(1).
"the appointed day"—*ibid*.
"contribution-based jobseeker's allowance"—*ibid*.
"jobseeker's allowance"—*ibid*.
"the JSA Regulations 1996"—*ibid*.
"the JSA Regulations 2013"—*ibid*.
"new style JSA award"—*ibid*.
"old style JSA award"—*ibid*.

GENERAL NOTE

3.147   This makes transitional provisions for the continuity of jobseeking periods where a person has a new style JSA award and previously had an old style JSA award. Article 13 deals with the converse position.

Note, however, that art.10 of the No.11 Commencement Order amends and modifies this provision with respect to certain cases that are to occur after that Order is made.

Continuity of jobseeking period in case of transition from new style JSA

3.148   **13.**—(1) Paragraph (2) applies where—

(a) a person is entitled to an old style JSA award and they were previously entitled to a new style JSA award that was not in existence immediately before the first day on which the person in question is entitled to the old style JSA award; or

(b) article 6(2) applies in relation to a new style JSA award (such that it continues as an old style JSA award).

(2) Where this paragraph applies, regulation 47 of the JSA Regulations 1996 (jobseeking period) is to be read as if—

(a) any reference in the regulation to the jobseeking period in relation to a claimant included a reference to any period that, under regulation 37 of the JSA Regulations 2013 (jobseeking period), forms part of such a jobseeking period; and

(b) in paragraph (4) of that regulation, the reference to any day that is to be treated as a day in respect of which the claimant was entitled to a contribution-based jobseeker's allowance is to be read as if it included a reference to a day that, under regulation 37(3) of the JSA Regulations 2013 (jobseeking period), is to be treated as a day in respect of which the claimant was entitled to a jobseeker's allowance.

DEFINITIONS

"contribution-based jobseeker's allowance"—art.2(1).
"jobseeker's allowance"—*ibid.*
"the JSA Regulations 1996"—*ibid.*
"the JSA Regulations 2013"—*ibid.*
"new style JSA award"—*ibid.*
"old style JSA award"—*ibid.*

GENERAL NOTE

This makes transitional provisions for the continuity of jobseeking periods where   **3.149**
a person has an old style JSA award and previously had a new style JSA award.
Article 12 deals with the converse position.
Note, however, that art.11 of the No.11 Commencement Order amends and modifies this provision with respect to certain cases that are to occur after that Order is made.

Sanctions: transition from old style ESA in case of a new award

14.—(1) This article applies where—   **3.150**
(a) a person is entitled to a new style ESA award and they were previously entitled to an old style ESA award that was not in existence immediately before the first day on which the person in question is entitled to the new style ESA award; and
(b) immediately before the old style ESA award terminated, payments were reduced under regulation 63 of the ESA Regulations 2008 (reduction of employment and support allowance).

(2) Where this article applies—
(a) the failure which led to reduction of the old style ESA award ("the relevant failure") is to be treated for the purposes of Part 8 of the ESA Regulations 2013, as a failure which is sanctionable under section 11J of the 2007 Act (sanctions);
(b) the new style ESA award is to be reduced in relation to the relevant failure, in accordance with the provisions of this article and Part 8 of the ESA Regulations 2013 as modified by this article; and
(c) the reduction referred to in sub-paragraph (b) is to be treated, for the purposes of the ESA Regulations 2013, as a reduction under section 11J of the 2007 Act.

(3) The reduction period for the purposes of the ESA Regulations 2013 is to be the number of days which is equivalent to the length of the fixed period applicable to the person under regulation 63 of the ESA Regulations 2008 in relation to the relevant failure, minus—
(a) the number of days (if any) in that fixed period in respect of which the amount of the old style ESA award was reduced; and
(b) the number of days (if any) in the period starting with the day after the day on which the old style ESA award terminated and ending

with the day before the first day on which the person is entitled to the new style ESA award.

(4) Accordingly, regulation 51 of the ESA Regulations 2013 (general principles for calculating reduction periods) applies in relation to the relevant failure as if—

(a) in paragraph (1), for the words "in accordance with regulations 52 and 53" there were substituted the words "in accordance with article 14 of the Welfare Reform Act 2012 (Commencement No. 9 and Transitional and Transitory Provisions and Commencement No. 8 and Savings and Transitional Provisions (Amendment)) Order 2013"; and

(b) in paragraph (3), for the words "in accordance with regulation 52 or 53" there were substituted the words "in accordance with article 14 of the Welfare Reform Act 2012 (Commencement No. 9 and Transitional and Transitory Provisions and Commencement No. 8 and Savings and Transitional Provisions (Amendment)) Order 2013".

DEFINTIONS

"the 2007 Act"—art.2(1).
"employment and support allowance"—*ibid*.
"the ESA Regulations 2008"—*ibid*.
"the ESA Regulations 2013"—*ibid*.
"new style ESA award"—*ibid*.
"old style ESA award"—*ibid*.

GENERAL NOTE

3.151   This makes transitional provision in relation to sanctions where a person has a new style ESA award and previously had an old style ESA award and was subject to sanctions.

Sanctions: transition from old style ESA in case of a continuing award

3.152   **15.**—(1) This article applies where—

(a) the amending provisions have come into force under article 4(1) in relation to the case of a claim for universal credit referred to in article 4(2)(b) to (d) (and any award that is made in respect of the claim) or an award of universal credit referred to in article 4(2)(e) or (f);

(b) the person in question had an old style ESA award immediately before the appointed day which consisted of or included a contributory allowance (which allowance therefore continues as a new style ESA award); and

(c) immediately before the appointed day, payments under that award were reduced in accordance with regulation 63 of the ESA Regulations 2008 (reduction of employment and support allowance).

(2) Where this article applies—

(a) the failure which led to reduction of the old style ESA award ("the relevant failure") is to be treated for the purposes of Part 8 of the ESA Regulations 2013, as a failure which is sanctionable under section 11J of the 2007 Act (sanctions);

(b) on and after the appointed day, the award (in its continuation as a new style ESA award) is to be reduced in relation to the relevant failure, in accordance with the provisions of this article and Part 8 of the ESA Regulations 2013 as modified by this article; and

(c) the reduction referred to in sub-paragraph (b) is to be treated, for the purposes of the ESA Regulations 2013, as a reduction under section 11J of the 2007 Act.

(3) The reduction period for the purposes of the ESA Regulations 2013 is to be the number of days which is equivalent to the length of the fixed period applicable to the person under regulation 63 of the ESA Regulations 2008 in relation to the relevant failure, minus the number of days (if any) in that period in respect of which the amount of the old style ESA award was reduced.

(4) Accordingly, regulation 51 of the ESA Regulations 2013 (general principles for calculating reduction periods) applies in relation to the relevant failure as if—

(a) in paragraph (1), for the words "in accordance with regulations 52 and 53" there were substituted the words "in accordance with article 15 of the Welfare Reform Act 2012 (Commencement No. 9 and Transitional and Transitory Provisions and Commencement No. 8 and Savings and Transitional Provisions (Amendment)) Order 2013"; and

(b) in paragraph (3), for the words "in accordance with regulation 52 or 53" there were substituted the words "in accordance with article 15 of the Welfare Reform Act 2012 (Commencement No. 9 and Transitional and Transitory Provisions and Commencement No. 8 and Savings and Transitional Provisions (Amendment)) Order 2013".

DEFINITIONS

"the 2007 Act"—art.2(1)
"the amending provisions"—*ibid.*
"the appointed day"—*ibid.*
"employment and support allowance"—*ibid.*
"the ESA Regulations 2008"—*ibid.*
"the ESA Regulations 2013"—*ibid.*
"new style ESA award"—*ibid.*

GENERAL NOTE

This makes transitional provision in relation to sanctions where a person has an award of universal credit and previously had an old style ESA award which was subject to sanctions.

Escalation of sanctions: transition from old style ESA

16.—(1) This article applies where a person is entitled to a new style ESA award and, at any time previously, the person was entitled to an old style ESA award.

(2) Where this article applies, for the purposes of determining the reduction period under regulation 52 of the ESA Regulations 2013 (low-level sanction) in relation to a sanctionable failure by the person to whom the new style award referred to in paragraph (1) was made, other than a failure which is treated as sanctionable under article 14 or 15—

(a) a reduction of a new style ESA award in accordance with article 14 or 15 as the case may be; and

3.153

3.154

(b) a reduction of an old style ESA award under the ESA Regulations 2008 which did not result in a reduction under article 14 or 15,

is, subject to paragraph (3), to be treated as arising from a sanctionable failure for which the reduction period which applies is the number of days which is equivalent to the length of the fixed period which applied under regulation 63 of the ESA Regulations 2008 (reduction of employment and support allowance).

(3) In determining a reduction period under regulation 52 of the ESA Regulations 2013 in accordance with paragraph (2), no account is to be taken of—

(a) a reduction of a new style ESA award in accordance with article 14 or 15, as the case may be, if, at any time after that reduction, the person was entitled to an old style ESA award, an old style JSA award or income support;

(b) a reduction of an old style ESA award under the ESA Regulations 2008 if, at any time after that reduction, the person was entitled to universal credit, a new style ESA award or a new style JSA award, and was subsequently entitled to an old style ESA award, an old style JSA award or income support.

DEFINITIONS

"employment and support allowance"—art.2(1).
"the ESA Regulations 2008"—*ibid.*
"the ESA Regulations 2013"—*ibid.*
"new style JSA award"—*ibid.*
"old style ESA award"—*ibid.*
"old style JSA award"—*ibid.*

GENERAL NOTE

3.155   This ensures that any previous old style ESA fixed period reductions are taken into account when deciding the appropriate reduction period for the purposes of new style ESA award.

Sanctions: transition from old style JSA in case of a new award

3.156   17.—(1) This article applies where—

(a) a person is entitled to a new style JSA award and they were previously entitled to an old style JSA award that was not in existence immediately before the first day on which the person in question is entitled to the new style JSA award;

(b) immediately before that old style award terminated, payments were reduced under section 19 (as it applied both before and after substitution by the Act) (before substitution: circumstances in which a jobseeker's allowance is not payable; after substitution: higher-level sanctions) or 19A (other sanctions) of the 1995 Act, or under regulation 69B of the JSA Regulations 1996 (the period of a reduction under section 19B : Claimants ceasing to be available for employment etc.); and

(c) if the old style JSA award was made to a joint-claim couple within the meaning of the 1995 Act and the reduction related to—

(i) in the case of a reduction under section 19 as it applied before substitution by the Act, circumstances relating to only one member of the couple; or

(ii) in the case of a reduction under section 19 as it applied after substitution by the Act, a sanctionable failure by only one member of the couple,

the new style JSA award was made to that member of the couple.

(2) Where this article applies—

(a) the circumstances or failure which led to reduction of the old style JSA award (in either case "the relevant failure") is to be treated, for the purposes of the JSA Regulations 2013, as—

    (i) a failure which is sanctionable under section 6J of the 1995 Act (higher-level sanctions), where the reduction was under section 19 of the 1995 Act; or

    (ii) a failure which is sanctionable under section 6K of the 1995 Act (other sanctions), where the reduction was under section 19A of the 1995 Act or regulation 69B of the JSA Regulations 1996;

(b) the award of new style JSA is to be reduced in relation to the relevant failure, in accordance with the provisions of this article and Part 3 of the JSA Regulations 2013 (sanctions), as modified by this article; and

(c) the reduction is to be treated, for the purposes of the JSA Regulations 2013, as a reduction under section 6J or, as the case may be, section 6K of the 1995 Act.

(3) The reduction period for the purposes of the JSA Regulations 2013 is to be the number of days which is equivalent to the length of the period of reduction of a jobseeker's allowance which is applicable to the person under regulation 69, 69A or 69B of the JSA Regulations 1996, minus—

(a) the number of days (if any) in that period in respect of which the amount of a jobseeker's allowance was reduced; and

(b) the number of days (if any) in the period starting with the day after the day on which the old style JSA award terminated and ending with the day before the first day on which the person is entitled to a new style JSA award.

(4) Accordingly, regulation 18 of the JSA Regulations 2013 (general principles for calculating reduction periods) applies in relation to the relevant failure as if—

(a) in paragraph (1), for the words "in accordance with regulations 19, 20 and 21", there were substituted the words "in accordance with article 17 of the Welfare Reform Act 2012 (Commencement No.9 and Transitional and Transitory Provisions and Commencement No. 8 and Savings and Transitional Provisions (Amendment)) Order 2013"; and

(b) in paragraph (3), for the words "in accordance with regulation 19, 20 or 21", there were substituted the words "in accordance with article 17 of the Welfare Reform Act 2012 (Commencement No. 9 and Transitional and Transitory Provisions and Commencement No. 8 and Savings and Transitional Provisions (Amendment)) Order 2013".

DEFINITIONS

"the Act"—art.2(1).
"the 1995 Act"—*ibid.*
"jobseeker's allowance"—*ibid.*
"the JSA Regulations 1996"—*ibid.*

"the JSA Regulations 2013"—*ibid.*
"new style JSA award"—*ibid.*
"old style JSA award"—*ibid.*

GENERAL NOTE

3.157　　This makes transitional provision in relation to sanctions where a person has a new style JSA award and previously had an old style JSA award and was subject to sanctions.

Sanctions: transition from old style JSA in case of a continuing award

3.158　　**18.**—(1) This article applies where—

(a) the amending provisions have come into force under article 4(1) in relation to the case of a claim for universal credit referred to in article 4(2)(b) to (d) (and any award that is made in respect of the claim) or an award of universal credit referred to in article 4(2)(e) or (f);

(b) the person in question had an old style JSA award immediately before the appointed day which consisted of or included a contribution-based allowance (which allowance therefore continues as a new style JSA award);

(c) immediately before the appointed day, payments under that award were reduced under section 19 (as it applied both before and after substitution by the Act) (before substitution: circumstances in which a jobseeker's allowance is not payable; after substitution: higher-level sanctions) or 19A (other sanctions) of the 1995 Act, or under regulation 69B of the JSA Regulations 1996) (the period of a reduction under section 19B : Claimants ceasing to be available for employment etc.); and

(d) if the old style JSA award was made to a joint-claim couple within the meaning of the 1995 Act and the reduction related to—

(i) in the case of a reduction under section 19 as it applied before substitution by the Act, circumstances relating to only one member of the couple; or

(ii) in the case of a reduction under section 19 as it applied after substitution by the Act, a sanctionable failure by only one member of the couple,

the new style JSA award was made to that member of the couple.

(2) Where this article applies—

(a) the circumstances or failure which led to reduction of the old style JSA award (in either case "the relevant failure") is to be treated, for the purposes of the JSA Regulations 2013, as—

(i) a failure which is sanctionable under section 6J of the 1995 Act (higher-level sanctions), where the reduction was under section 19 of the 1995 Act; or

(ii) a failure which is sanctionable under section 6K of the 1995 Act (other sanctions), where the reduction was under section 19A of the 1995 Act or regulation 69B of the JSA Regulations 1996;

(b) the award (in its continuation as a new style JSA award) is to be reduced in relation to the relevant failure, in accordance with the provisions of this article and Part 3 of the JSA Regulations (sanctions), as modified by this article; and

(c) the reduction is to be treated, for the purposes of the JSA Regulations

2013, as a reduction under section 6J or, as the case may be, section 6K of the 1995 Act.

(3) The reduction period for the purposes of the JSA Regulations 2013 is to be the number of days which is equivalent to the length of the period of reduction of a jobseeker's allowance which is applicable to the person under regulation 69, 69A or 69B of the JSA Regulations 1996, minus the number of days (if any) in that period in respect of which the amount of a jobseeker's allowance was reduced.

(4) Accordingly, regulation 18 of the JSA Regulations 2013 (general principles for calculating reduction periods) applies in relation to the relevant failure as if—

(a) in paragraph (1), for the words "in accordance with regulations 19, 20 and 21", there were substituted the words "in accordance with article 18 of the Welfare Reform Act 2012 (Commencement No. 9 and Transitional and Transitory Provisions and Commencement No. 8 and Savings and Transitional Provisions (Amendment)) Order 2013"; and

(b) in paragraph (3), for the words "in accordance with regulation 19, 20 or 21", there were substituted the words "in accordance with article 18 of the Welfare Reform Act 2012 (Commencement No. 9 and Transitional and Transitory Provisions and Commencement No. 8 and Savings and Transitional Provisions (Amendment)) Order 2013".

DEFINITIONS

"the Act"—art.2(1).
"the 1995 Act"—*ibid.*
"the amending provisions"—*ibid.*
"the appointed day"—*ibid.*
"jobseeker's allowance"—*ibid.*
"the JSA Regulations 1996"—*ibid.*
"the JSA Regulations 2013"—*ibid.*
"new style JSA award"—*ibid.*
"old style JSA award"—*ibid.*

GENERAL NOTE

This is the JSA equivalent to reg.15.

3.159

Escalation of sanctions: transition from old style JSA

19.—(1) This article applies where a person is entitled to a new style JSA award and, at any time previously, the person was entitled to an old style JSA award.

3.160

(2) Where this article applies, for the purposes of determining the applicable reduction period under regulation 19 (higher-level sanction), 20 (medium-level sanction) or 21 (low-level sanction) of the JSA Regulations 2013 in relation to a sanctionable failure by the person other than a failure which is treated as sanctionable by virtue of article 17 or 18—

(a) a reduction of a new style JSA award in accordance with article 17 or 18; and

(b) a reduction of an old style JSA award under section 19 (as it applied both before and after substitution by the Act) or 19A of the 1995

Act, or under regulation 69B of the JSA Regulations 1996, which did not result in a reduction under article 17 or 18,

is, subject to paragraph (3), to be treated as arising from a sanctionable failure for which the reduction period is the number of days which is equivalent to the length of the period which applied under regulation 69, 69A or 69B of the JSA Regulations 1996.

(3) In determining a reduction period under regulation 19 (higher-level sanction), 20 (medium-level sanction) or 21 (low-level sanction) of the JSA Regulations 2013 in accordance with paragraph (2), no account is to be taken of—

(a) a reduction of a new style JSA award in accordance with article 17 or 18 if, at any time after that reduction, the person was entitled to an old style JSA award, an old style ESA award or income support;

(b) a reduction of an old style JSA award under section 19 (as it applied both before and after substitution by the Act) or 19A of the 1995 Act, or under regulation 69B of the JSA Regulations 1996, if, at any time after that reduction, the person was entitled to universal credit, a new style JSA award or a new style ESA award, and was subsequently entitled to an old style JSA award, an old style ESA award or income support.

DEFINITIONS

"the Act"—art.2(1).
"the 1995 Act"—*ibid.*
"the JSA Regulations 1996"—*ibid.*
"the JSA Regulations 2013"—*ibid.*
"new style JSA award"—*ibid.*
"old style ESA award"—*ibid.*
"old style JSA award"—*ibid.*

GENERAL NOTE

3.161   This is the JSA equivalent to reg.16.

Termination of sanctions under a new style ESA or JSA award

3.162   **20.**—(1) Paragraph (2) applies where—

(a) a new style ESA award or new style JSA award terminates while there is an outstanding reduction period (within the meaning of regulation 55 of the ESA Regulations 2013 (reduction period to continue where award of employment and support allowance terminates) or regulation 23 of the JSA Regulations 2013 (reduction period to continue where award of jobseeker's allowance terminates)) and the claimant becomes entitled to an old style ESA award, an old style JSA award or income support during that period; or

(b) article 6(2) applies to a new style ESA award or new style JSA award (such that it continues as an old style ESA award or an old style JSA award) and there is such an outstanding reduction period on the last day of the period of the new style ESA award or new style JSA award.

(2) Where this paragraph applies—

(a) regulation 55 of the ESA Regulations 2013 or regulation 23 of the JSA Regulations 2013, as the case may be, are to cease to apply; and

(b) the reduction period is to terminate on the first day of entitlement to an old style ESA award, old style JSA award or income support as the case may be.

DEFINITIONS

"employment and support allowance"—art.2(1).
"the ESA Regulations 2013"—*ibid.*
"jobseeker's allowance"—*ibid.*
"the JSA Regulations 2013"—*ibid.*
"new style ESA award"—*ibid.*
"new style JSA award"—*ibid.*
"old style JSA award"—*ibid.*

GENERAL NOTE

This provides that where a claimant has a new style ESA (or new style JSA) award, is subject to sanctions and subsequently becomes entitled to an old style ESA (or old style JSA) award or income support, then the sanctions cease to have effect. **3.163**

Transitory provisions: appeals

21.—(1) Paragraph (2) applies where— **3.164**
  (a) the amending provisions have come into force under article 4(1) in relation to the case of a claim referred to in article 4(2)(a) to (d) (and any award that is made in respect of the claim) or the case of an award referred to in article 4(2)(e) or (f);
  (b) the person is sent notice of a decision relating to a new style ESA award or a new style JSA award; and
  (c) the date of notification with respect to that decision is before 28th October 2013.

(2) Where this paragraph applies, the provisions mentioned in paragraph (3) apply for the purposes of any appeal in relation to that decision as if regulation 55 of the Decisions and Appeals Regulations 2013 (consequential amendments) did not apply in that person's case.

(3) The provisions referred to are the following provisions of the Social Security and Child Support (Decisions and Appeals) Regulations 1999—
  (a) regulation 32 (late appeals);
  (b) regulation 33 (notice of appeal); and
  (c) regulation 34 (death of a party to an appeal).

(4) For the purposes of paragraph (1), "the date of notification" means the date on which the decision notice was posted to the person's last known address by the Secretary of State.

DEFINITIONS

"the amending provisions"—art.2(1).
"the Decisions and Appeals Regulations 2013"—*ibid.*
"new style JSA award"—*ibid.*

GENERAL NOTE

This makes limited transitory provision with respect to appeals where a person is sent a notice relating to a new style ESA award or a new style JSA award before October 29, 2013. **3.165**

Transitional provision: references to contributory employment and support allowance and contribution-based jobseeker's allowance

3.166   **22.** Where the amending provisions have come into force under article 4(1) in relation to the case of a claim referred to in article 4(2)(a) to (d) (and any award that is made in respect of the claim) or the case of an award referred to in article 4(2)(e) or (f), then, in relation to such a case, any reference in the Social Security Administration Act 1992 or the Social Security Contributions and Benefits Act 1992 to—

    (a) a contributory employment and support allowance is to be read as if it included a reference to a new style ESA award; and

    (b) a contribution-based jobseeker's allowance is to be read as if it included a reference to a new style JSA award.

DEFINITIONS

"the amending provisions"—*ibid.*
"contribution-based jobseeker's allowance"—*ibid.*
"contributory employment and support allowance"—*ibid.*
"new style JSA award"—*ibid.*

GENERAL NOTE

3.167   This provision seeks to ensure that new style ESA and JSA awards are to be treated to all intents and purposes as awards of a contributory employment or support allowance or to a contribution-based jobseeker's allowance respectively. It does so by providing that, in relation to a case with respect to which art.4(1)(a)–(c) have come into force, references in the SSAA 1992 and the SSCBA 1992 are to be construed as if they included a reference to a new style ESA award or to a new style JSA award respectively.

Amendment of the Welfare Reform Act 2012 (Commencement No.8 and Savings and Transitional Provisions) Order 2013

3.168   **23.**—(1) Article 5 of the Welfare Reform Act 2012 (Commencement No 8 and Savings and Transitional Provisions) Order 2013 (appointed day and saving for provisions relating to overpayments) is amended as follows.

(2) In paragraph (3)(a), at the beginning insert "subject to paragraph (3A),".

(3) After paragraph (3) insert—

"(3A) In so far as section 105(1) of the 2012 Act inserts section 71ZB(1) (b) and (c) of the 1992 Act, those paragraphs come into force on 29th April 2013 only in so far as they relate respectively to a new style JSA award and a new style ESA award.".

(4) In paragraph (6), for "those benefits have been claimed before 29th April 2013" substitute "they relate respectively to an old style JSA award and an old style ESA award".

(5) After paragraph (6) add—

"(7) In this article, "old style JSA award", "new style JSA award", "old style ESA award" and "new style ESA award" have the same meaning as in article 2(1) of the Welfare Reform Act 2012 (Commencement No. 9 and Transitional and Transitory Provisions and Commencement No. 8 and Savings and Transitional Provisions (Amendment)) Order 2013.".

DEFINITIONS

"the appointed day"—art.2(1).
"new style JSA award"—*ibid.*
"old style ESA award"—*ibid.*
"old style JSA award"—*ibid.*

GENERAL NOTE

This amends art.5 of the Commencement No.8 Order as regards overpayments. It **3.169**
is intended to make it clear that the new rules applying to overpayments of employment and support allowance and of jobseeker's allowance under the WRA 2012
apply only to overpayments of a new style ESA award and a new style JSA award
respectively (para.(3)). The amendments also clarify that the old rules relating to
overpayments of those benefits will continue to apply to overpayments of an old
style ESA award and an old style JSA award respectively (para.(4)).

SCHEDULE 1

POSTCODE DISTRICTS

1. M43
2. OL6
3. OL7
4. SK16

Article 3(2)

SCHEDULE 2

UNIVERSAL CREDIT PROVISIONS COMING INTO FORCE IN RELATION TO
CERTAIN CLAIMS AND AWARDS

1. Section 1 (universal credit).
2. Section 2(1) (claims).
3. Section 3 (entitlement).
4. Section 4(1) and (4) (basic conditions).
5. Section 5 (financial conditions).
6. Section 6 (restrictions on entitlement).
7. Section 7(1) and (4) (basis of awards).
8. Section 8 (calculation of awards).
9. Section 9(1) (standard allowance).
10. Section 10(1) (responsibility for children and young persons).
11. Section 11(1) and (2) (housing costs).
12. Section 12(1) and (2) (other particular needs or circumstances).
13. Section 13 (work-related requirements: introductory).
14. Section 14 (claimant commitment).
15. Section 15(1) and (4) (work-focused interview requirement).
16. Section 16 (work preparation requirement).
17. Section 17(1), (2), (3)(a) to (e), (4) and (5) (work search requirement).
18. Section 18 (work availability requirement).
19. Section 19(1), (2)(a) to (c), (5) and (6) (claimants subject to no work-related requirements).
20. Section 20 (claimants subject to work-focused interview requirement only).
21. Section 21 (claimants subject to work preparation requirement).
22. Section 22 (claimants subject to all work-related requirements).
23. Section 23 (connected requirements).
24. Section 24(2), (3) and (4) (imposition of requirements).
25. Section 26(1) to (5) (higher-level sanctions).
26. Section 27(1) to (3) and (6) to (8) (other sanctions).

3.170

SCHEDULE 3

COMMENCEMENT OF REPEALS IN PART 1 OF SCHEDULE 14 TO THE ACT

Short title and chapter	Extent of repeal
Jobseekers Act 1995 (c.18)	Section 1(2A) to (2D) and (4). In section 2, in subsection (3C)(d), "contribution-based". Sections 3 to 3B. In section 4— (a) in subsection (1), "contribution-based"; (b) subsections (3), (3A) and (6) to (11A). Section 4A. In section 5— (a) in the heading and in subsection (1) "contribution-based"; (b) in subsection (2), "contribution-based" in the first two places; (c) in subsection (3), "contribution-based". Section 13. Sections 15 to 17. In section 17A(10), the definition of "claimant". Section 23. Sections 26. In section 35(1)— (a) in the definition of "claimant", the words from "except" to the end; (b) the definitions of "contribution-based jobseeker's allowance", "income-based jobseeker's allowance", "income-related employment and support allowance", "joint-claim couple", "joint-claim jobseeker's allowance" and "the nominated member". In section 38— (a) in subsections (3) and (4), "contribution-based"; (b) subsection (6). In Schedule 1— (a) in paragraph 6(1), "contribution-based"; (b) paragraphs 8 and 8A; (c) paragraphs 9 to 10; (d) in paragraph 11(1), "contribution-based"; (e) in paragraph 16(1) and (2)(d), "contribution-based"; (f) paragraph 18(b) and (c).
Welfare Reform and Pensions Act 1999 (c.30)	In Schedule 7, paragraphs 2(3) and (4), 4, 5(3) and (4), 6, 9 to 11, 15 and 16. In Schedule 8, paragraph 29(2).
State Pension Credit Act 2002 (c.16)	In Schedule 2, paragraphs 36 to 38.

Short title and chapter	Extent of repeal
Income Tax (Earnings and Payments) Act 2003 (c.1)	In Schedule 6, paragraphs 228 to 230.
Civil Partnership Act 2004 (c.33)	In Schedule 24, paragraphs 118 to 122.
Welfare Reform Act 2007 (c.5)	In section 1— (a) in subsection (2), in the opening words, "either"; (b) in subsection (2)(a), "Part 1 of" and "that Part of"; (c) subsection (2)(b) and the preceding "or"; (d) in subsection (3)(f), the words from "(and" to "allowance)"; (e) in subsection (3A), "Part 1 of"; (f) in subsection (6), the definition of "joint-claim jobseeker's allowance"; (g) subsections (6A) and (7). In subsection 1A— (a) in the heading "contributory"; (b) in subsections (1) (in both places), (3) and (4), "Part 1 of". Section 1B(2). In section 2, in the heading, "contributory". In section 3, in the heading, "contributory". Sections 4 to 6. Section 23. In section 24(1), the definitions of "contributory allowance" and "income-related allowance". In section 26(1)(a), "or 4(4)(c) or (5)(c)". Section 27(2)(a) and (4). In Schedule 1— (a) the heading to Part 1; (b) Part 2. In Schedule 2— (a) in the headings to paragraphs 6 and 7, "Contributory allowance:"; (b) paragraph 8; (c) paragraph 11(b) and (c); (d) paragraph 12, so far as not otherwise repealed.
Welfare Reform Act 2009 (c.24)	In Part 3 of Schedule 7, the entry relating to the Civil Partnership Act 2004.

Article 9

SCHEDULE 4

3.171

MODIFICATIONS OF THE 2010 TRANSITIONAL REGULATIONS

1. The 2010 Transitional Regulations are to be read as if the amendments set out in this Schedule were made.

2. (1) Regulation 2 (interpretation) is amended as follows:

(2) In paragraph (1)—

(a) insert at the appropriate places in the alphabetical order of the definitions—

""the Claims and Payments Regulations" means the Universal Credit, Personal Independence Payment, Jobseeker's Allowance and Employment and Support Allowance (Claims and Payments) Regulations 2013;";

""the Decisions and Appeals Regulations" means the Universal Credit, Personal Independence Payment, Jobseeker's Allowance and Employment and Support Allowance (Decisions and Appeals) Regulations 2013;";

""the ESA Regulations" means the Employment and Support Allowance Regulations 2013;";

(b) omit—

(i) the definition of "income-related allowance";

(ii) paragraphs (a) to (d) of the definition of "relevant deduction";

(c) in the definition of "benefit week", for "the 2008 Regulations" substitute "the ESA Regulations".

(3) In paragraph (3), omit "or awards".

3. In regulation 4 (the notice commencing the conversion phase), omit paragraph (6).

4. In regulation 5 (deciding whether an existing award qualifies for conversion)—

(a) in paragraph (1), omit "or awards";

(b) in paragraph (2)(a), for "or awards qualify" substitute "qualifies";

(c) in paragraph (2)(b), for "or awards do" substitute "does";

(d) in paragraph (6)(b), omit "or awards".

5. In regulation 6(2) (application of certain enactments for purpose of making conversion decisions)—

(a) for sub-paragraphs (b) and (c), substitute—

"(b) the ESA Regulations;

(c) regulation 38(2) and (3) of the Claims and Payments Regulations (evidence and information in connection with an award);";

(b) for sub-paragraph (e), substitute—

"(e) the Decisions and Appeals Regulations."

6. In regulation 7 (qualifying for conversion)—

(a) in paragraph (1)—

(i) omit "or awards";

(ii) for "qualify" substitute "qualifies";

(b) in paragraphs (2)(b) and (3)(b), for "regulation 30 of the 2008 Regulations" substitute "regulation 26 of the ESA Regulations".

7. In regulation 8(1) (amount of an employment and support allowance on conversion), for "the 2008 Regulations" substitute "the ESA Regulations".

8. In regulation 9(1) (determining entitlement to a transitional addition)—

(a) for "or awards qualify" substitute "qualifies";

(b) omit "or 11(2) (transitional addition: income support)".

9. In regulation 10 (transitional addition: incapacity benefit or severe disablement allowance)—

(a) in paragraph (1), omit "(and for these purposes it is irrelevant whether the person is also entitled to any existing award of income support)";

(b) in paragraph (4)(a), for "paragraph (2) of regulation 67 of the 2008 Regulations (prescribed amounts for purpose of calculating a contributory allowance)" substitute "paragraph (1) of regulation 62 of the ESA Regulations (prescribed amounts)".

10. Omit regulation 11 (transitional addition: income support).

11. In regulation 12 (regulations 10 and 11: supplementary)—

(a) in the title, for "Regulations 10 and 11" substitute "Regulation 10";

(b) in paragraph (1), for "regulations 10 and 11" substitute "regulation 10";

(c) in paragraph (2), for "Amounts A and C are" substitute "Amount A is" and for "Amounts B and D are" substitute "Amount B is";

(d) for paragraph (3)(a), substitute—

"(a) by virtue of an order made under section 150 of the Administration Act (annual up-rating of benefits), there is an increase in the weekly rate which, in accordance with regulation 10(3) (transitional addition: incapacity benefit or severe disablement allowance), is to be used to calculate Amount A; and";

(e) in paragraph (4)(a), for "paragraph (3)(a)(i) or (ii)" substitute "paragraph (3)(a)";

(f) in paragraphs (3) and (4), omit "or C" and "or applicable amount (as the case may be)".

12. In regulation 13(3) (the effective date of a conversion decision), omit "or awards".
13. In regulation 14 (conversion decision that existing award qualifies for conversion)—
  (a) in paragraph (1)—
     (i) for "Subject to paragraph (2A), paragraphs (2) to (6)" substitute "Paragraphs (2) to (5)";
    (ii) for "or awards qualify" substitute "qualifies";
  (b) for paragraph (2), substitute—
    "(2) On the effective date of the conversion decision P's existing award is by virtue of this paragraph converted into, and shall have effect on and after that date as, a single award of an employment and support allowance of such amount as is specified in the conversion decision.";
  (c) omit paragraphs (2A), (2B) and (6);
  (d) in paragraph (4), omit "or awards";
  (e) for paragraph (7), substitute—
    "(7) In this regulation paragraphs (2) to (5) are subject to regulation 17 (changes of circumstances before the effective date).".
14. In regulation 15 (conversion decision that existing award does not qualify for conversion)—
  (a) in paragraph (1)—
     (i) for "Subject to paragraphs (2A) and (4), paragraphs (2), (3) and (6)" substitute "Subject to paragraph (4), paragraphs (2) and (3)";
    (ii) for "or awards do" substitute "does";
  (b) for paragraph (2), substitute—
    "(2) P's entitlement to an existing award of incapacity benefit or severe disablement allowance shall terminate by virtue of this paragraph immediately before the effective date of P's conversion decision.";
  (c) omit paragraphs (2A), (2B) and (6);
  (d) in paragraph (4)(a)—
     (i) for "the 2008 Regulations" substitute "the ESA Regulations";
    (ii) in paragraph (i), for "regulation 22(1) (failure to provide information or evidence requested in relation to limited capability for work)" substitute "regulation 18(1) (failure to provide information in relation to limited capability for work)";
    (iii) in paragraph (ii), for "regulation 23(2) (failure to attend for a medical examination to determine whether the claimant has limited capability for work)" substitute "regulation 19(2) (claimant may be called for a medical examination to determine whether the claimant has limited capability for work)";
  (e) in paragraph (5)—
     (i) in sub-paragraph (c), omit "or awards";
    (ii) in sub-paragraph (d), omit "or those existing awards";
  (f) for paragraph (7), substitute—
    "(7) In this regulation paragraphs (2) and (3) are subject to regulation 17 (changes of circumstances before the effective date).".
15. In regulation 16 (application of other enactments applying to employment and support allowance)—
  (a) in paragraph (1A)(b), for "regulation 145(1) of the 2008 Regulations" substitute "regulation 86 of the ESA Regulations";
  (b) in paragraph (2)(e)(ii), for "the 2008 Regulations" substitute "the ESA Regulations";
  (c) in paragraph (2)(e)(iii), omit "(being regulations consequentially amended by regulations made under Part 1 of the 2007 Act)".
16. In regulation 17 (changes of circumstances before the effective date)—
  (a) omit "or awards" in both places where it occurs;
  (b) in paragraph (a)(ii)—
     (i) omit "regulation 14(2B)(a) (termination of an existing award of incapacity benefit or severe disablement allowance where entitlement to award of income support continues),";
    (ii) for "(termination of existing awards which do not qualify for conversion)" substitute "(termination of an existing award which does not qualify for conversion)";
  (c) omit paragraph (c).
17. In regulation 18 (reducing the transitional addition: general rule), for paragraph (2) substitute—

"(2) For the purposes of paragraph (1), a relevant increase is an increase in any amount applicable to the person under regulation 62(1) or (2) of the ESA Regulations, which is not excluded by paragraph (3).".

18. In regulation 21 (termination of transitional addition)—

    (a) in paragraph (1)(b)—

        (i) for ", (3), (3A) and (4)" substitute ", (3) and (3A)"and (4)";

        (ii) omit "an employment and support allowance (entitlement to which arises from sections 1(2)(a) or 1(2)(b) of the 2007 Act), or to" and "or to an income-related allowance";

    (b) omit paragraph (4);

    (c) in paragraph (5)(a), for "regulation 145(1) of the 2008 Regulations (linking rules)" substitute "regulation 86 of the ESA Regulations (linking period)";

    (d) in paragraph (5)(c)(ii), for "regulation 30 of the 2008 Regulations" substitute "regulation 26 of the ESA Regulations";

    (e) in paragraph (5A)(c), for "regulation 145(1) of the 2008 Regulations (linking rules)" substitute "regulation 86 of the ESA Regulations (linking period)";

    (f) omit paragraph (6);

    (g) in paragraph (7)—

        (i) for ", 1A and 2" substitute "and 1A";

        (ii) omit "or additions, as the case may be," in both places where it occurs;

        (iii) for "an allowance which is referred to in paragraph (1)(b)" substitute "a contributory allowance".

19. In regulation 22 (disapplication of certain enactments following conversion decision), omit paragraphs (c) and (d).

20. In Schedule 1 (modification of enactments: making conversion decisions)—

    (a) in paragraph 2(a), for the modified section 1(2) substitute—

        "(2) Subject to the provisions of this Part, a notified person is entitled to an employment and support allowance if the person satisfies the basic conditions and is entitled to an existing award of incapacity benefit or severe disablement allowance.";

    (b) for paragraph 6, substitute—

        "6. Schedule 1 to the 2007 Act is to be read as if paragraphs 1 to 6 were omitted.";

    (c) in the heading to Part 2, for "the 2008 Regulations" substitute "the ESA Regulations";

    (d) in paragraph 10, for "Regulation 30" substitute "Regulation 26";

    (e) omit paragraph 10A;

    (f) in paragraph 11, for "Regulation 75" substitute "Regulation 68";

    (g) in paragraph 12, for "Regulation 144" substitute "Regulation 85";

    (h) in the sub-heading to Part 3, for "Social Security (Claims and Payments) Regulations 1987" substitute "The Claims and Payments Regulations";

        (i) in paragraph 13—

        (i) for "Regulation 32 of the Social Security (Claims and Payments) Regulations 1987" substitute "Regulation 38 of the Claims and Payments Regulations";

        (ii) in sub-paragraph (a), for "paragraph (1)" substitute "paragraph (2)";

        (iii) in sub-paragraph (b), for "paragraph (1A)" substitute "paragraph (3)".

21. (1) Schedule 2 (modification of enactments: after the conversion phase) is amended as follows.

(2) In paragraph 2—

    (a) in sub-paragraph (a), in the modified section 1(2)—

        (i) in paragraph (a), for "or awards into a single award of an employment and support allowance;" substitute "into an award of an employment and support allowance; and";

        (ii) omit paragraph (c) and for "; and" at the end of paragraph (b) substitute ",";

    (b) in sub-paragraph (b) in the modified section 1(7)—

        [¹ (i) for the definition of "contributory allowance" substitute-

        "employment and support allowance" means an employment and support allowance to which a person is entitled by virtue of the Employment and Support Allowance (Transitional Provisions, Housing Benefit and Council Tax Benefit) (Existing Awards)(No.2) Regulations 2010 which was based on an award of incapacity benefit or severe disablement allowance to which the person was entitled.] and for "; and" following that definition substitute ".".];

        (ii) omit the definition of "income-related allowance".

[¹ (2A) In paragraph 2A—

    (a) in paragraph (1), omit "contributory"; and

    (b) in paragraph (2), in the substituted section 1A

      (i) in paragraphs (1) and (3) to (5), for "a contributory allowance" substitute "an employment and support allowance"; and

      (ii) in paragraph (3), omit "Part 1 of".]

(3) In paragraph 3(b), for "regulation 147A of the 2008 Regulations" substitute "regulation 87 of the ESA Regulations".

(4) Omit paragraphs 4 and 4A.

(5) In paragraph 6A—

  (a) in sub-paragraph (a), after paragraph (iv) insert "and";

  (b) in sub-paragraph (b), for "; and" substitute ".";

  (c) omit sub-paragraph (c).

(6) In the heading to Part 3, for "the 2008 Regulations" substitute "the ESA Regulations".

(7) In paragraph 8, for "regulation 147A of the 2008 Regulations" substitute "regulation 87 of the ESA Regulations".

(8) In paragraph 10, for "regulation 30" substitute "regulation 26".

"(9) For paragraph 11, substitute—

    11. Regulation 39 (exempt work) is to be read as if, in the definition of "work period" in paragraph (6), after "referred to in paragraph (1)(c)", in both places where it occurs, there were inserted ", or any work done in accordance with regulation 17(4) (a) of the Social Security (Incapacity for Work)(General) Regulations 1995.

(10) For paragraph 12, substitute—"

    "**12.** Regulation 62 (prescribed amounts) is to be read as if, in paragraph (1), for sub-paragraphs (a) and (b) there were substituted—

      (a) (i)where the claimant satisfies the conditions set out in section 2(2) or (3) of the Act, £71.70; or

          (ii) where the claimant does not satisfy the conditions set out in section 2(2) or (3) of the Act—

             (aa) where the claimant is aged not less than 25, £71.70; or

             (bb) where the claimant is aged less than 25, £56.80; and

      (b) the amount of any transitional addition to which the person is entitled under regulation 10 of the Employment and Support Allowance (Transitional Provisions, Housing Benefit and Council Tax Benefit) (Existing Awards) (No.2) Regulations 2010."

(9) Omit paragraph 13.

(10) In paragraph 14—

  (a) for "Regulation 75" substitute "Regulation 68";

  (b) for "paragraph 38" substitute "paragraph 11".

(11) In paragraph 15—

  (a) in the introductory words, for "Regulation 147A" substitute "regulation 87";

  (b) in the inserted regulation—

      (i) in the description of the number of the regulation, for "147A.—" substitute "87.—";

      (ii) in paragraph (2), for "regulation 19" substitute "regulation 15";

      (iii) in paragraph (4)(a), for "regulation 22 or 23" substitute "regulation 18 or 19";

      (iv) for "regulation 30", in all places where it occurs, substitute "regulation 26";

      (v) in paragraph (5)(c), for the words from ", struck out" to "(notice of appeal)", substitute "or struck out";

      (vi) in paragraph (5A), for "either—" and sub-paragraphs (a) and (b), substitute "receives the First-tier Tribunal's notification that the appeal is dismissed, withdrawn or struck out.".

(12) Omit paragraph 16.

(13) In the sub-heading before paragraph 17, for "Social Security (Claims and Payments) Regulations 1987" substitute "The Claims and Payments Regulations".

(14) In paragraph 17, for "The Social Security (Claims and Payments) Regulations 1987" substitute "The Claims and Payments Regulations".

(15) For paragraph 18 substitute—

    "**18.** Regulation 7 (claims not required for entitlement to an employment and support allowance in certain cases) is to read as if—

      (a) the existing provisions were renumbered as paragraph (1);

      (b) after paragraph (1) there were inserted—

          (2) It is also not to be a condition of entitlement to an employment and support allowance that a claim be made for it where any of the following conditions are met—

          (a) the claimant—

(i) has made and is pursuing an appeal against a conversion decision made by virtue of the Employment and Support Allowance (Transitional Provisions, Housing Benefit and Council Tax Benefit) (Existing Awards) (No. 2) Regulations 2010 which embodies a determination that the beneficiary does not have limited capability for work; or

(ii) was entitled to an employment and support allowance by virtue of the Employment and Support Allowance (Transitional Provisions, Housing Benefit and Council Tax Benefit) (Existing Awards) (No. 2) Regulations 2010 and has made and is pursuing an appeal against a later decision which embodies a determination that the claimant does not have limited capability for work; or

(b) the claimant is entitled to an existing award which is subject to conversion under the Employment and Support Allowance (Transitional Provisions, Housing Benefit and Council Tax Benefit) (Existing Awards) (No. 2) Regulations 2010."

(16) In paragraph 19, for "regulation 26C" substitute "regulation 51".

(17) In paragraph 20—

(a) for "regulation 32(1B)" substitute "regulation 38(4)";

(b) in sub-paragraph (a), for the words "sub-paragraph (a)" substitute "sub-paragraph (b)";

(c) in sub-paragraph (b), for "(ab)" substitute "(bb)".

(18) Omit paragraph 21.

(19) In paragraph 22, for "Schedule 9B" substitute "Schedule 7".

(20) In paragraph 22A, in the inserted text omit paragraph (2B).

(21) In paragraph 23, in the inserted text omit paragraph (2B).

(22) In paragraph 24, in the inserted text omit paragraph (2B).

(23) In paragraph 25, in the inserted text omit paragraph (2B).

(24) In the sub-heading before paragraph 25A, for "Social Security and Child Support (Decisions and Appeals) Regulations 1999" substitute "Universal Credit, Personal Independence Payment, Jobseeker's Allowance and Employment and Support Allowance (Decisions and Appeals) Regulations 2013".

(25) In paragraph 25A—

(a) in sub-paragraph (1), for "Regulation 3 of the Social Security and Child Support (Decisions and Appeals) Regulations 1999 (revision of decisions)" substitute "Regulation 5 of the Universal Credit, Personal Independence Payment, Jobseeker's Allowance and Employment and Support Allowance (Decisions and Appeals) Regulations 2013 (revision on any grounds)";

(b) in sub-paragraph (1)(b), for "paragraph (9)(a)" substitute "paragraphs (2)(a) and (b)";

(c) for sub-paragraph (1)(c), substitute—

"(c) in paragraph (2)(a), for "in the case of an advance award under regulation 32, 33 or 34 of the Claims and Payment Regulations 2013" there were substituted, "in the case of an advance award under regulation 32, 33 or 34 of the Claims and Payment Regulations 2013 or a conversion decision within the meaning of regulation 5(2)(a) of the Employment and Support Allowance (Transitional Provisions, Housing Benefit and Council Tax Benefit) (Existing Awards) (No. 2) Regulations 2010".";

(d) for sub-paragraph (2), substitute—

"(2) Regulation 23(1)(a) of those Regulations (change of circumstances) is to be read as if for "in the case of an advance award under regulation 32, 33 or 34 of the Claims and Payments Regulations 2013" there were substituted "in the case of an advance award under regulation 32, 33 or 34 of the Claims and Payments Regulations 2013 or a conversion decision within the meaning of regulation 5(2)(a) of the Employment and Support Allowance (Transitional Provisions, Housing Benefit and Council Tax Benefit) (Existing Awards) (No. 2) Regulations 2010.""

(26) Omit paragraph 27.

22. In Schedule 3—

(a) for "The Social Security (Claims and Payments) Regulations 1987" substitute "the Claims and Payments Regulations";

(b) for "The Social Security and Child Support (Decisions and Appeals) Regulations 1999" substitute "the Decisions and Appeals Regulations".

AMENDMENT

1. Welfare Reform Act 2012 (Commencement No.11 and Transitional and Transitory Provisions and Commencement No.9 and Transitional and Transitory Provisions (Amendment)) Order 2013 (SI 2013/1511) art.7 (July 1, 2013).

Welfare Reform Act 2012 (Commencement No. 11 and Transitional and Transitory Provisions and Commencement No. 9 and Transitional and Transitory Provisions (Amendment)) Order 2013

(SI 2013/1511) (c.60)

The Secretary of State, in exercise of the powers conferred by section 150(3)   3.172
and (4)(a), (b)(i) and (c) of the Welfare Reform Act 2012, makes the following
Order:

ARRANGEMENT OF ARTICLES

GENERAL NOTE

This Commencement Order ("the Commencement No.11 Order") extends the   3.173
universal credit scheme to certain postcode districts in Wigan ("the No.2 relevant
districts") and Manchester, Oldham and Warrington ("the No.3 relevant districts")
as from July 1, 2013. The Order accordingly brings into force provisions of the WRA
2012 that relate to both the introduction of universal credit and the abolition of
income-related employment and support allowance and income-based jobseeker's
allowance. This is achieved by reference to the specific categories of cases set out
in arts 3 and 4. In addition, of course, the claimant must fall within the Pathfinder
Group, i.e. be a person who meets the requirements of regs 5–12 of the Transitional
Provisions Regulations 2013.

An award of employment and support allowance under P1 of the Welfare Reform
Act 2007, in a case where income-related ESA has been abolished, is referred to

as a "new style ESA award". Likewise an award of a jobseeker's allowance under the Jobseekers Act 1995, in a case where income-based JSA has been abolished, is referred to as a "new style JSA award". Conversely an award of employment and support allowance under Pt 1 of the Welfare Reform Act 2007, in a case where income-related ESA has not been abolished, is referred to as an "old style ESA award". Similarly an award of JSA under the Jobseekers Act 1995, in a case where income-based JSA has not been abolished, is referred to as an "old style JSA award".

This Order also amends certain transitional provisions in the Commencement No.9 Order.

Citation

3.174   **1.** This Order may be cited as the Welfare Reform Act 2012 (Commencement No. 11 and Transitional and Transitory Provisions and Commencement No. 9 and Transitional and Transitory Provisions (Amendment)) Order 2013.

Interpretation

3.175   **2.**—(1) In this Order—

"the Act" means the Welfare Reform Act 2012;

"the 1995 Act" means the Jobseekers Act 1995;

"the 2007 Act" means the Welfare Reform Act 2007;

"the amending provisions" means the provisions referred to in article 4(1)(a) to (c) of the No. 9 Order (day appointed for the abolition of income-related employment and support allowance and income-based jobseeker's allowance);

"appointed day" means the day appointed for the coming into force of the amending provisions in accordance with article 4(3) of the No. 9 Order;

"contribution-based jobseeker's allowance" means a contribution-based allowance under the 1995 Act as it has effect apart from the amendments made by Part 1 of Schedule 14 to the Act that remove references to an income-based allowance;

"contributory employment and support allowance" means a contributory allowance under Part 1 of the 2007 Act as it has effect apart from the amendments made by Schedule 3, and Part 1 of Schedule 14, to the Act that remove references to an income-related allowance;

"employment and support allowance" means an employment and support allowance under Part 1 of the 2007 Act;

"jobseeker's allowance" means an allowance under the 1995 Act;

"joint-claim couple" has the meaning given in section 1(4) of the 1995 Act;

"new style ESA award" means an award of an employment and support allowance under Part 1 of the 2007 Act as amended by the provisions of Schedule 3, and Part 1 of Schedule 14, to the Act that remove references to an income-related allowance;

"new style JSA award" means an award of a jobseeker's allowance under the 1995 Act as amended by the provisions of Part 1 of Schedule 14 to the Act that remove references to an income-based jobseeker's allowance;

"No. 2 relevant districts" means the postcode districts and part-districts specified in Part 1 of the Schedule;

"No. 3 relevant districts" means the postcode districts and part-districts specified in Part 2 of the Schedule;

"the No. 9 Order" means the Welfare Reform Act 2012 (Commencement No. 9 and Transitional and Transitory Provisions and Commencement No. 8 and Savings and Transitional Provisions (Amendment)) Order 2013;

"old style ESA award" means an award of an employment and support allowance under Part 1 of the 2007 Act as it has effect apart from the amendments made by Schedule 3, and Part 1 of Schedule 14, to the Act that remove references to an income-related allowance;

"old style JSA award" means an award of a jobseeker's allowance under the 1995 Act as it has effect apart from the amendments made by Part 1 of Schedule 14 to the Act that remove references to an income-based jobseeker's allowance;

"the Transitional Regulations" means the Universal Credit (Transitional Provisions) Regulations 2013.

(2) For the purposes of this Order, a reference to a person falling within the Pathfinder Group is a reference to a person who meets the requirements of regulations 5 to 12 of the Transitional Regulations.

GENERAL NOTE   3.176

Para. (2)   3.177
On membership of the Pathfinder Group, see also the notes to regs 3 and 4 of the Transitional Provisions Regulations 2013.

Day appointed for commencement of the universal credit provisions in Part 1 of the Act

3.—(1) The day appointed for the coming into force of the provisions   3.178
of the Act listed in Schedule 2 to the No. 9 Order, in so far as they are not already in force, in relation to the case of a claim referred to in paragraph (2), and any award that is made in respect of the claim, is the day appointed in accordance with paragraph (3).

(2) The claims referred to are—

(a) a claim for universal credit that is made or treated as made on or after 1st July 2013 in respect of a period that begins on or after 1st July 2013 by a person who, on the day on which the claim is made or treated as made, resides in one of the No. 2 relevant districts;

(b) a claim for universal credit that is made or treated as made by a person on or after 1st July 2013 in respect of a period that begins on or after 1st July 2013, where—

 (i) the person does not reside in one of the No. 2 relevant districts on the day on which the claim is made or treated as made;

 (ii) in connection with the claim, the person gives incorrect information regarding their residence in such a district; and

 (iii) after a decision is made that the person is entitled to universal credit and one or more payments have been made in respect of the person, the Secretary of State discovers that the person gave that incorrect information;

(c) a claim for universal credit that is made or treated as made on or after 29th July 2013 in respect of a period that begins on or after 29th July

2013 by a person who, on the day on which the claim is made or treated as made, resides in one of the No. 3 relevant districts;

(d) a claim for universal credit that is made or treated as made on or after 29th July 2013 by a person in respect of a period that begins on or after 29th July 2013, where—

(i) the person does not reside in one of the No. 3 relevant districts on the day on which the claim is made or treated as made;

(ii) in connection with the claim, the person gives incorrect information regarding their residence in such a district; and

(iii) after a decision is made that the person is entitled to universal credit and one or more payments have been made in respect of the person, the Secretary of State discovers that the person gave that incorrect information.

(3) The day appointed in relation to the case of a claim referred to in paragraph (2), and any award that is made in respect of the claim, is the first day of the period in respect of which the claim is made or treated as made.

(4) Article 3(5) of the No. 9 Order applies for the purposes of paragraph (2) as it applies for the purposes of article 3(3)(a) and (b) of the No. 9 Order.

(5) Article 3(6) of the No. 9 Order applies for the purposes of paragraph (3) as it applies for the purposes of article 3(4)(a) of the No. 9 Order.

DEFINITIONS

"the Act"—art.2(1).
"No.2 relevant districts"—*ibid.*
"No.3 relevant districts"—*ibid.*
"the No.9 Order"—*ibid.*

GENERAL NOTE

Para. (1)

3.179   This brings into force provisions relating to universal credit in Pt 1 of the WRA 2012, as set out in Sch.2 to the Commencement No.9 Order in relation to the four different categories of case set out in para.(2).

Para. (2) (a)

3.180   This covers the making of a claim for universal credit on or after July 1, 2013 in respect of a period that begins on or after that date where a person lives in a "No.2 relevant district" at the time that the claim is made. The "No.2 relevant districts" are those Wigan postcodes described in Pt 1 of the Schedule. The other conditions for making a claim for universal credit, known as the "Pathfinder Group conditions", are set out in the Transitional Provisions Regulations 2013.

Para. (2) (b)

3.181   This relates to the making of a claim for universal credit on or after July 1, 2013 in respect of a period that begins on or after that date but provides incorrect information as to their residence in a No.2 relevant district (Pt 1 of Schedule), and this is only discovered once payments of universal credit have been made. Such a claim remains within the universal credit regime despite the error.

Para. (2) (c)

3.182   This is the equivalent to para.(2)(a) for those who lives in a "No.3 relevant district" at the time that the claim is made. The "No.3 relevant districts", described in Pt 2 of the Schedule, cover certain postcodes in Manchester, Oldham and Warrington.

Para. (2) (d)
This is the equivalent to para.(2)(b) for those who incorrectly stated that they live   3.183
in a "No.3 relevant district" at the time that the claim is made.

Para. (3)
The day appointed for the commencement of the universal credit provisions in   3.184
the above cases is the first day of the period in respect of which the claim is made
(or treated as made).

Para. (4)
Article 3(5) of the Commencement No.9 Order provides that the Claims and   3.185
Payments Regulations 2013 apply for the purpose of deciding whether and when a
claim for universal credit is made or is to be treated as made.

Para. (5)
Article 3(6) of the Commencement No.9 Order deals with the situation where   3.186
there is an extension of time for making a claim.

Day appointed for the abolition of income-related employment and support allowance and income-based jobseeker's allowance

4.—(1) The day appointed for the coming into force of the amending   3.187
provisions, in relation to the case of a claim referred to in paragraph (2),
and any award that is made in respect of the claim, is the day appointed in
accordance with paragraph (3).
(2) The claims referred to are—
   (a) a claim for universal credit, an employment and support allowance
       or a jobseeker's allowance that is made or treated as made on or
       after 1st July 2013 in respect of a period that begins on or after 1st
       July 2013 by a person who, on the day on which the claim is made
       or treated as made, resides in one of the No. 2 relevant districts
       and falls within the Pathfinder Group;
   (b) a claim for universal credit that is made or treated as made by a
       person on or after 1st July 2013 in respect of a period that begins
       on or after 1st July 2013 where—
       (i) the person does not reside in one of the No. 2 relevant districts
           or does not fall within the Pathfinder Group on the day on
           which the claim is made or treated as made;
       (ii) in connection with the claim, the person gives incorrect infor-
           mation regarding their residence in such a district or their
           falling within the Pathfinder Group; and
       (iii) after a decision is made that the person is entitled to universal
           credit and one or more payments have been made in respect of
           the person, the Secretary of State discovers that the person gave
           that incorrect information;
   (c) a claim for universal credit, an employment and support allowance
       or a jobseeker's allowance that is made or treated as made on or after
       29th July 2013 in respect of a period that begins on or after 29th
       July 2013 by a person who, on the day on which the claim is made
       or treated as made, resides in one of the No. 3 relevant districts and
       falls within the Pathfinder Group; and

(d) a claim for universal credit that is made or treated as made by a person on or after 29th July 2013 in respect of a period that begins on or after 29th July 2013 where—
  (i) the person does not reside in one of the No. 3 relevant districts or does not fall within the Pathfinder Group on the day on which the claim is made or treated as made;
  (ii) in connection with the claim, the person gives incorrect information regarding their residence in such a district or their falling within the Pathfinder Group; and
  (iii) after a decision is made that the person is entitled to universal credit and one or more payments have been made in respect of the person, the Secretary of State discovers that the person gave that incorrect information.

(3) The day appointed in relation to the case of a claim referred to in paragraph (2), and any award that is made in respect of the claim, is the first day of the period in respect of which the claim is made or treated as made.

(4) Paragraphs (4) and (5) of article 4 of the No. 9 Order apply in relation to an award of universal credit that is made in respect of a claim for universal credit referred to in paragraph (2) as they apply in relation to an award of universal credit that is made in respect of a claim for universal credit referred to in article 4(2)(a) or (b) of the No. 9 Order.

(5) Paragraphs (1) and (2) of article 5 of the No. 9 Order apply for the purposes of paragraph (2)(a) and (c) as they apply for the purposes of article 4(2)(a) of the No. 9 Order.

(6) Article 5(3) of the No. 9 Order applies for the purposes of paragraph (2) as it applies for the purposes of article 4(2)(a) to (d) of the No. 9 Order.

(7) Article 5(4) of the No. 9 Order applies for the purposes of paragraph (3) as it applies for the purposes of article 4(3)(a) of the No. 9 Order.

DEFINITIONS

"the amending provisions"—art.2(1).
"contributory employment and support allowance"—*ibid.*
"employment and support allowance"—*ibid.*
"jobseeker's allowance"—*ibid.*
"No.2 relevant districts"—*ibid.*
"No.3 relevant districts"—*ibid.*
"the No.9 Order"—*ibid.*

3.188   GENERAL NOTE

Para. (1)
3.189   This brings into force provisions relating to the abolition of income-related employment and support allowance and of income-based jobseeker's allowance where one of the four different categories of case set out in para.(2) applies.

Para. (2) (a)
3.190   This provides that the new provisions come into force in relation to a claim for (and any subsequent award of) universal credit, employment and support allowance or jobseeker's allowance, where a person makes such a claim on or after July 1, 2013 for a period that begins on or after that date and, at the time that the claim is made, the claimant both lives in a No.2 relevant district (see Pt 1 of Schedule) and meets the Pathfinder Group conditions.

Para. (2) (b)

This provides that the new provisions come into force in relation to a claim for (and any subsequent award of) universal credit where a person claims universal credit, again on or after July 1, 2013 for a period that begins on or after that date, but provides incorrect information as to either their residence in a No.2 relevant district or as to their meeting the Pathfinder Group conditions, but this is only discovered once payments of universal credit have been made. As with reg.3(2)(b), such a claim remains within the universal credit regime despite the error.

3.191

Para. (2) (c)

This makes identical provision to para.(2)(a) for those living in a No.3 relevant district (Pt 2 of Schedule).

3.192

Para. (2) (d)

This makes identical provision to para.(2)(a) for those who state incorrectly that they are living in a No.3 relevant district (Pt 2 of Schedule).

3.193

Para. (3)

The day appointed for the coming into force of the amending provisions in the above cases is the first day of the period in respect of which the claim is made or treated as made.

3.194

Para. (4)

Article 4(4) and (5) of the Commencement No.9 Order extend the universal credit provisions to include certain claims and awards that follow on from the conversion process that applies to recipients of incapacity benefit and severe disablement allowance.

3.195

Para. (5)

Article 5(1) of the Commencement No.9 Order provides that the Claims and Payments Regulations 1987 determine whether and when a claim for employment and support allowance or jobseeker's allowance is made or is treated as made. Article 5(2) simply deems any reference in regs 5–12 of the Transitional Provisions Regulations 2013 to a claim for universal credit as including a claim to employment and support allowance or jobseeker's allowance as appropriate.

3.196

Para. (6)

Article 5(3) of the Commencement No.9 Order provides that the Claims and Payments Regulations 2013 apply for the purpose of deciding whether and when a claim for universal credit is made or is to be treated as made.

3.197

Para. (7)

Article 5(4) of the Commencement No.9 Order deals with the circumstances where there is an extension of time for making a claim.

3.198

Application of the No. 9 Order

5. Articles 6 and 9 to 22 of the No. 9 Order apply in connection with the coming into force of the amending provisions in relation to the case of a claim referred to in article 4(2), and any award made in respect of the claim, as they apply in connection with the coming into force of the amending provisions in relation to the case of a claim referred to in article 4(2)(a) and (b) of the No. 9 Order and any award made in respect of the claim.

3.199

"the amending provisions"—art.2(1).
"the No. 9 Order"—*ibid.*

GENERAL NOTE

3.200   Articles 6–9 of the No.9 Order deal respectively with the following issues:

- Transitional provision: where the abolition of income-related employment and support allowance and income-based jobseeker's allowance is treated as not applying (art.6).

- Day appointed for commencement of provisions relating to claimant responsibilities with respect to employment and support allowance and jobseeker's allowance, and transitional provisions (art.7).

- Transitional provision: conversion of incapacity benefits (art.8).

- Day appointed for commencement of provisions concerning consideration of revision before appeal (art.9).

Amendment of article 7 of the No. 9 Order—transitional provisions in relation to claimant responsibilities with respect to employment and support allowance and jobseeker's allowance

3.201   **6.**—(1) Paragraph (3) applies in relation to a case where, under any secondary legislation, in relation to a new style JSA award, the 1995 Act applies as though the amending provisions had not come into force (which award therefore continues as an old style JSA award) and where the day with effect from which the 1995 Act so applies occurs on or after 1st July 2013.

(2) Paragraph (4) applies in relation to a case where, under any secondary legislation, in relation to a new style ESA award, Part 1 of the 2007 Act applies as though the amending provisions had not come into force (which award therefore continues as an old style ESA award) and where the day with effect from which Part 1 of the 2007 Act so applies occurs on or after 1st July 2013.

(3) In relation to a case to which this paragraph applies, for article 7(2) of the No. 9 Order substitute—

"(2) Where, under any secondary legislation, in relation to a new style JSA award, the 1995 Act applies as though the amending provisions had not come into force, then, with effect from the day on which the 1995 Act so applies, the 1995 Act, the Social Security Administration Act 1992 and the Social Security Act 1998 are to apply in relation to the award as though the provisions referred to in paragraph (1)(a), (b) and (e) had not come into force."

(4) In relation to a case to which this paragraph applies, for article 7(3) of the No. 9 Order substitute—

"(3) Where, under any secondary legislation, in relation to a new style ESA award, Part 1 of the 2007 Act applies as though the amending provisions had not come into force, then, with effect from the day on which Part 1 of the 2007 Act so applies, Part 1 of the 2007 Act and the Welfare Reform Act 2009 are to apply in relation to the award as though the provisions referred to in paragraph (1)(c), (d) and (f) had not come into force."

(5) For the purposes of this article, "secondary legislation" means an instrument made under an Act.

DEFINITIONS

"the 1995 Act"—art.2(1).
"the 2007 Act"—*ibid.*
"the amending provisions"—*ibid.*
"employment and support allowance"—*ibid.*
"new style ESA award"—*ibid.*
"new style JSA award"—*ibid.*
"the No. 9 Order"—*ibid.*
"old style ESA award"—*ibid.*
"old style JSA award"—*ibid.*
"secondary legislation"—para.(5)

GENERAL NOTE

Article 7 of the Commencement No.9 Order (claimant responsibilities with **3.202** respect to ESA and JSA) provides for the appointed day and transitional provisions for the measures in the 2012 Act that relate to claimant responsibilities in relation to a new style ESA or new style JSA awards. By virtue of art.7 of the Commencement No.9 Order, those new provisions come into force in relation to any case with respect to which the provisions of art.4(1)(a)–(c) of that Order come into force.

This provision amends Art.7 of the Commencement No.9 Order with respect to certain cases that are to occur after the Order is made. In relation to the case where, under any secondary legislation, Pt 1 of the WRA 2007 or the Jobseekers Act 1995 applies in relation to a new style ESA award or a new style JSA award respectively as though the amending provisions had not come into force, then the amendments clarify that such awards remain governed by the previous primary legislation.

Amendment of Schedule 4 to the No. 9 Order

7. With effect from 1st July 2013, Schedule 4 to the No. 9 Order (modifi- **3.203** cations of the 2010 Transitional Regulations) is amended as follows—
  (a) for paragraph 21(2)(b)(i) substitute—
       "(i) for the definition of "contributory allowance" substitute—
       "employment and support allowance" means an employment and support allowance to which a person is entitled by virtue of the Employment and Support Allowance (Transitional Provisions, Housing Benefit and Council Tax Benefit)(Existing Awards)(No.2) Regulations 2010 which was based on an award of incapacity benefit or severe disablement allowance to which the person was entitled.",
       and for "; and" following that definition substitute "."; "; and
  (b) after paragraph 21(2) insert—
       "(2A) In paragraph 2A—
           (a) in paragraph (1), omit "contributory"; and
           (b) in paragraph (2), in the substituted section 1A
               (i) in paragraphs (1) and (3) to (5), for "a contributory allowance" substitute "an employment and support allowance"; and
               (ii) in paragraph (3), omit "Part 1 of".".

DEFINITIONS

"employment and support allowance"—art.2(1).
"the No.9 Order"—*ibid.*

3.204   This simply amends Sch.4 to the Commencement No.9 Order to ensure consistency between the wording of ss.1 and 1A of the WRA 2007 as modified by the Transitional Provisions Regulations 2010, and the wording of that Act as amended by the provisions of Sch.3, and Pt 1 of Sch.14, to the WRA 2012 (that remove references to an income-related allowance).

Amendment of the No. 9 Order—transition from old style ESA to new style ESA

3.205   **8.**—(1) Paragraph (2) applies in relation to a case where—
    (a) (i) a person makes, or is treated as making, a claim for an employment and support allowance;
       (ii) under article 4 of the No. 9 Order, Part 1 of the 2007 Act, as amended by the provisions of Schedule 3, and Part 1 of Schedule 14, to the Act that remove references to an income-related allowance, applies in relation to the claim; and
       (iii) the claim is made or treated as made on or after 1st July 2013; or
    (b) (i) a person has an old style ESA award immediately before the appointed day in relation to a case of a claim for universal credit referred to in article 4(2)(a) to (d) of the No. 9 Order (and any award made in respect of the claim), or an award of universal credit referred to in article 4(2)(e) or (f) of the No. 9 Order;
       (ii) the old style ESA award consists of or includes a contributory employment and support allowance (which allowance therefore continues as a new style ESA award); and
       (iii) the first day on which the person is entitled to an employment and support allowance under the new style ESA award occurs on or after 1st July 2013.
    (2) Where this paragraph applies, article 10 of the No. 9 Order is amended as follows—
    (a) for the title substitute "Transition from old style ESA";
    (b) for paragraph (1) substitute—
       "(1) This article applies where a person—
          (a) makes, or is treated as making, a claim for an employment and support allowance and, under article 4, Part 1 of the 2007 Act, as amended by the provisions of Schedule 3, and Part 1 of Schedule 14, to the Act that remove references to an income-related allowance, applies in relation to the claim; or
       (b) (i) has an old style ESA award immediately before the appointed day in relation to a case of a claim for universal credit referred to in article 4(2)(a) to (d) (and any award made in respect of the claim), or an award of universal credit referred to in article 4(2)(e) or (f); and
          (ii) the old style ESA award consists of or includes a contributory employment and support allowance (which allowance therefore continues as a new style ESA award),
       and, in the case of sub-paragraph (a), the condition referred to in paragraph (1A) is satisfied.
       (1A) The condition is that—
          (a) the person previously made, or was treated as having made, a claim for an employment and support allowance

and Part 1 of the 2007 Act, as it has effect apart from the provisions of Schedule 3, and Part 1 of Schedule 14, to the Act that remove references to an income-related allowance, applied in relation to the claim;

(b) a notice was issued to the person under regulation 4 of the 2010 Transitional Regulations and Part 1 of the 2007 Act, as that Part has effect apart from the provisions of Schedule 3, and Part 1 of Schedule 14, to the Act that remove references to an income-related allowance, applied in relation to the notice; or

(c) the person previously had a new style ESA award and article 6(2) applied in relation to the award (which award therefore continued as an old style ESA award).";

(c) after paragraph (2)(g) omit "and" and insert—

"(ga) in regulation 39(6) (exempt work), the reference to an employment and support allowance included a reference to an old style ESA award;

(gb) in regulation 85(2)(a) (waiting days), where a claimant was entitled to an old style ESA award with effect from the first day of a period of limited capability for work by virtue of regulation 144(2)(a) of the ESA Regulations 2008 and, with effect from the second or third day of that period, that award continued as a new style ESA award in the circumstances referred to in paragraph (1)(b) of this article, the reference to an employment and support allowance included a reference to the old style ESA award;";

(d) after paragraph (2)(h) insert—

"(i) in regulation 89 (short absence), where—

(i) a claimant had an old style ESA award in the circumstances referred to in paragraph (1)(b) of this article;

(ii) a temporary absence from Great Britain commenced when regulation 152 of the ESA Regulations 2008 applied to the claimant; and

(iii) the first 4 weeks of the temporary absence had not ended immediately before the first day of entitlement to the new style ESA award,

the initial words of regulation 89 included a reference to the claimant being entitled to the new style ESA award during the remainder of the first 4 weeks of the temporary absence that commenced when regulation 152 of the ESA Regulations 2008 applied to the claimant;

(j) in regulation 90 (absence to receive medical treatment), where—

(i) a claimant had an old style ESA award in the circumstances referred to in paragraph (1)(b) of this article;

(ii) a temporary absence from Great Britain commenced when regulation 153 of the ESA Regulations 2008 applied to the claimant; and

(iii) the first 26 weeks of the temporary absence had not ended immediately before the first day of entitlement to the new style ESA award,

the initial words of paragraph (1) of regulation 90 included a reference to the claimant being entitled to the new style ESA award during the remainder of the first 26 weeks of the temporary absence that commenced when regulation 153 of the ESA Regulations 2008 applied to the claimant;

(k) in regulation 93 (disqualification for misconduct etc)—

(i) in paragraph (3), for "Paragraph (2) does" there were substituted "Paragraphs (2) and (5) do"; and

(ii) after paragraph (4) there were inserted—

"(5) Subject to paragraph (3), a claimant is to be disqualified for receiving an employment and support allowance for any period determined by the Secretary of State under regulation 157(2) of the Employment and Support Allowance Regulations 2008 less any days during that period on which those Regulations applied to the claimant.

(6) Where paragraph (5) applies to a claimant, paragraph (2) is not to apply to that claimant with respect to any matter referred to in paragraph (1) that formed the basis for the claimant's disqualification under regulation 157(2) of the Employment and Support Allowance Regulations 2008.";

(l) in regulation 95 (treating a claimant as not having limited capability for work), the existing words became paragraph (1) and—

(i) at the beginning of paragraph (1), there were inserted "Subject to paragraph (2),"; and

(ii) after paragraph (1), there were inserted—

"(2) A claimant is to be treated as not having limited capability for work if-

(a) under Part 1 of the Act as it has effect apart from the amendments made by Schedule 3, and Part 1 of Schedule 14, to the Welfare Reform Act 2012 that remove references to an income-related allowance ("the former law"), the claimant was disqualified for receiving a contributory employment and support allowance during a period of imprisonment or detention in legal custody;

(b) Part 1 of the Act as amended by the provisions of Schedule 3, and Part 1 of Schedule 14, to the Welfare Reform Act 2012 that remove references to an income-related allowance ("the current law") applied to the claimant with effect from a day that occurred during the period of imprisonment or detention in legal custody referred to in sub-paragraph (a) and during the period of six weeks with effect from the day on which the claimant was first disqualified as referred to in sub-paragraph (a); and

(c) the total of—

(i) the period for which the claimant

was disqualified for receiving a contributory employment and support allowance during the period of imprisonment or detention in legal custody when the former law applied to the claimant; and

(ii) the period for which the claimant was disqualified for receiving an employment and support allowance during the period of imprisonment or detention in legal custody when the current law applied to the claimant,

amounts to more than six weeks.".".; and

(e) after paragraph (2) insert—

"(3) Subject to paragraph (4), where this article applies, the 2007 Act is to be read as though—

(a) the reference to an employment and support allowance in section 1A(1) and (4) to (6);

(b) the first reference to an employment and support allowance in section 1A(3); and

(c) the first reference to an employment and support allowance in section 1B,

included a reference to a contributory employment and support allowance.

(4) Where this article applies and the 2010 Transitional Regulations apply to a person, paragraph (3)(c) becomes paragraph (3)(b) and, for paragraph (3)(a) and (b), there is substituted—

"(a) in section 1A as substituted by the 2010 Transitional Regulations—

(i) the reference to an employment and support allowance in section 1A(1), (4) and (5); and

(ii) the first reference to an employment and support allowance in section 1A(3); and".

(5) Where this article applies and a claimant—

(a) had an old style ESA award in the circumstances referred to in paragraph (1)(b); and

(b) the old style ESA award had not been preceded by a new style ESA award in the circumstances referred to in paragraph (1A)(c),

the 2007 Act is to be read as if, in section 24(2), the beginning of the assessment phase (subject to section 24(3)) was the first day of the period for which the claimant was entitled to the old style ESA award.".

DEFINITIONS

"the Act"—art.2(1).
"the 2007 Act"—*ibid*.
"appointed day"—*ibid*.
"contributory employment and support allowance"—*ibid*.
"employment and support allowance"—*ibid*.
"new style ESA award"—*ibid*.
"the No.9 Order"—*ibid*.
"old style ESA award"—*ibid*.

3.206   This Article, together with arts 9–11, amends arts 10 and 11 of the Commencement No.9 Order, and substitute new arts 12 and 13 of the Commencement No.9 Order (transition from old style ESA to new style ESA and vice versa, and old style JSA to new style JSA and vice versa) with respect to claims that are made on or after July 1, 2013 and awards of old style ESA or JSA that continue as awards of new style ESA or JSA (or vice versa) on or after that date. The amendments are intended to clarify the cases to which the modifications made by those articles apply and provide for additional modifications of legislation governing ESA and JSA.

Transition from new style ESA to old style ESA

3.207   **9.**—(1) Paragraph (2) applies in relation to a case where—

(a) (i) a person makes, or is treated as making, a claim for an employment and support allowance;

(ii) Part 1 of the 2007 Act as it has effect apart from the provisions of Schedule 3, and Part 1 of Schedule 14, to the Act that remove references to an income-related allowance, applies in relation to the claim; and

(iii) the claim is made or treated as made on or after 1st July 2013; or

(b) (i) a person has a new style ESA award and article 6(2) of the No. 9 Order applies in relation to the award (which award therefore continues as an old style ESA award); and

(ii) the first day on which the person in question is entitled to an employment and support allowance under the old style ESA award occurs on or after 1st July 2013.

(2) Where this paragraph applies, article 11 of the No. 9 Order is amended as follows—

(a) for the title substitute "Transition from new style ESA";

(b) for paragraph (1) substitute—

"(1) This article applies where a person—

(a) makes, or is treated as making, a claim for an employment and support allowance and Part 1 of the 2007 Act, as it has effect apart from the provisions of Schedule 3, and Part 1 of Schedule 14, to the Act that remove references to an income-related allowance, applies in relation to the claim; or

(b) has a new style ESA award and article 6(2) applies in relation to the award (which award therefore continues as an old style ESA award),

and, in the case of sub-paragraph (a), the condition referred to in paragraph (1A) is satisfied.

(1A) The condition is that—

(a) the person previously made, or was treated as having made, a claim for an employment and support allowance and, under article 4, Part 1 of the 2007 Act, as amended by the provisions of Schedule 3, and Part 1 of Schedule 14, to the Act that remove references to an income-related allowance, applied in relation to the claim;

(b) a notice was issued to the person under regulation 4 of the 2010 Transitional Regulations and, under article 4, Part 1 of the 2007 Act, as amended by the provisions of Schedule 3, and Part 1 of Schedule 14, to the Act that remove references to an income-related allowance, applied in relation to the notice; or

(c) the person previously—
    (i) had an old style ESA award immediately before the appointed day in relation to a case of a claim for universal credit referred to in article 4(2)(a) to (d) (and any award made in respect of the claim), or an award of universal credit referred to in article 4(2)(e) or (f); and
    (ii) the old style ESA award consisted of or included a contributory employment and support allowance (which allowance therefore continued as a new style ESA award).";
(c) after paragraph (2)(g), omit "and" and insert—
"(ga) in regulation 45(10) (exempt work), the reference to an employment and support allowance included a reference to a new style ESA award;
(gb) in regulation 144(2)(a) (waiting days), where the claimant was entitled to a new style ESA award with effect from the first day of a period of limited capability for work by virtue of regulation 85(2)(a) of the ESA Regulations 2013 and, with effect from the second or third day of that period, that award continued as an old style ESA award in the circumstances referred to in paragraph (1)(c) of this article, the reference to an employment and support allowance included a reference to the new style ESA award;";
(d) after paragraph (2)(h), insert—
"(i) in regulation 152 (short absence), where—
    (i) a claimant had a new style ESA award in the circumstances referred to in paragraph (1)(b) of this article;
    (ii) a temporary absence from Great Britain commenced when regulation 89 of the ESA Regulations 2013 applied to the claimant; and
    (iii) the first 4 weeks of the temporary absence had not ended immediately before the first day of entitlement to the old style ESA award,
the initial words of regulation 152 included a reference to the claimant being entitled to the old style ESA award during the remainder of the first 4 weeks of the temporary absence that commenced when regulation 89 of the ESA Regulations 2013 applied to the claimant;
(j) in regulation 153 (absence to receive medical treatment)—
    (i) a claimant had a new style ESA award in the circumstances referred to in paragraph (1)(b) of this article;
    (ii) a temporary absence from Great Britain commenced when regulation 90 of the ESA Regulations 2013 applied to the claimant; and
    (iii) the first 26 weeks of the temporary absence had not ended immediately before the first day of entitlement to the old style ESA award,
the initial words of paragraph (1) of regulation 153 included a reference to the claimant being entitled to the old style ESA award during the remainder of the first 26 weeks of the temporary absence that commenced when regulation 90 of the ESA Regulations 2013 applied to the claimant;
(k) in regulation 157 (disqualification for misconduct etc)—

405

(i) in paragraph (3), for "Paragraph (2) does" there were substituted "Paragraphs (2) and (4) do"; and

(ii) after paragraph (3) there were inserted—

"(4) Subject to paragraph (3), a claimant is to be disqualified for receiving an employment and support allowance for any period determined by the Secretary of State under regulation 93(2) of the Employment and Support Allowance Regulations 2013 less any days during that period on which those Regulations applied to the claimant.

(5) Where paragraph (4) applies to a claimant, paragraph (2) is not to apply to that claimant with respect to any matter referred to in paragraph (1) that formed the basis for the claimant's disqualification under regulation 93(2) of the Employment and Support Allowance Regulations 2013."; and

(l) in regulation 159 (treating a claimant as not having limited capability for work), the existing words became paragraph (1) and—

(i) at the beginning of paragraph (1), there were inserted "Subject to paragraph (2),"; and

(ii) after paragraph (1), there were inserted—

"(2) A claimant is to be treated as not having limited capability for work if—

(a) under Part 1 of the Act as amended by the provisions of Schedule 3, and Part 1 of Schedule 14, to the Welfare Reform Act 2012 that remove references to an income-related allowance ("the former law"), the claimant was disqualified for receiving an employment and support allowance during a period of imprisonment or detention in legal custody;

(b) Part 1 of the Act as it has effect apart from the amendments made by Schedule 3, and Part 1 of Schedule 14, to the Welfare Reform Act 2012 that remove references to an income-related allowance ("the current law") applied to the claimant with effect from a day that occurred during the period of imprisonment or detention in legal custody referred to in sub-paragraph (a) and during the period of six weeks with effect from the day on which the claimant was first disqualified as referred to in sub-paragraph (a); and

(c) the total of—

(i) the period for which the claimant was disqualified for receiving an employment and support allowance during the period of imprisonment or detention in legal custody when the former law applied to the claimant; and

(ii) the period for which the claimant was disqualified for receiving a contributory employment and support allowance during the period of imprisonment or detention in legal custody when the current law applied to the claimant,

amounts to more than six weeks."."; and

(e) after paragraph (2) insert—

"(3) Subject to paragraph (4), where this article applies, the 2007 Act is to be read as though—

(a) the reference to a contributory allowance in section (1A)(1) and (4) to (6);

(b) the first reference to a contributory allowance in section (1A)(3); and

(c) the first reference to a contributory allowance in section 1B, included a reference to a new style ESA award.

(4) Where this article applies and the 2010 Transitional Regulations apply to a person, paragraph (3)(c) becomes paragraph (3)(b) and, for paragraph (3)(a) and (b), there is substituted—

"(a) in section 1A as substituted by the 2010 Transitional Regulations—

(i) the reference to a contributory allowance in section 1A(1), (4) and (5); and

(ii) the first reference to a contributory allowance in section 1A(3); and".

(5) Where this article applies and a claimant—

(a) had a new style ESA award in the circumstances referred to in paragraph (1)(b); and

(b) the new style ESA award had not been preceded by an old style ESA award in the circumstances referred to in paragraph (1A)(c),

section 24(2) of the 2007 Act is to be read as if the beginning of the assessment phase (subject to section 24(3)) was the first day of the period for which the claimant was entitled to the new style ESA award.".

DEFINITIONS

"the Act"—art.2(1).
"the 2007 Act"—*ibid.*
"appointed day"—*ibid.*
"contributory employment and support allowance"—*ibid.*
"employment and support allowance"—*ibid.*
"new style ESA award"—*ibid.*
"the No.9 Order"—*ibid.*
"old style ESA award"—*ibid.*

Transition from old style JSA to new style JSA

10.—(1) Paragraph (2) applies in relation to the case where—   3.208

(a)   (i) a person makes, or is treated as making, a claim for a jobseeker's allowance;

(ii) under article 4 of the No. 9 Order, the 1995 Act as amended by the provisions of Part 1 of Schedule 14 to the Act that remove references to an income-based jobseeker's allowance, applies in relation to the claim; and

(iii) the claim is made or treated as made on or after 1st July 2013; or

(b) (i) a person has an old style JSA award (whether or not the award was made to the person as a member of a joint-claim couple) immediately before the appointed day in relation to a case of a claim for universal credit referred to in article 4(2)(a) to (d) of the No. 9 Order (and any award made in respect of the claim) or an award of universal credit referred to in article 4(2)(e) or (f) of the No. 9 Order;

(ii) the old style JSA award consists of or includes a contributory employment and support allowance (which allowance therefore continues as a new style JSA award); and

(iii) the first day on which the person in question is entitled to a jobseeker's allowance under the new style JSA award occurs on or after 1st July 2013.

(2) Where this paragraph applies, for article 12 of the No. 9 Order substitute—

"Transition from old style JSA

3.209   **12.**—(1) This article applies where a person—

(a) makes, or is treated as making, a claim for a jobseeker's allowance and, under article 4, the 1995 Act, as amended by the provisions of Part 1 of Schedule 14 to the Act that remove references to an income-based jobseeker's allowance, applies in relation to the claim; or

(b) (i) has an old style JSA award (whether or not the award was made to the person as a member of a joint-claim couple) immediately before the appointed day in relation to a case of a claim for universal credit referred to in article 4(2)(a) to (d) (and any award made in respect of the claim), or an award of universal credit referred to in article 4(2)(e) or (f); and

(ii) the old style JSA award consists of or includes a contribution-based jobseeker's allowance (which allowance therefore continues as a new style JSA award),

and, in the case of sub-paragraph (a), the condition referred to in paragraph (2) is satisfied.

(2) The condition is that the person previously—

(a) made, or was treated as having made, a claim for a jobseeker's allowance (whether or not as a member of a joint-claim couple) and the 1995 Act, as it has effect apart from the provisions of Part 1 of Schedule 14 to the Act that remove references to an income-based jobseeker's allowance, applied in relation to the claim; or

(b) had a new style JSA award and article 6(2) applied in relation to the award (which award therefore continued as an old style JSA award).

(3) Where this article applies, the JSA Regulations 2013 are to be read as if—

(a) in regulation 15(3)(b) (victims of domestic violence), the reference to regulation 15 applying to the claimant included a reference to the claimant having been treated as being available for employment under regulation 14A(2) or (6) of the JSA Regulations 1996;

(b) in regulation 36(1) (waiting days), where a person was entitled to an old style JSA award with effect from the first day of a jobseeking period by virtue of regulation 46(1)(a) of the JSA Regulations 1996 and, with effect from the second or third day of that period, that award continued as a new style JSA award in the circumstances referred to in paragraph (1)(b) of this article, the reference to a jobseeker's allowance included a reference to the old style JSA award;

(c) in regulation 37 (jobseeking period)—

(i) the jobseeking period in relation to a claimant included any period that, under regulation 47 of the JSA Regulations 1996 (jobseeking period), forms part of the jobseeking period for the purposes of the 1995 Act; and

(ii) in paragraph (3), the reference to a day that is to be treated as a day in respect of which the claimant was entitled to a job-seeker's allowance included a reference to any day that, under regulation 47(4) of the JSA Regulations 1996, is to be treated as a day in respect of which the claimant was entitled to a contribution-based jobseeker's allowance;

(d) in regulation 41 (persons temporarily absent from Great Britain), where a person had an old style JSA award in the circumstances referred to in paragraph (1)(b) of this article, the reference in paragraph (2)(b), (3)(a) and (c), (5)(a) and (6)(b) to entitlement to a jobseeker's allowance included a reference to the old style JSA award; and

(e) in regulation 46 (short periods of sickness), after paragraph (5) there were inserted—

"(6) Where—

(a) a person has been treated under regulation 55(1) of the Jobseeker's Allowance Regulations 1996 as capable of work or as not having limited capability for work for a certain period; and

(b) these Regulations apply to that person with effect from a day ("the relevant day") within that period,

the person is to be treated for the part of that period that begins with the relevant day as capable of work or as not having limited capability for work.

(7) Where paragraph (6) applies to a person and the conditions in paragraph (1)(a) to (c) are fulfilled in relation to that person on any day within the part of a period referred to in paragraph (6), the requirement of paragraph (1) to treat the person as capable of work or as not having limited capability for work is to be regarded as satisfied with respect to the fulfilment of those conditions on that day.

(8) For the purposes of paragraph (3), where paragraph (6) applies to a person, paragraph (3) is to apply to the person as though the preceding provisions of this regulation had applied to the person with respect to the person having been treated for a period, under regulation 55(1) of the Jobseeker's Allowance Regulations 1996 and paragraph (6), as capable of work or as not having limited capability for work.".

(4) Where this article applies, the 1995 Act is to be read as though, in section 5 of the 1995 Act, the reference to a jobseeker's allowance in subsection (1) and the first reference to a jobseeker's allowance in subsection (2) included a reference to a contribution-based jobseeker's allowance.

(5) For the purposes of this article, "joint-claim couple" has the meaning given in section 1(4) of the 1995 Act.".

DEFINITIONS

"the Act"—art.2(1).
"the 1995 Act"—*ibid.*
"appointed day"—*ibid.*
"contribution-based jobseeker's allowance"—*ibid.*
"contributory employment and support allowance"—*ibid.*

"jobseeker's allowance"—*ibid.*
"joint-claim couple"—*ibid.*
"new style JSA award"—*ibid.*
"the No.9 Order"—*ibid.*
"old style JSA award"—*ibid.*

Transition from new style JSA to old style JSA

3.210   **11.**—(1) Paragraph (2) applies in relation to a case where—
(a)   (i) a person makes, or is treated as making, a claim for a job-seeker's allowance (whether or not as a member of a joint-claim couple);
(ii) the 1995 Act, as it has effect apart from the provisions of Part 1 of Schedule 14 to the Act that remove references to an income-based jobseeker's allowance, applies in relation to the claim; and
(iii) the claim is made or treated as made on or after 1st July 2013; or
(b)   (i) a person has a new style JSA award and article 6(2) of the No. 9 Order applies in relation to the award (which award therefore continues as an old style JSA award); and
(ii) the first day on which the person in question is entitled to a jobseeker's allowance under the old style JSA award occurs on or after 1st July 2013.
(2) Where this paragraph applies, for article 13 of the No. 9 Order substitute—

"Transition from new style JSA

3.211   **13.**—(1) This article applies where a person—
(a) makes, or is treated as making, a claim for a jobseeker's allowance (whether or not as a member of a joint-claim couple) and the 1995 Act, as it has effect apart from the provisions of Part 1 of Schedule 14 to the Act that remove references to an income-based jobseeker's allowance, applies in relation to the claim; or
(b) has a new style JSA award and article 6(2) applies in relation to the award such that it continues as an old style JSA award,
   and, in the case of sub-paragraph (a), the condition referred to in paragraph (2) is satisfied.
(2) the condition is that the person previously—
(a) made, or was treated as having made, a claim for a jobseeker's allowance and, under article 4, the 1995 Act, as amended by the provisions of Part 1 of Schedule 14 to the Act that remove references to an income-based jobseeker's allowance, applied in relation to the claim; or
(b)   (i) had an old style JSA award immediately before the appointed day in relation to a case of a claim for universal credit referred to in article 4(2)(a) to (d) (and any award made in respect of the claim), or an award of universal credit referred to in article 4(2)(e) or (f); and
(ii) the old style JSA award consisted of or included a contributory employment and support allowance (which allowance therefore continued as a new style JSA award).

(3) Where this article applies, the JSA Regulations 1996 are to be read as if—

(a) in regulation 14A (victims of domestic violence), for the purposes of paragraph (3)(b) of that regulation, a person had been treated as available for employment on a day (under paragraph (2) of that regulation) where regulation 15 of the JSA Regulations 2013 applied to that person on that day;

(b) in regulation 46 (waiting days)—

(i) where a person was entitled to a new style JSA award with effect from the first day of a jobseeking period by virtue of regulation 36(1) of the JSA Regulations 2013 and, with effect from the second or third day of that period, that award continued as an old style JSA award in the circumstances referred to in paragraph (1)(b) of this article, the reference to a jobseeker's allowance in paragraph (1)(a) included a reference to the new style JSA award; and

(ii) the second reference to a jobseeker's allowance in paragraph (1)(d) included a reference to a new style JSA award;

(c) in regulation 47 (jobseeking period)—

(i) the jobseeking period in relation to a claimant included any period that, under regulation 37 of the JSA Regulations 2013 (jobseeking period) forms part of the jobseeking period for the purposes of the 1995 Act; and

(ii) in paragraph (4), the reference to any day that is to be treated as a day in respect of which the claimant was entitled to a contribution-based jobseeker's allowance included a reference to a day that, under regulation 37(3) of the JSA Regulations 2013 (jobseeking period), is to be treated as a day in respect of which the claimant was entitled to a jobseeker's allowance;

(d) in regulation 50 (persons temporarily absent from Great Britain), where a person had a new style JSA award in the circumstances referred to in paragraph (1)(b) of this article, the reference in paragraph (2)(b), (3)(a) and (c), (5)(a) and (c), (6AA)(a) and (6D)(b) to entitlement to a jobseeker's allowance included a reference to the new style JSA award; and

(e) in regulation 55 (short periods of sickness), after paragraph (5) there were inserted—

"(6) Where—

(a) a person has been treated under regulation 46(1) of the Jobseeker's Allowance Regulations 2013 as capable of work or as not having limited capability for work for a certain period; and

(b) these Regulations apply to that person with effect from a day ("the relevant day") within that period,

the person is to be treated for the part of that period that begins with the relevant day as capable of work or as not having limited capability for work.

(7) Where paragraph (6) applies to a person and the conditions in paragraph (1)(a) to (c) are fulfilled in relation to that person on any day within the part of a period referred to in paragraph (6), the requirement of paragraph (1) to treat the person as capable of work or as not having limited capability for work is

411

to be regarded as satisfied with respect to the fulfilment of those conditions on that day.

(8) For the purposes of paragraph (3), where paragraph (6) applies to a person, paragraph (3) is to apply to the person as though the preceding provisions of this regulation had applied to the person with respect to the person having been treated for a period, under regulation 46(1) of the Jobseeker's Allowance Regulations 2013 and paragraph (6), as capable of work or as not having limited capability for work.".

(4) Where this article applies, the 1995 Act is to be read as though, in section 5 of the 1995 Act, the reference to a contribution-based jobseeker's allowance in subsection (1) and the first reference to a contribution-based jobseeker's allowance in subsection (2) included a reference to a new style JSA award.

(5) For the purposes of this article, "joint-claim couple" has the meaning given in section 1(4) of the 1995 Act.".

DEFINITIONS

"the Act"—art. 2(1).
"the 1995 Act"—*ibid.*
"appointed day"—*ibid.*
"contribution-based jobseeker's allowance"—*ibid.*
"contributory employment and support allowance"—*ibid.*
"jobseeker's allowance"—*ibid.*
"joint-claim couple"—*ibid.*
"new style JSA award"—*ibid.*
"the No.9 Order"—*ibid.*
"old style JSA award"—*ibid.*

Article 2(1)

SCHEDULE

PART I

THE NO.2 RELEVANT DISTRICTS

1. WN1 1 and WN1 2.
2. WN2 1 to WN2 5.
3. WN3 0.
4. WN3 4 to WN3 6.
5. WN5 0.
6. WN5 6 to WN5 9.
7. WN6 0.
8. WN6 7 to WN6 9.

PART II

THE NO.3 RELEVANT DISTRICTS

1. M35 0 to M35 4.
2. M35 6 and M35 7.
3. M35 9.
4. OL1 0 to OL1 6.
5. OL1 8 and OL1 9.
6. OL2 1.
7. OL2 3 to OL2 9.

8. OL3 1.
9. OL3 5 to OL3 7.
10. OL3 9.
11. OL4 0 to OL4 5.
12. OL8 and OL9.
13. WA1 and WA2.
14. WA3 4 to WA3 7.
15. WA4 and WA5.
16. WA13 0.
17. WA13 9.

Welfare Reform Act 2012 (Commencement No. 13 and Transitional and Transitory Provisions) Order 2013

(SI 2013/2657) (c.103)

The Secretary of State, in exercise of the powers conferred by section 150(3) and (4)(a), (b)(i) and (c) of the Welfare Reform Act 2012, makes the following Order: **3.212**

ARRANGEMENT OF ARTICLES

1. Citation
2. Interpretation
3. Day appointed for commencement of the universal credit provisions in Part 1 of the Act
4. Day appointed for the abolition of income-related employment and support allowance and income-based jobseeker's allowance
5. Amendment of the No. 9 Order
6. Application of the No. 9 Order

Schedule: The No. 4 relevant districts

GENERAL NOTE

This Commencement Order ("the Commencement No.13 Order") extends the universal credit scheme to certain postcode districts in West London, Manchester and Wigan ("the No.4 relevant districts") as from October 28, 2013. In addition, of course, the claimant must fall within the Pathfinder Group, i.e. be a person who meets the requirements of regs 5–12 of the Transitional Provisions Regulations 2013.   **3.213**

Citation

1. This Order may be cited as the Welfare Reform Act 2012 (Commencement No.13 and Transitional and Transitory Provisions) Order 2013.   **3.214**

Interpretation

2. (1) In this Order—
"the Act" means the Welfare Reform Act 2012;   **3.215**

"the amending provisions" means the provisions referred to in article 4(1)(a) to (c) of the No. 9 Order (day appointed for the abolition of income-related employment and support allowance and income-based jobseeker's allowance);

"employment and support allowance" means an employment and support allowance under Part 1 of the Welfare Reform Act 2007;

"jobseeker's allowance" means a jobseeker's allowance under the Jobseekers Act 1995;

"No. 4 relevant districts" means the postcode part-districts specified in the Schedule;

"the No. 9 Order" means the Welfare Reform Act 2012 (Commencement No. 9 and Transitional and Transitory Provisions and Commencement No. 8 and Savings and Transitional Provisions (Amendment)) Order 2013.

(2) For the purposes of this Order, a reference to a person who falls within the Pathfinder Group is a reference to a person who meets the requirements of regulations 5 to 12 of the Universal Credit (Transitional Provisions) Regulations 2013.

GENERAL NOTE

Para. (2)

3.216   On membership of the Pathfinder Group, see also the notes to regs 3 and 4 of the Transitional Provisions Regulations 2013.

Day appointed for commencement of the universal credit provisions in Part 1 of the Act

3.217   **3.** (1) The day appointed for the coming into force of the provisions of the Act listed in Schedule 2 to the No. 9 Order, in so far as they are not already in force, in relation to the case of a claim referred to in paragraph (2), and any award that is made in respect of the claim, is the day appointed in accordance with paragraph (3).

(2) The claims referred to are—

(a) a claim for universal credit that is made or treated as made on or after 28th October 2013 in respect of a period that begins on or after 28th October 2013 by a person who, on the day on which the claim is made or treated as made, resides in one of the No. 4 relevant districts; and

(b) a claim for universal credit that is made or treated as made by a person on or after 28th October 2013 in respect of a period that begins on or after 28th October 2013, where—

(i) the person does not reside in one of the No. 4 relevant districts on the day on which the claim is made or treated as made;

(ii) in connection with the claim, the person gives incorrect information regarding their residence in such a district; and

(iii) after a decision is made that the person is entitled to universal credit and one or more payments have been made in respect of the person, the Secretary of State discovers that the person gave that incorrect information.

(3) The day appointed in relation to the case of a claim referred to in paragraph (2), and any award that is made in respect of the claim, is the first day of the period in respect of which the claim is made or treated as made.

(4) Article 3(5) of the No. 9 Order applies for the purposes of paragraph (2) as it applies for the purposes of article 3(3)(a) and (b) of the No. 9 Order.

(5) Article 3(6) of the No. 9 Order applies for the purposes of paragraph (3) as it applies for the purposes of article 3(4)(a) of the No. 9 Order.

DEFINITIONS

"the Act"—art.2(1).
"the No.4 relevant districts"—*ibid.*
"the No.9 Order"—*ibid.*

GENERAL NOTE

Para. (1)

This brings into force provisions relating to universal credit in Pt 1 of the WRA 2012, as set out in Sch.2 to the Commencement No.9 Order, in so far as they are not already in force, in relation to the two further categories of case set out in para.(2).   **3.218**

Para. (2) (a)

This covers the making of a claim for universal credit on or after October 28, 2013, in respect of a period that begins on or after that date, where a person lives in a "No.4 relevant district" at the time that the claim is made. The "No.4 relevant districts" are those Manchester, Wigan but principally West London postcodes (the latter mainly dealt with by Hammersmith Jobcentre) set out in the Schedule. The other conditions for making a claim for universal credit, known as the "Pathfinder Group conditions", are set out in regs 5–12 of the Transitional Provisions Regulations 2013.   **3.219**

Para. (2) (b)

This relates to the making of a claim for universal credit on or after October 28, 2013 in respect of a period that begins on or after that date but provides incorrect information as to their residence in a No.4 relevant district, and this is only discovered once payments of universal credit have been made. Such a claim remains within the universal credit regime despite the error.   **3.220**

Para. (3)

The day appointed for the commencement of the universal credit provisions in the above cases is the first day of the period in respect of which the claim is made (or treated as made).   **3.221**

Para. (4)

Article 3(5) of the Commencement No.9 Order provides that the Claims and Payments Regulations 2013 apply for the purpose of deciding whether and when a claim for universal credit is made or is to be treated as made.   **3.222**

Para. (5)

Article 3(6) of the Commencement No.9 Order deals with the situation where there is an extension of time for making a claim.   **3.223**

Day appointed for the abolition of income-related employment and support allowance and income-based jobseeker's allowance

4. (1) The day appointed for the coming into force of the amending provisions, in relation to the case of a claim referred to in paragraph (2), and any award that is made in respect of the claim, is the day appointed in accordance with paragraph (3).   **3.224**

(2) The claims referred to are—

(a) a claim for universal credit, an employment and support allowance or a jobseeker's allowance that is made or treated as made on or after 28th October 2013 in respect of a period that begins on or after 28th October 2013 by a person who, on the day on which the claim is made or treated as made, resides in one of the No. 4 relevant districts and falls within the Pathfinder Group; and

(b) a claim for universal credit that is made or treated as made by a person on or after 28th October 2013 in respect of a period that begins on or after 28th October 2013 where—

    (i) the person does not reside in one of the No. 4 relevant districts or does not fall within the Pathfinder Group on the day on which the claim is made or treated as made;

    (ii) in connection with the claim, the person gives incorrect information regarding their residence in such a district or their falling within the Pathfinder Group; and

    (iii) after a decision is made that the person is entitled to universal credit and one or more payments have been made in respect of the person, the Secretary of State discovers that the person gave that incorrect information.

(3) The day appointed in relation to the case of a claim referred to in paragraph (2), and any award that is made in respect of the claim, is the first day of the period in respect of which the claim is made or treated as made.

(4) Paragraphs (4) and (5) of article 4 of the No. 9 Order apply in relation to an award of universal credit that is made in respect of a claim for universal credit referred to in paragraph (2) as they apply in relation to an award of universal credit that is made in respect of a claim for universal credit referred to in article 4(2)(a) or (b) of the No. 9 Order.

(5) Paragraphs (1) and (2) of article 5 of the No. 9 Order apply for the purposes of paragraph (2)(a) as they apply for the purposes of article 4(2)(a) of the No. 9 Order.

(6) Article 5(3) of the No. 9 Order applies for the purposes of paragraph (2) as it applies for the purposes of article 4(2)(a) and (b) of the No. 9 Order.

(7) Article 5(4) of the No. 9 Order applies for the purposes of paragraph (3) as it applies for the purposes of article 4(3)(a) of the No. 9 Order.

DEFINITIONS

"the amending provisions"—art.2(1)
"employment and support allowance"—*ibid.*
"jobseeker's allowance"—*ibid.*
"the No.4 relevant districts"—*ibid.*
"the No.9 Order"—*ibid.*
"a person who . . . . falls within the Pathfinder Group"—art.2(2).

GENERAL NOTE

Para. (1)

3.225   This brings into force provisions relating to the abolition of income-related employment and support allowance and of income-based jobseeker's allowance where the case falls within one of the two categories set out in para.(2) (see also the incorporation by reference of other provisions as made by paras (4)–(6) below).

Para.(2)(a)

This provides that the new provisions come into force in relation to a claim for (and any subsequent award of) universal credit, employment and support allowance or jobseeker's allowance, where a person makes such a claim on or after October 28, 2013 for a period that begins on or after that date and, at the time that the claim is made, the claimant both lives in a No.4 relevant district (see Schedule) and meets the Pathfinder Group conditions.

3.226

Para.(2)(b)

This provides that the new provisions come into force in relation to a claim for (and any subsequent award of) universal credit where a person claims universal credit, again on or after October 28, 2013 for a period that begins on or after that date, but provides incorrect information as to either their residence in a No.4 relevant district (see Schedule) or as to their meeting the Pathfinder Group conditions, but this is only discovered once payments of universal credit have been made. As with reg.3(2)(b), such a claim remains within the universal credit regime despite the error.

3.227

Para.(3)

The day appointed for the coming into force of the amending provisions in the above cases is the first day of the period in respect of which the claim is made or treated as made.

3.228

Para.(4)

Article 4(4) and (5) of the Commencement No.9 Order extend the universal credit provisions to include certain claims and awards that follow on from the conversion process that applies to recipients of incapacity benefit and severe disablement allowance.

3.229

Para.(5)

Article 5(1) of the Commencement No.9 Order provides that the Claims and Payments Regulations 1987 determine whether and when a claim for employment and support allowance or jobseeker's allowance is made or is treated as made. Article 5(2) simply deems any reference in regs 5–12 of the Transitional Provisions Regulations 2013 to a claim for universal credit as including a claim to employment and support allowance or jobseeker's allowance as appropriate.

3.230

Para.(6)

Article 5(3) of the Commencement No.9 Order provides that the Claims and Payments Regulations 2013 apply for the purpose of deciding whether and when a claim for universal credit is made or is to be treated as made.

3.231

Para.(7)

Article 5(4) of the Commencement No.9 Order deals with the circumstances where there is an extension of time for making a claim.

3.232

Amendment of the No. 9 Order

5. With effect from 29th October 2013—
   (a) in article 11(2)(f)(ii) of the No. 9 Order, for "paragraph (2)(b)(iii)" substitute "paragraph (4)(c)"; and
   (b) in article 5 of the Welfare Reform Act 2012 (Commencement No. 11 and Transitional and Transitory Provisions and Commencement No. 9 and Transitional and Transitory Provisions (Amendment)) Order 2013(1), the reference to article 11 of the No. 9 Order is a reference to article 11 as amended by paragraph (a).

3.233

3.234   This article makes a minor amendment to the Commencement No.9 Order (which is noted in the statutory text above) and makes a consequential clarification of the effect of a provision in the Commencement No.11 Order.

Application of the No. 9 Order

3.235   **6.** Articles 6 and 9 to 22 of the No. 9 Order apply in connection with the coming into force of the amending provisions in relation to the case of a claim referred to in article 4(2), and any award made in respect of the claim, as they apply in connection with the coming into force of the amending provisions in relation to the case of a claim referred to in article 4(2)(a) and (b) of the No. 9 Order and any award made in respect of the claim.

DEFINITION

"the amending provisions"—art. 2(1).

GENERAL NOTE

3.236   This is in the same terms as art.5 of the Commencement No.11 Order.

Article 2(1)

3.237   SCHEDULE

THE NO. 4 RELEVANT DISTRICTS

1. M35 5.
2. W6 0.
3. W6 6 to W6 9.
4. W14 0.
5. W14 4.
6. W14 8 and W14 9.
7. WN1 3.

Welfare Reform Act 2012 (Commencement No. 14 and Transitional and Transitory Provisions) Order 2013

(SI 2013/2846) (c.114)

3.238   *The Secretary of State, in exercise of the powers conferred by section 150(3) and (4)(a), (b)(i) and (c) of the Welfare Reform Act 2012, makes the following Order:*

ARRANGEMENT OF ARTICLES

1.   Citation
2.   Interpretation
3.   Day appointed for commencement of the universal credit provisions in Part 1 of the Act
4.   Day appointed for the abolition of income-related employment and support allowance and income-based jobseeker's allowance
5.   Application of the No. 9 Order

Schedule: The No. 5 relevant districts

GENERAL NOTE

This Commencement Order ("the Commencement No.14 Order") extends the   3.239
universal credit scheme to certain postcode districts in Rugby, Inverness and Perth
("the No.5 relevant districts") as from November 25, 2013. In addition, of course,
the claimant must fall within the Pathfinder Group, i.e. be a person who meets the
requirements of regs 5–12 of the Transitional Provisions Regulations 2013.

Citation

1. This Order may be cited as the Welfare Reform Act 2012   3.240
(Commencement No. 14 and Transitional and Transitory Provisions)
Order 2013.

Interpretation

2.—(1) In this Order—   3.241
"the Act" means the Welfare Reform Act 2012;
"the amending provisions" means the provisions referred to in article
   4(1)(a) to (c) of the No. 9 Order (day appointed for the abolition of
   income-related employment and support allowance and income-based
   jobseeker's allowance);
"employment and support allowance" means an employment and support
   allowance under Part 1 of the Welfare Reform Act 2007;
"jobseeker's allowance" means a jobseeker's allowance under the
   Jobseekers Act 1995;
"No. 5 relevant districts" means the postcode part-districts specified in
   the Schedule;
"the No. 9 Order" means the Welfare Reform Act 2012 (Commencement
   No. 9 and Transitional and Transitory Provisions and Commencement
   No. 8 and Savings and Transitional Provisions (Amendment)) Order
   2013.
(2) For the purposes of this Order, a reference to a person who falls
within the Pathfinder Group is a reference to a person who meets the
requirements of regulations 5 to 12 of the Universal Credit (Transitional
Provisions) Regulations 2013.

GENERAL NOTE   3.242

Para. (2)
On membership of the Pathfinder Group, see also the notes to regs 3 and 4 of the   3.243
Transitional Provisions Regulations 2013.

Day appointed for commencement of the universal credit provisions in Part 1 of the Act

3.—(1) The day appointed for the coming into force of the provisions   3.244
of the Act listed in Schedule 2 to the No. 9 Order, in so far as they are not
already in force, in relation to the case of a claim referred to in paragraph
(2), and any award that is made in respect of the claim, is the day appointed
in accordance with paragraph (3).
(2) The claims referred to are—
(a) a claim for universal credit that is made or treated as made on or
   after 25th November 2013 in respect of a period that begins on or
   after 25th November 2013 by a person who, on the day on which the

claim is made or treated as made, resides in one of the No. 5 relevant districts; and

(b) a claim for universal credit that is made or treated as made on or after 25th November 2013 by a person in respect of a period that begins on or after 25th November 2013, where—

    (i) the person does not reside in one of the No. 5 relevant districts on the day on which the claim is made or treated as made;

    (ii) in connection with the claim, the person gives incorrect information regarding their residence in such a district; and

    (iii) after a decision is made that the person is entitled to universal credit and one or more payments have been made in respect of the person, the Secretary of State discovers that the person gave that incorrect information.

(3) The day appointed in relation to the case of a claim referred to in paragraph (2), and any award that is made in respect of the claim, is the first day of the period in respect of which the claim is made or treated as made.

(4) Article 3(5) of the No. 9 Order applies for the purposes of paragraph (2) as it applies for the purposes of article 3(3)(a) and (b) of the No. 9 Order.

(5) Article 3(6) of the No. 9 Order applies for the purposes of paragraph (3) as it applies for the purposes of article 3(4)(a) of the No. 9 Order.

DEFINITIONS

    "the Act"—art. 2(1).
    "the No.5 relevant districts"—*ibid.*
    "the No.9 Order"—*ibid.*

3.245 GENERAL NOTE

Para. (1)

3.246 This brings into force provisions relating to universal credit in Pt 1 of the WRA 2012, as set out in Sch.2 to the Commencement No.9 Order, in so far as they are not already in force, in relation to the two further categories of case set out in para.(2).

Para. (2) (a)

3.247 This covers the making of a claim for universal credit on or after November 25, 2013, in respect of a period that begins on or after that date, where a person lives in a "No.5 relevant district" at the time that the claim is made. The "No.5 relevant districts" are those postcodes in Rugby, Inverness and Perth set out in the Schedule. The other conditions for making a claim for universal credit, known as the "Pathfinder Group conditions", are set out in the Transitional Provisions Regulations 2013.

Para. (2) (b)

3.248 This relates to the making of a claim for universal credit on or after November 25, 2013 in respect of a period that also begins on or after that date but where the claimant provides incorrect information as to their residence in a No.5 relevant district, and this is only discovered once payments of universal credit have been made. Such a claim remains within the universal credit regime despite the error.

Para. (3)

3.249 The day appointed for the commencement of the universal credit provisions in the above cases is the first day of the period in respect of which the claim is made (or treated as made).

Para. (4)

3.250 Article 3(5) of the Commencement No.9 Order provides that the Claims and Payments Regulations 2013 apply for the purpose of deciding whether and when a claim for universal credit is made or is to be treated as made.

Para. (5)

Article 3(6) of the Commencement No.9 Order deals with the situation where there is an extension of time for making a claim.

3.251

Day appointed for the abolition of income-related employment and support allowance and income-based jobseeker's allowance

4.—(1) The day appointed for the coming into force of the amending provisions, in relation to the case of a claim referred to in paragraph (2), and any award that is made in respect of the claim, is the day appointed in accordance with paragraph (3).

3.252

(2) The claims referred to are—

(a) a claim for universal credit, an employment and support allowance or a jobseeker's allowance that is made or treated as made on or after 25th November 2013 in respect of a period that begins on or after 25th November 2013 by a person who, on the day on which the claim is made or treated as made, resides in one of the No. 5 relevant districts and falls within the Pathfinder Group; and

(b) a claim for universal credit that is made or treated as made by a person on or after 25th November 2013 in respect of a period that begins on or after 25th November 2013 where—

   (i) the person does not reside in one of the No. 5 relevant districts or does not fall within the Pathfinder Group on the day on which the claim is made or treated as made;

  (ii) in connection with the claim, the person gives incorrect information regarding their residence in such a district or their falling within the Pathfinder Group; and

 (iii) after a decision is made that the person is entitled to universal credit and one or more payments have been made in respect of the person, the Secretary of State discovers that the person gave that incorrect information.

(3) The day appointed in relation to the case of a claim referred to in paragraph (2), and any award that is made in respect of the claim, is the first day of the period in respect of which the claim is made or treated as made.

(4) Paragraphs (4) and (5) of article 4 of the No. 9 Order apply in relation to an award of universal credit that is made in respect of a claim for universal credit referred to in paragraph (2) as they apply in relation to an award of universal credit that is made in respect of a claim for universal credit referred to in article 4(2)(a) or (b) of the No. 9 Order.

(5) Paragraphs (1) and (2) of article 5 of the No. 9 Order apply for the purposes of paragraph (2)(a) as they apply for the purposes of article 4(2)(a) of the No. 9 Order.

(6) Article 5(3) of the No. 9 Order applies for the purposes of paragraph (2) as it applies for the purposes of article 4(2)(a) and (b) of the No. 9 Order.

(7) Article 5(4) of the No. 9 Order applies for the purposes of paragraph (3) as it applies for the purposes of article 4(3)(a) of the No. 9 Order.

DEFINITIONS

    "the amending provisions"—art.2(1).
    "employment and support allowance"—*ibid.*
    "jobseeker's allowance"—*ibid.*
    "the No.4 relevant districts"—*ibid.*

"the No.9 Order"—*ibid.*
"a person who . . . falls within the Pathfinder Group"—art.2(2).

GENERAL NOTE

Para. (1)

3.253   This brings into force provisions relating to the abolition of income-related employment and support allowance and of income-based jobseeker's allowance where the case falls within one of the two categories set out in para.(2) (see also the incorporation by reference of other provisions as made by paras (4)–(6) below).

Para. (2) (a)

3.254   This provides that the new provisions come into force in relation to a claim for (and any subsequent award of) universal credit, employment and support allowance or jobseeker's allowance, where a person makes such a claim on or after November 25, 2013 for a period that begins on or after that date and, at the time that the claim is made, the claimant both lives in a No.5 relevant district (see Schedule) and meets the Pathfinder Group conditions.

Para. (2) (b)

3.255   This provides that the new provisions come into force in relation to a claim for (and any subsequent award of) universal credit where a person claims universal credit, again on or after November 25, 2013 for a period that begins on or after that date, but provides incorrect information as to either their residence in a No.5 relevant district (see Schedule) or as to their meeting the Pathfinder Group conditions, but this is only discovered once payments of universal credit have been made. As with reg.3(2)(b), such a claim remains within the universal credit regime despite the error.

Para. (3)

3.256   The day appointed for the coming into force of the amending provisions in the above cases is the first day of the period in respect of which the claim is made or treated as made. See further the inclusion of late claims, where time has been extended, by virtue of para.(7) below.

Para. (4)

3.257   Article 4(4) and (5) of the Commencement No.9 Order extend the universal credit provisions to include certain claims and awards that follow on from the conversion process that applies to recipients of incapacity benefit and severe disablement allowance.

Para. (5)

3.258   Article 5(1) of the Commencement No.9 Order provides that the Claims and Payments Regulations 1987 determine whether and when a claim for employment and support allowance or jobseeker's allowance is made or is treated as made. Article 5(2) simply deems any reference in regs 5–12 of the Transitional Provisions Regulations 2013 to a claim for universal credit as including a claim to employment and support allowance or jobseeker's allowance as appropriate.

Para. (6)

3.259   Article 5(3) of the Commencement No.9 Order provides that the Claims and Payments Regulations 2013 apply for the purpose of deciding whether and when a claim for universal credit is made or is to be treated as made.

Para. (7)

3.260   Article 5(4) of the Commencement No.9 Order deals with the circumstances where there is an extension of time for making a claim.

Application of the No. 9 Order

5. Articles 6 and 9 to 22 of the No. 9 Order apply in connection with the   **3.261**
coming into force of the amending provisions in relation to the case of a
claim referred to in article 4(2), and any award made in respect of the claim,
as they apply in connection with the coming into force of the amending
provisions in relation to the case of a claim referred to in article 4(2)(a) and
(b) of the No. 9 Order and any award made in respect of the claim.

DEFINITION

"the amending provisions"—art.2(1).

GENERAL NOTE

This provision is in the same terms as art.5 of the Commencement No.11 Order.   **3.262**

Article 2(1)

SCHEDULE

THE NO. 5 RELEVANT DISTRICTS

1. CV21 1 to CV21 4.
2. CV21 9.
3. CV22 5 to CV22 7.
4. IV1 1.
5. IV1 3.
6. IV1 9.
7. IV2 3 to IV2 7.
8. IV3 5.
9. IV3 8.
10. IV4 7.
11. IV5 7.
12. IV8 8.
13. IV9 8.
14. IV10 8.
15. IV11 8.
16. IV12 4 and IV12 5.
17. IV12 9.
18. IV13 7.
19. IV21 2.
20. IV22 2.
21. IV26 2.
22. IV54 8.
23. IV63 6 and IV63 7.
24. PH19 1.
25. PH20 1.
26. PH21 1.
27. PH22 1.
28. PH23 3.
29. PH24 3.
30. PH25 3.
31. PH26 3.
32. PH26 9.
33. PH32 4.

PART V

UNIVERSAL CREDIT: CLAIMS & PAYMENTS AND DECISIONS & APPEALS

Universal Credit, Personal Independence Payment, Jobseeker's Allowance and Employment and Support Allowance (Claims and Payments) Regulations 2013

(SI 2013/380)

The Secretary of State, in exercise of the powers conferred upon him by the provisions set out in Schedule 1 to these Regulations, makes the following Regulations.

In accordance with section 172(1) of the Social Security Administration Act 1992, the Secretary of State has referred the proposals for these Regulations to the Social Security Advisory Committee.

The Secretary of State has consulted with organisations representing qualifying lenders likely to be affected by the fee specified in paragraph 9(2) of Schedule 5 to the Regulations (direct payment to lender of deductions in respect of interest on secured loans).

In accordance with section 176(2)(b) of the Social Security Administration Act 1992 and in so far as these Regulations relate to housing benefit, the Secretary of State has obtained the agreement of organisations appearing to him to be representative of the authorities concerned that proposals in respect of these Regulations should not be referred to them.

ARRANGEMENT OF REGULATIONS

PART I

General

PART II

CLAIMS

PART III

EVIDENCE, INFORMATION AND NOTIFICATION OF CHANGES OF CIRCUMSTANCES

PART IV

PAYMENTS

PART V

THIRD PARTIES

PART VI

MOBILITY COMPONENT OF PERSONAL INDEPENDENCE PAYMENT

General Note

4.2   An annotated version of these Regulations is included in Vol.III. However, the provisions relating to universal credit, new-style ESA and new-style JSA had not come into force by the cut-off date for that volume and so were omitted. The Regulations (as amended) are now reproduced in full below (except for Sch.3 which made consequential amendments to other legislation). The provisions which relate to universal credit are annotated in this volume. Those relating to new-style ESA and JSA will be annotated in the forthcoming Supplement to the main volumes. Readers are referred to Vol.III for commentary on the provisions which relate to personal independence payment or are of general application. These Regulations are in force from April 8, 2013 in relation to personal independence payment and April 29, 2013 in relation to universal credit, new-style ESA and new-style JSA.

Part I

General

Citation and commencement

4.3   **1.**—(1) These Regulations may be cited as the Universal Credit, Personal Independence Payment, Jobseeker's Allowance and Employment and Support Allowance (Claims and Payments) Regulations 2013.

(2) For the purpose of personal independence payment these Regulations come into force on 8th April 2013.

(3) For the purposes of universal credit, jobseeker's allowance and employment and support allowance these Regulations come into force on 29th April 2013.

Interpretation

4.4   **2.** In these Regulations—
"the 1991 Act" means the Child Support Act 1991;
"the 2012 Act" means the Welfare Reform Act 2012;
"the Administration Act" means the Social Security Administration Act 1992;
"the Contributions and Benefits Act" means the Social Security Contributions and Benefits Act 1992;
"the Jobseeker's Allowance Regulations" means the Jobseeker's Allowance Regulations 2013;
"the Personal Independence Payment Regulations" means the Social Security (Personal Independence Payment) Regulations 2013;
"the Universal Credit Regulations" means the Universal Credit Regulations 2013;
"appropriate office" means—
(a)   an office of the Department for Work and Pensions or any other place designated by the Secretary of State in relation to any case or class of case as a place to, or at which, any claim, notice, document,

evidence or other information may be sent, delivered or received for the purposes of these Regulations and includes a postal address specified by the Secretary of State for that purpose; or

(b) in the case of a person who is authorised or required by these Regulations to use an electronic communication for any purpose, an address to which such communications may be sent in accordance with Schedule 2;

"assessment period" has the meaning given by regulation 21 of the Universal Credit Regulations;

"attendance allowance" means an allowance payable by virtue of section 64 of the Contributions and Benefits Act;

"benefit", except in regulation 60 and Schedules 5 and 6, means universal credit, personal independence payment, a jobseeker's allowance or an employment and support allowance;

"child" has the meaning given by section 40 of the 2012 Act;

"claimant" in relation to—

(a) universal credit, has the meaning given by section 40 of the 2012 Act;

(b) personal independence payment, means any person who is a claimant for the purposes of regulations made under Part 4 (personal independence payment) of that Act;

(c) a jobseeker's allowance, has the meaning given by section 35(1) of the Jobseekers Act 1995; and

(d) an employment and support allowance, has the meaning given by section 24(1) of the Welfare Reform 2007 Act;

"couple" has the meaning given by section 39 of the 2012 Act;

"disability living allowance" means an allowance payable by virtue of section 71 of the Contributions and Benefits Act;

"earned income" has the meaning given by regulation 52 of the Universal Credit Regulations;

"electronic communication" has the meaning given by section 15(1) of the Electronic Communications Act 2000;

"employment and support allowance" means an allowance under Part 1 of the Welfare Reform Act 2007 as amended by the provisions of Schedule 3, and Part 1 of Schedule 14, to the 2012 Act that remove references to an income-related allowance;

"jobseeker's allowance" means an allowance under the Jobseekers Act 1995 as amended by the provisions of Part 1 of Schedule 14 to the 2012 Act that remove references to an income-based allowance;

"limited capability for work" has the meaning given by section 1(4) of the Welfare Reform Act 2007;

"local authority" has the meaning given by section 191 of the Administration Act;

"maternity allowance" means an allowance payable by virtue of section 35 of the Contributions and Benefits Act;

"official computer system" means a computer system maintained by or on behalf of the Secretary of State to—

(a) send or receive any claim or information; or

(b) process or store any claim or information;

"partner" means one of a couple;

"personal independence payment" means the allowance under Part 4 of the 2012 Act;

"qualifying young person" has the meaning given by regulation 5 of the Universal Credit Regulations;

"regular and substantial caring responsibilities for a severely disabled person" has the meaning given by regulation 30 of the Universal Credit Regulations;

"universal credit" means the benefit under Part 1 of the 2012 Act;

"writing" includes writing produced by means of electronic communications used in accordance with Schedule 2.

Use of electronic communications

4.5   **3.** Schedule 2 makes provision as to the use of electronic communications.

DEFINITION

"electronic communication"—see reg.2.

Consequential amendments

4.6   **4.** Schedule 3 makes amendments to other regulations which are consequential upon these Regulations.

Disapplication of section 1(1A) of the Administration Act

4.7   **5.** Section 1(1A) of the Administration Act (requirements in respect of a national insurance number) is not to apply to a child or a qualifying young person in respect of whom universal credit is claimed.

DEFINITIONS

"the Administration Act"—see reg.2.
"universal credit"—*ibid.*

PART II

CLAIMS

Claims not required for entitlement to universal credit in certain cases

4.8   **6.**—(1) It is not to be a condition of entitlement to universal credit that a claim be made for it where all the following conditions are met—

    (a) a decision is made as a result of the change of circumstances, whether as originally made or as revised, that the person ("former claimant") is not entitled to universal credit in a case where, but for the receipt of earned income, the former claimant would have continued to be entitled to an amount of universal credit;

    (b) at the date of notification to an appropriate office of the change of circumstances referred to in sub-paragraph (a), the former claimant was in receipt of earned income;

(c) not more than six months have elapsed since the last day of entitlement to universal credit;

(d) the former claimant provides such information as to their income at such times as the Secretary of State may require and the Secretary of State is satisfied that the former claimant has provided such information as may be required by the Secretary of State to determine whether an award may be made and if so, the amount;

(e) since the last day of entitlement to universal credit the former claimant's circumstances have changed such that, if the former claimant were entitled to universal credit, the amount payable would not be less than the minimum amount in regulation 17 of the Universal Credit Regulations.

(2) It is not to be a condition of entitlement to universal credit that a claim be made for it where all the following conditions are met—

(a) the former claimant made a claim for universal credit and a decision is made, whether as originally made or as revised, that the former claimant is not entitled to universal credit in a case where, but for the receipt of earned income, the former claimant would have been entitled to an amount of universal credit;

(b) at the time the decision referred to in sub-paragraph (a) was made, the former claimant was in receipt of earned income;

(c) not more than six months have elapsed since the date of that claim;

(d) the former claimant provides such information as to their income at such times as the Secretary of State may require and the Secretary of State is satisfied that the former claimant has provided such information as may be required by the Secretary of State to determine whether an award may be made and if so, the amount;

(e) the former claimant's circumstances have changed such that, if the former claimant were entitled to universal credit, the amount payable would not be less than the minimum amount in regulation 17 of the Universal Credit Regulations.

DEFINITIONS

"the Universal Credit Regulations"—see reg.2.
"claimant"—*ibid.*
"earned income"—see reg.2 and Universal Credit Regulations., reg.52.
"universal credit"—see reg.2.

GENERAL NOTE

SSAA 1992 s.1(1) provides that except in such cases as may be prescribed, **4.9** no person shall be entitled to any benefit unless, in addition to satisfying any other conditions of entitlement, he or she "makes a claim for it in the manner, and within the time, prescribed in relation to that benefit by regulations" under SSAA Pt 1. Regulation 6 is made under the power to prescribe exceptions in s.1(1) SSAA. In the circumstances set out in paras (1) and (2), entitlement to universal credit can arise (or, more accurately—because both paragraphs require the existence of a previous entitlement—revive) without a claim being made.

Claims not required for entitlement to an employment and support allowance in certain cases

4.10   **7.** It is not to be a condition of entitlement to an employment and support allowance that a claim be made for it where the following conditions are met—

(a) the claimant has made, and is pursuing, an appeal against a decision of the Secretary of State that embodies a determination that the claimant does not have limited capability for work; and

(b) the appeal relates to a decision to terminate or not to award an employment and support allowance for which a claim was made.

DEFINITIONS

"claimant"—see reg.2.
"employment and support allowance"—*ibid.*

Making a claim for universal credit

4.11   **8.**—(1) Except as provided in paragraph (2), a claim for universal credit must be made by means of an electronic communication in accordance with the provisions set out in Schedule 2 and completed in accordance with any instructions given by the Secretary of State for that purpose.

(2) A claim for universal credit may be made by telephone call to the telephone number specified by the Secretary of State if the claim falls within a class of case for which the Secretary of State accepts telephone claims or where, in any other case, the Secretary of State is willing to do so.

(3) A claim for universal credit made by means of an electronic communication in accordance with the provisions set out in Schedule 2 is defective if it is not completed in accordance with any instructions of the Secretary of State.

(4) A claim made by telephone in accordance with paragraph (2) is properly completed if the Secretary of State is provided during that call with all the information required to determine the claim and the claim is defective if not so completed.

(5) If a claim for universal credit is defective the Secretary of State must inform the claimant of the defect and of the relevant provisions of regulation 10 relating to the date of claim.

(6) The Secretary of State must treat the claim as properly made in the first instance if—

(a) in the case of a claim made by telephone, the person corrects the defect; or

(b) in the case of a claim made by means of an electronic communication, a claim completed in accordance with any instructions of the Secretary of State is received at an appropriate office,

within one month, or such longer period as the Secretary of State considers reasonable, from the date on which the claimant is first informed of the defect.

DEFINITIONS

"appropriate office"—see reg.2.
"claimant"—*ibid.*
"electronic communication"—*ibid.*
"universal credit"—*ibid.*

GENERAL NOTE

Regulation 8 and Sch.2 prescribe the manner in which a claim for universal credit must be made. The general rule (in accordance with the aspiration that universal credit is to be "digital by default") is that the claim must be made by "an electronic communication" in accordance with Sch.2. In brief, the claim must be made by completing and submitting an online claim form (para.(1)). However, a claim may instead be made by telephone if the Secretary of State is prepared to accept it in that form (para.(2)). An online claim that is not completed in accordance with the Secretary of State's instructions, or a telephone claim where the Secretary of State is not provided with all the information required to determine the claim during the phone call, is defective (paras (3) and (4)). On receipt of a defective claim, the Secretary of State must inform the claimant of the defect and of the relevant provisions of reg.10 (i.e., para.(2) of that regulation) (para.(5)). If the claimant then corrects the defect within a month (or longer if the Secretary of State considers it reasonable), then the claim is treated as having been properly made in the first place (para.(6)).

4.12

Claims for universal credit by members of a couple

9.—(1) Where a person is a member of a couple and may make a claim as a single person by virtue of regulation 3(3) (couples) of the Universal Credit Regulations, but instead makes a claim for universal credit jointly, that claim is to be treated as a claim made by that person as a single person.

4.13

(2) Where a claim for universal credit is made jointly by a member ("M1") of a polygamous marriage with another member of the polygamous marriage ("M2"), that claim is to be treated as a claim made by M1 as a single person where—

(a) M1 is not a party to an earlier marriage in the polygamous marriage, and

(b) any party to an earlier marriage is living in the same household as M1 and M2.

(3) In paragraph (2) "polygamous marriage" means a marriage during which a party to it is married to more than one person and which took place under the laws of a country which permits polygamy.

(4) The Secretary of State may treat a claim made by members of a couple as single persons as a claim made jointly by the couple where it is determined by the Secretary of State that they are a couple.

(5) Where the Secretary of State considers that one member of a couple is unable to make a joint claim with the other member of that couple, the other member of the couple may make a claim jointly for both of them.

(6) Where an award of universal credit to joint claimants is terminated because they cease to be a couple, it is not to be a condition of entitlement to universal credit that a claim be made for it by the member of the former couple who—

(a) does not notify the Secretary of State that they have ceased to be a couple, where the other former member of the couple has already so notified; or

(b) is the second of them to notify the Secretary of State that they have ceased to be a couple.

(7) Where awards of universal credit to two single claimants are terminated because they form a couple who are joint claimants, it is not to be a condition of entitlement to universal credit that the couple make a claim for it and universal credit may be awarded to them jointly.

(8) A couple who are joint claimants are to be treated as making a claim for universal credit where—

(a) one of them was entitled to universal credit as a single person and ceased to be so entitled on becoming a member of the couple; and

(b) the other member of the couple did not have an award of universal credit as a single person before formation of the couple

[¹ and the claim is to be treated as made on the day after the member of the couple mentioned in sub-paragraph (a) ceased to be entitled to universal credit.]

(9) In relation to an award which may be made by virtue of paragraph (6) or (7) without a claim being required, a claimant and every person by whom or on whose behalf, sums by way of universal credit are receivable must supply in such manner and at such times as the Secretary of State may determine such information or evidence as the Secretary of State may require in connection with the formation or dissolution of a couple.

(10) Where an award of universal credit to joint claimants is terminated because one of them has died it is not to be a condition of entitlement to universal credit that the surviving partner makes a claim for it.

DEFINITIONS

"couple"—see reg.2 and WRA 2012, s.39.
"universal credit"—see reg.2.

AMENDMENT

1. Social Security (Miscellaneous Amendments) (No.2) Regulations 2013 (SI 2013/1508) reg.6(1) and (2) (July 29, 2013).

GENERAL NOTE

4.14   See the commentary to reg.3 of the Universal Credit Regulations.

Date of claim for universal credit

4.15   **10.**—(1) Where a claim for universal credit is made, the date on which the claim is made is—

(a) subject to sub-paragraph (b), in the case of a claim made by means of an electronic communication in accordance with regulation 8(1), the date on which the claim is received at an appropriate office;

(b) in the case of a claim made by means of an electronic communication in accordance with regulation 8(1), where the claimant receives assistance at home or at an appropriate office from the Secretary of State, or a person providing services to the Secretary of State, which is provided for the purpose of enabling that person to make a claim, the date of first notification of a need for such assistance;

(c) subject to sub-paragraph (d), in the case of a claim made by telephone in accordance with regulation 8(2), the date on which that claim is properly completed in accordance with regulation 8(4); or

(d) where the Secretary of State is unable to accept a claim made by telephone in accordance with regulation 8(2) on the date of first notification of intention to make the claim, the date of first notification, provided a claim properly completed in accordance with regulation 8(4) is made within one month of that date, or the first day in respect of which the claim is made if later than the above.

(2) In the case of a claim which is defective by virtue of regulation 8, the date of claim is to be the first date on which the defective claim is received or made but is treated as properly made in the first instance in accordance with regulation 8(6).

DEFINITIONS

"appropriate office"—see reg.2.
"claimant"—*ibid.*
"electronic communication"—*ibid.*
"universal credit"—*ibid.*

GENERAL NOTE

Regulation 10 identifies the date on which a claim for universal credit is made. Online claims are made when received by the DWP (para.(1)(a)), unless the person received assistance to complete the form from an officer of the Department (or a contractor providing services to the Secretary of State) in which case the date of claim is the date on which the Secretary of State was told that assistance was needed (para.(1)(b)). A telephone claim is made on the day reg.8(4) is satisfied (i.e., when the Secretary of State is provided with all the information required to determine the claim) (para.(1)(c)). But if the Department cannot accept a telephone claim on the same day as the claimant first notifies it that it would like to make one, then the claim is made on that day as long as a properly completed telephone claim is made within a month of that day (para.(1)(d)).

4.16

Paragraph (2) applies where a defective claim is treated as properly made in the first instance under reg.8(6). Such a claim is made on the first date the defective claim was received.

Making a claim for personal independence payment

11.—(1) A claim for personal independence payment must be made—

4.17

(a) in writing on a form authorised by the Secretary of State for that purpose and completed in accordance with the instructions on the form;

(b) by telephone call to the telephone number specified by the Secretary of State; or

(c) by receipt by the claimant of a telephone call from the Secretary of State made for the purpose of enabling a claim for personal independence payment to be made,

unless in any case or class of case the Secretary of State decides only to accept a claim made in one of the ways specified in paragraph (a), (b) or (c).

(2) In the case of a claim made in writing the claim must be sent to or received at the appropriate office.

(3) A claim for personal independence payment made in writing is defective if it is not completed in accordance with any instructions of the Secretary of State.

(4) A claim made by telephone in accordance with paragraph (1) is properly completed if the Secretary of State is provided during that call with all the information required to determine the claim and the claim is defective if not so completed.

(5) If a claim for personal independence payment is defective the Secretary of State must inform the claimant of the defect and of the relevant provisions of regulation 12 relating to the date of claim.

(6) The Secretary of State must treat the claim as properly made in the first instance if a claim completed in accordance with any instructions of the Secretary of State is received within one month, or such longer period as the Secretary of State may consider reasonable, from the date on which the claimant is first informed of the defect.

(7) Paragraph (8) applies where—

(a) a person ("P1") makes a claim for personal independence payment on behalf of another person ("P2") whom P1 asserts to be a person unable for the time being to act; and

(b) the Secretary of State makes a decision not to appoint P1 under regulation 57.

(8) The Secretary of State must treat the claim made by P1 as properly made by P2 in the first instance if a further claim made by P2 is received within one month, or such longer period as the Secretary of State may consider reasonable, from the date the Secretary of State notified the decision not to appoint P1 under regulation 57.

DEFINITIONS

"claimant"—see reg.2.
"personal independence payment"—*ibid.*
"writing"—*ibid.*

Date of claim for personal independence payment

4.18

12.—(1) Subject to paragraph (4), where a claim for personal independence payment is made in accordance with regulation 11 the date on which the claim is made is—

(a) in the case of a claim in writing made by means of an electronic communication in accordance with the provisions set out in Schedule 2, the date on which the claim is received at the appropriate office;

(b) in the case of a claim made by telephone, the date on which a claim made by telephone is properly completed; or

(c) where a person first notifies an intention to make a claim and provided that a claim made in writing produced other than by means of an electronic communication is properly completed and received at the appropriate office designated by the Secretary of State in that claimant's case within one month or such longer period as the Secretary of State considers reasonable of the date of first notification, the date of first notification,

or the first day in respect of which the claim is made if later than the above.

(2) In the case of a claim which is defective by virtue of regulation 11(3) or (4)—

(a) subject to sub-paragraph (b) and paragraph (4), the date of claim is to be the first date on which the defective claim is received or made but is treated as properly made in the first instance in accordance with regulation 11(6);

(b) the date of claim is to be the date of first notification of an intention to make a claim where a claim made by a person to whom paragraph (1)(c) applies is defective but is treated as properly made in the first instance in accordance with regulation 11(6).

(3) In the case of a claim which is treated as properly made by the claimant in accordance with regulation 11(8), the date on which the claim is made is the date on which it was received in the first instance.

(4) Where a further claim made by a person ("P2") in the circumstances set out in regulation 11(8) is defective and that further claim is treated as properly made in the first instance in accordance with regulation 11(6), the date of claim is to be the date on which the claim made by the person ("P1") whom the Secretary of State decided not to appoint under regulation 57 was received in the first instance.

(5) In a case where the Secretary of State decides not to award personal independence payment following a claim for it being made on behalf of another expressly on the ground of terminal illness (which has the meaning given by section 82(4) of the 2012 Act), the date of claim is to be—

(a) the date that claim was made if a further claim, made in accordance with regulation 11, is received within one month, or such longer period as the Secretary of State may consider reasonable, from the date the Secretary of State notified the decision not to award personal independence payment on the ground of terminal illness; or

(b) the date that claim was made where the further claim is defective but is treated as properly made in the first instance in accordance with regulation 11(6).

DEFINITIONS

"appropriate office"—see reg.2.
"claimant"—*ibid.*
"electronic communication"—*ibid.*
"personal independence payment"—*ibid.*
"writing"—*ibid.*

Making a claim for an employment and support allowance by telephone

13.—(1) Except where the Secretary of State directs in any case or class of case that a claim must be made in writing, a claim for an employment and support allowance may be made by telephone call to the telephone number specified by the Secretary of State.

(2) Where the Secretary of State, in any particular case, directs that the person making the claim approves a written statement of the person's circumstances provided for the purpose by the Secretary of State, a telephone claim is not a valid claim unless the person complies with the direction.

(3) A claim made by telephone in accordance with paragraph (1) is properly completed if the Secretary of State is provided during that call with all the information required to determine the claim and the claim is defective if not so completed.

(4) Where a telephone claim is defective, the Secretary of State must advise the person making it of the defect and of the effect on the date of claim of the provisions of regulation 14.

(5) If the person corrects the defect so that the claim then satisfies the requirements of paragraph (3) and does so within one month, or such longer period as the Secretary of State considers reasonable, of the date the Secretary of State first drew attention to the defect, the Secretary of State must treat the claim as if it had been properly made in the first instance.

4.19

"employment and support allowance"—see reg.2.

Date of claim for an employment and support allowance where claim made by telephone

4.20   **14.** In the case of a telephone claim, the date on which the claim is made is to be the first date on which—

(a) a claim made by telephone is properly completed;

(b) a person first notifies the Secretary of State of an intention to make a claim, provided that a claim made by telephone is properly completed within one month or such longer period as the Secretary of State considers reasonable of first notification; or

(c) a defective claim is received but is treated as properly made in the first instance in accordance with regulation 13(5),

or the first day in respect of which the claim is made if later than the above.

Making a claim for an employment and support allowance in writing

4.21   **15.**—(1) A claim for an employment and support allowance may be made to the Secretary of State in writing on a form authorised by the Secretary of State for that purpose and must be completed in accordance with the instructions on the form.

(2) A written claim for an employment and support allowance, which is made on the form approved for the time being, is properly completed if completed in accordance with the instructions on the form and defective if not so completed.

(3) If a written claim is defective when first received, the Secretary of State must advise the person making it of the defect and of the effect on the date of claim of the provisions of regulation 16.

(4) If the person corrects the defect so that the claim then satisfies the requirements of paragraph (2) and does so within one month, or such longer period as the Secretary of State considers reasonable, of the date the Secretary of State first drew attention to the defect, the Secretary of State must treat the claim as if it had been properly made in the first instance.

DEFINITIONS

"employment and support allowance"—see reg.2.
"writing"—*ibid.*

Date of claim for an employment and support allowance where claim made in writing

4.22   **16.** In the case of a written claim for an employment and support allowance, the date on which the claim is made is to be the first date on which—

(a) a properly completed claim is received in an appropriate office;

(b) a person first notifies an intention to make a claim, provided that a properly completed claim form is received in an appropriate office within one month, or such longer period as the Secretary of State considers reasonable, of first notification; or

(c) a defective claim is received but is treated as properly made in the first instance in accordance with regulation 15(4), or the first day in respect of which the claim is made if later than the above.

DEFINITIONS

"appropriate office"—see reg.2.
"employment and support allowance"—*ibid.*

Claims for an employment and support allowance where no entitlement to statutory sick pay

17.—(1) Paragraph (2) applies to a claim for an employment and support   4.23
allowance for a period of limited capability for work in relation to which the
claimant gave the claimant's employer a notice of incapacity under regulation 7 of the Statutory Sick Pay (General) Regulations 1982 and for which
the claimant has been informed in writing by the employer that there is no
entitlement to statutory sick pay.

(2) A claim to which this paragraph applies is to be treated as made on
the date accepted by the claimant's employer as the first day of incapacity,
provided that the claimant makes the claim within the period of 3 months
beginning with the day on which the claimant is informed in writing by the
employer that the claimant was not entitled to statutory sick pay.

DEFINITIONS

"claimant"—see reg.2.
"employment and support allowance"—*ibid.*
"limited capability for work"—*ibid.*
"writing"—*ibid.*

Special provisions where it is certified that a woman is expected to be confined or where she has been confined

18. Where, in a certificate issued or having effect as issued under the   4.24
Social Security (Medical Evidence) Regulations 1976, it has been certified that it is to be expected that a woman will be confined and she makes
a claim for maternity allowance in expectation of that confinement, any
such claim may, unless the Secretary of State otherwise directs, be treated
as a claim for an employment and support allowance, made in respect of
any days in the period beginning with either—
(a) the beginning of the sixth week before the expected week of confinement; or
(b) the actual date of confinement,
whichever is the earlier, and ending in either case on the 14th day after
the actual date of confinement.

(2) Where, in a certificate issued under the Social Security (Medical
Evidence) Regulations 1976 it has been certified that a woman has been
confined and she claims maternity allowance within three months of the date
of her confinement, her claim may be treated in the alternative or in addition
as a claim for an employment and support allowance for the period beginning with the date of her confinement and ending 14 days after that date.

DEFINITIONS

"employment and support allowance"—see reg.2.
"maternity allowance"—*ibid.*

Making a claim for a jobseeker's allowance: attendance at an appropriate office

4.25 **19.** A person wishing to make a claim for a jobseeker's allowance, unless the Secretary of State otherwise directs, is required to attend for the purpose of making a claim for that allowance, in person at an appropriate office or such other place, and at such time, as the Secretary of State may specify in that person's case.

DEFINITIONS

"appropriate office"—see reg.2.
"jobseeker's allowance"—*ibid.*

Date of claim where a person claiming a jobseeker's allowance is required to attend at an appropriate office

4.26 **20.**—(1) Subject to regulation 29(6), where a person is required to attend in accordance with regulation 19, if the person subsequently attends for the purpose of making a claim for a jobseeker's allowance at the place and time specified by the Secretary of State and, if so requested, provides a properly completed claim form at or before the time when the person is required to attend, the claim is to be treated as made on whichever is the later of the date of first notification of intention to make that claim or the first day in respect of which the claim is made.

(2) Where a person who is required to attend in accordance with regulation 19 without good cause fails to attend at either the place or time specified in that person's case, or does not, if so requested, provide a properly completed claim form at or before the time when the person is required to attend, the claim is to be treated as made on the first day on which the person does attend at the specified place or time or does provide a properly completed claim form, or if later the first day in respect of which the claim is made.

(3) The Secretary of State may direct that the time for providing a properly completed claim form may be extended to a date no later than the date one month after the date of first notification of intention to make that claim.

DEFINITION

"jobseeker's allowance"—see reg.2.

Making a claim for a jobseeker's allowance in writing

4.27 **21.**—(1) Except where a person is required to attend in accordance with regulation 19, a claim for a jobseeker's allowance may be made in writing on a form authorised by the Secretary of State for that purpose and may be delivered or sent to the Secretary of State at an appropriate office.

(2) A claim made in accordance with paragraph (1) must be completed in accordance with the instructions on the form.

(3) A written claim for a jobseeker's allowance made under this regulation or regulation 20, which is made on the form approved for the time being, is properly completed if completed in accordance with the instructions on the form and defective if not so completed.

(4) If a written claim made under this regulation is defective when first received, the Secretary of State must advise the person making it of the

defect and of the effect on the date of claim of the provisions of regulation 22.

(5) If that person corrects the defect so that the claim then satisfies the requirements of paragraph (3) and does so within one month, or such longer period as the Secretary of State considers reasonable, from the date the Secretary of State first drew attention to the defect, the claim must be treated as having been properly made in the first instance.

DEFINITIONS

"appropriate office"—see reg.2.
"jobseeker's allowance"—*ibid.*
"writing"—*ibid.*

Date of claim for a jobseeker's allowance where claim made in writing

22. Subject to regulation 29(6), in the case of a written claim for a job-   4.28
seeker's allowance made under regulation 21, the date on which the claim is made or treated as made is to be the first date on which—

(a) a properly completed claim is received in an appropriate office;

(b) a person first notifies an intention to make a claim, provided that a properly completed claim form is received in an appropriate office within one month or such longer period as the Secretary of State considers reasonable of first notification; or

(c) a defective claim is received but is treated as properly made in the first instance in accordance with regulation 21(5),

or the first day in respect of which the claim is made if later than the above.

DEFINITIONS

"appropriate office"—see reg.2.
"jobseeker's allowance"—*ibid.*

Making a claim for a jobseeker's allowance by telephone

23.—(1) Except where a person is required to attend in accordance   4.29
with regulation 19, or where the Secretary of State in any case directs that the claim must be made in writing in accordance with regulation 21, a claim for a jobseeker's allowance may be made by telephone call to the telephone number specified by the Secretary of State where such a claim falls within a class of case for which the Secretary of State accepts telephone claims or in any other case where the Secretary of State is willing to do so.

(2) A claim made by telephone in accordance with paragraph (1) is properly completed if the Secretary of State is provided during that call with all the information required to determine the claim and the claim is defective if not so completed.

(3) Where a telephone claim is defective, the Secretary of State must advise the person making it of the defect and of the effect on the date of claim of the provisions of regulation 24.

(4) If the person corrects the defect so that the claim then satisfies the requirements of paragraph (2) and does so within one month, or such longer period as the Secretary of State considers reasonable, of the date the

Secretary of State first drew attention to the defect, the Secretary of State must treat the claim as if it had been properly made in the first instance.

DEFINITIONS

"jobseeker's allowance"—see reg.2.
"writing"—*ibid.*

Date of claim for a jobseeker's allowance where claim made by telephone

4.30   **24.** Subject to regulation 29(6), in the case of a telephone claim made under regulation 23, the date on which the claim is made or treated as made is to be the first date on which—

(a) a claim made by telephone is properly completed;

(b) a person first notifies an intention to make a claim, provided that a claim made by telephone is properly completed within one month or such longer period as the Secretary of State considers reasonable of first notification; or

(c) a defective claim is received but is treated as properly made in the first instance in accordance with regulation 23(4),

or the first day in respect of which the claim is made if later than the above.

Interchange with claims for other benefits

4.31   **25.**—(1) The Secretary of State may treat a claim for an employment and support allowance by a woman in addition or in the alternative as a claim for maternity allowance.

(2) The Secretary of State may treat a claim for a maternity allowance in addition or in the alternative as a claim for an employment and support allowance.

(3) Where it appears that a person who has made a claim for personal independence payment is not entitled to it but may be entitled to disability living allowance or attendance allowance, the Secretary of State may treat any such claim alternatively, or in addition, as a claim for either disability living allowance or attendance allowance as the case may be.

(4) Where it appears that a person who has made a claim for disability living allowance or attendance allowance is not entitled to it but may be entitled to personal independence payment, the Secretary of State may treat any such claim alternatively, or in addition, as a claim for personal independence payment.

(5) In determining whether the Secretary of State should treat a claim as made alternatively or in addition to another claim ("the original claim") under this regulation the Secretary of State must treat the alternative or additional claim, whenever made, as having been made at the same time as the original claim.

DEFINITIONS

"attendance allowance"—see reg.2.
"disability living allowance"—*ibid.*
"employment and support allowance"—*ibid.*
"maternity allowance"—*ibid.*
"personal independence payment"—*ibid.*

Time within which a claim for universal credit is to be made

26.—(1) Subject to the following provisions of this regulation, a claim for universal credit must be made on the first day of the period in respect of which the claim is made.

(2) Where the claim for universal credit is not made within the time specified in paragraph (1), the Secretary of State is to extend the time for claiming it, subject to a maximum extension of one month, to the date on which the claim is made, if—

(a) any one or more of the circumstances specified in paragraph (3) applies or has applied to the claimant; and

(b) as a result of that circumstance or those circumstances the claimant could not reasonably have been expected to make the claim earlier.

(3) The circumstances referred to in paragraph (2) are—

(a) the claimant was previously in receipt of a jobseeker's allowance or an employment and support allowance and notification of expiry of entitlement to that benefit was not sent to the claimant before the date that the claimant's entitlement expired;

(b) the claimant has a disability;

(c) the claimant has supplied the Secretary of State with medical evidence that satisfies the Secretary of State that the claimant had an illness that prevented the claimant from making a claim;

(d) the claimant was unable to make a claim in writing by means of an electronic communication used in accordance with Schedule 2 because the official computer system was inoperative;

(e) where an award of universal credit has been terminated in the circumstances specified in regulation 9(6) and the person who first notifies the Secretary of State makes a further claim to universal credit as a single person;

(f) where—

(i) the Secretary of State decides not to award universal credit to members of a couple jointly because one of the couple does not meet the basic condition in section 4(1)(e) of the 2012 Act;

(ii) they cease to be a couple; and

(iii) the person who did meet the basic condition in section 4(1)(e) makes a further claim as a single person;

(g) where—

(i) an award of universal credit to joint claimants has been terminated because one of the couple does not meet the basic condition in section 4(1)(e) of the 2012 Act;

(ii) they cease to be a couple; and

(iii) the person who did meet the basic condition in section 4(1)(e) makes a further claim as a single person.

(4) In the case of a claim for universal credit made by each of joint claimants, the prescribed time for claiming is not to be extended under paragraph (2) unless both claimants satisfy that paragraph.

DEFINITIONS

"the 2012 Act"—see reg.2.
"benefit"—*ibid.*
"claimant"—*ibid.*

"couple"—see reg.2 and WRA 2012, s.39.
"jobseeker's allowance"—see reg.2.
"universal credit"—*ibid.*

GENERAL NOTE

4.33   A claim for universal credit must normally be made on the first day for which the claimant wishes to receive it (para.(1)). However, under para.(2), the Secretary of State must extend that time limit by up to one month (but no more) if at least one circumstances in para.(3) applies, or has applied, to the claimant; and, as a result of that circumstance or those circumstances, the claimant could not reasonably have been expected to make the claim earlier. In the case of joint claimants, both must satisfy para.(2) before the time limit can be extended (para.(4)). See reg.21(5) and (6) of the Universal Credit Regulations for details of how the first assessment period is identified in cases where time has been extended and how the payment of universal credit for that period is calculated.

Time within which a claim for personal independence payment is to be made

4.34   **27.** A claim for personal independence payment must be made on the first day of the period in respect of which the claim is made.

DEFINITION

"personal independence payment"—see reg.2.

Time within which a claim for an employment and support allowance is to be made

4.35   **28.** A claim for an employment and support allowance must be made on the first day of the period in respect of which the claim is made or within the period of three months immediately following that day.

DEFINITION

"employment and support allowance"—see reg.2.

Time within which a claim for a jobseeker's allowance is to be made

4.36   **29.**—(1) Subject to paragraphs (2) and (4), a claim for a jobseeker's allowance must be made on the first day of the period in respect of which the claim is made.

(2) In a case where the claim is not made within the time specified in paragraph (1), the Secretary of State is to extend the time for claiming a jobseeker's allowance, subject to a maximum extension of three months, to the date on which the claim is made, where—

(a) any one or more of the circumstances specified in paragraph (3) applies or has applied to the claimant; and

(b) as a result of that circumstance or those circumstances the claimant could not reasonably have been expected to make the claim earlier.

(3) The circumstances referred to in paragraph (2) are—

(a) the claimant has difficulty communicating because—

(i) the claimant has learning, language or literacy difficulties; or

(ii) the claimant is deaf or blind,

and it was not reasonably practicable for the claimant to obtain assistance from another person to make the claim;

(b) the claimant was caring for a person who is ill or disabled and it was not reasonably practicable for the claimant to obtain assistance from another person to make the claim;

(c) the claimant was given information by an officer of the Department for Work and Pensions which led the claimant to believe that a claim for a jobseeker's allowance would not succeed;

(d) the claimant was given written advice by a solicitor or other professional adviser, a medical practitioner, a local authority or a person working in a Citizens Advice Bureau or a similar advice agency, which led the claimant to believe that a claim for a jobseeker's allowance would not succeed;

(e) the claimant was required to deal with a domestic emergency affecting the claimant and it was not reasonably practicable for the claimant to obtain assistance from another person to make the claim; or

(f) the claimant was prevented by adverse weather conditions from attending an appropriate office.

(4) In a case where the claim is not made within the time specified in paragraph (1), the prescribed time for claiming a jobseeker's allowance is to be extended, subject to a maximum extension of one month, to the date on which the claim is made, where—

(a) any one or more of the circumstances specified in paragraph (5) applies or has applied to the claimant; and

(b) as a result of that circumstance or those circumstances the claimant could not reasonably have been expected to make the claim earlier.

(5) The circumstances referred to in paragraph (4) are—

(a) the appropriate office where the claimant would be expected to make a claim was closed and alternative arrangements were not available;

(b) the claimant was unable to attend the appropriate office due to difficulties with the claimant's normal mode of transport and there was no reasonable alternative available;

(c) there were adverse postal conditions;

(d) the claimant was previously in receipt of an employment and support allowance and notification of expiry of entitlement to that benefit was not sent to the claimant before the date that the entitlement expired;

(e) the claimant had ceased to be a member of a couple within the period of one month before the claim was made;

(f) during the period of one month before the claim was made a close relative of the claimant had died and for this purpose "close relative" means partner, parent, son, daughter, brother or sister;

(g) the claimant was unable to make telephone contact with the appropriate office where the claimant would be expected to notify an intention of making a claim because the telephone lines to that office were busy or inoperative;

(h) the claimant was unable to make contact by means of an electronic communication used in accordance with Schedule 2 where the claimant would be expected to notify an intention of making a claim because the official computer system was inoperative.

(6) In a case where the time for claiming a jobseeker's allowance is extended under paragraph (2) or (4), the claim is to be treated as made on the first day of the period in respect of which the claim is, by reason of the operation of those paragraphs, timeously made.

DEFINITIONS

> "appropriate office"—see reg.2.
> "claimant"—*ibid.*
> "electronic communication"—*ibid.*
> "jobseeker's allowance"—*ibid.*
> "official computer system"—*ibid.*
> "partner"—*ibid.*

Amendment of claim

4.37   **30.**—(1) A person who has made a claim for benefit may amend it at any time before a determination has been made on the claim by notice in writing received at an appropriate office, by telephone call to a telephone number specified by the Secretary of State or in such other manner as the Secretary of State may decide or accept.

(2) Any claim amended in accordance with paragraph (1) may be treated as if it had been so amended in the first instance.

DEFINITIONS

> "benefit"—see reg.2.
> "writing"—*ibid.*

Withdrawal of claim

4.38   **31.**—(1) A person who has made a claim for benefit may withdraw it at any time before a determination has been made on it by notice in writing received at an appropriate office, by telephone call to a telephone number specified by the Secretary of State or in such other manner as the Secretary of State may decide or accept.

(2) Any notice of withdrawal given in accordance with paragraph (1) has effect when it is received.

DEFINITION

> "appropriate office"—see reg.2.

Advance claim for and award of universal credit

4.39   **32.**—(1) This regulation applies where—

(a) although a person does not satisfy the conditions of entitlement to universal credit on the date on which a claim is made, the Secretary of State is of the opinion that unless there is a change of circumstances that person will satisfy those conditions for a period beginning on a day not more than one month after the date on which the claim is made; and

(b) the case falls within a class for which Secretary of State accepts advance claims or is a case where Secretary of State is otherwise willing to do so.

(2) The Secretary of State is to treat the claim as if made on the first day of that period.

(3) The Secretary of State may award universal credit accordingly, subject to the requirement that the person satisfies the conditions for entitlement on the first day of that period.

DEFINITION

"universal credit"—see reg.2.

GENERAL NOTE

Regulation 32 permits claims for universal credit to be made up to one month in advance.

4.40

Advance claim for and award of personal independence payment

33.—(1) Where, although a person does not satisfy the requirements for entitlement to personal independence payment on the date on which the claim is made, the Secretary of State is of the opinion that unless there is a change of circumstances the person will satisfy those requirements for a period beginning on a day ("the relevant day") not more than 3 months after the date on which the decision on the claim is made, the Secretary of State may award personal independence payment from the relevant day subject to the condition that the person satisfies the requirements for entitlement on the relevant day.

4.41

(2) A person who has an award of personal independence payment may make a further claim for personal independence payment during the period of 6 months immediately before the existing award expires.

(3) Where a person makes a claim in accordance with paragraph (2) the Secretary of State may—

(a) treat the claim as if made on the first day after the expiry of the existing award; and

(b) award personal independence payment accordingly, subject to the condition that the person satisfies the requirements for entitlement on that first day after the expiry of the existing award.

DEFINITION

"personal independence payment"—see reg.2.

Advance claim for and award of an employment and support allowance or a jobseeker's allowance

34. Where, although a person does not satisfy the requirements of entitlement to an employment and support allowance or a jobseeker's allowance on the date on which a claim is made, the Secretary of State is of the opinion that unless there is a change of circumstances that claimant will satisfy those requirements for a period beginning on a day ("the relevant day") not more than three months after the date on which the claim is made, then the Secretary of State may—

4.42

(a) treat the claim as if made for a period beginning with the relevant day; and

(b) award an employment and support allowance or a jobseeker's allowance accordingly, subject to the condition that the person satisfies the requirements for entitlement when those benefits become payable under an award.

DEFINITIONS

"employment and support allowance"—see reg.2.
"jobseeker's allowance"—*ibid.*

Attendance in person

4.43   **35.** Except in a case where regulation 9 of the Personal Independence Payment Regulations applies, every person who makes a claim for benefit, other than a jobseeker's allowance, or any person entitled to benefit, other than a jobseeker's allowance, and any other person by whom, or on whose behalf, payments by way of such a benefit are receivable, must attend at such place and on such days and at such times as the Secretary of State may direct, for the purpose of supplying any information or evidence under regulations 37, 38, 39 and 41, if reasonably so required by the Secretary of State.

DEFINITIONS

"benefit"—see reg.2.
"jobseeker's allowance"—*ibid.*

Duration of awards

4.44   **36.**—(1) A claim for universal credit is to be treated as made for an indefinite period and any award of universal credit on that claim is to be made for an indefinite period.

(2) The provisions of Schedule 4 are to have effect in relation to claims for a jobseeker's allowance made during periods connected with public holidays.

GENERAL NOTE

4.45   Under para.(1), claims for universal credit are treated as made for an indefinite period and any award made is also for an indefinite period. However, this does not prevent the Secretary of State from revising the decision making the award, or from superseding that decision so as to change the award or bring it to an end if there is a subsequent change of circumstances. For revision and supersession of decisions about universal credit see ss.9 and 10 SSA 1998 and regs. 5–37 of the Decisions and Appeals Regulations 2013.

PART III

EVIDENCE, INFORMATION AND NOTIFICATION OF CHANGES OF
CIRCUMSTANCES

DEFINITION

"universal credit"—see reg.2.

Evidence and information in connection with a claim

4.46   **37.**—(1) Subject to regulation 8 of the Personal Independence Payment Regulations, paragraphs (2) and (3) apply to a person who makes a claim for benefit, other than a jobseeker's allowance, or on whose behalf a claim is made.

(2) The Secretary of State may require the person to supply information or evidence in connection with the claim, or any question arising out of it, as the Secretary of State considers appropriate.

(3) The person must supply the Secretary of State with the information or evidence in such manner as the Secretary of State determines within one month of first being required to do so or such longer period as the Secretary of State considers reasonable.

(4) Where joint claimants have made a claim for universal credit, information relating to that claim may be supplied by the Secretary of State to either or both members of the couple for any purpose connected with the claim.

(5) Where a person is a member of a couple and may make a claim as a single person by virtue of regulation 3(3) (couples) of the Universal Credit Regulations and entitlement to or the amount of any universal credit is or may be affected by the circumstances of their partner, the Secretary of State may require the partner to do any of the following, within one month of being required to do so or such longer period as the Secretary of State may consider reasonable—

(a) to confirm the information given about the partner's circumstances;

(b) to supply information or evidence in connection with the claim, or any question arising out of it, as the Secretary of State may require.

(6) The Secretary of State may require a landlord or a rent officer to supply information or evidence in connection with a claim for universal credit that may include in the calculation of an award an amount in respect of housing costs, and any information or evidence so requested must be supplied within one month of the request or such longer period as the Secretary of State considers reasonable.

(7) Every person providing relevant childcare as defined in regulation 35 of the Universal Credit Regulations, in a case where the calculation of a claimant's award of universal credit may include an amount in respect of childcare costs under regulation 31 of those Regulations, must supply such information or evidence in connection with the claim made by the claimant, or any question arising out of it, as may be required by the Secretary of State, and must do so within one month of being required to do so or such longer period as the Secretary of State may consider reasonable.

(8) In this regulation any reference to a person or joint claimants making a claim for a benefit, other than a jobseeker's allowance, is to be interpreted as including a person or joint claimants in a case where it is not a condition of entitlement to benefit that a claim be made for it.

(9) In this regulation any reference to a claim for a benefit, other than a jobseeker's allowance, is to be interpreted as including a potential award of benefit in a case where it is not a condition of entitlement to benefit that a claim be made for it.

DEFINITIONS

"the Personal Independence Payment Regulations"—see reg.2.
"the Universal Credit Regulations"—*ibid.*
"benefit"—*ibid.*
"claimant"—*ibid.*
"couple"—see reg.2 and WRA 2012, s.39.
"jobseeker's allowance"—see reg.2.
"partner"—*ibid.*
"personal independence payment"—*ibid.*
"universal credit"—see reg.2.

Evidence and information in connection with an award

38.—(1) This regulation, apart from paragraph (7), applies to any person entitled to benefit, other than a jobseeker's allowance, and any other person by whom, or on whose behalf, payments by way of such a benefit are receivable.

(2) Subject to regulation 8 of the Personal Independence Payment Regulations, a person to whom this regulation applies must supply in such manner as the Secretary of State may determine and within the period applicable under regulation 45(4)(a) of the Universal Credit, Personal Independence Payment, Jobseeker's Allowance and Employment and Support Allowance (Decisions and Appeals) Regulations 2013 such information or evidence as the Secretary of State may require for determining whether a decision on the award of benefit should be revised under section 9 of the Social Security Act 1998 or superseded under section 10 of that Act.

(3) A person to whom this regulation applies must supply in such manner and at such times as the Secretary of State may determine such information or evidence as the Secretary of State may require in connection with payment of the benefit awarded.

(4) A person to whom this regulation applies must notify the Secretary of State of any change of circumstances which the person might reasonably be expected to know might affect—

(a) the continuance of entitlement to benefit;

(b) the amount of benefit awarded; or

(c) the payment of benefit,

as soon as reasonably practicable after the change occurs.

(5) A notification of any change of circumstances under paragraph (4) must be given—

(a) in writing or by telephone (unless the Secretary of State determines in any case that notice must be given in a particular way or to accept notice given otherwise than in writing or by telephone); or

(b) in writing if in any class of case the Secretary of State requires written notice (unless the Secretary of State determines in any case to accept notice given otherwise than in writing),

and must be sent or delivered to, or received at, the appropriate office.

(6) Where universal credit has been awarded to joint claimants, information relating to that award may be supplied by the Secretary of State to either or both members of the couple for any purpose connected with that award.

(7) Every person providing relevant childcare as defined in regulation 35 of the Universal Credit Regulations, in a case where the claimant's award of universal credit includes an amount in respect of childcare costs under regulation 31 of those Regulations, must supply such information or evidence in connection with the award, or any question arising out of it, as the Secretary of State may require, and must do so within one month of being required to do so or such longer period as the Secretary of State may consider reasonable.

(8) Where the calculation of an award of universal credit includes, by virtue of regulation 29 of the Universal Credit Regulations, an amount in respect of the fact that a claimant has regular and substantial caring responsibilities for a severely disabled person, the Secretary of State may

require a person to whom this regulation applies to furnish a declaration signed by such severely disabled person confirming the particulars respecting the severely disabled person which have been given by that person.

DEFINITIONS

"the Universal Credit Regulations"—see reg. 2.
"benefit"—*ibid.*
"claimant"—*ibid.*
"jobseeker's allowance"—*ibid.*
"personal independence payment"—*ibid.*
"regular and substantial caring responsibilities for a severely disabled person"—*ibid.*
"universal credit"—*ibid.*
"writing"—*ibid.*

Alternative means of notifying changes of circumstances

39. In such cases and subject to such conditions as the Secretary of State   4.48
may specify, the duty in regulation 38(4) to notify a change of circumstances may be discharged by notifying the Secretary of State as soon as reasonably practicable—

(a) where the change of circumstances is a birth or death, through a local authority, or a county council in England, by personal attendance at an office specified by that authority or county council, provided the Secretary of State has agreed with that authority or county council for it to facilitate such notification; or

(b) where the change of circumstances is a death, by telephone to a telephone number specified for that purpose by the Secretary of State.

DEFINITION

"local authority"—see reg. 2.

Information to be provided to rent officers

40.—(1) The Secretary of State must provide to the rent officer such   4.49
information as the rent officer may reasonably require to carry out functions under section 122 of the Housing Act 1996.

(2) The information referred to in paragraph (1) may include information required to make a determination under the Rent Officers Order and may include—

(a) the name and address of a universal credit claimant in respect of whom the Secretary of State has applied for a determination;

(b) the amount of any rent (within the meaning of paragraph 2 of Schedule 1 to the Universal Credit Regulations) (meaning of payments in respect of accommodation);

(c) the amount of any service charge payments (within the meaning of paragraph 2 of Schedule 1 to the Universal Credit Regulations);

(d) the number of bedrooms in the accommodation in respect of which a determination is made;

(e) the name and address of a claimant's landlord.

(3) A landlord must provide to the rent officer such information or evidence as the rent officer may reasonably require to make a determination in

accordance with the Rent Officers Order and which the rent officer is not able to obtain from the Secretary of State.

(4) The evidence referred to in paragraph (3) may include evidence as to whether a property is let at an Affordable Rent within the meaning in Schedule 2 to the Rent Officers Order.

(5) In this regulation and regulation 37 "landlord" means any person to whom a claimant or partner is liable to make payments in respect of the occupation of the claimant's accommodation.

(6) In this regulation "the Rent Officers Order" means the Rent Officer (Universal Credit Functions) Order 2013.

DEFINITIONS

"the Universal Credit Regulations"—see reg.2.
"claimant"—*ibid.*
"universal credit"—*ibid.*

Evidence and information required from pension fund holders

4.50

41.—(1) Where a claimant or the claimant's partner is aged not less than 60 and is a member of, or a person deriving entitlement to a pension under a personal pension scheme or an occupational pension scheme, such a person must, where the Secretary of State so requires, furnish the following information—

(a) the name and address of the pension fund holder;

(b) such other information including any reference or policy number as is needed to enable the personal pension scheme or occupational pension scheme to be identified.

(2) Where the pension fund holder receives from the Secretary of State a request for details concerning the personal pension scheme or occupational pension scheme relating to a person to whom paragraph (1) refers, the pension fund holder must provide the Secretary of State with any information to which the following paragraph refers.

(3) The information to which this paragraph refers is—

(a) where the purchase of an annuity under a personal pension scheme or occupational pension scheme has been deferred, the amount of any income which is being withdrawn from the personal pension scheme or occupational pension scheme;

(b) in the case of—

(i) a personal pension scheme or occupational pension scheme where income withdrawal is available, the maximum amount of income which may be withdrawn from the scheme; or

(ii) a personal pension scheme or occupational pension scheme where income withdrawal is not available, the maximum amount of income which might be withdrawn from the fund if the fund were held under a personal pension scheme or occupational pension scheme where income withdrawal was available,

calculated by or on behalf of the pension fund holder by means of tables prepared from time to time by the Government Actuary which are appropriate for this purpose.

(4) In this regulation any reference to a claimant is to be interpreted as including a person in a case where it is not a condition of entitlement to benefit that a claim be made for it.

(5) This regulation does not apply to a person claiming personal independence payment.

(6) In this regulation—

(a) "pension fund holder" means with respect to a personal pension scheme or an occupational pension scheme, the trustees, managers or scheme administrators of the scheme concerned;

(b) "personal pension scheme" means—

    (i) a personal pension scheme as defined by section 1 of the Pension Schemes Act 1993;

    (ii) an annuity contract or trust scheme approved under section 620 or 621 of the Income and Corporation Taxes Act 1988 or a substituted contract within the meaning of section 622(3) of that Act which is treated as having become a registered pension scheme by virtue of paragraph 1(1)(f) of Schedule 36 to the Finance Act 2004;

    (iii) a personal pension scheme approved under Chapter 4 of Part 14 of the Income and Corporation Taxes Act 1988 which is treated as having become a registered pension scheme by virtue of paragraph 1(1)(g) of Schedule 36 to the Finance Act 2004;

(c) "occupational pension" means any pension or other periodical payment under an occupational pension scheme but does not include any discretionary payment out of a fund established for relieving hardship in particular cases.

DEFINITIONS

"claimant"—see reg.2.
"partner"—*ibid.*

Notification for purposes of sections 111A and 112 of the Administration Act

42. Regulations 43 to 44 below prescribe the person to whom, and manner in which, a change of circumstances must be notified for the purposes of sections 111A(1A) to (1G) and 112(1A) to (1F) of the Administration Act (offences relating to failure to notify a change of circumstances).   4.51

DEFINITION

"the Administration Act"—see reg.2.

Notification of changes of circumstances affecting a jobseeker's allowance or an employment and support allowance for purposes of sections 111A and 112 of the Administration Act

43.—(1) Subject to paragraphs (2) and (3), where the benefit affected by the change of circumstances is a jobseeker's allowance or an employment and support allowance, notice must be given to the Secretary of State at the appropriate office—   4.52

(a) in writing or by telephone (unless the Secretary of State determines in any case that notice must be in writing or may be given otherwise than in writing or by telephone); or

(b) in writing if in any class of case the Secretary of State requires written notice (unless the Secretary of State determines in any case to accept notice given otherwise than in writing).

(2) Where the notice in writing referred to in paragraph (1) is given or sent by an electronic communication that notice must be given or sent in accordance with the provisions set out in Schedule 2 to these Regulations (electronic communications).

(3) In such cases and subject to such conditions as the Secretary of State may specify, the duty in regulation 38(4) of these Regulations or regulation 31(4) of the Jobseeker's Allowance Regulations to notify a change of circumstances may be discharged by notifying the Secretary of State as soon as reasonably practicable—

(a) where the change of circumstances is a birth or death, through a local authority, or a county council in England, by personal attendance at an office specified by that authority or county council, provided the Secretary of State has agreed with that authority or county council for it to facilitate such notification; or

(b) where the change of circumstances is a death, by telephone to a telephone number specified for that purpose by the Secretary of State.

DEFINITIONS

"the Jobseeker's Allowance Regulations"—see reg.2.
"appropriate office"—*ibid.*
"benefit"—*ibid.*
"electronic communication"—*ibid.*
"employment and support allowance"—*ibid.*
"jobseeker's allowance"—*ibid.*
"writing"—*ibid.*

Notification of changes of circumstances affecting personal independence payment or universal credit for purposes of sections 111A and 112 of the Administration Act

4.53   **44.**—(1) Subject to paragraphs (2) and (3), where the benefit affected by the change of circumstances is personal independence payment or universal credit, notice must be given to the Secretary of State ("S") at the appropriate office—

(a) in writing or by telephone (unless S determines in any case that notice must be in writing or may be given otherwise than in writing or by telephone); or

(b) in writing if in any class of case S requires written notice (unless S determines in any case to accept notice given otherwise than in writing).

(2) Where the notice in writing referred to in paragraph (1) is given or sent by an electronic communication that notice must be given or sent in accordance with the provisions set out in Schedule 2 to these Regulations (electronic communications).

(3) In such cases and subject to such conditions as the Secretary of State may specify, the duty in regulation 38(4) to notify a change of circumstances may be discharged by notifying the Secretary of State as soon as reasonably practicable—

(a) where the change of circumstances is a birth or death, through a local authority, or a county council in England, by personal attendance at an office specified by that authority or county council, provided the Secretary of State has agreed with that authority or county council for it to facilitate such notification; or

(b) where the change of circumstances is a death, by telephone to a telephone number specified for that purpose by the Secretary of State.

DEFINITIONS

"the Administration Act"—see reg.2.
"electronic communication"—*ibid.*
"local authority"—*ibid.*
"personal independence payment"—*ibid.*
"universal credit"—*ibid.*
"writing"—*ibid.*

GENERAL NOTE

SSAA ss.111A(1A) to (1F) and 112(1A) to (1D) create various offences where   4.54
a person "fails to give a prompt notification of [a change of circumstances] in the
prescribed manner to the prescribed person". The main difference between the two
sections is that offences under s.111A require proof of dishonesty whereas those
under s.112 do not. Regulation 44 provides that the "prescribed person" to whom
notice must be given is the Secretary of State and that the "prescribed manner" of
giving notice is as set out in paras (1)–(3). The general rule (para.(1)) is that notice
may be given by telephone or in writing unless the Secretary of State requires notice
to be given in writing. That is subject to the special rules about reporting births and
deaths in para.(3). Written notices that are "given or sent by an electronic communication" (i.e., by email and, when the technology permits, online) must satisfy the
rules in Sch.2 (para.(2)).

PART IV

PAYMENTS

Time of payment: general provision

45. Subject to the other provisions of this Part, benefit is to be paid in   4.55
accordance with an award as soon as is reasonably practicable after the
award has been made.

DEFINITION

"benefit"—see reg.2.

Direct credit transfer

46.—(1) The Secretary of State may arrange for benefit to be paid by way   4.56
of direct credit transfer into a bank or other account—
(a) in the name of the person entitled to benefit, the person's partner, a
person appointed under regulation 57(1) or a person referred to in
regulation 57(2);
(b) in the joint names of the person entitled to benefit and the person's
partner;
(c) in the joint names of the person entitled to benefit and a person
appointed under regulation 57(1) or a person referred to in regulation 57(2); or
(d) in the name of such persons as are mentioned in regulation 57(2).

(2) A Jobseeker's Allowance or an Employment and Support Allowance are to be paid in accordance with paragraph (1) within seven days of the last day of each successive period of entitlement.

DEFINITIONS

"benefit"—see reg.2.
"partner"—*ibid.*

Payment of universal credit

4.57

47.—(1) Universal credit is payable monthly in arrears in respect of each assessment period unless in any case or class of case the Secretary of State arranges otherwise.

(2) Where universal credit is to be paid in accordance with regulation 46, it is to be paid within seven days of the last day of the assessment period but if it is not possible to pay universal credit within that period of seven days, it is to be paid as soon as reasonably practicable thereafter.

(3) In respect of an award of universal credit which is the subject of an arrangement for payment under regulation 46, the Secretary of State may make a particular payment by credit transfer otherwise than is provided by paragraph (2), if it appears to the Secretary of State appropriate to do so for the purpose of—

(a) paying any arrears of benefit; or

(b) making a payment in respect of a terminal period of an award or for any similar purpose.

(4) Where the Secretary of State has arranged for universal credit to be paid in accordance with regulation 46, joint claimants may nominate a bank or other account into which that benefit is to be paid.

(5) Where joint claimants of universal credit have not nominated a bank or other account into which that benefit is to be paid, the Secretary of State may nominate a bank or other account.

(6) The Secretary of State may, in any case where the Secretary of State considers it is in the interests of—

(a) the claimants;

(b) a child or a qualifying young person for whom one or both of the claimants are responsible; or

(c) a severely disabled person, where the calculation of an award of universal credit includes, by virtue of regulation 29 of the Universal Credit Regulations, an amount in respect of the fact that a claimant has regular and substantial caring responsibilities for that severely disabled person,

arrange that universal credit payable in respect of joint claimants be paid wholly to only one member of the couple or be split between the couple in such proportion as the Secretary of State considers appropriate.

(7) Where a superseding decision takes effect in accordance with paragraph 26 of Schedule 1 to the Universal Credit, Personal Independence Payment, Jobseeker's Allowance and Employment and Support Allowance (Decisions and Appeals) Regulations 2013, the amount payable in respect of that last assessment period is to be calculated as follows—

$$N \times \frac{(A \times 12)}{(365)}$$

where N is the number of days in the period and A is the amount calculated in relation to that period as if it were an assessment period of one month.

DEFINITIONS

"assessment period"—see reg.2 and Universal Credit Regs, reg.21.
"benefit"—see reg.2.
"child"—see reg.2 and WRA 2012 s.40.
"couple"—see reg.2 and WRA 2012, s.39.
"employment and support allowance"—see reg.2.
"jobseeker's allowance"—*ibid.*
"qualifying young person"—*ibid.*
"regular and substantial caring responsibilities for a severely disabled person"—*ibid.*
"universal credit"—*ibid.*

GENERAL NOTE

Regulation 47 contains important rules about the payment of universal credit.   **4.58**

Para. (1)
Universal credit is normally paid monthly in arrears after the end of the relevant assessment period. This is in contrast to the rules for income support, income-based JSA and income-related ESA. The change in policy is linked to the provisions under which earned income for each assessment period is taken to be the amount reported to HMRC by the claimant's (or claimants') employers. Monthly payment in arrears after the end of the assessment period is intended to ensure that no payment is made until after changes in circumstances relating to earned income have been reported and that overpayments will be reduced.

Paras (2) to (5)
These apply where universal credit is paid by direct transfer under reg.46 which will be the usual method of payment. They are largely administrative. However, the rule in para.(2) that payment by direct transfer must be paid within seven days of the last day of the assessment period or as soon as reasonably practicable thereafter will be important to claimants.

Para. (6)
Allows the Secretary of State pay universal credit to one of two joint claimants or to split that payment between them in the circumstances specified. See also reg.58(1).

Para. (7)
Changes of circumstance relating to universal credit normally take effect from the first day of the assessment period in which they occur. However, Sch.1, para.26 of the Decisions and Appeals Regulations 2013 provides that where a claimant reaches the qualifying age for state pension credit during an assessment period and has made an advance claim for SPC, the change in circumstances takes effect when it occurs. In those circumstances, it is necessary to make a payment which covers less than a full assessment period and para.(7) specifies how that payment is to be calculated. The rule is the same as that which applies under reg.21(6) of the Universal Credit Regulations where a payment has to be made covering less than a full assessment period because the time limit for claiming has been extended and entitlement therefore begins before the date of claim.

Payment of personal independence payment

48.—(1) Subject to the following provisions of this regulation and regulation 50, personal independence payment is to be paid at intervals of four weeks in arrears.   **4.59**

(2) In the case of any person to whom section 82 of the 2012 Act (terminal illness) applies, the Secretary of State may arrange that personal independence payment is to be paid at intervals of one week in advance.

(3) Where the amount of personal independence payment payable is less than £5.00 a week the Secretary of State may arrange that it is to be paid in arrears at such intervals as may be specified not exceeding 12 months.

DEFINITION

"personal independence payment"—see reg.2.

Days for payment of personal independence payment

4.60   **49.**—(1) Subject to the following provisions of this regulation, a personal independence payment is payable on the day of the week on which the Secretary of State makes a decision to award that benefit, except that where that decision is made on a Saturday or a Sunday the benefit is to be paid on such day of the week as the Secretary of State may direct in any case.

(2) The Secretary of State may, in any case or class of case, arrange that personal independence payment or any part of it be paid on any day of the week.

(3) Where personal independence payment is in payment to any person and the day on which it is payable is changed, it is to be paid at a daily rate of 1/7th of the weekly rate in respect of any of the days for which payment would have been made but for that change.

(4) Where there is a change in the amount of any personal independence payment payable, or where entitlement to personal independence payment ends, and these events do not occur on the day of the week referred to in paragraph (1) or (2), personal independence payment is to be paid at a daily rate of 1/7th of the weekly rate.

DEFINITIONS

"benefit"—see reg.2.
"personal independence payment"—*ibid.*

Payment of personal independence payment at a daily rate between periods in hospital or other accommodation

4.61   **50.**—(1) Personal independence payment is to be paid in respect of any person, for any day falling within a period to which paragraph (2) applies, at the daily rate (which is to be equal to 1/7th of the weekly rate) and personal independence payment payable in pursuance of this regulation is to be paid weekly or as the Secretary of State may direct in any case.

(2) This paragraph applies to any period which is not a period of residence—

(a) but which commences immediately following such a period; and

(b) on the first day of which it is expected that, before the expiry of the term of 28 days beginning with that day, the person will commence another period of residence.

(3) Where paragraph (2) applies, the period referred to in that paragraph is to end—

(a) at the expiry of the term of 28 days beginning with the first day of the period referred to in that paragraph; or

(b) if earlier, on the day before the day which is the first day of a period of residence.

(4) In this regulation a "period of residence" means a period of residence where—

(a) the person is a resident of a care home, as defined in section 85(3) of the 2012 Act, and no amount of personal independence payment which is attributable to the daily living component is payable in respect of the person by virtue of regulation 28(1) of the Personal Independence Payment Regulations; or

(b) the person is undergoing medical or other treatment as an in-patient at a hospital or similar institution and no amount of personal independence payment which is attributable to the daily living component or the mobility component is payable in respect of the person by virtue of regulation 29 of the Personal Independence Payment Regulations,

and such period is to be deemed to begin on the day after the day on which the person enters the care home, hospital or similar institution and to end on the day before the day on which the person leaves the care home, hospital or similar institution.

DEFINITIONS

"the 2012 Act"—see reg.2.
"the Personal Independence Payment Regulations"—*ibid.*
"personal independence payment"—*ibid.*

Payment of an employment and support allowance

51.—(1) Subject to paragraphs (3) to (8), an employment and support allowance paid in accordance with regulation 46 is to be paid fortnightly in arrears on the day of the week determined in accordance with paragraph (2).   **4.62**

(2) The day specified for the purposes of paragraph (1) is the day in column (2) which corresponds to the series of numbers in column (1) which includes the last two digits of the claimant's national insurance number—

(1)	(2)
00 to 19	Monday
20 to 39	Tuesday
40 to 59	Wednesday
60 to 79	Thursday
80 to 99	Friday

(3) The Secretary of State may, in any case or class of case, arrange that the claimant be paid otherwise than fortnightly.

(4) In respect of an award of an employment and support allowance which is the subject of an arrangement for payment under regulation 46, the Secretary of State may make a particular payment by credit transfer otherwise than as provided by paragraph (1), if it appears to the Secretary of State appropriate to do so for the purpose of—

(a) paying any arrears of benefit; or

(b) making a payment in respect of a terminal period of an award or for any similar purpose.

(5) The Secretary of State may, in any case or class of case, arrange that an employment and support allowance be paid on any day of the week and where it is in payment to any person and the day on which it is payable is changed, it is to be paid at a daily rate of 1/7th of the weekly rate in respect of any of the days for which payment would have been made but for that change.

(6) Where the weekly amount of an employment and support allowance is less than £1.00 it may be paid in arrears at intervals of not more than 13 weeks.

(7) Where the weekly amount of an employment and support allowance is less than 10 pence that allowance is not payable.

(8) Where an employment and support allowance is normally payable in arrears and the day on which that benefit is payable by reason of paragraph (2) is affected by office closure, it may for that benefit week be paid wholly in advance or partly in advance and partly in arrears and on such day as the Secretary of State may direct.

(9) Where under paragraph (8) an employment and support allowance is paid either in advance or partly in advance and partly in arrears it is for any other purposes to be treated as if it were paid in arrears.

(10) For the purposes of paragraph (8), "benefit week" means a period of seven days beginning or ending with such day as the Secretary of State may direct.

(11) For the purposes of paragraph (8), "office closure" means a period during which an appropriate office is closed in connection with a public holiday.

(12) For the purposes of paragraph (11), "public holiday" means—

(a) in England and Wales, Christmas Day, Good Friday or a bank holiday under the Banking and Financial Dealings Act 1971;

(b) in Scotland, a bank holiday under the Banking and Financial Dealings Act 1971 or a local holiday.

DEFINITIONS

"appropriate office"—see reg.2.
"benefit"—*ibid.*
"claimant"—*ibid.*
"employment and support allowance"—*ibid.*

Payment of a jobseeker's allowance

4.63   **52.**—(1) Subject to paragraphs (2) to (4), a jobseeker's allowance paid in accordance with regulation 46 is to be paid fortnightly in arrears unless in any case or class of case the Secretary of State arranges otherwise.

(2) In respect of an award of a jobseeker's allowance which is the subject of an arrangement for payment under regulation 46, the Secretary of State may make a particular payment by credit transfer otherwise than as provided by paragraph (1), if it appears to the Secretary of State appropriate to do so for the purpose of—

(a) paying any arrears of benefit; or

(b) making a payment in respect of a terminal period of an award or for any similar purpose.

(3) Where the amount of a jobseeker's allowance is less than £1.00 a week the Secretary of State may direct that it is to be paid at such intervals, not exceeding 13 weeks, as may be specified in the direction.

(4) Where a jobseeker's allowance is normally payable in arrears and the day on which that benefit is normally payable is affected by office closure, it may for that benefit week be paid wholly in advance or partly in advance and partly in arrears and on such day as the Secretary of State may direct.

(5) Where under paragraph (4) a jobseeker's allowance is paid either in advance or partly in advance and partly in arrears it is for any other purposes to be treated as if it were paid in arrears.

(6) For the purposes of paragraph (4), "benefit week" means a period of seven days ending with a day determined in accordance with the definition of that term in regulation 2(2) (general interpretation) of the Jobseeker's Allowance Regulations.

(7) For the purposes of paragraph (4), "office closure" means a period during which an appropriate office is closed in connection with a public holiday.

(8) For the purposes of paragraph (7), "public holiday" means—
(a) in England and Wales, Christmas Day, Good Friday or a bank holiday under the Banking and Financial Dealings Act 1971;
(b) in Scotland, a bank holiday under the Banking and Financial Dealings Act 1971 or a local holiday.

DEFINITIONS

"benefit"—see reg.2.
"jobseeker's allowance"—*ibid.*

Fractional amounts of benefit

53. Where the amount of any benefit payable would, but for this regula-   **4.64** tion, include a fraction of a penny, that fraction is to be disregarded if it is less than half a penny and is otherwise to be treated as a penny.

DEFINITION

"benefit"—see reg.2.

Payment to persons under age 18

54. Where a benefit is paid to a person under the age of 18, a direct credit   **4.65** transfer under regulation 46 into any such person's account, or the receipt by the person of a payment made by some other means, is sufficient discharge for the Secretary of State.

Extinguishment of right to payment if payment is not obtained within the prescribed period

55.—(1) The right to payment of any sum by way of benefit is to be extin-   **4.66** guished where payment of that sum is not obtained within the period of 12 months from the date on which the right is treated as having arisen.

(2) For the purposes of this regulation, the right to payment of any sum by way of benefit is to be treated as having arisen—
(a) where notice is given or sent that the sum contained in the notice is

ready for collection, on the date of the notice or, if more than one
such notice is given or sent, the date of the first such notice;

(b) in relation to any such sum which the Secretary of State has arranged
to be paid by means of direct credit transfer in accordance with regulation 46 into a bank or other account, on the due date for payment
of the sum or in the case of universal credit on the date of payment
of the sum; or

(c) in relation to any such sum to which neither sub-paragraph (a) or (b)
applies, on such date as the Secretary of State determines.

(3) The giving or sending of a notice under paragraph (2)(a) is effective
for the purposes of that paragraph, even where the sum contained in that
notice is more or less than the sum which the person concerned has the
right to receive.

(4) Where a question arises whether the right to payment of any sum by
way of benefit has been extinguished by the operation of this regulation and
the Secretary of State is satisfied that—

(a) the Secretary of State first received written notice requesting
payment of that sum after the expiration of 12 months from the date
on which the right is treated as having arisen;

(b) from a day within that period of 12 months and continuing until the
day the written notice was given, there was good cause for not giving
the notice; and

(c) no payment has been made under the provisions of regulation 46
(direct credit transfer),

the period of 12 months is extended to the date on which the Secretary
of State decides that question, and this regulation is to apply accordingly as
though the right to payment had arisen on that date.

(5) This regulation applies to a person appointed under regulation 57(1)
to act on behalf of a claimant or a person referred to in regulation 57(2) as
it applies to a claimant.

DEFINITIONS

"benefit"—see reg.2.
"claimant"—*ibid.*

Payments on death

4.67   **56.**—(1) On the death of a person who has made a claim for benefit, the
Secretary of State may appoint such person as the Secretary of State thinks
fit to proceed with the claim and any related issue of revision, supersession
or appeal under the Social Security Act 1998.

(2) Subject to paragraphs (6) and (7), any sum payable by way of benefit
which is payable under an award on a claim proceeded with under paragraph (1) may be paid or distributed by the Secretary of State to or amongst
persons over the age of 16 claiming as personal representatives, legatees,
next of kin or creditors of the deceased and the provisions of regulation 55
(extinguishment of right to payment if payment is not obtained within the
prescribed period) are to apply to any such payment or distribution.

(3) Subject to paragraphs (2), (6) and (7), any sum payable by way of
benefit to the deceased, payment of which the deceased had not obtained
at the date of the deceased's death, may, unless the right to payment was
already extinguished at that date, be paid or distributed to or amongst any

persons mentioned in paragraph (2), and regulation 55 is to apply to any such payment or distribution, except that, for the purpose of that regulation, the period of 12 months is to be calculated from the date on which the right to payment of any sum is treated as having arisen in relation to any such person and not from the date on which that right is treated as having arisen in relation to the deceased.

(4) A direct credit transfer under regulation 46 into an account in the name of any person mentioned in paragraph (2), or the receipt by such a person of a payment made by some other means, is sufficient discharge for the Secretary of State for any sum so paid.

(5) Where the Secretary of State is satisfied that any sum payable by way of benefit under paragraph (2) or (3), or part of it, is needed for the well-being of any person under the age of 16, the Secretary of State may obtain sufficient discharge for it by paying the sum or part of it to a person over that age who satisfies the Secretary of State that that person will apply the sum so paid for the well-being of the person under the age of 16.

(6) Paragraphs (2) and (3) are not to apply in any case unless written application for the payment of any sum is made to the Secretary of State within 12 months from the date of the deceased's death or within such longer period as the Secretary of State may allow in any case.

(7) The Secretary of State may dispense with strict proof of the title of any person claiming in accordance with the provisions of this regulation.

(8) In paragraph (2) "next of kin" means—

(a) in England and Wales, the persons who would take beneficially on an intestacy;

(b) in Scotland, the persons entitled to the moveable estate of the deceased on intestacy.

DEFINITION

"benefit"—see reg.2.

PART V

THIRD PARTIES

Persons unable to act

57.—(1) Where a person ("P1") is, or may be, entitled to benefit (whether or not a claim for benefit has been made by P1 or on P1's behalf) but P1 is unable for the time being to act, the Secretary of State may, if all the conditions in paragraph (2) and the additional conditions in paragraph (3) are met, appoint a person ("P2") to carry out the functions set out in paragraph (4).

4.68

(2) The conditions are that—

(a) no deputy has been appointed by the Court of Protection under Part 1 of the Mental Capacity Act 2005;

(b) no receiver has been appointed under Part 7 of the Mental Health Act 1983 who is treated as a deputy by virtue of the Mental Capacity Act 2005 with power to claim or receive benefit on P1's behalf;

(c) no attorney with a general power, or a power to claim or receive benefit, has been appointed by P1 under the Powers of Attorney Act 1971, the Enduring Powers of Attorney Act 1985, the Mental Capacity Act 2005 or otherwise; and

(d) in Scotland, P1's estate is not being administered by a judicial factor or any guardian acting or appointed under the Adults with Incapacity (Scotland) Act 2000 who has power to claim or receive benefit on P1's behalf.

(3) The additional conditions are that—

(a) P2 has made a written application to the Secretary of State to be appointed; and

(b) if P2 is a natural person, P2 is over the age of 18.

(4) The functions are exercising on behalf of P1 any right to which P1 may be entitled and receiving and dealing on behalf of P1 with any sums payable to P1.

(5) Anything required by these Regulations to be done by or in relation to P1 may be done by or in relation to P2 or any person mentioned in paragraph (2).

(6) Where a person has been appointed under regulation 82(3) of the Housing Benefit Regulations 2006 by a relevant authority within the meaning of those Regulations to act on behalf of another in relation to a benefit claim or award, the Secretary of State may, if the person so appointed agrees, treat that person as if the Secretary of State had appointed that person under paragraph (1).

(7) A direct credit transfer under regulation 46 into the account of P2 or any person mentioned in paragraph (2), or the receipt by such a person of a payment made by some other means, is sufficient discharge for the Secretary of State for any sum paid.

(8) An appointment under paragraph (1) or (6) comes to an end if—

(a) the Secretary of State at any time revokes it;

(b) P2 resigns P2's office having given one month's notice in writing to the Secretary of State of an intention to do so; or

(c) the Secretary of State is notified that any condition in paragraph (2) is no longer met.

DEFINITION

"benefit"—see reg.2.

Payment to another person on the claimant's behalf

4.69   **58.**—(1) The Secretary of State may direct that universal credit be paid wholly or in part to another person on the claimant's behalf if this appears to the Secretary of State necessary to protect the interests of—

(a) the claimant;

(b) their partner;

(c) a child or qualifying young person for whom the claimant or their partner or both are responsible; or

(d) a severely disabled person, where the calculation of the award of universal credit includes, by virtue of regulation 29 of the Universal Credit Regulations, an amount in respect of the fact that the claimant has regular and substantial caring responsibilities for that severely disabled person.

(2) The Secretary of State may direct that personal independence payment be paid wholly to another person on the claimant's behalf if this appears to the Secretary of State necessary to protect the interests of the claimant.

DEFINITIONS

"the Universal Credit Regulations"—see reg. 2.
"claimant"—*ibid.*
"partner"—*ibid.*
"regular and substantial caring responsibilities for a severely disabled person"—*ibid.*
"universal credit"—*ibid.*

GENERAL NOTE

Para. (1)
Universal credit may be paid to third parties in the specified circumstances. 4.70

Direct payment to lender of deductions in respect of interest on secured loans

59. Schedule 5 has effect where section 15A(1) of the Administration Act (payment out of benefit of sums in respect of mortgage interest etc.) applies in relation to a case where a claimant is entitled to universal credit. 4.71

GENERAL NOTE

Where an award of universal credit includes the housing costs element based on loan interest payments, that part of the award will normally be paid directly to the lender under the provisions of Sch.5. 4.72

Deductions which may be made from benefit and paid to third parties

60. Except as provided for in regulation 59 and Schedule 5, deductions may be made from benefit and direct payments may be made to third parties on behalf of a claimant in accordance with the provisions of Schedule 6 and Schedule 7. 4.73

DEFINITIONS

"benefit"—see reg. 2.
"claimant"—*ibid.*
"personal independence payment"—*ibid.*

GENERAL NOTE

Regulation 60 gives effect to Schs 6 and 7. Under Sch.6, the Secretary of State may make deductions from certain benefits (including universal credit) and pay them to third parties where the claimant is in arrears of mortgage payments, rent or service charge, charges for fuel, water charges, or the payments due under certain loans. It also allows deductions to be made in respect of payments in lieu of child support due under s.43 Child Support Act 1991 and reg.28 Child Support (Maintenance Assessments and Special Cases) Regulations 1992, and to recover integration loans made to refugees. 4.74

Under Sch.7, deductions from universal credit may be made to enforce payment of child support maintenance due under the Child Support Act 1991. Deductions under that schedule are then paid to the person with care of the qualifying child.

PART VI

MOBILITY COMPONENT OF PERSONAL INDEPENDENCE PAYMENT

Cases where mobility component of personal independence payment not payable

4.75   **61.**—(1) Subject to the following provisions of this regulation, personal independence payment by virtue of entitlement to the mobility component is not payable to any person who would otherwise be entitled to it during any period in respect of which that person has received, or is receiving, any payment—

(a) by way of grant under section 5 of, and paragraph 10 of Schedule 1 to, the National Health Service Act 2006, section 5 of, and paragraph 10 of Schedule 1 to, the National Health Service (Wales) Act 2006 or section 46 of the National Health Service (Scotland) Act 1978 towards the costs of running a private car;

(b) of mobility supplement under—

(i) the Naval, Military and Air Forces etc., (Disablement and Death) Service Pensions Order 2006;

(ii) the Personal Injuries (Civilians) Scheme 1983; or

(iii) the Order referred to in paragraph (i) by virtue of the War Pensions (Naval Auxiliary Personnel) Scheme 1964, the Pensions (Polish Forces) Scheme 1964, the War Pensions (Mercantile Marine) Scheme 1964 or an Order of Her Majesty in relation to the Home Guard dated 21st or 22nd December 1964 or in relation to the Ulster Defence Regiment dated 4th January 1971; or

(c) out of public funds which the Secretary of State is satisfied is analogous to a payment under sub-paragraph (a) or (b).

(2) Paragraph (3) applies where a person in respect of whom personal independence payment is claimed for any period has received any such payment as is referred to in paragraph (1) for a period which, in whole or in part, covers the period for which personal independence payment is claimed.

(3) Such payment referred to in paragraph (1) is to be treated as an aggregate of equal weekly amounts in respect of each week in the period for which it is made and, where in respect of any such week a person is treated as having a weekly amount so calculated which is less than the weekly rate of mobility component of personal independence payment to which, apart from paragraph (1), they would be entitled, any personal independence payment to which that person may be entitled for that week is to be payable at a weekly rate reduced by the weekly amount so calculated.

Payment of personal independence payment on behalf of a claimant (Motability)

62.—(1) This regulation applies where—

(a) personal independence payment is payable in respect of a claimant by virtue of entitlement to the mobility component at the enhanced rate; and

(b) under arrangements made or negotiated by Motability, an agreement has been entered into by or on behalf of the claimant for the hire or hire-purchase of a vehicle.

(2) Where this regulation applies, the Secretary of State may arrange that any personal independence payment by virtue of entitlement to the mobility component at the enhanced rate be paid in whole or in part on behalf of the claimant in settlement of liability for payments due under the agreement mentioned in paragraph (1).

(3) Subject to regulations 63 and 64, in the case of the hire of a vehicle, an arrangement made by the Secretary of State under paragraph (2) terminates—

(a) where the vehicle is returned to the owner at or before the expiration of the term of hire or any agreed extension of the term of hire, on expiry of the period of the term or extended term;

(b) where the vehicle is retained by or on behalf of the claimant with the owner's consent after the expiration of the term of hire or any agreed extension of the term of hire, on expiry of the period of the term or extended term; or

(c) where the vehicle is retained by or on behalf of the claimant otherwise than with the owner's consent after the expiration of the term of hire or any agreed extension of the term of hire, or its earlier termination, on expiry of whichever is the longer of the following periods—

  (i) the period ending with the return of the vehicle to the owner; or

  (ii) the period of the term of hire or any agreed extension of the term of hire.

(4) Subject to regulations 63 and 64 in the case of a hire-purchase agreement, an arrangement made by the Secretary of State under paragraph (2) terminates—

(a) on the purchase of the vehicle; or

(b) where the vehicle is returned to, or is repossessed by, the owner under the terms of the agreement before the completion of the purchase, at the end of the original period of the agreement.

(5) In this regulation "Motability" means the company, set up under that name as a charity and originally incorporated under the Companies Act 1985 and subsequently incorporated by Royal Charter.

Power for the Secretary of State to terminate an arrangement (Motability) 63. The Secretary of State may terminate an arrangement under regulation 62(2) on such date as the Secretary of State decides—

(a) if requested to do so by the owner of the vehicle to which the arrangement relates; or

(b) if it appears to the Secretary of State that the arrangement is causing undue hardship to the claimant and that it should be terminated earlier than provided for by regulation 62(3) or (4).

Restriction on duration of arrangements by the Secretary of State (Motability) 64. The Secretary of State must terminate an arrangement under regulation 62(2) where the Secretary of State is satisfied that—

(a) the vehicle to which the arrangement relates has been returned to the owner; and

(b) the expenses of the owner arising out of the hire or hire-purchase agreement have been recovered following the return of the vehicle.

Definitions

"claimant"—see reg.2.
"personal independence payment"—*ibid.*

Preamble

Schedule 1

Powers Exercised in Making these Regulations

1. The following provisions of the Administration Act—
 (a) section 1(1), (1C);
 (b) section 5(1)(a), (b), (c), (d), (g), (i), (j), (k), (l), (m), (p), (q), (1A), (2A), (2B), (2C), (3B);
 (c) section 7A(2)(b);
 (d) section 15A(2);
 (e) section 111A(1A)(d), (1B)(d), (1D)(c), (1E)(c);
 (f) section 112(1A)(d), (1B)(d), (1C)(c), (1D)(c);
 (g) section 189(1) and (5) to (6);
 (h) section 191.
2. Paragraph 7A of Schedule 2 to the Abolition of Domestic Rates etc. (Scotland) Act 1987.
3. Paragraph 6 of Schedule 4 to the Local Government Finance Act 1988.
4. Section 24(2)(b), (c) and (d) and section 30 of the Criminal Justice Act 1991.
5. Section 43(2) of the 1991 Act.
6. Paragraphs 1 and 6(2)(b) of Schedule 4 and paragraph 6 of Schedule 8 to, the Local Government Finance Act 1992.
7. Sections 32 and 92 of, and paragraph 3(1)(a), (b), (2)(a), (b) and (c) of Schedule 1 to the 2012 Act.

Definitions

"the Administration Act"—see reg.2.
"electronic communication"—*ibid.*

Regulation 3

Schedule 2

Electronic Communications

Part I

Use of Electronic Communications

Use of electronic communications by the Secretary of State
4.76   **1.** The Secretary of State may use an electronic communication in connection with claims for, and awards of, any benefit.

Conditions for the use of electronic communications by other persons
4.77   **2.**—(1) A person other than the Secretary of State may use an electronic communication in connection with the matters referred to in paragraph 1 if the conditions specified in sub-paragraphs (2) to (5) are satisfied.
 (2) The first condition is that the person is for the time being permitted to use an electronic communication for the purpose in question by an authorisation given by means of a direction of the Secretary of State.
 (3) The second condition is that the person uses an approved method of—
  (a) authenticating the identity of the sender of the communication where required to do so;
  (b) electronic communication;

(c) authenticating any claim or information delivered by means of an electronic communication; and

(d) subject to sub-paragraph (6), submitting any claim or information to the Secretary of State.

(4) The third condition is that any claim or information sent by means of an electronic communication is in an approved form.

(5) The fourth condition is that the person maintains such records as may be specified in a direction given by the Secretary of State.

(6) Where the person uses any method other than the method approved by the Secretary of State of submitting any claim or information, it is to be treated as not having been submitted.

(7) In this paragraph "approved" means approved by means of a direction given by the Secretary of State for the purposes of this Schedule.

Use of intermediaries

3. The Secretary of State may use intermediaries in connection with—   4.78

(a) the delivery of any claim or information by means of an electronic communication; and

(b) the authentication or security of anything transmitted by such means,

and may require other persons to use intermediaries in connection with those matters.

PART II

EVIDENTIAL PROVISIONS

Effect of delivering information by electronic communications

4.—(1) Any claim or information which is delivered by means of an electronic communica-   4.79
tion is to be treated as having been delivered in the manner or form required by any provision
of these Regulations on the day on which the conditions imposed—

(a) by this Schedule; and

(b) by or under an applicable enactment (except to the extent that the condition thereby imposed is incompatible with this Schedule), are satisfied.

(2) The Secretary of State may, by a direction, determine that any claim or information is to be treated as delivered on a different day (whether earlier or later) from the day specified in sub-paragraph (1).

(3) Any claim or information is not to be taken to have been delivered to an official computer system by means of an electronic communication unless it is accepted by the system to which it is delivered.

Proof of delivery

5.—(1) The use of an approved method of electronic communication is to be presumed,   4.80
unless the contrary is proved, to have resulted in delivery—

(a) in the case of any claim or information falling to be delivered to the Secretary of State, if the delivery of that claim or information is recorded on an official computer system; or

(b) in the case of any information that falls to be delivered by the Secretary of State, if the despatch of that information is recorded on an official computer system.

(2) The use of an approved method of electronic communication is to be presumed, unless the contrary is proved, not to have resulted in delivery—

(a) in the case of any claim or information falling to be delivered to the Secretary of State, if the delivery of that claim or information is not recorded on an official computer system; or

(b) in the case of information that falls to be delivered by the Secretary of State, if the despatch of that information is not recorded on an official computer system.

(3) The time and date of receipt of any claim or information sent by an approved method of electronic communication is to be presumed, unless the contrary is proved, to be that recorded on an official computer system.

Proof of identity

6.—(1) The identity of—   4.81

(a) the sender of any claim or information delivered by means of an electronic communication to an official computer system; or

(b) the recipient of any claim or information delivered by means of an electronic communication from an official computer system, is to be presumed, unless the contrary is proved, to be the person whose name is recorded as such on that official computer system.

(2) Any claim or information delivered by an approved method of electronic communication on behalf of another person ("P") is to be deemed to have been delivered by P unless P proves that it was delivered without P's knowledge or connivance.

Proof of content

4.82   **7.** The content of any claim or information sent by means of an electronic communication is to be presumed, unless the contrary is proved, to be that recorded on an official computer system.

DEFINITIONS

"electronic communication"—see reg.2.
"official computer system"—*ibid*.

Regulation 36(2)

SCHEDULE 4

SPECIAL PROVISIONS RELATING TO CLAIMS FOR A JOBSEEKER'S ALLOWANCE
DURING PERIODS CONNECTED WITH PUBLIC HOLIDAYS

1. In this Schedule and regulation 36(2)—
  (a) "public holiday" means—
      (i)   in England and Wales, Christmas Day, Good Friday or a bank holiday under the Banking and Financial Dealings Act 1971,
      (ii) in Scotland, a bank holiday under the Banking and Financial Dealings Act 1971 or a local holiday;
  (b) "Christmas and New Year holidays" means—
      (i)   in England and Wales, the period beginning at the start of Christmas Day and terminating at the end of New Year's Day, or if New Year's Day is a Sunday at the end of 2nd January,
      (ii) in Scotland, the period beginning at the start of Christmas Day and terminating at the end of 2nd January, or where New Year's Day is a Saturday or a Sunday terminating at the end of 3rd January;
  (c) "Easter Holidays" means the period beginning at the start of Good Friday and terminating at the end of Easter Monday;
  (d) "office closure" means a period during which an appropriate office is closed in connection with a public holiday.
2. Where a claim for a jobseeker's allowance is made during any period set out in paragraph 3, the Secretary of State may treat that claim as a claim for a period, to be specified in a decision of the Secretary of State, not exceeding—
  (a) 35 days after the date of the claim where the claim is made during the period specified in sub-paragraph (a) of paragraph 3; or
  (b) 21 days after the date of claim where the claim is made during the period specified in either sub-paragraph (b) or (c) of paragraph 3.
3. For the purposes of paragraph 2 the periods are—
  (a) in the case of Christmas and New Year holidays, a period beginning with the start of the 35th day before the first day of office closure and terminating at the end of the last day of office closure;
  (b) in the case of Easter Holidays, a period beginning with the start of the 16th day before the first day of office closure and terminating at the end of the last day of office closure;
  (c) in the case of any other public holiday, a period beginning with the start of the 14th day before the first day of office closure and terminating at the end of the last day of office closure.

DEFINITIONS

"appropriate office"—see reg.2.
"jobseeker's allowance"—*ibid*.

SCHEDULE 5

DIRECT PAYMENT TO LENDER OF DEDUCTIONS IN RESPECT OF INTEREST ON
SECURED LOANS

Interpretation

    1.—(1) In this Schedule—   **4.83**

"housing costs element" means an amount in respect of housing costs which is included in a claimant's award of universal credit under section 11(1) of the 2012 Act;

"qualifying lender" means (subject to paragraph 10)—

    (a) the bodies or persons listed in paragraphs (a) to (g) of section 15A(3) of the Administration Act;

    (b) the Regulator of Social Housing;

    (c) the Greater London Authority; and

    (d) any body incorporated under the Companies Act 1985, the main objects of which include the making of loans secured by—

        (i) a mortgage of or charge over land, or

        (ii) in Scotland a heritable security;

"loan interest payments" has the meaning given by paragraph 5 of Schedule 1 to the Universal Credit Regulations;

"relevant claimant" has the meaning given in paragraph 2(1);

"specified benefits", in relation to a relevant claimant, means the benefits specified in paragraph 2(2)—

    (a) to which the relevant claimant is entitled; or

    (b) where the relevant claimant is a member of a couple, to which the other member of the couple is entitled;

"standard rate" means the standard rate of interest determined under paragraph 12 of Schedule 5 to the Universal Credit Regulations.

    (2) References in this Schedule to a relevant claimant who meets the payment condition or the liability condition are to a claimant who meets those conditions in accordance with regulation 25 of the Universal Credit Regulations (the housing costs element).

Relevant claimants and benefits from which payments are to be made

    2.—(1) For the purposes of this Schedule, "relevant claimant" means a claimant—   **4.84**

    (a) who is entitled to universal credit;

    (b) whose maximum amount for the purposes of universal credit includes the housing costs element; and

    (c) whose amount of housing costs element is calculated by reference to loan interest payments (whether or not that amount is calculated by reference to any other description of payment).

    (2) Direct payments of loan interest may be made under paragraph 3 from any of the following benefits—

    (a) universal credit; and

    (b) if the maximum amount to which the relevant claimant is entitled for the purposes of universal credit is insufficient for the purposes of this Schedule—

        (i) a jobseeker's allowance, or

        (ii) an employment and support allowance.

Circumstances in which direct payments of loan interest to be made

    3.—(1) If the circumstances set out in sub-paragraph (2) apply to a relevant claimant in   **4.85**
respect of a loan, the Secretary of State is to pay part of the specified benefits directly to the qualifying lender to whom the loan interest payments in respect of the loan are payable.

    (2) The circumstances are that—

    (a) a loan was made in respect of which loan interest payments are payable to a qualifying lender;

    (b) the relevant claimant (or either joint claimant) meets the payment condition and liability condition in respect of loan interest payments on the loan;

    (c) those payments are taken into account in calculating the amount of housing costs element to be included in the relevant claimant's award of universal credit; and

    (d) the amount included in respect of those payments is calculated by reference to the standard rate.

(3) The part of the specified benefits which is to be paid under sub-paragraph (1) is the amount calculated under paragraphs 4 and 5 in respect of the relevant claimant.

Determining the amount to be paid to a qualifying lender

4.86   **4.**—(1) Where the circumstances set out in paragraph 3(2) apply to a relevant claimant in respect of one loan only, the amount that is to be paid under paragraph 3 directly to the qualifying lender is to be calculated as follows.

Step 1

Find the amount in respect of the loan interest payments which is calculated under paragraph 10 of Schedule 5 to the Universal Credit Regulations (amount in respect of interest on loans).

Step 2

Deduct from the amount resulting from step 1 a sum equivalent to so much of any amount payable in the circumstances described in sub-paragraph (2) as represents payments in respect of loan interest.

(2) This sub-paragraph applies where a payment is being made under a policy of insurance taken out by a relevant claimant to insure against the risk of not being able to maintain repayments of loan interest to a qualifying lender.

(3) The amount to be paid directly to the qualifying lender in respect of the relevant claimant is—

    (a) the amount resulting from sub-paragraph (1); or

    (b) where the aggregate amount of all of the specified benefits is less than the amount resulting from sub-paragraph (1), the aggregate amount of all those benefits less one penny.

Determining the amount to be paid to a qualifying lender: more than one loan

4.87   **5.**—(1) Where the circumstances set out in paragraph 3(2) apply to a relevant claimant in respect of more than one loan, the amount that is to be paid under paragraph 3 directly to each of the qualifying lenders to whom loan interest payments are payable is to be calculated as follows.

(2) Where loan interest payments on two or more loans are payable to the same qualifying lender, the amount to be paid directly to that lender is found by—

    (a) in respect of each of those loans, calculating an amount in accordance with Steps 1 and 2 of paragraph 4(1); and

    (b) adding those amounts together.

(3) Where loan interest payments are payable to more than one qualifying lender, the amount to be paid directly to each lender is found by—

    (a) where loan interest payments are payable to a qualifying lender in respect of one loan only, calculating an amount in accordance with Steps 1 and 2 of paragraph 4(1) in respect of the loan;

    (b) where loan interest payments are payable to a qualifying lender in respect of more than one loan, calculating an amount in accordance with sub-paragraph (2).

(4) The amount to be paid directly to the qualifying lender in respect of the relevant claimant is—

    (a) the amount resulting from sub-paragraph (2) or (3) in respect of that lender; or

    (b) where the aggregate amount of all of the specified benefits is less than the sum of the amounts resulting from sub-paragraph (2) or (3), the amount determined under sub-paragraph (5).

(5) For the purposes of sub-paragraph (4)(b)—

    (a) the overall total of the amounts to be paid directly to the qualifying lenders is the aggregate amount of all of the specified benefits less one penny; and

    (b) that amount is to be paid directly to qualifying lenders as follows—

        (i) the qualifying lender in whose case the amount resulting from sub-paragraph (2) or (3) is the largest is to be paid first,

        (ii) if anything remains, the qualifying lender in whose case the amount resulting from sub-paragraph (2) or (3) is next largest is to be paid next, and so on until nothing remains.

(6) In the application of sub-paragraph (5)(b) in any case where the amount resulting from sub-paragraph (2) or (3) is the same in respect of two or more qualifying lenders, the available amount is to be divided equally between them.

Qualifying lenders to apply direct payments in discharge of borrower's liability

6. Where a direct payment is made under paragraph 3 to a qualifying lender in respect **4.88**
of a relevant claimant, the lender must apply the amount of the payment towards discharging the liability to make loan interest payments in respect of which the direct payment was made.

Application by qualifying lenders of any amount which exceeds liability

7.—(1) This paragraph applies where, in respect of a relevant claimant— **4.89**
  (a) any direct payment is made under paragraph 3 to a qualifying lender; and
  (b) the amount paid exceeds the amount of the loan interest payments payable.
(2) Unless sub-paragraph (3) applies, the qualifying lender must apply the amount of the excess as follows—
  (a) first, towards discharging the amount of any liability of the relevant claimant for arrears of loan interest payments in respect of the loan in question; and
  (b) if any amount of the excess is then remaining, towards discharging any liability of the relevant claimant to repay—
      (i) the principal sum in respect of the loan, or
      (ii) any other sum payable by the relevant claimant to that lender in respect of the loan.
(3) Where loan interest payments on two or more loans are payable to the same qualifying lender, the lender must apply the amount of the excess as follows—
  (a) first, towards discharging the amount of any liability of the relevant claimant for arrears of loan interest payments in respect of the loan in respect of which the excess amount was paid; and
  (b) if any amount of the excess is then remaining, towards discharging any liability of the relevant claimant to repay—
      (i) in respect of the loan referred to in paragraph (a), the principal sum or any other sum payable by the relevant claimant to that lender, or
      (ii) in respect of any other loan, any sum payable by the relevant claimant to that lender where the liability to pay that sum has not already discharged under this Schedule.

Time and manner of payments

8. Direct payments under paragraph 3 are to be made in monthly instalments in arrears. **4.90**

Fees payable by qualifying lenders

9.—(1) A fee is payable by a qualifying lender to the Secretary of State for the purpose of **4.91**
meeting the expenses of the Secretary of State in administering the making of direct payments to qualifying lenders under paragraph 3.
(2) The fee is £0.35 in respect of each occasion on which a direct payment is made to the qualifying lender.

Election not to be regarded as a qualifying lender

10.—(1) A body or person who would otherwise be within the definition of "qualifying **4.92**
lender" in paragraph 1(1)—
  (a) may elect not to be regarded as such by giving notice to the Secretary of State in writing; and
  (b) may revoke any such notice by giving a further notice in writing.
(2) In respect of any financial year, a notice under sub-paragraph (1) which is given not later than the 1st February before the start of the financial year takes effect on 1st April following the giving of the notice.
(3) Where a body or person becomes a qualifying lender in the course of a financial year—
  (a) any notice of an election by the body or person under sub-paragraph (1)(a) must be given within 6 weeks ("the initial period") of the date of their becoming a qualifying lender; and
  (b) no direct payments may be made under paragraph 3 to the body or person before the expiry of the initial period.
(4) But sub-paragraph (3)(b) does not apply in any case where—
  (a) the body or person gives the Secretary of State notice in writing that that provision should not apply; and
  (b) that notice is given before the start of the initial period or before that period expires.
(5) In relation to a notice under sub-paragraph (1)—
  (a) where the notice is given by an electronic communication, it must be given in accordance with the provisions set out in Schedule 2 (electronic communications);

(b) where the notice is sent by post, it is to be treated as having been given on the day the notice was received.

Provision of information

4.93   **11.**—(1) A qualifying lender must, in respect of a relevant claimant, provide the Secretary of State with information as to—

(a) the loan interest payments in respect of which the relevant claimant meets the payment condition and the liability condition;

(b) the amount of the loan;

(c) the purpose for which the loan was made;

(d) the amount outstanding on the loan;

(e) the amount of arrears of loan interest payments due in respect of the loan;

(f) any change in the amount of the loan interest payable; and

(g) the redemption of the loan.

(2) The information referred to in sub-paragraph (1)(a) to (e) must be provided at the request of the Secretary of State where—

(a) a claim is made for universal credit; or

(b) the housing costs element is to be included in an award of universal credit otherwise than on the making of a claim,

and loan interest payments payable to the qualifying lender are taken into account in determining the amount of the relevant claimant's housing costs element.

(3) The information referred to in sub-paragraph (1)(f) must be provided at such times, or in the case of the information referred to in sub-paragraph (1)(d) at such other times, as the Secretary of State may determine.

(4) The information referred to in sub-paragraph (1)(g) must be provided to the Secretary of State immediately once the qualifying lender has received notice that the loan is to be redeemed.

Recovery of sums wrongly paid

4.94   **12.**—(1) In the following circumstances, a qualifying lender must at the request of the Secretary of State repay any amount paid to the lender under paragraph 3 which ought not to have been paid.

(2) Those circumstances are that, in respect of a relevant claimant—

(a) an amount calculated by reference to loan interest payments payable to the qualifying lender ceases to be included in the relevant claimant's housing costs element;

(b) a specified benefit ceases to be paid to a relevant claimant;

(c) the loan in respect of which loan interest payments are payable has been redeemed; or

(d) both of the conditions set out in sub-paragraphs (3) and (4) are met.

(3) The first condition is that the amount of the relevant claimant's housing costs element is reduced as a result of—

(a) the standard rate having been reduced; or

(b) the amount outstanding on the loan having been reduced.

(4) The second condition is that no corresponding reduction was made to the amount calculated in respect of the qualifying lender under paragraph 4 or 5.

(5) A qualifying lender is not required to make a repayment in the circumstances described in sub-paragraph (2)(a) or (b) unless the Secretary of State's request is made before the end of the period of two months starting with the date on which the thing described in that provision ceased.

Definitions

"the 2012 Act"—see reg.2.

"benefit"—*ibid.*

"claimant"—*ibid.*

"couple"—see reg.2 and WRA 2012, s.39.

"electronic communication"—see reg.2.

"universal credit"— *ibid.*

"the Universal Credit Regulations"—*ibid.*

"writing"—*ibid.*

Regulation 60

SCHEDULE 6

DEDUCTIONS FROM BENEFIT AND DIRECT PAYMENT TO THIRD PARTIES

Interpretation

1. [²(1)] In this Schedule—   4.95
"assessment period" has the meaning given by regulation 21 (assessment periods) of the Universal Credit Regulations;
"the work allowance" means, in relation to any claimant, the amount applicable to that claimant under regulation 22(2) (deduction of income and work allowance) of the Universal Credit Regulations;
"child element" means, in relation to any claimant, any amount included in the claimant's award of universal credit under regulation 24 (the child element) of the Universal Credit Regulations;
"the Community Charges Regulations" means the Community Charges (Deductions from Income Support) (No. 2) Regulations 1990;
"the Community Charges (Scotland) Regulations" means the Community Charges (Deductions from Income Support) (Scotland) Regulations 1989;
"the Council Tax Regulations" means the Council Tax (Deductions from Income Support) Regulations 1993;
"the Fines Regulations" means the Fines (Deductions from Income Support) Regulations 1992;
"standard allowance" means, in relation to any claimant, any amount included in the claimant's award of universal credit under section 9(1) of the 2012 Act;
"water charges" means—
   (a) as respects England and Wales, any water and sewerage charges under Chapter 1 of Part 5 of the Water Industry Act 1991;
   (b) as respects Scotland, any such charges established by Scottish Water under a charges scheme made under section 29A of the Water Industry (Scotland) Act 2002;
   [² ...]
[² (2) For the purposes of this Schedule, where the relevant percentage of the standard allowance results in a fraction of a penny, that fraction is to be disregarded if it is less than half a penny and otherwise it is to be treated as a penny.]

General

2.—(1) The Secretary of State may deduct an amount from a claimant's award of universal   4.96
credit and pay that amount to a third party in accordance with the following provisions of this Schedule to discharge (in whole or part) a liability of the claimant to that third party.
(2) A payment made to a third party in accordance with this Schedule may be made at such intervals as the Secretary of State may direct.

Limitations applicable to deductions made under this Schedule

3.—(1) The Secretary of State may not deduct an amount from a claimant's award of uni-   4.97
versal credit under this Schedule and pay that amount to a third party if, in relation to any assessment period, that would—
   (a) reduce the amount payable to the claimant to less than one penny; or
   (b) result in more than three deductions being made, in relation to that assessment period, under one or more of the provisions mentioned in sub-paragraph (2).
(2) The provisions are—
   (a) paragraph 6 (housing costs) of this Schedule;
   (b) paragraph 7 (rent and service charges included in rent) of this Schedule;
   (c) paragraph 8 (fuel costs) of this Schedule;
   (d) paragraph 9 (water charges) of this Schedule;
   (e) paragraph 10 (payments in place of payments of child support maintenance) of this Schedule;
   (f) paragraph 11 (eligible loans) of this Schedule;
   (g) paragraph 12 (integration loans) of this Schedule;
   (h) regulation 3 (deductions from income support etc.) of the Community Charges Regulations;
   (i) regulation 3 (deductions from income support etc.) of the Community Charges (Scotland) Regulations;

477

(j) regulation 5 (deduction from debtor's income support etc.) of the Council Tax Regulations; and

(k) regulation 4 (deductions from offender's income support etc.) of the Fines Regulations.

(3) The aggregate amount deducted from a claimant's award of universal credit in relation to any assessment period and paid to a third party under paragraphs 8 (fuel costs) and 9 (water charges) of this Schedule must not, without the claimant's consent, exceed a sum equal to [² 25%] of the aggregate of the standard allowance and any child element.

Maximum amount

4.98

4.—(1) Except as provided for in sub-paragraph (4), the Secretary of State may not deduct an amount from a claimant's award of universal credit under a provision mentioned in paragraph 5(2) of this Schedule if, in relation to any assessment period, that would result in the Secretary of State deducting an amount in excess of [² 40%] of the standard allowance ("the maximum amount") from the claimant's award under one or more relevant provisions.

(2) The relevant provisions are—

(a) those mentioned in paragraph 5(2) of this Schedule;

(b) section 26 (higher-level sanctions) of the 2012 Act;

(c) section 27 (other sanctions) of the 2012 Act;

(d) section 71ZG (recovery of payments on account) of the Administration Act;

(e) section 6B of the Social Security Fraud Act 2001 ("the 2001 Act");

(f) section 7 of the 2001 Act; and

(g) section 9 of the 2001 Act.

(3) For the purposes of determining whether the maximum amount would be exceeded, no account is to be taken of any liability for continuing need mentioned in—

(a) paragraph 8(4)(b) (fuel costs) of this Schedule; or

(b) paragraph 9(6)(b) or (7)(b)(water charges) of this Schedule.

(4) Subject to paragraph 3 of this Schedule, the Secretary of State may deduct an amount from the claimant's award under paragraph 6 (housing costs), paragraph 7 (rent and service charges included in rent) or paragraph 8 (fuel costs) of this Schedule and pay that amount to a third party where the deduction appears to the Secretary of State to be in the claimant's best interests, even though the deduction would result in the maximum amount being exceeded.

Priority as between certain debts

4.99

5.—(1) This paragraph applies to a claimant ("C") where, in relation to any assessment period—

(a) a deduction could otherwise be made from C's award under more than one of the provisions mentioned in sub-paragraph (2); and

(b) the amount of universal credit payable to C in relation to that assessment period is insufficient to enable the Secretary of State to meet all of the liabilities for which in C's case deductions may be made under those provisions or the deduction, were it to be made, would mean that the maximum amount referred to in paragraph 4(1) would be exceeded.

(2) The provisions are—

(a) paragraph 6 (housing costs) of this Schedule;

(b) paragraph 7 (rent and service charges included in rent) of this Schedule;

(c) paragraph 8 (fuel costs) of this Schedule;

(d) regulation 3 (deductions from income support etc.) of the Community Charges Regulations, regulation 3 (deductions from income support etc.) of the Community Charges (Scotland) Regulations or (because no such payments are being made in C's case) regulation 5 (deduction from debtor's income support etc.) of the Council Tax Regulations;

(e) regulation 4 (deductions from offender's income support etc.) of the Fines Regulations where the amount of the deduction equals 5% of the standard allowance;

(f) paragraph 9 (water charges) of this Schedule;

(g) paragraph 10 (payments in place of child support maintenance) of this Schedule;

(h) Schedule 7 (deductions from benefit in respect of child support maintenance and payment to persons with care) to these Regulations;

(i) section 78(2) (recovery of social fund awards) of the Administration Act;

(j) section 71ZH(1)(a) or (b) (recovery of hardship payments etc.) of the 2012 Act;

(k) section 115A (penalty as alternative to prosecution) of the Administration Act where an overpayment is recoverable from a person by, or due from a person to, the Secretary of State or an authority under or by virtue of section 71 (overpayments – general), section 75 (overpayments of housing benefit) or section 71ZB (recovery of overpayments of certain benefits) of that Act;

(l) section 71 (overpayments – general), section 71ZC (deduction from benefit) or section 75(4) (overpayments of housing benefit) of the Administration Act or an overpayment of working tax credit or child tax credit, where in each case, the overpayment (or part of it) is the result of fraud;

(m) section 115C(4) (incorrect statements etc.) and section 115D(4) (failure to disclose information) of the Administration Act;

(n) section 71 (overpayments – general), section 71ZC (deduction from benefit) or section 75(4) (overpayments of housing benefit) of the Administration Act or an overpayment of working tax credit or child tax credit, where in each case, the overpayment (or part of it) is not the result of fraud;

(o) paragraph 12 (integration loans) of this Schedule;

(p) paragraph 11 (eligible loans) of this Schedule;

(q) regulation 4 (deductions from offender's income support etc.) of the Fines Regulations where the amount of the deduction exceeds the minimum amount that may be deducted in accordance with those Regulations.

(3) Where this paragraph applies to a claimant, the Secretary of State must make a deduction under any of the provisions mentioned sub-paragraph (2) in accordance with sub-paragraphs (4) and (5).

(4) The Secretary of State must give priority to any such deductions in the order in which they are listed in sub-paragraph (2), with housing costs having the priority.

(5) Where two or more provisions mentioned in any single paragraph of sub-paragraph (2) apply to the claimant, unless the Secretary of State directs otherwise, those deductions have equal priority with each other and the amount of such deductions are to be apportioned accordingly.

(6) For the purposes of sub-paragraph (2)(l) and (n), an overpayment is the result of fraud if, in relation to that overpayment or that part of it, the claimant—

(a) has been found guilty of an offence whether under statute or otherwise;

(b) made an admission after caution of deception or fraud for the purpose of obtaining benefit under the Administration Act, or in the case of a tax credit, under the Tax Credits Act 2002; or

(c) agreed to pay a penalty under section 115A of the Administration Act (penalty as an alternative to prosecution) and the agreement has not been withdrawn.

Housing costs

6.—(1) This paragraph applies where the following condition is met.   **4.100**

(2) The condition is that in any assessment period the claimant is in debt for any item of housing costs which is included in the claimant's award of universal credit under Schedule 5 (housing costs element for owner-occupiers) to the Universal Credit Regulations.

(3) Where this paragraph applies, but subject to sub-paragraph (4), the Secretary of State may, in such cases and circumstances as the Secretary of State may determine, in relation to that assessment period deduct an amount from the claimant's award equal to 5% of the standard allowance in respect of any debt mentioned in sub-paragraph (2) and pay that amount or those amounts to the person to whom any such debt is owed.

(4) Before the Secretary of State may commence (or re-commence) making deductions in respect of any such debt, the claimant's earned income (or in the case of joint claimants their combined earned income) in relation to the previous assessment period must not exceed the work allowance.

(5) No amount may be deducted under this paragraph in respect of owner-occupier payments within the meaning of paragraph 4 of Schedule 1 (meaning of payments in respect of accommodation) to the Universal Credit Regulations in any case where those payments—

(a) are required to be paid directly to a qualifying lender under regulation 59 of these Regulations; or

(b) would have been required to be paid to a body which, or a person who, would otherwise have been a qualifying lender but for an election given under paragraph 10 of Schedule 5 to these Regulations.

(6) As between liability for items of housing costs to which this paragraph applies, liabilities in respect of owner-occupier payments (within the meaning of paragraph 4(1) of Schedule 1 (meaning of payments in respect of accommodation) to the Universal Credit Regulations) are to have priority over all other items.

Rent and service charges included in rent

7.—(1) This paragraph applies where all of the following conditions are met.   **4.101**

(2) The first condition is that in any assessment period the claimant—

(a) has an award of universal credit which includes an amount under Schedule 4 (housing costs element for renters) to the Universal Credit Regulations; or

(b) occupies exempt accommodation and has an award of housing benefit under section 130 (housing benefit) of the Contributions and Benefits Act.

(3) The second condition is that the claimant is in debt for any—

(a) rent payments;

(b) service charges which are paid with or as part of the claimant's rent.

(4) The third condition is that the claimant occupies the accommodation to which the debt relates.

(5) Where this paragraph applies, but subject to sub-paragraphs (6) and (7), the Secretary of State may, in such cases and circumstances as the Secretary of State may determine, deduct in relation to that assessment period an amount from the claimant's award equal to 5% of the standard allowance and pay that amount to the person to whom the debt is owed.

(6) Before the Secretary of State may commence (or re-commence) making deductions in respect of such a debt, the claimant's earned income (or in the case of joint claimants their combined earned income) in relation to the previous assessment period must not exceed the work allowance.

(7) The Secretary of State must stop making such deductions if, in relation to the three assessment periods immediately preceding the date on which the next deduction could otherwise be made, the claimant's earned income (or in the case of joint claimants their combined earned income) equals or exceeds the work allowance.

(8) In this paragraph—

"exempt accommodation" has the meaning given by paragraph 1 of Schedule 1 (interpretation) to the Universal Credit Regulations;

"rent payments" includes any elements included in the claimant's rent which would not fall to be treated as rent under the Housing Benefit Regulations 2006 or as rent payments under the Universal Credit Regulations;

"service charges" includes any items in a charge for services in respect of the accommodation occupied by the claimant which would not fall to be treated as service charges under the Universal Credit Regulations.

Fuel costs

4.102   8.—(1) This paragraph applies where the following condition is met.

(2) The condition is that in any assessment period the claimant is in debt for any [¹ fuel item].

(3) Where this paragraph applies, but subject to sub-paragraphs (5) and (6), the Secretary of State may, in such cases and circumstances as the Secretary of State may determine, deduct in relation to that assessment period the following amounts from the claimant's award and pay them to the person to whom the payment is due.

(4) The amount which may be deducted in respect of any fuel item is—

(a) an amount equal to 5% of the standard allowance; and

(b) an additional amount which the Secretary of State estimates is equal to the average monthly cost necessary to meet the claimant's continuing need for [¹ the fuel in respect of which the debt arose, plus such monthly amount as is required to meet any payments required to be made under a green deal plan within the meaning of section 1 of the Energy Act 2011 ("the 2011 Act")], except where current consumption is paid for by other means such as a pre-payment meter.

(5) Before the Secretary of State may commence (or re-commence) making deductions in respect of such a debt, the claimant's earned income (or in the case of joint claimants their combined earned income) in relation to the previous assessment period must not exceed the work allowance.

(6) The Secretary of State must stop making such deductions if, in relation to the three assessment periods immediately preceding the date on which the next deduction could otherwise be made, the claimant's earned income (or in the case of joint claimants their combined earned income) equals or exceeds the work allowance.

(7) As between liabilities for items of gas or electricity, the Secretary of State must give priority to whichever liability the Secretary of State considers it would, having regard to the circumstances and to any requests of the claimant, be appropriate to discharge.

[¹(8) In this paragraph, "fuel item" means—

(a) any charge for mains gas, including for the reconnection of mains gas;

(b) any charge for mains electricity and including any charge for the disconnection and reconnection of mains electricity and including any payments required to be made under a green deal plan within the meaning of section 1 of the 2011 Act.]

Water charges

   9.—(1) This paragraph applies where the following condition is met.

   (2) The condition is that in any assessment period the claimant is in debt for water charges, including any charges for reconnection ("the original debt").

   (3) Where this paragraph applies, but subject to sub-paragraphs (4) and (5), the Secretary of State may, in such cases and circumstances as the Secretary of State may determine, deduct an amount from the claimant's award in accordance with sub-paragraphs (6) to (8) and pay it to a water undertaker to whom the payment is due or to the person or body authorised to collect water charges for that undertaker.

   (4) Before the Secretary of State may commence (or re-commence) making deductions in respect of such a debt, the claimant's earned income (or in the case of joint claimants their combined earned income) in relation to the previous assessment period must not exceed the work allowance.

   (5) The Secretary of State must stop making such deductions if, in relation to the three assessment periods immediately preceding the date on which the next deduction could otherwise be made, the claimant's earned income (or in the case of joint claimants their combined earned income) equals or exceeds the work allowance.

   (6) Where water charges are determined by means of a water meter, the amount to be deducted under this paragraph in relation to any assessment period is to be—

    (a) an amount equal to 5% of the standard allowance towards discharging the original debt; and

    (b) an additional amount which the Secretary of State estimates to be the average monthly cost necessary to meet the claimant's continuing need for water consumption.

   (7) Where water charges are determined otherwise than by means of a water meter, the amount to be deducted in relation to any assessment period under this paragraph is to be—

    (a) the amount referred to in sub-paragraph (6)(a); and

    (b) an additional amount equal to the cost necessary to meet the continuing need for water consumption in that assessment period.

   (8) Where the claimant is in debt to two water undertakers—

    (a) only one amount under sub-paragraph (6)(a) or (7)(a) may be deducted;

    (b) a deduction in respect of an original debt for sewerage may only be made after the whole debt in respect of an original debt for water has been paid; and

    (c) deductions in respect of continuing charges for both water and for sewerage may be made at the same time.

   (9) In this paragraph "water undertaker" means—

    (a) in relation to any area in England and Wales, a company holding an appointment as a water undertaker or a sewerage undertaker under the Water Industry Act 1991; or

    (b) in relation to any area in Scotland, Scottish Water.

Payments in place of payments of child support maintenance

   10.—(1) This paragraph applies where the Secretary of State has determined that section 43 (contribution to maintenance by deduction from benefit) of the 1991 Act and regulation 28 (contribution to maintenance by deduction from benefit) of the Child Support (Maintenance Assessments and Special Cases) Regulations 1992 apply in relation to the claimant.

   (2) Where this paragraph applies, the Secretary of State must, if satisfied that there is sufficient universal credit in payment (but subject to paragraphs 1, 4 and 5 of this Schedule), determine that an amount is to be deducted from the claimant's award for transmission to the person or persons entitled to receive that amount under or by virtue of the 1991 Act.

   (3) Not more than one deduction may be made under this paragraph in relation to any assessment period.

   (4) The amount of universal credit which may be deducted in relation to any assessment period and paid to a third party under this paragraph is to be an amount equal to 5% of the standard allowance.

Eligible loans

   11.—(1) This paragraph applies where both of the following conditions are met:

   (2) The first condition is that in any assessment period the claimant is in arrears in respect of a loan agreement entered into (whether solely or jointly) with an eligible lender in respect of an eligible loan.

   (3) The second condition is that, as at the date on which the Secretary of State receives an application for deductions to be made under this paragraph, no deductions are being made from any eligible benefit awarded to the claimant in respect of an amount recoverable under—

4.103

4.104

4.105

(a) section 71 (overpayments—general) or 71ZB (recovery of overpayments of certain benefits) of the Administration Act 1992; or

(b) section 78 (recovery of social fund awards) of that Act.

(4) Where the claimant has an award of universal credit, the Secretary of State may, in such cases and circumstances as the Secretary of State may determine, deduct in relation to the assessment period referred to in sub-paragraph (2) an amount from the claimant's award equal to 5% of the standard allowance and pay that amount to the eligible lender towards discharging the amount owing under the loan agreement.

(5) In a case where the claimant has an award of universal credit but the amount payable to the claimant in relation to that assessment period is insufficient to enable such a deduction to be made, the Secretary of State may instead deduct a weekly amount equal to 5% of the personal allowance for a single claimant aged not less than 25 from any employment and support allowance or jobseeker's allowance awarded to the claimant and pay that amount to the eligible lender.

(6) In a case where the claimant does not have an award of universal credit, but has an award of an employment and support allowance or a jobseeker's allowance, the Secretary of State may deduct a weekly amount equal to 5% of the personal allowance for a single claimant aged not less than 25 from any such award and pay that amount to the eligible lender.

(7) The Secretary of State must not make deductions from a claimant's employment and support allowance or a jobseeker's allowance under this paragraph if that would reduce the amount payable to the claimant to less than 10 pence.

(8) In this paragraph—

"eligible benefit" means—

(a) an employment and support allowance;

(b) a jobseeker's allowance;

(c) universal credit;

"eligible lender" means—

(a) a body registered under section 1 (societies which may be registered) of the Industrial and Provident Societies Act 1965;

(b) a credit union within the meaning of section 1 (registration under the Industrial and Provident Societies Act 1965) of the Credit Unions Act 1979;

(c) a charitable institution within the meaning of section 58(1) (interpretation of Part 2) of the Charities Act 1992;

(d) a body entered on the Scottish Charity Register under section 3 (Scottish Charities Register) of the Charities and Trustee Investment (Scotland) Act 2005;

(e) a community interest company within the meaning of Part 2 of the Companies (Audit, Investigations and Community Enterprise) Act 2004,

which, except for a credit union, is licensed under the Consumer Credit Act 1974 and which the Secretary of State considers is an appropriate body to which payments on behalf of the claimant may be made in respect of loans made by that body;

"eligible loan" means a loan made by a lender who is, at the time the loan agreement is made, an eligible lender, to a claimant except a loan which—

(a) is secured by a charge or pledge;

(b) is for the purpose of business or self-employment; or

(c) was made by means of a credit card;

"loan agreement" means an agreement between the eligible lender and the claimant in respect of an eligible loan;

"5% of the personal allowance" means 5% of the personal allowance applicable in the claimant's case, rounded up (in any case where that calculation produces a result which is not a multiple of five pence) to the next higher multiple of five pence.

Integration loans

4.106   **12.**—(1) This paragraph applies where both of the following conditions are met.

(2) The first condition is that the claimant has an integration loan which is recoverable by deductions.

(3) The second condition is that, as at the date on which the Secretary of State receives an application for deductions to be made under this paragraph, no deductions are being made from the claimant's universal credit in respect of an amount recoverable under—

(a) section 71 (overpayments – general) or 71ZB (recovery of overpayments of certain benefits) of the Administration Act; or

(b) section 78 (recovery of social fund awards) of that Act.

(4) Where this paragraph applies, the amount payable by deductions in any assessment period is to be equal to 5% of the standard allowance.

(5) In this paragraph, "integration loan which is recoverable by deductions" means an integration loan which is made under the Integration Loans for Refugees and Others Regulations 2007 and which is recoverable from the claimant by deductions from the claimant's award of universal credit under regulation 9 of those Regulations.

AMENDMENTS

1. Social Security (Miscellaneous Amendments) Regulations 2013 (SI 2013/443) reg.10 (April 29, 2013).
2. Social Security (Miscellaneous Amendments) (No. 2) Regulations 2013 (SI 2013/1508) reg.6(1) and (3) (July 29, 2013).

DEFINITIONS

"the 1991 Act"—see reg.2.
"the 2012 Act"—*ibid.*
"the Administration Act"—*ibid.*
"assessment period"—see reg.2 and Universal Credit Regs., reg.21.
"benefit"—see reg.2.
"child" —see reg.2 and WRA 2012 s.40.
"claimant"—see reg.2.
"earned income"—see reg.2 and Universal Credit Regs., reg.52.
"employment and support allowance"—see reg.2.
"jobseeker's allowance"—*ibid.*
"universal credit"—*ibid.*
"the Universal Credit Regulations"— *ibid.*

Regulation 60

SCHEDULE 7

DEDUCTIONS FROM BENEFIT IN RESPECT OF CHILD SUPPORT MAINTENANCE AND PAYMENT TO PERSONS WITH CARE

Interpretation
   1. In this Schedule—   **4.107**
"beneficiary" means a person who has been awarded a specified benefit;
"maintenance", except in paragraph 3, means child support maintenance which a non-resident parent is liable to pay under the 1991 Act at a flat rate (or would be so liable but for a variation having been agreed to) where that rate applies (or would have applied) because the non-resident parent falls within paragraph 4(1)(b), (c) or (2) of Schedule 1 to the 1991 Act, and includes such maintenance payable at a transitional rate in accordance with regulations made under section 29(3)(a) of the Child Support, Pensions and Social Security Act 2000;
"person with care" has the same meaning as in section 3 (meaning of certain terms used in this Act) of the 1991 Act;
"specified benefit" means—
    (a) an employment and support allowance;
    (b) a jobseeker's allowance;
    (c) universal credit.

Deductions
   2.—(1) Subject to the following provisions of this paragraph and to paragraph 5 (flat rate   **4.108**
maintenance), the Secretary of State may deduct from any specified benefit awarded to a beneficiary, an amount equal to the amount of maintenance which is payable by the beneficiary and pay the amount deducted to or among the person or persons with care in discharge (in whole or in part) of the liability to pay maintenance.
   (2) A deduction may only be made from one specified benefit in respect of the same period.
   (3) No amount may be deducted under this Schedule from any employment and support

allowance or any jobseeker's allowance awarded to the claimant if that would reduce the amount of the benefit payable to the claimant to less than 10 pence.

(4) No amount may be deducted from any universal credit awarded to the claimant under this Schedule if that would reduce the amount payable to the claimant to less than one penny.

Arrears

4.109

3.—(1) Except where universal credit is awarded to the beneficiary, the Secretary of State may deduct the sum of £1 per week from any employment and support allowance or jobseeker's allowance which the beneficiary has been awarded and, subject to sub-paragraph (2), pay the amount deducted to or among the person or persons with care in discharge (in whole or in part) of the beneficiary's liability to pay arrears of maintenance.

(2) Deductions made under sub-paragraph (1) may be retained by the Secretary of State in the circumstances set out in regulation 8 of the Child Support (Arrears, Interest and Adjustment of Maintenance Assessments) Regulations 1992.

(3) In sub-paragraph (1) "maintenance" means child support maintenance as defined by section 3(6) of the 1991 Act whether before or after the amendment of the definition of such maintenance by section 1(2)(a) of the Child Support, Pensions and Social Security Act 2000, and includes maintenance payable at a transitional rate in accordance with regulations made under section 29(3)(a) of that Act.

Apportionment

4.110

4. Where maintenance is payable to more than one person with care, the amount deducted must be apportioned between the persons with care in accordance with paragraphs 6, 7 and 8 of Schedule 1 (maintenance assessments) to the 1991 Act.

Flat rate maintenance

4.111

5.—(1) This paragraph applies where the beneficiary and that person's partner are each liable to pay maintenance at a flat rate in accordance with paragraph 4(2) of Schedule 1 to the 1991 Act and either of them has been awarded universal credit (whether as a single claimant or as joint claimants).

(2) Where this paragraph applies, an amount not exceeding an amount equal to the flat rate of maintenance may be deducted from such an award in respect of the total liability of both partners to pay maintenance, in the proportions described in regulation 4(3) of the Child Support (Maintenance Calculations and Special Cases) Regulations 2001 or regulation 44(3) of the Child Support Maintenance Calculation Regulations 2012 and must be paid in discharge (in whole or in part) of the respective liabilities to pay maintenance.

Notice

4.112

6. Where the Secretary of State commences making deductions under this Schedule, the Secretary of State must notify the beneficiary in writing of the amount and frequency of the deduction and the benefit from which the deduction is made and must give further such notice when there is a change to any of the particulars specified in the notice.

DEFINITIONS

"the 1991 Act"—see reg.2.
"beneficiary"—see para.(1).
"benefit"—see reg.2.
"child"—see reg.2 and WRA 2012 s.40.
"claimant"—see reg.2.
"employment and support allowance"—*ibid.*
"jobseeker's allowance"—*ibid.*
"maintenance"—see para.(1).
"person with care"—*ibid.*
"specified benefit"—*ibid.*
"universal credit"—see reg.2.

Universal Credit, Personal Independence Payment, Jobseeker's Allowance and Employment and Support Allowance (Decisions and Appeals) Regulations 2013

(SI 2013/381)

The Secretary of State makes the following Regulations in exercise of the powers conferred by sections: 5(1A), 159D(1) and (6), 189(1), (4) to (6) and section 191 of the Social Security Administration Act 1992; 9(1), (4) and (6), 10(3) and (6), 10A, 11(1), 12(2), (3), (3A), (3B), (6) and (7)(b), 16(1), 17, 18(1), 21(1) to (3), 22 and 23, 25(3)(b) and (5)(c), 26(6)(c), 28(1), 31(2), 79(1) and (4) to (7) and 84 of, and paragraph 9 of Schedule 2, paragraphs 1, 4 and 9 of Schedule 3 and Schedule 5 to, the Social Security Act 1998. **4.113**

A draft of this instrument was laid before and approved by a resolution of each House of Parliament in accordance with section 80(1) of the Social Security Act 1998.

The Social Security Advisory Committee has agreed that the proposals in respect of these Regulations should not be referred to it.

ARRANGEMENT OF REGULATIONS

PART I

GENERAL

PART II

REVISION

CHAPTER 1

REVISION ON ANY GROUNDS

CHAPTER 2

REVISION ON SPECIFIC GROUNDS

CHAPTER 3

PROCEDURE AND EFFECTIVE DATE

PART III

SUPERSESSIONS

CHAPTER 1

GROUNDS FOR SUPERSESSION

CHAPTER 2

SUPERSEDING DECISIONS: LIMITATIONS AND PROCEDURE

CHAPTER 3

EFFECTIVE DATES FOR SUPERSESSIONS

PART IV

OTHER MATTERS RELATING TO DECISION- MAKING

PART V

SUSPENSION

PART VI

TERMINATION

PART VII

APPEALS

GENERAL NOTE

4.114   An annotated version of these Regulations is included in Vol. III. They are repeated in this volume so as to provide a complete text of the law governing universal credit. Readers are referred to Vol. III for commentary on the individual provisions. These Regulations are in force from April 8, 2013 in relation to personal independence payment and April 29, 2013 in relation to universal credit, new-style employment and support allowance and new-style jobseeker's allowance.

PART I

GENERAL

Citation, commencement and application

4.115   **1.**—(1) These Regulations may be cited as the Universal Credit, Personal Independence Payment, Jobseeker's Allowance and Employment and Support Allowance (Decisions and Appeals) Regulations 2013.

(2) They come into force—

(a) in so far as they relate to personal independence payment and for the purposes of this regulation, on 8th April 2013;

(b) for all remaining purposes, on 29th April 2013.

(3) These Regulations apply in relation to—

(a) an employment and support allowance payable under Part 1 of the 2007 Act as amended by Schedule 3 and Part 1 of Schedule 14 to the 2012 Act (to remove references to an income-related allowance);

(b) a jobseeker's allowance payable under the Jobseekers Act as amended by Part 1 of Schedule 14 to the 2012 Act (to remove references to an income-based allowance);

(c) personal independence payment; and

(d) universal credit.

Interpretation

2. In these Regulations—   4.116

"the 1998 Act" means the Social Security Act 1998;

"the 2007 Act" means the Welfare Reform Act 2007;

"the 2012 Act" means the Welfare Reform Act 2012;

"the Administration Act" means the Social Security Administration Act 1992;

"appeal", except where the context otherwise requires, means an appeal to the First-tier Tribunal established under the Tribunals, Courts and Enforcement Act 2007;

"appropriate office" means—

(a) in the case of a contributions decision which falls within Part 2 (contributions decisions) of Schedule 3 (decisions against which an appeal lies) to the 1998 Act, any National Insurance Contributions office of HMRC or any office of the Department for Work and Pensions; or

(b) in any other case, the office of the Department for Work and Pensions, or other place, the address of which is specified on the notification of the original decision referred to in regulation 5(1) (revision on any grounds);

"assessment period" is to be construed in accordance with regulation 21 (assessment periods) of the Universal Credit Regulations;

"benefit" means a benefit or an allowance in relation to which these Regulations apply;

"benefit week" has the same meaning as in—

(a) regulation 2 (interpretation) of the Employment and Support Allowance Regulations 2013 in the case of an employment and support allowance;

(b) regulation 2 (general interpretation) of the Jobseeker's Allowance Regulations 2013, in the case of a jobseeker's allowance;

"child" means a person under the age of 16;

"claimant" means—

(a) any person who has claimed—

  (i) an employment and support allowance;

  (ii) a jobseeker's allowance;

  (iii) personal independence payment;

(b) in the case of universal credit, any person who is a claimant for the purposes of section 40 (interpretation) of the 2012 Act; and

(c) any other person from whom an amount of benefit is alleged to be recoverable;

"the Claims and Payments Regulations 2013" means the Universal Credit, Personal Independence Payment, Jobseeker's Allowance and Employment and Support Allowance (Claims and Payments) Regulations 2013;

"the Contributions and Benefits Act" means the Social Security Contributions and Benefits Act 1992;

"the date of notification", in relation to a decision of the Secretary of State, means the date on which the notification of the decision is treated as having been given or sent in accordance with—

(a) regulation 3 (service of documents); or

(b) where the notification is given or sent using an electronic communication, Schedule 2 (electronic communications) to the Claims and Payments Regulations 2013;

"designated authority" means—

(a) the Secretary of State; or

(b) a person providing services to the Secretary of State;

"electronic communication" has the same meaning as in section 15(1) of the Electronic Communications Act 2000;

"employment and support allowance" means an employment and support allowance in relation to which these Regulations apply;

"the Fraud Act" means the Social Security Fraud Act 2001;

"fraud penalty", in relation to any claimant of an employment and support allowance, a jobseeker's allowance or universal credit, means any period during which the provisions of section 6B, 7 or 9 of the Fraud Act apply to the award;

"family" means the claimant's partner and any—

(a) child; or

(b) qualifying young person, within the meaning of regulation 5 (meaning of "qualifying young person") of the Universal Credit Regulations, who is a member of the same household as the claimant and for whom the either the claimant or their partner is, or both of them are, responsible;

"HMRC" means Her Majesty's Revenue and Customs;

"the Jobseekers Act" means the Jobseekers Act 1995;

"jobseeker's allowance" means a jobseeker's allowance in relation to which these Regulations apply;

"limited capability for work" has the same meaning as in—

(a) section 1(4) of the 2007 Act in relation to an employment and support allowance;

(b) section 37(1) of the 2012 Act in relation to universal credit;

"limited capability for work determination" means—

(a) where the determination relates to an employment and support allowance, a determination whether a person has limited capability for work following a limited capability for work assessment in accordance with regulation 15(1) (determination of limited capability for work) of the Employment and Support Allowance Regulations 2013, or a determination that a person is to be treated as having limited capability for work in accordance with regulation 16 (certain claimants to be treated as having limited capability for work) or 25 (exceptional circumstances) of those Regulations;

(b) where the determination relates to universal credit, a determination whether a person has limited capability for work following a limited capability for work assessment referred to in regulation 39(2) (limited capability for work) of the Universal Credit Regulations, or a determination that a person is to be treated as having limited capability for work in accordance with regulation 39(6) of those Regulations;

"official error" means an error made by—

(a) an officer of the Department for Work and Pensions or HMRC acting as such which was not caused or materially contributed to by any person outside the Department or HMRC;

(b) a person employed by, and acting on behalf of, a designated authority which was not caused or materially contributed to by any person outside that authority,

but excludes any error of law which is shown to have been such by a subsequent decision of the Upper Tribunal, or of the court as defined in section 27(7) of the 1998 Act;

"partner" means one of a couple within the meaning of section 39 (couples) of the 2012 Act;

"personal independence payment" means an allowance payable under Part 4 (personal independence payment) of the 2012 Act;

"relevant benefit" has the same meaning as in Chapter 2 (social security decisions and appeals) of Part 1 (decisions and appeals) of the 1998 Act;

"the Rent Officers Order 2013" means the Rent Officers (Universal Credit Functions) Order 2013;

"terminally ill", in relation to a claimant, means that the claimant is suffering from a progressive disease and that death in consequence of that disease can reasonably be expected within 6 months;

"the Tribunal Procedure Rules" means the Tribunal Procedure (First-tier Tribunal) (Social Entitlement Chamber) Rules 2008;

"the Universal Credit Regulations" means the Universal Credit Regulations 2013;

"universal credit" means the benefit payable under Part 1 (universal credit) of the 2012 Act;

"writing" includes writing produced by means of electronic communications used in accordance with regulation 4 (electronic communications).

Service of documents

3.—(1) Where, under any provision of these Regulations, any notice or other document is given or sent by post to the Secretary of State, it is to be treated as having been given or sent on the day on which it is received by the Secretary of State.

(2) Where, under any provision of these Regulations, the Secretary of State sends a notice or other document by post to a person's last known address, it is to be treated as having been given or sent on the day on which it was posted.

4.117

Electronic communications

4. Schedule 2 (electronic communications) to the Claims and Payments Regulations 2013 applies to the delivery of electronic communications to or by the Secretary of State for the purposes of these Regulations in the same manner as it applies to the delivery of electronic communications for the purposes of the Claims and Payments Regulations 2013.

4.118

DEFINITIONS

"the Claims and Payments Regulations 2013"—see reg. 2.
"electronic communication"—*ibid.*

PART II

REVISION

CHAPTER 1

REVISION ON ANY GROUNDS

Revision on any grounds

4.119   **5.**—(1) Any decision of the Secretary of State under section 8 or 10 of the 1998 Act ("the original decision") may be revised by the Secretary of State if—

(a) the Secretary of State commences action leading to the revision within one month of the date of notification of the original decision; or

(b) an application for a revision is received by the Secretary of State at an appropriate office within—

    (i) one month of the date of notification of the original decision (but subject to regulation 38(4)(correction of accidental errors));

    (ii) 14 days of the expiry of that period if a written statement of the reasons for the decision is requested under regulation 7 (consideration of revision before appeal) or regulation 51 (notice of a decision against which an appeal lies) and that statement is provided within the period specified in paragraph (i);

    (iii) 14 days of the date on which that statement was provided if the statement was requested within the period specified in paragraph (i) but was provided after the expiry of that period; or

    (iv) such longer period as may be allowed under regulation 6 (late application for a revision).

(2) Paragraph (1) does not apply—

(a) in respect of a relevant change of circumstances which occurred since the decision had effect or, in the case of an advance award under regulation 32, 33 or 34 of the Claims and Payments Regulations 2013, since the decision was made;

(b) where the Secretary of State has evidence or information which indicates that a relevant change of circumstances will occur;

(c) in respect of a decision which relates to an employment and support allowance or personal independence payment where the claimant is terminally ill, unless the application for a revision contains an express statement that the claimant is terminally ill.

DEFINITIONS

"appeal"—see reg.2.
"claimant"—*ibid.*
"the date of notification"—*ibid.*
"personal independence payment"—*ibid.*
"terminally ill"—*ibid.*

Late application for a revision

6.—(1) The Secretary of State may extend the time limit specified in regulation 5(1) (revision on any grounds) for making an application for a revision if all of the following conditions are met.

(2) The first condition is that the person wishing to apply for the revision has applied to the Secretary of State at an appropriate office for an extension of time.

(3) The second condition is that the application—

(a) explains why the extension is sought;

(b) contains sufficient details of the decision to which the application relates to enable it to be identified; and

(c) is made within 13 months of the latest date by which the application for revision should have been received by the Secretary of State in accordance with regulation 5(1)(b)(i) to (iii).

(4) The third condition is that the Secretary of State is satisfied that it is reasonable to grant the extension.

(5) The fourth condition is that the Secretary of State is satisfied that due to special circumstances it was not practicable for the application for revision to be made within the time limit specified in regulation 5(1)(b)(i) to (iii) (revision on any grounds).

(6) In determining whether it is reasonable to grant an extension of time, the Secretary of State must have regard to the principle that the greater the amount of time that has elapsed between the end of the time limit specified in regulation 5(1)(b)(i) to (iii) (revision on any grounds) and the date of the application, the more compelling should be the special circumstances on which the application is based.

(7) An application under this regulation which has been refused may not be renewed.

4.120

DEFINITION

"appropriate office"—see reg.2.

Consideration of revision before appeal

7.—(1) This regulation applies in a case where—

(a) the Secretary of State gives a person written notice of a decision under section 8 or 10 of the 1998 Act (whether as originally made or as revised under section 9 of that Act); and

(b) that notice includes a statement to the effect that there is a right of appeal in relation to the decision only if the Secretary of State has considered an application for a revision of the decision.

(2) In a case to which this regulation applies, a person has a right of appeal under section 12(2) of the 1998 Act in relation to the decision only if the Secretary of State has considered on an application whether to revise the decision under section 9 of that Act.

(3) The notice referred to in paragraph (1) must inform the person—

(a) of the time limit under regulation 5(1) (revision on any grounds) for making an application for a revision; and

(b) that, where the notice does not include a statement of the reasons for the decision ("written reasons"), the person may, within one month of the date of notification of the decision, request that the Secretary of State provide written reasons.

4.121

(4) Where written reasons are requested under paragraph (3)(b), the Secretary of State must provide that statement within 14 days of receipt of the request or as soon as practicable afterwards.

(5) Where, as the result of paragraph (2), there is no right of appeal against a decision, the Secretary of State may treat any purported appeal as an application for a revision under section 9 of the 1998 Act.

DEFINITIONS

"the 1998 Act"—see reg.2.
"appeal"—*ibid.*

CHAPTER 2

REVISION ON SPECIFIC GROUNDS

Introduction

4.122   **8.** A decision of the Secretary of State under section 8 or 10 of the 1998 Act may be revised at any time by the Secretary of State in any of the cases and circumstances set out in this Chapter.

Official error, mistake etc.

4.123   **9.** A decision may be revised where the decision—
(a) arose from official error; or
(b) was made in ignorance of, or was based on a mistake as to, some material fact and as a result is more advantageous to a claimant than it would otherwise have been.

DEFINITION

"official error"—see reg.2.

Decisions against which no appeal lies

4.124   **10.** A decision may be revised where the decision is one which is—
(a) specified in Schedule 2 (decisions against which no appeal lies) to the 1998 Act; or
(b) prescribed by regulation 50(2) (decisions which may or may not be appealed).

DEFINITIONS

"the 1998 Act"—see reg.2.
"appeal"—*ibid.*

Decisions where there is an appeal

4.125   **11.**—(1) A decision may be revised where there is an appeal against the decision within the time prescribed by the Tribunal Procedure Rules but the appeal has not been decided.
(2) Where—

494

(a) the Secretary of State makes a decision under section 8 or 10 of the 1998 Act or such a decision is revised under section 9(1) of the 1998 Act ("decision A");
(b) the claimant appeals against decision A;
(c) after the appeal has been made, but before it results in a decision by the First-tier Tribunal, the Secretary of State makes another decision ("decision B") which—
  (i) supersedes decision A; or
  (ii) decides a further claim by the claimant;
(d) after the making of decision B, the First-tier Tribunal makes a decision on the appeal ("decision C"); and
(e) the Secretary of State would have made decision B differently if, at the time, the Secretary of State had been aware of decision C,
the Secretary of State may revise decision B.

DEFINITIONS

"the 1998 Act"—see reg.2.
"appeal"—*ibid.*
"claimant"—*ibid.*

Award of another benefit

12. Where—   4.126
(a) the Secretary of State makes a decision to award a benefit to a claimant ("the original award"); and
(b) an award of another relevant benefit or of an increase in the rate of another relevant benefit is made to the claimant or, in the case of universal credit, to a member of their family, for a period which includes the date on which the original award took effect,
the Secretary of State may revise the original award.

DEFINITIONS

"benefit"—see reg.2.
"claimant"—*ibid.*
"relevant benefit"—*ibid.*
"universal credit"—*ibid.*

Advance awards etc.

13. A decision pursuant to regulation 32, 33 or 34 of the Claims and   4.127
Payments Regulations 2013 to make an advance award of benefit may be revised if the conditions for entitlement are found not to have been satisfied at the start of the period for which the claim is treated as having been made.

DEFINITION

"the Claims and Payments Regulations 2013"—see reg.2.

Sanctions cases etc.

14.—(1) The following decisions may be revised—   4.128
(a) a decision that the amount of an employment and support allowance is to be reduced by virtue of section 11J(1) (sanctions) of the 2007 Act;

 (b) a decision that the amount of a jobseeker's allowance is to be reduced by virtue of section 6J (higher-level sanctions) or 6K(1) (other sanctions) of the Jobseekers Act;

 (c) a decision that the amount of universal credit is to be reduced by virtue of section 26(1) (higher-level sanctions) or 27(1) (other sanctions) of the 2012 Act.

 (d) A decision under section 6B, 7 or 9 ("the loss of benefit provisions") of the Fraud Act that benefit ceases to be payable or falls to be reduced as a result of the person—

 (e) being convicted of an offence; or

 (f) agreeing to pay a penalty as an alternative to prosecution,

may be revised where that conviction is quashed or set aside by a court or where the person withdraws the agreement to pay the penalty.

DEFINITIONS

"the 2007 Act"—see reg.2.
"benefit"—*ibid.*
"employment and support allowance"—*ibid.*
"the Fraud Act"—*ibid.*
"the Jobseekers Act"—*ibid.*
"jobseeker's allowance"—*ibid.*

Other decisions relating to an employment and support allowance

4.129 **15.**—(1) A decision awarding an employment and support allowance may be revised in any of the following circumstances.

(2) The first circumstance is where—

 (a) the decision was made on the basis that the claimant had made and was pursuing an appeal against a decision of the Secretary of State that the claimant did not have limited capability for work ("the original decision"); and

 (b) the appeal in relation to the original decision is successful.

(3) The second circumstance is where—

 (a) the decision incorporates a determination that the conditions in regulation 26(2) (conditions for treating claimant as having limited capability for work until a determination about limited capability for work has been made) of the Employment and Support Allowance Regulations 2013 are satisfied;

 (b) those conditions were not satisfied when the claim was made; and

 (c) a decision falls to be made concerning entitlement to that award in respect of a period before the date on which the award took effect.

(4) The third circumstance is where the claimant's current period of limited capability for work is treated as a continuation of another such period under regulation 86 (linking period) of the Employment and Support Allowance Regulations 2013.

(5) A decision terminating a person's entitlement to an employment and support allowance may be revised where—

 (a) that entitlement was terminated because of section 1A (duration of contributory allowance) of the 2007 Act; and

 (b) it is subsequently determined, in relation to the period of entitlement before that decision, that the person had or is treated as having had limited capability for work-related activity.

DEFINITIONS
"appeal"—see reg.2.
"claimant"—*ibid.*
"employment and support allowance"—*ibid.*
"limited capability for work"—*ibid.*

Other decisions relating to a jobseeker's allowance

16.—(1) A decision awarding a jobseeker's allowance may be revised in any of the following circumstances.   4.130

(2) The first circumstance is where—

(a) the Secretary of State makes a conversion decision (within the meaning of regulation 5(2)(b) of the Employment and Support Allowance (Transitional Provisions, Housing Benefit and Council Tax Benefit) (Existing Awards) (No. 2) Regulations 2010 (deciding whether an existing award qualifies for conversion)) in respect of a person;

(b) the person appeals against that decision;

(c) before or after the appeal is made, there is a decision to award a jobseeker's allowance as the result of a claim being made by that person; and

(d) the appeal in relation to the conversion decision referred to in sub-paragraph (a) is successful.

(3) The second circumstance is where—

(a) a person's entitlement to an employment and support allowance is terminated because of a decision which embodies a determination that the person does not have limited capability for work;

(b) the person appeals against that decision;

(c) before or after the appeal is made, there is a decision to award a jobseeker's allowance as the result of a claim being made by that person; and

(d) the appeal in relation to the termination decision referred to in sub-paragraph (a) is successful.

DEFINITIONS
"appeal"—see reg.2.
"benefit"—*ibid.*
"employment and support allowance"—*ibid.*
"jobseeker's allowance"—*ibid.*

Contributions cases

17.—(1) A decision ("the original decision") may be revised where—   4.131

(a) on or after the date of the original decision—

(i) a late paid contribution is treated under regulation 5 (treatment of late paid contributions where no consent, connivance or negligence by the primary contributor) of the Social Security (Crediting and Treatment of Contributions and National Insurance Numbers) Regulations 2001 ("the Crediting Regulations") as paid on a date which falls on or before the date on which the original decision was made;

(ii) a direction is given under regulation 6 (treatment of contributions paid late through ignorance or error) of those Regulations that a late paid contribution is to be treated as paid on a date which falls on or before the date on which the original decision was made; or

(iii) an unpaid contribution is treated under regulation 60 (treatment of unpaid contributions where no consent, connivance or negligence by the primary contributor) of the Social Security (Contributions) Regulations 2001 as paid on a date which falls on or before the date on which the original decision was made; and

(b) either an award of benefit would have been made or the amount of benefit awarded would have been different.

(2) A decision may be revised where, by virtue of regulation 6C (treatment of Class 3 contributions paid under section 13A of the Act) of the Crediting Regulations, a contribution is treated as paid on a date which falls on or before the date on which the decision was made.

DEFINITION

"benefit"—see reg.2.

Other decisions relating to personal independence payment

4.132   **18.**—(1) Where the Secretary of State makes a decision awarding personal independence payment which takes effect immediately after the expiry of an existing award under regulation 33(3) (advance claim for and award of personal independence payment) of the Claims and Payments Regulations 2013, that decision may be revised if the requirements for entitlement are found not to have been met on the date on which the decision takes effect.

(2) A decision that personal independence payment is not payable to a person for any period may be revised where—

(a) the Secretary of State determines that the person meets the condition in section 85(2) of the 2012 Act (care home residents where the costs of qualifying services are borne out of local or public funds) on incomplete evidence in accordance with regulation 39(5); and

(b) after that determination is made, any of the costs of the qualifying services are recovered from the person for whom they are provided.

(3) A decision of the Secretary of State made in consequence of a negative determination may be revised at any time if it contains an error to which the claimant did not materially contribute.

DEFINITIONS

"the 2012 Act"—see reg.2.
"personal independence payment"—*ibid.*

Other decisions relating to universal credit

4.133   **19.**—(1) Where the Secretary of State has reduced the amount of an award of universal credit as a consequence of regulation 81 (reduction of universal credit) of the Universal Credit Regulations, that decision may be revised.

(2) A decision in relation to universal credit which adopts a determi-

nation made under the Rent Officers Order 2013 may be revised at any time in consequence of a rent officer's redetermination made under that Order which resulted in an increase in the amount which represents rent for the purposes of calculating the housing costs element in universal credit.

DEFINITIONS

"the Universal Credit Regulations"—see reg.2.
"universal credit"—*ibid.*

CHAPTER 3

PROCEDURE AND EFFECTIVE DATE

Procedure for making an application for a revision

20.—(1) The Secretary of State may treat an application for a supersession under section 10 of the 1998 Act as an application for a revision under section 9 of that Act.

4.134

(2) The following paragraph applies where the Secretary of State, in order to consider all the issues raised by the application, requires further evidence or information from a person who has applied for a revision ("the applicant").

(3) The Secretary of State must notify the applicant that—

(a) the further evidence or information specified in the notification is required;

(b) if the applicant provides the relevant evidence or information within one month of the date of notification or such longer period as the Secretary of State may allow, the decision may be revised taking such evidence or information into account; and

(c) if the applicant does not provide such evidence or information within that period, the decision may be revised using such evidence or information as was submitted with the application for revision.

DEFINITION

"the date of notification"—see reg.2.

Effective date of a revision

21. Where, on a revision under section 9 of the 1998 Act, the Secretary of State decides that the date from which the decision under section 8 or 10 of that Act ("the original decision") took effect was wrong, the revision takes effect from the date from which the original decision would have taken effect had the error not been made.

4.135

DEFINITION

"the 1998 Act"—see reg.2.

PART III

SUPERSESSIONS

CHAPTER 1

GROUNDS FOR SUPERSESSION

Introduction

4.136   **22.** Subject to regulation 32 (decisions which may not be superseded), the Secretary of State may make a decision under section 10 ("a superseding decision") of the 1998 Act in any of the cases and circumstances set out in this Chapter.

Changes of circumstances

4.137   **23.**—(1) The Secretary of State may supersede a decision in respect of which—

(a) there has been a relevant change of circumstances since the decision to be superseded had effect or, in the case of an advance award under regulation 32, 33 or 34 of the Claims and Payments Regulations 2013, since it was made; or

(b) it is expected that a relevant change of circumstances will occur.

(2) The fact that a person has become terminally ill is not a relevant change of circumstances for the purposes of paragraph (1) unless an application for supersession is made which contains an express statement that the person is terminally ill.

DEFINITIONS

"the Claims and Payments Regulations 2013"—see reg.2.
"terminally ill"—*ibid.*

Error of law, ignorance, mistake etc.

4.138   **24.** A decision of the Secretary of State, other than one to which regulation 25 (decisions against which no appeal lies) refers, may be superseded where—

(a) the decision was wrong in law, or was made in ignorance of, or was based on a mistake as to, some material fact; and

(b) an application for a supersession was received, or a decision was taken by the Secretary of State to act on the Secretary of State's own initiative, more than one month after the date of notification of the decision to be superseded or after the expiry of such longer period as may have been allowed under regulation 6 (late application for a revision).

Decisions against which no appeal lies

4.139   **25.** A decision specified in Schedule 2 (decisions against which no appeal lies) to the 1998 Act or prescribed in regulation 50(2) (decisions which may or may not be appealed) may be superseded.

DEFINITIONS

"the 1998 Act"—see reg.2.
"appeal"—*ibid.*

Medical evidence and limited capability for work etc.

26.—(1) An employment and support allowance decision, a personal independence payment decision or universal credit decision may be superseded where, since the decision was made, the Secretary of State has—

    (a) received medical evidence from a healthcare professional or other person approved by the Secretary of State; or

    (b) made a determination that the claimant is to be treated as having limited capability for work in accordance with regulation 16, 21, 22 or 29 of the Employment and Support Allowance Regulations 2013 or Part 5 (capability for work or work-related activity) of the Universal Credit Regulations.

(2) The decision awarding personal independence payment may be superseded where there has been a negative determination.

(3) In this regulation—

"an employment and support allowance decision", "personal independence payment decision" and "universal credit decision" each has the meaning given in Schedule 1 (effective dates for superseding decisions made on the ground of a change of circumstances);

"healthcare professional" means—

    (a) a registered medical practitioner;

    (b) a registered nurse; or

    (c) an occupational therapist or physiotherapist registered with a regulatory body established by an Order in Council under section 60 (regulation of health professions, social workers, other care workers etc.) of the Health Act 1999.

4.140

DEFINITIONS

"claimant"—see reg.2.
"employment and support allowance"—*ibid.*
"limited capability for work"—*ibid.*
"personal independence payment"—*ibid.*
"universal credit"—*ibid.*

Sanctions cases

27.—(1) A decision as to the amount of an award of benefit may be superseded where the amount of that award is to be reduced by virtue of—

    (a) section 11J(1) (sanctions) of the 2007 Act;

    (b) section 6J(1) (higher-level sanctions) or 6K(1) (other sanctions) of the Jobseekers Act; or

    (c) section 26(1) (higher-level sanctions) or 27(1) (other sanctions) of the 2012 Act.

(2) A decision reducing an award of benefit by virtue of any of those provisions may be superseded where the reduction falls to be suspended or terminated.

4.141

DEFINITIONS

"the 2007 Act"—see reg.2.
"benefit"—*ibid.*

Loss of benefit cases

4.142   **28.** A decision that a benefit is payable to a claimant may be superseded where that benefit ceases to be payable or falls to be reduced by virtue of section 6B, 7 or 9 of the Fraud Act (loss of benefit provisions).

DEFINITION

"benefit"—see reg.2.

Contributions cases

4.143   **29.** The Secretary of State may supersede a decision ("the original decision") where, on or after the date on which the decision is made, a late or an unpaid contribution is treated as paid under—

  (a) regulation 5 of the Social Security (Crediting and Treatment of Contributions and National Insurance Numbers) Regulations 2001 (treatment of late paid contributions where no consent, connivance or negligence by the primary contributor) on a date which falls on or before the date on which the original decision was made;

  (b) regulation 6 of those Regulations (treatment of contributions paid late through ignorance or error) on a date which falls on or before the date on which the original decision was made; or

  (c) regulation 60 of the Social Security (Contributions) Regulations 2001 (treatment of unpaid contributions where no consent, connivance or negligence by the primary contributor) on a date which falls on or before the date on which the original decision was made.

Housing costs: universal credit

4.144   **30.**—(1) A decision in relation to universal credit which adopts a determination made under the Rent Officers Order 2013 may be superseded where, in consequence of a rent officer's redetermination made in under that Order, the amount which represents rent for the purposes of calculating the housing costs element in universal credit is reduced.

DEFINITIONS

"the Rent Officers Order 2013"—see reg.2.
"universal credit"—*ibid.*

Tribunal decisions

4.145   **31.** The Secretary of State may supersede a decision of the First-tier Tribunal or Upper Tribunal which—

  (a) was made in ignorance of, or was based upon a mistake as to, some material fact; or

  (b) in a case where section 26(5) (appeals involving issues that arise in other cases) of the 1998 Act applies, was made in accordance with section 26(4)(b)of that Act.

CHAPTER 2

SUPERSEDING DECISIONS: LIMITATIONS AND PROCEDURE

Decisions which may not be superseded

32. A decision which may be revised under section 9 of the 1998 Act may 4.146
not be superseded under Chapter 1 of this Part unless—
  (a) circumstances arise in which the Secretary of State may revise the
      decision under Part 2; and
  (b) further circumstances arise in relation to that decision which—
      (i) are not set out in that Part; but
      (ii) are set out in Chapter 1 of this Part or are ones where a supersed-
           ing decision may be made in accordance with regulation 33(3).

DEFINITION

  "the 1998 Act"—see reg.2.

Procedure for making an application for a supersession

33.—(1) The Secretary of State may treat an application for a revision 4.147
under section 9 of the 1998 Act, or a notification of a change of circumstances, as an application for a supersession under section 10 of that Act.

(2) The following paragraph applies where the Secretary of State, in
order to consider all the issues raised by the application, requires further
evidence or information from a person who has applied for a supersession
("the applicant").

(3) The Secretary of State must notify the applicant that—
  (a) the further evidence or information specified in the notification is
      required;
  (b) if the applicant provides the relevant evidence or information within
      one month of the date of notification or such longer period as the
      Secretary of State may allow, the decision may be superseded taking
      such information or evidence into account; and
  (c) if the applicant does not provide such evidence or information within
      that period, the decision to be superseded may be superseded taking
      into account only such evidence or information as was submitted
      with the application for a supersession.

DEFINITION

  "the date of notification"—see reg.2.

CHAPTER 3

EFFECTIVE DATES FOR SUPERSESSIONS

Introduction

34. This Chapter and Schedule 1 (effective dates for superseding 4.148
decisions made on the ground of a change of circumstances) contains

exceptions to the provisions of section 10(5) of the 1998 Act as to the date from which a decision under section 10 of that Act which supersedes an earlier decision takes effect.

DEFINITION

"the 1998 Act"—see reg.2.

Effective dates: Secretary of State decisions

4.149   **35.**—(1) Schedule 1 (effective dates for superseding decisions made on the ground of a change of circumstances) makes provision for the date from which a superseding decision takes effect where there has been, or it is anticipated that there will be, a relevant change of circumstances since the earlier decision took effect.

(2) This paragraph applies where the Secretary of State supersedes a decision—

(a) on the ground that the decision was wrong in law, or was made in ignorance of, or was based on a mistake as to, some material fact, in accordance with regulation 24 (error of law, ignorance, mistake etc.); or

(b) under regulation 25 (decisions against which no appeal lies).

(3) In a case where paragraph (2) applies and the superseding decision relates to a jobseeker's allowance or an employment and support allowance, the superseding decision takes effect from the first day of the benefit week in which the superseding decision, or where applicable, the application for supersession, was made.

(4) In a case where paragraph (2) applies and the superseding decision relates to universal credit, the superseding decision takes effect from the first day of the assessment period in which the superseding decision, or where applicable, the application for supersession, was made.

(5) A superseding decision made in consequence of a decision which is a relevant determination for the purposes of section 27 of the 1998 Act (restrictions on entitlement to benefit in certain cases of error) takes effect from the date of the relevant determination.

(6) In the case of an employment and support allowance, a superseding decision made in accordance with regulation 26(1) (medical evidence and limited capability for work etc.), following an application by the claimant, that embodies a determination that the claimant has limited capability for work-related activity, takes effect from the date of the application.

(7) In the case of an employment and support allowance, a superseding decision made on the Secretary of State's own initiative in accordance with regulation 26(1) that embodies a determination that the claimant has—

(a) limited capability for work; or

(b) limited capability for work-related activity; or

(c) limited capability for work and limited capability for work-related activity,

takes effect from the beginning of the 14th week of entitlement where the determination is the first such determination.

(8) In the case of an employment and support allowance where regulation 6 of the Employment and Support Allowance Regulations 2013 (assessment phase – previous claimants) applies, a superseding decision

made in accordance with regulation 26(1) of these Regulations that embodies a determination that the claimant has—

   (a) limited capability for work; or

   (b) limited capability for work-related activity; or

   (c) limited capability for work and limited capability for work-related activity,

takes effect from the beginning of the 14th week of the claimant's continuous period of limited capability for work.

(9) In the case of universal credit, a superseding decision made in accordance with regulation 26(1) that embodies a determination that the claimant has limited capability for work or limited capability for work and work-related activity takes effect—

   (a) in a case to which regulation 28(1) (period for which the LCW or LCWRA element is not to be included) of the Universal Credit Regulations applies, from the beginning of the assessment period specified in that paragraph; or

   (b) in any other case, from the beginning of the assessment period in which the decision (if made on the Secretary of State's own initiative) or the application for a supersession was made.

(10) A superseding decision to which regulation 27(1) (sanctions cases: reduction in an award) applies takes effect from the beginning of the period specified in—

   (a) regulation 54 of the Employment and Support Allowance Regulations 2013, where the decision relates to the start of a reduction in the amount of an employment and support allowance;

   (b) regulation 56 of the Employment and Support Allowance Regulations 2013, where the decision relates to ending the suspension of a such a reduction where a fraud penalty ceases to apply;

   (c) regulation 22 of the Jobseeker's Allowance Regulations 2013, where the decision relates to the start of a reduction in the amount of a jobseeker's allowance;

   (d) regulation 24 of the Jobseeker's Allowance Regulations 2013, where the decision relates to ending the suspension of such a reduction where a fraud penalty ceases to apply;

   (e) regulation 106 of the Universal Credit Regulations, where the decision relates to the start of a reduction in the amount of universal credit;

   (f) regulation 108 of the Universal Credit Regulations, where the decision relates to ending the suspension of such a reduction where a fraud penalty ceases to apply.

(11) A superseding decision to which regulation 27(2) (sanctions cases: suspension and termination of a reduction) applies takes effect from the beginning of the period specified in—

   (a) regulation 56 of the Employment and Support Allowance Regulations 2013, where the decision relates to the start of a suspension where a fraud penalty applies;

   (b) regulation 57 of the Employment and Support Allowance Regulations 2013, where the decision relates to the termination of a reduction in the amount of an employment and support allowance;

   (c) regulation 24 of the Jobseeker's Allowance Regulations 2013, where the decision relates to the start of a suspension where a fraud penalty applies;

   (d) regulation 25 of the Jobseeker's Allowance Regulations 2013, where the decision relates to the termination of a reduction in the amount of a jobseeker's allowance;

   (e) regulation 108 of the Universal Credit Regulations, where the decision relates to the start of a suspension where a fraud penalty applies;

   (f) regulation 109 of the Universal Credit Regulations, where the decision relates to the termination of a reduction in the amount of an award of universal credit.

(12) A superseding decision to which regulation 28 (loss of benefit provisions) applies takes effect from the date prescribed for the purposes of section 6B or 7 of the Fraud Act.

(13) Where a decision is superseded in accordance with regulation 29 (contributions cases), the superseding decision takes effect from the date referred to in regulation 29(a), (b) or (c) on which the late or unpaid contribution is treated as paid.

(14) A superseding decision made in consequence of a redetermination in accordance with regulation 30 (housing costs: universal credit) takes effect on the first day of the first assessment period following the day on which that redetermination is received by Secretary of State.

DEFINITIONS

   "assessment period"—see reg.2 and Universal Credit Regs., reg.21.
   "benefit"—see reg.2.
   "claimant"—*ibid.*
   "employment and support allowance"—*ibid.*
   "the Fraud Act"—*ibid.*
   "fraud penalty"—*ibid.*
   "jobseeker's allowance"—*ibid.*
   "limited capability for work"—*ibid.*
   "the Universal Credit Regulations"—*ibid.*
   "universal credit"—*ibid.*

Effective dates for superseding decisions where changes notified late

4.150   **36.**—(1) For the purposes of regulation 35(1) (effective dates: Secretary of State decisions) and paragraphs 6, 14 and 21 of Schedule 1 (effective dates for superseding decisions made on the ground of a change of circumstances), the Secretary of State may extend the time allowed for a person ("the applicant") to give notice of a change of circumstances in so far as it affects the effective date of the change if all of the following conditions are met.

(2) The first condition is that an application is made to the Secretary of State at an appropriate office for an extension of time.

(3) The second condition is that the application—

   (a) contains particulars of the change of circumstances and the reasons for the failure to give notice of the change of circumstances on an earlier date; and

   (b) is made—

      (i) within 13 months of the date on which the change occurred; or

     (ii) in the case of personal independence payment where a notification is given under paragraph 15 of Part 2 of Schedule 1 (effective dates for superseding decisions made on the ground of a change of circumstances), within 13 months of the date on which the claimant first satisfied the conditions of entitlement to the particular rate of personal independence payment.

(4) The third condition is that the Secretary of State is satisfied that it is reasonable to grant the extension.

(5) The fourth condition is that the change of circumstances notified by the applicant is relevant to the decision which is to be superseded.

(6) The fifth condition is that the Secretary of State is satisfied that, due to special circumstances, it was not practicable for the applicant to give notice of the change of circumstances within the relevant notification period.

(7) In determining whether it is reasonable to grant an extension of time—

(a) the Secretary of State must have regard to the principle that the greater the amount of time that has elapsed between the end of the relevant notification period and the date of the application, the more compelling should be the special circumstances on which the application is based;

(b) no account must be taken of the fact that the applicant or any person acting for them was unaware of, or misunderstood, the law applicable to the case (including ignorance or misunderstanding of the time limits imposed by these Regulations); and

(c) no account must be taken of the fact that the Upper Tribunal or a court has taken a different view of the law from that previously understood and applied.

(8) An application under this regulation which has been refused may not be renewed.

(9) In this regulation, "the relevant notification period" means—

(a) in the case of universal credit, the assessment period in which the change of circumstances occurs; or

(b) in any other case, a period of one month, beginning with the date on which the change of circumstances occurred.

Definition

"personal independence payment"—see reg.2.

Effective dates: tribunal cases

37.—(1) This paragraph applies where—   4.151

(a) the Secretary of State supersedes a decision of the First-tier Tribunal or the Upper Tribunal on the ground that it is made in ignorance of, or based on a mistake as to, a material fact in accordance with regulation 31(a) (tribunal decisions), and

(b) as a result of that ignorance or mistake, the decision to be superseded was more advantageous to the claimant than it would otherwise have been.

(2) In a case where paragraph (1) applies where the decision relates to—

(a) a jobseeker's allowance;

(b) personal independence payment,

the superseding decision takes effect from the date on which the decision of the First-tier Tribunal or the Upper Tribunal took, or was to take, effect.

(3) In a case where paragraph (1) applies and the decision relates to an employment and support allowance or universal credit where—

(a) the material fact does not relate to a limited capability for work determination embodied in or necessary to the decision; or

(b) the material fact does relate to such a determination and the Secretary of State is satisfied that at the time the decision was made the claimant knew or could reasonably be expected to know of it and that it was relevant,

the superseding decision takes effect from the first day of the benefit week or (as the case may be) the assessment period in which in the Tribunal's decision took or was to take effect.

(4) Where the Secretary of State supersedes a decision of the First-tier Tribunal or the Upper Tribunal in accordance with regulation 31(b) (tribunal decisions), the decision takes effect—

(a) if the decision relates to personal independence payment, from the date on which the decision of the First-tier Tribunal or the Upper Tribunal would have taken effect had it been decided in accordance with the determination of the Upper Tribunal or the court in the appeal referred to in section 26(1)(b) of the 1998 Act;

(b) if the decision relates to a jobseeker's allowance or an employment and support allowance, from the first day of the benefit week in which the Tribunal's decision would have taken effect had it been so decided;

(c) if the decision relates to universal credit, from the first day of the assessment period in which the Tribunal's decision would have taken effect had it been so decided.

(5) Paragraph (6) applies where—

(a) the Upper Tribunal, or the court as defined in section 27(7) (restrictions on entitlement to benefit in certain cases of error) of the 1998 Act, determines an appeal as mentioned in subsection (1)(a) of that section ("the relevant determination");

(b) the Secretary of State makes a decision of the kind specified in subsection (1)(b) of that section;

(c) there is an appeal against the relevant determination;

(d) after the Secretary of State's decision, payment is suspended in accordance with regulation 44 (suspension in prescribed cases); and

(e) on appeal a court, within the meaning of section 27, reverses the relevant determination in whole or part.

(6) A consequential decision by the Secretary of State under section 10 of the 1998 Act which supersedes an earlier decision of the Secretary of State under paragraph (5)(b) takes effect from the date on which the earlier decision took effect.

DEFINITIONS

"the 1998 Act"—see reg.2.
"appeal"—*ibid.*
"assessment period"—see reg.2 and Universal Credit Regs., reg.21.
"benefit"—see reg.2.
"benefit week"—*ibid.*
"claimant"—*ibid.*
"employment and support allowance"—*ibid.*
"jobseeker's allowance"—*ibid.*
"personal independence payment"—*ibid.*
"universal credit"—*ibid.*

PART IV

OTHER MATTERS RELATING TO DECISION- MAKING

Correction of accidental errors

38.—(1) An accidental error in a decision of the Secretary of State, or in any record of such a decision, may be corrected by the Secretary of State at any time.

(2) Such a correction is to be treated as part of that decision or of that record.

(3) The Secretary of State must give written notice of the correction as soon as practicable to the person to whom the decision was given.

(4) In calculating the time within which an application may be made under regulation 5 (revision on any grounds) for a decision to be revised, no account is to be taken of any day falling before the day on which notice of the correction was given.

4.152

Determinations on incomplete evidence

39.—(1) The following provisions of this regulation apply for the purposes of a decision under section 8 or 10 of the 1998 Act.

(2) Where—
(a) a determination falls to be made by the Secretary of State concerning the matter mentioned in paragraph (3); and
(b) it appears to the Secretary of State that the Secretary of State is not in possession of all of the evidence or information which is relevant for the purposes of the determination,

the Secretary of State must make the determination on the assumption that the relevant evidence or information which is not in the Secretary of State's possession is adverse to the claimant.

(3) The matter is whether, for the purposes of regulation 45 (relevant education) of the Jobseeker's Allowance Regulations 2013 a person is by virtue of that regulation to be treated as receiving relevant education.

(4) Where—
(a) a determination falls to be made by the Secretary of State as to what costs are to be included in claimant's award of universal credit under section 11 (housing costs) of the 2012 Act; and
(b) it appears to the Secretary of State that the Secretary of State is not in possession of all of the evidence or information which is relevant for the purposes of the determination,

the Secretary of State may make the determination on the assumption that the costs to be included in the claimant's award under that section are those that the Secretary of State is able to determine using such evidence or information as is in the Secretary of State's possession.

(5) Where, in the case of personal independence payment—
(a) a determination falls to be made by the Secretary of State as to whether a person meets the condition in section 85(2) (care home residents where the costs of qualifying services are borne out of local or public funds) of the 2012 Act; and
(b) it appears to the Secretary of State that, having made reasonable

4.153

enquiries, the Secretary of State is not in possession of all of the evidence or information which is or could be relevant for the purposes of the determination,

the Secretary of State may make the determination using such information or evidence as is in the Secretary of State's possession.

DEFINITIONS

"the 2012 Act"—see reg.2.
"claimant"—*ibid.*

Determinations as to limited capability for work

4.154   **40.**—(1) Where, in relation to an award of an employment and support allowance, the Secretary of State makes a determination (including a determination made following a change of circumstances) whether a person—

(a) has or does not have limited capability for work; or

(b) is to be treated as having or not having limited capability for work,

which is embodied in or necessary to a decision under Chapter 2 of Part 1 of the 1998 Act (decisions and appeals) or on which such a decision is based, that determination is to be conclusive for the purposes of any further decision relating to such an allowance.

(2) Paragraph (1) applies to determinations made in relation to universal credit as it applies in the case of an employment and support allowance.

(3) Where, in relation to any purpose for which Part 1 (employment and support allowance) of the 2007 Act or Part 1 (universal credit) of the 2012 Act applies, a determination falls to be made as to whether a person—

(a) is, or is to be treated as, having or not having limited capability for work; or

(b) is terminally ill,

that issue is to be determined by the Secretary of State, notwithstanding the fact that any other matter falls to be determined by another authority.

DEFINITIONS

"the 1998 Act"—see reg.2.
"employment and support allowance"—*ibid.*
"limited capability for work"—*ibid.*
"universal credit"—*ibid.*

Effect of alterations affecting universal credit

4.155   **41.**—(1) Subject to paragraph (3), an alteration in the amount of a person's employed earnings (within the meaning of regulation 55(1) of the Universal Credit Regulations) made in accordance with Chapter 2 of Part 6 (earned income) of the Universal Credit Regulations in consequence of information provided to the Secretary of State by HMRC is prescribed for the purposes of section 159D(1)(b)(vi) (effect of alterations affecting universal credit) of the Administration Act.

(2) For the purposes of this regulation, "alteration" means an increase or decrease in such earnings.

(3) Where the person disputes the figure used in accordance with regulation 55 (employed earnings) of the Universal Credit Regulations to calculate employed earnings in relation to any assessment period, the Secretary of State must—

    (a) inform the person that they may request that the Secretary of State gives a decision in relation to the amount of universal credit payable in relation to that assessment period; and

    (b) where such a decision is requested, give it within 14 days of receiving the request or as soon as practicable afterwards.

    (4) Paragraph (3) does not affect the validity of anything done under section 159D(2) or (3) of the Administration Act in relation to the person's award.

    (5) A decision made in accordance with paragraph (3) takes effect on the date on which the alteration under section 159(D)(2) or (3) came into force in relation to the person.

DEFINITIONS

    "the Administration Act"—see reg.2.
    "assessment period"—see reg.2 and Universal Credit Regs., reg.21.
    "the Universal Credit Regulations"—see reg.2.
    "universal credit"—*ibid.*

Issues for HMRC

    42.—(1) Where, on consideration of any claim or other matter, it appears to the Secretary of State that an issue arises which, by virtue of section 8 of the Transfer Act, falls to be decided by an officer of HMRC, the Secretary of State must refer that issue to HMRC.   4.156

    (2) Where—

    (a) the Secretary of State has decided any claim or other matter on an assumption of facts—

        (i) which appeared to the Secretary of State not to be in dispute, but

        (ii) concerning which, had an issue arisen, that issue would have fallen, by virtue of section 8 of the Transfer Act, to be decided by HMRC;

    (b) an application for a revision or supersession is made, or an appeal is brought, in relation to that claim or other matter; and

    (c) it appears to the Secretary of State on receipt of that application or appeal that such an issue arises,

the Secretary of State must refer that issue to HMRC.

    (3) Pending the final decision of any issue which has been referred to HMRC in accordance with paragraph (1) or (2), the Secretary of State may—

    (a) determine any other issue arising on consideration of the claim, application or other matter,

    (b) seek a preliminary opinion from HMRC on the issue referred and decide the claim, application or other matter in accordance with that opinion; or

    (c) defer making any decision on the claim, application or other matter.

    (4) On receipt by the Secretary of State of the final decision of an issue which has been referred to HMRC under paragraph (1) or (2), the Secretary of State must—

    (a) in a case where the Secretary of State made a decision under paragraph (3)(b), decide whether to revise the decision under section 9 of the 1998 Act or to supersede it under section 10 of that Act;

    (b) in a case to which paragraph (3)(a) or (c) applies, decide the claim, application or other matter in accordance with the final decision of the issue so referred.

(5) In this regulation—

(a) "final decision" means the decision of HMRC under section 8 (decisions by officers of Board) of the Transfer Act or the determination of any appeal in relation to that decision; and

(b) "the Transfer Act" means the Social Security Contributions (Transfer of Functions, etc.) Act 1999.

DEFINITIONS

"appeal"—see reg.2.
"HMRC"—*ibid.*

Appeals raising issues for HMRC

4.157   **43.**—(1) This regulation applies where—

(a) a person has appealed to the First-tier Tribunal and it appears to the First-tier Tribunal that an issue arises which, by virtue of section 8 of the Transfer Act, falls to be decided by HMRC; and

(b) the tribunal has required the Secretary of State to refer that issue to HMRC.

(2) Pending the final decision of any issue which has been referred to HMRC in accordance with paragraph (1), the Secretary of State may revise the decision under appeal under section 9 of the 1998 Act, or make a further decision under section 10 of that Act superseding that decision, in accordance with the Secretary of State's determination of any issue other than one which has been so referred.

(3) On receipt by the Secretary of State of the final decision of an issue which has been referred to HMRC in accordance with paragraph (1), the Secretary of State must consider whether the decision under appeal ought to be revised or superseded under the 1998 Act, and—

(a) if so, revise it or make a further decision which supersedes it; or

(b) if not, invite the First-tier Tribunal to determine to appeal.

(4) In this regulation, "final decision" and "Transfer Act" have the same meaning as in regulation 42 (issues for HMRC).

DEFINITIONS

"the 1998 Act"—see reg.2.
"appeal"—*ibid.*
"HMRC"—*ibid.*

PART V

SUSPENSION

Suspension in prescribed cases

4.158   **44.**—(1) The Secretary of State may suspend, in whole or part, payment of any benefit to a person ("P") in the circumstances described in paragraph (2).

(2) The circumstances are where—

(a) it appears to the Secretary of State that—

    (i) an issue arises whether the conditions for entitlement to the benefit are or were fulfilled;

    (ii) an issue arises whether a decision relating to an award of the benefit should be revised under section 9 or superseded under section 10 of the 1998 Act,

    (iii) an issue arises whether any amount of benefit paid to P is recoverable under or by virtue of section 71ZB, 71ZG or 71ZH of the Administration Act,

    (iv) the last address notified to the Secretary of State of P is not the address at which P resides,

(b) an appeal is pending in P's case against a decision of the First-tier Tribunal, the Upper Tribunal or a court; or

(c) an appeal is pending against a decision given by the Upper Tribunal or a court in a different case and it appears to the Secretary of State that, if the appeal were to be decided in a particular way, an issue would arise as to whether the award of any benefit to P (whether the same benefit or not) ought to be revised or superseded.

(3) For the purposes of section 21(2)(c) (suspension in prescribed circumstances) of the 1998 Act, where an appeal against the decision has not been brought or an application for permission to appeal against the decision has not been made but the time for doing so has not yet expired, an appeal is pending in the circumstances described in paragraph (4).

(4) The circumstances are where a decision of the First-tier Tribunal, the Upper Tribunal or a court has been made and the Secretary of State—

(a) is awaiting receipt of that decision; or

(b) in the case of a decision of the First-tier Tribunal, is considering whether to apply for a statement of reasons for the decision or has applied for such a statement and is awaiting receipt; or

(c) has received that decision or, if it is a decision of the First-tier Tribunal has received the statement of reasons for it, and is considering whether to apply for permission to appeal, or where permission to appeal has been granted, is considering whether to appeal.

(5) Where payment of any benefit is suspended as the result of paragraph (2)(b) or (c), the Secretary of State must, as soon as reasonably practicable, give written notice to P of any proposal to—

(a) request a statement of the reasons for a tribunal decision;

(b) apply for permission to appeal; or

(c) make an appeal.

Definitions

"the 1998 Act"—see reg.2.
"appeal"—*ibid.*
"benefit"—*ibid.*

Provision of information or evidence

45.—(1) This regulation applies where the Secretary of State requires information or evidence from a person mentioned in paragraph (2) ("P") in order to determine whether a decision awarding a benefit should be revised under section 9 of the 1998 Act or superseded under section 10 of that Act.   4.159

(2) The persons are—

(a) a person in respect of whom payment of any benefit has been suspended in the circumstances set out in regulation 44(2)(a) (suspension in prescribed cases);

(b) a person who has made an application for a decision of the Secretary of State to be revised or superseded;

(c) a person from whom the Secretary of State requires information or evidence under regulation 38(2) (evidence and information in connection with an award) of the Claims and Payments Regulations 2013;

(d) a person from whom the Secretary of State requires documents, certificates or other evidence under regulation 31(3) (evidence and information) of the Jobseeker's Allowance Regulations 2013;

(e) a person whose entitlement to an employment and support allowance or universal credit is conditional on their having, or being treated as having, limited capability for work.

(3) The Secretary of State must notify P of the requirements of this regulation.

(4) P must either—

(a) supply the information or evidence within—

(i) a period of 14 days beginning with the date on which the notification under paragraph (3) was given or sent to P or such longer period as the Secretary of State allows in that notification, or

(ii) such longer period as P satisfies the Secretary of State is necessary in order to comply with the requirements, or

(b) satisfy the Secretary of State within the period applicable under sub-paragraph (a)(i) that either—

(i) the information or evidence does not exist, or

(ii) it is not possible for P to obtain it.

(5) In relation to a person to whom paragraph (2)(d) refers, paragraph (4)(a)(i) has effect as if for "14 days" there were substituted "7 days".

(6) The Secretary of State may suspend the payment of a benefit, in whole or part, to any person to whom paragraph (2)(b), (c), (d) or (e) applies who fails to satisfy the requirements of paragraph (4).

(7) In this regulation, "evidence" includes evidence which a person is required to provide in accordance with regulation 2 (evidence of incapacity for work, limited capability for work and confinement) of the Social Security (Medical Evidence) Regulations 1976.

DEFINITIONS

"benefit"—see reg.2.
"jobseeker's allowance"—*ibid.*
"limited capability for work"—*ibid.*

Making of payments which have been suspended

4.160   **46.** The Secretary of State must pay a benefit which has been suspended where—

(a) in a case where regulation 44(2)(a) (suspension in prescribed cases) applies, the Secretary of State is satisfied that the benefit is properly payable and that there are no outstanding issues to be resolved;

(b) in a case to which regulation 45(6) (provision of information or evidence) applies, the Secretary of State is satisfied that the benefit is properly payable and that the requirements of regulation 45(4) have been satisfied;

(c) in a case to which regulation 44(2)(b) (suspension in prescribed cases) applies, the Secretary of State—

    (i) does not, in the case of a decision of the First-tier Tribunal, apply for a statement of the reasons for that decision within the period specified under the Tribunal Procedure Rules;

    (ii) does not, in the case of a decision of the First-tier Tribunal, the Upper Tribunal or a court, make an application for permission to appeal or (where permission to appeal is granted) make the appeal within the time prescribed for the making of such application or appeal;

    (iii) withdraws an application for permission to appeal or withdraws the appeal; or

    (iv) is refused permission to appeal, in circumstances where it is not open to the Secretary of State to renew the application for permission or to make a further application for permission to appeal;

(d) in a case to which regulation 44(2)(c) (suspension in prescribed cases) applies, the Secretary of State, in relation to the decision of the Upper Tribunal or a court in a different case—

    (i) does not make an application for permission to appeal or (where permission to appeal is granted) make the appeal within the time prescribed for the making of such application or appeal;

    (ii) withdraws an application for permission to appeal or withdraws the appeal;

    (iii) is refused permission to appeal, in circumstances where it is not open to the Secretary of State to renew the application for permission or to make a further application for permission to appeal.

DEFINITIONS

"appeal"—see reg. 2.
"benefit"—*ibid.*
"the Tribunal Procedure Rules"—*ibid.*

PART VI

TERMINATION

Termination for failure to furnish information or evidence

47.—(1) This regulation applies where payment of a benefit to a person ("P") has been suspended in full under—   4.161

(a) regulation 44 (suspension in prescribed cases) and P subsequently fails to comply with a requirement for information or evidence under regulation 45 (provision of information or evidence) and more than one month has elapsed since the requirement was made; or

(b) regulation 45(6) and more than one month has elapsed since the first payment was suspended.

(2) In a case to which this regulation applies, except where entitlement

ceases on an earlier date other than under this regulation, the Secretary of State must decide that P ceases to be entitled to that benefit with effect from the date on which the payment of the benefit was suspended.

DEFINITION

"benefit"—see reg.2.

Termination in the case of entitlement to alternative benefits

4.162   **48.**—(1) This paragraph applies where an award of a jobseeker's allowance ("the existing benefit") exists in favour of a person and, if that award did not exist and a claim was made by that person for an employment and support allowance ("the alternative benefit"), an award of the alternative benefit would be made on that claim.

(2) This paragraph applies where an award of an employment and support allowance ("the existing benefit") exists in favour of a person and, if that award did not exist and a claim was made by that person for a jobseeker's allowance ("the alternative benefit"), an award of the alternative benefit would be made on that claim.

(3) In a case where paragraph (1) or (2) applies, if a claim for the alternative benefit is made, the Secretary of State may bring to an end the award of the existing benefit if satisfied that an award of the alternative benefit will be made.

(4) Where the Secretary of State brings an award of the existing benefit to an end under paragraph (3), the Secretary of State must end the award on the day immediately preceding the first day on which an award of the alternative benefit takes effect.

(5) Where an award of a jobseeker's allowance is made in accordance with this regulation, paragraph 4 of Schedule 1 to the Jobseekers Act (waiting days) does not apply.

(6) Where an award of an employment and support allowance is made in accordance with this regulation, paragraph 2 (waiting days) of Schedule 2 (supplementary provisions) to the 2007 Act does not apply.

DEFINITIONS

"the 2007 Act"—see reg.2.
"benefit"—*ibid.*
"employment and support allowance"—*ibid.*
"the Jobseekers Act"—*ibid.*
"jobseeker's allowance"—*ibid.*

PART VII

APPEALS

Other persons with a right of appeal

4.163   **49.** In addition to the claimant, but subject to regulation 7 (consideration of revision before appeal), the following persons have the right of appeal under section 12(2) of the 1998 Act—

(a) any person appointed by the Secretary of State under regulation 56 (payments on death) of the Claims and Payments Regulations 2013 to proceed with the claim of a person who claimed benefit and subsequently died;

(b) any person appointed by the Secretary of State under regulation 57 (persons unable to act) of those Regulations to act on behalf of another;

(c) any person claiming personal independence payment on behalf of another under section 82(5) of the 2012 Act (terminal illness); and

(d) in the case of a decision under section 71ZB, 71ZG or 71ZH of the Administration Act to recover any amount paid by way of benefit, any person from whom such an amount is recoverable, but only if their rights, duties or obligations are affected by that decision.

DEFINITIONS

"the 1998 Act"—see reg.2.
"the 2012 Act"—*ibid.*
"the Administration Act"—*ibid.*
"appeal"—*ibid.*
"benefit"—*ibid.*
"the Claims and Payments Regulations 2013"—*ibid.*
"personal independence payment"—*ibid.*

Decisions which may or may not be appealed

50.—(1) An appeal lies against a decision set out in Schedule 2 (decisions against which an appeal lies).

(2) No appeal lies against a decision set out in Schedule 3 (decisions against which no appeal lies).

(3) In paragraph (2) and Schedule 3, "decision" includes a determination embodied in or necessary to a decision.

4.164

DEFINITION

"appeal"—see reg.2.

Notice of a decision against which an appeal lies

51.—(1) This regulation applies in the case of a person ("P") who has a right of appeal under the 1998 Act or these Regulations.

(2) The Secretary of State must—

(a) give P written notice of the decision and of the right to appeal against that decision; and

(b) inform P that, where that notice does not include a statement of the reasons for the decision, P may, within one month of the date of notification of that decision, request that the Secretary of State provide a written statement of the reasons for that decision.

(3) If the Secretary of State is requested under paragraph (2)(b) to provide a written statement of reasons, the Secretary of State must provide such a statement within 14 days of the request or as soon as practicable afterwards.

4.165

DEFINITION

"appeal"—see reg.2.

Appeals against decisions which have been revised

4.166   **52.**—(1) An appeal against a decision of the Secretary of State does not lapse where—

(a) the decision is revised under section 9 of the 1998 Act before the appeal is decided; and

(b) the decision of the Secretary of State as revised is not more advantageous to the appellant than the decision before it was revised.

(2) In a case to which paragraph (1) applies, the appeal must be treated as though it had been brought against the decision as revised.

(3) The Secretary of State must inform the appellant that they may, within one month of the date of notification of the decision as revised, make further representations as to the appeal.

(4) After the end of that period, or within that period if the appellant consents in writing, the appeal to the First-tier Tribunal must proceed, except where—

(a) the Secretary of State further revises the decision in light of further representations from the appellant; and

(b) that decision is more advantageous to the appellant than the decision before it was revised.

(5) Decisions which are more advantageous for the purpose of this regulation include those where—

(a) the amount of any benefit payable to the appellant is greater, or any benefit is awarded for a longer period, as a result of the decision;

(b) the decision would have resulted in the amount of benefit in payment being greater but for the operation of any provision of the Administration Act or the Contributions and Benefits Act restricting or suspending the payment of, or disqualifying a claimant from receiving, some or all of the benefit;

(c) as a result of the decision, a denial or disqualification for the receipt of any benefit is lifted, wholly or in part;

(d) the decision reverses a decision to pay benefit to a third party instead of to the appellant;

(e) in consequence of the decision, benefit paid is not recoverable under section 71ZB, 71ZG or 71ZH of the Administration Act or regulations made under any of those sections, or the amount so recoverable is reduced; or

(f) a financial gain accrued or will accrue to the appellant in consequence of the decision.

DEFINITIONS

"the 1998 Act"—see reg.2.
"the Administration Act"—*ibid.*
"appeal"—*ibid.*
"benefit"—*ibid.*
"claimant"—*ibid.*
"the date of notification"—*ibid.*
"writing"—*ibid.*

Decisions involving issues that arise on appeal in other cases

4.167   **53.**—(1) For the purposes of section 25(3)(b) of the 1998 Act (prescribed cases and circumstances in which a decision may be made on a prescribed basis)—

(a) a prescribed case is a case in which the claimant would be entitled to the benefit to which the decision relates, even if the other appeal referred to in section 25(1)(b) of the 1998 Act were decided in a way which is the most unfavourable to the claimant; and

(b) the prescribed basis on which the Secretary of State may make the decision is as if—

    (i) the other appeal referred to in section 25(1)(b) of the 1998 Act had already been decided; and

    (ii) that appeal had been decided in a way which is the most unfavourable to the claimant.

(2) For the purposes of section 25(5)(c) of the 1998 Act (appeal treated as pending against a decision in a different case, even though an appeal against the decision has not been brought or an application for permission to appeal against the decision has not been made but the time for doing so has not yet expired), the prescribed circumstances are that the Secretary of State—

(a) certifies in writing that the Secretary of State is considering appealing against that decision; and

(b) considers that, if such an appeal were to be decided in a particular way—

    (i) there would be no entitlement to benefit in that case; or

    (ii) the appeal would affect the decision in that case in some other way.

DEFINITIONS

    "the 1998 Act"—see reg. 2.
    "appeal"—*ibid.*
    "benefit"—*ibid.*
    "claimant"—*ibid.*

Appeals involving issues that arise in other cases

54. For the purposes of section 26(6)(c) of the 1998 Act (appeal is treated as pending against a decision in a different case, even though an appeal against the decision has not been brought or an application for permission to appeal has not been made but the time for doing so has not yet expired) the prescribed circumstances are that the Secretary of State—   **4.168**

(a) certifies in writing that the Secretary of State is considering appealing against that decision; and

(b) considers that, if such an appeal were already decided, it would affect the determination of the appeal referred to in section 26(1)(a) of the 1998 Act.

DEFINITIONS

    "the 1998 Act"—see reg. 2.
    "appeal"—*ibid.*
    "writing"—*ibid.*

Consequential amendments

55. [Omitted]   **4.169**

SCHEDULE 1

EFFECTIVE DATES FOR SUPERSEDING DECISIONS MADE ON THE
GROUND OF A CHANGE OF CIRCUMSTANCES

PART I

EMPLOYMENT AND SUPPORT ALLOWANCE AND JOBSEEKER'S ALLOWANCE

1. Subject to the following provisions of this Part and to Part 4, in the case of an employment and support allowance or a jobseeker's allowance, a superseding decision made on the ground of a change of circumstances takes effect from the first day of the benefit week in which the relevant change of circumstances occurs or is expected to occur.

2. Paragraph 1 does not apply where—

(a) the superseding decision is not advantageous to the claimant; and

(b) there has been an employment and support allowance decision where the Secretary of State is satisfied that, in relation to a limited capability for work determination, the claimant—

(i) failed to notify an appropriate office of a change of circumstances which the claimant was required by regulations under the Administration Act to notify; and

(ii) could not reasonably have been expected to know that the change of circumstances should have been notified.

3. Where a relevant change of circumstances results, or is expected to result, in a reduced award and the Secretary of State is of the opinion that it is impracticable for a superseding decision to take effect from the day set out in paragraph 1, that superseding decision takes effect—

(a) where the relevant change has occurred, from the first day of the benefit week following that in which that superseding decision is made; or

(b) where the relevant change is expected to occur, from the first day of the benefit week following that in which that change of circumstances is expected to occur.

4. Where entitlement ends, or is expected to end, as the result of a change of circumstances, the superseding decision takes effect from the day on which the relevant change of circumstances occurs or is expected to occur.

5. In the case of an employment and support allowance where a person who is subject to—

(a) section 45A or 47 of the Mental Health Act 1983 (power of higher courts to direct hospital admission; removal to hospital of persons serving sentences of imprisonment etc.);

(b) section 59A (hospital direction) of the Criminal Procedure (Scotland) Act 1995; or

(c) section 136 (transfer of prisoners for treatment for mental disorder) of the Mental Health (Care and Treatment) (Scotland) Act 2003,

ceases, or is expected to cease, to be detained in a hospital (as defined in the Act, or the Act of the Scottish Parliament, to which the person is subject) for a period of less than a week, a superseding decision related to that person's departure from, or return to, hospital takes effect from the day on which that change of circumstances occurs or is expected to occur.

6. Where the superseding decision is advantageous to the claimant and the change of circumstances was notified to an appropriate office more than one month after the change occurred or after the expiry of such longer period as may be allowed under regulation 36 (effective dates for superseding decisions where changes notified late), the superseding decision takes effect from the beginning of the benefit week in which the notification was given.

7. In the case of an employment and support allowance decision where the Secretary of State is satisfied that, in relation a limited capability for work determination, the claimant—

(a) failed to notify an appropriate office of a change of circumstances which the claimant was required by regulations under the Administration Act to notify; and

(b) could reasonably have been expected to know that the change of circumstances should have been notified,

the superseding decision takes effect in accordance with paragraph 8.

8. The superseding decision takes effect—

(a) from the date on which the claimant ought to have notified the change of circumstances; or

(b) if more than one change has taken place between the date from which the decision to be superseded took effect and the date of the superseding decision, from the date on which the first change ought to have been notified.

9. In the case of a claimant who makes an application for a supersession which contains an express statement that they are terminally ill, the superseding decision takes effect from the date on which the claimant became terminally ill.

10. Where the superseding decision is advantageous to the claimant and is made on the Secretary of State's own initiative, the decision takes effect from the beginning of the benefit week in which the Secretary of State commenced action with a view to supersession.

11. In this Part—

"employment and support allowance decision" means a decision to award an employment and support allowance embodied in or necessary to which is a determination that the claimant has, or is to be treated as having, limited capability for work;

"week" means a period of 7 days, beginning with midnight between Saturday and Sunday.

PART II

PERSONAL INDEPENDENCE PAYMENT

12. Subject to the following provisions of this Part and to Part 4, in the case of personal independence payment, a superseding decision made on the ground of a change of circumstances takes effect on the date on which the relevant change of circumstances occurs or is expected to occur.

13. Paragraph 12 does not apply where—
  (a) the superseding decision is not advantageous to the claimant; and
  (b) there has been a personal independence payment decision where the Secretary of State is satisfied that, in relation to such a decision, the claimant—
      (i) failed to notify an appropriate office of a change of circumstances which the claimant was required by regulations under the Administration Act to notify; and
      (ii) could not reasonably have been expected to know that the change of circumstances should have been notified.

14. Except in a case where paragraph 15 or 31 applies, where the superseding decision is advantageous to the claimant and the change of circumstances was notified to an appropriate office more than one month after the change occurred or after the expiry of such longer period as may be allowed under regulation 36 (effective dates for superseding decisions where changes notified late), the superseding decision takes effect from the date of notification of the change.

15. Where—
  (a) the change is relevant to entitlement to a particular rate of personal independence payment; and
  (b) the claimant notifies an appropriate office of the change no later than one month after the date on which they first satisfied the conditions of entitlement to that rate or within such longer period as may be allowed by regulation 36 (effective dates for superseding decisions where changes notified late),
the superseding decision takes effect from the date on which the claimant first satisfied those conditions.

16. Where the Secretary of State is satisfied that, in relation to a personal independence payment decision, the claimant—
  (a) failed to notify an appropriate office of a change of circumstances which the claimant was required by regulations under the Administration Act to notify; and
  (b) could reasonably have been expected to know that the change of circumstances should have been notified,
the superseding decision takes effect in accordance with paragraph 17.

17. The superseding decision takes effect—
  (a) from the date on which the claimant ought to have notified the change of circumstances; or
  (b) if more than one change has taken place between the date from which the decision to be superseded took effect and the date of the superseding decision, from the date on which the first change ought to have been notified.

18. Where the superseding decision is advantageous to the claimant and is made on the Secretary of State's own initiative, the decision takes effect from the date on which the Secretary of State commenced action with a view to supersession.

19. In paragraphs 13 and 16, "personal independence payment decision" means a decision to award personal independence payment, embodied in or necessary to which is a determination whether the claimant satisfies any of the requirements in section 78(1) and (2) (daily living component) or section 79(1) and (2) (mobility component) of the 2012 Act.

PART III

UNIVERSAL CREDIT

20. Subject to the following paragraphs and to Part 4, in the case of universal credit, a superseding decision made on the ground of a change of circumstances takes effect from the first day of the assessment period in which that change occurred or is expected to occur.

21. Except in a case to which paragraph 22 or 31 applies, where the superseding decision is advantageous to the claimant and the change of circumstances was notified to an appropriate office after the end of the assessment period in which the change occurred or after the expiry of such longer period as may be allowed under regulation 36 (effective dates for superseding decisions where changes notified late), the superseding decision takes effect from the first day of the assessment period in which the notification was given.

22. In the case of a person to whom regulation 61 (information for calculating earned income) of the Universal Credit Regulations applies, where—

    (a) the relevant change of circumstances is that the person's employed earnings are reduced; and

    (b) the person provides such information for the purposes of calculating those earnings at such times as the Secretary of State may require,

the superseding decision takes effect from the first day of the assessment period in which that change occurred.

23. In the case of a universal credit decision where the Secretary of State is satisfied that, in relation to a limited capability for work determination, the claimant—

    (a) failed to notify an appropriate office of a change of circumstances which the claimant was required by regulations under the Administration Act to notify; and

    (b) could reasonably have been expected to know that the change of circumstances should have been notified,

the superseding decision takes effect in accordance with paragraph 24.

24. The superseding decision takes effect—

    (a) from the first day of the assessment period in which the claimant ought to have notified the change of circumstances; or

    (b) if more than one change has taken place between the date from which the decision to be superseded took effect and the date of the superseding decision, from the first day of the assessment period in which the first change ought to have been notified.

25. Where—

    (a) the superseding decision is not advantageous to the claimant; and

    (b) there has been a universal credit decision where the Secretary of State is satisfied that, in relation to a limited capability for work determination, the claimant—

    (i) failed to notify an appropriate office of a change of circumstances which the claimant was required by regulations under the Administration Act to notify; and

    (ii) could not reasonably have been expected to know that the change of circumstances should have been notified,

the superseding decision takes effect on the first day of the assessment period in which the Secretary of State makes that decision.

26. Where, in any assessment period, a claimant—

    (a) reaches the qualifying age for state pension credit under the State Pension Credit Act 2002; and

    (b) has made an advance claim for an award of state pension credit,

a superseding decision made in consequence of the person reaching that age takes effect on the date on which that change of circumstances occurs or is expected to occur.

27. A superseding decision of the Secretary of State to make or to cease making a hardship payment takes effect in accordance with regulation 117 (period of hardship payments) of the Universal Credit Regulations.

28. In the case of a claimant who makes an application for a supersession which contains an express statement that they are terminally ill, the superseding decision takes effect from the first day of the assessment period in which the claimant became terminally ill.

29. Where the superseding decision is advantageous to a claimant and is made on the Secretary of State's own initiative, it takes effect from the first day of the assessment period in which the Secretary of State commenced action with a view to supersession.

30. In this Part, "a universal credit decision" means a decision to award universal credit embodied in or necessary to which is a determination that the claimant has or is to be treated as having limited capability for work.

PART IV

COMMON PROVISIONS

31.—(1) This paragraph applies in relation to an award of personal independence payment or universal credit where the change of circumstances is that the claimant or, in the case of universal credit, a member of their family, becomes entitled to another relevant benefit, ceases so to be entitled or the rate of another such benefit alters.

(2) Where this paragraph applies, the superseding decision takes effect from—

   (a) where the superseding decision concerns universal credit, the first day of the assessment period in which—

      (i) the entitlement to the other benefit arises;

      (ii) the entitlement to the other benefit ends; or

      (iii) entitlement to a different rate of the other benefit arises;

   (b) where the superseding decision concerns personal independence payment, the date on which—

      (i) the entitlement to the other benefit arises;

      (ii) the entitlement to the other benefit ends; or

      (iii) entitlement to a different rate of the other benefit arises.

(3) For the purpose of sub-paragraph (1), where the superseding decision relates to personal independence payment, "relevant benefit" includes any payment made under any of the provisions mentioned in regulation 61(1) (cases where mobility component of personal independence payment not payable) of the Claims and Payments Regulations 2013.

32. Where the change of circumstances is that there has been a change in the legislation in relation to any benefit, the superseding decision takes effect from the date on which that change in the legislation had effect.

33. Where the change of circumstances is the expected coming into force of a change in the legislation in relation to any benefit, the superseding decision takes effect from the date on which that change in the legislation takes effect.

DEFINITIONS

    "the Administration Act"—see reg.2.

    "appropriate office"—*ibid.*

    "assessment period"—see reg.2 and Universal Credit Regulations, reg.21.

    "benefit week"—see reg.2.

    "benefit"—*ibid.*

    "claimant"—*ibid.*

    "employment and support allowance"—*ibid.*

    "family"—*ibid.*

    "jobseeker's allowance"—*ibid.*

    "limited capability for work determination"—*ibid.*

    "limited capability for work"—*ibid.*

    "personal independence payment"—*ibid.*

    "relevant benefit"—*ibid.*

    "terminally ill"—*ibid.*

    "universal credit"—*ibid.*

Regulation 50(1)

SCHEDULE 2

DECISIONS AGAINST WHICH AN APPEAL LIES

1. A decision as to whether a person is entitled to a benefit for which no claim is required by virtue of regulation 6, 7 or 9(6) and (7) of the Claims and Payments Regulations 2013.

DEFINITIONS

"appeal"—see reg.2.
"the Claims and Payments Regulations 2013"—*ibid.*

Regulation 50(2)

SCHEDULE 3

DECISIONS AGAINST WHICH NO APPEAL LIES

Claims and Payments

4.170   **1.** A decision under any of the following provisions of the Claims and Payments Regulations 2013—
- (a) regulation 18 (special provisions where it is certified that a woman is expected to be confined or where she has been confined);
- (b) regulation 25 (interchange with claims for other benefits);
- (c) regulation 37 (evidence and information in connection with a claim);
- (d) regulation 46 (direct credit transfer);
- (e) regulation 47 (payment of universal credit);
- (f) regulation 48 (payment of personal independence payment);
- (g) regulation 49 (days for payment of personal independence payment);
- (h) regulation 50(1) (payment of personal independence payment at a daily rate between periods in hospital or other accommodation);
- (i) regulation 51 (payment of an employment and support allowance);
- (j) regulation 52 (payment of a jobseeker's allowance);
- (k) regulation 55, except a decision under paragraph (4) (extinguishment of right to payment if payment is not obtained within the prescribed period);
- (l) regulation 56 (payments on death);
- (m) regulation 57 (persons unable to act);
- (n) regulation 58 (payment to another person on the claimant's behalf);
- (o) regulation 59 (direct payment to lender of deductions in respect of interest on secured loans);
- (p) Part 6 (mobility component of personal independence payment).

Other Jobseeker's Allowance Decisions

4.171   **2.** A decision made in accordance with regulation 39(2) (jobseeker's allowance determinations on incomplete evidence) of these Regulations.

Other Decisions relating to Universal Credit

4.172   **3.** A decision in default of a nomination under regulation 21(4) (assessment periods) of the Universal Credit Regulations.

4. A decision in default of an election under regulation 29 (award to include the carer element) of the Universal Credit Regulations.

5. A decision as to the amount of universal credit to which a person is entitled, where it appears to the Secretary of State that the amount is determined by reference to the claimant's entitlement to an increased amount of universal credit in the circumstances referred to in section 160C(2) (implementation of increases in universal credit due to attainment of a particular age) of the Administration Act.

6. So much of a decision as adopts a decision of a rent officer under an order made by virtue of section 122 of the Housing Act 1996 (decisions of rent officers for the purposes of universal credit).

Suspension

7. A decision of the Secretary of State relating to suspending payment of benefit, or to the payment of a benefit which has been suspended, under Part 5 (suspension) of these Regulations.

4.173

Decisions Depending on Other Cases

8. A decision of the Secretary of State in accordance with section 25 or 26 of the 1998 Act (decisions and appeals depending on other cases).

4.174

Expenses

9. A decision of the Secretary of State whether to pay travelling expenses under section 180 of the Administration Act.

4.175

Deductions

10. A decision of the Secretary of State under the Fines (Deductions from Income Support) Regulations 1992, other than a decision whether benefit is sufficient for a deduction to be made.

4.176

11. Any decision of the Secretary of State under the Community Charges (Deductions from Income Support) (No. 2) Regulations 1990, the Community Charges (Deductions from Income Support) (Scotland) Regulations 1989 or the Council Tax (Deductions from Income Support) Regulations 1993, except a decision—

(a) whether there is an outstanding sum due of the amount sought to be deducted;

(b) whether benefit is sufficient for the deduction to be made; or

(c) on the priority of the deductions.

Loss of Benefit

12.—(1) In the circumstances referred to in sub-paragraph (2), a decision of the Secretary of State that a sanctionable benefit as defined in section 6A(1) of the Fraud Act is not payable (or is to be reduced) pursuant to section 6B, 7 or 9 of that Act as a result of—

4.177

(a) a conviction for one or more benefit offences in one set of proceedings;

(b) an agreement to pay a penalty as an alternative to prosecution;

(c) a caution in respect of one or more benefit offences; or

(d) a conviction for one or more benefit offences in each of two sets of proceedings, the later offence or offences being committed within the period of 5 years after the date of any of the convictions for a benefit offence in the earlier proceedings.

(2) The circumstances are that the only ground of appeal is that any of the convictions was erroneous, or that the offender (as defined in section 6B(1) of the Fraud Act) did not commit the benefit offence in respect of which there has been an agreement to pay a penalty or a caution has been accepted.

Payments on Account, Overpayments and Recovery

13. In the case of personal independence payment, a decision of the Secretary of State under the Social Security (Payments on account, Overpayments and Recovery) Regulations 1988, except a decision of the Secretary of State under the following provisions of those Regulations—

4.178

(a) regulation 5, as to the offsetting of a prior payment against a subsequent award;

(b) regulation 11(1), as to whether a payment in excess of entitlement has been credited to a bank or other account;

(c) regulation 13, as to the sums to be deducted in calculating recoverable amounts.

14. A decision of the Secretary of State under the Social Security (Payments on Account of Benefit) Regulations 2013, except a decision under regulation 10 (bringing payments on account of benefit into account) of those Regulations.

15. A decision of the Secretary of State under the Social Security (Overpayments and Recovery) Regulations 2013, except a decision of the Secretary of State under the following provisions of those Regulations—

(a) regulation 4(3), as to the person from whom an overpayment of a housing payment is recoverable;

(b) regulation 7, as to the treatment of capital to be reduced;

(c) regulation 8, as to the sums to be deducted in calculating recoverable amounts;

(d) regulation 9 (sums to be deducted: change of dwelling).

Reciprocal Agreements

16. A decision of the Secretary of State made in accordance with an Order made under section 179 (reciprocal agreements with countries outside the United Kingdom) of the Administration Act.

4.179

European Community Regulations

4.180   17. An authorisation given by the Secretary of State in accordance with Article 22(1) or 55(1) of Council Regulation (EEC) No 1408/71 on the application of social security schemes to employed persons, to self-employed persons and to members of their families moving within the European Union.

Up-rating

4.181   18. A decision of the Secretary of State relating to the up-rating of benefits under Part 10 (review and alteration of benefits) of the Administration Act.

DEFINITIONS

"the Administration Act"—see reg.2.

"assessment period"—see reg.2 and Universal Credit Regs., reg.21.

"benefit"—see reg.2.

"claimant"—*ibid.*

"the Fraud Act"—*ibid.*

"jobseeker's allowance"—*ibid.*

"personal independence payment"—*ibid.*

"universal credit"—*ibid.*

"the Universal Credit Regulations"—*ibid.*

INDEX

LEGAL TAXONOMY
FROM SWEET & MAXWELL

This index has been prepared using Sweet and Maxwell's Legal Taxonomy. Main index entries conform to keywords provided by the Legal Taxonomy except where references to specific documents or non-standard terms (denoted by quotation marks) have been included. These keywords provide a means of identifying similar concepts in other Sweet & Maxwell publications and online services to which keywords from the Legal Taxonomy have been applied. Readers may find some minor differences between terms used in the text and those which appear in the index. Suggestions to *sweetandmaxwell.taxonomy@thomson.com*.

(All references are to paragraph number)

Additional statutory paternity pay
  meaning, 2.6
Adjustment
  recovery of overpayments, 1.14–1.15
Advance claims
  generally, 4.39–4.40
Advance payments
  generally, 3.63–3.64
Alcoholism
  work-related requirements, 2.224
Alternative finance arrangements
  See Islamic finance
Appeals
  decisions, against
    appealable decisions, 4.164,
      4.169–4.181
    appellants,, 4.163
    benefit decisions, 1.25
    contributions decisions, 1.26
    decisions involving issues arise in other
      cases, 4.167
    excluded decisions, 1.24
    generally, 1.22
    notice of appeal, 4.165
    persons with right, 4.163
    Regulations, 4.163–4.169
    revised decisions, against, 4.166
  transitional provisions, 3.61–3.62,
    3.164–3.165
Armed forces personnel
  entitlement, 2.30–2.31
Assessment periods
  See Awards
Attendance allowance
  benefit cap, 2.178
  meaning, 2.6
Awards
  amounts
    generally, 2.102–2.103
    run-on after death, 2.104–2.105
  assessment periods
    Regulations, 2.59–2.64

  statutory provisions, 1.52–1.53
  basis, 1.52–1.53
  calculation, 1.54–1.55
  capability for work
    generally, 2.78–2.80
    period for which element not to be
      included, 2.81–2.83
    Regulations, 2.78–2.83
    statutory provisions, 1.62–1.63
  carer element
    amount, 2.102–2.103
    generally, 2.84–2.85
    'regular and substantial caring
      responsibilities for a severely
      disabled person', 2.86–2.87
    Regulations, 2.84–2.87
    statutory provisions, 1.62–1.63
  child element
    amount, 2.102–2.103
    introduction, 2.70
    Regulations, 2.71–2.72
    statutory provisions, 1.58–1.59
  childcare costs element
    amount, 2.102–2.103
    calculation, 2.96–2.98
    childcare costs condition, 2.92–2.93
    introduction, 2.70
    generally, 2.88–2.89
    Regulations, 2.88–2.102
    'relevant children', 2.99–2.102
    statutory provisions, 1.58–1.59
    work condition, 2.90–2.91
  deduction of income, 2.65–2.68
  elements
    amounts, 2.102–2.105
    carers, 2.84–2.87
    child, 2.71–2.72
    childcare costs, 2.88–2.102
    housing costs, 2.73–2.77
    introduction, 2.69–2.70
    limited capability for work,
      2.78–2.83

527